Communication

FIFTH EDITION

COMMUNICATION

MAKING CONNECTIONS

STUDY EDITION

William J. Seiler
University of Nebraska at Lincoln

Melissa L. Beall
University of Northern Iowa

Boston • New York • San Francisco
Mexico City • Montreal • Toronto • London • Madrid • Munich • Paris
Hong Kong • Singapore • Tokyo • Cape Town • Sydney

Editor in Chief: Karen Hanson
Senior Editor: Karon Bowers
Developmental Editor: Carol Alper
Editorial Assistant: Sarah Kelly
Marketing Manager: Jacqueline Aaron
Editorial-Production Service: Omegatype Typography, Inc.
Composition and Prepress Buyer: Linda Cox
Manufacturing Buyer: Megan Cochran
Cover Administrator: Linda Knowles
Interior Designer: Carol Somberg
Cover Designer: Studio Nine
Electronic Composition: Omegatype Typography, Inc.
Photo Researcher: Laurie Frankenthaler

Previous editions were published under *Communication: Making Connections,* Fifth Edition, copyright © 2002, 1999 by Allyn and Bacon, *Communication: Foundations, Skills, and Applications,* Third Edition, © 1996 by HarperCollins Publishers, Inc., and *Introduction to Speech Communication,* Second Edition, © 1992 by HarperCollins; © 1998 by Scott Foresman.

ISBN 0-205-36539-6

Printed in the United States of America

10 9 8 7 6 5 4 3 2 1   RRD-OH   08 07 06 05 04 03 02

*To Kathi, with my love, for being in my life
and for allowing me time to golf.*

W. J. S.

*To Hugh, with gratitude—thanks for your love,
friendship, support, and always being here.*

M. L. B.

CONTENTS

PART ONE   Making Connections Through Communication

Connecting Process and Principles   2

Connecting Perceptions and Communication   32

Connecting Self and Communication   58

Connecting Through Verbal Communication   82

5   Connecting Through Nonverbal Communication   **114**

Connecting Listening and Thinking in the Communication Process   146

PART TWO   Connecting in the Public Context

Selecting a Topic and Relating to the Audience   168

8   Gathering and Using Information   198

9   Organizing and Outlining Your Speech   222

10 Managing Anxiety and Delivering Your Speech   258

11 Informative Speaking   296

12 Persuasive Speaking 326

PART THREE Connecting in Relational Contexts

13 Interpersonal Communication 360

14   Developing Relationships   388

15   Group and Team Communication (General)   422

Participating in Groups and Teams *(Specifics → Read ch.16 first)*   **446**

 APPENDIX
Employment Interviewing: Preparing for Your Future   **A-1**

Glossary   G-1

Index   I-1

Practice Tests   PT-1

BOXED FEATURES

Making Connections

PREFACE

This book is about the way communication connects people in their everyday lives. The authors of this textbook came together because we both have a love for the introductory communication course and have similar backgrounds, but many different experiences in teaching the introductory course. We are extremely pleased that so many instructors have used our previous editions in their classes. When the fourth edition was published, you may have noticed substantial changes in the book's design and in its content. We also changed the title to reflect that communication is the one central force in our lives that allows us to make connections with those around us. Because communication is the link to everything people do, our overall theme remains "showing students how to make connections between communication and their daily lives." We believe that communication is all about connecting. We have continued and strengthened this focus in the fifth edition.

We also further integrated technology, diversity, ethics, and communication competency throughout this edition to emphasize their influences on our everyday lives. It is important for all of us to be able to make connections with a diverse and ever-changing society in the twenty-first century. Those who are able and willing to make these connections will find themselves well positioned for success, not only today but also tomorrow.

We believe that it is important for students to read about communication, to think critically about it, and to make connections with the way communication affects their lives. Our purpose in this edition, as in previous editions, is to help students learn about communication principles, public speaking, and interpersonal and group communication. This edition, like its predecessors, provides a solid foundation for the understanding of communication along with information to develop and improve students' communication competencies.

 ## Our Goal

The goal of the fifth edition is to provide students with a comprehensive, practical, readable, enjoyable, and, most important, intellectually sound book from which to learn about communication. As a result, the fifth edition of *Communication: Making Connections* is adaptable to the teaching styles of beginning instructors, who will be assisted by its thoroughness, pertinent and student-oriented examples, and well-organized pedagogy, as well as of experienced teachers, who will complement its content with their personal knowledge and experience.

As both authors and educators with combined experience of more than fifty years teaching the basic course, we know how important it is to have an introductory book with content and pedagogy that balance theory, research, and skills. We have made every effort to provide a reasonable and very practical connection among theory, research, and skills so that students are challenged but not overwhelmed.

In this edition, we made every effort to ensure that social diversity is integrated throughout the book's content. For example, we included examples of people with different ethnic backgrounds, ages, physical and mental abilities, and other important differences such as gender and sexual orientation. We believe differences in people help to shape the world around us as well as influence our everyday communication; our differences help us understand each other. We encourage students to appreciate diversity as part of our cultural life as it connects to and influences our communication.

Changes in the Fifth Edition

The fifth edition, like its predecessors, represents input from many talented and helpful individuals. We listened to instructors and students in the communication discipline and made many changes in this edition:

- **We have integrated even more information and activities and added links to websites related to technology.** Our last edition was considered by many to be a leader and a model for other texts; in this edition, there are even more sections exclusively related to the practical applications of technology to help students to learn its influences and effects on their lives. We have thoroughly examined each website for its usefulness and ensured that each Internet address is accurate and accessible as of this printing. You will find links and periodic updates on our website (www.ablongman.com/seiler).

- **We have expanded coverage of gender, cultural diversity, ethics, and critical thinking.** These topics are relevant to a wide range of students, including nontraditional students. There is more information about gender differences as they relate to interpersonal, presentational, and small group communication; more about critical thinking and listening; and much more balanced coverage of cultural and ethical issues throughout the text to provide a better understanding of the communication competencies needed to succeed in our global environment. Critical thinking exercises and many new thought-provoking questions are integrated throughout the text and in many new end-of-chapter discussion questions.

- **New and expanded Making Connections boxes appear in every chapter.** We reviewed each Making Connections box, examining its relevancy and how it would aid students in becoming better critical thinkers and competent communicators. The boxes are placed whenever possible to avoid interrupting the flow of the text and to enhance students' understanding of the communication theories, concepts, and principles they are reading about.

- **Additional information throughout helps students improve communication competence.** The text emphasizes understanding what it means to be a competent communicator. We discuss competence throughout the text, provide examples of competent communicators, ask students to assess their ability to communicate effectively in a variety of situations, and provide guidelines for communicating competently.

- **Meaningful quotations and scenarios, many new in this edition, introduce each chapter.** These are all student oriented to show the relevance of communication to their lives, to attract their attention, and to make the chapters more meaningful.

■ **New photos and updated contemporary examples of communication situations are included.** These bolster existing examples and make the content relevant to all students.

■ **This edition provides the most recent research.** When appropriate, current research studies and the names of important researchers have been added to help students understand the relationship between content and the research it supports.

■ **Electronic information sources—Using the Internet for Research—are new to this edition in Chapter 8.** Many students, for better or worse, use the Internet as a default option for researching their speeches. This section explains how to find information by using a search engine. Instructors who want to give even greater attention to the Internet can do so with *Speech Communication on the 'Net,* which is available as a supplement to *Communication: Making Connections.* Taken together, these resources provide the most up-to-date, thorough, and helpful coverage of the Internet available with any introductory textbook.

■ **The expanded and revised section on public communication includes more student-oriented examples, information on topic selection, and broader coverage of organization and outlining.** We have provided more about the use of computer searches to obtain information, expanded coverage of vocal delivery, and engaged in more discussion of speech anxiety and how to eliminate it. A new section on technology and the development of visuals also has been added to aid students in using the most up-to-date technology in their speeches. Finally, we have provided new student sample speeches and commentary as well as an accompanying video library of student speeches as part of the supplement package to aid students in developing their own speeches.

■ **Chapter 15, Group and Team Communication, and Chapter 16, Participating in Groups and Teams, now include online discussion.** We cover the research relevant to online discussions and how they can be used. We also discuss their advantages and disadvantages. The information provided instructs students on how to make the most of online discussions.

■ **The Appendix, Employment Interviewing: Preparing for Your Future, has been updated to include more information about online job searches, preparation for the employment interview, and many other aspects of the employment interview.** It contains information specifically written for first- or second-year students to help prepare them for their futures. Nevertheless, the information in the appendix is useful to all students because it addresses many of the important issues of preparing for and participating in the employment interview. It also has one of the best sections on using the Internet for job searches and résumé development of any introductory communication textbook.

■ **Two new chapters—Chapter 17, Connecting to Mediated and Mass Communication, and Chapter 18, Connecting in the Organizational Context—are now available on the Internet.** These two chapters can be accessed with the PIN code available with every new copy of the book, as of spring 2002.

■ Finally, our online ***Interactive Companion Website*** (www.abinteractive.com/login), accessed with a PIN code, contains a transcript of an interview that Bill Seiler conducted with Mr. Gary Danek, a retired account executive with Fortune 500 company Proctor & Gamble for more than thirty years. During that time Danek recruited and hired hundreds of students. In addition, you can email your questions about the interview or anything related to employment interviews, and Mr. Danek will respond.

Specific Changes in the Fifth Edition

Part One: Making Connections Through Communication

- The section on what communication is contains a new emphasis on historical perspective, including additional reasons it is important to study communication and the role communication plays in having a successful career.

- A new section on understanding perception includes awareness, cognitive processing, and the influence of language on perception. New sections on attribution discuss attribution error, ethnocentrism, and cultural relativism.

- A new model helps explain the eight components of self-concept, and an expansion and update of relevant research related to gender and self-concept has been included.

- A new listing of the key principles of nonverbal communication, new research related to eye gaze, a new model on space and how it connects to and influences communication, and an expanded discussion of deceptive communication all provide the latest information available.

- New sections cover the role of remembering, guidelines for effective and competent listening, and critical listening and thinking skills.

Part Two: Connecting in the Public Context

- New examples apply to students of all ages who come from a variety of occupational backgrounds.

- A new informative speech with commentary provides a model for students to read.

- A new section on electronic information sources offers tips on researching your speech.

- A helpful section describes how to determine the source and purpose of a web page by looking at its URL (e.g., edu denotes an educational institution, whose purpose is to provide factual information).

- Updated information explains how to evaluate web sources.

- A new section on guidelines and caveats shows how to use computer-generated presentational aids.

- Updated websites help students find information for speeches.

- Additional guidelines for using the Web help students find topics and information.

- New website addresses provide additional information on communication apprehension.

- Websites provide examples of persuasive and other notable speeches and debates.

- Updated topic suggestions are included for informative and persuasive speeches.

Part Three: Connecting in Relational Contexts

- New sections provide the latest information on social exchange theory, online relationships, self-disclosure and privacy, coming together on the Internet, dialectical theory, causes of conflict, and conflict management strategies.

■ New sections describe individuals and collectivistic orientations, why some group members fail to share information, disadvantages of small groups, technology and groups, team building, roles of group members, applying reflec-tive thinking to problem solving and decision making, and brainstorming via technology.

■ New sections cover researching a company via the Internet, behavioral-based interview questions, and how to email your résumé.

Features

Effectiveness in speech communication is an acquired skill. Although natural speaking ability is an asset, any person's capabilities in communication can be improved through (1) an understanding of communicative theories and principles, (2) training in its basic principles, (3) practice, and (4) improving communication competence. This edition meets students' needs in all four areas by providing:

■ Simply stated and specific learning objectives at the beginning of each chapter

■ Thorough and systematic explanations of basic principles

■ Clear, concrete, student-oriented examples, photos, cartoons, and other visual materials that support and expand on key concepts

■ Thought-provoking Making Connections boxes that encourage students' active involvement throughout each chapter

■ Guidelines boxes with lists of down-to-earth hints and recommendations for transforming theory into practice

■ Thorough end-of-chapter summaries that review key terms and concepts

■ Discussion questions at the end of each chapter

■ Complete glossary of key terms at the end of the book

Organization

The chapters are arranged to provide a practical and workable approach to teaching the fundamentals of communication. Part One, Making Connections Through Communication, provides the necessary background and basic principles for all communication. Part Two, Connecting in the Public Context, helps students develop speaking skills as they learn to select a topic, analyze an audience, gather and use supporting and clarifying materials, organize and outline speech material, deliver a speech with confidence, and effectively inform and persuade an audience. Part Three, Connecting in Relational Contexts, describes communication in relationships and small groups and teams.

Public communication skills are discussed early, before interpersonal communication, because we believe that they are fundamental to all communication. All communication is goal oriented. Therefore, in order to communicate effectively throughout life—whether socially or on the job, in one-to-one situations, in small groups, or before an audience—a person must be able to communicate with confidence, support and clarify his or her thoughts, organize information, analyze those with whom he or she is communicating, and inform and persuade effectively. This sequence of presentation is based on the recognition that students in an introductory communication course must master a great deal of basic information before they give a speech, yet because of time constraints, they need to begin preparing and presenting speeches as early in the term as possible. Introducing public speaking skills first provides a more even balance between speech presentations and other activities and alleviates the tendency to focus on speechmaking exclusively at the end of the term.

Considerable demands are placed on the introductory communication course, and as a result, there is a wide variety of ways to teach it—with emphasis on interpersonal communication, with emphasis on public speaking, with equal emphasis on all types of communication, and so forth. To meet these differing needs, each chapter is completely self-contained so that an instructor can easily arrange the sequence to meet the demands of the specific teaching situation.

The Instructor's Resource Manual

The **Instructor's Resource Manual** is authored by Melissa Beall and Marilyn Shaw, University of Northern Iowa, with contributions from Mary Bort and Bill Seiler. It provides nuts-and-bolts information about designing and developing an introductory communication course and methods for aiding instruction. Included in the manual are suggestions for managing and organizing the course; exercises and assignments for use in the classroom as well as outside the classroom; resources for instruction, including additional readings, games, simulations, and films; a section on evaluating speeches; a section on training and working with part-time instructors and graduate teaching assistants; and finally, a section on the Personalized System of Instruction (PSI), which is an efficient and effective method for teaching the introductory course.

Other Instructor's Supplements

- The **Test Bank,** by Scott Titsworth of Minnesota State University, Moorhead, contains multiple-choice, true/false, and short-answer questions for each chapter. All questions are referenced by text chapter and page number and include an indicator of difficulty.

- The **Computerized Testing Program** is an ideal test-generation system that features all test items in the *Test Bank,* with answers keyed to the text. Users can easily mix, scramble, edit, or create questions of their own.

- **A Guide for New Teachers of Introduction to Communication,** prepared by Susanna G. Porter of Kennesaw State University, helps new teachers teach the introductory course effectively. It covers such topics as preparing for the term, planning and structuring the course, evaluating speeches, utilizing the textbook, integrating technology into the classroom, and much more.

- **The ESL Guide for Public Speaking** provides strategies and resources for instructors teaching in a bilingual or multi-lingual classroom. It also includes suggestions for further reading and a listing of related websites.

- **The Blockbuster Approach: Teaching Interpersonal Communication with Video,** Second Edition, by Thomas E. Jewell, Marymount College, provides lists and descriptions of commercial videos that can be used in the classroom to illustrate interpersonal concepts and complex interpersonal relationships. Sample activities are available.

- A **PowerPoint Presentation** (on the Web) written and developed especially for this text by Paul Lakey and Jennifer Pulley at Abilene Christian University includes teaching outlines as well as a set of slides to enhance and enrich lectures. It is available on our website at www.ablongman.com/ppt.

- A **PowerPoint Presentation for Introduction to Communication** (on the Web) is a package of approximately fifty PowerPoint slides that cover a range of communication topics: public speaking, interpersonal communication, group communication, mass media, and interviewing. It is available on our website at www.ablongman.com/ppt.

- A **PowerPoint Presentation for Public Speaking** (on the Web) includes 125 slides and a brief User's Guide. It is available on our website at www.ablongman.com/ppt.

- **The Allyn & Bacon Communication Studies Digital Media Archive CD-ROM,** Version 2, is a collection of communication media images and sound bites available on CD-ROM that illustrates concepts in all areas of communication. It includes more than two hundred still images, thirty video excerpts, web links, and a complete set of lecture resources.

- **The Allyn & Bacon Public Speaking Transparency Package,** including 100 full-color transparencies created with PowerPoint, provides visual support for classroom lectures and discussion.

- **The Allyn & Bacon Student Speeches Video Library** includes student speeches covering a wide range of informative and persuasive topics (including a sample speech that is annotated in the text). Some restrictions apply.

- **The Allyn & Bacon Communication Video Library** includes a collection of videotapes highlighting a wide variety of communication topics, such as body language, group decision making, and presentation skills. Restrictions apply. Please contact your Allyn & Bacon representative for details.

- **The Allyn & Bacon Public Speaking Video** includes excerpts of classic and contemporary speeches as well as student speeches to illustrate the speaking process.

- **Video: Interpersonal Communication,** with Guidebook, includes eight scenarios that illustrate various concepts in interpersonal communication.

- **The Allyn & Bacon Interpersonal Communication Video,** with User's Guide, contains three scenarios that illustrate concepts in interpersonal communication.

- **The Allyn & Bacon Public Speaking Key Topics Video Library** contains three videos that address core topics covered in the classroom: Critiquing Student Speeches, Speaker Apprehension, and Addressing Your Audience. Some restrictions apply.

- **CourseCompass** (available spring 2002), powered by Blackboard, is the most flexible online course management system on the market today. By using this powerful suite of online tools in conjunction with Allyn & Bacon's pre-loaded textbook and testing content, you can create an online presence for your course in under thirty minutes. Log on at www.coursecompass.com, and find out how you can get the most out of this dynamic teaching resource.

Student Supplements

- The ***Companion Website with Online Practice Tests,*** (www.ablongman.com/seiler) offers an array of study materials.

- ***The Allyn & Bacon Communication Studies Website*** provides enrichment materials and activities. Access this site at www.ablongman.com/commstudies.

- ***iSearch: Speech Communication (with ContentSelect access code),*** by Terrence Doyle, Northern Virginia Community College, contains material on the basics of using the Internet, conducting web searches, and critically evaluating and documenting Internet sources. It contains material specific to using the Internet in the study of speech communication through Internet activities and lists of URLs related to the discipline. The book also includes an access code for ContentSelect, our online research database.

- The ***Speech Preparation Workbook,*** by Jennifer Dreyer and Gregory H. Patton, San Diego State University, takes students through the various stages of speech creation—from audience analysis to writing the speech—and provides guidelines, tips, and easy-to-fill-in pages.

- ***Public Speaking in the Multicultural Environment,*** Second Edition, by Devorah A. Lieberman, helps students think about the effects of the diverse backgrounds of audience members, not only on how speeches are prepared and delivered but also on how those speeches are perceived. It will help students learn to analyze the cultural diversities within their audiences and provide them with specific tools to adapt their presentations.

- The ***Interactive Speechwriter,*** Version 1.1, by Martin R. Cox, provides supplemental material and enhances students' understanding of key concepts discussed in the text. It includes tutorials, self-test questions, sample speeches, and templates for writing outlines as well as informative, persuasive, and motivated sequence speeches. (It is available for Windows and Macintosh platforms.)

- ***Preparing Visual Aids for Presentations,*** Second Edition, by Dan Cavanaugh, provides a host of ideas for using today's multimedia tools to improve presentations, including suggestions for how to plan a presentation, guidelines for designing visual aids, storyboarding, and a walkthrough that shows how to prepare a visual display using PowerPoint.

- The ***Outlining Workbook,*** by Reeze L. Hanson and Sharon Condon, Haskell Indian Nations University, includes activities, exercises, and answers and will help students develop and master the critical skill of outlining.

- ***The Speech Writer's Workshop CD-ROM,*** Version 2, will assist students with speech preparation and enable them to write better speeches. The software includes four separate features: (1) a speech handbook with tips for researching and preparing speeches plus information about grammar, usage, and syntax; (2) a speech workshop that guides students through the speech writing process while displaying a series of questions at each stage; (3) a topics dictionary that gives students hundreds of ideas for speeches—all divided into subcategories to help students with outlining and organization; and (4) a citation database that formats bibliographic entries in MLA or APA style.

■ *PSI-Study Guide Manual* provides students with questions and exercises to aid them in studying. The manual is designed for use at the University of Nebraska at Lincoln but can be modified to meet different uses. For a sample manual, contact Bill Seiler, Department of Communication Studies, University of Nebraska at Lincoln, Lincoln, Nebraska 68588-0329 or call 402-472-2069. His email address is bseiler@unl.edu.

The Authors

Bill Seiler is currently Professor and Chair of the Department of Communication Studies, University of Nebraska at Lincoln, where he has taught since 1972. He received his doctorate from Purdue University and has an adjunct appointment in Teachers College as a professor of curriculum and instruction. Professionally trained in the areas of business and organizational communication, instructional communication, psycholinguistics, statistics, and speech communication, Dr. Seiler is an experienced educator, consultant, researcher, and author. He has published numerous monographs, articles, and educational materials in the area of communication.

In addition, Dr. Seiler has presented lectures and speeches throughout the Midwest. He has published two other textbooks, *Communication in Business and Professional Organizations* and *Communication for the Contemporary Classroom.* He has served on the editorial boards for several of his discipline's major research journals and has held a variety of offices in his discipline's professional associations.

Dr. Seiler has been honored as an Outstanding Educator of America and Outstanding University and College Teacher by the Nebraska Communication Association; received the Outstanding Young Alumni and Distinguished Alumni Awards from the University of Wisconsin at Whitewater (the only person to receive both awards in the university's history); and is listed in the International Who's Who in Education.

Dr. Seiler is also the director of the basic communication course at the University of Nebraska at Lincoln. He has been directing the course since his arrival there some twenty-nine years ago. Dr. Seiler was one of the first people in the nation to use a Personalized System of Instruction (PSI) in a large, multiple-section basic communication course. Currently, the University of Nebraska teaches over a thousand students a year using the PSI method in the basic communication course.

Melissa Beall is a professor in the Communication Studies Department at the University of Northern Iowa. She came to UNI in 1990 as the basic course director and is also a member of the teacher education faculty. An avid Husker fan, she always wears red and white on football Saturdays. Dr. Beall received all three of her degrees from the University of Nebraska at Lincoln and appreciates having two home states, Iowa and Nebraska. Her expertise includes communication education, listening, communication and technology, intercultural communication, and communication theory, but she considers herself a generalist in the field of communication. She has taught at all levels, pre-kindergarten through adult education, and loves to teach. When she was a high school teacher in Nebraska, she taught English, theater, speech, and debate; directed plays; and coached the speech and debate teams. In her "spare time," she taught classes at UNL and Doane College–Lincoln. At UNI, she presents weekly lectures to two hundred students in the basic course (Oral Communication) and also teaches courses such as Public Speaking, Critical Thinking in Communication, Listening, Organizational Communication, Communication Education: College Teaching, Communication and Technology, Language and Communication, and Communication Theory.

Dr. Beall was selected as a Scottish Rite Distinguished Educator, an Outstanding Young High School Teacher by the Nebraska Speech Communication and Theatre Association, the National Communication Association's Marcella E. Oberle Outstanding K–12 Teacher, and a Master Teacher by the National Communication Association, Central States Communication Association, and Western States Communication Association. She has served on numerous editorial boards and has presented more than three hundred papers, programs, and workshops for professional organizations. She also presents technology, listening, and critical thinking workshops for schools, departments, and business organizations. Dr. Beall is a past president of the Central States Communication Association and is a former National Communication Association Administrative Committee member and a past Chair of the Educational Policies Board. She also serves on the executive boards of both the International Listening Association and the World Communication Association.

Acknowledgments

Numerous people have contributed to the previous editions as well as this edition of the book. First and foremost, we are grateful to the students who have shared their time and learning experiences with us, the instructors who patiently taught us about communication and life, the colleagues who have shared their expertise with us, the many graduate students who have worked in our basic speech course over the past twenty-three years, and the hundreds of undergraduate assistants and assistant supervisory instructors who have worked in our Personalized System of Instruction basic communication course during the past fourteen years.

With any project of this proportion, there are many to thank who helped in making this edition possible. We would like especially to thank Dr. Larry Routh, the Director of Career Planning and Placement at the University of Nebraska, for his review and guidance in the writing of the employment interview appendix.

Special thanks go to Marilyn Shaw, instructor of the introductory communication course at the University of Northern Iowa, for assisting and writing the *Instructor's Resource Manual*. We would also like to thank B. Scott Titsworth, Moorhead State University, for his help in revising the *Test Bank*. In addition to Marilyn and Scott, there have been many other faculty and graduate students—especially Diane Badzinski, Mary Bort, Dawn Braithwaite, Ann Burnett, John Caughlin, Jeff Cook, Susan Cusmano-Reans, Linda Dickmeyer, Gus Friedrich, Bobbi Harry, Jack Kay, Rob Paterson, Drew McGukin, Carol Morgan, Jack Sargent, Paul Schrodt, Shawn Wahl, and Nicole Zumbach—who have helped us by providing ideas and suggestions too numerous to mention here. Finally, thanks to all of the undergraduate and graduate students as well as the forensics students at the University of Nebraska at Lincoln who provided resources and examples.

We are also grateful to Carol Alper, Allyn & Bacon, for her guidance and editing and developmental skills. It was Carol, more than any other individual, who made the fifth edition come together. Thanks are also extended to Karon Bowers, our editor, and Karen Hanson, Editor in Chief, at Allyn & Bacon, for their willingness to take on this project.

The publishing of any book requires people dedicated to quality, and this book is no exception. We thank all those who participated in the review process of the first four editions of the book:

Philip M. Backlund, Central Washington University

William Patrick Barlow, Madison Area Technical College

Barbara L. Breaclen, Lane Community College

Allan R. Broadhurst, Cape Cod Community College

Michael Bruner, University of North Texas

Diane O. Casagrande, West Chester University

Patricia Comeaux, University of North Carolina at Wilmington

Juanita E. Dailey, Univesity of Rio Grande

Terrence Doyle, Northern Virginia Community College

Skip Eno, University of Texas at San Antonio

Jeanine Fassl, University of Wisconsin at Whitewater

Mary C. Forestieri, Lane Community College

Anne Grissom, Mountain View College

Ted Hindermarsh, Brigham Young University

Mary Lee Hummert, University of Kansas

David D. Hudson, Golden West College

Karla Kay Jensen, Nebraska Wesleyan University

Donald L. Loeffler, Western Carolina University

Sharry Messer, Hawkeye Community College

Mary Y. Mandeville, Oklahoma State University

Kay E. Neal, University of Wisconsin, Oshkosh

Sandra E. Presar, West Virginia Wesleyan College

Richard G. Rea, University of Arkansas

Marc E. Routhier, Frostburg State College

Thomas E. Ruddick, Edison Community College

Marilyn M. Shaw, University of Northern Iowa

Cheri J. Simonds, Illinois State University

Colleen Hogan-Taylor, University of Washington

Beth Waggenspack, Virginia Polytechnic Institute and State University

Catherine Egley Waggoner, Ohio State University

Kathie A. Webster, Northwest Missouri State University

Larry A. Weiss, University of Wisconsin at Oshkosh

Cherie C. White, Muskingum Area Technical College

Finally, thanks to those who provided analysis of the fourth edition, suggested changes, and reviewed the fifth edition:

Scott Britten, Tiffin University

Carley H. Dodd, Abilene Christian University

Julia Fennell, Community College of Allegheny County, South Campus

Robert E. Frank, Morehead State University

Kelby K. Halone, Clemson University

Stephen K. Hunt, Illinois State University

Kathryn C. Jones, Northern Virginia Community College, Annandale Campus

Charles J. Korn, Northern Virginia Community College

Nan Peck, Northern Virginia
    Community College
Marlene M. Preston, Virginia Tech
    University

Bill Seiler
Department of Communication Studies
University of Nebraska–Lincoln
Lincoln, Nebraska 68588-0329
402-472-2069
bseiler@unl.edu

Gretchen Aggertt Weber, Horry-
    Georgetown Technical College

Melissa Beall
Department of Communication Studies
University of Northern Iowa
Cedar Falls, Iowa 50614-0357
319-273-2992
Melissa.Beall@uni.edu

Communication

CHAPTER 1

Connecting Process and Principles

"Communication is a process (either verbal or nonverbal) of sharing information with another person in such a way that s/he understands what you are saying. Talking and listening and understanding are all involved in the process of communication."

—Dr. H. Norman Wright

- Define communication.
- Become aware of how communication can affect your career development.
- Become aware of how ethical behavior, culture, and technology can affect communication.
- Understand four basic principles of communication.
- Learn the essential components of the communication process.
- Distinguish among intrapersonal, interpersonal, and public communication.
- Identify five common myths about communication.

SCENARIO

Jared: Nikki, I just don't understand you anymore. You said you wanted a few weeks to think about things and to see other people, and then we could get back together to discuss our relationship. We've both gone out with others, we've had three weeks to think about things, and I want to continue to date others for a while. Now, you're upset. I thought that was what this whole "experiment" was all about. What's wrong with you? I just don't get it. It was *your* idea. Just because I want to continue to date others, you're upset. This is what you wanted to find out in the first place. And, don't tell me I'm wrong. You know I'm always open-minded and fair about things, even if you're not. I remember our discussion perfectly.

Nikki: Jared, that's just it! You *never* understand. You always think you know what everyone else is thinking, and you don't listen to everything they say. People start something and you have to finish their sentences, and whether you're right or not, you believe only your own views. You never pay any attention to the way people say things or the way they behave when they say things around you. When are you going to wake up? You just don't get it. You have such an elevated view of yourself and how *right* you always are. Maybe I should forget I ever knew you at all. ■

In this scenario, Jared and Nikki seem to be on different wavelengths about their relationship and, perhaps, about their views of the world. How many times have you been on another wavelength when conversing with family or friends? Most of us feel that way at some time or another, and sometimes we feel at odds more often than at other times, for example, with dates, friends, family, co-workers, other students, and even teachers.

Jared thinks Nikki is unreasonable. Nikki claims that Jared does not *listen,* fills in what he *thinks* others are going to say, is unaware of nonverbal communication, and

Technology allows us to make connections with each other and with the world. Technology is indeed changing our way of communicating and how we relate with others.

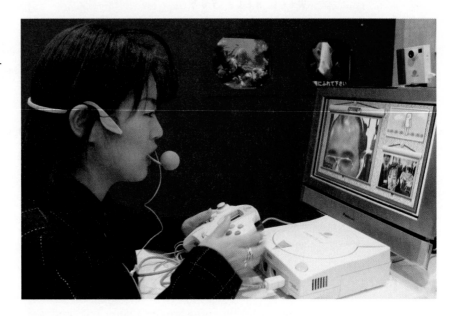

is not open or receptive to others' views. Unless both Nikki and Jared can talk through their problems, there seems to be little hope for their relationship, either as friends or as a couple. Both Nikki and Jared need to discuss clearly and candidly their relationship.

Communication helps us make connections with each other and with the world. Technology is changing our world so rapidly that some people believe they cannot keep pace with the changes. Others welcome change, and still others are totally baffled by the way computers, the Internet, and other forms of mediated communication (see Chapter 17, available on the Internet at www.ablongman.com/seiler/, for a more complete explanation of mediated and mass communication) are changing the way we live, work, socialize, and communicate. **Mediated communication** is any communication transmitted by some kind of mechanistic means, such as radio, television, telephone, or the Internet, and it may be one-on-one communication. **Mass communication,** however, generally means that someone is communicating with or to a large number of people. Radio, television, newspapers, magazines, books, the World Wide Web, movies, recordings, DVD, and CD-ROM are types of mass communication—they are the means by which messages of some type are directed to a large group (a mass) of people. It becomes confusing when we use some form of media to communicate with large numbers, or masses, of people, and, despite the popularity of mass communication, there is very little interaction between the sender and the receiver of the communications.

With the most current software and gadgets, we can email pictures to one another, or even actually sit at the computer with digital cameras and have "face-to-face conversations" with little lag time. We can meet people on the computer hours and miles away and recognize them when we meet face to face. (For a comprehensive view of the Internet, its technologies, and usage, check out this website: http://livinginternet.com/.) The advent of new technologies does not really change one thing: Communication is the process that helps us *make connections.* Communication is a learned tool that helps us in our personal and family lives, our social lives, our work lives, and in our roles as citizens of the world. Although it is a necessary skill, people often overlook the significant impact effective communication has on us.

This book and the class for which you have registered will help you understand the importance of effective communication and will provide suggestions and strategies for effective communication in a variety of settings and situations. The authors and publisher realize that people have different learning styles and a variety of preferred ways to study and learn. (In fact, we consider different ways of learning, listening, and thinking in Chapter 6.) For that reason, some of you may choose to supplement this text with the Interactive Companion. You may seek out the web links you find there. Some of you may reread these words numerous times, whereas others may read them through very quickly. We hope that the variety of approaches we use for this text will help you learn more about the exciting ways people *make connections* through communication.

This chapter presents the underlying principles and process of effective communication in everyday life. In particular, we examine the essential components and principles of communication, the types and contexts of communication, and the myths about communication. You will have the opportunity to think about the role of communication in an increasingly multicultural and technological world. We provide some hands-on activities to help you apply these principles to your personal life and to use communication to *make connections* in all areas of your life.

What Is Communication?

What then, you may ask, is communication? To answer this question, we need to ask and answer a series of questions concerning definitions and situations. What do we mean when we say that communication occurs? How do we know when we have effectively communicated? Can we send what we believe is a perfectly clear message yet not be understood by those for whom the message was intended? We must examine many factors to answer these questions. Does the relationship among the people communicating with each other influence the outcome? Do cultural differences have an impact on how effectively we communicate? How do electronic media influence what and how we communicate? How does the computer affect communication? Will email take the place of direct, face-to-face communication? Why do some people seem to know what to say, how to say it, and when to say it, whereas others do not? What do cultural awareness and sensitivity have to do with effective communication? How do ethical perspectives concern us in communication? How can we use communication to help us make connections in our lives?

The answers to these questions require an understanding of the principles, process, and concepts as well as some guidelines for successful interactions. Britannica. com (an online encyclopedia) defines com·mu'·ni·ca·tion as "the exchange of meanings between individuals through a common system of symbols."[1] In many dictionary definitions, communication is described as a process, because it reflects an active and changing event or set of behaviors. The terms *transmit* and *impart* are often used to suggest that during this process something is sent. But is sending a message truly the essence of communication? In the following situations, a message is definitely sent, but it is questionable whether communication has occurred:

- While her son plays Nintendo, a mom asks him to mow the lawn. He nods affirmatively.

- A professor tells her students that a paper is due at the next session of the class, but nobody meets the deadline.

■ A wife plays computer solitaire while her husband watches television. He comments on the news and she says, "Oh, that's interesting," and continues her game.

A review of speech communication textbooks quickly reveals the lack of a universally accepted definition of communication. Definitions can be long and complex or brief. They may take the view of the initiator, the receiver, or both in describing this phenomenon. Our purpose is not to argue whether one definition is better than another but to provide a starting point for discussing this concept. We define **communication** as the simultaneous sharing and creating of meaning through human symbolic action. (The terms used in this definition will be explained in more detail throughout the book.) We might also state the obvious, because it is worth emphasizing: Communication is complex. If it were simple, we would have no difficulties with it and, certainly, would not need to read a textbook about it! But this challenging process is essential to all relationships from the professional to the romantic. In fact, to make meaningful connections in any area of life, people need communication skills.

Because of its importance, communication has long been studied by scholars and recognized as a powerful means of influencing people. As a discipline, communication has existed for thousands of years. In ancient Greece and Rome, classical rhetoricians studied the principles of communicating effectively, including ways of composing and delivering persuasive speeches. In the Middle Ages in western Europe, religious leaders developed written and spoken means of communication, such as letter writing and preaching, in order to spread the Christian faith. Public speaking, narratives, and debate have long been important means of urging political action and swaying public opinion; they have shaped society in many ways. Well-known practitioners of this art include Abraham Lincoln, Susan B. Anthony, Winston Churchill, Barbara Jordan, Mohandas Gandhi, Mother Theresa, Mao Tse-tung, Fidel Castro, and Martin Luther King Jr.

As previously noted, technology has a major impact on the ways we connect with other people. And as technology continues to develop, communication will change to reflect those changes, as it has in the past.

Making Connections

What Is Communication?

Effective communicators are aware of the concepts and practices related to communication. Now that we have provided a definition, you should stop and think for a moment about the communication process. Respond to each of the following statements with either "true" or "false." Explain and justify your answers on a separate sheet of paper. Then compare your responses with those of a classmate or the class as a whole, or ask a co-worker to complete the exercise and compare notes.

1. Communication can solve all of our problems.
2. The more we communicate, the better.
3. Meanings are in words.
4. Communication is a natural ability.
5. Communication is reversible.

Discuss your answers and explanations for each statement with others. The answers for this exercise may be found on page 30. Be sure to discuss any questions you may have with your instructor.

The style and content of effective communication have evolved over time. Today we may not easily be drawn into the long, detailed campaign speeches given by political candidates of the nineteenth century. And we can only guess how nineteenth-century audiences would react to televised town meetings and talk radio. Technology continues to transform the ways in which people interact today to share information, spur action, sell a product, or simply enjoy one another's company.

Speech communication is a subcategory of the field of communication and forms the main emphasis of this book. We often think about speech communication simply as the practice and study of giving speeches. When we take a communication class, we go into the class thinking that we will be giving numerous speeches. Speech communication, however, involves much more than this. The Association for Communication Administrators defines the **speech communication** discipline as

> a humanistic and scientific field of study, research, and application. Its focus is upon how, why, and with what effects people communicate through spoken language and associated nonverbal messages. Just as political scientists are concerned with political behavior and economists with economic behavior, the student of speech communication is concerned with communicative behavior.[2]

Communication, the singular form, refers to the process by which we create and share meanings. **Communications,** however, is the word generally used to denote the delivery systems for mediated and mass communication. People often confuse the two words, but they are quite different. Communication is what you and your friend do when you discuss the next speech assignment. Communications involve ways of disseminating information, as in, "The Internet is a vital communications link for students and office workers."

According to this definition, speech communication involves a range of behaviors and occurs in a variety of situations: public and private, business and social, home and school, formal and informal. The diverse situations are all connected by one common thread—*human symbolic interaction,* or, people using a symbol system (language) to share thoughts, feelings, beliefs, attitudes, customs, and ideas. As you read this text, you will learn about human symbolic interaction as it occurs within and among individuals, groups, organizations, cultures, and co-cultures. You will learn more about the nature of the communication *process:* listening, thinking, speaking in public settings, speaking in small-group settings, and speaking with one or two, or a small number of people, in your interpersonal relationships. Your ability to communicate by using speech will be one of the determining factors in your success in the classroom, in the workplace, and in your personal life. Being an effective communicator saves time, makes life more enjoyable, allows people to establish and maintain relationships successfully, and facilitates accomplishing personal goals. The humorist James Thurber may have said it best: "Precision of communication is important, more important

Making Connections

Communication and the Workforce

We have suggested that communication skills are essential in the workplace. Employers advise that communication skills are critical to finding and holding jobs and meeting the requirements of many careers. Peruse the Help Wanted in your local newspaper.

1. What kinds of skills are identified?
2. How many of the ads specify speaking, listening, thinking, and group or people skills?
3. What are some of the other requirements?

than ever, in our era of hair-trigger balances, when a false, or misunderstood word may create as much disaster as a sudden thoughtless act."[3]

Why Should We Study Communication?

Although you have communicated for many years, you probably have not had the opportunity to learn about **communication competence,** the ability to take part in effective communication, which is characterized by skills and understandings that enable communication partners to exchange messages successfully. The ability to communicate may seem natural because unless there are disabilities, most of us readily develop speaking skills. But the ability to *communicate* (not simply to utter words) is learned, and learning to be a competent communicator is a difficult, lifelong project. You can make progress quickly, however, if you work hard to learn the principles and concepts and then apply them in practice situations. Think about your life experiences, then connect the chapter material, class applications, and discussions to your life. These skills will reap benefits for you in career development, ethical behavior, and the promotion of positive relationships among people of diverse cultural backgrounds. As previously noted, we live in a time of rapid technological change. Put simply, effective communication is critical to living successfully in today's society.

Communication and Career Development

Most of us aspire to succeed in our chosen careers. We enter college in order to better ourselves and to prepare for satisfying jobs. Communication plays an important role in career success. Leaders in education, business, and industry have identified several critical life skills necessary to function successfully in the workforce, and communication is one of the most valued areas of expertise. For example, several recent studies[4] reinforce what previous research had already demonstrated: Employers want workers at all levels who know how to communicate. These studies specifically recommend the following:

- Speak effectively.
- Listen carefully and efficiently.
- Think critically.
- Get along well with others.
- Be aware of and sensitive to differences in cultural perspectives.
- Make good decisions, individually and in groups.

In other words, effective workplace communicators can explain ideas clearly and give good directions. Effective communicators are good listeners who work well with others and represent their companies well in small- and large-group settings. Too often, employers believe that these skills are lacking in their employees. Introductory courses in communication, such as the one for which you are reading this text, focus on these skills.

Personnel directors have described their needs in prospective employees as follows: "Send me people who know how to speak, listen, and think, and I'll do the rest. I can train people in their specific job responsibilities, as long as they listen well, know how

Making Connections

Your Communication Effectiveness

In the surveys cited in the text, executives indicated that all employees need to improve their communication skills. The executives also noted that greater flexibility and higher ethical standards should be a focus of career preparation. If a prospective employer asked you the following questions, how would you respond?

1. Are you an effective communicator? Why? Why not?
2. What are five of your "communication concerns"?
3. What anxieties about communication do you have? (James McCroskey and his colleagues at West Virginia University developed the Perceived Report of Communication Apprehension (PRCA) to help identify the strength of one's communication anxiety. You might wish to look at Dr. McCroskey's web page (http://www. as.wvu.edu/~jmccrosk/special.htm) for more information; try a web search on communication apprehension, and complete a PRCA form found on the Web. We discuss communication apprehension more fully in Chapter 10.)
4. What areas of communication do you need to improve? How do you know you need to work on these areas?
5. Describe one instance in which you found yourself wishing that you were a better listener.
6. What were you doing the last time you found yourself wishing you were a better communicator? What did you mean by the term?
7. In what recent situations did you find yourself wondering how to be more effective in interpersonal relationships?

to think, and can express themselves well."[5] In fact, most careers involve contact with others and require the ability to communicate effectively with them. Business and industry often look for the most competent communicators when they hire new employees. So, although some companies provide on-the-job training in communication skills, it is by far most advantageous to develop excellent speaking, listening, and analytical abilities before applying for the exciting job that could launch or enhance your career.

Communication and Ethical Behavior

All societies hold certain ethical standards—ideals concerning what is right and what is wrong—and unethical behavior often carries a penalty. People have been removed from political office, lost their jobs, or been publicly chastised for violating ethical standards and codes. Such behaviors often involve unethical acts related to communication. Financiers have received prison terms for participating in insider trading—using illegally obtained information to make money on the stock market. Sharing such information constitutes an illegal act of communication. Another such behavior is telling lies, whether done to hurt someone else or to protect or enhance one's own position. Though politicians spring to mind as typical offenders in this category, other examples show that the problem is more widespread, for example, enhancing one's résumé to increase the chances of being hired or "borrowing" a friend's old term paper in order to pass a course.

The long-running Napster controversy is an example of an ethical dilemma played out on the Net and in the courts. The music industry believes that Napster is a ring of digital music thieves. Others believe Napster is simply providing a service that allows users to download software to search for specific songs to sample. One thing is certain: The Internet has made plagiarism a much greater possibility because of the ease with which people can access information. There are so many sites with so much information that people often believe they can access sites, take what they want, and never be caught. Unfortunately, plagiarism, in whatever form and however accessible, is still unethical, and it can result in students' failing courses and even being removed from their colleges and universities. In the workplace, plagiarism and other unethical behaviors can result in the loss of one's job or a demotion. In recent years, newspaper reporters have been in the news for fabricating stories and losing their jobs. Ethics and plagiarism are discussed throughout the text and are defined here. **Ethics** refers to an individual's system of moral principles. **Plagiarism** is the use of another person's information, language, or ideas without citing the originator and making it appear that the user is the originator.

The ethical communicator speaks responsibly and gives credit to any sources that contribute to the message being conveyed. An ethical communicator does not plagiarize and does not equivocate. Aristotle, a Greek rhetorician (384–322 B.C.), suggested that communication was most powerful when the speaker's character, or *ethos* (ethical appeal), was engaged in presenting the truth.[6] (Chapter 10 further develops this concept.) Quintilian (A.D.ca. 35–ca. 100), another rhetorician, stated (before the days of inclusive language) that communication needed to be presented by "a good man speaking well."[7]

An important distinction to make here is that unethical communication may, in fact, constitute effective communication. If one person persuades another to do something morally wrong, the communication has been effective, but it is not virtuous. Unethical communication should never be condoned, even when it has appeared to succeed. A good deal of critical thinking is needed as we attempt to be effective *and* ethical communicators and as we evaluate others' communication to determine its ethical content.

Today, many colleges and universities offer ethics classes to encourage students to take ethical responsibilities seriously and to remind them that the need for responsible, ethical behavior pervades all aspects of life. Throughout this text, examples of ethical dilemmas and perspectives will help you become aware of the need for ethical communication behaviors.

Communication and Our Multicultural Society

Job transfers, changes in economic and political conditions, and numerous other factors cause people to move from place to place, often leaving their country of birth to put down roots elsewhere. United States society reflects an increase in this trend. What was once a population with a white majority of northern European roots is now a diverse mosaic of people of different ethnic and cultural backgrounds. In this environment, we can all grow to appreciate the distinctions that make each culture unique as well as the interconnectedness shared by all, sometimes described as the "global village." But a great deal of knowledge, flexibility, and sensitivity are necessary if people of diverse cultural backgrounds are to communicate successfully and live well together.

Making Connections

Ethical Communication

Read this account of a student's ethical dilemma, and then answer the questions that follow.

Sundee was about ready to graduate from college and was ready to get out on her own. Because she did not complete certain academic requirements until her junior year, she was unable to declare her major. Because she was not yet declared, she was ineligible to take the final six hours of course work in her major in time to graduate when she had planned to, though she could participate in the commencement exercises. Sundee's parents insisted that they could no longer afford to pay for her tuition, because her younger sister was graduating from high school and also wanted to go to college. Because the family could afford to pay for the college expenses of only one child at a time, Sundee agreed that she would find work close to her college and complete the final six hours as she worked to pay her own way.

When Sundee interviewed for jobs, prospective employers asked about her educational background. To her dismay, Sundee discovered that her lack of a completed college degree kept her from being hired for the positions she really liked. Yet her four years of college education made her appear overqualified in the minds of prospective employers who offered work that did not require such education.

Sundee was desperate to find work. She confided to her friend Pat that she really needed a job immediately so that she could both complete her degree and get on with her life. Pat suggested that in future interviews, she should fudge the facts just a tiny bit. Why not state that she was in fact graduating, because in a sense she was—right? She would be involved in the commencement ceremonies. Wasn't it just a tiny little technicality?

1. What is Sundee's ethical dilemma?
2. If you were Sundee, what would you do? Why?
3. How might Sundee convince the prospective employer that she sincerely intends to finish college and has most of the qualifications represented by the degree, even though she has not yet completed all the requirements?
4. What might happen if Sundee does as Pat suggests? What if the employer discovers, six months after hiring her, that Sundee has hedged the truth? Does her employer have the right to fire her? Why or why not? Does the employer have the right to dock her pay?
5. How can Sundee be an effective and ethical communicator in this situation?

Current demographic trends and projections in the United States make it not an option, but a necessity, to interact successfully with people of all racial, ethnic, cultural, and religious heritage. The U.S. Census Bureau reports the following demographic breakdown by race (all ages) in 2000:

32,832,000 Hispanic Origin (any race)

196,929,000 White, Not Hispanic

33,619,000 Black, Not Hispanic

2,059,000 American Indian, Eskimo, and Aleut, Not Hispanic

10,620,000 Asian and Pacific Islander, Not Hispanic[8]

This translates to roughly the following percentages: 71 percent of the population is White; 12 percent, Hispanic; 12 percent, Black; 4 percent, Asian and Pacific Islander; and 1 percent, American Indian. Projections suggest a significant increase in Hispanic, Black, and Asian numbers in the near future, with a decline or stable percentage for Whites. The changes in "how we look" are already occurring in elementary schools and high schools, as well as college and university classrooms. Language differences complicate communication within many schools. Some kindergarten through twelfth-grade schools on the East and West coasts and in such populous areas as Chicago, Cincinnati, and St. Louis have students representing fifty to one hundred or more different native languages. College and university classrooms, too, have increasing numbers of students whose first language is not English, and each one's cultural and ethnic background affects the way these students communicate in the classroom, the residence hall, the supermarket or grocery store, and the workplace.

Language structure itself influences and is influenced by culture. Nonverbal communication behaviors, such as physical stance, eye contact, style of speaking, and so on, are also largely determined by cultural background. It takes a great deal of patience, understanding, and respect to learn to communicate effectively in situations involving different language backgrounds and different social and conversational customs. Thus, it is important to learn all we can about the backgrounds of the people with whom we relate at work or in the community, to consider how our own customs might seem unusual to a person of a different heritage, and to cultivate an open mind and a good sense of humor. These attitudes will facilitate communication and will also enrich our lives.

Communication and Our Technological Society

The world seems to be getting smaller, because so many people travel and because the mass media bring the world to our living rooms, residence hall rooms, offices, and even our automobiles. Only a few years ago it took a day or so to get news from one part of the world to another. Now, however, advancements in technology often make

Advancements in technology, such as the satellie communication used here, often make it possible for us to make immediate contact. Messages by way of email, fax, or telephone can be sent to almost any part of the world.

Making Connections

Communication and Technology

The Internet is a potent force in our lives. We use the Internet in the classroom, in the workplace, and in our homes. Some are concerned that people will forget how to relate to others because so much of our time is spent at the computer. Think about your own Internet or intranet use and answer these questions.

1. Have you (or do you know someone who has) experienced a cyber relationship?
2. How did the relationship develop?
3. What rules did you or your friend follow in establishing this relationship?
4. What concerns do you have about this type of relationship? Why?
5. How is your cyber communication easier or more difficult than face-to-face communication with your friends or family?

Discuss these questions and your answers with (1) others who do not use the Internet very often and (2) those who spend a great deal of time on the Internet? What are the similarities and differences in the answers between the two?

it possible for us to experience historic events not only moments after they occur, but sometimes even *while* they occur. We can communicate with people in almost any part of the world; we can send messages via email, fax, and telephone. We can use digital cameras at our computers and visit face to face with people around the world. We can turn on the television and see and hear what is happening anywhere in the world or even in space. Interviews with world leaders, celebrities, and ordinary people are broadcast on television and radio every day. If you happen to be in the right place at the right time, witnessing a news event or simply crossing the path of a reporter looking for a story, your image, words, or voice may be instantaneously transmitted to your community, the nation, or the world.

The way technology has sped the pace of communication adds to the challenge of both presenting and receiving meaningful messages. Flashing images and sound bites can be hard to interpret. The sheer volume of communication presented through electronic media can seem overwhelming. Yet technological developments are exciting in that they increase the avenues through which communication can occur and make the process quick and easy. Those who take time to learn and practice the principles of sound communication will be able to use to the best advantage these technological means of sending and receiving messages. (See Chapter 17, available on the Internet, for more information on mediated and mass communication.)

Principles of Communication

To appreciate the true nature of communication, it is important to understand four fundamental principles:

1. Communication is a process.
2. Communication is a system.
3. Communication is both interactional and transactional.
4. Communication can be intentional or unintentional.

These principles are readily applicable to life beyond the classroom (and they improve interactions within the classroom as well). No doubt, situations from your personal life—work experiences, family relationships, or your participation in sports teams, music groups, social clubs, or political or community action organizations—will come to mind as we discuss the dynamics of communication. An understanding of these principles should make a difference in your life, building greater understanding and cooperation into relationships at any level.

Communication Is a Process

Communication is considered a **process,** because it involves a series of actions that has no beginning or end and is constantly changing.[9] It is not an object that you can hold to examine or dissect. It is like the weather, which changes constantly.[10] Sometimes the weather is warm, sunny, and dry, and other times it is cold, cloudy, and wet. The weather is a result of complex interrelationships among variables, such as high and low pressure systems, the position of the earth, and ocean currents, that can never be exactly duplicated. Communication is similarly an ongoing, constantly changing process.

Communication also involves variables that can never be duplicated. The interrelationships among people, environments, skills, attitudes, status, experiences, and feelings all determine communication at any given moment. Think about a relationship you developed with someone recently. How did it occur? It may have happened by chance (striking up a conversation with someone you met while walking to class) or it may have been a prearranged meeting (a business meeting with a prospective client). No two relationships are developed in the same way. And like the weather, some relationships are warm and others cold.

Communication is both ever-changing and capable of effecting change. Saying something that you wish you hadn't said is an excellent example of this principle. No matter how hard you try to take back your comment, you cannot. It has made its impact and has, in all likelihood, affected your relationship with another person in some way. The change may not be immediate or significant, but it does take place as a result of your communication.

Furthermore, the communication and the changes it produces may not have a clearly identifiable beginning or end. Certain events led up to it, and, as we noted, results of the communication will follow in its wake. Communication generally is not characterized by abrupt endings and beginnings, but rather it takes place within a flow. If you were to stop in mid-conversation and walk away, that conversation would still have an effect on you; it would not end. You would carry away some new information or at least a general impression, whether positive or negative. If you understand that communication is a process, you will be able to see how events and relationships constantly change and yet also have continuity.

Communication Is a System

Simply stated, a **system** is a combination of parts interdependently acting to form a whole. The human body is an excellent example of a system. All parts of the body are interdependent and work together to form one complex system. If something is not functioning correctly, some response usually occurs either to correct what has gone wrong or to warn that something is going wrong. When you have a headache, it affects not only your head but also the rest of your body, including the thinking process and emotions. You may find that you have trouble seeing and even walking. You may not wish to eat, because your head pain seems to have taken over your body. If you have a severe headache, you may have trouble thinking clearly because of the pounding in your head. You may also have difficulty explaining something to your co-workers or friends. Because each part of the system is connected, your ability to think clearly, speak clearly, or listen effectively leads to ineffective communication.

Systems also exist in the workplace, in the family, and in the classroom. If your supervisor has had a fight at home, that event may affect the supervisor's relationship with the workers; the supervisor may be irritable and snap at you and others. Although you don't know what has caused the irritability, it does affect all who must deal with it and other behaviors. In other words, the supervisor's domestic squabble has an impact not only on the home system but also on the system at work. In a similar sense, the communication process is a system and occurs only when the necessary components interact. If all components of communication malfunction or are absent, communication is prevented or ineffective.

Communication Is Interactional and Transactional

The interactional and transactional aspects of communication are closely related and should be considered together. **Interaction** is an exchange of communication in which people take turns sending and receiving messages. It is similar to playing catch. Someone throws a ball. Another person catches it and throws it back. Each throw and each catch is a separate action. It is, however, necessary for the ball to get to the other person before it can be thrown back. Figure 1.1 illustrates this interaction. In interaction, there is a distinct time delay between each message being sent. An example of communication as an interaction is a phone conversation between two people. Person A speaks and Person B listens, then Person B speaks and Person A listens, and so on. Each message is a separate action. Even though there is a reaction to each message being sent, the reaction and message are not simultaneous.

Most face-to-face communication does not occur as a series of distinctly separate actions. Thus, the term **transaction** is used to extend the concept of interaction to include simultaneous actions. Persons involved in transaction engage in sending (encoding) and receiving (decoding) messages at the same time (see Figure 1.2). For example, when teachers communicate to their students, or supervisors to their employees, they not only send information but also receive information at the same time. The teacher and students and supervisor and employees are sending and receiving

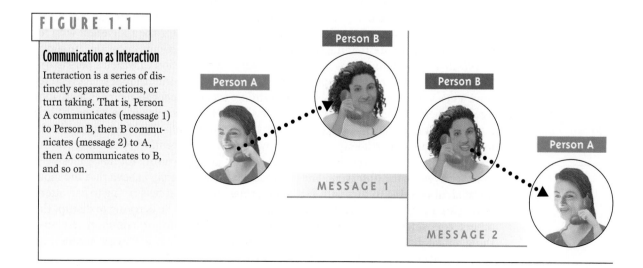

FIGURE 1.1

Communication as Interaction

Interaction is a series of distinctly separate actions, or turn taking. That is, Person A communicates (message 1) to Person B, then B communicates (message 2) to A, then A communicates to B, and so on.

Person A

Person B

MESSAGE 1

Person B

Person A

MESSAGE 2

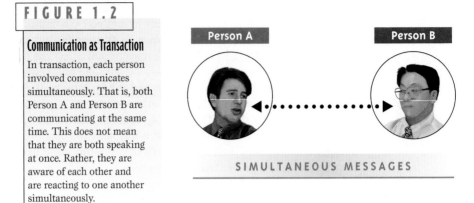

FIGURE 1.2

Communication as Transaction

In transaction, each person involved communicates simultaneously. That is, both Person A and Person B are communicating at the same time. This does not mean that they are both speaking at once. Rather, they are aware of each other and are reacting to one another simultaneously.

messages simultaneously. This does not necessarily mean they are talking at the same time; it does mean, however, that two-way communication is taking place. Your handshake communicates a message that another person interprets at the same time that you are receiving and interpreting the message in the handshake that you are receiving. In addition, you both are simultaneously receiving feedback about the message your own handshake is sending.

Without simultaneous actions, face-to-face communication would be impossible or extremely limited, like sending a letter to someone and then having to wait a week or two for a response. In face-to-face communication, each person affects the other and shares in the process simultaneously. Thus, communication transaction can be seen as the simultaneous exchange by which we share our reality with others. The principle of transaction is more fully depicted in Figure 1.4 on page 18.

Communication Can Be Intentional or Unintentional

Communication can occur regardless of whether it is intended. Generally, when one person communicates with another, he or she intends that specific messages with specific purposes and meanings be received. **Intentional communication** is a message that is purposely sent to a specific receiver. **Unintentional communication** is a message that was not intended to be sent or was not intended for the individual who received it. Based on intent or the lack of intent, four possible communication situations can occur, as shown in Figure 1.3. Arrow 2 indicates a situation in which a person unintentionally communicates something to someone who is intentionally trying to receive a message or messages. This situation arises every time someone reads more into a communication than was intended by the source. For example, when a student in a quiet classroom gets up to sharpen a pencil, the eyes of the other students immediately focus on the moving student, who may have no specific intention of communicating anything. The mere movement, however, provides an opportunity for many messages to be received by the observers. For instance, one observer may believe that the moving student is trying to flirt with her, another may think that he's trying to call attention to his attractiveness, and the instructor may think that he is trying to disrupt the others' concentration. Despite the student's lack of intention to communicate anything, others have read meaning into his movement, and in one way or another, he may have to contend with their interpretations.

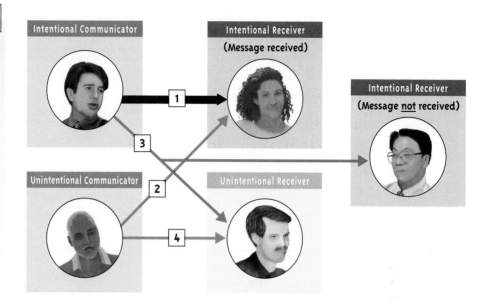

FIGURE 1.3

Types of Intentional and Unintentional Communication

Communication occurs both intentionally and unintentionally. Thus, we must be aware that even when we do not intend it, communication can occur. Can you recall any instances in which you unintentionally communicated to another person?

Arrow 3 illustrates the opposite situation. Here the source intends to send a message, but the person for whom the message is intended is not consciously or intentionally receiving it. Such a situation arises when a parent tries to communicate to a child who intentionally does not want to hear. It also happens in the classroom when students daydream while the instructor is lecturing.

Arrow 4 shows that communication can be unintentional for both the source and the receiver and can occur without anyone intentionally sending or receiving a message. Communication that is not intended, or that is at least not consciously sent and received, is usually nonverbal. Nonverbal communication is any information that is expressed without words. For example, the clothing a person wears might not be worn to communicate any specific message, and persons observing the clothing might not intentionally or consciously receive any message through it, but they do see it. Thus, communication occurs even though neither the person nor the observer has any intention of communicating.

Essential Components of Communication

Although there is no exhaustive list of the myriad components of communication, eight of the most basic elements are worth examining in detail:

1. Source	**5.** Receiver
2. Message	**6.** Feedback
3. Interference	**7.** Environment
4. Channel	**8.** Context

Figure 1.4 illustrates how these components interact when two people are communicating, yet it depicts each element's movement and interdependence on the other

Making Connections

Communication in the Workplace

Shenita and Jason work together at a local retail store and have learned that good communication is essential to their success as employees. Even though the positions they now hold are not directly related to their career goals, both Shenita and Jason believe that their success in this position will help them achieve career goals. In fact, their supervisor suggested that they enroll in a communication course at the local college to help them now and in the future. Both are taking a communication class and have been asked to make a five-minute informal presentation in front of the class to discuss a communication concept they discovered was important outside the classroom.

Focus on a workplace experience of your own as you answer these questions.

1. What communication concept would you choose to talk about? Why?
2. How do you find that the principles of communication relate to your role as a communicator inside and outside the classroom?
3. Which of the four principles of communication identified in the text is clearly involved in your communication roles outside the classroom?
4. How does communication help you to make connections between this class and other areas of your life?

elements only in a limited way. During actual communication, these components are constantly in flux as the communicators react to each other. The model also shows that communication is a process, that the components work together as a system, that interaction and transaction are both possible modes of communication, and that intentional and unintentional communication can occur—thus illustrating the principles of communication that we have already discussed.

FIGURE 1.4

Schematic Model of the Essential Components of Communication

The essential components of the transactional communication process are constantly changing, ongoing, and dynamic, and they affect one another.

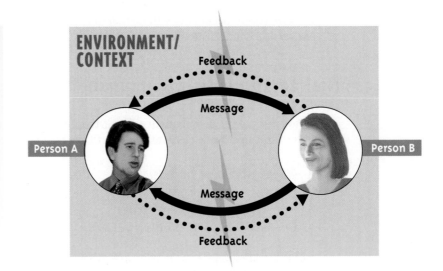

Now that you can see how these elements relate during communication, we will discuss each one separately.

Source

The **source** is the creator of the message. Because communication usually involves more than one person, more than one source of communication can exist at one time. In the model in Figure 1.4, both persons function as a source. Likewise, both the teacher and the students in a classroom can function as sources, sending messages simultaneously to one another—teacher to students, students to teacher, and students to students.

The communication source performs four roles: He or she determines the meaning of what is to be communicated, encodes the meaning into a message, sends the message, and perceives and reacts to a listener's response to the message. Person A, when acting as source, also brings into play the communicative skills, knowledge, attitudes, and sociocultural background that make him or her a unique individual. No two communicators are identical in their abilities to communicate, nor do they see others, events, or situations in exactly the same way. The greater the differences between Person A and Person B, the more effort and skill it will take for Person A to effectively communicate with Person B. Respecting another person's views, even when they differ from one's own, is the first step to communicating well in such situations.

Determining Meanings.   A source has many decisions to make in creating a message. The meaning of some communication messages is relatively simple, but others can be extremely complex and difficult. For example, telling someone about a high grade you received on a recent speech entails making a decision about the meaning you wish to convey. Do you want the other person to know that this is the highest grade you have ever received on a speech or merely that you got a high grade? Do you want the person to know what you did to get the high grade?

Encoding.   Once a source has chosen a meaning, she or he **encodes** it. In other words, a source translates the thoughts or feelings into words, sounds, and physical expressions, which make up the actual message that is to be sent. According to symbolic interactionism, a theory created by George Mead and his students, the most human and humanizing activity people engage in is talking with one another. It is our conversations with others, our participation in the communication process in social settings, that allow us to construct meaning. According to social interactionism, the meaning we attribute in those interactions is determined by our language choices. Furthermore, symbolic interactionism also explains that we talk to ourselves (intrapersonal communication) as we sort through difficult circumstances, solve problems, and make decisions.

Sending.   The source then sends the message, which involves the source's ability to communicate overtly, that is, to use voice and body to express the intended meaning accurately. For example, if your internal meaning is to tell the other person how pleased you are to receive a high grade on your speech, then you must use words and actions to illustrate what you are feeling and thinking.

Reacting.   Finally, a source must interpret the receiver's response to the message. A source's perception of a receiver's response in most communication situations is simultaneous with the response. For example, the person you are telling about the high grade will be sending you messages (smiles, nods of the head, eye contact) as you speak in reaction to what you are saying. If you interpret that response as positive, you will probably continue to tell more about your high grade.

Message

A **message** is the stimulus produced by the source. It is comprised of words, grammar, organization of thoughts, physical appearance, body movement, voice, aspects of the person's personality and self-concept, and personal style. Environment and noise can also shape the message. Any stimulus that affects a receiver is a message from the source, regardless of whether the source intended to send it. Hence, if a teacher tells a student that everything appears to be fine while frowning in an expression of deep concern, he or she might be communicating more to the student than was intended, even if the teacher's facial expression has nothing to do with the student.

Remember, each message is unique. Even if the same message were to be created over and over again, it would differ in each instance because messages cannot be repeated or received in exactly the same way or in the same context. To illustrate this, imagine reading the headline "The World Has Been Invaded by Small Green People!" in a comic book and then in your local newspaper. Although the words might be the same, the messages conveyed would be quite different.

Interference

Anything that changes the meaning of an intended message is called **interference.** It is included in our model because it is present, to one degree or another, in every communication environment.

Interference can be external and physical, such as noise caused by the slamming of a door or the blasting of a stereo. Other examples of external interference include an unpleasant environment, such as a smoke-filled room or a room that is too cool or too hot; an odor, such as that of overly strong perfume; or distracting characteristics of the speaker, such as too much makeup, a speech impediment, talk that is too fast or too slow, mumbling pronunciation, or weird clothing.

Interference can also be internal and psychological. For example, thoughts going through a person's mind can interfere with the reception or creation of a message. A person who speaks in a loud voice to get someone's attention may create both physical and psychological interference. If the receiver perceives the loudness as anger, the loud voice creates not only a distraction from attending but also a distortion of interpretation. If the receiver responds accordingly, the sender may be quite surprised. Essentially, interference is anything that reduces or distorts the clarity, accuracy, meaning, understanding, or retention of a message.

Channel

A **channel** is the route by which messages flow between sources and receivers. The usual communication channels are light waves and sound waves, which allow us to see and hear one another. The medium through which the light and sound waves travel, however, may differ. For example, when two people are talking face to face, light and sound waves in the air serve as the channels. If a letter is sent from one person to another, light waves serve as the channel, but the paper and the writing itself serve as the means by which the message is conveyed. Books, films, videotapes, tele-

Making Connections

Recognizing Sources of Interference

In what way could these things interfere with communication?

- Chewing gum while conversing
- A hot, sticky room
- Shyness
- A personal bias
- A foreign accent
- An inappropriate choice of words
- Numerous mispronounced words
- One person checking email
- A speaker with a cold

- A darkened room where you must take notes
- Wearing sunglasses
- The playing of a stereo
- A cold room
- Ethnic background
- Computer beeping to signal new mail
- One person conducting a web search

Write a one- or two-page paper about the responsibilities of communicators to ensure that the meaning of a message is received.

---

vision sets, computers, radios, magazines, newspapers, and pictures are media through which messages may be conveyed.

We also receive communication by smelling, touching, and tasting. We sometimes take these senses for granted, but imagine walking into a bakery and not being able to smell the aroma or taste the flavors. All you have to do is hug someone you care about to recognize how important touch is as a means of communicating. All five senses, therefore, contribute to communication.

Receiver

Both persons function as receivers in the model depicted in Figure 1.4. A **receiver** analyzes and interprets messages, in effect translating them into meaning. This process is called **decoding.** *You are simultaneously a receiver and a source.* As you listen to another person's message, you react with body movements and facial expressions, and the person sending the message receives the information conveyed by your physical reactions. Like the source, a receiver has several roles: to receive (hear, see, touch, smell, or taste) the message; to attend to the message; to interpret and analyze the message; to store and recall the message; and to respond to the source, message, channel, environment, and noise. In addition, Person B also has communication skills, knowledge, attitudes, and a sociocultural background that differ from those of Person A. The greater the differences between Person A and Person B, the more effort Person B must make to be a competent receiver.

Feedback

Another component in the communication process is **feedback,** the response to a message that a receiver sends back to a source. Feedback enables a sender to determine

Making Connections

Feedback in Communication

In class, ask a classmate to listen carefully (not read along) as you read the following story aloud. Use a monotone voice, and do not vary your speaking rate. When you are finished, ask the listener to repeat the story back to you. Then, the two of you should answer the questions following the story.

Homer Garrison, a schoolteacher, unexpectedly inherited $60,000. He decided that he would invest his money in a restaurant.

He spent $18,000 for a down payment on an old house in his hometown of Greenwood. He did not want a showplace, just a nice family-style restaurant. He used the remaining por-

tion of the money to purchase equipment and to convert the house. Soon his restaurant became the talk of the small town.

1. How much detail did the listener remember?
2. Why did the person remember some things and forget others?
3. What could you as a speaker do to help the listener to recall information?
4. What could the listener do to improve his or her memory?

Discuss in class what this exercise taught you about communication and the importance of feedback.

---

whether the communication has been received and understood as intended. To share meaning accurately, the sender must correct faulty messages and misconceptions, repeat missed meanings, and correct responses as necessary.

Feedback is a natural extension of effective receiving. Receivers have the responsibility of attending to, decoding, and determining a message's intended meaning. The next logical step is to provide responses (feedback) that let the sender know that the message was received and understood. It is then up to the sender to decide if the feedback provides enough information to judge whether the receiver accurately interpreted the message. Thus, feedback serves as a kind of control mechanism in the communication process. Unfortunately, we too often fail to monitor our own communication and, more important, others' reactions to it, so that we are not heard or are misunderstood. To imagine the consequences, consider what would happen to the temperature in a room if the heater and the thermostat acted independently of each other.

Feedback is an essential component of the communication process, because it is not only a corrective device but also a means by which we learn about ourselves. It helps us adjust to others and assess ourselves. Giving feedback to others is just as important as receiving it, making the communication truly a shared process.

Feedback offers other advantages. A classic study found that when feedback is increased, reception of information is enhanced.[11] The experiment required four groups of students to construct geometric patterns that were described by a teacher under conditions that differed for each group: (1) zero feedback—the teacher's back was turned to the students, and students were not allowed to ask questions or make noise; (2) visible audience feedback—the students could see the teacher's face but could not ask questions; (3) limited verbal feedback—the students were allowed to ask the teacher questions, but the teacher could respond only with yes or no; (4) free feedback—all channels of communication were open, with no limits placed on the type of questions asked of the teacher or the depth of response the teacher could provide. Students provided with no opportunity to receive feedback from the teacher fared poorly, whereas each increasing level of feedback produced better results. This study resulted in two important findings: (1) as the amount of feedback increases, so does the accuracy of communication and (2) as the amount of feedback increases, so does the recipient's confidence in performance.

Environment

The **environment,** or atmosphere, refers to the psychological and physical surroundings in which communication occurs. The environment encompasses the attitudes, feelings, perceptions, and relationships of the communicators as well as the characteristics of the location in which communication takes place, for example, the size, color, arrangement, decoration, and temperature of the room.

The environment affects the nature and quality of the communication. For example, it is much easier to carry on an intimate conversation in a private, quiet, and comfortable setting than in a public, noisy, and uncomfortable setting. Most of us find it easier to communicate with someone we know than with someone we do not know. Some environments appear to foster communication, whereas others seem to inhibit it. Consider these contrasting environments:

> The room is clean, painted light blue, and has quiet music playing in the background. Two people, seated in soft, comfortable chairs, are facing each other, smiling, and one is gently touching the other. They show genuine concern for each other. Their communication is open and caring.
>
> The room is dirty, painted dark brown, and has loud music playing in the background. Two people, seated ten feet apart on folding chairs, are staring at each other. They show little respect or concern for each other. Their communication is guarded.

How does the appearance of the room ultimately affect the negative communication? Both effective and ineffective communication are, in part, products of their environments. Effective communication can occur anywhere and under most circumstances, but pleasing, comfortable environments (along with open, trusting relationships) are more likely to produce positive exchanges.

Context

The broad circumstances or situation in which communication occurs is called the **context.** Communication does not occur in a vacuum. It takes place in informal and formal settings such as between two friends, among five colleagues in a business meeting, or between a minister and a congregation. The number of people, the type of communication, and the situation in which the communication occurs all lend themselves to the context. Each context affects what we say and how we say it. Contexts also influence environment and vice versa. They also help to determine the type of communication that would be used.

Types of Communication

Type of communication is usually distinguished by the number of people involved, by the purpose of the communication, and by the degree of formality in which it occurs.

Each type of communication involves certain verbal and nonverbal behaviors that are considered appropriate. Four types of communication are discussed in this text: intrapersonal, interpersonal, small group and team, and public. We also refer to elements of mass, or mediated, communication throughout the text.

Intrapersonal Communication

To communicate with others, we must first understand how we communicate with ourselves. This process of understanding information within oneself is called **intrapersonal communication.** As we mature, we learn a lot about ourselves and our surroundings. Much of what we learn is gained from our own experiences. Even though there are many things we are taught by others, there are many things we must learn through our own experiences and can learn no other way. For example, the first time you experience the sensation of warmth coming over your chilled body is a form of intrapersonal communication. If the warmth is coming from a fire, the fire is the source of heat, but that heat is not really known to you until it is felt by your body and is eventually registered in your brain. Your skin senses the heated air and transmits the sensation through your central nervous system to your brain, which records it as warmth. In this sense you are communicating within yourself.

Intrapersonal communication also occurs anytime we evaluate or attempt to understand the interaction that occurs between us and anything that communicates a message to us. We are involved in intrapersonal communication as we receive, attend to, interpret and analyze, store and recall, or respond in some fashion to any message. Thus, communication between two individuals is far more complex than it appears on the surface.

Intrapersonal communication includes diverse internal activities such as thinking, problem solving, conflict resolution, planning, emotion, stress, evaluation, and relationship development. All messages that we create first occur within us. This makes communication a personal event, because we can never divorce ourselves from our interaction with others, no matter how neutral or empathic we may think we are. We say, "I understand your feelings," to someone, but we understand another's feelings only after they are filtered through our own feelings and perceptions. Ultimately, all communication takes place within each of us as we react to communication cues. Intrapersonal communication may occur without the presence of any other type of communication, but all other types of communication cannot occur without it. In fact, intrapersonal communication is occurring almost always, and yet we don't often think about it as a type of communication.

Interpersonal Communication

The informal exchange of information between two or more people is referred to as **interpersonal communication.** It is similar to intrapersonal communication in that it helps us share information, solve problems, resolve conflicts, understand our perception of self and of others, and establish relationships with others. (In Chapters 13 and 14, interpersonal relationships and our relationships with friends and family members are discussed in more detail.)

A subcomponent of interpersonal communication is dyadic communication. **Dyadic communication** is simply defined as an exchange of information between two people. It includes informal conversations, such as talks with a parent, spouse, child, friend, acquaintance, or stranger, as well as more formal conversations, such

Informal exchanges in which two people are involved are referred to as dyadic communication. They include informal conversations, such as talks with a parent, spouse, child, friend, acquaintance, or stranger, as well as more formal conversations, such as interviews.

as interviews. An **interview** is a carefully planned and executed question-and-answer session designed to exchange desired information between two parties. (Chapter 8 and the Appendix discuss, respectively, information and employment interviews.)

Another subcomponent of interpersonal communication is **small-group communication,** which is an exchange of information among a relatively small number of persons, ideally, five to seven, who share a common purpose, such as doing a task, solving a problem, making a decision, or sharing information. (Chapters 15 and 16 discuss the purposes, characteristics, leadership, participation, decision making, problem solving, and evaluation of communication in small groups.)

Public Communication

In **public communication,** a message is transmitted from one person to a number of individuals who listen. The most widely used form of public communication is the public speech. We find ourselves on the listening end of a public speech in lecture classes, political rallies, group meetings, convocations, and religious services.

Although there are many similarities between public speaking and other types of communication, there are also some differences. Public speaking almost always is more highly structured than the other types. It demands, if it is to be done well, much detailed planning and preparation by the speaker. Unlike participants in other types of communication, listeners do not regularly interrupt the speaker with questions or comments. It is the responsibility of the public speaker to anticipate questions that listeners may have and to attempt to answer them.

Public speaking almost always requires a more formal use of language and a more formal delivery style than the other types. The use of jargon, poor grammar, or slang is usually not accepted or tolerated in public speeches. The public speaker must use language precisely and must speak clearly in order to be heard throughout the audience. This may require that the speaker eliminate distracting vocal and physical mannerisms that might be tolerated in other types of communication.

Public speeches are often presented for three purposes: to inform, to persuade, and to entertain. They are also presented to introduce, to pay tribute, and to welcome. (Chapters 7 through 12 consider public speaking in detail.)

Misconceptions About Communication

Several misconceptions keep many of us from examining *our* own communication more closely. Notice the emphasis on *our* own! Most of us who have problems communicating tend to look for the fault in places other than ourselves. Becoming aware that these misconceptions exist and that many people accept them as truths should help us to understand why the study of communication is necessary. Here are some of the most common myths that interfere with people's improving their own communication skills.

Myth 1: Communication Is a Cure-All

The first misconception is the notion that communication has the magical power to solve all of our problems. The act of communicating with others does not carry any guarantees. Obviously, without communication we cannot solve our problems, but sometimes communication can create more problems than it solves.

You can probably provide several personal experiences that prove this point. Let one of us provide one of our own. A friend was writing an important paper for his boss and was struggling to get it right. He asked for my constructive criticism of the paper. I read it, suggested that he needed to clearly present his position at the beginning of the paper, and also that he needed to maintain that focus throughout the paper, because it did not come through clearly. He responded that I had obviously not read the paper carefully and that others had told him that his position was an important one to take. What I thought were simple descriptive statements created a significant problem between us. What could I have done differently to have prevented the problem?

Communication can help to eliminate or reduce our problems, but it is not a panacea. Communicating itself does not make the difference; the message that is communicated does.

Myth 2: Quantity Means Quality

Most of us assume that the more we communicate, the better off we will be. Within limits, people who communicate a great deal are often perceived to be more friendly, competent, and powerful and to have more leadership potential than those who do not. However, quantity of communication is not the same as quality. One of the authors of this text had a discussion with a colleague about the colleague's poor teacher evaluations, and the more we communicated, the more we disagreed with one another and the more negative our discussion became. Hence, as in the case of the first myth, it isn't the act or the amount of communication, but the content of communication that makes the difference.

Myth 3: Meaning Is in the Words We Use

If your sister told you that she doesn't feel well, what would that mean to you? That she is sick? That she has a cold? That she has an upset stomach? That her feelings have been hurt? It could mean any number of things, for, without context and more information, the statement is not all that clear. If she told you that she has a cold and doesn't feel well, is that message clear? Well, at least it would narrow the choices a little. Confusion may arise because the statement "I don't feel well" is relative; that is, it may not mean the same thing to you that it does to her. Some people use the statement to refer to a a minor discomfort, whereas others mean they are more seriously ill. The words themselves could refer to many degrees or types of conditions. Thus, *meanings are in people and not in the words they use.*

The notion that words contain meanings is probably the most serious misconception of all. Words have meaning only when we give them meanings. *No two people share the same meanings for all words, because no two people completely share the same background and experiences.* Thus, the meaning of a word cannot be separated from the person using it.

Myth 4: We Have a Natural Ability to Communicate

Many people believe that because we are born with the physical and mental equipment needed to communicate, communication must be a natural ability. This simply is not true. The ability to communicate, like almost everything we do, is learned. Most of us possess the physical ability to tie our shoes, but we still have to learn how the strings go together. Similarly, most of us are born with the ability to see, but that does not make us able to read. Reading requires knowledge of the alphabet, the acquisition of vocabulary, and practice. The ability to communicate requires not only that we be capable but also that we understand how human communication works and that we have an opportunity to use that knowledge.

Myth 5: Communication Is Reversible

All of us sometimes make a blunder in communication. We may think that we can take something back, but that is impossible. Once something is said, it is out there; the listener will have to deal with that message, and the speaker will have to try to explain and compensate for what was said. For example, in a moment of anger we say something that we regret and later ask the other person to "forget that I even said that." Although the other person may forgive us for speaking in anger, it is not likely that he or she will ever forget what was said. When we communicate through writing, we can take things back until we let someone else see what we've written. When we send oral messages, others can hear and will respond to what we say, even if we don't really mean to say things the way they come out. It is important, therefore, to carefully organize our thoughts and choose our words before we utter them to others. As you study this textbook and the communication process in class, you will learn more about communication competence.

Improving Communication Competence

To be competent communicators, we must understand the role of communication in our lives and be aware of the complexity of the communication process and different types of communication. We also need to realize that myths about communication may hinder our ability to develop effective communication.

This successful career woman, in addition to other qualifications, has developed a broad communication repertoire—a wide range of communication behaviors from which to choose. Competent communicators are able to coordinate several communication tasks simultaneously.

Throughout this chapter we have referred to the concept of communication competence. We discuss it throughout the text, provide examples of such competence, and ask you to evaluate your ability to communicate effectively in a variety of situations. Earlier in the text we described communication competence as the ability to engage in effective communication. Communication competence, however, is another of those concepts that various authors have defined in various ways. One noteworthy definition is provided by Dan O'Hair, Gustav Friedrich, John Wiemann, and Mary Wiemann, who state that "communication competencies are skills and understandings that enable communication partners to exchange messages appropriately and effectively."[12] This chapter has only introduced the types of skills and understandings necessary to successful communication. One such skill is the ability to select and implement the most appropriate communication behavior for a particular situation. Good communicators have developed a broad communication **repertoire,** a range of communication behaviors from which to choose.[13] Another hallmark of communication competence is the ability to evaluate the effectiveness of a given communication after the fact.[14]

Competence is also characterized by the ability to coordinate several communication tasks simultaneously. For example, a competent communicator will, at the same time, choose a way of conveying a message, consider what the receiver's various responses might be, and plan a way to restate the message if the first attempt is not effective.

Consider the last time you asked a question or responded to another student or your professor in a classroom. What did you think about before you raised your hand or before you spoke? How did the reactions of your professor or classmates as you spoke affect the way you presented your ideas? What would you do differently the next time? Reflecting on your answers to these questions can help you find ways to become a better communicator.

Through practice and study you will become comfortable with communicating in a variety of situations. Background knowledge about communication, practical experience, and feedback given in the classroom will help you think on your feet and make better decisions as you communicate. You will also gain confidence and the ability to evaluate your skills as your work in this course progresses.

Summary

The *speech communication* discipline is a humanistic and scientific field of study that focuses on how, why, and with what effect people communicate using spoken language and associated nonverbal messages. Communicating effectively is important in our everyday lives, affecting relationships, the ability to make connections with people from other cultures, and career effectiveness.

Communication is defined as the simultaneous sharing and creating of meaning through *human symbolic action,* a process by which verbal and nonverbal symbols are sent, received, and given meaning. There are eight basic components of communication: source, message, interference, channel, receiver, feedback, environment, and context. Each is integral to effective communication. The *source* (creator of messages) uses *encoding* (the process of changing thoughts or feelings into words that become *messages,* or *stimulus*). The *channel* is the route that allows messages to flow between source and receiver. The *receiver,* after obtaining the message, uses *decoding* (the process of translating the message into thoughts and feelings). The receiver then gives positive or negative *feedback,* indicating his or her reaction to the message. Although it takes time and effort to provide and receive feedback, the result is usually that communication is more effective. The *environment* is the physical and psychological climate in which communication occurs. Communication always takes place in a *context* (circumstances or situation in which communication occurs). *Interference* (anything that changes the meaning of a message) is always present to one degree or another in all communication. In this chapter and throughout the text, the authors suggest that competent communicators need to be aware of *ethics* (an individual's system of moral principles) and *plagiarism* (use of another person's information, language, or ideas without citing the originator and making it appear that the user is the originator). Ethical concerns are increasingly important in today's society and students should reflect on the role of those concerns in their own lives.

Communication is described as a *process,* because it is dynamic and has no specific beginning or end. Communication is a *system* made up of several interdependent components. Communication may be interactional or transactional, intentional or unintentional. *Interaction* is an exchange of communication in which communicators take turns sending and receiving messages (similar to what might be done using email or sending a letter and receiving one back); *transaction* is the simultaneous sending and receiving of messages. *Intentional communication* is purposely sent to a specific receiver, whereas *unintentional communication* is a message that either was not intended to be sent or was not intended for the individual who received it. A message received that is not intended is often sent unconsciously and is usually *nonverbal communication* (information expressed without words).

Three types of communication are discussed in this chapter. *Intrapersonal communication* is the process of understanding oneself. Intrapersonal communication is a prerequisite for all other forms of communication. *Interpersonal communication* is the informal exchange of information between two or more people. This type also includes *dyadic communication, the interview,* and *small-group communication. Public communication* involves the transmission of a message from one person speaking to a number of individuals who listen.

Some common myths keep many of us from examining and improving our own communication. Communication cannot solve all problems, and, when used improperly, it can create more problems than it solves. Merely increasing the quantity of communication cannot improve relationships or situations, and, in fact, it may lead to more confusion and misunderstanding. Problems stem from communicators, not from communication. We tend to believe that we can take back something we regret saying; unfortunately, communication is not reversible. Communication is a tool and, as such, is neither good nor bad; it is how we use communication that makes it either effective or ineffective.

We should strive to increase our *communication competence,* remembering that an effective communicator seeks the most appropriate strategy for each encounter, has a broad *repertoire* of communication behaviors, and is aware that every communication situation is unique and requires a customized approach. By studying and practicing communication, receiving and giving feedback, and taking time to evaluate our communication efforts, we can make great strides toward improving our communication competence.

DISCUSSION STARTERS

1. Why is it so difficult to agree on a single definition of communication?
2. Which current national or international leader do you believe to be the most effective oral communicator? Why?
3. What distinguishes an effective from an ineffective communicator?
4. Why is our society so dependent on communication?
5. Explain how communication can be both a process and a system at the same time.
6. Who is responsible for effective oral communication—the source or the receiver? Why?
7. What would happen to our communication if there were no feedback?
8. Drawing on your own experiences, describe how feedback can be both a motivator and an inhibitor of behavior.
9. In what ways can the environment help and hinder communication?
10. Explain the difference between interaction and transaction. Why do you think communication scholars disagree about these two terms?
11. Why is it helpful to understand that communication is a transaction?
12. What can you do to improve communication with members of another culture?
13. What effect has technology had on communication in your life?
14. How do you think the Internet and email will significantly change the way we communicate? Why?
15. Which misconception about communication do you think can cause us the most difficulty when communicating with others?
16. How do you think computers and the Internet affect you as a student? As a communicator?

ANSWERS AND EXPLANATIONS

Making Connections:
What Is Communication?

1. **F** Communication can help solve our problems, but it is not a cure-all. In fact, sometimes more communication can create more problems than it can solve.
2. **F** Quantity does not equate with quality. Thus it is not the amount of communication but the content that is communicated.
3. **F** Meanings are in people—the words we use are symbols but do not contain meaning until we give them meaning.
4. **F** Many believe that communication is a natural phenomena, because there are some individuals for whom it appears to be so easy. However, like most everything we do, it is learned.
5. **F** Once something is said, it is said and it cannot be taken back. That does not mean that you cannot say you're sorry or make a correction to what you have said. It does, however, mean that no matter what you say, you cannot change the fact that you said it.

NOTES

1. *Encyclopaedia Britannica,* online version, see http://www.britannica.com, 1999–2000, "definition of communication."

2. *Association for Communication Administrators, Communication Careers* (Falls Church, Va.: Association for Communication Administrators, 1981).

3. J. Thurber, "Friends, Romans, Countrymen, Lend Me Your Ear Muffs," in *Lanterns and Lances* (New York: Harper & Row, 1960), 40.

4. *Spanning the Chasm: Corporate and Academic Cooperation to Improve Work-Force Preparation* (Washington, D.C.: American Council on Education, 1997). Also, "Survey by the National Association of Colleges and Employers," in Work Week, *Wall Street Journal,* February 8, 2000; and the 21st Century Workforce Commission Report, June 2000.

5. Personal conversations with business executives, personnel managers, and recruiters, May 2000.

6. Aristotle, *The Rhetoric and Poetics of Aristotle,* trans. W. R. Roberts and I. Bywater (New York: The Modern Library, 1954), 24–25.

7. W. M. Smail, *Quintilian on Education,* Book XII, Chapter 1 (Oxford: Clarendon Press, 1938) 108.

8. U.S. Census Bureau, "Resident Population Estimates of the United States by Sex, Race, and Hispanic Origin: April 1, 1990 to July 1, 1999, with Short-Term Projection to November 1, 2000," http://www.census.gov/population/www/estimates/nation/intfile3-1.txt. Internet release date: January 2, 2001; accessed February 12, 2001.

9. D. K. Berlo, *The Process of Communication* (New York: Holt, Rinehart and Winston, 1960), 23.

10. J. T. Masterson, S. A. Beebe, and N. H. Watson, *Speech Communication Theory and Practice* (New York: Holt, Rinehart and Winston, 1983), 6–7.

11. H. J. Leavitt and R. Mueller, "Some Effects of Feedback on Communication," *Human Relations* 4 (1951): 401–10.

12. D. O'Hair, G. W. Friedrich, J. M. Wiemann, and M. O. Wiemann, *Competent Communication,* 2nd ed. (New York: St. Martin's Press, 1997), 21.

13, B. S. Wood, ed., *Development of Functional Communication Competencies: Grades 7–12* (Urbana, Ill.: ERIC Clearinghouse on Reading and Communication Skills and Speech Communication Association, 1977), 5.

14. Ibid., 5–6.

Connecting Perceptions and Communication

"Resemblances are the shadows of differences. Different people see different similarities and similar differences."

—Vladimir Nabokov

■ Describe the connection between perception and communication competence.

■ Discuss what perception is and how it functions.

■ Explain why perception differs from one person to another.

■ Suggest ways to alter and improve perception as well as communication competence.

SCENARIO

Jason's mother sees him as a warm, tender, loving son. He is the kind of kid, according to his mother, who would do anything to help others. "He's so thoughtful when he comes home and he always has nice things to say to me," says his mother.

Jason's brother sees him as a real competitor, someone that no one is going to push around. "He is tough, ruthless, and unstoppable. He is not going to let anyone get in his way in his quest to be the best. He is determined and will do whatever it takes to get what he wants. He is always putting me down—I can't talk with him about anything, because he's only interested in himself," says his brother.

Jason's girlfriend isn't really sure who is right. "There are times when he is caring and thoughtful, but there are also times when he is abusive, not in a physical way but in his actions and what he says. He is really a contradiction, and you're never sure which Jason will appear. I have to watch what I say to him all the time, because I never know when he is going to get upset," says his girlfriend.

Jason's best friend sees him as a hardworking, dedicated kind of guy, a real team player. The kind of guy you can count on when things are down. "You can talk to Jason and he really listens. He is a great friend. He is always there and is a guy you can really lean on and talk to," says his best friend.

Jason's dad sees him as a guy that has no direction in life. Jason, according to his dad, is always trying to get something for nothing. "He doesn't want to earn anything by doing the work—he thinks everyone owes him something. You can't trust him, because he will stab you in the back the first chance he gets. You can never be sure if he is telling the truth about anything. You can't talk to Jason—he simply won't listen," says his father. ■

These descriptions illustrate five different perceptions of Jason. Which one is correct? Would Jason's perception of himself match any of those described? How would the descriptions influence your impressions of Jason even though you have never met him? There should be no doubt that there is a connection between perception and its influence on our communication. **Perception** is the process of selecting, organizing, and interpreting information in order to give personal meaning to the communication we receive. What we perceive about ourselves, others, objects, and events gives meanings to our experiences, and it is these meanings, based on our perception, that we communicate to others. The meanings we give to our experiences almost always originate in us and do not reflect a totally objective account of the experiences themselves. No two people have internalized identical meanings for the same words, messages, or experiences. Communication is indeed personal! In this chapter we discuss perception and how it is connected to communication. In Chapter 3 we focus on self-concept.

Perception is at the heart of all communication. It can also be argued that without communication, perceptions could not exist. Thus, the statement that communication is at the heart of all perceptions is equally true. Robert L. Scott, a communication scholar, writes, "Nothing is clear in and of itself but in some context for some persons."[1] A difference between two people's perceptions, for example, does not necessarily make the perception of one person more correct or accurate than that of the other. It does, however, mean that communication between individuals who see things differently may require more understanding, negotiation, persuasion, and tolerance of those differences.

Perception, like communication, is a complex phenomenon. It is impossible to form perceptions without communication and vice versa. Because perception is a part of everything we do, it is very easy to dismiss it as unimportant—after all, it is something that happens automatically, and it seems as if we have little control over it. However, as stated earlier, perception is an integral part of our communication. Perception does influence our reactions as indicated in the opening scenario where each description of Jason would influence our communication and behavior toward him. We also know that perceptions are relative. There is no way to view people, situations, events, or objects objectively. For example, when someone says to another person, "I understand your feelings," the statement is based on perceptions of those feelings—not an identical experiencing of them. It is virtually impossible for one person to actually feel what another person feels; we perceive those feelings based on communication. Thus, it is extremely important to understand how perception influences our communication.

The 2000 presidential election demonstrations illustrated a controversial issue in which perception was at the heart of communication. When different people view the outcome of a situation in different ways, such as in this election, we need to stress understanding, negotiation, persuasion, and tolerance of our differences.

Understanding Perception

Perception as defined previously involves selecting, organizing, and interpreting, which are related to our cognitive abilities and how we internalize and process information. Perceiving in and of itself sounds and appears simple enough. After all, we do it every day, and it seems so natural that we hardly give our perceptions a thought. We just do it, think little about it, and move on. But perception is a very complex process that, if not understood, could lead to a variety of problems, some of which could be quite costly. In order to perceive our surroundings, we must first be aware of them. Second, we must process them cognitively, and then, finally, we must classify them via our use of language.

Awareness

Imagine walking into the student union on your campus for the first time. What do you notice? More than likely your senses are fully engaged and you observe people moving in all directions. You see the food courts, the ATM, the beautiful carvings in the entrance, the signs that lead to various sections of the building, the bookstore, and so on. Being aware of your surroundings and taking in the sights, sounds, smells, and so on is basically paying attention to what's going on, absorbing each detail as if it were something at which to marvel. It is especially true when the situation is new or novel. However, we are creatures of habit, and when others behave in routine ways or when something is very predictable, we are more likely to gloss over the details of the other person or situation and become unaware or mindless.

Cognitive Process

Our cognitive processes have a profound effect on how we perceive others, how we talk with them, and how they respond to us. The way we process our experiences and the type of knowledge schemata that we use to organize and interpret those experiences differ for each of us. The level of our **cognitive complexity** is measured by the number of mental structures we use, how abstract they are, and how elaborately they interact to shape perceptions. For example, most children have simple cognitive systems in which to classify what they experience. When children see another person, they are likely to focus on concrete aspects, such as a person's height (tall or short), attractiveness (pretty or not pretty), or race (the same or different), rather than on abstract psychological aspects, such as sincerity, honesty, and so on. In addition, children often do not perceive relationships among multiple perceptions, such as how sincerity may relate to honesty or vice versa. For example, if a child sees an animal with four legs for the first time and is told that it is a dog (doggie), because of the child's low level of cognitive complexity, he or she will call every animal with four legs a dog (doggie) until taught otherwise. Young children cannot cognitively distinguish among four-legged animals until they are taught to make those distinctions.

Of course, as we mature and become adults, we learn to distinguish between and among different experiences, all of which help to develop our cognitive abilities. The more cognitively complex we are, the more sophisticated our level of perception. You might notice that a person talks a lot, dresses well, tells good jokes, and is attractive in appearance. At an abstract, psychological level you might infer that the behaviors you observe reflect an extroverted, sincere, secure, and self-confident personality. This level of assessment is a sophisticated explanation, because it involves perceptions of why the person acts as he or she does, and it is not based solely on concrete observations.

People who have high levels of cognitive complexity are likely to be flexible in interpreting complicated events and situations and are able to integrate new information into their perceptions. Also, people who are cognitively complex are likely to use "person-centered" messages when communicating with others. These individuals are likely to take multiple considerations into their perspective when communicating with others. For example, those with high degrees of cognitive complexity are able to take into account others' values, beliefs, and emotional needs and incorporate them into their messages. Being able to do this allows those with high levels of cognitive complexity to be effective communicators, because they are able to understand and process multiple perspectives at one time. Individuals who have less complex cognitive abilities, however, are unable to process multiple perspectives and, thus, often ignore information that does not fit their past experiences. They may even throw out their old perceptions completely and replace them with new ones.

Language

How language affects our thoughts and how it influences our ability to think about the world are considered in Chapter 4. The opening scenario of this chapter illustrates that what people say and how they say it can influence our perception of others. For example, the language used by those describing Jason depicts extremely different ideas about who Jason is and what he is like. You may wonder if those describing him are actually referring to the same person. Whose description is the correct one? Is there a correct description? How would each description affect your perception of him? How would the language used to describe Jason affect your communication with him?

It is the words used to describe Jason that create your perception of him and the image you have of him. The image you form of Jason, however, depends on whose description you hear, their credibility, their ability to communicate their perceptions of him to you, and the image you form based on your understanding of the language they used to describe him. Thus, your image of Jason is created through words and not through any action or behavior of Jason's.

Perceptions do change; it is not unusual for the initial impressions we form about someone to change or become disconfirmed after subsequent interactions. We often set expectations for what we think someone is like based on what we have heard or observed, but after time and additional interaction, we either find our initial perceptions to be true or we change them. Let's assume you recently visited Jason's girlfriend and she told you how much she loved Jason, but that he was difficult to understand. You then met a friend of Jason's girlfriend who informed you that he was abusive to her. How would that information affect your perceptions of Jason, and, more important, how would it influence your communication should you encounter him in person? In order to answer these questions, we need to know how the perception process works and how it influences everything we do.

The Perception Process

Our lack of awareness of how perception operates can lead us to misunderstand and misjudge others' ideas and behavior. Many people imagine the brain to be similar in operation to a camera or tape recorder; information enters through the eyes or ears and is stored in the brain. Actually, far too much information exists for the brain to absorb at once, so the brain ignores much of it. It accepts a certain amount of information and organizes it into meaningful patterns. It discards a tremendous amount of information. Much of what we know about the way we perceive events, objects, and people seems to involve how we select, organize, and interpret information. All of these connections happen in milliseconds.

Selection

Because it is impossible to attend to, sense, perceive, retain, and give meaning to every stimulus we encounter, we narrow our focus. A **stimulus** incites or quickens action, feeling, or thought. Although we are exposed to millions of bits of stimuli, or data, at one time, the mind can process only a small fraction of them. On both the unconscious level of the nervous system and the conscious level of directing attention, **selection** occurs as the brain sorts one stimulus from another, based on criteria formed by our previous experiences. There are three kinds of selection: selective exposure, selective attention, and selective retention.

Selective Exposure.   The deliberate choices we make to experience or to avoid experiencing particular stimuli are referred to as **selective exposure.** For example, you may dislike violent and sexist lyrics in the music you listen to, so you avoid purchasing tapes by certain individuals or groups known for such lyrics. When we choose to communicate with certain individuals instead of others, we are also using selective exposure.

Selective Attention.   Focusing on specific stimuli while ignoring or downplaying other stimuli is called **selective attention.** That is, you concentrate on the data you wish to attend to, in order to eliminate or reduce the effects of all extraneous stimuli. This task is often easier said than done. Paying attention to something usually requires decisive effort, but even the best attempts to concentrate may be interrupted by distractions. For example, a book dropped in a quiet classroom, a loud sneeze, background talking, a siren, a baby's cry, a call for help, an odor, or a movement can avert our attention from the task in which we are involved. Continuing to attend to the original task may require extra effort. Similarly, when we converse with someone in a crowded lounge with loud music playing in the background, we focus on each other's words more attentively and ignore the other sounds. This blocking out of all extraneous stimuli to concentrate on the other person is an instance of selective attention. To make sense out of the multitude of stimuli that surrounds us, we learn to focus our senses on a few stimuli at a time.

Selective Retention.   Because we cannot possibly remember all the stimuli we encounter, we also select the information we will retain. **Selective retention** occurs when we process, store, and retrieve information that we have already selected, organized, and interpreted. We are more likely to remember information that agrees with our views and to selectively forget information that does not. Also, after perceiving and selecting certain stimuli, we may retain only a portion of them. For example, how many times have you listened to someone tell you how to do something, and later, after thinking that you had completed the task, found that you had done only a portion of it? Chances are that you retained the pleasant parts of the task and forgot the not-so-pleasant parts. Selection plays an important role in what, why, and how we communicate.

Making Connections

Overreacting or Seeing Things as They Really Are?

Vershawn [walks out of his psychology class after the first day with fear showing on his face]: Man, I'm dropping psychology. It's too hard; the prof's a geek, and she thinks I am a screw off.

Maria: You said that about the last psychology class, and you aced it. Besides, I think the prof is cool. You *can't* drop it. It's a requirement and it's not going to be that hard. Besides, the prof doesn't even know you yet. So hang in there.

Vershawn: I don't know. It's the way she looks at me and she knows that I am a jock. It's pretty clear she doesn't like jocks.

Maria: She never said anything about sports or jocks. What makes you think she's going to give you a hard time?

Vershawn: It's the way she talks and looks at me—as if I am nothing.

This type of exchange is not uncommon, because it is the perception of what is said as well as how it is said that leads us to either similar or different interpretations about people, events, and objects.

1. Why is the perception of what happened to Vershawn seen differently from Maria's viewpoint?
2. Which interpretation is correct, Maria's or Vershawn's?
3. Why doesn't Maria's perception of the classroom interaction agree with Vershawn's?
4. What role, if any, might cultural, gender, or age difference play in the differing interpretations of what happened?
5. Are any ethical concerns involved in evaluating whose perception is more accurate?

Organization

We categorize stimuli in our environment in order to make sense of them. This **organization** of data plays an important role in how we perceive and communicate about events, objects, and people.

Figure and Ground Organization.   Probably the most common way to organize stimuli is to distinguish between figure and ground. **Figure and ground organization** is the ordering of perceptions so that some stimuli are in focus and others recede into the background. Examine Figure 2.1. What do you see? It may not be immediately apparent, but Figure 2.1 is a map. When we look at a map, we usually expect the water area to form the background for the land. However, many nautical maps do just the opposite. In Figure 2.1 the black area (the figure) represents water—the Mediterranean Sea. The boot shape is Italy. Once we have associated what we see with something familiar, it is difficult to shift figure and ground to perceive something else. Our first perception of the illustration will not usually persist after we recognize the Mediterranean Sea.

This example of figure and ground organization illustrates how our perceptions influence what we hear and what we communicate. For example, a student who was unhappy about a grade on an assignment asked how to earn a higher grade. The professor

FIGURE 2.1

Figure and Ground: Water or Land?

Once we recognize that the white portion represents the land (or figure) and the dark represents the water (or ground), the figure becomes dominant. Thus, our understanding of what is represented in the figure helps us to organize our perception of it. How is communication influenced by how we organize our perceptions and views of events?

J. R. Block and H. E. Yuker, *Can You Believe Your Eyes?* New York: Brunner/Mazel, 1989. Reprinted by permission.

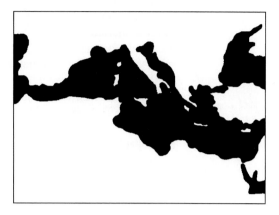

began to discuss ways for the student to improve work on the next assignment. The student, however, didn't really want to talk about improvement, but simply wanted a higher grade on the assignment at hand. For the student, the grade was the figure and improvement was the ground. For the instructor, improvement on the next assignment was the figure and the grade was the ground. The communication message was influenced by how each person organized thoughts regarding how to improve the grade.

Closure.   Another way to organize the stimuli around us is through **closure.** We tend to fill in missing pieces and to extend lines in order to finish or complete figures. This completion process is called closure. In Figure 2.2 we see a figure—a tree—that doesn't really exist in the printed material. This occurs because we are always trying to make meaningless material meaningful. We perceive the image of the tree by mentally connecting the white spaces. Interestingly, such illusory figures often seem to stand out in front of the disconnected shapes that suggest them, thus appearing to be closer to the viewer than the paper on which they are printed.

Filling in the blank spaces or missing information helps us categorize, label, and make sense of the things we see and hear. We sometimes do the same thing as we try

FIGURE 2.2

Closure: Tree or Incomplete Circles?

The partial outlines of this shape lead us to fill in the missing lines so that we can make sense of it. This organizing of the visual data allows us to give meaning to the drawing.

J. R. Block and H. E. Yuker, *Can You Believe Your Eyes?* New York: Brunner/Mazel, 1989. Reprinted by permission.

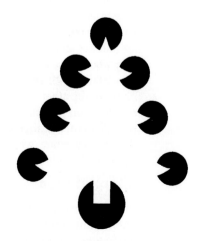

to understand people. For example, if we don't know someone or the person is from a different ethnic or cultural background, we sometimes fill in unknown information in order to make sense of the person. Unfortunately, what we fill in may be based on biases and ignorance. When supplying missing information, we must remain aware of what we are doing and remember to distinguish between what we know and what we don't. Otherwise we increase our chances of forming a wrong or at least inaccurate perception of who the person really is. Our inaccurate perceptions about others can adversely affect communication, and that can be costly.

Proximity and Similarity. Two additional concepts involved in organizing stimuli are proximity and similarity. **Proximity** is the grouping of two or more stimuli that are close to one another, based on the assumption that because objects or people appear together, they are basically the same. This, of course, is not always true. For example, people who live close to each other do not necessarily behave in the same way, and for us to assume that they do would be inaccurate.

Organization based on **similarity** involves the grouping of stimuli that resemble one another in size, shape, color, or other traits. For example, Shelly, who likes baseball, might believe that others who enjoy baseball resemble her in other ways as well. Thus, if Shelly likes both baseball and opera, she might assume that others who like baseball will also like opera. Of course, this may be wishful thinking on her part, but just because two people are similar in one attribute doesn't automatically mean they will be similar in another. We sometimes make perceptual assumptions, such as Shelly's, when we see people from different cultures. We tend to assume that because people are similar in appearance, they must behave similarly as well.

How Organization Works. To help you understand how we organize stimuli and its effect on communication, consider what happens when you enter a room filled with people. When you first walk in, you begin to sort and organize people into groups or categories. Chances are you will first begin to look for people whom you know; by doing so you are categorizing the people in the room according to those you know (figure) and those you don't know (ground). People whom you know and who happen to be nearest to you (proximity) are those whom you will likely visit first. It is also likely that you will spend more time with those whom you perceive to be like you (similarity) than those who are not.

In the crowd, a woman spots a man she has been interested in but whom she has met only briefly at another gathering. As she moves through the crowd toward him, another woman moves next to the man and places her arm around him. He also places his arm around her, and they engage in what seems to be intimate conversation (closure). The first woman quickly moves back into the crowd so as not to be noticed by him and begins talking with another friend, but her mind is still concentrating on the image of the man and the other woman. Her thoughts of him drift off as she tries to involve herself in conversation with her friend. From this example, it is clear that the way we organize the stimuli around us affects our choices concerning with whom we communicate, what we communicate, how we communicate, and why we communicate with others.

Interpretation

Interpretation of what we see and hear is an integral part of how our perceptions influence our communication. **Interpretation** is the assigning of meaning to stimuli. We use our experiences, both past and present, as well as the opinions of others to aid us in interpreting the meaning of stimuli.

Making Connections

The Internet and Perception

Open your college or university's home page and randomly select three or four department home pages. Briefly examine the department websites by opening at least several of their links, for example, faculty, majors, course offerings, and so on. Answer the following questions:

1. What impressions did you form about the department based on what you saw on its home page?
2. Does the department's website give you the perception that it is friendly or unfriendly? Organized or unorganized? High or low quality? Professional or unprofessional? Personal or impersonal?

3. Based on your impressions (regardless of your major), would you want to visit the department to learn more about it? Why or why not?
4. If you met the department chair after seeing the website, would your interaction with him or her be affected? If so, how?
5. How does the appearance of the website influence your perceptions?
6. What did you learn about perception and communication from this Making Connections exercise?

Interpretation Based on Past Experience.   Our interpretations of stimuli depend on our past experiences. The more familiar you are with objects, events, and people, the less ambiguous your interpretations of them will be. For example, when you first arrived on campus, you probably either asked for help or consulted a map in order to locate various buildings and classrooms. Your perception of the campus layout was a bit unclear. With each passing day, however, you probably found it much easier to get around and probably even discovered shortcuts from one place to another. In similar ways, all of our experiences provide contexts that help us make sense of the world around us.

Figure 2.3 demonstrates the connection between communication and perception. The figure also illustrates how our perceptions guide our interpretations of what we believe to be reality and how we communicate that reality. Look at part (a), and describe what you see. Do you see a person? If so, of what sex is the person? How old is the person? What is the person wearing? How easy would it be to communicate with the person you see? Did you see a young woman in the picture? An old woman? Or both? If you saw only one woman, look again until you see both the young woman (b) and the old woman (c) in part (a).

Although part (a) is designed to create an illusion, it does point out how easy it is for us to misinterpret what we see and to assume that we see the full picture. If you were shown only part (b) or only part (c) before you saw part (a), you would probably see the image you were first exposed to as you looked at ambiguous part (a). Try a little experiment by showing some of your friends part (b) first and some of your friends part (c) first. Then ask them to look at part (a). Do they see only the image to which they were first exposed? Tell them there is a second image and what it is. Can they find the second image? What does this tell you about how perception is connected to communication?

FIGURE 2.3

Interpreting Perception: Young Woman or Old Woman?

There is a distinct relationship between our perceptions and communication. This figure points out the importance of validating our perceptions and the experiences in which our perceptions are based before we communicate them to someone else. There may be more than one way to look at something and, thus, more than one interpretation of it.

(a)   (b)   (c)

Interpretation Based on New Situations.   Good communicators understand that others may not always agree with their view. They know that almost every issue has many sides and that if they don't want to be misunderstood, they must be careful to examine an issue from as many angles as possible before they try to pass on their views about it to others. They also know that jumping to conclusions can be a useless exercise, especially if those conclusions are not based on fact.

Although past experiences become a basis for our interpretations of stimuli, we must be careful not to let these experiences keep us from finding fresh meanings in new situations or events. For example, having an experience with an incompatible roommate does not automatically mean that your next roommate experience will be the same. Sometimes past experiences can act as blinders and thus produce inaccurate perceptions.

Each of us perceives the world through our own set of lenses or filters. We can never see precisely the same river, tree, mountain, person, or event, or hear the same message in exactly the same way that others do. We are different from one another.

Making Connections

Is This a Snow Job?

The anecdote in the text about the snowstorm in Washington, D.C., leads us to ask the following questions:

1. Which headline would you choose to communicate to your friends in different parts of the country? Why?
2. What can we do to ensure that the perceptions of others that are communicated to us represent what really happened?
3. What are some ethical concerns for newspaper editors to consider as they report such news? Explain.

Often people think that information by itself constitutes communication. It is not unusual to hear people say, "The truth doesn't lie," "Seeing is believing," or "The facts speak for themselves." This approach to communication is unfounded. Any information, regardless of the form in which it is received, must always be interpreted to be meaningful. Because interpretation is based on the experiences of the person who is receiving the information, often different people who receive exactly the same information will disagree about what it means, what it entails, or what conclusions can be drawn from it.

Each of us perceives the world through our own set of "lenses" or "filters." We can never see precisely the same river, tree, mountain, person, or event or hear the same message in exactly the same way that others do. We are different from one another. The scenario at the beginning of this chapter illustrates this quite clearly. One interpretation about Jason is not necessarily more accurate than another, but it is important to recognize the differences and how these differences affect communication.

Interpretations Based on Others' Opinions.   Our perceptions are often altered or influenced by how and what others communicate to us. Much of what we learn about our world comes from magazines, newspapers, and television. Through these media many of our perceptions of reality are formed. Often the world we know is shaped and created for us by the perceptions others have formed about the world.

A few years ago Washington, D.C., had several major snowstorms. One day the headlines in two different newspapers read "Blizzard Paralyzes Capital" and "Snow Gives 300,000 Day Off in D.C." Both headlines were factually correct, but as you can see, they gave quite different interpretations of the same event. If you read the first headline, you would get one impression of the storm; if you read the second, you would get an entirely different message. Thus, the perceptions and experiences of the authors of the headlines would shape your understanding of the snowstorm's effects on the city.

Perceptual Differences

Because communication takes place within each of us and because each of us is different, our perceptions of incoming messages may differ from what others perceive. Sometimes those differences are small and have no appreciable effect on the meaning of a specific message. In some situations, however, the differences between individuals and the circumstances in which they receive a message can actually reverse the communication's intended meaning or seriously distort it.

Our past experiences, our physical makeup, our cultural background, and our current psychological state determine what we perceive; how we interpret, evaluate, and organize our perceptions; and what actions we might take in response to them. The following sections discuss how our perceptions are influenced by these factors.

Perceptual Set

When we ignore new information and instead rely on past experiences—fixed, previously determined views of events, objects, and people—to interpret information, we are using a **perceptual set.**[2] A perceptual set allows our past experiences to control or focus our perceptions so that we ignore information that is different or has changed about an event, object, or person. It is a form of stereotyping. **Stereotyping** refers to the categorizing of events, objects, and people without regard to unique individual characteristics and qualities. Stereotyping, for example, exists in nearly every intercultural situation. Stereotyping is pervasive because of the human psychological need to categorize and classify information. Through stereotyping we pigeonhole people. This tendency may hamper our communication, because it may cause us to overlook individual characteristics. Also, stereotypes often oversimplify, overgeneralize, or exaggerate traits or qualities and, thus, are based on half-truths, distortions, and false premises—hardly fertile ground for successful communication. Finally, stereotypes repeat and reinforce beliefs until they come to be taken as the truth. Stereotypes ultimately perpetuate inaccuracies about people and, thus, impede communication. Although many stereotypes are negative, there are positive stereotypes as well. For example, to stereotype men as decisive or women as sensitive projects positive images that should be equally applicable to both genders.

Perceptual sets and stereotypes both involve selective attention and selective retention. The difference between a stereotype and a perceptual set is that a stereotype uses categories and perceptual set does not. To illustrate perceptual set, quickly read the statements inside the triangles in Figure 2.4. Look again. Did you notice two *as* and two *the*s in the statements the first time you read them? If you didn't, you are not alone. Most people don't notice these extra words for several reasons: (1) the statements are familiar and common, (2) most of us have learned to read groups of words rather than each individual word, (3) the words are placed in an unusual setting and in an unusual arrangement, and (4) we have been conditioned to ignore certain types of errors to achieve speed and efficiency in processing information. But perceptual set can interfere with communication. For example, some parents communicate with their offspring as if they were still children, even though they are adults. Their perceptual set may be the belief that "they are our children, and they will always be our children." Therefore, the parents are unwilling to communicate with them as adults.

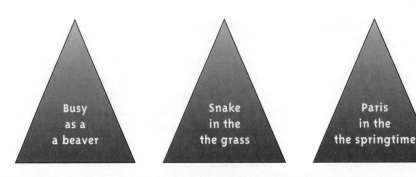

FIGURE 2.4

Perceptual Set

Sometimes we see only what we want to see. Once we are familiar with something, we tend not to look closely to see if it differs from our expectations. How does this figure reveal how perceptual set affects us?

Busy
as a
a beaver

Snake
in the
the grass

Paris
in the
the springtime

Making Connections

It Just Doesn't Add Up, or Does It?

Use a sheet of paper to cover the numbers listed below. Move the paper slowly downward to reveal one number at a time, and add the numbers aloud as they appear, for example, "one thousand, two thousand, two thousand twenty," and so on.

> 1,000
> 1,000
> 20
> 1,000
> 40
> 1,000
> 30
> 1,000
> 10

What did you get for a total? 6,000? 6,100? 5,010? 6,010? If you did, you are wrong! The correct answer and explanation can be found on page 57. If you did select one of the above answers, why do you think this happened? What can this exercise tell us about how we communicate with others?

J. Wenburg and W. Wilmot, *The Personal Communication Process* (New York: Wiley, 1973), 115. The "counting game" was adapted by Wenburg and Wilmot from an exercise used in AIDS Communication Seminars, Michigan State University.

Perceptual set may prevent us from seeing things that differ from what we expect to see and from noticing changes in things. Massimo Piattelli-Palmarini, in his book *Inevitable Illusions: How Mistakes of Reason Rule Our Minds,* uses the example of the St. Louis arch to illustrate the point that "the eye sees what it sees, even when we know what we know."[3] He points out that the arch is as wide as it is tall, yet it appears to be taller than it is wide. According to Piattelli-Palmarini, this inability to see the similarity between the arch's height and width demonstrates that our minds are unable to adjust their perceptions even when we know the facts. He says these errors, or cognitive illusions, occur without our being aware of them. Perceptual sets operate in a similar manner. Differences between what we do, what happens to us, and what is innate within us create bias, something that all of us have.[4] Our brain's ability to process information, therefore, is based on our experiences. Thus, we should always make sure, or at least try to make sure, that what we see or hear or both see and hear represents reality rather than assumptions that may be false. A nineteenth-century humorist, Artemus Ward put it: "It ain't the things we don't know that hurt us. It's the things we do know that ain't so." We are all at times victims of unconsciously making fallacious assumptions that can insidiously affect our encoding and decoding of messages.

Perceptual sets, like stereotypes, do not always limit or hinder us. Sometimes they help us to make decisions more efficiently. We could not make sense of the world without perceptual sets. They provide us with expectations of how things, events, or people should be, and they enable us to compare our expectations with the reality of the moment and to respond accordingly. The key is to avoid the assumption that perceptual sets will always be accurate. Many communication scholars believe that *the greatest single problem with human communication is the assumption that our perceptions are always correct.*[5] The fact is, people do not always act in prescribed ways in similar situations. Thus, it is necessary for us to adapt to each individual circumstance.

Making Connections

The Opposite Sex and Shyness

An attractive young man, age seventeen, came to the attention of a certain clinic as a voluntary case. For several years his parents had been concerned over the abnormal shyness that he exhibited in the presence of young women or girls. In the presence of members of the opposite sex he would blush violently and lapse into a nervous silence after a few stammered remarks. His behavior was arrogant when he was with guys his own age and at least confident in the presence of adult men.

The medical findings were negative. . . . The social investigation revealed nothing in the home environment at the moment that would seem to be responsible for his mental condition. But social investigation did yield the significant fact that his shyness had developed quite suddenly three years before. The parents had no explanation to offer as to the possible cause of the condition.

The psychologist talked with the boy in a friendly and informal manner. In the course of the conversation it was observed that, although he discussed sports and school activities quite freely, he would invariably become emotional when the subject of girls was mentioned. . . .

Little by little the following story unraveled: Three years before, at a children's party, the boy had been playing with some girls. In some manner he caught his fingers in a door when it was slammed shut. This caused the child such extreme pain that he became ill and vomited. The incident was quickly forgotten by everybody but the little boy himself, to whom it remained a crushing misfortune. Although he tried not to think of it, the bitter memory was always there to be reinstated by the presence of girls!

This case clearly points out how events of the past influence perceptions and how those perceptions can be transferred to future communication with others.

1. What advice would you give the young man?
2. Describe some perceptual sets that have affected you recently.
3. How might you train yourself to avoid using perceptual sets inappropriately?

Adapted from F. L. Ruch, *Psychology and Life,* 3rd ed. (Chicago: Scott, Foresman, 1948), quoted in W. V. Haney, *Communication and Organizational Behavior: Text and Cases,* 3rd ed. (Homewood, Ill.: Irwin, 1973), 392.

Attribution Error

It is human nature to attribute, or assign, causes to people's behavior. **Attribution** is the complex process through which we attempt to understand the reasons behind others' behaviors. There are two sets of reasons that allow us to assign attributions about our own and others' behavior: the *situation* (environment) and the *disposition* (traits of the person). We are always trying to explain why people behave the way they do, and in order to do this, we must make assumptions. For example, imagine that you witness the following scene. A man arrives at a meeting one hour late. On entering, he drops his notes on the floor. While he is trying to pick them up, his glasses fall out of his coat pocket and break. Later, he spills coffee all over his tie. How would you explain these events? The chances are good that you would reach conclusions such as "This person is disorganized and clumsy." Are such attributions accurate? Perhaps. But it is also possible that the man was late because of unavoidable delays at the airport, dropped his notes because the paper was slick, and spilled his coffee because the cup was too hot to hold. Research shows that we are more likely to overestimate dispositional causes and underestimate situational causes of others' actions. This bias is referred to as the fundamental attribution error.[6] **Attribution error** occurs when we perceive others as acting as they do because they are "that kind of person" rather than because of any external factors that may have influenced their behavior.

Suppose, as actually happened during 1997 and 1998, a woman accuses the president of the United States of sexual harassment—for example, of making unwanted sexual advances to her. Why would she do this? One possible reason is that she was very upset at the time and believed it was her duty to call this inappropriate (and illegal) behavior by the president to public attention. But now suppose that soon after she made her claim, a reporter discovers that the woman had an affair with the president and was upset about being dumped by him. So another possible explanation for her action is revenge—perhaps she wanted retribution for what she perceived as mistreatment. After learning of this second potential cause, how would you view the first cause (her desire to do her duty and warn other women)? The chances are good that you will view it as a less likely or less important cause. Our tendency is to attribute dispositional causes to others' behaviors (she did it for revenge) and to attribute situational causes to our own behavior (I did it because I wanted to warn other women).

Now, in contrast, imagine the same situation involving the president with one difference—the woman makes her claim of sexual harassment even though she strongly supported the president and worked vigorously for his election in the past. What will you conclude about her claim now? You will probably believe that it is true and that it is motivated by the woman's desire to warn the public about the president's behavior. The difference in our perception of the woman depends on what we already know about the woman and to what we attribute to her behavior.

Physical Characteristics

A person's weight, height, body shape, health, strength, and ability to use his or her five senses account for the way he or she takes in perceptual differences. For example, a person who is visually impaired experiences the world in ways that a sighted person finds difficult to comprehend or even imagine. Sighted people may not automatically take such differences into account, thus making communication more difficult.

Short persons and tall persons sometimes perceive events differently. Consider this situation. Two young boys were walking to a neighborhood store when two older boys threatened them with a knife and demanded their money. Afterward, the police asked the victims to describe their assailants. One boy gave the robbers' heights as about five feet six inches and five feet ten inches and estimated their ages to be about sixteen and twenty. The other boy described them as about five feet ten inches and six feet two inches and guessed their ages to be about twenty and twenty-seven. The first boy

The age and physical height differences between the son and the father clearly affect their perception of the snow depth. However, the father has not taken this difference into account in his communication.

Reprinted by permission of Jerry Marcus.

was six years old and five feet tall; the other was nine years old and just over four feet tall. Of course, the smaller boy perceived the robbers as much taller and older.[7]

The cartoon on page 47 depicts much the same situation. Whose perception is right? A similar situation has probably happened to each of us. Our perceptions usually change with experience; it is difficult to see a situation through someone else's eyes, even if we were once in the very same position. Our experiences can help us solve problems or see things more clearly, but they can also limit our view of events and people, hinder us in solving problems, and create barriers to effective communication.

Psychological State

Another factor that can influence or alter our perceptions of people, events, and things is our state of mind. All information that we receive goes through various filters and screens that sort and color what we receive and how we perceive it. Obviously, when everything is going well and we are in a positive frame of mind, we view things, events, and people much more positively than when our mind-set is negative. When we are under a great deal of stress or if we have a poor self-image, these conditions will influence how we perceive the world around us. Sometimes this distortion is small and temporary and has no appreciable effect on communication. At other times, our state of mind can actually reverse meaning or alter a message, changing how we select, organize, and interpret it. It is undeniable that psychological disposition can color or alter perceptions and, ultimately, communication. Think about how you feel when you are upset, angry, or frustrated with someone or something and when you are not. How does your disposition affect your perception of that person or event? Our perceptions depend on our state of mind and how we see ourselves. In the next chapter the connections between self-concept and perception are discussed in more detail.

Cultural Background

Cultural background can also affect the way in which people perceive other people, events, and things. To many people, culture can be explained as a status issue concerning manners, music, art, and types of food. Some historians, sociologists, archaeologists, and anthropologists use the term *culture* to describe particular early civilizations characterized by certain artifacts or practices. There are many different definitions of culture. Researchers Larry A. Samovar, Richard E. Porter, and Lisa A. Stefani define **culture** as "the deposit of knowledge, experience, beliefs, values, actions, attitudes, meanings, hierarchies, religion, notions of time, roles, spatial relations, concepts of the universe, and artifacts acquired

Making Connections

What Does This Mean to You?

Think about the two examples of interpretation that are described in the text: Two boys are accosted on their way to a neighborhood store and give contrasting descriptions of the assailants. A father and son depicted in the cartoon perceive the same physical conditions, the deep snow, in very different ways.

Now identify a set of physical characteristics in your own life that might be interpreted differently by you than by someone else.

1. How likely are your different interpretations of the same physical characteristics to influence your interaction with others?
2. Are some of the characteristics that you identified more likely to influence men's communication than women's, or vice versa? Why do you think so?
3. Ask students in your class who come from various cultural backgrounds to discuss their responses to questions 1 and 2. What were the differences, if any? Why are there differences?

Making Connections

Perceptions of Groups

Consider the following groups: Korean Americans, homosexuals, Jews, Cuban Americans, African Americans, homeless people. Suppose you were asked to list the traits most characteristic of each. Would you find this a difficult task? Probably not. You would probably be able to construct a list for each group; and, moreover, you could probably do so even for groups with whom you have had limited or no personal contact.

1. Why?
2. How do the characteristics you listed affect your perceptions?
3. In what ways would the list you constructed influence how you communicated about individuals in these groups?
4. In what ways would the list you constructed influence your communication with individuals from these groups?

by a group of people in the course of generations through individual and group striving."[8] How do you think we learn about our culture? N. L. Gage and David C. Berliner, two educational psychologists, suggest that differences that characterize individuals (such as intelligence, cognitive development, personality, and sex roles) are defined in the context of culture. Culture, according to Gage and Berliner, is powerful because it influences all of us in ways that we are often unaware of.[9]

Culture is an integral part of each of us and determines many of our individual characteristics. Culture identifies us as members of a particular group and shapes our values and biases. Much cultural influence occurs without our realizing it; typically, we are not conscious of the fact that much of our behavior is conditioned by our culture. The way we greet others, the way we use language, our opinions about what and when to eat, and many of our personal preferences are all culturally conditioned.[10]

The connection between culture and communication is crucial to understanding communication. In fact, it is through the influence of culture that we learn to communicate at all according to Richard Porter and Larry Samovar, two intercultural communication scholars. For example, a Korean, an Egyptian, or an American learns to communicate like other Koreans, Egyptians, or Americans. Each knows that certain behaviors convey certain meanings, because they are learned and shared in their respective cultures.[11] Just as they behave in a certain way, people also perceive and organize their thoughts, observations, and values according to the dictates of their culture. For example, in a purely scientific sense, the moon is a rocky sphere; yet when they look at the moon, many Americans see the "man in the moon." Some Native Americans view this same image as a rabbit, the Chinese interpret it as a lady fleeing her husband, and Samoans see in it the shape of a woman weaving.[12] These particular differences may not seem significant, but they point to the way that people from different cultures may view the same phenomenon quite differently. When cultural differences are apparent, it requires sensitivity, patience, and tolerance in order to avoid or reduce misunderstandings that can create barriers to effective communication and to relationship development.

Effective communication between people of diverse backgrounds can be limited or impossible if either party is unwilling to recognize that there is more than one correct viewpoint. Those who understand that they hold only one of many possible views are more likely to be tolerant and understanding when they encounter differences. Communicators must be willing to make appropriate adjustments when communicating with people from different cultures.

Those who cannot appreciate ideas, customs, or beliefs that differ from those of their own cultural background and who automatically assume that their own view is superior to that of any other culture are ethnocentric. **Ethnocentric** persons go

People from one culture may perceive people from other cultures as behaving with different sets of values. The way we greet each other, speak, choose what and when to eat, and many other personal preferences are all culturally conditioned.

beyond pride in their heritage or background to the conviction that they know more and are better than those of different cultures. Those who lack interaction or contact with other cultures may find it hard to understand that other cultures and their practices may be as acceptable as our own. Even if we know of weaknesses in our own culture (too competitive, too materialistic, too informal, and so on), we are unlikely to criticize our culture when comparing it to others.

Ethnocentrism is a learned belief that our own culture is superior to all others. This is not necessarily a bad thing, but it does alter our perceptions and often colors how we look at others who are different from us. We learn to behave through our culture, and the way we behave, most of us believe, is the way everyone else should behave. We use our culture and our cultural behaviors as a yardstick by which we judge all other cultures and people who are different from us. The difference between a person's own culture and other cultures is often judged on a superiority–inferiority scale. People often view cultures that are different from their own as inferior. The greater the differences, the more people perceive other cultures to be inferior to their own.

The idea behind cultural sensitivity training is to make each of us more sensitive to different cultures. Cultural sensitivity is not intended to change cultural behaviors, but it is intended to move people from a narrow view of the world to a broader worldview. Cultural sensitivity is understanding that being different doesn't mean being inferior. When people take on a broader worldview and open their minds to different cultures as merely being different, and not judging them as inferior because they are different, they are accepting the philosophy of **cultural relativism.** People who have a cultural relativistic attitude strive to understand differences rather than to judge them so that intercultural relations can develop. Cultural relativism is "we-oriented," whereas ethnocentrism is "me-oriented." Cultural relativists are willing to put themselves in the place of others who have a different culture in order to understand it without making judgments about it. Understanding differences, however, does not require accepting those differences or even condoning them. Of course, anything or anyone who violates the basic human rights of others should not be supported or defended.

Making Connections

Thinking About What We Want

Many men honestly do not know what women want, and women honestly do not know why men find what they want so hard to comprehend.

1. Do you agree with the above statement? Why?
2. What will have to happen in order for men and women to better understand each other?

D. Tannen, *You Just Don't Understand: Women and Men in Conversation* (New York: Morrow, 1990), 81.

Gender

Another factor that colors the way we perceive the world is gender. Unlike biological sex, **gender** is a social construct related to masculine and feminine behaviors that are learned. Some theorists believe that women and men learn to perceive the world around them differently, resulting in different ways of communicating.

It has been shown, in groups containing both females and males, that males tend to talk for longer periods of time, take more turns at speaking, exert more control over the topic of conversation, and interrupt females more frequently than females interrupt males. Also, what males say appears to be taken more seriously than what females say.[13]

These communication differences may occur because of how females and males perceive their roles and how the roles are defined by culture.

There remains a great deal of uncertainty about what causes the differences in the roles of men and women in our society. We are told about "the gender gap" and that men and women don't understand each other or speak the same language. Men are often confused when women want to continue to talk about something that they think has been settled; women often find themselves frustrated when men don't seem to listen or respond to what they say. The perceptions that men and women have of each other and of themselves is not always clear, especially in this time of transition in which the roles of men and women are changing. Men are no longer the sole breadwinners, nor are women solely responsible for taking care of the home, as was once the traditional arrangement. Most of us today believe that there is no reason why both men and women cannot pursue careers or that both cannot be involved in homemaking and child care. Americans, as a group, have to some extent enlarged their perspectives on the roles and abilities of both men and women.

Media

Sometimes other people influence our perceptions deliberately. Advertisers, government leaders, political advocates, and many others attempt to shape our views. Advertisers have mastered techniques to encourage us to think and behave in ways that will benefit their clients.

Have you ever wondered how much the media influence our perceptions? In recent elections, candidates have hired people often referred to as "handlers" or "spin doctors." Their job is to create a positive image of the candidates and to protect them from any exposure that might create a negative image.

What about the shows we watch on television? Do they create or alter our perceptions? Although family sitcoms, for example, present families that are generally atypical, regardless of race or ethnic background, they still influence our image of families. Network news shows select events from all the reports they receive and present them to us in a half-hour broadcast, which, when the commercials are removed, amounts to approximately 24 minutes of actual news. The information we see is not

Making Connections

Media and Ethics

Bob, a photographer, was hired to create a positive image for a motel in a large city. His job is to take photographs that will make the motel appear attractive in a brochure. Bob discovers quickly that the motel is located in an undesirable part of town, parking is difficult, and there are few attractions nearby. Thus, he does not take any shots that show the motel's surroundings. He photographs a model dressed to look like a distinguished businessperson approaching the newly remodeled entrance. He takes photos of a few attractive models in the pool. He takes a shot of one of the rooms using a wide-angle lens to give the illusion of spaciousness. Thus, Bob creates the impression that the motel attracts businesspeople, its customers are attractive, and its

rooms are spacious. Bob's brochure is successful in influencing our perceptions of the motel.

1. Did Bob capture a sense of the real motel?
2. Can we assume that because "pictures don't lie," we should accept Bob's interpretation of what the motel is?
3. If Bob had taken his photographs without the attractive models, shown more of the surrounding area, and not used a wide-angle lens, would we have the same image of the motel? Would the brochure have been printed?
4. Are advertisers obligated to present their products in a completely truthful way?

only limited but also selected and edited for our consumption, affecting our perceptions of the world.

These examples show that the media mold our perceptions in powerful ways. You may believe there is nothing wrong with this, but think about how we depend on the media for information and how literally so many people accept what is presented to them. There can be a great deal of difference between reality and what is presented to us.

Improving Perception Competencies

In order for us to be competent communicators, we must understand the impact that perceptions have on us, how we communicate with others, and what we accept as reality through the communication we receive. We tend to take the validity of our perceptions for granted and fail to look beneath the surface. But if we analyze specific personal experiences, we can begin to recognize and identify misperceptions that create communication problems for us.

Become an Active Perceiver

First, we must be *active* as perceivers. We must be willing to seek out as much information as possible about a given person, subject, event, or situation. The more information we obtain, the deeper our understanding and the more accurate our perceptions will be. We must question our perceptions to determine how accurate they are. By considering the possibility that we may misinterpret information, we prompt ourselves to confirm facts and impressions before we draw conclusions. Taking the time to gather more information and to recheck the accuracy of our perceptions is well worth the effort.

Recognize That Each Person's Frame of Reference Is Unique

Second, we must recognize the uniqueness of our own frame of reference. We must remember that our view of things may be only one of many views. Each of us has a unique window to the world, as well as a unique system of understanding and storing data. Some of us make judgments about people based on appearance, whereas others base their judgments on ability, income, education, gender, ethnicity, or other factors. This variety of approaches shows that all of us operate on different perceptual systems, and it is wrong to assume that one system is better than another.

Distinguish Facts from Inferences

A third way to improve our perceptions and interpretations is to distinguish facts from inferences or assumptions. A fact is something put forth as objectively real that can be verified (proved), for example, which building is the world's tallest, that Gina has been late to class five times this semester, or that person *X* received more votes than person *Y*. An inference is an interpretation that goes beyond what we know to be factual. For example, Bonnie is always late to group meetings, she always stares off into space, and generally does not give her opinion. The members of the group see her as lazy, unprepared, and rude. Saying that she is lazy, unprepared, and rude goes beyond the facts; she may be late because of other commitments, she may stare off into space because she feels unwanted in the group, and she may not give her opinion because she is extremely shy.

Because facts and inferences are often extremely difficult to distinguish, it is very easy to confuse them. We sometimes treat inferences as if they are facts. A statement such as "Bonnie is lazy" sounds factual, and we tend to accept those types of statements as truth rather than communicating to find out what is fact and what is inference. We need to label our statements as our inferences when we communicate them. For example, saying "Bonnie seems to be lazy" is much more tentative and is not stated as a fact or certainty.

Recognize That People, Objects, and Situations Change

A fourth way to improve our perceptions and interpretations is to recognize the fact that people, objects, and situations change. We must, therefore, be prepared to evaluate our own perceptions over time. We cannot assume that today's accurate perception will remain accurate forever.

Become Aware of the Role Perceptions Play in Communication

A fifth way to improve our perceptions and interpretations is to be aware of the role that perceptions play in communication, take others' perceptions into account, and avoid the tendency to assume too much about what we perceive. To make the most

Making Connections

Checking Your Perceptions

From what you have read and studied in this chapter, are you convinced that our perceptions play a significant role in our communication? Below are two examples of situations where the accuracy of perception is important to the outcome and future communication.

Sue runs into the room crying. She can barely speak, but there is anger written all over her face. Sam, her boyfriend, knows from past experience that when Sue behaves in this way he should leave her alone.

Bob's eyes begin to drift over to Joan's paper. He begins to appear self-conscious and a little shifty in his behavior. The teacher observes Bob and begins to question Bob's honesty.

In both situations, the observer's initial perception may be wrong. To verify the accuracy of such perceptions, it is counterproductive to rush to judgment or to assume the worst. Discuss in class the following issues:

1. What questions might Sam ask of Sue to check his perceptions of her behavior?
2. What questions might the teacher ask Bob to confirm or to counter initial perceptions of Bob's behavior?
3. Write a brief paper describing a situation in which you have been involved where your initial perception of someone's behavior was incorrect. Also describe how the misperception was brought to your attention and what you did to correct the situation.

of the information that we receive, we must first evaluate it. We should check the source of the information and the context in which the information was acquired. We should make sure we are not reading too much into the information. To help ensure that our perceptions are accurate, we should ask questions and obtain feedback whenever possible. We cannot determine whether our perceptions are accurate without testing them.

Keep an Open Mind

A sixth way to improve our perceptions and interpretations is to keep an open mind and remind ourselves that our perceptions may not be complete or totally accurate. Thus, we must continue to make observations, seek out additional information, be willing to describe what we observe mentally and out loud, state what a given observation means to us, and put our perceptions into words to test their logic and soundness.

Check Your Perceptions

1. Learn to separate facts from assumptions.
2. Hold off evaluation until you have ample information.
3. Remember that perceptions, especially first impressions, are not always accurate.

4. Learn to recognize your personal biases.

5. Recognize that people from different cultural backgrounds do not always attach the same meanings to events, objects, and people.

6. Remember that perceptions are a function of the perceiver, the perceived, and the situation in which the perception occurs.

7. Recognize that people, events, and places change over time.

8. Be willing to change your misperceptions.

 ## Summary

Perception is the process of selecting, organizing, and interpreting information in order to give it personal meaning. It lies at the heart of the communication process. Our perceptions of events, people, ideas, and things become our reality.

Perception is a part of everything we do, and thus it is important to understand how it influences our communication. For us to be perceptive to our surroundings we must first be aware of them, cognitively process them, and finally classify them via our language. Our ability to process information and how we think about the world around us has to do with our cognitive complexity. *Cognitive complexity* is the number of mental structures used, how abstract they are, and how elaborately they interact to share our perceptions.

Selection involves the sorting of one *stimulus* (something that incites or quickens action, feeling, or thought) from another. We use three kinds of selection—*selective exposure, selective attention,* and *selective retention*—to deliberately choose to experience or to avoid particular stimuli; to focus on some stimuli and ignore or downplay other stimuli; and to process, store, and retrieve information that we have already selected, organized, and interpreted.

Organization is the categorizing of stimuli so that we can make sense of them. *Figure and ground* (focusing on certain stimuli, allowing other stimuli to become background), *closure* (the filling in of details), *proximity* (grouping of two or more stimuli that are close to another), and *similarity* (grouping of stimuli that resemble one another in size, shape, or another trait) are all ways in which we organize our perceptions.

Interpretation is the assigning of meaning to stimuli. The meanings we choose are usually based on our past experiences. We must, therefore, take care that our past experiences do not create blinders that distort our perceptions.

Differences in people's perceptions result from each individual's state of mind, physiological makeup, cultural background, gender, and media exposure. These differences occur because we are all psychologically and physically different from one another, and our experiences are not identical, even when we participate in the same events. A common phenomenon that can distort our perception of reality is a *perceptual set,* a fixed, previously determined view of people, things, or events. People tend to see things they expect to see and to look on people, things, and events as if they will never change. Perceptual set is a form of stereotyping. *Stereotyping* refers to the categorizing of events, objects, and people without regard to their unique individual characteristics and qualities.

Perceptual set and stereotyping and our desire to attribute causes to people's behavior can also lead to inaccuracies in our perceptions and ultimately in our communication. *Attribution* is the complex process through which we attempt to understand the reasons behind others' behavior. *Attribution error* occurs when we perceive others as acting as they do because they are "that kind of person," rather than because of any external factors that may have influenced their behavior.

When the sender and receiver have different cultural backgrounds, their communication can become more complicated. *Culture* is defined as the deposit of knowledge, experience, beliefs, values, actions, attitudes, meanings, hierarchies, religion, notions of time, roles, spatial relations, concepts of the universe, and artifacts acquired by a group of people in the course of generations through individual and group striving. People from different cultural groups behave differently, perceive differently, and organize their values differently. People whose pride in their heritage or background leads to the conviction that they know more and are better than those who differ is *ethnocentric*. It is when we take a broader worldview and open our minds to different cultures as merely being different and not judging them as inferior because they are different that we are accepting the philosophy of *cultural relativism*.

Communication between men and women is also shaped by culture. Unlike biological sex, *gender* is a social construct related to masculine and feminine behaviors that are learned. Because our communication is grounded in our experiences and because our experiences exist within a culture, people who come from different cultural backgrounds bring a variety of perspectives and worldviews to their interactions with others. Common experiences shared between people increase the likelihood that words and other meanings are likely to be similar. People tend to believe that their own perception of the world is the only correct one. This, of course, is not so. Because perception is so subjective, one person's perception of a situation may be no more correct than another person's.

To improve our communication, we must constantly remember that no one way of perceiving anything can be considered completely right or wrong; perceptions reflect how we have learned to view the world and ourselves.

DISCUSSION STARTERS

1. What does it mean to be perceptive?
2. Explain why it is helpful to understand the role of perception in our communication.
3. What are the lessons that can be learned about perception as it relates to the opening scenario?
4. Describe the role that cognitive complexity has in determining our perception of the world around us?
5. Describe a personal experience that illustrates attribution error. How did the error affect perceptions?
6. List ways that perceptual set can interfere with communication. How can perceptual set aid our communication?
7. How does ethnocentrism affect perception? Communication?
8. How would you describe a person who is a cultural relativist?
9. Explain what role media may have in influencing our perceptions? Does the media have too much influence? If so, why?
10. What is the most important principle, idea, or concept that you learned in Chapter 2.

ANSWERS AND EXPLANATIONS

Making Connections:
It Just Doesn't Add Up, or Does It?

The correct answer is 5,100. How is it possible to have obtained anything other than 5,100? The error is probably caused by perceptual set. Since grade school, you have been taught to add one column at a time and to carry the re-mainder to the next column. This time you were asked to move the paper down the numbers, which changed your perception and may have led you to obtain an incorrect total.

NOTES

1. R. L. Scott, "On Viewing Rhetoric as Epistemic: Ten Years Later," *The Central States Speech Journal* (winter 1976): 258–66.

2. W. V. Haney, *Communication and Organizational Behavior: Text and Cases,* 3rd ed. (Homewood, Ill.: Irwin, 1973), 289–408.

3. M. Piattelli-Palmarini, *Inevitable Illusions: How Mistakes of Reason Rule Our Minds* (New York: Wiley, 1994), 17.

4. Ibid., 18–19.

5. C. Stewart and W. Cash, *Interviewing: Principles and Practices,* 9th ed. (New York: McGraw-Hill, 2000), 31.

6. S. Kassin, *Psychology* (Upper Saddle River, N.J.: Prentice Hall, 1998); D. T. Gilbert and P. S. Malone, "The Correspondence Bias," *Psychological Bulletin* 117 (1995): 21–28; F. Van Overwalle, "Dispositional Attributions Require the Joint Application of the Methods of Difference and Agreement," *Personality and Social Psychology Bulletin* 23 (1997): 974–80; and E. E. Jones, "The Rocky Road from Acts to Dispositions," *American Psychologist* 34 (1979): 107–17.

7. J. Pearson and P. Nelson, *Understanding and Sharing: An Introduction to Speech Communication,* 3rd ed. (Dubuque, Iowa: Brown, 1985), 27.

8. L. A. Samovar, R. E. Porter, and Lisa A. Stefani, *Communication Between Cultures,* 3rd ed. (Belmont, Calif.: Wadsworth, 1998), 36.

9. N. L. Gage and D. C. Berliner, *Educational Psychology,* 6th ed. (Boston: Houghton Mifflin, 1998), 151.

10. Ibid., 152–53.

11. R. E. Porter and L. A. Samovar, "An Introduction to Intercultural Communication," in *Intercultural Communication: A Reader,* 8th ed., edited by L. A. Samovar and R. E. Porter (Belmont, Calif.: Wadsworth, 1997), 20.

12. N. Dresser, *Multicultural Manners* (New York: Wiley, 1996), 89–90.

13. L. P. Stewart, P. J. Cooper, A. D. Stewart, and S. A. Friedley, *Communication and Gender,* 3rd ed. (Scottsdale, Ariz.: Gorsuch Scarisbrick, 1996), 51–56.

CHAPTER

3

Connecting
Self and
Communication

"The world's best reformers are those

who begin on themselves."

—*George Bernard Shaw*

■ Characterize the connection between self-concept and perception.

■ Describe how self-concept is developed.

■ Explain how self-concept is related to communication.

■ Explain how culture and gender affect self-concept.

■ Suggest ways to improve self-concept.

SCENARIO

For an exercise in their communication class, Jason and another student have been discussing self-concept and its connection to communication. As part of the class exercise, they are to describe how they think others see them and how they see themselves. Recall the opening scenario in Chapter 2 where Jason was described by five people who know him as five very different individuals. Who then is Jason? Is he the person that others describe or is he someone entirely different?

How does Jason believe others perceive him?

Jason thinks others see him as a leader, a team player, competitive, outgoing, easy to talk to, attractive in appearance, sensitive, smart, and fun.

How does Jason see himself?

When describing himself, Jason sees himself the same way he believes others see him.

Who is the real Jason? ■

Who is the real me? This is a question that all of us ask about ourselves, but seldom can we find a complete or entirely accurate or satisfying answer to this question. Each of us is an extremely complex person. Very early in our lives, we begin learning who we are, or at least, who we think we are. We develop a social identity, or self-definition, that includes how we conceptualize ourselves, including how we evaluate ourselves. For each of us, this identity includes our sex (male or female), relationships (daughter, son, spouse, single parent), vocation or avocation (such as student, nontraditional student, musician, consultant, sales associate, athlete), political or ideological affiliation (feminist, conservative, liberal, environmentalist, Democrat, Republican), and an aspect of the self of which we rightly feel proud (such as religion, race, sexual orientation, or ethnic background).

Thinking about oneself is an unavoidable human activity—most of us are self-centered. That is, the self is the center of each of our social universes. Our self-identity, or self-concept, is acquired through interactions with other people—beginning with immediate family members and then broadening to interactions with others outside of the family.

In order to become competent communicators, we must understand that our image of self plays a significant role in how we communicate with others and how others communicate with us, and therefore we must understand what self-concept is and how it connects to our communication with others.

Many psychologists believe there are many selves—a social self, a psychological self, a physical self, and so on. Each of these aspects of self contributes to a larger general view of self, which is in essence our identity. Each aspect is discussed in more detail in this chapter.

Who then are you? How would you describe yourself? Before you read further, try to give ten different answers to these questions. Would you say that you are an effective speaker, a good listener, well organized, a good writer, happy, outgoing, responsible, lovable, attractive, warm, sensitive, caring, tall, thin, intelligent, and interesting? Or would you choose other adjectives to describe yourself? The next question is this: What makes you think your description actually describes the real you?

Self-Concept and Its Connection to Communication

Our **self-concept** or self-identity is our mental picture and evaluation of our physical, social, and psychological attributes. Self-concept is determined by our experiences and communication with others, the roles and values we have selected for ourselves, and how we believe others see us (see Figure 3.1). Self-concept consists of two components: **self-image** is our mental picture of ourselves or our social identity, and **self-esteem** is our feelings and attitudes toward ourselves or how we evaluate ourselves.

We spend a lot of time and effort thinking about ourselves. To some extent, we literally tend to be self-centered. That is, the self is the center of each person's social universe.

"Who am I?" Two researchers asked 200 college students to give twenty responses to that question.[1] Through statistical analysis they found the students' responses could be placed in eight distinct categories, each making up components of the self-concept (see Figure 3.2). Though different people tend to use the same categories in describing themselves, the specific content of each category varies from person to person according to the researchers.

Self-concept and perception are very closely related, so it is difficult to separate them. They constantly interact. For example, what you think about yourself shapes, and in many ways determines, what you do and say. What you think about yourself

FIGURE 3.1

The Self-Concept

Self-concept is determined by our experiences and communication with others, the roles and values we have selected for ourselves, and our perception of how others see us.

self-esteem

Our experiences and communication with others

The roles and values we have selected for ourselves

self-image

SELF-CONCEPT

Our perception of how others see us

Making Connections

Discovering Your Self-Esteem Level on the Internet

Go to http://www.queendom.com/tests/health/self_esteem.html. On this website you will find a test that is designed to evaluate your general level of self-esteem. Follow the instructions and you will get a score and a brief interpretation of what the score means.

1. How would you explain the score you received?
2. What factors or events in your life do you think contributed most to your self-esteem?
3. What are the things that you would change about yourself if you could?
4. How can taking a test such as this one help you to better understand the role your self-esteem has in your communication with others?
5. Using an Internet search engine, search using the words *self-concept, self-identity, self-esteem,* or *self-image.* What do you find?

is influenced by the information you receive from others, which helps you create an image of who you are. If you think of yourself as a good piano player, you would take positive comments made about your piano playing as affirmation of your ability and skill. If, however, someone made a disparaging comment, you probably would dismiss

FIGURE 3.2

Who Am I? Eight Components of Self-Concept

More than 200 college students were asked to respond to the question "Who am I?" twenty times in a row; they gave a different answer each time. Statistical analysis produced eight distinct categories. Categories were labeled by the researchers as shown in the figure.

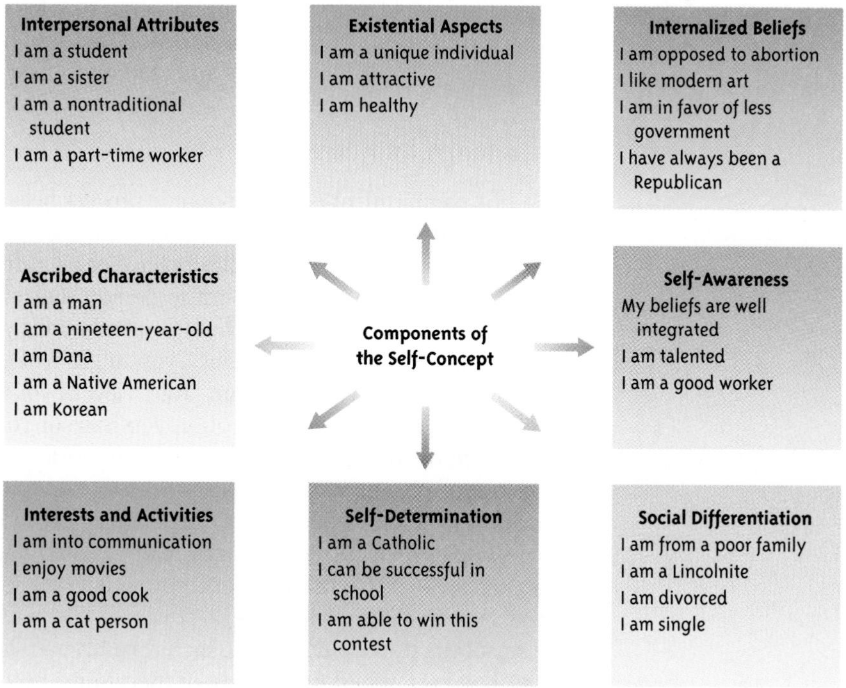

Interpersonal Attributes
I am a student
I am a sister
I am a nontraditional student
I am a part-time worker

Existential Aspects
I am a unique individual
I am attractive
I am healthy

Internalized Beliefs
I am opposed to abortion
I like modern art
I am in favor of less government
I have always been a Republican

Ascribed Characteristics
I am a man
I am a nineteen-year-old
I am Dana
I am a Native American
I am Korean

Components of the Self-Concept

Self-Awareness
My beliefs are well integrated
I am talented
I am a good worker

Interests and Activities
I am into communication
I enjoy movies
I am a good cook
I am a cat person

Self-Determination
I am a Catholic
I can be successful in school
I am able to win this contest

Social Differentiation
I am from a poor family
I am a Lincolnite
I am divorced
I am single

Making Connections

How Do You See Yourself?

Write a brief response to the following questions. Your answers should address a variety of aspects of your self, such as appearance, personality, ability, and intelligence.

1. How do you see yourself as a student, a friend, a son or daughter, a parent, a communicator?
2. How do you believe others see you in these roles?

Ask a friend to write a brief response indicating his or her perceptions of you based on the same questions. Compare your friend's responses to yours.

■ What did you learn about yourself?
■ Does your friend see you as you see yourself?
■ If there are differences, why do you think your friend sees you differently?

it as not reflecting your notion of how well you play the piano. In fact, you may interpret the comment as a sign of jealousy or humor, or simply that the person who made the comment simply doesn't know you.

The messages that we communicate, intentionally or unintentionally, relate directly to the way we feel about and view ourselves. Who and what we perceive ourselves to be influence how we present ourselves to others. What and how we communicate with others and the reactions of others toward us help develop our self-image and self-esteem, both of which ultimately make up our self-concept. Each of us has a unique identity and a special sense of who we are.

Why is it important for us to understand the connection between communication and self-concept? Think about this and read on to find an answer to the question.

Self-Concept as a Process

We describe communication as a dynamic process because it has no beginning or end and is constantly changing. In the same sense, self-concept is also a process. Self-perceptions, and the perceptions others have of us, differ from time to time, from situation to situation, and from person to person. For example, your view of yourself may vary somewhat according to how you feel about yourself at a given time. If you receive a high grade in a difficult class, you might feel good about yourself, or at least about your effectiveness as a student. Your view of yourself might differ if you receive a low grade. In addition, the perception you have of yourself as a student is probably different from the one you have of yourself at work, at church, or at home.

The notion that self-concept is a process is illustrated by how we perceive others and their view of us, and how this affects our view of ourselves. In the opening scenario in Chapter 2, Jason's friends and relatives provided their view of him, and in the opening scenario of this chapter, Jason provided his view of himself. Is Jason the person others perceive him to be, or is he the person he perceives himself to be? Jason may not be any of the persons described, including his own description of himself. The perceptions, however, whether accurate or inaccurate, become *Jason the person* as seen by others and himself. Jason's self-concept consists of his and others' perceptions and is

In Papua New Guinea, two Huli children see themselves in an instant photograph. We see ourselves based on how we think we look and on how we think others see us. Our self-image and self-esteem are often based on these interactions.

determined by the beliefs he holds about those perceptions. Perceptions of Jason held by others may not be accurate or completely known to him, but nevertheless, they affect him and he must deal with them. Consider the perception that Jason's brother has of him (he is ruthless, tough, and arrogant). If Jason knows that is what his brother thinks of him, how will that affect Jason's self-concept? How will it affect his communication with his brother?

The perceptions we believe others have of us affect how we receive their communication and influence our responses, and vice versa. Equally, our view of ourselves influences how we communicate with others. Communication and self-concept are inseparable and both involve process—continuous change with no beginning or end.

Development of Self-Concept

As children, our first communication involves sensing our environment—all the sights, sounds, tastes, and smells that surround us. We learn about ourselves as others touch us and speak to us. Their responses to us help determine how we view ourselves. Parental communication, both verbal and nonverbal, generally has an extremely strong impact on the initial development of self-concept. For example, the clothes and toys that they provide and what and how they communicate to us affect who we become in some way. As we age and expand our environment and relationships, the communication of others may reinforce or alter our perceptions of self. In her book *Old Is Not a Four-Letter Word: A Midlife Guide,* Anne Gerike writes that there are advantages to aging. For example, she says that aging brings increased self-confidence, a more reliable inner voice or "gut feeling," an acceptance of not being perfect, a sense of perspective that difficult situations get worked out, an acceptance that life isn't fair, and a willingness to accept responsibility instead of directing the blame elsewhere.[2] Assuming that Gerike's observations are correct, why do you think such developments occur with age?

Making Connections

The Ideal Communicator

Based on your perceptions of what you believe an ideal communicator should be, mark the scales below.

Expert	___	___	___	___	___	___	Incompetent
Intelligent	___	___	___	___	___	___	Unintelligent
Qualified	___	___	___	___	___	___	Unqualified
Interesting	___	___	___	___	___	___	Boring
Nervous	___	___	___	___	___	___	Poised
Calm	___	___	___	___	___	___	Anxious
Honest	___	___	___	___	___	___	Dishonest
Kind	___	___	___	___	___	___	Cruel
Undependable	___	___	___	___	___	___	Dependable
Powerful	___	___	___	___	___	___	Powerless
Bold	___	___	___	___	___	___	Timid
Silent	___	___	___	___	___	___	Talkative
Aggressive	___	___	___	___	___	___	Meek
Organized	___	___	___	___	___	___	Disorganized
Unpleasant	___	___	___	___	___	___	Pleasant
Irritable	___	___	___	___	___	___	Good-natured
Cheerful	___	___	___	___	___	___	Gloomy

Now mark the form as you perceive yourself. Compare the results. Discuss in small groups what you have learned.

From "An Instrument for Measuring Source Credibility of Basic Speech Communication Instructors," by J. C. McCroskey, W. Holdridge, and J. K. Toomb, *Speech Teacher* 23 (1974), p. 30. Used by permission of the National Communication Association.

Social psychologist Daryl J. Bem believes that sometimes we don't know our own attitudes, feelings, or emotions directly. We, therefore, focus on others to obtain such information.[3] Bem does, however, indicate that we learn a great deal about ourselves by observing our own behaviors. He suggests that what we do or how we act is a guide to what is happening inside us and how we feel about ourselves. Further, according to Bem, we draw inferences about ourselves in the same manner that we do about others. Thus, the process through which we come to know ourselves is very similar to the process through which we come to know others.

Our self-concept, which develops through an extremely complex process, usually consists of many images that we place on a continuum, ranging from negative to positive. There is no way to predict which image will dominate because our view of ourselves is a composite of all the self-images, which is ever in a state of flux. Self-concept is affected not only by how we perceive ourselves but also by how we perceive others, how others perceive us, and how we think others perceive us. Self-concept is based on both past and present experiences, which affect how we will perceive ourselves in the

Making Connections

What Others Say Can Influence Who We Are

You're pathetic. You can't do anything right!

Get outta here! I'm sick of looking at your face.

You're more trouble than you are worth. I wish you'd never been born.

You're so talented. You do everything so well!

I enjoy having you around! Your smile makes me feel good!

You're so helpful and easy to love. I am glad you are here.

People often believe what others tell them. Stop and listen to what you're saying. You might be surprised at some of the messages you've been sending to people for whom you care or should care.

1. In what way does our communication help form others' concepts of themselves?
2. In what way does our communication reflect who we are?
3. Why is it that putting other people down seems to be so fashionable in our society?

future. It is also determined by the values, attitudes, and beliefs we possess; how we attribute these qualities to others; and how they connect them to us. Such values, attitudes, and beliefs also form the basis for cognitive processes such as memory, reasoning, making inferences, judgment, and so on.

The actions and characteristics of others influence us in many ways. For example, say you are standing in line at a grocery store; suddenly, another person walks up and cuts in line in front of you. The person you've been dating exclusively for six months suddenly and unexpectedly says, "I think we should see other people." You make a presentation in one of your classes; after it's over, the instructor remarks, "That was terrific—best speech I've heard in years!" Will these actions by others have any impact on you? Indeed they will. Clearly, we are often strongly affected by the actions of others.

Possessions are part of the self.

Values. General, relatively long-lasting ideals that guide our behavior are called **values.** Values can be classified into broad categories, such as aesthetic, religious, humanitarian, intellectual, and material. Each category determines our behavior as well as our communication and is reflected in our self-concept. For

Making Connections

The Excuse?

Suppose that you are meeting a friend, and this person is late. In fact, after forty minutes, you begin to suspect that your friend will never arrive. Finally, your friend appears on the scene and says, "Sorry, our meeting just slipped my mind!" How would you react?

Imagine that your friend instead says, "I am really sorry for being late. There was a terrific accident, and there was a huge backup of traffic for miles." Now how would you react?

If, however, your friend is always late and has used similar excuses before, you may well be suspicious about whether this explanation is true.

Or, in contrast, if this is the first time your friend has been late for an appointment or your friend has never used this type of an excuse before, you may accept the explanation as true.

1. On what will your reaction to this situation depend?
2. On what will your judgment regarding the real reason for your friend's lateness depend?
3. How will your communication be affected by the values, attitudes, and beliefs you hold regarding your friend?

example, if material objects are important to us, we tend to judge ourselves by what we do or do not possess. A desire to have the finer things in life is not unusual, at least in our society, but the strength of the desire can greatly affect our behavior. Possessions can become so important for some people that they ignore other concerns (see the cartoon on page 65). They may pursue high income at the expense of job satisfaction, family life, leisure time, and personal health. Thus values can have both positive and negative influences on how we behave and communicate.

Attitudes.   Evaluative dispositions, feelings, or positions about oneself, others, events, ideas, or objects are called **attitudes.** Attitudes help determine self-concept, but unlike values, they are more narrowly defined. The relationship between values and attitudes is close because values are reflected in attitudes. For example, your attitude might be that the federal government is spending too much money on defense, especially at the expense of social programs. Your attitude says something about your value system; in other words, you value helping those in need above building a strong military program.

Beliefs.   Closely related to attitudes are beliefs. A **belief** is a conviction or confidence in the truth of something that is not based on absolute proof. We have, for example, beliefs about history, religion, schools, events, people, and ourselves. We say, "Space exploration is helpful to humanity," "God is good to us," "Speech class is important," "We will win the Orange Bowl game," "I know Sally loves me," or "I am going to get a high grade on my next speech." These statements and hundreds of similar statements that we make daily could begin with "I believe . . ." or "There is evidence that. . . ."

Our beliefs, like our attitudes and values, have a hierarchy of importance. That is, some are much more important to us than others are. Our most important beliefs, such as those about religion, education, and family life, do not change easily, but our less important beliefs, such as those about today's weather or the outcome of a sports event, are only momentary in duration.

Making Connections

Thinking About Attitudes and Values

Now, be honest: Have you ever felt uneasy in the presence of a person with a physical disability? Do you ever behave differently toward a highly attractive person than toward a less attractive person? Toward elderly persons than toward young ones? Toward persons belonging to racial and ethnic groups different from your own? Your answers to some of these questions are probably yes, for we are often strongly influenced by the visible characteristics and appearance of others. These reactions may be unconscious and not recognized by us until they are pointed out. How-

ever, our actions, regardless of whether they are conscious, do communicate our attitudes and values.

1. What do these statements say about how values and attitudes connect to our communication with others?
2. Why do we form values and attitudes similar to those described?
3. What can we do to ensure that we communicate with sensitivity in situations such as those mentioned here?

Making clear and absolute distinctions among values, attitudes, and beliefs is difficult because they are interrelated. Consider, for example, the close relationship among the following three statements:

> *Value (ideal):* People should love one another.
> *Attitude (feeling or position):* Love is good.
> *Belief (conviction):* Love is important in our lives.

Attitudes differ from beliefs in that attitudes include an evaluation of whether someone or something is good or bad. Beliefs, in turn, reflect the perception of whether something is true or false. Your attitudes and beliefs about love may change as a result of your experiences, but the value you place on love endures. Table 3.1 provides definitions and examples of values, attitudes, and beliefs.

The Hierarchy of Self-Concept

Like the beliefs we hold, the components of our self-concept may be organized into a hierarchy, as shown in Figure 3.3. At the highest level is our general self-concept, a set of beliefs we hold about ourselves. These beliefs are well established and relatively difficult to modify. At the second level are the principal components of self-concept—self-esteem and self-image.

The next level consists of the elements that form our self-esteem and self-image—psychological self-concept, social self-concept, and physical self-concept. On the lowest level are self-concepts related to specific characteristics, such as interpersonal attributes, existential aspects, internalized beliefs, interests and activities, self-determination, self-awareness, ascribed characteristics, and social differentiation.

The further we travel down the hierarchy, the more specific and the more susceptible to change the elements become. On the lowest level, the elements are not only

TABLE 3.1	Values, Attitudes, and Beliefs	
	DEFINITION	**EXAMPLE**
Values	Broad-based ideals that are relatively long lasting	Everyone should have an education.
Attitudes	Evaluative dispositions, feelings, or positions about ourselves, other persons, events, ideas, or objects	Our educational system, as it operates today, is too costly.
Beliefs	Convictions or confidence in the truth of something that lacks absolute proof	Even though it has its faults, our educational system is the best in the world.

susceptible to change but also often vary from situation to situation, develop over time, and impact our self-concept in positive or negative ways. For example, during high school the academic self-concept of one of the author's daughters was heavily based on her grades and the teacher feedback she received about her work and attitude. Her athletic self-concept was heavily dependent on her play during a given game; on how the coach, teammates, and her friends reacted to that play; and on her perceptions of her own play. During the past several years, her self-concept regarding her academic ability has changed dramatically from modestly positive to extremely positive since she has graduated from college. Yet her perceptions of her intelligence and academic ability seem to vary somewhat from one day to the next, depending on how successful she perceives herself to be. However, her success in athletics as a high school

FIGURE 3.3

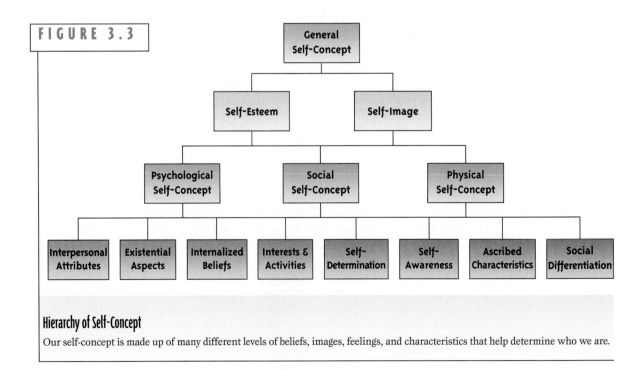

Hierarchy of Self-Concept

Our self-concept is made up of many different levels of beliefs, images, feelings, and characteristics that help determine who we are.

student brought her self-confidence and respect from her peers and coaches. Her athletic self-concept has been quite positive and remains that way even though she is no longer involved in formal athletics.

Communication and Self-Concept

A reciprocal connection seems to exist between self-concept and the way we communicate: Communication affects the self-concept, and self-concept affects how and what we communicate. A model developed by social psychologist John W. Kinch[4] demonstrates this relationship (see Figure 3.4). Our perceptions of how others respond to us (P) affect our self-concept (S). Our self-concept affects how we behave (B). Our behavior is directly related to how others react to our behavior (A). The actual responses of others relate to our perceptions of others' responses (P), and so we have come full circle.

According to William W. Wilmot, a leading communication scholar, "each person's view of himself affects his as well as his partner's behavior."[5] This means that each person's self-concept is influenced by interaction with the other person. How we perceive the communication that we receive from others has a direct impact on our self-concept and our subsequent communication. For example, people who have a weak self-concept are more likely to be depressed and less certain of their self-worth and are more affected by and concerned with derogative sources of negative feedback. Individuals with a strong self-concept usually exhibit opposite behaviors. They are more likely to adjust. Generally, those with high self-esteem function better in social situations than those with a weak self-concept.

Personality theorists, such as the late Carl Rogers, believe that our self-concept is the single most important aspect of our personality. Our image of self determines our personality, which in turn determines our style of communication. It is generally agreed that those with high self-concepts function

When good things happen or when we are acknowledged, our self-concept improves. It is often important to associate with people who reinforce our success and who listen when we have problems. Support from others is essential for creating a strong self-image.

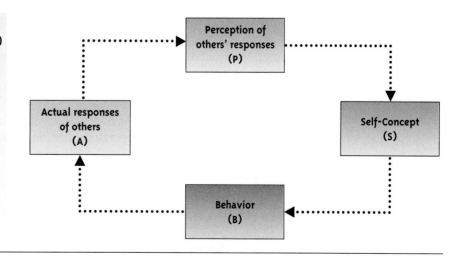

FIGURE 3.4

Kinch's Model of the Relationship Between Self-Concept and Communication

Kinch illustrates the relationship between self-concept and communication. Our self-concept is based on our communication with others.

J. Kinch, "A Formalized Theory of the Self-Concept," *American Journal of Sociology* 68 (January 1963): 481–86. University of Chicago Press. Reprinted by permission.

better in interpersonal situations than do those with low self-concepts. In other words, our view of self determines our communication style as seen by others and internalized by us, which in turn affects how we communicate with others.

There is some evidence that how others see us relates to our style of communication, which in turn is a reflection of our self-concept. One study examining the relationship between preschool children's style of communication and their attractiveness as perceived by their teachers and peers found that the higher children were rated on communication style, the more attractive they were to others. Those who were rated as less attractive were seen as having lower "communicator image," that is, were less "open, dramatic, contentious, animated, or impression leaving."[6]

Also relevant to style of communication is the notion of communication apprehension, which also relates directly to self-concept. **Communication apprehension** is "an anxiety syndrome associated with either real or anticipated communication with another person or persons."[7] Fear of communicating with others is a learned behavior usually based on how we think others will respond to our communication and to us. Communication apprehension can involve a fear not only of public speaking, but also of any form of communication. Some highly apprehensive people avoid talking, but others talk incessantly or inappropriately because of their nervousness. The fear of communicating with others also forms a part of self-concept, and thus communication apprehension affects how we interact with others and how they interact with us. Those who have a high level of anxiety are often perceived as unwilling to communicate, shy, withdrawn, less intelligent, less social, less attractive, less competitive, lower in self-esteem, lower in credibility, and so forth. These perceptions may not reflect reality. This problem can also reinforce itself over time. If we expect ourselves to be anxious in a particular situation, we are likely to be anxious. For those who have little communication apprehension, the opposite would likely be true. For more on communication apprehension, see Chapter 10.

Expectations that others have of us play an important role in determining our self-concept because others often behave and communicate with us based on their expectations. Thus, our self-concept is formed to a large extent by the communication we receive from others.

Self-Fulfilling Prophecy and Impression Management

In addition to values, attitudes, and beliefs, expectations determine how we behave, who we eventually become, and what we communicate to others and ourselves. Our own expectations and those of others influence our perceptions and behavior. Thus, our self-concept is affected by our past experiences, our interactions with others, the expectations others have of us, and how we present ourselves to create an image.

Self-Fulfilling Prophecy.   Expectations we have of ourselves or that others have of us help create the conditions that lead us to act in predictable ways. The expectation becomes a **self-fulfilling prophecy**.[8] A research study of college students who were either characteristically optimistic or generally pessimistic were asked to describe their future selves.[9] Both types of students, according to the research, could imagine a positive future, but the optimistic students had higher expectations about actually attaining a positive possible self than did those who were pessimistic. Thus, we are more likely to succeed if we believe that we have the potential for success. By the same token, we are more likely to fail if we believe ourselves to be failures.

Self-esteem can have significant effects on the prophecies people make about themselves. It is a matter of attribution—people with positive or high self-esteem confidently attribute their success to past successes; therefore, they expect to succeed again in the future. People with low self-esteem, however, attribute any success they might have had to luck and so prophesize that they will not necessarily succeed again unless they are lucky. The images we have of ourselves and how we describe ourselves influence our expectations.

Others also influence our expectations and affect how we ultimately perform. For example, if your professor tells you that she has heard that you are a very good speaker and expects that you will give an excellent oral report to the class, and if you believe your professor's prophecy, it is likely that you will act in a way that is consistent with the professor's expectation. If you believe the expectation, it is likely that you will give an effective oral report. Of course, the opposite could also happen if your instructor tells you that she doesn't expect the oral report to be very good. She is setting up you and the other students for meeting her expectation of giving inadequate oral reports. Thus, it is important that we communicate high expectations to others rather than place unnecessary limitations on them. The lesson from this should be clear: We are likely to get from others what we expect to get from them.

Impression Management.   The creation of a positive image of oneself in order to influence the perceptions of others is referred to as **impression management.** As your own experiences probably have suggested, impression management can take many forms. Most fall into two major categories: self-enhancement (efforts to boost your own image) and other-enhancement (efforts to make a target person feel good in your presence).

Specific tactics of self-enhancement include efforts to improve appearance. Often this is accomplished through careful choices in what to wear, personal grooming (cosmetics, hairstyles, the use of perfume or aftershave lotion), and the sensible use of nonverbal cues. Research findings indicate that all of these tactics seem to work, at least under some conditions. For example, women who dress in a professional manner for interviews (business suit or tailored dress, subdued jewelry) are often evaluated more favorably for management positions than women who dress in a more traditionally feminine manner.[10] Similarly, eyeglasses have been found to create impressions of intelligence, and long hair for women or beards for men tend to reduce such impressions.[11]

A variety of other-enhancement tactics can induce positive moods and reactions in others. Among the most commonly used and most important of these tactics is flattery—heaping praise on target persons, even if they don't deserve it; expressing agreement with their views; showing a high degree of interest in them (hanging on their every word); doing small favors for them; asking for their advice and feedback;[12] and expressing liking for them, either verbally or nonverbally.[13] All of these tactics appear to work, at least to a degree. They do cause the target person to experience positive reactions. These, in turn, can promote positive impressions of the person using the tactics. Through impression management, we can attempt to build a positive self-image and thereby strengthen our self-concept.

Culture and Self-Concept

Culture has a broad, all-encompassing effect on each of us. Self-concept involves our perception of self, our culture, our perception of our culture, and others' perception of

Making Connections

It's Me, Me, All Me!

In North American culture, the individual occupies a very important place. If you listen to how people raised in North America communicate, you will hear the word *I* fairly often. Other cultures do not necessarily share this perception of the self as being at the center of the universe.

1. How often do you and those with whom you communicate use *I* in conversations? Keep a log over a one- or two-day period and note the number of times you and others use this word in your conversations. Are your findings consistent with the statement that North Americans use *I* fairly often?

2. Talk to people from cultures different from your own to discover how much value they place on self.

3. In your discussions with people from other cultures, use the saying "the squeaky wheel gets the grease" (explain its meaning if you have to), and ask them if this statement would hold true in their culture. Report your findings to the class.

To conclude this exercise, discuss in class what adjustments, if any, you should make when interacting with people from cultures that do not place such emphasis on the self.

us and our culture. These views, in some combination, determine our self-concept. The development of self-concept varies from one culture to another and is determined by a specific combination of cultural norms and behaviors. Within a culture, social, institutional, and personal norms and beliefs related to self-concept are considered universal and not bound to a particular culture. This view is reinforced when two people from the same culture communicate within the context of their own culture. For instance, a white Anglo-Saxon Protestant in American society or a Japanese in Japanese society would have a stable self-concept with relatively few problems.

But when individuals are taken out of the context of their own culture and placed in a totally different society and culture, problems can arise. One's long-standing views and expectations no longer "fit" in the new culture. For example, if two people with different cultural backgrounds are communicating, they each will have different expectations of the other. This situation can create a cultural conflict and may eventually lead to a redefining of self-concept, which then allows the person to function more comfortably in the new culture. Being able to communicate with individuals from different cultural backgrounds requires both an understanding of their culture and of culture's influence on self-concept and the ability to adapt communication to accommodate differences.

To succeed in such communication requires developing a way to sense when messages have been successfully conveyed. It may also require overcoming fear. One African American woman stated one reason why such communication is difficult: "If people don't share the same life experiences, they can't be expected to understand each other. If whites haven't been exposed to blacks, there will be a 'fear of the unknown.' "[14] This same "fear" or potential for misunderstanding can happen whenever people from different backgrounds or experiences come together. Interestingly, in today's global village our self-concept is in part established through social interaction with others both inside and outside of our culture. This ongoing trend may bode well for the future, because it familiarizes us with those whose ways differ from our own. Contact with other cultures in the early development of self-concept may help us avoid some of the communication problems that occur when people of different backgrounds get together.

Gender and Self-Concept

It seems that the most pervasive element of our personal identity is that aspect of social identity in which we categorize ourselves as either female or male. That is, you may or may not pay much attention to your social class or ethnic identity, but it would be extremely rare for you to be unaware and unconcerned about being male or being female. In hundreds of ways, we are reminded each day of our gender by how we dress, how we act, and how others respond to us.

The terms *sex* and *gender* are often used interchangeably. We defined gender in Chapter 2 as a social construct related to learned masculine and feminine behaviors. **Sex** is defined in biological terms as the anatomical and physiological differences between males and females that are genetically determined.[15] Note, however, that these definitions are not universally accepted.

The origin of gender differences is sometimes a matter of dispute, but we are willing to assume that most gender attributes are based entirely on what one learns (such as an association between hairstyle and femininity), whereas other attributes may be based entirely on biological determinants (such as the presence of facial hair). Each of us has a gender identity: A key part of our self-concept is the label of "male" or "female." For the vast majority of people, biological sex and gender identity coincide, though there is a relatively small proportion of the population in which gender identity differs from sex.

From the moment of birth, no other characteristic of the self slants the treatment we receive more directly than our biological sex. The behavior of children begins to be shaped by their very first pink or blue blanket. It appears that these initial influences placed on children lead to gender stereotypes and expectations that strongly influence a person's self-concept. Each of us has a gender identity; that is, we label ourselves as male or female. In most instances, a person's biological sex and gender identity correspond. Issues related to sex and gender are still very much debated by psychologists. When psychologists speak of sex, they are usually referring to anatomical and physiological differences between males and females that are based on genetic differences present at conception. Gender is usually used to describe other attributes and behaviors associated with sex that are acquired on the basis of cultural expectations or a combination of biological and cultural factors, some of which are unknown to us.

Some male and female differences may be explained by biological differences in brain structure and development. According to Julia T. Wood, research indicates that, although both men and women use both lobes of the brain, each tends to specialize in one. Wood says that men generally exhibit greater development of the left lobe of the brain (the locus of mathematical abilities, analytical thought, and sequential information processing), whereas women manifest greater development of the right lobe of the brain (the locus of intuitive thought, imaginative and artistic activity, and some visual and spatial tasks). To support this theory, she states that research reported in 1995 suggests that women are more likely to use both sides of the brain to do language tasks, whereas men are more likely to depend on the left side of the brain. Women's brains, according to Wood, work less hard than men's to understand emotions.[16]

Other research disputes the influence of biology on gender, and considerable controversy exists concerning the degree and strength of biological influence in determining differences between women and men. Psychoanalytic theorists suggest that our development of and sense of self and gender identity occur when we are infants, as we internalize the responses of others around us. Wood suggests that "infants who are lovingly nurtured by a mother tend to incorporate the mother's view into their own sense of self, and they regard themselves as valuable and worthy."[17] This may also be true of fathers who lovingly nurture their children. Regardless of who does the nurturing, children who are well attended to, given affection, and so on are more likely to internalize similar capacities, and thus those attributes become a part of their self-concept.

Gender identity occurs when gender becomes a part of one's self-concept. We develop a sense of self that includes maleness and femaleness,[18] and somewhere between the ages of four and seven, the concept of gender consistency (the sense that one is permanently male or female) develops. We begin to accept the principle that gender is a basic attribute of a person. As soon as these attributes become known to us and are firmly in place, our perceptions of self are affected by what we believe about gender.

Gender Stereotypes. A research study found that when children (ages five to nine) and adolescents (age fifteen to college age) are shown videotapes of four nine-month-old infants, both age groups agree that the babies identified as female (named Karen or Sue) appear to be smaller, more beautiful, nicer, and softer than those identified as male (named William or Matthew).[19] Actually, the experimenters had assigned a male or female name to infants of both sexes. For example, each male baby was identified correctly as a boy for half the participants and incorrectly as a girl for the other half; similarly, each female baby was identified for half the participants as a girl and as a boy for the other half. The findings illustrate that gender stereotypes determined how the infants were perceived.

Even though our society has taken great strides to reduce stereotypical thinking about males and females, stereotypes and narrowly defined role expectations are still accepted by many in our culture and even more so in certain other cultures. These stereotypes affect communication behavior. There are many similarities in the communication behaviors of men and women. For example, there are soft-spoken men and verbally aggressive women; many men discuss their families and friends, and many women discuss sports and investments. It is, however, commonly accepted in our society that men and women communicate differently and prefer to discuss certain subjects. In addition, in some situations men and women are expected to communicate differently because of imposed cultural norms.

Females have often been the objects of stronger and more persistent stereotypes than males. That is not to say that there are no stereotypes assigned to males—they, too, are perceived as being "all alike" in possessing certain traits. Female stereotypes, however, are often more negative in content than those applied to males. The positive stereotypes of feminine behaviors include characteristics such as nurturance, sensitivity, and personal warmth. The traits are believed by some to be less desirable and less suited for the valued roles of leadership and authority than the gender stereotype for males.[20]

Are the stereotypes about males and females accurate? Are the traits assigned to feminine behaviors less desirable than those assigned to masculine behaviors? Do men and women really differ in the ways that stereotypes suggest? The answers to these questions are complex, for such differences between males and females, even if observed, may be based more on the perceived stereotype itself than actual differences between men and women. Research does seem to imply that when differences are observed between sexes, those differences tend to be overstated. Overall, the magnitude of such differences is far less than prevailing stereotypes imply.

Gender Expectations.   An overwhelming body of evidence demonstrates that sex differences in communication are the result of gender expectations. According to psycholinguist Deborah Tannen, men and women do see themselves as different, and as a result, they communicate differently. She says, "In this world [the man's] conversations are negotiations in which people try to achieve and maintain the upper hand if they can and protect themselves from others' attempts to put them down and push them around. Life, then, is a contest, a struggle to preserve independence and avoid failure." The man's world is a hierarchical social order in which people are either one-up or one-down. In the women's world, according to Tannen, "conversations are negotiations for closeness in which people try to seek and give confirmation and support and to reach consensus. They try to protect themselves from others' attempts to push them away. Life, then, is a community, a struggle to preserve intimacy and avoid isolation." The women's world is also hierarchical, but the order is related more to friendship than to power and accomplishment.[21] Are we really different?

According to one researcher's perspective, "the two sexes are essentially similar and . . . the differences linked to sexual functions are not related to psychological traits or social roles."[22] He further believes that most gender differences are relatively superficial and that differences that are perceived to exist are socially constructed in one's cultural upbringing. The differences between males and females, therefore, are more or less learned in and reinforced by culture.

When asked to describe themselves, males and females differ in their descriptions. Males tend to mention qualities such as ambition, energy, power, initiative, instrumentality, and control rather than external events. They are likely to discuss their success in sports and with females. Females, however, typically list qualities such as

When compared to men, women are much more likely to be concerned about body image and about physical appearance in general. One explanation may be that from infancy on, other people place more emphasis on the appearance of females than of males.

Men and women seemingly view body image differently.

generosity, sensitivity, consideration, and concern for others.[23] Males, it seems, are expected to be powerful and authoritative, whereas females are expected to be concerned with relationships and expressiveness. The accompanying cartoon illustrates some of the problems that may occur when men and women communicate and negotiate differences.

Despite some strides toward equality of the sexes, there is still a cultural bias in favor of masculinity. But because communication behaviors are learned and are culturally defined, they can also be unlearned and changed over time. To some extent, this has happened. The roles women play today are significantly different from their roles a few decades ago. For a time in our society, women expected and were expected by others to stay home and rear their children, whereas men were expected to be breadwinners. Today, it is estimated that between 70 and 80 percent of married women work outside the home. The U.S. Women's Bureau of the Department of Labor indicates on its website http://www.dol.gov/dol/wb/welcome.html that more than 70 million jobs were added between 1964 and 1999, more than doubling the 1964 figure. Of these 70 million new jobs, 43 million were filled by women, almost double those filled by men. There is also a significant population of single parents who work outside the home. Along with these changes in roles and responsibilities come changes in the way we communicate with one another. Though young girls in the United States today are performing better in school and avoiding unwanted sexual activity more than was true a decade ago, they are significantly more depressed than boys.[24] The most predominant factor linked to their unhappiness is a pervasive worry about their appearance.

When compared to men, women are much more likely to be concerned about body image and physical appearance in general. Furthermore, the male–female differences in body image satisfaction has increased from the pre-1970s era to the 1990s.[25] Columnist and humorist Dave Barry, in an article in the *Miami Herald* (January 30, 1998) titled "Beauty and the Beast," describes the gender differences as follows: Men think of themselves as average looking, and average is fine; in contrast women, evaluate their appearances as "not good enough." If you'd like to read more about what Barry has to say regarding gender differences go to his website http://www.herald.com/davebarry/.

Why is appearance such a major issue for women? One explanation is that from infancy on, other people place more emphasis on the appearance of females than of males. College women report a high frequency of childhood experiences in which they were teased by peers and siblings about how they looked and how much they weighed.[26] Unbelievable as it might seem, even parents discriminate against overweight daughters, but not overweight sons, by being less willing to give them financial support for college.[27] Presumably, the assumption—perhaps unconscious—is that an overweight female will not do well at either finding a husband or getting a job, so, why waste the money?

In spite of changes in gender roles, many communication behaviors are still considered more appropriate for one sex than the other. For example, research suggests that women in our society learn to talk more about their relationships with others, whereas men learn to talk about sports and finances. Women learn to express their emotions, whereas men learn to repress them. Women learn to be patient and wait for promotions, whereas men are expected to be more assertive in their careers.[28] If men and women are to break the stereotypes and expectations attributed to them, we must avoid categorizing behaviors as exclusively male or female.

Psychologists indicate that women and men who are **androgynous**—who have both male and female traits—are more likely to be successful in their interactions and careers than people who are totally masculine or feminine in their behaviors. For example, as you move from interactions with co-workers to interactions with your family, you may move from more "masculine" behaviors to more "feminine" behaviors. If you are a manager or owner of a business, you are expected to be assertive or task oriented;

Making Connections

Body Image and Self-Concept

Presumably because of societal pressures, women are usually much more concerned with body image than men, especially regarding weight. The cartoon on page 76 can be interpreted in a number of ways: as ridiculing gender stereotypes, as pointing out the insensitivity of a (typical?) egocentric man, as showing the oversensitivity and self-depreciation of women, or as a sexist attack.

1. What do you think this cartoon illustrates? Why?
2. Explain the relationship between body image and self-concept.
3. Should cultural differences be considered when discussing body image and self-concept? Give examples.
4. Why is it assumed that body image is more important to women than it is to men?
5. How do people discriminate based on body image?
6. How does body image influence our communication?

but when you spend time taking care of your children, you are expected to be patient and loving.

Improving the Self-Concept

Changing a self-concept is not easy. It usually begins with a concentrated effort to change behavior. Sometimes dramatic events may force a change in behavior and thus alter the self-concept. For example, getting married or having a first child may drastically change people's behavior, thus modifying their self-concept. Or a change in situation may change their view of roles, thus affecting their behavior.

To alter the self-concept requires a strong desire to change and a belief that you can succeed. A defeatist attitude diminishes anyone's chances for improvement. You must make the self-fulfilling prophecy work in your favor. But just thinking about success won't make you successful; you must take action. Anytime you act, you run the risk of failure, but successful people learn how to learn from failure and to avoid similar situations in the future. When you understand your shortcomings, learn how to deal with them, and believe that you can succeed, you will begin to see yourself in a more positive light.

Improving Your Self-Concept

1. *Decide what you would like to change about yourself.* In order to begin the process of improvement, you must know what needs to be changed. Describe, as accurately and specifically as you can, what you are unhappy about or what you don't like about yourself.

2. *Describe why you feel the way you do about yourself.* Is your problem brought on by yourself or by others? Many students, for example, do not really want to be in college. They are there because their parents or their friends put pressure on them. Although they'd rather be doing something else, they are afraid to take a stand. Before they can begin to feel better about themselves, they must recognize why they are unhappy and who is contributing to their problem. You may feel that you are not capable of earning good grades in a certain subject or that you are too shy to make friends easily. Ask yourself why you feel that way. Are you living out a self-fulfilling prophecy?

3. *Decide that you are going to do something to change your feelings about yourself.* If you can describe your problem, you can almost always find a solution—that is, if you want to find one. If you are unhappy about your appearance, make plans to change it. If you feel inadequate about meeting people, plan some ways to build your confidence. Nothing will ever change unless you want it to change.

4. *Set reasonable goals for yourself.* You must be reasonable in setting your goals. You may be able to change some things overnight, but other things may require a long-term effort. For example, you may decide that you are going to improve your grades by studying for several hours every night. You can begin your new study schedule immediately, but actually raising your grades may take much longer.

Sometimes a problem becomes more manageable if it is solved step by step. For example, you may feel hesitant to visit your professor in his or her office. Why not start by speaking briefly with your professor before or after class? You might begin by asking a question about your progress. Once you begin to feel comfortable, ask for an appointment or stop in to visit during office hours. If you continue such visits, you will gradually gain more confidence in yourself.

5. *Associate with people who will support and help you.* Try to surround yourself with people you like and trust. That will make it much easier to discuss your problems and ask for support. When others know what you are trying to do and how you need help, they can provide support to make your behavioral changes easier.

Summary

Our *self-concept*, or self-identity, is our mental picture and evaluation of our physical, social, and psychological attributes. Self-concept consists of our *self-image*, which is our mental picture of ourselves or our social identity, and *self-esteem,* which is our feelings and attitudes toward ourselves or how we evaluate ourselves. Self-concepts are affected by how we perceive ourselves, how we perceive others, how others perceive us, and how we think others perceive us. Like communication, self-concept is a process that has no beginning or end and is constantly changing. Self-perception and other people's perceptions of us change from time to time, from situation to situation, and from person to person.

Our self-concept is based on our values, attitudes, and beliefs. *Values* are general ideas that are relatively stable over time; *attitudes* are evaluative dispositions or feelings that relate to ourselves, others, events, or objects; and *beliefs* are convictions about the truth of something.

The components of self-concept may be organized into a hierarchy. The lower in the hierarchy a particular component is, the easier it is to change. *Communication apprehension* is anxiety associated with either real or anticipated communication with another person or persons and directly relates to our self-concept. Our expectations of ourselves can become *self-fulfilling prophecies* that determine how we behave, who we eventually become, and what we communicate to others and ourselves. *Impression management,* involving self-enhancement or other-enhancement techniques, can be used to bolster our image in order to create a positive outcome of communication with others.

Our cultural background affects the development of our self-concept through its norms and expected behaviors. Self-concept involves our perception of our own culture and others' perception of us and our culture. The view of self-concept within our own culture is generally stable, but when we enter into different cultures, problems may arise. The problems are often due to the fact that our views and expectations of how things are done in our own culture may no long work or fit in the new culture. Thus, communicating with people from different cultural backgrounds requires understanding of other cultures and an ability to adapt to them.

Gender in our society plays a significant role in determining our self-concept and how we communicate with others. Even though our society has taken great strides to reduce stereotypical thinking about males and females, the stereotypes and narrowly defined role expectations are still accepted. Gender stereotypes affect communication behavior of both males and females. A person who has both male and female traits is referred to as *androgynous.* They are more likely to be successful in their interactions and careers than people who are totally masculine or feminine in their behaviors.

Although it is not easy to alter our self-concept, we can achieve progress through hard work, a desire to improve, and the belief that we are and will be successful. Following are specific steps we can take to help ourselves: (1) decide what we want to change, (2) describe why we feel the way we do, (3) decide that we are going to take action, (4) set reasonable goals, and (5) surround ourselves with supportive people.

DISCUSSION STARTERS

1. How does self-concept affect communication? Give both a positive and a negative example.
2. How is self-concept determined?
3. How do expectations influence self-concept and ultimately communication? How have your expectations helped or hindered you?
4. How does culture affect self-concept?
5. How does gender affect self-concept?
6. What role does style of communication have in determining self-concept?
7. What can a person do to alter his or her self-concept?
8. How can a person help to change another person's self-concept?
9. What is the most important thing you learned in this chapter about communication, perception, and self?

NOTES

1. J. R. Rentsch and T. S. Heffner, "Assessing Self-Concept: Analysis of Gordon's Coding Scheme Using 'Who Am I?' Responses," *Journal of Social Behavior and Personality* 9 (1994): 283–300.
2. A. Gerike, *Old Is Not a Four-Letter Word: A Midlife Guide* (Watsonville, Calif.: Papier Mâché Press, 1997).
3. D. J. Bem, "Self-Perception Theory," in *Advances in Experimental Social Psychology,* vol. 6, ed. L. Berkowitz (New York: Academic Press, 1972).
4. J. W. Kinch, "A Formalized Theory of Self-Concept," *American Journal of Sociology* 68 (January 1963): 481–86.
5. W. W. Wilmot, *Dyadic Communication,* 3rd ed. (New York: Random House, 1987), 61.
6. C. Stohl, "Perceptions of Social Attractiveness and Communicator Style: A Developmental Study of Preschool Children," *Communication Education* 30 (1981): 367–76.
7. J. C. McCroskey, "Classroom Consequences of Communication Apprehension," *Communication Education* 26 (1977): 27–28.
8. R. Rosenthal and L. Jacobson, *Pygmalion in the Classroom: Teacher Expectation and Pupils' Intellectual De-velopment* (New York: Holt, Rinehart & Winston, 1968,) vii; T. Good and J. Brophy, *Looking in Classrooms,* 4th ed. (New York: Harper & Row, 1987).
9. C. S. Carver, L. A. Kus, and M. F. Scheier, "Effects of Good Versus Bad Mood and Optimistic Versus Pessimistic Outlook on Social Acceptance Versus Rejection," *Journal of Social and Clinical Psychology* 13 (1994): 138–51.
10. S. Forsythe, M. F. Drake, and C. E. Cox, "Influence of Applicant's Dress on Interviewer's Selection Decision," *Journal of Applied Psychology* 70 (1985): 374–78.
11. R. L. Terry and J. H. Krantz, "Dimensions of Trait Attributions Associated with Eyeglasses, Men's Facial Hair, and Women's Hair Length," *Journal of Applied Social Psychology* 23 (1993): 1757–69.
12. E. W. Morrison and R. J. Bies, "Impression Management in the Feedback-Seeking Process: A Literature Review and Research Agenda," *Academy of Management Review* 16 (1991): 322–41.
13. S. J. Wayne and G. R. Ferris, "Influence, Tactics, and Exchange Quality in Supervisor–Subordinate Interactions: A Laboratory Experiment and Field Study," *Journal of Applied Psychology* 75 (1990): 487–99.

14. S. A. Ribeau, J. R. Baldwin, and M. L. Hecht, "An African-American Communication Perspective," in *Intercultural Communication: A Reader,* ed. L. A. Samovar and R. E. Porter (Belmont,Calif.: Wadsworth, 1994), 143.

15. J. B. Beckwith, "Terminology and Social Relevance in Psychological Research on Gender," *Social Behavior and Personality* 22 (1994): 329–36.

16. J. T. Wood, *Gendered Lives: Communication, Gender and Culture,* 3rd ed. (Belmont, Calif.: Wadsworth, 1999), 45.

17. Ibid., 48.

18. N. Grieve, "Beyond Sexual Stereotypes. Androgyny: A Model or an Ideal?" in N. Grieve and P. Grimshaw, eds., *Australian Women: Feminist Perspectives* (Melbourne, Australia: Oxford University Press, 1980), 247–57.

19. D. A. Vogel, M. A. Lake, S. Evans, and K. H. Karraker, "Children's and Adults Sex-Stereotyped Perceptions of Infants," *Sex Roles* 24 (1991): 601–16.

20. M. E. Heilman, R. F. Martell, and M. C. Simon, "The Vagaries of Sex Bias: Conditions Regulating the Underevaluation, Equivaluation, and Overevaluation of Female Job Applicants," *Organizational Behavior and Human Decision Processes* 41 (1988): 98–110.

21. D. Tannen, *You Just Don't Understand: Women and Men in Conversation* (New York: Morrow, 1990), 24–25.

22. C. E. Epstein, *Deceptive Distinctions: Sex, Gender, and the Social Order* (New Haven, Conn.: Yale University Press, 1988), 25.

23. M. R. Gunnar-Von Gnechten, "Changing a Frightening Toy into a Pleasant Toy by Allowing the Infant to Control Its Actions," *Developmental Psychology* 14 (1978): 157–62; J. H. Block, "Differential Premises Arising from Differential Socialization of the Sexes: Some Conjectures," *Child Development* 54 (1983): 1335–54; J. T. Spence and R. L. Helmreich, *Masculinity and Femininity: Their Psychological Dimension and Antecedents* (Austin: University of Texas Press, 1978).

24. D. Mathis, "Reports on Girls' Lives Offers Mixed Assessment," Gannett News Service, June 17, 1998.

25. P. Pliner, S. Chaiken, and G. L. Flett, "Gender Differences in Concern with Body Weight and Physical Appearance over Life Span," *Personality and Social Psychology Bulletin* 16 (1990): 263–73.

26. T. F. Cash, "Development Teasing About Physical Appearance: Retrospective Descriptions and Relationships with Body Image," *Social Behavior and Personality* 23 (1995): 123–30.

27. C. S. Crandall, "Do Parents Discriminate Against Their Heavyweight Daughters?" *Personality and Social Psychology Bulletin* 21 (1995): 724–35.

28. L. P. Stewart, P. J. Cooper, A. D. Stewart, and S. A. Friedley, *Communication and Gender,* 3rd ed. (Scottsdale, Ariz.: Gorsuch Scarisbrick, 1996), 12, 203–12.

CHAPTER

4

Connecting Through Verbal Communication

"Words have set whole nations in motion and upheaved the dry ground on which rests our social fabric. Give me the right word and the right accent and I will move the world."

—Joseph Conrad

WILL HELP YOU:

- Define language and discuss its role in the communication process.
- Understand the power of language.
- Understand that using language is using a set of symbols in a system.
- Realize that language is personal: We all use language in unique ways.
- Be aware that language influences perceptions, thought, and views of reality.
- Describe the four key elements of language.
- Identify language-based barriers to communication and suggest how they can be overcome.
- Discuss gender-inclusive language, the effects of sexist language, and how to avoid using sexist language.
- Demonstrate the effect of cultures and co-cultures on language use.
- Explain how accuracy, vividness, verbal immediacy, appropriateness, and the use of metaphors contribute to a speaker's effectiveness.

SCENARIO

Aje-Ori, Angel, Barbara, Catherine, Chikako, Dussadee, Elvinet, Julian, Lene, Leo, Leonid, Pajaree, Peder, Roman, Sergei, Siruluk, Takehite, Tania, Webster, Wun-Jen, Xiaofan, Yanawan, and Yanliu are all international students in a U.S. college communication studies program.

When faced with oral presentations in class, they all say nearly the same thing: "English is my second language. I am so worried I will say the wrong thing." In discussions with these students, it becomes clear that they feel comfortable when writing, partially because they have a second-language dictionary to which they can refer, but the vagaries of language use in the United States sometimes leave them baffled. Although they know the "denotative," or dictionary, meanings, they sometimes struggle with words for which there are multiple meanings and those that are used in a new way. Even the woman who is a translator for Chinese–U.S. diplomatic and business meetings in her home country says she gets quite confused at times, because she is more literal than the people whose words and meanings she is asked to translate. She also says this happens more in the college setting than in business or diplomatic situations in which she must translate to Chinese delegations.

One of the students, Xiaofan, conducted a survey of international students and received thirty-eight responses: five African, nineteen Asian, eleven European, and three Latino. Nearly 60 percent identified (1) the need to get "chances to share their own perspectives/experiences/knowledge with the class" and (2) the need for U.S. classmates to be "willing to interact [talk] with us."[1] ■

According to the Educational Testing Service, college campuses will become increasingly more diverse in the twenty-first century. During the next fifteen years, enrollment is projected to increase by 19 percent to sixteen million students enrolled in U.S. colleges and universities. Minority students are expected to account for 80 percent of the growth, with the proportion of African or African American students rising from 12.8 to 13.2 percent by 2015; the proportion of Hispanic students to increase from 10 to about 15 percent and the proportion of Asian students to increase from 5.4 to 8.4 percent. The proportion of white students who attend college is expected to decline from about 71 percent to about 62 percent.[2]

English is increasingly *the* language of higher education around the world. This trend is enhanced by the spread of technology because much of the available computer software is written in English and because of the growth of the Internet where the English language prevails.[3] And because as technology grows, the world seems to shrink, our careful use of language will become even more important than previously. As effective communicators, we must make appropriate language choices so that diverse groups of people can understand us.

Mark Twain once said, "The difference between the right word and the almost right words is the difference between lightning and the lightning bug." This quotation certainly illustrates this point: Word choice does make a difference. Because the language we use is a message in itself, our use of language can convey a positive image of us or it can damage and degrade us as well as others. The United States is primarily an English-speaking culture, and even though there are many co-cultures within our society, educated people need to know which forms of English are expected and appropriate for different settings. In many college classrooms and in many business meetings and other workplace settings, standard English use is dominant and expected, whereas different forms of language may be more suitable in more informal settings. Competent communicators must determine which form of language is appropriate for a particular situation and which is not.

Language is critically important to the communication process. In this chapter we examine what language is, some common barriers to effective language use, the use of inclusive language, the avoidance of stereotypes, and we provide suggestions about effective language use.

The Importance of Language

Language is a structured system of signs, sounds, gestures, or marks that is used and understood to express ideas and feelings among people within a community, nation, geographic area, or cultural tradition. In this chapter we concentrate on spoken language; in the next chapter we consider nonverbal communication. Without language, there would be little or no human communication as we now know it. Language allows us to encounter our world in meaningful ways, because it allows us to share meaning with others. Can you imagine what it would be like to be unable to tell someone what you know or think or feel? Language is a powerful tool! But it is only as effective and efficient as the person or persons using it. Despite the fact that we often believe that language is neutral, in actuality, it communicates much about what we are and what we think and thus must be carefully used.

Making Connections

Words Can Be Harmful

Too often language is viewed as neutral and innocent. But it can get you into trouble. . . . A supervisor overheard two employees discussing some customers who had just entered the store. One made a comment about that "really old guy" and wondered why he would even come into the store. The second responded, "Yeah, but what's even more interesting is that the old guy's companion is clearly a flaming gay."

The supervisor took the two workers aside and made it clear that the company would not tolerate disrespectful language about anyone, further cautioning the workers to think carefully about what they say and how they say it. The supervisor reminded the workers that company policy demanded that each customer be treated with respect. Talking about customers, even quietly or out of earshot, was rude. Future violations of this policy, he said, would result in termination.

1. Search a local newspaper, contemporary magazines, or the Internet, or simply listen to people's choices of words to locate other examples of language that could be considered degrading, hurtful, or disrespectful. Share what you find with your classmates and discuss why this type of communication occurs.
2. Discuss what you can do to help stop rude, insensitive, and degrading messages.
3. List words or phrases that offend you when they are used in your presence. Describe why they offend you—after all they are only words.
4. Discuss the following question with your classmates: How can we balance our right to free speech with our obligation to avoid language that is disrespectful or harmful to others?
5. Continue the discussion by responding to the following: Have we become too sensitive and too politically correct in our use of language? Explain.

Language Is Powerful

We depend not only on our own experiences to gain information but also on communicating with people we know and do not know. Because we use language and are able to communicate, we are not limited to experiencing the world only through our own personal experiences and knowledge. We can learn by talking with others, taking courses; watching television; and reading newspapers, magazines, books, and information posted on the Internet.

Using language allows us to change, to cooperate, to create, and to resolve conflicts. It can prevent wars or start them, create friends or enemies, and change our behavior or the behavior of others. Yet most of us take language for granted and ignore its potential effects. We regard language as a "mere matter of words," forgetting that words have the power to affect our minds, feelings, thoughts, will, actions, and being. Successful communicators respect language and have learned how to use it effectively.

Language Affects Thought

The misuse of language involves more than the misuse of words. Misused language also affects our ability to think. Thought and language are inseparable. But which comes first? As with the chicken and the egg, the answer is debatable, but most scholars agree that words help us form thoughts. For example, at times we may think we know what we want to say but find that we don't know how to say it. However, if we really knew what we wanted to say, we would probably have no trouble expressing it. At other times we speak and later realize that we did not say what we meant. This usually occurs either because we did not carefully think about what we were saying or we did not carefully choose the words to express our thoughts.

It is also important to consider word choice carefully *before* speaking. Erasing the effect of something already said is extremely difficult. You can correct or retract a statement, and you can even apologize for saying it, but you cannot eliminate the fact that you said it.

Those whose career success is profoundly affected by the ability to communicate expend great effort on weighting the potential effects of using certain words. Politicians, for example, often try to assess how others might interpret their words. They know that failure to do so may place them in an awkward position, cost them an election, or even jeopardize national security. The presidential elections of recent years provide numerous examples. Ross Perot, a 1992 third-party candidate, offended many when he used "you people" while addressing a group of prominent African Americans. George W. Bush and Al Gore, 2000 presidential candidates, were careful about word choice, and yet each one unwittingly alienated some voters with their verbal miscues. Regardless of what was actually said, many believed that Gore claimed to have invented the Internet and were turned off. Others heard about George W. Bush's use of "fuzzy numbers" and were concerned about his abilities to rule the United States if elected president. In their debates, both Bush and Gore were carefully coached to avoid certain words and certain concepts and, if pressed, to answer carefully. Although their language choices cannot be blamed for the closeness of the 2000 election, what was said, what was implied, and what was inferred on the part of the listeners probably made a difference in the way people voted.

When we communicate, we first form thoughts and then decide how we are going to express them. The experiment by Bernard Baars described in the Making

Politicians need to be careful about word choice when they speak and constantly assess how others might interpret their words. They know that failure to do so may place them in an awkward position, cost them an election, or even jeopardize national security.

Connections box on page 88 clearly indicates that the thoughts of the subjects influence what they said. Being an effective communicator begins with clear thinking, followed by language use that reflects an understanding of what language is and how it is used.

The Elements of Language

Language, speech, and communication are three different, but related, phenomena. *Language,* as we noted earlier, is a structured system of signs, sounds, gestures, or marks (in other words, *symbols*) that allows people to express ideas and feelings to others; *speech* is one vehicle used to transmit language; and *communication* involves the exchange of meanings. Language is one means by which we communicate, and speech is one way in which we use language. The fact that we process language does not automatically mean that we can communicate well, but we cannot communicate without language, and language would be useless if it did not convey meanings.

To more clearly differentiate these concepts, consider the fact that you can indicate an affirmative response to a question by nodding your head, thus using a gesture to communicate without speech. You can also indicate the same response by writing the word *yes,* thus using writing instead of speech as the vehicle to transmit language. If you were traveling in a foreign country and said "yes," you might use language and speech without communicating.

The goal is to coordinate language and speech in order to produce effective communication, which is the transfer of meaning as intended. You can learn more about language by examining four of its key elements: sounds, words, grammar, and meaning.

Sounds

Most of us learn to speak language before we learn to write it, and most of us are born with the physical mechanisms that enable us to make speech sounds. However, we do not all learn to produce the sounds in exactly the same way. Though using the same language, people of certain geographic regions or cultural groups may speak quite differently. Dialects and other speech patterns may complicate communication between people who speak the same language.

Words

Words are symbols that stand for objects and concepts. A word can represent an object, as the word *chair* represents an actual piece of furniture, or it can represent an abstract concept, as *freedom* represents the intangible qualities of self-determination and civil and political liberty.

Words are agreed-on sound combinations within a language community. For example, the sounds in the word *help* constitute a word because English speakers agree that they do. However, *zelp,* although it consists of common sounds in our language, is not a word, because this combination of sounds does not have an agreed-on meaning.

Grammar

Just as language has rules that govern how sounds may be joined into words, it also has rules that govern how words may be joined into phrases and sentences. This

Making Connections

The Link Between Language and Thought

Consider the following excerpt from an article about how thought might influence what we say:

We're constantly at war with our tongues. Who hasn't tried to say something, then was startled by saying something else?

And who hasn't occasionally wondered if a verbal gaffe is more than a mere mistake, a faint signal from our subconscious, perhaps a reminder of long-suppressed feelings and desires?

Many psychologists regard slips as "information processing" errors, brief breakdowns in the neural machinery that controls speech.

But many also follow Sigmund Freud's belief that slips are clues to a person's most intimate and repressed feelings.

Researcher Bernard J. Baars, seeking to assess the validity of Freud's ideas, developed a technique to induce volunteers to commit slips and another to affect the content of the slips by changing the context of the experiment.

Baars tries to "prime" a volunteer to think about a particular subject. The goal is to determine how the "priming" affects the content of the slips.

In one experiment, male subjects were divided into three groups. The first group was led by an attractive female experimenter, who vol-unteered to dress in a sexually spectacular fashion; the second group was told they might receive an electric shock during the experiment and was shown some impressive-looking equipment (no shock was given); and the third group received neither of these treatments.

The results were dramatic. Subjects were given different word pairs such as "lice legs" and "shad bok."

When exposed to the lovely female experimenter, they were more than twice as likely to mess up "lice legs" by saying "nice legs."

When threatened with a shock, they more than doubled their rate of saying "bad shock" instead of "shad bok."

Discuss this article with your classmates.

1. How do you think thought influences the use of language?
2. Have you ever had trouble saying something you were asked to say?
3. Do you think the subjects' thoughts controlled their language, or was it the other way around?

Adapted from Keay Davidson, "Programmed Loose Lips Think Slips," *Chicago Tribune,* 12 December 1986, secs. 5, 7.

---

second set of rules is called **grammar.** For example, the English grammar system requires that singular nouns take singular verb forms and plural nouns take plural verb forms (table *is;* tables *are*).

As we join sounds together to form words and join words together to form phrases, sentences, and paragraphs, we use language's sound and grammar systems simultaneously. The ability to use sounds and grammar correctly is crucial to competent communication. Grammar enables us to make complete sentences and to understand the sentences made by others.

Despite the many rules that govern language, there is virtually no limit to the number of different messages that can be created. It has been estimated that in the English language, it is possible to create ten quintillion twenty-word sentences.[4] This does not include sentences either shorter or longer than twenty words. Thus, the number of possible sentences and messages is nearly infinite.

Meaning

The study of meaning, or the association of words with ideas, feelings, and contexts, is called **semantics.** If language did not have meaning, it would serve little or no purpose. Because words and word patterns can be used to exchange meanings between persons and even between generations, language is a useful tool for communication.

Do Words Contain Meaning?
We tend to associate language symbols (words) with specific meanings and to take that relationship for granted. But it is important to understand that, in fact, language by itself has no meaning.

This notion may seem to contradict our entire discussion so far. You may wonder how language can be a system involving rules and meanings, yet still have no meaning itself. Actually, it is entirely arbitrary that the word *cat* represents those four-legged felines that some of us love and some of us hate. There is nothing about the letters *c, a,* and *t* that is essentially related to the being of a cat. When we see or hear the symbol, we fill in the meaning.

Words are symbols that merely represent people, objects, concepts, and events; the word is not actually the person, object, concept, or event. For example, *chair, car, snake, communication, tall, black, money,* and *freedom* are merely words and not the entities they symbolize. It is easy to miss this distinction. Even though words are symbols, try screaming "Spider!" in front of someone who dislikes spiders, and you will quickly see how words cause reactions—as if they were the actual thing!

The belief that words have meaning in themselves is widespread. During the past several years we have asked students in beginning communication classes whether words have meaning. The data, though not scientifically collected, suggest that more than 75 percent of the students believe words do have meaning. But the simple fact is that words do *not* contain meanings by themselves. They only acquire meaning through the context in which they are used and the fact that those who use them give them meaning. Figure 4.1 shows how two different people attach different meanings to the word *house.*

The following scene from Lewis Carroll's *Through the Looking Glass* illustrates this notion. Humpty Dumpty and Alice become involved in an argument about language and meaning:

> "I don't know what you mean by 'glory,' " Alice said.
>
> Humpty Dumpty smiled contemptuously. "Of course you don't—till I tell you. I meant there's a nice knock-down argument for you!"
>
> "But 'glory' doesn't mean 'a nice knock-down argument,' " Alice objected.
>
> "When I use a word," Humpty Dumpty said, in a rather scornful tone, "it means just what I choose it to mean—neither more nor less."
>
> "The question is," said Alice, "whether you can make words mean so many different things."
>
> "The question is," said Humpty Dumpty, "which is to be master—that's all."[5]

Which is the master—you, words, or the meaning you give words? The answer is *you.* You control which words you use, the meaning you wish to give them, and, if you have mastered the art of communication, how people react to them. But though everyone has the same ability to impart meaning to words, not everyone does so in the same way. Thus, a sender may intend one meaning for a message, but the receiver may

FIGURE 4.1

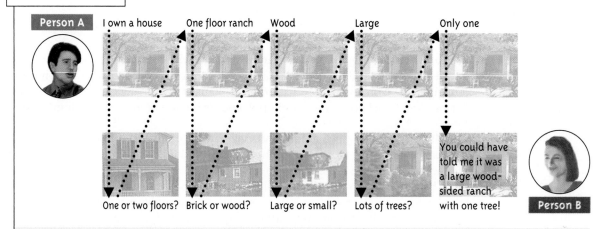

Meanings Are Not in Words, But Are in People

We cannot assume that using words that we consider appropriate and adequate to convey a particular message will succeed with every listener. As this figure illustrates, different people associate different meanings with even the simplest words. This is because words are symbols only—people fill in the meaning.

either intentionally or unintentionally give the message a different meaning. Disparity between meaning sent and meaning received may be a greater problem when the sender and receiver have different cultural backgrounds or even different experiences and knowledge. For example, people who keep up with computers and technology may use specialized language that is unfamiliar to someone lacking much knowledge about computers. Care in choosing words is especially important in such situations.

Words Have Denotative and Connotative Meanings.   **Denotation** is the core meaning associated with a word—its standard dictionary definition. Denotative meanings are usually readily understood. Many people use words as if they had only a denotative or specific meaning, but this is not the case. Although commonly understood dictionary definitions (denotative meanings) do exist, when we communicate we usually use words connotatively.

Connotation is the subjective meaning of a word, what a word suggests because of feelings or associations it evokes. The connotative meaning is based on the context in which the word is used, how the meaning is expressed verbally (tone of voice, facial expression of the speaker, and so on), and the understanding of the person who is receiving it. The competent communicator can differentiate between denotative and connotative meanings and understands which is being used in a given situation. Connotative meanings may be generally accepted by most of the people who use the language, by people within a particular group, or by an individual. For example, to one city person, the word *farm* may mean a place where crops are grown and animals are kept, but to a particular rural person, *farm* may represent a livelihood, a workplace, or a home.

Words Can Be Concrete or Abstract.   **Concrete words** are symbols for specific things that can be pointed to or physically experienced (seen, tasted, smelled, heard, or touched). For example, words such as *car, book, keys,* and *dog* are concrete words. They represent specific, tangible objects, and therefore their meanings are usually quite clear. Consequently, communication based on concrete words leaves little room for misunderstanding, and typically any disagreement can be resolved by referring to the objects themselves.

Abstract words, however, are symbols for ideas, qualities, and relationships. Because they represent things that cannot be experienced through the senses, their meanings depend on the experiences and intentions of the persons using them. For instance, words such as *right, freedom, truth,* and *trust* stand for ideas that mean different things to different people. Thus, the use of abstract words can easily lead to misunderstandings and result in ineffective communication, as illustrated by the following conversation:

Student: Your tests are unfair.

Instructor: Why do you say that?

Student: They're unfair, and it's impossible to get a high grade on them.

Instructor: Do they include material that wasn't covered in class or in our readings?

Student: No.

Instructor: Do you mean the wording is too ambiguous for you to understand?

Student: No.

Instructor: What's unfair about them?

Making Connections

Language and Meaning

"When people talk to each other, the actual meanings of the words stated convey a very small part of the meaning of the conversation."

—*Deborah Tannen, psychologist and author*

In small groups, discuss the following:

1. What is Dr. Tannen saying about spoken language?
2. Create and present a conversation in which meanings of words themselves are not the main carriers of meaning. Role-play the conversation to the class to see if others outside of your group can determine your intended meaning.
3. What did you discover about communication from participating in this exercise?

This conversation is problematic because the student expects the instructor to understand what the student meant by the word *unfair.* But because *unfair* is an abstract word, its meaning can vary greatly from person to person and from situation to situation. To clarify what he or she means by *unfair,* the student needs to use more concrete language, for instance, "Your tests are unfair because they contain too many items to complete in the time allotted." It is always a good idea to define or illustrate any abstract word that may be misunderstood in a conversation.

Figure 4.2 represents the "ladder of abstraction" first described by Alfred Korzybski in 1933 and expanded on by S. I. Hayakawa in 1964.[6] Figure 4.2 illustrates the varying degrees of concreteness among related words. *Cynthia* is the most tangible word because it refers to a specific individual named Cynthia. You can see that as the words move from concrete to abstract, they become less specific.

Meaning Depends on Commonalities. The more communicators have in common in terms of background, experience, and attitudes, the more

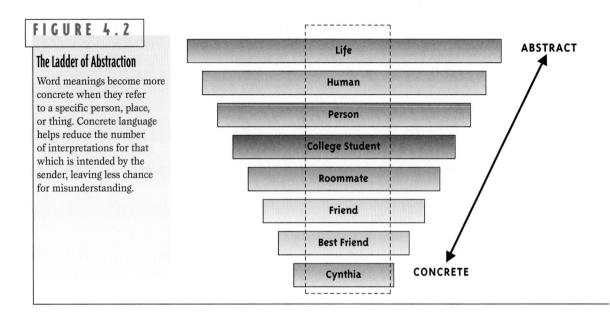

FIGURE 4.2

The Ladder of Abstraction

Word meanings become more concrete when they refer to a specific person, place, or thing. Concrete language helps reduce the number of interpretations for that which is intended by the sender, leaving less chance for misunderstanding.

ABSTRACT — Life — Human — Person — College Student — Roommate — Friend — Best Friend — Cynthia — CONCRETE

likely they are to hold similar meanings for the words they exchange. However, competent communicators should not assume too much about how others will interpret their messages; they should continuously refine messages based on the feedback they receive. Individuals' personally held connotations can skew their interpretations of messages that are made up of words that seem straightforward and concrete. Consider the following situation:

> Jill and her parents are discussing college. When the subject switches to Jill's boyfriend and the word *sex* is mentioned, Jill immediately stops the discussion because she knows her parents' views on sex are much different from her own. The word simply has different meanings for Jill and her parents.

Jill cannot talk about sex with her parents because the word conjures up different connotations that promote misinterpretation and distrust. What can be done to prevent this kind of obstacle to communication? Who is at fault? Why?

Different experiences, backgrounds, and ages of the communicators, as well as their relationship to one another, can influence word choice of the sender and the meanings understood by the receiver. Jill knows that her parents attach a different meaning to the word *sex,* so she chooses to avoid communication with them on this topic—it just seems too difficult. This difficulty derives from different (even incompatible) connotations, even though the denotative meaning of *sex* is somewhat constant and generally understood. In this situation the connotations are far more powerful than the denotation. They reflect the fact that Jill and her parents lack common ground on this issue—perhaps their values, behaviors, beliefs, or knowledge differ. It takes great skill to bridge such a gap.

Language Can Obscure Meanings.   Word meanings vary from person to person, based on each one's experience and the direct relationship of those experiences to particular words. For example, the term *myocardial infarction* has limited meaning for most people, whereas the term *heart attack* is understood by almost everyone to denote a serious health crisis related to the heart. However, a doctor, a patient, a relative of a patient,

Making Connections

Using Language in Your Role as Student

Imagine that you have been assigned to write a brief research paper and then to use that same topic for an informative speech three weeks later. Because language use should vary according to the time, the place, the situation, and the mode of communication, think about the similarities and differences between the language used in written reports and oral presentations.

1. List the characteristics of language appropriate to writing a paper.
2. List the characteristics of the language appropriate to making an oral presentation on the same topic.
3. Together with a classmate, compare and contrast the two lists. What differences do you note between language suited to writing and to speaking?

Now, consider different audiences:

4. You are speaking to a group of high school students. How will that affect your use of words? List the characteristics of language appropriate to this audience.
5. How will your language use change if you are speaking to a group of people over the age of sixty-five? List the characteristics of language appropriate to this audience.
6. Together with a classmate, compare and contrast the two lists. Why should language use vary according to context?

and a statistician in a hospital will understand the term quite differently. The doctor thinks of procedures that will help the patient. The patient thinks, "Will I live or die?" The family members ask, "What can I do?" The statistician sees a probability related to life and death. The medical doctor knows that using the term *myocardial infarction* may confuse the patient and family members, so the more common "lay term" must be used. Employing the wrong language in such a sensitive situation can lead to misunderstanding and confusion.

Also, the meanings of words, like words themselves, change from time to time and from place to place. It is easy to forget that the meaning we have for a word may not match those held by others. For example, ask a person over age sixty the meanings of these words: *grass, geek, speed, pot, joint, gay, high,* or *stoned.* What words do we use now that might change in meaning over the next twenty years? We also are constantly adding words to our language, especially those related to new technologies. Consider *email, snail mail, fax, CD-ROM, compact disc, cell phone, ATM, spamming, surfing the Web, netiquette, download, upload,* and so on.

Word meanings also vary from region to region. For example, in some regions of the United States, if you ask for "pop" at a store, the clerk will not understand you until you rephrase your question and ask for "soda" or a "Coke." In Nebraska and Iowa, people get a drink of water from the drinking fountain, but in Wisconsin, people use a bubbler. Regional word use can lead to misunderstandings, and we must be sensitive to such potential differences. Also, cultures and co-cultures hold differing meanings for certain words. For example, for most Americans "very dear" means something that is highly valued or loved, whereas in Ireland "very dear" means very expensive and has nothing to do with value or love.

Language, or jargon, used by a particular group or discipline may be too specialized or technical to be understood by the general public. In order to understand what is being said here, one would have to have specific knowledge about the group or subject.

Subpopulations of a language community sometimes use words or phrases in special ways unique to their group. Such language is referred to as **slang** or jargon. For example, language used by people selling cars includes slang terms such as *flea* for a person who is out to get a great bargain. A prisoner refers to a knife or to stab with a knife as *shank,* and a real estate agent might use the term *handyman's special* to refer to a house in need of repair.[7] Professor Judi Sanders and her students in the Department of Communication at California State Polytechnic University in Pomona have a College Slang Research Project that is accessible on the Web. Here are the top five slang terms on the 1999 College Slang Page:

> *Dope*—good; very good
>
> *Chill*—to relax
>
> *Tight*—good
>
> *Cool*—good
>
> *Phat*—good; very good

Other popular slang terms among college students across the nation included the following:

> *Dis*—to disrespect
>
> *As if*—Yeah, right,; that's not true
>
> *Baggin' up*—laughing uncontrollably
>
> *Live park*—the act of waiting in traffic or driving around the block while someone runs an errand.[8]

Are these slang words still commonly used? Have new slang words replaced them? Such words are constantly being discarded and new ones invented—sometimes just to make sure that people outside a particular group will not catch on to their meanings. All kinds of groups, including members of a given profession, college students, ethnic groups, and gangs, develop and use slang terms.[9]

Language is used to share meaning, but it also can be used to obscure, distort, or hide meaning. One way to obscure meaning is to use a euphemism. A **euphemism** is an inoffensive or mild expression given in place of one that may offend, cause embarrassment, or suggest something unpleasant. Our society also uses euphemisms to avoid taboo subjects or words that can trigger negative reactions. Employing euphemisms can defuse the emotional charge associated with controversial or difficult concepts. For example, when a person has died, we use a euphemism such as "passed away" instead of blunter words. The phrase "passed away" seems to make a difficult, complex situation more approachable.

Euphemisms can also be used to enhance something, to make it seem a little more glamorous than it actually is. In our society, we have become so concerned with labels that we have renamed many things in order to give them a more positive connotation. For example, we rarely use the term *salesman* because, apart from its being sexist, it also conjures up a negative image not exactly characterized by scrupulous business ethics. This unfavorable connotation has been fostered by the media and sometimes by personal experience. Thus, referring to a person who sells merchandise as a sales associate, sales consultant, or sales representative sounds more positive. Sometimes the term "trash collector" or "garbage man" is recast as "sanitation engineer," which makes the job seem more attractive.

Language can also be used to create deliberately ambiguous messages. William Lutz, a professor at Rutgers University, says he can live with ordinary euphemisms, but his teeth are set on edge when a worker is told he has been "dehired" because the firm is experiencing "negative employee retention." Actually, the employee has been fired in a layoff. But no one is willing to say so, laments Lutz, who wrote *Doublespeak,* a book denouncing the use of words to conceal meaning. **Doublespeak** is the deliberate misuse of language to distort meaning.

"It is going just too far," says Lutz, when the Pentagon refers to bombs that accidentally kill civilians as "incontinent ordinance" or when lawyers write off a plane crash as "the involuntary conversion of a 727." That, he says, is language "designed to distort reality and corrupt thought."[10] Lutz thinks the practice is disgraceful, dangerous to democracy, perverse, and pervasive. It's hard work, too. Doublespeak isn't just the natural work product of the bureaucratic mind; it is invented painstakingly by committees laboring to cloak meaning. Doublespeak is not a slip of the tongue or language used improperly because of ignorance. It is a tool used by the powerful to achieve their ends without clearly communicating with those who may be affected by their actions or who may foot the bill for them. According to Lutz and other scholars, doublespeak is particularly harmful when it makes something inappropriate or negative appear to be appropriate or positive.

As you can see, language and meaning are inseparable parts of communication. They mesh together smoothly in successful communication. Unfortunately, a type of communication also occurs when a message is misunderstood.

Language-Based Barriers to Communication

Although it takes little physical effort to say something to someone, it does take mental effort to ensure that what we say conveys our intended meaning. Even if we create

Making Connections

Dictionary.com

Web searches on different language topics can provide interesting and exciting information. Some sites help you learn more about words, their usage, and their definitions. Dictionary.com is one such site. When you key in a word, seeking a definition, the search engine provides several definitions from different dictionaries so you can compare meanings. The site features "Dr. Dictionary" so you can ask questions relating to words and grammar and will translate anything from a phrase to an entire web page from one major European language, including English, to another.

1. Access Dictionary.com by keying in http://www.dictionary.com.

2. Seek the definition of a word of your choice (try to find a word with which you are relatively unfamiliar that you recently read or one you heard from someone else). If you can't think of a word, try one of these: *etymology, homophily, multiculturalism, panacea,* or *volition.*

3. Compare the definitions returned. How are they similar? How different? How would you know which was the "best" definition?

4. Go to Dr. Dictionary in Dictionary.com and ask a question about a word or phrase (e.g., "What is the word meaning 'to throw out of a window'?").

5. Share what you've learned with other students.

what we *think* is the perfect message, the possibility always exists that the receiver will misinterpret the message or find it ambiguous. Thus, the receiver must also make an effort to receive the intended message.

"There are over 300 different languages in everyday use in the United States. This number includes more than 200 Native American languages, the languages of the colonizers (English, French, and Spanish), languages of immigrants—both old and new—and a variety of dialects spoken in various regions of the country."[11] We must recognize that communication is a symbolic interaction rich in subtlety. It will never be strictly concrete or objective and thus always carries the potential for misunderstanding. Misunderstandings occur for numerous physical, mental, and cultural reasons. Ineffective use of language is one reason. Among the most common language-based barriers to effective communication are bypassing, indiscrimination, and polarization.[12]

Meanings Can Be Misunderstood

What is *meant* by a speaker and what is *heard* and *understood* by the listener often differ. Such misunderstanding between a sender and a receiver is called **bypassing.** How many times have we said to someone, "But that's not what I meant"? Here is a classic illustration of bypassing:

A motorist was driving down a highway when her engine suddenly stalled. She quickly determined that her battery was dead and managed to stop another driver, who consented to push her car to get it started.

"My car has an automatic transmission," she explained to the other driver, "so you'll have to get up to 15 to 20 miles per hour to get me started."

The man smiled and walked back to his car. The motorist climbed into her own and waited for him to line up his car behind hers. She waited—and waited. Finally, she turned around to see what was wrong. There was the man—coming at her car at 15 to 20 miles per hour!

The damage to her car amounted to over $1,000![13]

That result could not have been anticipated by either driver, given each one's understanding of the message. The driver of the stalled vehicle thought she knew exactly what she had asked of the other driver, but the meanings of the message sent and the message received obviously were different. Bypassing took place.

Bypassing usually results from the false belief that each word has only one meaning and that words have meaning in themselves. But a glimpse at our everyday language quickly illustrates that most words have multiple uses and meanings. For example, the *Random House Dictionary of the English Language* provides sixty different definitions for the word *call,* thirty for *fast,* twenty-two for *seat,* twenty-nine for *see,* and ninety-six for *turn.* Words acquire these many meanings because they change over time, are used and understood differently in various cultures and regions, and often reflect the knowledge and situation of the user. Thus it is crucial that all of us as communicators, both senders and receivers, stay alert to the fact that words can be interpreted differently by different people.

The interpretation of words becomes even more complex when people from different cultures exchange everyday communication. The problem is magnified when someone uses common phrases that are unfamiliar to non-native speakers of English. For example, consider this sentence: "Won't you have some tea?" The non-native speaker of English listens to the literal meaning of the question and would answer no if he or she did in fact want tea. Because they use this wording so frequently, native English speakers forget that it contains a double negative. But a non-native speaker may not know that, in practice, "Won't you have some tea?" and "Will you have some tea?" mean the same thing. In this situation bypassing occurred because of cultural differences between the two speakers.[14]

Some speakers deliberately invite bypassing by using euphemisms or doublespeak to soften or distort meanings. It is important to be aware of this. Politicians and advertisers sometimes will say one thing in order to get people to believe or accept something else. Listeners should critically examine what is being said. Both speaking and listening involve ethical considerations. Issues of conscience—what is right or wrong and what is beneficial or harmful—are everyone's responsibility.

Reducing Bypassing[15]

1. *Be person-minded, not word-minded.* Think about words and their meanings, but also consider the persons using the words and the meanings they might give to them. Constantly question your own interpretation: "This is what the word means to me, but what does it mean to the others?"

2. *Query and paraphrase.* Ask questions and paraphrase your message or the meaning you've derived from others' messages, whenever there is a potential for misunderstanding. Differences in background, age, gender, occupation, culture, attitudes, knowledge, and perceptions may affect communication. If you are uncertain, ask others to explain. Restating a message in your own words gives you and the sender a chance to check that you received a similar

message to what was sent. As the importance and complexity of a message increases, so does the need for asking questions and paraphrase.

3. *Be approachable.* Encourage open and free communication. The most frequent barrier to effective communication is an unwillingness to listen to others. Allow others to question and paraphrase your messages, and show respect for what they say. Being receptive is not always easy, but the effort will ensure a clear exchange of information.

4. *Be sensitive to contexts.* Consider the verbal and situational contexts in which communication occurs. The meaning of a word can be more precisely interpreted by considering the words, sentences, and paragraphs that precede and follow it and the setting in which communication takes place.

Language Can Shape Our Attitudes

Indiscrimination is the neglect of individual differences and the overemphasis of similarities. Indiscrimination is a form of perceptual set (see Chapter 2) in which a person chooses to ignore differences and changes in events, things, and people. Language plays a significant role in our tendency to see similarities between things, even when they don't exist. Nouns that categorize people *(teenager, divorcé, student, professor, African American, southerner, liberal, friend, government official, politician, salesperson)* encourage us to focus on similarities. Statements such as "Politicians are crooks" and "Students cheat in school" may be interpreted to include all politicians and all students, instead of some politicians and some students. They fail to distinguish between individuals. Such categorization often results in stereotyping.

A stereotype, as defined in Chapter 2, is a categorizing of events, objects, and people without regard to unique individual characteristics and qualities. Stereotypes are often negative, but they may also be positive, for example, "All liberals are hardworking," "All conservatives want peace," "All teachers are dedicated professionals," "All environmentalists are concerned citizens." Whether the stereotype is negative or positive, the problem is the same: Individual qualities are ignored. Stereotyping is quick and easy to do because it does not require analysis, investigation, or thought. By precluding distinctions, stereotypes give us neat, oversimplified categories that facilitate our evaluation of people, situations, and events.

There are ways to reduce indiscrimination in our communication. **Indexing** points up differences that distinguish various members of a group and thus reduces indiscrimination. Indexing identifies the specific person, idea, event, or object to which a statement refers. When you hear someone say, "Politicians are corrupt," "College men are oversexed," "Homosexuals have perverted values," "Athletes are dumb," or any statement that lumps persons, ideas, events, or objects into a single category, immediately ask, "Which ones are you talking about?" No matter what people may think, not all politicians are corrupt. Politician A is different from politician B, and politician B is different from politician C. The same is true of college men, homosexuals, and athletes. They may belong to a class or group that has an identity and whose members have similarities, but the group is composed of individuals, each different from the other.

Dating, another technique for reducing indiscrimination, is a form of indexing that sorts people, ideas, events, and objects according to time. By telling when something occurred, we acknowledge that things change over time and add specificity to a statement. As an example of how important dating is, indicate the year in which you think each of the following news bulletins was probably made:

Pope Condemns Use of New "Horror" Weapons

Vatican City—Prompted by widespread fears that new weapons of mass destruction might wipe out Western civilization, the Pope today issued a bulletin forbidding the use of these weapons by any Christian state against another, whatever the provocation.

Moral Rot Endangers Land, Warns General

Boston—The head of the country's armed forces declared here today that if he had known the depth of America's moral decay, he would never have accepted his command. "Such a dearth of public spirit," he asserted, "and want of virtue, and fertility in all the low arts to obtain advantages of one kind or another, I never saw before and hope I may never be witness to again."[16]

The thoughts expressed in these two paragraphs could easily apply to what is happening today, but, in fact, the first paragraph pertains to a statement made by Pope Innocent II in 1139 and the second quotes a comment made by George Washington in 1775.

Did you think that these news bulletins referred to recent events? If so, you fell victim to indiscrimination. Why do such errors occur? How can we avoid or prevent them? The contexts of the statements in these news bulletins could be greatly clarified merely by adding dates: Vatican City, 1139, and Boston, 1775. Dating gives listeners valuable information that can increase their understanding of the intended message.

Language Can Cause Polarization

Polarization is the tendency to view things in terms of extremes—rich or poor, beautiful or ugly, large or small, high or low, good or bad, intelligent or stupid—even though most things exist somewhere in between. This either–or, black-or-white way of thinking is aggravated by aspects of language.

Polarization can be destructive, escalating conflict to the point that two parties simply cannot communicate. This escalation is referred to as the **pendulum effect.** The pendulum represents a person's perception of reality, which includes feelings, attitudes, opinions, and value judgments about the world. When the pendulum is hanging in the center, a person's perception is considered to be realistic, virtuous, intelligent, sane, honest, and honorable. Of course, most of us believe that our pendulums are at or near the center most of the time. When two individuals disagree in their perceptions of reality, their pendulums begin to move in opposite directions. The distance the pendulum swings represents their differences in opinion or conviction. As the conversation intensifies, each remark provokes a stronger reaction from the party to whom it is directed, until both parties are driven to positions at opposite extremes. For example, when two roommates argue over whose turn it is to clean, one may begin by saying, "It's your turn. I did it the last time." The other is likely to respond, "No, I did it the last time. Now it's your turn." If the disagreement continues and no solution is found, both will become more entrenched in their positions, and their comments may turn into personal attacks: "You're always so messy and lazy." "And you're always so picky and critical." The situation may degenerate to the point that one or

Polarization is the tendency to view things in terms of extremes—rich or poor, beautiful or ugly, large or small, high or low, good or bad, intelligent or stupid—even though most things exist somewhere between. This either–or, black-or-white way of thinking is aggravated by aspects of language.

the other threatens to move out. Such an extreme outcome is typical of a discussion driven by the pendulum effect. Emotions may eventually run so high that the differences between the parties may seem insurmountable and a mutually agreeable settlement may seem unattainable.

Speakers can avoid the dangers of polarization by recognizing the potential for misunderstanding and by making statements that do not represent unnuanced extremes. For example, a noncontroversial statement such as "Nebraska is hot in the summer" is not as meaningful as it could be because the word *hot* represents a generalized extreme. Further information will prevent misunderstanding: What is the basis of comparison (Florida or Minnesota)? Are Nebraska summers all the same, or do they vary from year to year? Is a Nebraska summer the same in all parts of the state, or does it vary from north to south? What is the average summer temperature? The problem of making an incorrectly overgeneralized and extreme statement is avoided here: "Nebraska summers can be hot. The average temperature is 85 degrees Fahrenheit, with lows around 74 degrees and highs around 105 degrees." Such clarification is especially important when the topic at hand is likely to provoke emotional, defensive, or unpredictable reactions.

Language Can Be Sexist

There is a difference in how men and women may use language and converse with one another (as indicated in Chapter 3). Deborah Tannen, for example, suggests that men use language to assert status, whereas women use language to establish and maintain social relationships.[17] Tannen says that, rather than use language to dominate another, women employ it to establish closeness and support. Men, however, use language to dominate or compete. The result, according to Tannen, is that the game of communication for men and women is the same, but the rules are different. When men and women communicate with each other, there is the potential for clash and conflict because of different language use. The problem is magnified when sexist language is used either consciously or unconsciously. Our goal should be to use **gender-inclusive language**—language that does not discriminate against males or females.

Unfortunately, the English language is structured with an inherent bias in favor of men. There are, for example, no singular gender-neutral pronouns in the English language. Thus, traditionally, the masculine pronouns *(he, him, his)* have been used to refer to people in general, even if the referent could be a male or female. Use of the masculine pronoun is not incorrect grammatically, but its use in generic situations is a social issue. Language sets expectations that at times discriminate against and stereotype women. According to traditional usage, the omnipresence of *he* and *him,* and the general absence of *she* and *her,* subtly but powerfully gives the impression that men hold important roles, whereas women do not. Thus, our language creates the expectation that males are active and have important roles, whereas females are inactive and do not hold important roles.

Making Connections

Language Clarifies Meaning

Competent speakers demonstrate the ability to use language that clarifies, persuades, or inspires while respecting differences in listeners' backgrounds (race, ethnicity, age, etc.).* Competent speakers also remember who their listeners are and can place themselves in their listeners' perspectives. In order to work on your communication competence, respond to the following as you think about how a speaker's language affects listeners.

1. Identify three specific language choices you have made in the past because you were aware of your listeners and their perspectives (e.g., speaking to a professor, a grandparent, a friend):

   A.

   B.

   C.

2. Identify three specific language choices you made in preparing for a class presentation:

   A.

   B.

   C.

3. Identify three language considerations you will keep in mind for future presentations in this class, based on your knowledge of both speakers and listeners:

   A.

   B.

   C.

*(*Competent Communicators K–12 Speaking, Listening, and Media Literacy Standards and Competency Statements* (Annandale, Va.: National Communication Association, 1998), 14.

Sexual stereotypes and the assumption that the male gender is superior to the female characterize **sexist language**.[18] In our society, sexist language involves an attitude as much as the use of specific words. Words with a positive connotation are used to describe males—*independent, logical, strong, confident, aggressive;* females are associated with words having negative connotations—*dependent, illogical, weak, gullible, timid.* Sexist language suggests that men are more important than and superior to women. Language used to discriminate against women can be quite subtle. Consider these statements: "She is president of the company and she's a woman"; "Wanda got that position because she's a woman." They describe women who have risen to high authority positions, but they also imply that women do not typically hold these positions or that the only reason Wanda got the position was

Making Connections

Using Language to Understand the World

Five-year-old Jamie and her mother were watching a television documentary on mammals of the ocean. The narrator talked about the size of whales and said, "Don't worry. Whales do not eat men."

Jamie was immediately alarmed and became agitated. Her mother said, "What's wrong, Jamie?"

Jamie asked, "Do whales eat women?"

Her mother answered, "No, the man just said that whales don't eat men, and that means that whales don't eat people."

"But Mom, he just said that whales don't eat men, but he did not say that whales don't eat women."

"But Jamie, what he meant was that whales don't eat people."

"Why didn't he say that? Doesn't he know that girls might get frightened if they hear that whales don't eat men, but he doesn't say that they don't eat women?"

1. How would you explain the use of the generic term *men* to Jamie?
2. How might you use this situation to help others understand the power of language?
3. How can we make others understand that using inclusive language involves more than being "politically correct"?
4. Identify similar situations in which misunderstandings occurred because of inappropriate word choices.

This true story was related by Pam Cooper, communication professor at Northwestern University, and is used with her permission.

because she's a woman. In other words, they imply that women are less qualified than men.

Stereotypes do not occur in a social vacuum. On the contrary, they often exert powerful influence on the lives of those who are stereotyped. Gender stereotypes influence perceptions and behaviors of both men and women. Stereotypes of women affect both how they are treated in society and how they think of themselves. Language is one significant means of perpetuating these stereotypes. Avoiding sexist language and substituting gender-inclusive terms represent a positive step toward doing away with them.

Other stereotypes are reinforced in the use of homophobic language. When someone asks another to "tell me what to look for so I can recognize gays or lesbians and then avoid them," the speaker is demonstrating both insensitivity to individuals and a general negative categorization of a group of people, each of whom is unique.

Metaphors used in our culture to describe men and women are often sexist. A **metaphor** is a figure of speech that associates two things or ideas, not commonly linked, as a means of description. These stereotypical animal metaphors illustrate the use of sexist language: Men are likely to be described as aggressive (*wolf, tomcat, stud*) and women as harmless pets (*kitten, lamb, chick*) or as unattractive barnyard animals (*cow, pig, dog*). The effective communicator must avoid such negative metaphorical stereotyping, find more positive metaphors related to women, and use inclusive language in general.

Using Gender-Inclusive Language

1. Commit yourself to removing sexism from your communication.

2. Practice and reinforce nonsexist communication patterns until they become habitual. The ultimate goals are to use nonsexist language effortlessly in private conversation and to think in nonsexist terms.

3. Use familiar language whenever possible, but if you must choose between sexist language and an unfamiliar phrase, choose the unfamiliar phrase and practice it until it becomes familiar.

4. Do not arouse negative reactions in receivers by using awkward, cumbersome, highly repetitive, or unnecessary words. There are so many graceful and controlled ways to state your message inclusively that you need not use bland or offensive constructions.

5. Ascertain whether roots and meanings of words need to be changed before doing so.

6. Check every outgoing message—written, oral, nonverbal, and email—for sexism before sending it.[19]

It is important that the language we use be inclusive and not demeaning to any group of individuals. Language influences how we see others around us. Inappropriate language causes perceptual and social problems that should not be tolerated in our society.

Culture Affects Language Use

Just as there are differences in the ways men and women use language, there are also cultural differences in the use of language. As we saw in the opening scenario, people visiting from other nations often are reluctant to speak in front of groups in classrooms, social gatherings, and the workplace, because they are concerned that they will not use the "correct" words and might embarrass themselves by communicating ineffectively. According to the **Sapir-Whorf hypothesis,** our perception of reality is determined by our thoughts, and our language influences our thought processes. According to Sarah Trenholm, this hypothesis involves two theories: **linguistic determinism** (the theory that language determines thought) and **linguistic relativity** (the theory that people from different language communities perceive the world differently).[20] Together they suggest that culture helps create variations in communication. In other words, according to the Sapir-Whorf hypothesis, language is more than simply attaching labels to the world around us. Language shapes our reality. We only "know" the world in terms of the language we have at our command, and that language determines our cultural reality. If we don't have the words to explain something, we

Making Connections

Understanding the Difference Between High- and Low-Context Cultures

Aleta is from China (high-context culture). Her neighbor, Jennifer, is from the United States (low-context culture). Jennifer's daughter is learning to play the piano and practices early in the morning, after school, and in the evening before bedtime.

One night at 9 P.M., Aleta knocked on Jennifer's door and said, "You must be so proud of your daughter. She practices the piano so much. You must plan to have her become a concert pianist."

"Why, no." Jennifer responded, "She's just beginning to play the piano."

"You must be proud that she practices early in the morning, after school, and into the night. She is certainly a dedicated student. She plays the piano so many hours." And, with that, Aleta turned around and went into her own apartment.

1. What's the difference between the language use in high- and low-context cultures?
2. What was the "real" message here?
3. Does Jennifer get the message?
4. If the neighbor had been another person from the United States, what do you suppose would have been said?

don't really "know" it, and it doesn't exist. When we can use words to explain the concept, event, or idea, it takes on meaning that can be shared. Judith Martin and Thomas Nakayama suggest that the relationship between communication and culture can be viewed in three complementary ways: (1) Culture influences communication, (2) culture is enacted through communication, and (3) communication is a way of contesting and resisting the dominant culture.[21]

And further, anthropologist Edward T. Hall suggests that for some cultures, the situation in which a particular communication occurs tells us a great deal about its meaning.[22] In a **high-context culture** the meaning of the communication act is inferred from the situation or location. In Japan (a high-context culture), for example, businesspeople do not conduct business in a social setting, although they may refer to their business interests. If one visits Japan on business and is invited out to dinner, there is no "hidden agenda"—the objective for the evening is to eat a meal together, not to conduct business. Business is saved for "the office" or the meeting place. Also, in a high-context culture, language is indirect, nonspecific, and not very assertive. In a **low-context culture** the meaning of the communication act is inferred from the messages being sent and not the location where the communication occurs. According to Hall, the United States is a low-context culture in which businesspeople are as likely to conduct business on the golf course, in a restaurant, or at a reception as they are in the workplace. People in a low-context culture typically are more assertive and more direct. They get immediately to the point. Because understanding such distinctions is essential to sending and receiving messages successfully, the competent communicator will learn as much about language and cultural differences as possible.

Neil Postman, in *Technopoly,* says that technology redefines culture through its control over and elevation of information. "The uncontrolled growth of technology destroys the vital sources of our humanity."[23] Given the rapid growth of technology, it is likely that some changes will occur simply because of the technological advances. Language, however, will still influence thought, and Martin and Nakayama's third point (communication is a way of contesting and resisting the dominant culture) may well be more needed than ever before.

How to Use Language Effectively

People of all ages, cultures, and educational levels use language every day. Nevertheless, the ability to use language efficiently and effectively requires years of practice and study. Although many variables influence the effectiveness of language use, five aspects of language merit special attention. They are accuracy, vividness, immediacy, appropriateness, and metaphor.

Use Accurate Language

Using accurate language is as critical to a speaker as giving accurate navigational directions is to an air traffic controller. Choosing a wrong word can distort your intended message, misguide your receiver, and undermine your credibility. When you speak, your goal should be precision. Don't leave room for misinterpretation. You should constantly ask yourself, "What do I want to say?" and "What do I mean?" When necessary, consult a dictionary to be sure you have chosen the correct word to express your message.

The more words you can use accurately, the more likely it is that you will find the one you need to make your meaning clear. You must expand your vocabulary. Two of the best ways to do this are through listening to others and reading. Pay attention to words that you don't understand. Whenever you come across an unfamiliar word, determine the context in which it is used and consult a dictionary to find its meaning. Once you have learned a new word, try to put it to use. Words that are not used are typically forgotten. Expanding your vocabulary takes effort and time, but with practice, it can become part of your daily routine.

One word of warning: As you develop your vocabulary, avoid the temptation to use long or little-known words when short or common words serve the purpose. Also be sure you know the shades of meaning and connotations of new words before you use them; and remember that words may have different meanings for different people.

Sometimes a message is unclear because it was not structured effectively. Poor sentence structure and word usage can wreak havoc with a statement's clarity. For example, classified ads in newspapers frequently are so condensed that their intended meaning becomes distorted or obscured. The result may be "1989 Cadillac hearse for sale—body in good condition" and "Wanted to rent—four-room apartment by careful couple; no children." Obviously, these advertisers knew what they intended to communicate, but their failure to phrase their messages accurately interfered with conveying their intended meaning.

When conversing, we can easily clear up misunderstandings caused by scrambled sentence structure or poor word choice. But to do so, we must first be aware of listeners'

Making Connections

Using Language Effectively

Compare the two following messages. The first was made by President Franklin D. Roosevelt. The second expresses a similar thought, though in a different way.

> *I see one-third of a nation ill-housed, ill-clad, ill-nourished.*

> *It is evident that a substantial number of persons within the continental boundaries of the United States have inadequate financial resources with which to purchase the products of agricultural communities and industrial establishments. It would appear that, for a considerable segment of the population,*

perhaps as much as 33.333 percent of the total, there are inadequate housing facilities, and an equally significant proportion is deprived of the proper types of clothing and nourishment.*

1. How would you describe the word choice in each message?
2. How does each message affect your emotions?
3. What impression do you have of each speaker?

*Excerpt from *Power of Words,* copyright 1954, 1953 and renewed 1982, 1981 by Stuart Chase, reprinted by permission of Harcourt, Inc.

reactions to what we are saying. If they appear confused or ask a question, we should rephrase the message more clearly.

Effective speakers do not assume that what is clear to them will necessarily be clear to listeners. They are especially aware of this potential problem in situations such as public speeches, during which listeners may not be able to ask questions. To ensure comprehension, such speakers strive to make their meaning clear by, among other things, using familiar and concrete rather than abstract language and by being aware of the connotations associated with particular words.

Use Vivid Language

To communicate effectively, make your message animated and interesting. Direct, fresh language given in the active voice can bring a sense of excitement, urgency, and forcefulness to what you say. Such **vividness** tells your audience that they had better listen because what you have to say is important.

For example, suppose an organization is trying to raise money for homeless people. It could take one of two approaches in seeking a donation from you: (1) present statistics to illustrate the number of people who are believed to be homeless in our society or (2) present cases of actual individuals who are homeless, including children and their families. The first approach is rational, informative, abstract, and emotionally distant. The second approach is emotional, urgent, concrete, and forceful. The vividness of the second approach is likely at least to get your attention and perhaps influence you to contribute.

To narrate this ceremony in a Vietnamese temple, the language should vividly and animatedly highlight the event, what people are wearing, the background ornamentation, and so forth. People tend to listen more completely when language is alive and remember more accurately when they are able to recall mental images.

According to social psychologists, vivid language affects us in several ways. It is more persuasive than a flat, pallid presentation of information, because it is more memorable and has an emotional impact. Vivid messages are more likely to create readily retained and recalled mental images. Finally, people tend to listen more attentively to vivid messages than to uninspiring or uninteresting messages.[24]

To increase a message's vividness, fill in details and use interesting, but not obscure, words. Use active verbs, and vary the sentence structures. The sentence "They had realized their most cherished dream; they discovered the ancient tomb of the Egyptian king they had sought for so long" shows action and conveys a sense of excitement. Note how much more animated and energetic it is than this dry and passive statement: "The old tomb was found by the explorers."

You should also avoid using clichés such as "happy as a lark," "blind as a bat," and "fit as a fiddle." Such overused, unimaginative phrases lack impact. You are more likely to hold your audience's attention by using fresh language to present your ideas in a new and exciting way.

Use Immediate Language

Verbal immediacy identifies and projects the speaker's feelings and makes the message more relevant to the listener. Verbal immediacy draws listeners in and involves them in the subject at hand. The following statements illustrate different levels of verbal immediacy. The first sentence displays a high immediacy level, and the last, a low level:

1. We certainly will enjoy the baseball game.
2. You and I will enjoy the baseball game.
3. I think you and I may enjoy baseball.
4. People often enjoy baseball games.

Making Connections

Technology and Language Use

The language we use is important in initiating web searches. The way you use words to search and the specific search engine you use will affect the results of your search. You need to know whether to ask a question (such as on ask.com or Ask Jeeves), put quotation marks around each separate word, or put *and, or,* or other joining words with the concepts for which you're searching. Here are some general guidelines to help you quickly find the information you are seeking.

1. The search entry form usually consists of an empty space or rectangular box in which you type in search criteria, either words or phrases, or both.
2. The "Search," "Submit," or "Go" button activates the search.
3. Click on the "Help," "Options," or "Tips" icon to learn how to put your words and punctuation marks together for the most effective search.
4. Some search engines use plus (+) when you require the words and minus (–) when you prohibit words.
5. When you use AltaVista (http://www.altavista.com), use quotation marks to separate words in the topic. This search engine considers each word independently unless you identify a group of words as a phrase within quotation marks. If you're looking for information on *lesson plans for health and nutrition,* you should enter the words as follows: + health + "lesson plans" + nutrition (or + nutri*, which tells the search engine that you will accept any form of the word that begins with the five letters *nutri*).
6. When you use Yahoo!, you should set your options before you begin the search. The Yahoo! search engine gives you the option of restricting how far into the past you wish to search. To use this option you must make a selection from a drop-down menu from three years to one day. You can tell Yahoo! to handle the text you type into the search entry form as a group of single words or as a phrase. This is accomplished by using *or* or *and* as your connecting words.
7. You can save yourself a great deal of time by checking the specific search engine to learn how to use words most effectively to search the Web.
8. If one word or term does not provide results, think of synonyms, key in those words, and search again. There is much information on the Web. You must choose your words carefully to get the most from your search.

The first statement is directly related to the speaker, the listener, and the situation. It is assertive, and the speaker makes a connection with the listener by using the word *we*. In each successive statement, the speaker decreases the intensity of this association with the listener and the event. The language becomes less immediate, more distant in tone.

Verbal immediacy also makes the speaker appear relaxed, confident, competent, and effective. Also, receivers tend to view messages characterized by immediacy as similar to their own beliefs more readily than those cast in language unrelated to the speaker, topic, or receiver.[25]

Use Appropriate Language

Each time you speak, your listeners have specific expectations about the kind of language you will use. Different kinds of language are appropriate to different situations. For example, the language you would use in addressing the president of your college or university would be much more formal than the language you would use when chatting with friends. You would be unlikely to call the president by a nickname, and you would be equally unlikely to call a friend Dr. or Mr. or Ms., except in jest.

Using language inappropriate for a given situation damages your credibility, and your message may be misinterpreted or disregarded. It is, therefore, crucial to assess each speaking situation and adjust your language accordingly. In public situations, profanity, improper grammar, and slang are always inappropriate.

Use Metaphorical Language

According to some language scholars, our way of looking at the world around us is fundamentally metaphorical in nature. Metaphors help us to structure what we think, how we perceive things, and what we do. Metaphorical language pervades our everyday language and our thoughts. A metaphor is a figure of speech in which a word or phrase relates one object or idea to another that is not commonly linked to it. A successful metaphor makes an object or idea more clear and vivid. Jesse Jackson, for example, at the 1988 National Democratic Convention, used a quilt

Making Connections

Making Meaning with Metaphorical Language

Suzanne McCorkle, a communication scholar at Boise State University, has used metaphors to examine managing interpersonal conflict and to teach critical thinking and the ethical implications of language use.* She asks students to think about metaphorical language as a tool. In this activity, think about common terms and find new ways to explain them using metaphorical language. Complete the following:

1. College is . . . (fill in your metaphor) because . . . (give an explanation).
2. Communication is like the game of . . . because. . . .
3. Discuss your metaphorical choices with your classmates, family members, or friends.
4. Defend your choices.
5. What other metaphors or analogies might you have chosen?
6. Why did you choose these instead of the other ones?
8. Listen for others' use of analogies and metaphors. Write them down and bring them to class with you so that the whole group can discuss metaphorical ways of looking at things.

*S. M. McCorkle, "Metaphor in the Classroom: A Patchwork of Inconsistency," *Speech Communication Teacher* (Annandale, Va.: National Communication Association, summer 1999), 9–10.

metaphor to make his point that the United States is made up of many different people, ideas, and lifestyles:

> America's not a blanket woven from one thread, one color, one cloth. When I was a child, growing up in Greenville, South Carolina, and Grandmother could not afford a blanket, she didn't complain and we did not freeze. Instead, she took pieces of old cloth—patches, wool, silk, gabardine—barely good enough to wipe off your shoes with.
>
> But they didn't stay that way very long. With sturdy hands and a strong cord, she sewed them together into a quilt, a thing of beauty and power and culture.
>
> Now, Democrats, we must build such a quilt.[26]

Metaphorical language is culture bound, and most metaphors have meaning only within a specific language community. If your receivers cannot identify with a particular metaphor you use, it will be meaningless to them. Also, as we pointed out earlier in the chapter, avoid metaphors that negatively or unfairly categorize a specific person or group of people.

As a student, you probably can think of many metaphors that describe your college experiences. For example, some students have said that college life is like a roller-coaster ride. There are many ups and downs, as well as turns. What are some other metaphors that vividly express your college experience?

 ## Summary

Learning how to use language is important for effective communication in any situation. Our ability to use language determines our success, makes communication personal, and allows us to translate our thoughts, feelings, and experiences into messages.

Language is a structured system of signs, sounds, gestures, and marks used and understood to express ideas and feelings. The misuse of language is more than simply a matter of misusing words; it also affects our ability to think. Thought and language, according to most scholars, are inseparable. When we cannot find the words to express a thought, perhaps our thinking is not clear. If our thoughts are not expressed clearly and accurately, misunderstanding is inevitable.

Language is made up of four key elements: sounds, words, grammar, and meaning. Speech sounds convey spoken language. When sounds are joined together in agreed-on combinations, they form *words,* symbols that stand for the objects and concepts they name. Words, in turn, can be joined together to form phrases and sentences. The rules that govern how phrases and sentences must be constructed form a language's *grammar.* A language's sound and grammar systems work simultaneously to ensure effective and efficient communication.

The goal of communication is to exchange meanings. The study of meaning, or the association of words with ideas, feelings, and contexts, is called *semantics.* If language did not have meaning, it would serve little or no purpose.

We tend to associate words with specific meanings and to take that relationship for granted, but in reality words have been arbitrarily paired with meanings. Words are not actual objects or ideas, but symbols that represent them. Meanings, therefore, are not in words but in people. Words have a *denotative* meaning (dictionary definition) and a *connotative* meaning (social or personal definition). Words can be *concrete* (specific) or they can be *abstract* (general).

Language can also obscure, distort, or hide meaning. When words and phrases are used in special ways by subpopulations of a language community, they are referred to as *slang.* A *euphemism* is the use of an inoffensive or mild expression in place of one that may offend, cause embarrassment, or suggest something unpleasant. *Doublespeak* is the deliberate misuse of language to distort meaning.

Three common language-based barriers to effective communication are bypassing, indiscrimination, and polarization. *Bypassing* is the misunderstanding that occurs between a sender and a receiver, usually as a result of the belief that a word has only one meaning. Actually, words may mean different things to different people. To reduce the frequency of bypassing, we should be focused on the receiver, approachable, and sensitive to contexts, and we should ask questions to make sure we've been understood and paraphrase our messages when necessary.

Indiscrimination is the neglect of individual differences and the overemphasis of similarities concerning a certain group of people. Indiscrimination can lead to stereotyping—developing a fixed mental picture of a group and attributing such characteristics to an individual, without regard to individual unique characteristics and qualities. To help reduce the misunderstandings caused by indiscrimination, we can use *dating* (identifying the time at which a given point held true) and *indexing* (asking which specific person or thing an overly general statement refers to) to add distinguishing detail.

Polarization is the tendency to view things in terms of extremes. Polarizations can give rise to the *pendulum effect,* escalating conflict between people that stems from their use of polar terms to describe and defend their perceptions of reality.

Gender-inclusive language does not discriminate against males or females. Unfortunately, the English language is structured to have an inherent bias in favor of men. When sexual stereotypes or the superiority of one gender over another is expressed, the language used is *sexist.* Similarly, homophobia may influence language use and may unfairly stereotype gay and lesbian people. Clear thinking and careful choice of words can help communicators avoid placing negative, overgeneralized labels on individuals or groups of people who may differ from one's own group.

Language, culture, and thought are bound together. Effective communicators are aware of how to interact with people from other cultures. Avoiding unfamiliar words, sensitivity toward another person's culture and command of the language, and patient effort characterize such interactions. The *Sapir-Whorf hypothesis* indicates that our language influences our perception of reality. The hypothesis involves *linguistic determinism* (language determines thought) and *linguistic relativity* (people from different language communities perceive the world differently). Culture also influences the nature of a communication, where it might occur, and under what circumstances. In a *high-context culture,* for example, meaning is inferred from the situation or location in which the communication occurs. Whereas in a *low-context culture,* the message is more important than the location or context in which it occurs.

Effective use of language requires practice and study. Among the most important areas to consider are accuracy, vividness, verbal immediacy, appropriateness, and metaphorical language. Accuracy helps prevent misinterpretation. *Vividness* makes messages come alive and grabs listeners' attention. *Verbal immediacy* projects the speaker's feelings and makes the message more relevant to the listener. Appropriateness ensures that a speaker's choice of words and manner of speaking suit the situation. *Metaphor* is a figure of speech in which a word or phrase relates one object or idea to another object or idea in a fresh way, making ideas and points clearer and more meaningful.

DISCUSSION STARTERS

1. Why is language so powerful?
2. How are thought and language related?
3. Why are language and communication not synonymous?
4. How is it possible that language can have rules and still be arbitrary?
5. The notion that meanings are in people is extremely important to the understanding of how we use language. Why is this so?
6. Which of the language barriers discussed in this chapter is the most likely to occur in everyday conversations? Why?
7. What advice would you give to someone about indexing and dating their communications?
8. How can language increase or reduce credibility?
9. What does it mean to say that you use language effectively?
10. How does technology affect language?

NOTES

1. X. Liao, "Effective Communication in Multicultural Classrooms." Paper presented at the National Communication Association Annual Convention, November, 2000.
2. Educational Testing Service Study on College Enrollment. Reported in *The Chronicle of Higher Education,* May 26, 2000: A35–A37.
3. *The Chronicle of Higher Education,* September 8, 2000.
4. G. A. Miller, *The Psychology of Communication* (Baltimore: Penguin, 1967).
5. L. Carroll, *Alice's Adventures in Wonderland, Through the Looking Glass, and The Hunting of the Smark* (New York: Modern Library, 1925), 246–47.
6. A. Korzybski, *Science and Sanity: An Introduction to Non-Aristotelian Systems and General Semantics* (Lancaster, Pa.: Science Press Printing, 1933).
7. P. Dickson, *Slang!* (New York: Pocket Books, 1990).
8. J. Sanders, "College Slang Page," from the College Slang Research Project, Department of Communication, California State Polytechnic University, Pomona, http://www.csupomona.edu/~jasanders/slang/. Professor Sanders may be contacted at < jasanders@csupomona.edu >
9. P. Dickson.
10. W. Lutz, *Doublespeak: From "Revenue Enhancement" to "Terminal Living": How Government, Business, Advertisers, and Others Use Language to Deceive You.* (New York: Harper & Row, 1987), 3–4.
11. K. Cushner, A. McClelland, and P. Safford, *Human Diversity in Education: An Integrative Approach* (New York: McGraw-Hill, 1992), 159.
12. Adapted from W. V. Haney, *Communication and Organizational Behavior,* 3rd ed. (Homewood, Ill.: Irwin, 1973), 211–330; and *Communication and Interpersonal Relations,* 5th ed. (Homewood, Ill.: Irwin, 1986), 213–405.
13. W. V. Haney, *Communication and Organizational Behavior,* 246.
14. L. M. Barna, "Stumbling Blocks in Intercultural Communication," in *Intercultural Communication: A Reader,* 7th ed., eds. L. A. Samovar and R. E. Porter (Belmont, Calif.: Wadsworth Publishing, 1994), 340.
15. Adapted from Haney, 232–33.
16. News bulletins from W. R. Espy, "Say When," *This Week,* 13 July 1952, quoted in W. V. Haney, *Communication and Organizational Behavior,* 396.
17. D. Tannen, *You Just Don't Understand* (New York: Morrow, 1990).
18. C. Miller and K. Swift, *The Handbook on Nonsexist Writing,* 2nd ed. (New York: Harper & Row, 1988).
19. Adapted from B. D. Sorrels, *Nonsexist Communicator: Solving the Problem of Gender and Awkwardness*

in Modern English (Englewood Cliffs, N.J.: Prentice-Hall, 1983), 17.

20. S. Trenholm, *Thinking Through Communication* (Boston: Allyn and Bacon, 2000), 87.

21. J. N. Martin and T. K. Nakayama, *Intercultural Communication in Contexts* (Mountain View, Calif.: Mayfield Publishing Co., 1997), 59.

22. E. T. Hall, *The Hidden Dimension* (Garden City, N.Y.: Doubleday, 1966).

23. N. Postman, *Technopoly* (New York: Alfred A. Knopf, 1992), 4.

24. S. T. Fiske and S. E. Taylor, *Social Cognition* (Reading, Mass.: Addison-Wesley, 1984), 190–94.

25. J. J. Bradac, J. W. Bowers, and J. A. Courtright, "Three Language Variables in Communication Research: Intensity, Immediacy, and Diversity," *Human Communication Research* 5 (1979): 257–69.

26. J. Jackson, "Common Ground and Common Sense," *Vital Speeches of the Day* 54 (1988): 649–53.

CHAPTER 5

Connecting Through Nonverbal Communication

"There is no such thing as an empty space or an empty time. There is always something to see, something to hear. In fact, try as we may to make a silence, we cannot."

—John Cage

- Define nonverbal communication.
- Tell why six key characteristics of nonverbal communication are crucial to using and interpreting it.
- Describe different types of nonverbal communication and their connection to cultural and gender uses.
- Cite five common functions of nonverbal communication.
- Explain why nonverbal communication is difficult to interpret and understand.
- Suggest ways to improve both the interpretation and use of nonverbal communication.

SCENARIO

"Hi, did you see the game last night? I'm done—it's your turn to speak."

"No, but I did go to the dance recital. Your turn—I am done."

"Thanks, the game was really great. Dana was really hot. She must have made . . . "

"Do you mind? I'd like to say something."

"Oh! You want to talk about the recital some more—sure, go ahead." ■

Unusual conversation you say, but is it? Actually, if our conversations did not include unspoken cues, this is very similar to what they would be like. Keep in mind that we would have no vocal or bodily cues to help express ourselves, and there would be no way of knowing when one person was finished speaking and the other should start. In other words, our communication would be verbal only and monotone in sound. At best it would be very difficult for us to carry on a conversation without unspoken cues. Unspoken cues are what most communication scholars refer to as nonverbal communication.

Nonverbal communication includes all behaviors, attributes, or objects (except words) that communicate messages that have social meaning. Nonverbal communication includes tone of voice, facial expressions, posture, gestures, and appearance, all of which are used to communicate messages. Nonverbal communication supplements words, such as when tone of voice, volume, or facial expression adds emphasis to the meaning of a word. Nonverbal communication can compliment our messages by helping make them clearer and more effective. Unfortunately, nonverbal communication can also change the intended meaning of a message or make it confusing and unclear. Nonverbal communication can also be intentional or unintentional, serving a variety of functions. It literally has an impact on all facets of our lives—social interactions, relationships, and careers. It does not include, however, gestures that represent words, such as American Sign Language (ASL), written words, or words transmitted

This child is talking to his mother by signing. Signing is a complete language with symbols and gestures that allow people who are deaf or hearing impaired to communicate with shared meaning. Each culture or community has a signing language based on its area's traditions.

electronically. To hearing persons, sign language is often seen as nonverbal communication. However, to persons who are hearing impaired, sign language is verbal because the signs, movements, and facial expressions are signals for words, phrases, and emphasis.

The inclusion of nonverbal behavior in the study of communication is relatively recent. We tend to take nonverbal communication for granted because it is so basic, but its importance is unmistakable and its connection to communication is undeniable. Research indicates that in most situations, we spend more of our time communicating nonverbally than verbally and that our nonverbal messages carry more meaning than our verbal messages. Studies have estimated, for example, that the average person speaks for only ten to eleven minutes per day and that the average spoken sentence spans about 2.5 seconds. In a normal two-person conversation, 60 to 93 percent of communicative meaning is transmitted through nonverbal behaviors.[1]

Jeffrey Philpott, a communication professor, in his 1983 master's thesis summarized nonverbal research. He concluded that 65 percent of the meaning of our interactions comes from nonverbal cues and attributed 35 percent to verbal communication.[2] Although the percentages that verbal and nonverbal messages contribute to the meaning of a communication can vary dramatically, they are indicators of the role each plays in our everyday conversations. Even if we assume the lowest percentage of meaning at 60 percent, nonverbal communication plays an important role in our communication with others. People do indeed reveal much about their current moods, preferences, and emotions through nonverbal communication; however, the process of reading and deciphering such information is far more complex and subtle than it appears on the surface.[3]

A review by Mark Knapp and Judith Hall of nonverbal research concluded that some people depend more heavily on verbal messages, whereas others seem to rely more on nonverbal messages.[4] Another research study found that nonverbal behaviors were twelve to thirteen times more powerful in impact compared to the accompanying verbal message.[5] These findings indicate the importance and impact of nonverbal behaviors. Our communication must be viewed as a whole and not simply as verbal or nonverbal messages. What is your preference—nonverbal or verbal communication? Why?

Without realizing it, you often use nonverbal communication as the basis for many daily decisions. For example, whether you approach your professor about turning in an overdue paper might depend on your perception of his or her nonverbal behavior. If he or she has an open office door and is smiling, you would probably conclude that the professor is friendly and approachable at the moment and that this would be an appropriate time to discuss your late paper.

Even though our culture is highly verbally oriented, more and more scholars and teachers are recognizing the significant connection of nonverbal behavior to the communication process. In this chapter we examine nonverbal characteristics, forms, functions, and interpretation, as well as how individuals can improve their nonverbal communication.

Characteristics of Nonverbal Communication

We can better interpret and use nonverbal communication if we understand some of its basic characteristics. Think, for example, of the far-reaching implications of the fact that through our nonverbal behavior, we are always communicating something, regardless of whether we intend to. We must also consider that the interpretation of nonverbal cues depends on the context, that nonverbal communication is more believable than verbal communication, that nonverbal communication is our primary way of expressing our feelings and attitudes toward others, that culture affects nonverbal communication, and that nonverbal communication is ambiguous in nature.

Nonverbal Communication Occurs Constantly

When another person is present, you have to communicate. Whether you make eye contact, smile, frown, or try to totally ignore the other person, you are communicating something. Sometimes what is said is less important than what is not said. For example, not attending a meeting at which you were expected, coming late to an employment interview, wearing jeans when you were expected to dress formally, wearing a suit when jeans were expected, talking about a sad situation with a smirk on your face, and speaking to someone but never looking him or her in the eye all convey strong messages. We all believe we can tell a great deal about people based on their facial expression, appearance (sex, race, physique), clothing, willingness to make eye contact, body movements, and posture.

To illustrate that we are always communicating, whether intentionally or unintentionally, consider the following example. Jack is always perfectly groomed and smells of expensive aftershave lotion. George has shoulder-length hair and always wears sweatshirts and jeans. By simply looking at them, we cannot really tell what the two men actually intend to communicate. Jack may simply be neat and use aftershave lotion because it feels good, or he may really want to communicate that designer clothes and expensive aftershave lotion are important to him. Similarly, George may simply like to dress comfortably, or he may be attempting to communicate that he disdains society's seeming obsession with outward appearances. Ultimately, it's not so much what Jack and George intend to communicate as what others perceive. Both students, whether they want to, are communicating something about themselves through appearance.

Nonverbal Communication Depends on Context

The context in which nonverbal communication occurs plays a crucial role in its interpretation. Pounding on a table to make a point during a speech means something entirely different than pounding on the table in response to someone's calling you a liar. Direct eye contact with a stranger can mean something entirely different from direct eye contact with a close friend.

When you communicate, your nonverbal and verbal cues usually supplement and support each other. Your appearance, tone of voice, eye movement, posture, and facial expression provide cues about the communication relationship. For example, when you talk to a friend, your relaxed tone of voice, eye contact, and posture reveal much about your friendship. Your nonverbal cues can tell your friends how much you value them, how comfortable you feel, and how intimate your relationships have become.

Such nonverbal communication is interpreted within the context of your friendships and is complemented by casual and personal conversations.

Without understanding the context in which communication occurs, it is almost impossible to tell what a specific nonverbal behavior may mean. In fact, misunderstandings can occur even when the context is fully understood. That is why we must think twice about our interpretation of others' nonverbal behavior and their possible interpretations of ours.

Nonverbal Communication Is More Believable Than Verbal Communication

Most of us tend to believe nonverbal communication, even when it contradicts the accompanying verbal message. Consider this conversation between a mother and her daughter regarding the daughter's husband:

> "What's wrong? Are you upset with Chad?" asks Jess's mother.
> (Stare and frown) "Whatever, I'm not upset, why should I be?" responds Jess.
> "You seem to be in a funk, and you are avoiding talking to me—so what's wrong—did you and Chad have a fight?" asks Jess's mother.
> "I SAID NOTHING IS WRONG—LEAVE ME ALONE—EVERYTHING IS FINE!"

Throughout the conversation Jess seems upset, snappy in tone, and to be sending a signal to her mother that she isn't telling the whole story. It seems clear from the interaction and the mother's intuition that Jess is hiding something, hence the second inquiry. Indeed, the real story is that Jess and her husband have not been getting along lately. They have been fighting over money and the mother could sense that something was on Jess's mind. Nonverbal messages are much more difficult to control than verbal messages because nonverbal cues are more representative of our emotions, which are more difficult to control. Is the nonverbal or the verbal communication more likely to be truer? Verbal communication as we suggested in Chapter 4 is more conscious; it involves more processing of thoughts and impulses into words. Although nonverbal messages can be conscious and deliberate, they often, as we have suggested, are unintentional and subconsciously generated. It is almost always easy to determine what you are going to say, but it is very difficult for most of us to control our voices, facial expressions, and other body movements when we are upset, hurt, or angry. Jess's mother interpreted her daughter's nonverbal communication as a more accurate reflection of Jess's feelings than her verbal communication. See Table 5.1 for key principles of nonverbal communication. Later in this chapter we discuss nonverbal behaviors and deception in more detail.

Nonverbal Communication Is a Primary Means of Expression

We can often detect other people's feelings of frustration, anger, sadness, resentment, or anxiety without their actually saying anything. We can detect others' emotions because nonverbal communication is so powerful. Almost all of our feelings and attitudes are expressed through our nonverbal behavior. For example, at a graduation party attended by many young children, one little girl entered with her parents and spotted a neighbor. She turned up her nose and walked away. Her mother, running after her, asked why she had suddenly left, to which the girl replied, "I don't

TABLE 5.1

Key Principles of Nonverbal Communication

- Nonverbal communication is overwhelmingly important because it carries most of the meaning of a message.
- Nonverbal communication is a frequent source of misunderstanding.
- Nonverbal communication is not governed by rules.
- Nonverbal communication is not a language.
- Nonverbal communication is multichanneled, complicated, and ever-changing.
- Nonverbal communication is context and culture bound.
- Nonverbal communication is more likely than verbal communication to be spontaneous and unintentional.
- Nonverbal communication is powerful and is more believable than verbal communication.
- Nonverbal communication is learned (not always consciously).

like that girl over there." The nonverbal communication really didn't need much explanation—it was obvious what the little girl was saying through her actions, whether intentionally or unintentionally.

Nonverbal Communication Is Related to Culture

Culture contributes significantly to differences in nonverbal behavior. Norms and rules that govern the management of behavior differ from culture to culture. Yet because human beings around the world share common biological and social functions, it should not be too surprising to also find areas of similarity in nonverbal communication. For example, studies comparing facial expressions have found that certain universal expressions, such as those indicating sadness and fear, are easily understood across varying cultures. Although much outward behavior is innate (such as smiling, touching, eye contact, moving), we are not born knowing what meanings such nonverbal messages communicate. Most scholars would agree that cultures formulate display rules that dictate when, how, and with what consequences nonverbal expressions are exhibited. For instance, all of us are born with the capacity to cry, yet what makes us cry and who is allowed to see us cry need to be learned within cultural boundaries.

Nonverbal Communication Is Ambiguous

Because nonverbal messages are always present, we must recognize their importance or impact yet also be very careful when interpreting them. Like verbal communication, nonverbal behavior can be ambiguous, abstract, and arbitrary. We can not assume that nonverbal messages have only one meaning. For example, does crying always signify grief or sadness, or could it also express joy or pain? Interpreting nonverbal behavior requires understanding the context in which it takes place and the cultural norms governing it. Yet even when a person understands these dynamics, it

Making Connections

Emotion and Emphasis via Electronic Communication

The messages we communicate are given more meaning and emphasis through our nonverbal communication. But how can you use nonverbal expressions to illustrate emotions if you are communicating mainly via email with someone? When we write to others, we can put certain words in all capitals to emphasize their importance or to convey a strong meaning, such as, frustration or anger. For instance, "CALL ME SOON!" illustrates a stronger message than simply "call me soon."

To emphasize that we are happy or sad about something we sometimes use visual images, such as a happy, smiling face or an unhappy, sad face, on a letter or message to the make the point that we are pleased or displeased with something. There are symbols that convey a variety of emotions, which can be used when sending email messages, that have become popular. The most common emotions are conveyed by combining a colon, dash, and other symbols to relay nonverbal messages (they are referred to as "emoticons"). Here are some common ones.

:-(Depressed or upset by a remark

:-l Straight face

:-o Surprise

1. What are some other symbols that convey emotions or feelings that might be used when communicating electronically?
2. Do you accept these symbols as nonverbal communication? Why or why not?

is still very easy to misperceive nonverbal behaviors. For example, does the yawn of a fellow student signal boredom or fatigue? Does a speaker tremble because of nervousness or excitement? Most nonverbal behaviors have a multitude of possible meanings, and to automatically assume that you have grasped the only possible meaning could lead to a serious misunderstanding. There are no consistent rules for using nonverbal communication.

Types of Nonverbal Communication

When you dress in a suit for a meeting, smile at someone, sit in a specific seat in class, use your hands while talking, play with a pen or pencil while listening, dim the lights to create a romantic atmosphere, play music loudly, look someone directly in the eyes, or burn incense to create a pleasant odor, you are communicating nonverbally. Every day we perform a wide range of nonverbal behaviors without even thinking about them, yet such behaviors can convey definite messages to others. Because nonverbal communication is so diverse, complex, common, and informative, we need to be sensitive to its many manifestations. In the following pages, we examine some of the more significant forms of nonverbal communication, such as kinesics (body movements, including gestures, facial expressions, and eye behavior), physical characteristics, haptics (touch), proxemics (space), chronemics (time), paralanguage, artifacts, and environment.

Facial Expressions and Body Movements

We use body movements—gestures, facial expressions, and eye behavior—to create an infinite number of nonverbal messages. For our purposes, we define **kinesics,** which is sometimes referred to as "body language," as any movement of the face or body that communicates a message. Two particularly significant categories of kinesics are eye behavior and facial expressions. **Eye behavior** is a subcategory of facial expressions that includes any movement or behavior of the eyes and is also referred to as **oculesics,** which is the study of eye movement or eye behavior. The eyes, through eye contact with others, have the primary function of establishing relationships. **Facial expressions** include configurations of the face that can reflect, augment, contradict, or appear unrelated to a speaker's spoken message.

Eye Behavior or Oculesics.   According to some researchers, eye behavior is the first and primary characteristic noticed by people. The researchers found that during interactions people spend about 45 percent of the time looking at each other's eyes.[6] Through eye behavior we establish relationships with others. Eyes also convey a variety of other important messages. We notice a speaker's eye contact, share mutual glances with friends, and feel uncomfortable when stared at. Eye behavior, according to one communication scholar, can serve one of six important communicative functions: (1) influence attitude change and persuasion; (2) indicate degree of attentiveness, interest, and arousal; (3) express emotions; (4) regulate interaction; (5) indicate power and status; and (6) form impressions in others.[7]

Eye gaze at the interpersonal level communicates sincerity, trustworthiness, and friendliness. Romantic partners are more likely to gaze into each other's eyes for prolonged periods when expressing their affection for one another.[8] Members of groups or teams use eye contact to build their relationships and to show unity or a sense of belonging to the group or team. In Chapter 10, we discuss the importance of eye contact between a speaker and an audience. In general, effective speakers use more frequent eye contact with their audiences than less effective speakers. Eye contact is also important for those of us who are listeners, because looking at the speaker indicates our interest in what is being said and is a sign of respect for the speaker.

Have you ever had a conversation with someone wearing dark glasses? If you have, you know that it is a bit uncomfortable, because you can't completely see how the other person is reacting to you. Ancient poets described the eyes as "windows to the soul," and in one sense they were correct. We do learn much about other's feelings and emotions from their eyes. For example, we associate a high level of gaze or indirect eye contact from another as a sign of liking or friendliness.[9] In contrast, if others avoid making eye contact with us, we are likely to

Making Connections

The Eyes Have It

Try the following experiment. Get on an elevator—the more people on it, the better—and try to be the last person on it. Then, instead of facing the door, face the people and look at each of them directly. Do not talk; look directly at the people. After fifteen or twenty seconds, look down slightly, but still try to observe the people's reactions to you.

1. What did you notice about people's behavior when you looked directly at them?
2. Describe any changes in the people's behavior when you looked down.
3. How did you feel during the experiment?
4. What does this experiment tell you about oculesics (eye movement)?

conclude that they are unfriendly, don't like us, or are simply shy.[10] Although a high level of eye contact can be interpreted as positive, there are some exceptions to this rule. If people look at us continuously and maintain the eye contact regardless of actions we take, they are said to be staring. When confronted by unwanted staring, most of us tend to withdraw from the situation.[11] Generally, people find being stared at an unpleasant experience; it makes most of us nervous and tense.[12] This is especially true of what is referred to as a "cold stare," because it is a form of intimidation, and unwanted stares are often interpreted in our society as a sign of hostility and anger.[13] This is one reason experts on road rage—highly aggressive driving by motorists, sometimes followed by actual assaults—recommend that drivers avoid eye contact with people who are disobeying traffic laws and rules of the road.

Facial Expression. Facial expressions typically display emotions, but because of their complexity, they can be difficult to interpret. As we communicate, we trade visual information by making facial expressions and interpreting those made by others. The human face is said to produce more than a thousand different expressions.[14] Most are displayed by distinct areas of the face and can be identified with different emotions.

The face is one of the most important sources of emotional information. For example, after studying numerous videotapes of couples fighting, psychologists Robert Levenson of the University of California and John Gottman of the University of Washington concluded that facial expressions of fear and disgust during marital conflicts seemed to indicate the union would fail within four years.[15] The key, explained Levenson, is that the presence of facial expressions associated with emotional distance—fear and disgust—seem to predict marital failure. Facial expressions have an extremely powerful role in communication and relationships. Of all the body motions, facial expressions convey the most information. Researchers have examined the judgments we make regarding the facial expressions of others and have found that not only do we judge emotions but we also make judgments about personality, such as the tendency to be friendly or unfriendly, harsh or kind, based on facial expressions.[16] We perceive

Our facial expressions typically display our emotions, but because of their complexity, these emotions can be difficult to interpret. Researchers have identified more than a thousand different expressions of the human face.

people who have relaxed facial expressions as having more power and being more in control than people whose facial expressions seem nervous.[17]

Although observers are able to determine the specific emotional content of certain expressions with high accuracy, the meanings associated with other facial expressions differ from culture to culture. For example, expressions of happiness or sadness but not other facial expressions can be interpreted quite accurately as to intensity and meaning by observers from differing cultural backgrounds.[18] Interpretation of emotions is learned and usually conforms to specific cultural expectations. When observing the facial expressions of members of other cultures, we must remember that there are cultural differences in the circumstances that produce an emotion, the effect of the emotion, and the rules that govern the use of a particular facial expression in a specific social situation.

However, despite cultural rules, our faces often communicate feelings and emotions spontaneously in reaction to a situation. For example, if you open the door to your house, and a group of your friends hiding in the dark turn on the lights and yell, "Congratulations!" your face will probably automatically and unconsciously express surprise. If you open the door and they yell, "Boo," your face will probably show fear or anxiety.

Although many facial expressions are unconscious, involuntary reactions to certain stimuli, researchers have found that facial cues may be only partially reliable in terms of what they express. Michael Motley, a communication researcher, in a study confirms that facial expressions are often ambiguous and may be only relevant and interpretable as they relate to the particular conversation and context in which they occur.[19] In addition, people learn to conceal their real feelings.[20] They learn to control their facial muscles in order to hide inappropriate or unacceptable responses. Such controlling behaviors are referred to as **facial management techniques.** Facial management techniques may be used to intensify, deintensify, neutralize, or mask a felt emotion.[21]

Intensifying is a facial behavior response that exaggerates expressions in order to meet the expectation of others. If someone gives you a gift, regardless of whether you like the gift, you are likely to try to look completely surprised, excited, and delighted. We exaggerate facial behaviors to meet the expectations of others, to avoid giving offense, and to maintain positive relationships.

Deintensifying is a facial behavior response that understates reactions in order to maintain favorable relationships with others. For example, you and your best friend each give a speech in the same class. You get an A and your friend gets a C. You might tend to tone down your elation, just in case your friend feels bad about receiving a lower grade.

Neutralizing is the avoidance of any emotional expression in a situation—in other words, maintaining a "poker face" or nonexpressive facial behavior. Men and women may neutralize different emotional reactions to conform with cultural norms. In the United States, for example, experiencing fear and sadness is considered less than manly, so some men may try to neutralize facial displays that express those responses, even when they reflect their actual experience.

Making Connections

Learning on the Internet

Learn about nonverbal communication at http://zzyx.ucsc.edu/~archer/intro.html. See how good you are at identifying emotions displayed on the faces in the photos at the site. How well did you identify emotions on those faces that were from different cultural backgrounds than your own? What did you learn?

Masking is the replacing of one expression of an emotion with another considered more appropriate for the situation. We have all seen the moment in beauty contests on television when the winner is announced and all the other contestants smile and hug the winner. We know that the other contestants are not happy but are masking their real emotions.

Body Movements.   To make sense of thousands of different body movements, Paul Ekman and Wallace Friesen have devised a classification system based on the origins, functions, and coding of nonverbal behavior.[22] Their system divides body motions into five categories: emblems, illustrators, regulators, affect displays, and adaptors (see Table 5.2). Because there are so many body motions, many of which are interdependent, it is important to understand that the categories are not mutually exclusive. Some body motions may be classified under more than one category.

Body and facial movements that can be directly translated into words or phrases are called **emblems.** They include the hand signs for "OK," "I want a ride," "peace," "power," and the many other signs that we use as substitutes for specific words or phrases. The meanings of emblems are like the meanings of words in that they are arbitrary, subject to change with time, learned, and culturally determined.

Body motions that accent, reinforce, or emphasize an accompanying verbal message are called **illustrators.** An instructor who underlines a word on the chalkboard to emphasize it, a child who indicates how tall he is by holding his hand up, a softball player who swings her arms while describing a hit, children who use their thumbs and fingers as if they were guns—all these people are using illustrators.

Body motions that control, monitor, or maintain the back-and-forth interaction between speakers and listeners are **regulators.** Regulators include eye contact, shifts in posture, nodding of the head, and looking at a clock or wristwatch. These cues tell us when to stop, continue, repeat, hurry, elaborate, make things more interesting, or let someone else speak. The opening scenario in this chapter illustrates the importance of regulators.

Body movements that express emotions and feelings are **affect displays.** Although your face is the primary means of displaying affect, your body may also be used. For example, you may slouch when you are sad, slam your fist on a table when

TABLE 5.2

Categories of Body Movements and Facial Expressions

CATEGORY	CHARACTERISTICS	EXAMPLES
Emblems	Translate directly into words	Extended thumb of a hitchhiker
Illustrators	Accent, reinforce, or emphasize a verbal message	A child holding up his hands to indicate how tall he is while saying, "I'm a big boy"
Regulators	Control, monitor, or maintain interaction	Eye contact, shift in posture, nod of head
Affect displays	Express emotion and feelings	Sad face, slouching, jumping up and down
Adaptors	Help one feel at ease in communication situations	Scratching, playing with coins, moving toward someone

you are angry, and jump up and down when you are excited. Affect displays communicate messages that may repeat, contradict, supplement, replace, or not even relate to verbal messages.

Body motions that help us feel at ease in communication situations are **adaptors.** They are the most difficult nonverbal signals to interpret because interpreting them requires the most speculation. Scratching, playing with a pencil, sitting straight in a chair, grooming motions, and smoking are adaptors. People are especially likely to engage in such actions in stressful situations, such as those that involve trying to satisfy needs, manage emotions, or develop social contacts. Adaptors fall into three categories:

1. Self-adaptors are generally not directed at others but serve some personal need. They include common actions such as scratching, smoothing hair, and straightening clothes.

2. Object-adaptors involve the use of an object, such as a pencil, paper clip, coin, cigarette, or jewelry, for a purpose other than its intended function. Most object-adaptor behaviors are unconscious. They help to release excess energy and tend to occur only when people are nervous or anxious.

3. Alter-adaptors are body motions directed at others that are learned from past experiences and from the manipulation of objects. They include gestures used to protect oneself from others, such as putting the hands in front of the face; movements made to attack others, such as assuming a fighting position; actions intended to establish intimacy with others, such as moving closer to someone; and actions signaling withdrawal from a conversation, such as moving toward a door. Several authors of books on body language contend that alter-adaptors are performed unconsciously and reveal hidden desires or tendencies. For example, the way people cross their legs may indicate sexual invitation, introversion, or aggression. To date, however, there is not sufficient proof to support these claims.

Finally, body movements and posture can reveal much about our physical states (vigor, age) and perhaps the extent to which we possess certain traits.[23] Evidence from several research studies supports these conclusions. For example, one study investigating males and females in four age groups (five to seven, thirteen to fourteen, twenty-six to twenty-eight, and seventy-five to eighty years old) had the participants walk back and forth at a pace they felt was comfortable.[24] The walkers were videotaped and then shown to others who rated the walkers on various dimensions, such as gait, traits, age, and sex. By using adjustments and lighting techniques, the researchers were able to disguise the walkers so that the subjects saw only their gait.

The subjects made judgments about the walkers two different times. The first time, they rated the walkers' gait in terms of revealing certain traits (submissive or dominating, physically weak or physically strong, timid or bold, sad or happy, unsexy or sexy). The second time, they rated the walkers' gait in terms of several other characteristics (amount of hip sway, knee bending, forward or backward lean, slow or fast pace, stiff or loose-jointed gait, short or long strides). In addition, the subjects were asked to estimate each walker's age and guess whether each was female or male.

The study's results were very interesting and clearly indicate that people's gaits provide important nonverbal cues about them. For example, as predicted, ratings of traits and gaits did vary according to age. Ratings of sexiness did increase from children to adolescents and young adults but decreased for older adults. Further analysis

Making Connections

Walk the Walk, Talk the Talk

Consider the research studies about how gait influences perceptions. Then answer the following questions, and discuss your responses with a classmate.

1. Think of situations in which a person's gait influenced your perception of him or her. In what ways did the gait influence you?
2. Can you think of cultural or gender influences that have affected your perception of others, based on their gait?

revealed that possession of a youthful gait (one characterized by hip sway, knee bending, arm swing, loose-jointedness, and more steps per second) was strongly related to ratings of the walkers' happiness and power. Thus, persons with a youthful gait—regardless of their actual age—were rated more positively along several dimensions than persons with an older gait.

Another study used the same walkers but did not alter the videotape. Researchers found that, in spite of the rich array of nonverbal cues (age, gender) available to the raters, gait still influenced their ratings more than any of the other factors.[25] Again, walkers with a youthful gait were rated as more powerful and happier. These findings suggest that people's gaits are important determinants of the impression they make on others. Bounce in the step and smooth body motions, it seems, are definite pluses, especially in societies such as the United States, which value youth and physical vigor.

Physical Characteristics

Whereas body movements and facial expressions change quickly and can be controlled to some extent, physical characteristics, such as body type, attractiveness, height, weight, hair color, and skin tone, are fairly constant and more difficult to control, especially in the course of a single interaction.

Physical appearance and condition play a significant role in communication and relationships. In recent years, segments of our society have become obsessed with physical appearance and general health, spending billions of dollars each year on modifying, preserving, and decorating their bodies. One of the reasons for this concern with appearance is that we have acquired some stereotypes about body shapes that seem to influence how we react to and interact with each other. In one research study, participants were asked to rate silhouettes of people with three different body shapes—overweight, athletic, and thin—who were all the same height. The subjects consistently rated the overweight people as older, shorter, more old-fashioned, less attractive, more talkative, more warm-hearted and sympathetic, more good-natured and agreeable, more dependent, and more trusting of others. They rated athletic people as stronger, younger, taller, more masculine, better looking, more adventurous, more mature in behavior, and more self-reliant. They rated thin people as younger, taller, more ambitious, more suspicious of others, more tense and nervous, less masculine, more stubborn and inclined to be difficult, more pessimistic and quieter.[26]

Although this research suggests that people tend to make judgments about personality and behavior characteristics based on body shape, there is little proof that such judgments are accurate. As you learned in Chapter 3, making decisions and assumptions on the basis of stereotypes can lead to serious misunderstandings.

Physical attractiveness has an extremely powerful influence on everyday communication. In our society, attractive people are generally treated more positively than

Making Connections

Average Is Attractive

Alluring eyes and sunny smile are not enough. If you want to find an attractive face, a high-tech study suggests, look for one that is basically average. A computer was used to construct faces that blended facial features of up to thirty-two people, averaging out such features as nose length and chin prominence. In this way, the more faces that went into a composite, the more it represented an average face.

Although other factors may contribute to making movie stars handsome or beautiful, Judith Langlois of the University of Texas at Austin states, "I'll bet their faces have the fun-

damental attributes of averageness, and without that they would not be very attractive."

1. What does this information suggest about the nature of attractiveness?
2. Why does our mainstream culture place so much value on attractiveness?
3. Are there ethical considerations regarding attractiveness that ultimately affect our communication with others?

Adapted from "Attractiveness Discovered to Be Average Quality" New York (AP). Printed in *Lincoln Star* 27, March, 1990, 1, 7.

those who are not. It appears that both males and females are strongly influenced by attractiveness, though males seem to be more responsive to appearance than are females.[27] Numerous research studies have indicated that attractive people, when compared to unattractive people, are perceived to be more popular, successful, sociable, persuasive, sensual, and happy. One research study found that attractive students receive more interaction from their teachers,[28] unattractive defendants are less likely to be found innocent than attractive defendants in a court of law,[29] and attractiveness plays a predominant role in dating behaviors.[30] Attractiveness affects credibility and a person's ability to persuade others, to get a job, and to gain a higher salary. Handsome males are likely to be perceived as more masculine, whereas beautiful females are seen as more feminine, in comparison with those perceived as less attractive.[31]

In a few situations, attractiveness can be a disadvantage. Although attractiveness was found to be an asset for men throughout their executive careers, one research study found that being attractive could be a liability for women managers. Even when such women had reached top executive levels, their success was attributed to their looks rather than to their abilities, and they were consistently judged less capable than unattractive women managers.[32] Attractive females, in comparison to other women, are judged by some to be more vain, more materialistic, and less faithful to their husbands.[33] For both males and females, attractiveness is often considered the reason for their success, rather than their ability or hard work.[34]

We know that our society places a great deal of value on physical appearance, but do attractive individuals differ in behavior from others who are less attractive? The answer is no. In fact, attractive people do *not* seem to fit the stereotypes associated with them.[35] Surprisingly, self-esteem is not consistently high among those who are considered the most attractive. This could be because they believe that they are rewarded not for what they have done, but for how they look, thus diminishing their sense of self-worth.[36]

Touching is referred to as either tactile communication or haptics. The kind and amount of touching that is appropriate varies according to the individuals, their relationship, and the situation.

Touch

Touching is referred to as either tactile communication or **haptics.** Haptics is one of the most basic forms of communication. "Reach out and touch someone" is a slogan once used by a national phone company. Although the company's advertisement suggests touching in an abstract sense, the idea behind the advertisement is that touch is a personal and powerful means of communication. As one of our most primitive and yet sensitive ways of relating to others, touch is a critical aspect of communication. It plays a significant role in giving encouragement, expressing tenderness, and showing emotional support, and it can be more powerful than words. For example, when you've just received some bad news, a pat on the shoulder from a friend can be far more reassuring than many understanding words.

The kind and amount of touching that is appropriate varies according to the individuals, their relationship, and the situation. Some researchers have set up categories to describe these variations in touch. The categories are functional–professional, social–polite, friendship–warmth, love–intimacy, and sexual arousal.[37]

1. Functional–professional touch is an unsympathetic, impersonal, cold, or businesslike touch. For example, a doctor's touch during a physical examination or an athletic trainer's touch of an injured athlete serves a purely medical, functional purpose. A tailor who takes customers' measurements is another example of functional–professional touching. The person being touched is usually treated as an object or nonperson in order to prevent implying any other messages.

2. Social–polite touch acknowledges another person according to the norms or rules of a society. In our society, the handshake is the most predominant form of polite recognition of another. In many European countries, a kiss is used in place of the handshake to acknowledge another.

3. Friendship–warmth touch expresses an appreciation of the special attributes of others. Friendship–warmth touch is also the most misinterpreted type of touching behavior, because it can be mixed or confused with touching related to sex. For example, you see two men meet in an airport, hug, and walk off with their arms around each other. You would probably infer that these two men are close relatives or friends who have not seen each other for a while. Their touching conforms to social expectations about how friends behave in a public context. Their behavior expresses and reinforces the warm feelings they have for each other.

4. Love–intimacy touch usually occurs in romantic relationships between lovers and spouses. It includes caressing, hugging, embracing, kissing, and many other forms of intimate touch. It is highly communicative. Usually, this form of touch requires consent between both parties, although one person can initiate love–intimacy touch and the other person being touched may not always reciprocate.

Intimate touch conveys strong caring, devoted, enamored, and loving interpersonal messages. It also complements and validates verbal messages, such as "I love you" or "You are someone special in my life." Intimate touch does not necessarily imply sexual involvement. Sometimes confusion between intimate and sexual touch leads to dissatisfaction in some couples' special relationships.

5. Sexual-arousal touch is the most intimate level of personal contact with another. Sexual touch behavior, if mutually desired, is extremely pleasurable for most people, but it can also produce fear and anxiety. This category of touch expresses physical attraction between two consenting individuals.

The meaning of a particular touch depends on the type of touch, the situation in which the touch occurs, who is doing the touching, and the cultural background of those involved. Some cultures are more prone to touching behavior than others. Research has found that people in the United States are less touch-oriented when compared to persons in other cultures. For example, a study examining touching behavior

Making Connections

Whom Do You Touch?

A schoolteacher in Lincoln, Nebraska, loses her job for touching a student; a worker in Canton, Ohio, sues an employer for "improper" touching behavior; a person talks on the radio about touching behavior between male coaches and female athletes. Touching has many different meanings. When is it inappropriate, and when isn't it? Here are some situations to consider:

1. Does it mean the same thing when the boss places an arm around the secretary and when the secretary places an arm around the boss?

2. Does it mean the same thing when a teacher places a hand on a student's shoulder and when a student places a hand on a teacher's shoulder?

3. Does it mean the same thing when a doctor touches a patient and when a patient touches a doctor?

4. When is touch appropriate, and when isn't it?

5. How does the gender of the people affect your answer to these questions?

during a one-hour period in a coffeeshop found that people in San Juan, Puerto Rico, touched 180 times in an hour; those in Paris, France, touched 110 times; and those in Gainesville, Florida, touched only 2 times.[38]

Gender differences in touching behavior are also interesting to note. Men tend to touch more than women do, women tend to be touched more often than men, and women seem to value touch more than men do. Gender differences in touching behavior may be partially attributed to men's sexual aggressiveness in our culture and their expression of power and dominance. According to Nancy Henley, men have access to women's bodies, but women do not have the same access to men's bodies. This, according to the research, may be a man's way of exerting power because touch represents an invasion of another's personal space.[39]

Space

Statements such as "Give me some room to operate," signs that say "Keep Out," and the bumper sticker that reads "Keep Off My" followed by a picture of a donkey all are attempts to regulate the distance between people. Such behaviors are of special interest to researchers in **proxemics,** the study of how we use space and the distance we place between others and ourselves when communicating. Edward T. Hall, author of two classic books, *The Silent Language* and *The Hidden Dimension,* coined the term *proxemics.*[40] Hall was a pioneer in helping to explain how space is used in North American culture. In his study of proxemics, Hall identified four zones; they are illustrated in Figure 5.1. *Intimate space* is defined as the distance from no space between people to one-and-a-half feet between people. This zone is the most personal, and it is usually only open to those with whom we are well acquainted, unless such closeness is physically forced on us, such as in a crowded train or elevator.

The second zone is referred to as *personal space* and ranges from distances of one-and-a-half feet to four feet between people. It is not unusual for us to carry on conversations or other activities with close friends and relatives in this zone. If someone we don't know enters this zone, we are likely to feel uncomfortable or violated. The third zone is called *social space.* It ranges from four to twelve feet and is where most professional conversations occur, as well as group interactions, such as meetings. *Public space,* the fourth zone, includes twelve feet or more. This distance is not unusual for public speaking situations or other formal presentations. The actual distance or zone may be determined by the context and relationship of those involved in the interaction.

The need for us to identify certain amounts of space as our own is an aspect of proxemics called **territoriality.** We often position markers such as books, coats, pencils, papers, and other objects to declare our space. Some students become upset when someone else sits in a seat they usually occupy, even though seating is not assigned. This uneasiness stems from a strong desire to stake out and protect territory. Similar reactions occur when someone enters a room without knocking or tailgates when driving—it seems like an invasion of our territory.

We usually give little conscious attention to the role of space in our communication, yet the way in which others use space gives strong clues to what they are thinking and how they are reacting to us. There are many variables that influence our use of space when communicating—status, sex, culture, and context are but a few.

Status affects the distance that is maintained between communicators. Research shows that people of different status levels tend to stay farther apart than do individuals of equal status. Furthermore, people of higher status tend to close the distance be-

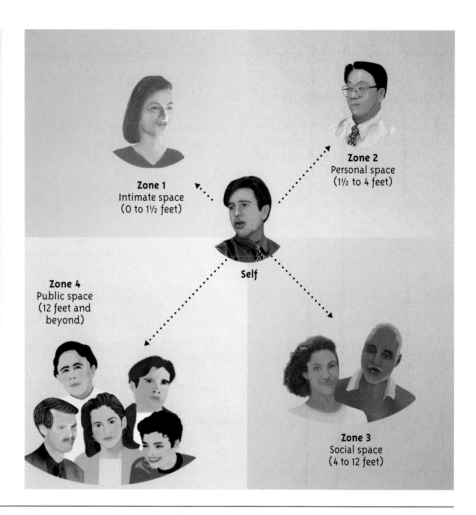

FIGURE 5.1

Edward T. Hall's Four Distance Zones

Zone 1
Intimate space
(0 to 1½ feet)

Zone 2
Personal space
(1½ to 4 feet)

Self

Zone 4
Public space
(12 feet and beyond)

Zone 3
Social space
(4 to 12 feet)

tween themselves and people of lower status, but seldom do people of lower status move to close the distance between themselves and a person of higher status.

Men and women tend to differ in their proxemic patterns. But the differences in part hinge on whether the interaction is with someone of the same or opposite sex. In same sex situations, men prefer, expect, and usually establish greater conversational distance than women do. Opposite-sex distancing depends on how intimate the relationship is.

Culture creates a wealth of differences in the way individuals use distance for communication. For example, people from the United States tend to stand farther apart during conversations than do people from many European and Middle Eastern cultures. Arabs, for example, consider it polite to stand close to the person with whom they are communicating. There are as many culture-based differences as there are cultures, and it is not unusual for one group to be perceived as cold and unfriendly and another as pushy and forward as a result of their use of space. The important thing is to recognize that not all cultures view distance in the same way.

Context also influences the space that is maintained between individuals. For example, people in line at an automated teller machine usually stand back far enough

Making Connections

Space—Who Needs It?

Edward Hall, a renowned scholar in the area of nonverbal communication, devised a system of identifying spatial zones based on interpersonal relationships. For example, he suggests that in professional–business or educational situations, the appropriate distance between communicators should be from four to twelve feet.

1. Go to the library, the student union, or some other place with a number of tables. Find a person sitting alone (someone of the other sex), and sit right next to the person. Notice the reaction and how the person looks at you. After a while—before the person leaves—tell him or her that you were doing an experiment for your communication class. Then ask what the person thought when you sat down close by, and how he or she felt.

2. Now do the same thing with someone of your own sex. What happened? How did you feel?

3. If you feel uncomfortable doing the experiments in items 1 and 2, try this: When sitting with a friend or friends at a table where there are salt and pepper shakers or other items, slowly but surely start pushing the items toward a friend. Move them very slowly and move as many items as you can—not all at once, but one at a time. Notice what happens. Discuss what the person was thinking as you kept moving items in his or her direction.

4. What do the results of these experiments tell you about how people treat space and its importance to them? Do men and women react to space considerations differently?

5. Do the results of your experiments match the findings of Hall? If not, why do you think your results were different?

to give the person using the machine the feeling that a transaction is not being observed. But passengers waiting to board a bus ordinarily stand close together to avoid losing their places.

Time

Chronemics is the study of how people perceive, structure, and use time as communication.[41] People in our society are preoccupied with time. Everything seems to have a starting time and an ending time. We worry about how long we have to wait for something and how long it takes to do something. We even go so far as to say that time is money. Because we place such a high value on time, it plays a significant role in our nonverbal communication. We are particularly sensitive to people and events that waste or make exceptional demands on our time. Consider your reaction, for instance, when your date keeps you waiting, when an instructor continues to lecture after the bell has signaled the end of class, or when you are given only one day's notice of an upcoming test. Your feelings may range from confusion to indignation to outrage, but you will almost certainly not be neutral. To some extent, your reaction will depend on who the other person is. You will probably be more tolerant if the offending party is a friend or someone who has great power over you. Thus, if a blind date keeps you waiting too long, you may decide to leave, but if your professor is late for an office appointment, you will probably suffer in silence and continue to wait for his or her arrival.

We tend to have many expectations about how time should be used, and we often judge people by their use of time. For example, students are expected to be on time for class. Thus, students who are punctual are more likely to create a positive impression, whereas those who are consistently late may be perceived as irresponsible, lazy, or uninterested. We must be constantly aware of the message we send through our use (and misuse) of time.

Individuals can differ in their approaches to time. For example, some people are always looking to the future, others long for the past, and still others live for the moment. Each approach communicates something about people and the ways they use time to communicate who they are. Each culture teaches its members about time expectations, and these expectations vary. In some cultures being punctual is expected, whereas in others, being punctual is not important and in fact it is expected that people will be late. In the U.S. culture, for example, you are expected to be on time for a dinner party, but being up to twenty minutes late is socially accepted and still considered on time. In some European countries, arriving late for a dinner party is considered an insult. Our use of time communicates messages about us, and it is important that we adhere to the time-related norms of the culture wherein we are communicating.

Paralanguage

Paralanguage is the way we vocalize, or say, the words we speak. Paralanguage includes not only speech sounds but also speech rate, accents, articulation, pronunciation, and silence. Sounds such as groans, yawns, coughs, laughter, crying, and yelping, which are nonsymbolic but can communicate very specific messages, are also included. Expressions such as "um," "uh-huh," "ya know," "like," and "OK" are referred to as vocal fillers and are considered paralanguage. Vocal fillers are often interspersed in conversations without forethought or a set order. They may reflect nervousness, speech patterns of a particular subculture, or a personal habit. In any case, the use of vocal fillers can influence our image positively or it can damage and degrade others and us.

The content of words is verbal communication, whereas the sound quality or volume that creates the words is a form of nonverbal communication. We rely more often on paralanguage than on the words themselves when interpreting another person's message. Note how the meaning of a sentence may vary according to the word that is emphasized:

1. *Jane's* taking Tom out for pizza tonight. (not Hilary or Dana)
2. Jane's taking *Tom* out for pizza tonight. (not Bill or Dave)
3. Jane's taking Tom *out* for pizza tonight. (not staying home)
4. Jane's taking Tom out for *pizza* tonight. (not seafood or hamburgers)
5. Jane's taking Tom out for pizza *tonight.* (not tomorrow or next weekend)[42]

Even though the words in each sentence are identical, each creates an entirely different message solely because of the emphasis placed on specific words.

Paralanguage includes pitch (how high or low the voice is), vocal force (intensity or loudness of the voice), rate (speed), quality (overall impression of the voice), and pauses or silence. The way we vary our voices conveys different meanings to receivers. For

Making Connections

It's Not What You Say, But How You Say It!

"My teacher is wonderful."

Read the preceding statement aloud in four different ways: (1) with no expression at all, (2) as if your teacher is really wonderful, (3) as if you actually think your teacher is anything but wonderful, and (4) as if you are really trying to convince someone that your teacher is wonderful. Note how you can change your meaning without changing the words.

1. What do you actually do with your voice to change the sentence's meaning?
2. What else do you notice about your behavior each time you try to create a different meaning?

From this exercise you should see the importance of vocal expression and its impact on the meaning of the message.

example, a person who speaks quickly may communicate a message that is different from a person who speaks slowly. Even when the words are the same, if the rate, force, pitch, and quality differ, the receiver's interpretations will differ. Researchers estimate that approximately 38 percent of the meaning of oral communication is affected by our use of voice, by *the way* in which something is said rather than by *what* is said.[43]

On the basis of paralanguage, we make many judgments about what is being said, the person saying it, the speaking and listening roles, and the credibility of the message. Of course, judgments about people based on paralanguage can be just as unreliable as judgments based on body type. We must, therefore, recognize the effect that paralanguage has on our communication and adjust our use of it accordingly.

Silence or vocal pauses are very communicative and are part of the paralinguistic features of our communication. Vocal pauses or hesitations are usually short in duration, whereas silence generally refers to extended periods of time. Vocal pauses can be used to emphasize a word or thought or to make a point. Hesitations are usually the result of gathering thought or nervousness. Silence is expected in certain contexts, for example, during a funeral or while listening to a speech presentation, or it can be self-imposed as a way of thinking or doing nothing at all. Silence has many possible meanings. The next time a good friend says "Hi," pause for five to ten seconds before reacting. You will quickly learn the effect silence can have as a message.

Artifacts

Artifacts are personal adornments or possessions that communicate information about a person. They include clothes, perfume, makeup, eyeglasses, hairstyles, beards, automobiles, briefcases, and the many hundreds of other material cues that we use to communicate our age, gender, status, role, class, group membership, personality, and relation to others.

Effective communicators learn to adapt their use of artifacts to a specific situation. In that way, they try to ensure that the message conveyed by the artifacts will be consistent with and reinforce their intended message and will not contradict the message or distract a receiver from the intended message. For example, dressing in a suit, dress, or other conservative clothing would be appropriate for a job interview in order to give the impression that you are a serious applicant.

Environment

Environment, as discussed in Chapter 1, is the psychological and physical surroundings in which communication occurs, including the furniture, architectural design, lighting conditions, temperature, smells, colors, and sounds of the location and the attitudes, feelings, perceptions, and relationships of the participants. The impact of the environment has a lot to do with the individuals, their backgrounds, and their perception of what is important to them at the time of the interaction. The best environment allows a speaker's intended message to be delivered accurately. Thus, soft background music, dim lights, a log burning in a fireplace, a tray of hors d'oeuvres, and two candles would create the perfect environment for a romantic encounter, but would fail to create the proper atmosphere for a pregame pep rally.

Functions of Nonverbal Communication

Nonverbal communication adds life to our exchanges by complementing, repeating, regulating, and substituting for our words. Sometimes we even use it to deceive others (see Table 5.3).

Complementing Verbal Behavior

Nonverbal cues can be used to complete, describe, or accent verbal cues. This use is called **complementing.** For example, a golfer, after shooting a chip shot from about seventy-five yards, tells her partner that she missed the cup by inches and uses her thumb and index finger to show the distance. When saying hello to a friend, you show your genuine interest by displaying a warm smile, maintaining steady eye contact, and holding the friend's hand.

We use complementary nonverbal cues to accent verbal behavior by emphasizing or punctuating our spoken words. For example, if a husband wants sympathy from his wife when he's not feeling well, he may tell her, in a weak voice, that he feels sick and may

TABLE 5.3

Functions of Nonverbal Communication

CATEGORY	CHARACTERISTICS	EXAMPLES
Complementing	Completes, describes, or accents a verbal message	A person needs help immediately, so he yells as loudly as he can
Repeating	Expresses a message identical to the verbal one	A person says yes and nods her head up and down
Regulating	Controls flow of communication	A person shakes his head up and down as a way of communicating "I am interested in what you are saying"—implying "tell me more"
Substituting	Replaces a verbal message with nonverbal signals to exchange thoughts	Two people use hand signals to communicate, because it is too loud to hear each other's voices
Deceiving	Nonverbal cues that purposely disguise or mislead to create a false impression	A doctor examining a patient discovers a serious problem, but the doctor's facial expressions remain neutral so as not to alarm the patient

give her a look that implies he is about to collapse. We often use our voices to highlight or accentuate what we are saying. A mother trying to get her children to quiet down may say quietly, "Will you please keep it down." If that doesn't work and the noise is really bothering her, she may raise her voice to indicate that she wants quiet immediately.

People who are excited or enthusiastic are more likely to use nonverbal cues for accenting their messages than are people who are restrained, having a difficult time expressing themselves, not paying attention, or not understanding what is being said. If used correctly in a public speech, that is, if accenting gestures and changes in tone of voice appear natural and flow smoothly with the message, they can be especially effective ways of making a point clearer to an audience.

Repeating Verbal Behavior

Whereas complementing behaviors help modify or elaborate verbal messages, repeating behavior expresses a message identical to the verbal one. For example, a father attempting to keep his child quiet at an adult gathering may place his index finger to his lips while saying, "Shush!" A speaker stating that she has two points to make may hold up two fingers. The actions of the father and the speaker are called **repeating** because they convey the same meaning as the verbal message.

Such repetition is especially common in sports. For instance, a referee on a basketball court shouts, "Traveling!" while rolling her arms in a circular motion, or a baseball umpire cries, "Strike," while raising his right arm. These repeating nonverbal signals are deliberately planned so that all players and spectators will know the official's call. But most repeating messages are sent without much thought. They are simply a natural part of our communicative behavior.

Regulating Verbal Behavior

Nonverbal cues can also be used for controlling the flow of communication, a behavior known as **regulating.** For example, we frequently use nonverbal signals to indicate that we want to talk, to stop another person from interrupting us when we are talking, or to show that we are finished talking and that the other person may take a turn. When we are listening, we may nod our head rapidly to suggest that the speaker hurry up and finish, or we may nod slowly to show that we want to hear more.

Senders may not even realize that they are sending regulating cues, but receivers are usually aware of such signals. In class, for example, a professor receives a clear message when students put on their coats or close their notebooks to indicate that class is over. Although the students are merely recognizing that it is time for them to leave, the message the professor receives is quite different.

Substituting for Verbal Behavior

Using nonverbal messages in place of verbal messages is known as **substituting.** It is common when speaking is impossible, undesirable, or inappropriate. For example, ramp controllers at airports use hand signals to guide planes to their unloading positions, because the noise level is too high for spoken communication; friends often exchange knowing looks when they want to communicate something behind another person's back; some people with hearing impairments use a sophisticated formal sign language in place of the spoken word.

Nonverbal messages can substitute when verbal ones are impossible. This man is signaling to the pilot, with batons that are used by day or night, where and when to bring the plane to a complete stop.

Deceiving

We may purposely mislead others by using nonverbal cues to create false impressions or to convey incorrect information. Among the most common of such *deceiving* nonverbal behaviors is the poker face that some use when playing cards. Masking is a form of deceiving. We may try to appear calm when we are really nervous or upset, and we often act surprised, alert, or happy when in fact we are feeling quite the opposite. In addition, we consciously try to manage our nonverbal behavior when we give a speech or attend a job interview in order to disguise our true purpose and emotions.

Deception research has identified a set of nonverbal cues that people display when they are not telling the truth. In one study it was found that people who lie make fewer hand movements and tend to look away from a person when they are not telling the truth. The research further found that liars' voices can also be a telling sign—there is a tendency to hesitate and to shift their pitch more often than those telling the truth.[44] Another study found that liars often try to control their voices, which often leads to sounding over- or undercontrolled indicating anxiety or deception.[45] In spite of what we know about people's nonverbal behaviors when they are not telling the truth, very

Making Connections

Telling the Truth—It's Not What You Say, It's How You Behave

There is a lot of guessing when it comes to people's honesty in relation to their nonverbal communication—are they telling the truth? Often we make assumptions about the truthfulness of people based on the inconsistencies of their nonverbal and verbal messages.

1. Why is or isn't it ethical to make assumptions about other's truthfulness based on their nonverbal messages?
2. What can we do to prevent premature judgment about the truthfulness of others' nonverbal messages?
3. Why is it that we assume we know when people are lying or being deceptive from their nonverbal messages?

Nonverbal messages unrelated to the verbal message are sometimes helpful in identifying deception.

By permission of Mell Lazarus and of Creators Syndicate, Inc.

few of us are able to detect or interpret these behaviors as signs of deception. People who can detect untruthfulness usually consider more than one nonverbal cue to determine whether someone is telling the truth. There is a very fine line between the nonverbal behaviors of someone who may be legitimately anxious and someone who is not being truthful. Therefore, there are no sure ways to confirm lying using nonverbal behaviors alone.

Interpreting Nonverbal Communication

If nonverbal communication is so credible and powerful and if we can define, categorize, describe, and observe it, why do we still have difficulty interpreting it? There are at least three good reasons:

1. *Nonverbal cues have multiple meanings.* Nonverbal communication is difficult to understand because a single behavior may have many potential meanings. For example, a frown may indicate unhappiness, sadness, anger, pain, thought, aggressiveness, disapproval, dejection, fear, fatigue, discouragement, disapproval, or a combination of some of these. Unlike words, nonverbal cues lack dictionary definitions.

Interpretations are unreliable because they depend so heavily on perceptions. Suppose, for example, that you have just walked out of a sad movie when you see a friend with tears in her eyes, talking to her sister. She might be reacting to the movie, or her crying could stem from breaking up with her boyfriend, hurting herself, or hearing about a death in the family. Her tears could even result from laughing hard at something that occurred after the movie. Of course, some nonverbal behaviors, such as nodding the head for yes and shaking it for no (in U.S. society), are consistent in both their meaning and their interpretation, but, unfortunately, such consistency is the exception rather than the rule.

2. *Nonverbal cues are interdependent.* The meaning of one nonverbal cue often depends on the correct interpretation of several other simultaneously occurring cues. For example, when we see someone enter a room, we begin to select certain cues about that person, such as gender, physical traits, facial expressions, voice characteristics, and clothing. Each cue intermeshes with the others and adds to the total picture. This interdependence of nonverbal behaviors and our inability to perceive all aspects of any one nonverbal communication make interpretation risky.

Looking for meaning by using more than one nonverbal message at a time is called the **functional approach.** The functional approach examines nonverbal behavior not by isolating nonverbal cues, but by seeing how each cue interacts and works with the others to perform various communicative functions.

3. *Nonverbal cues are subtle.* Many nonverbal behaviors are subtle and difficult to observe. A cue that one person notices immediately may be overlooked by another person, and thus multiple interpretations may be made in the same situation. For example, a friend tells you that a person whom you are interested in getting to know has been looking at you, but you haven't noticed the glances or you see the eye contact as more accidental than a deliberate message of interest in you.

Improving Our Interpretation of Nonverbal Communication

Nonverbal communication is complex, but there are some things that you can do to interpret it better. First, be observant of and sensitive to the nonverbal messages that you receive. Second, verify nonverbal messages that you are not sure of or that are inconsistent with other cues. Assume, for example, that a friend who used to visit regularly hasn't come over in several weeks. It might seem logical to conclude that she doesn't want to see you anymore, but then again, she may have become wrapped up in her studies, taken a part-time job, or fallen ill. To accurately interpret her behavior, consider all the possibilities and avoid jumping to conclusions. Because it is so tempting to make inferences based on nonverbal behavior, it is important to remember not to go beyond actual observations.

One method to help verify the meaning of a nonverbal message is to use **descriptive feedback,** which is the stating of the interpretation of the message received back to the sender. The other person can then clarify an intended meaning. Descriptive feedback is not always necessary, but when a message seems inconsistent with the situation or other behaviors or when you're not sure you have accurately interpreted an important message, you should verify your perceptions with the other person. When using descriptive feedback, do not express agreement or disagreement or draw conclusions; simply describe the message you believe was communicated. For example, if you think someone's behavior seems to indicate that he is uncomfortable around you, but you're not sure, don't ask, "Why are you so nervous when I'm around?" Rather, describe the situation nonjudgmentally: "Jim, I get the impression that you may not be comfortable around me. Is that the case?" This allows the other person to explain without feeling defensive, and it enables you to avoid inaccurate interpretations.

Improving the Nonverbal Communication We Send

We must be aware of the nonverbal messages we send to others. Fortunately, most of us do a good job of communicating nonverbally and thus do not need to make dramatic changes in the way we behave. Nonetheless, we cannot afford to ignore the effects of our nonverbal behavior or to allow the nonverbal messages that we send to go unexamined. If you find that others often misunderstand your intended meaning, you might want to consider how you communicate nonverbally. When you take action to show that you care about how others perceive your behavior, you are engaging in self-monitoring. **Self-monitoring** involves the willingness to change behavior to fit a given situation, an awareness of how we affect others, and the ability to regulate nonverbal cues and other factors to influence others' impressions. In Chapter 3 we discussed impression-management techniques that can enhance a person's image. Self-monitoring is similar, but it goes beyond impression management. It entails both concern with projecting the desired image and the ability to assess the effects of it.

Monitoring Your Nonverbal Communication

1. *Be aware of how people react to you.* If you notice that people react to you differently than you anticipate, you may be giving nonverbal messages that differ from your intentions.

2. *Ask friends or colleagues for their help.* It is very difficult to know if you are sending nonverbal messages that are being misunderstood unless you seek feedback.

3. *Videotape yourself to see how you appear to others.* Then review the videotape by yourself, with a friend, or with your teacher to analyze your nonverbal behaviors.

4. *Adapt to the context or situation in which you find yourself.* As you carry out different roles or find yourself in different communicative contexts, your nonverbal behavior should conform, when appropriate, to the expectations and norms associated with the role or the context. To learn about expectations related to various contexts, observe how others behave in them. For example, if everyone is always on time for a meeting and you are always late, chances are you are violating an established norm. Thus, you must make an effort to conform or you will find that your nonverbal behaviors will be perceived in ways that you might not want them to be.

There is no question that our nonverbal messages greatly influence how others perceive us and our communication. For example, an extremely bright and talented student was constantly being turned down for jobs that he should have been getting. When I asked why he thought this was happening, he replied that he had no idea. To find out, friends videotaped a mock interview in which he was interviewed by another student. When he reviewed the tape, he immediately noticed that he never looked at the interviewer. Instead, his gaze wandered about the room. The lack of direct eye contact by the student gave the impression that he lacked confidence and that he might not be totally candid in what he was saying. Once he knew why he was being rejected, he could try to change his behavior. To help him practice, his friends videotaped another interview session. This time, he was reminded to look at the interviewer each time his gaze wandered. After several such sessions, he grew relaxed about looking at the interviewer and consequently appeared more confident and truthful in his communication.

Although changing your nonverbal behavior is not simple, it can be done with a little effort and desire. The key is to examine conscientiously how your nonverbal cues may be undermining your intended message. If you realize that you have distracting mannerisms, such as smirking, playing with coins, twisting your hair, shuffling your feet, or saying "you know" or "OK" too much, you can ask others to call your attention to these things. Then you can make a conscious effort to change.

Summary

Nonverbal communication encompasses everything that we communicate to others without using words. It is not what we say, but how we say it with our tone of voice; body movements; appearance; and use of space, touch, and time.

We are always communicating something through our nonverbal behavior, regardless of whether we intend to. The interpretation of nonverbal cues depends on context. Nonverbal communication is more believable than verbal communication. Nonverbal communication is our primary way of expressing our feelings and attitudes toward others. Nonverbal communication is related to culture and is ambiguous.

There are eight types of nonverbal communication behaviors: kinesics, physical characteristics, haptics, proxemics, chronemics, paralanguage, artifacts, and environment. All are interdependent and, together with verbal communication, contribute to the total communication process. *Kinesics* refers to various types of body language. A body movement is any movement of the face, hands, feet, trunk, or other parts of the body that communicates a message. Two particularly significant categories of kinesics are (1) *eye behavior* or *oculesics* and (2) *facial expressions,* which include configurations of the face that can reflect, augment, contradict, or be unrelated to a speaker's vocal delivery. Eye contact assists in establishing relationships.

Facial management techniques can conceal inappropriate or unacceptable responses to others. The techniques are *intensifying* (responses that exaggerate facial expressions to meet the expectations of others), *deintensifying* (responses that understate reactions and emotions), *neutralizing* (the avoidance of any emotional facial expression), and *masking* (responses that replace an expression of emotion with another considered more appropriate).

Body movements may be classified as *emblems* (movements that can be translated directly into words or phrases), *illustrators* (body motions that accent, reinforce, or emphasize an accompanying verbal message), *regulators* (motions that control, monitor, or maintain the interaction), *affect displays* (movements that express emotion and feeling), and *adaptors* (body motions that increase a feeling of ease in communication situations). Adaptors can fall into one of three types: *self-adaptors* (usually serve some personal need), *object-adaptors* (involve use of an object for a purpose other than its intended function), and *alter-adaptors* (body motions directed at others that are learned from past experiences and from the manipulation of objects).

Physical characteristics (appearance) play significant roles in the way we interact with one another. Physical attractiveness is an influential variable in everyday communication.

Touch or *haptics* is one of the most personal and powerful means of communicating with others. The kind and amount of touching that is appropriate varies greatly from one situation to another and depends on the individuals and their relationship. Touch has been categorized as follows: *functional–professional touch,* an unsympathetic, impersonal, cold, or businesslike form of touch; *social–polite touch,* touch that acknowledges another according to the rules of a society; *friendship–warmth touch,* touch to express appreciation of the special attributes of others; *love–intimacy touch,* a variety of different forms of touch including personal stroking and the holding of another person; and *sexual-arousal touch,* the most intimate level of personal contact with another. Research has found that generally men touch more, and women are touched more often than men are. Touching behaviors differ from one culture to another.

The way we use space and the amount of distance we place between others and ourselves give strong clues about our thoughts and reactions. Researchers in *proxemics* are especially interested in *territoriality,* the need to identify certain amounts of space as our own. Status, culture, and context all influence our use of space when communicating.

Chronemics is the study of how people perceive, structure, and use time as communication. Because our culture places such a high value on time, it plays a significant role in our nonverbal communication. We often judge people by their use of time.

Verbal communication uses words to convey a message, and *paralanguage* is the way in which those words are said. We often depend more on paralanguage than on the words themselves when interpreting another person's message.

Artifacts are material cues, such as adornments and possessions, that we use to communicate information about our age, gender, status, personality, and relation to others. To ensure clear understanding, effective communicators learn to adapt their use of artifacts to the specific situation.

The impact of the environment in which communication takes place involves the individuals, their backgrounds, and their perception of what is important to them at the time of the interaction. The best environment allows an intended message to be communicated accurately.

Nonverbal communication adds life to our exchanges by *complementing, repeating, regulating,* and *substituting* for what we have to say. We sometimes use nonverbal communication to *deceive* others.

Nonverbal behavior may be interpreted differently by different people, because each cue has multiple meanings, the meaning of a nonverbal cue often depends on the correct interpretation of several other simultaneous cues, and some nonverbal cues are so subtle that they may be difficult to detect. The *functional approach* examines nonverbal behaviors by seeing how each cue interacts with others to perform various communicative functions. To avoid misinterpretation, we must be observant of and sensitive to the nonverbal messages we receive, consider all their possible meanings, and avoid jumping to conclusions. The surest way to determine the true meaning of a nonverbal message is to use *descriptive feedback,* which is the stating of the interpretation of the message received back to the sender.

We must also be aware of the nonverbal messages we send to others. *Self-monitoring* is the willingness to change our behavior to fit different situations, awareness of our effects on others, and the ability to regulate our nonverbal cues and other factors to influence others' impressions. Our nonverbal messages strongly influence how others perceive us. We should ask others for help in changing any distracting nonverbal behaviors we may have.

DISCUSSION STARTERS

1. What is nonverbal communication?
2. Why do you think that nonverbal communication was not seriously studied until recently?
3. How does eye contact serve to develop relationships?
4. Do you agree or disagree with the notion that you cannot *not* communicate? Explain your response.
5. Which nonverbal function do you think contributes the most to your understanding of a message? Why?
6. What is paralanguage?
7. In what ways do vocal cues help us to make judgments about others?
8. Why do you think that nonverbal communication is more believable than verbal communication?
9. What does it mean to say that the interpretation of nonverbal communication depends on the context in which it occurs?
10. How can we become more accurate in our interpretations of the nonverbal messages that we receive?

NOTES

1. M. L. Hickson III and D. W. Stacks, *Nonverbal Communication: Studies and Applications,* 3rd ed. (Dubuque, Iowa: Brown & Benchmark, 1993), 4; A. Mehrabian, *Silent Messages: Implicit Communication of Emotions and Attitudes,* 2nd ed. (Belmont, Calif.: Wadsworth, 1981), 77; R. L. Birdwhistell, *Kinesics and Context: Essays on Body Motion* (Philadelphia: University of Pennsylvania Press, 1970), 158; R. L. Birdwhistell, "Background to Kinesics," *ETC* 13 (1955): 10–18; A. Mehrabian and S. R. Ferris, "Inference of Attitudes from Nonverbal Communication in Two Channels," *Journal of Consulting Psychology* 31 (1967): 24–252.

2. J. S. Philpot, "The Relative Contribution to Meaning of Verbal and Nonverbal Channels of Communication: A Meta-Analysis," (master's thesis, University of Nebraska-Lincoln, 1983).

3. B. M. De Paulo, J. L. Stone, and G. D. Lassiter, "Deceiving and Detecting Deceit," in *The Self and Social Life,* ed. B. R. Schlenker (New York: McGraw-Hill, 1985), 323–70.

4. M. L. Knapp and J. Hall, *Nonverbal Communication in Human Interaction,* 4th ed. (New York: Harcourt Brace, 1997), 24.

5. M. Argyle, F. Alkema, and R. Gilmour, "The Communication of Friendly and Hostile Attitudes by Verbal and Nonverbal Signals," *European Journal of Social Psychology* 1 (1971): 385–402.

6. S. W. Janik, A. R. Wellens, J. L. Goldberg, and L. F. Dell'osso, "Eyes as the Center of Focus in the Visual Examination of Human Faces," *Perceptual and Motor Skills* 4 (1978): 857–58.

7. D. Leathers, *Successful Nonverbal Communication: Principles and Applications* (New York: Macmillan, 1986).

8. P. Andersen, *Nonverbal Communication: Forms and Functions* (Mountain View, Calif.: Mayfield, 1999).

9. C. L. Kleinke, "Gaze and Eye Contact: A Research Review," *Psychological Review* 100 (1986): 78–100.

10. P. G. Zimbardo, *Shyness: What Is It and What You Can Do About It* (Reading, Mass.: Addison-Wesley, 1977).

11. P. Greenbaum and H. W. Rosenfield, "Patterns of Avoidance in Responses to Interpersonal Staring and Proximity: Effects of Bystanders on Drivers at a Traffic Intersection," *Journal of Personality and Social Psychology* 36 (1978): 575–87.

12. P. C. Ellsworth and J. M. Carlsmith, "Eye Contact and Gaze Aversion in Aggressive Encounter," *Journal of Personality and Social Psychology* 33 (1973): 117–22.

13 Ibid.

14. P. Ekman, W. Friesen, and R. Ellsworth, *Emotion in the Human Face: Guidelines for Research and an Integration of Findings* (New York: Pergamon, 1972).

15. Research by R. Levenson and J. Gottman reported in news article, Cox News Service, *Lincoln Journal Star,* 16 October 1990, 10.

16. B. Knutson, "Facial Expression of Emotions Influence Interpersonal Trait Inferences," *Journal of Nonverbal Behavior* 20 (1996): 165–82.

17. H. Aguinis, M. Simonsen, and C. Pierce, "Effects of Nonverbal Behavior on Perceptions of Power

Bases," *Journal of Social Psychology* 138 (1998): 455–70.

18. P. Ekman and H. Oster, "Review and Prospect," in *Emotion in the Human Face,* 2nd ed., ed. P. Ekman (Cambridge: Cambridge University Press, 1982), 148.

19. M. T. Motley, "Facial Affect and Verbal Context in Conversation: Facial Expression as Interjection," *Human Communication Research* 20 (1993): 3–40.

20. M. Zukerman, D. T. Larrance, N. H. Spiegel, and R. Klorman, "Controlling Nonverbal Displays: Facial Expressions and Tone of Voice," *Journal of Experimental Social Psychology* 17 (1981): 506–24.

21. P. Ekman, W. V. Friesen, and P. Ellsworth, "Methodological Decisions," in *Emotion in the Human Face,* 2nd ed., ed. P. Ekman (Cambridge: Cambridge University Press, 1982), 7–21.

22. P. Ekman and W. V. Friesen, "The Repertoire of Nonverbal Behavior: Categories, Origins, Usage, and Coding," *Semiotica* 1 (1969): 49–98.

23. D. S. Berry and L. Zebrowitz-McAuthur, "Perceiving Character in Faces: The Impact of Age-Related Craniofacial Changes on Social Perception," *Psychological Bulletin* 100 (1986): 3–18.

24. J. M. Montepare and L. Zebrowitz-McAuthur, "Impressions of People Created by Age-Related Qualities of Their Gaits," *Journal of Personality and Social Psychology* 54 (1988): 547–56.

25. Ibid., 547–56.

26. W. Wells and B. Siegel, "Stereotyped Somatypes," *Psychological Reports* 8 (1961): 77–78.

27. T. F. Cash and R. N. Kilcullen, "The Aye of the Beholder: Susceptibility to Sexism and Beautyism in the Evaluation of Managerial Applicants," *Journal of Applied Social Psychology* 15 (1985): 591–605; A. Feingold, "Good-Looking People Are Not What We Think: An Integration of the Experimental Literature on Physical Attractiveness" (unpublished manuscript, Yale University, New Haven); V. S. Folkes, "Forming Relationships and the Matching Hypothesis," *Journal of Personality and Social Psychology* 8 (1982): 631–36; and E. Hatfield and S. Sprecher, *Mirror, Mirror . . . The Importance of Looks in Everyday Life* (Albany, N.Y.: SUNY Press, 1986).

28. V. P. Richmond, J. C. McCroskey, and S. K. Payne, *Nonverbal Behavior in Interpersonal Relations* (Englewood Cliffs, N.J.: Prentice-Hall, 1991).

29. M. G. Efran, "The Effect of Physical Appearance on the Judgment of Guilt, Interpersonal Attraction, and Severity of Recommended Punishment in a Simulated Jury Task," *Journal of Research in Personality* 8 (1974): 45–54.

30. E. H. Walster, E. Aronson, D. Abrahams, and L. Rohmann, "Importance of Physical Attractiveness in Dating Behavior," *Journal of Personality and Social Psychology* 4 (1966): 508–16.

31. B. Gillen, "Physical Attractiveness: A Determinant of Two Types of Goodness," *Personality and Social Psychology Bulletin* 7 (1981): 277–81.

32. "When Beauty Can Be Beastly," *Chicago Tribune,* 21 October 1986, 26a.

33. T. F. Cash and N. C. Duncan, "Physical Attractiveness Stereotyping Among Black College Students," *Journal of Social Psychology* 122 (1984): 71–77.

34. S. M. Kalick, "Physical Attractiveness as a Status Cue," *Journal of Experimental Social Psychology* 24 (1988): 469–89.

35. A. Feingold, "Gender Differences in Effects of Physical Attractiveness on Romantic Attraction: A Comparison Across Five Research Paradigms," *Journal of Personality and Social Psychology* 59 (1990): 981–93.

36. G. Maruyama and N. Miller, "Physical Attractiveness and Personality," in *Advances in Experimental Research in Personality,* ed. B. Maher (New York: Academic Press, 1981); B. Major, P. I. Carrington, and P. J. D. Carnevale, "Physical Attractiveness and Self-Esteem: Attributions for Praise from an Other-Sex Evaluator," *Personality and Social Psychology Bulletin* 10 (1984): 43–50.

37. R. Heslin and T. Alper, "Touch: A Bonding Gesture," in *Nonverbal Interaction,* eds. J. M. Wiemann and R. P. Harrison (Beverly Hills, Calif.: Sage, 1983), 47–75.

38. S. M. Jourard, *Disclosing Man to Himself* (Princeton, N.J.: Van Nostrand, 1968).

39. N. Henley, "Power, Sex, and Noverbal Communication," *Berkeley Journal of Sociology* 18 (1973–1974): 10–11.

40. E. T. Hall, *The Silent Language* (Greenwich, Conn.: Fawcett, 1959) and *The Hidden Dimension* (Garden City, N.Y.: Doubleday, 1969).

41. J. K. Burgoon, D. B. Buller, and W. G. Woodall, *Nonverbal Communication: The Unspoken Dialogue,* 2nd ed. (New York: Harper & Row, 1996), 122.

42. B. E. Gronbeck, R. E. McKerrow, D. Ehringer, and A. H. Monroe, *Principles and Types of Speech Communication,* 11th ed. (Glenview, Ill.: Scott Foresman, 1990), 325.

43. M. L. Knapp, *Essentials of Nonverbal Communication* (New York: Holt, Rinehart and Winston, 1980), 7; M. L. Knapp and J. Hall, *Nonverbal Communication*

in Human Interaction, 4th ed. (New York: Harcourt Brace, 1997), 10–11.

44. T. H. Feeley and M. A. Turck, "The Behavioral Correlates of Sanctioned and Unsanctioned Deceptive Communication," *Journal of Nonverbal Behavior* 22 (1998): 189–204; and A. Vrij, L. Akehurst, and P.

Morris, "Individual Differences in Hand Movemens During Deception," *Journal of Nonverbal Behavior* 21 (1997): 87–102.

45. L. Anolli and R. Ciceri, "The Voice of Deception: Vocal Strategies of Naïve and Able Liars," *Journal of Nonverbal Behavior* 21 (1997): 259–85.

Connecting Listening and Thinking in the Communication Process

"The reason why we have two ears and only one mouth is that we may listen the more and talk the less."

—Zeno of Citium

- ■ Explain why it is important to develop skills in listening.
- ■ Distinguish between hearing and listening.
- ■ Outline the six stages of the listening process.
- ■ Explain the role of feedback in listening.
- ■ Define and illustrate four functions of listening.
- ■ Identify six common barriers to effective listening.
- ■ Discuss two activities involved in listening critically.
- ■ Suggest specific guidelines for becoming a more effective listener.
- ■ Use technology to help you take better class notes.

SCENARIO

Jason: Hi, Dionne.

Dionne: Hi.

Jason: How are you?

Dionne: OK, but I'm in big trouble.

Jason: I'm OK, too, but I've really been busy. It seems as if every professor has doubled the homework.

Dionne: It looks as if I'm going to flunk calculus. My parents are going to kill me.

Jason: Oh! I know calc can be pretty rough. I've been so involved with my job that I've fallen way behind in my studies.

Dionne: Well, I'd better go to class.

Jason: What kind of problem are you having?

Dionne: Never mind. I'll tell you later. ■

Are Jason and Dionne *really* listening to each other? They may be hearing each other, but they are not actively listening. Listening requires effort and concentration, and it is difficult to know when someone is listening and when he or she is not. In the opening scenario conversation, Dionne and Jason *appear* to be conversing, but they are not really *listening* to each other and the conversation does not go anywhere. Both are more interested in talking about their own problems, and neither seems interested in listening to the other; thus Jason and Dionne are not effectively communicating. The failure to actively listen usually occurs when we are not ready to listen or when we have competing thoughts that interfere with our ability to listen.

Making Connections

Effective Listening

Look at the chapter opening scenario. We said that Jason and Dionne were not really listening to each other. Think about their communication, and answer the following questions:

1. What evidence is there that Jason and Dionne were not really listening to each other?
2. Have you ever found yourself in a similar situation? What was the result?
3. Have you ever said to someone, "You're not listening to me?" When? Why? What made you think the other person was not listening?
4. How do you behave when you're not really listening to someone else?

Skills in listening, analyzing, processing, and recording information are often neglected during formal education. Have you ever had any formal training in listening? If you are a typical college student, you have completed course work in reading, writing, and speaking, but few students have ever been presented with a systematic course in listening. Not only are there few opportunities for formal listening instruction but also informal listening training is not generally provided either. And yet, as students, you are expected to listen approximately 50 percent of the time—listening is proportionately the most used language skill.[1] In Chapter 1 we discussed several surveys from business executives who suggested that graduates need more work on communication skills; *listening* was high on all lists.[2] Listening scholars, Andrew Wolvin and Carolyn Coakley conducted a survey to determine the status of listening training in Fortune 500 corporations. They learned that more than 50 percent, including Boeing Aircraft and Qwest Communications (formerly U.S. West Communications), consider listening so essential that they provide special listening training for their employees.[3] Inefficient listening is a prevalent (and expensive) problem in our lives, in terms of time wasted, poor customer relations, and the need to redo many tasks. One specific professional organization is dedicated to the study of listening. The International Listening Association (ILA) is comprised of individuals who are dedicated to the study, application, and improvement of listening in every context. Visit the organization, whose members are dedicated to learning more about the impact that listening has on all human activity, at http://www.listen.org.

This chapter will help you become an effective listener and, as a result, an effective respondent. To enhance your listening competence, you will need to understand the importance of effective listening, the elements of listening, the functions of listening, the most common barriers to listening, how to analyze and evaluate what you listen to, and specific steps to improve your listening.

The Importance of Effective Listening

Most misunderstandings that arise in our daily lives, such as the conversation between Jason and Dionne in the opening scenario, occur because of poor listening habits. Poor listening skills can create serious personal, professional, and financial problems. For students, poor listening can result in incorrect assignments, missed appointments, misunderstood directions, lower grades, and lost job opportunities.

It may surprise you to realize how much of your waking day you spend listening—when you are not talking or reading, you are probably listening to something or someone. Communication scholar Larry Barker and several colleagues found that college

Effective listening is important to our success in all aspects of our lives. It may surprise you to realize how much of your waking day you spend listening, but when you are not talking or reading, you are probably listening to something or someone.

students spend nearly half of their communication time listening, almost one-third of it speaking, and less than one-third of it reading and writing (see Figure 6.1).[4] In a more recent study, communication researchers Owen Hargie, Christine Sauders, and David Dickson found similar results.[5] If, as is noted in Figure 6.1, the average person spends less than one-third of the communication day in speaking, you can see just how much time is left for listening to others, to television, to radio, to music, and to thousands of other sounds. If so much of our time is spent listening, why is it such a problem?

From the time we get up in the morning to the time we end the day, we are constantly listening to something. Yet most of us give little thought to the role that listening plays in our everyday experiences. Parents and children both complain, "They

FIGURE 6.1

Proportional Time Spent by College Students in Communication Activities

The graph indicates how typical college students spend their waking time. The proportions given in this graph are averages and, of course, can vary dramatically from person to person and situation to situation.

"An Investigation of Proportional Time Spent in Various Communicating Activities by College Students," L. Barker, R. Edwards, C. Gaines, et al., *Journal of Applied Communication Research 8* (1980): 101–109. Used by permission of the National Communication Association.

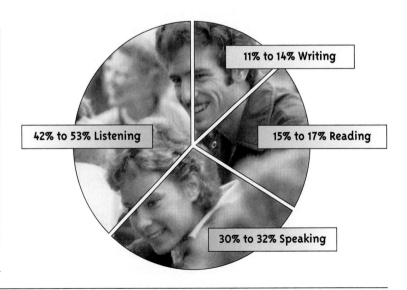

11% to 14% Writing

42% to 53% Listening

15% to 17% Reading

30% to 32% Speaking

Making Connections

The Art of Listening

The quotation at the beginning of this chapter states that there seems to be a reason why we have two ears and only one mouth. We do in fact spend more time listening than speaking. Think about effective listening behaviors and then do the following:

1. Describe in writing the behaviors of an effective listener.
2. In a conversation with another person observe as carefully as possible listening behaviors.
3. Were the listening behaviors consistent with that of a listener who shows skill and sensitivity? Explain.
4. How would you compare your listening behaviors to those of an effective listener and to the person you observed?

Before you go on with your reading, write a one-page paper discussing what you think you can do to improve your listening behavior.

don't listen to me." A similar refrain may be heard from relationship partners, workers and bosses, teachers and students. You may even have heard a friend say to you, "You really ought to listen to yourself." As simple as listening appears to be, many of us are not effective or efficient as listeners.

According to a nationwide survey of executives by Office Team, a leading staffing service in Menlo Park, California, 14 percent of each work week is wasted because of poor communication between staff and managers—amounting to seven weeks per year.[6] Jim Presley, vice president of professional services at SeeCommerce (www.seecommerce.com), a company that develops applications allowing customers to visualize supply chains and form collaborative groups, says that effective listening can improve sales by 30 to 40 percent.[7] Students, too, seem to have trouble as listeners. Informal surveys of our colleagues reveal that the instructors believe the "failure to listen" is one of the major problems in their students. There is little doubt that communicating, and in particular, listening, plays a significant role in society. Because we spend so much time as *consumers* of communication, we need to learn as much as we can about effective listening. In the global community in which we live and work, listening carefully to the messages conveyed by people of other cultures and backgrounds is a skill required to succeed in many areas of life.

Listening scholar Andrew D. Wolvin, author of *Listening in the Quality Organization* (1999), suggests that the individuals who make up organizations must be effective listeners. His book identifies the role of listening in the communication process and provides suggestions for how people can be more effective listeners. He concludes, "Quality listening, then is a benchmark for the quality organization of the twenty-first century. Some organizations have gotten there, while others are yet to develop a listening culture. . . . The challenge to get there is significant, but the rewards are tremendous. Indeed, our very economic, technological, political, and social lives depend on quality listening."[8]

Listening and Hearing: Is There a Difference?

Because most of us take listening for granted, we tend to think of it as a simple task. However, listening is actually quite complex. In fact, scholars still are not *exactly* sure how to define the concept and everything it entails. Scholars agree that listening, like communication in general, is a process and that it is closely linked to the thinking process. Wolvin and Coakley suggest that listening is a distinct behavior that is separate from other intellectual activities. They acknowledge, however, that much of the research closely links listening with reasoning, comprehension, and memory.[9] Wolvin suggests that further research in listening is needed.[10] Listening scholars and teachers do agree that hearing and listening are not the same. It is impossible to listen to sounds without first hearing them, but it is possible to hear sounds without listening to them. What distinguishes listening from hearing? The conversation in the opening scenario illustrates the difference. Both people certainly *heard* each other, but they weren't *listening* to each other.

Most scholars agree that the major difference between listening and hearing is expressed by the word *active*. **Listening** is the active process of receiving aural stimuli by hearing, selecting, attending, understanding, evaluating, and remembering whereas **hearing** is a passive physiological process in which sound is received by the ear.[11] Listening requires energy and desire. You must get involved and work at listening. Listening doesn't just happen; we must make it happen. Hearing, however, occurs with little or no effort when sound waves reach our ears. Thus, a person can have excellent hearing (the physical ability to hear sounds) but be a terrible listener. The ILA further elaborates on the definition of listening: "the process of receiving, constructing meaning from, and responding to spoken or nonverbal messages."[12] This definition takes into account some of the six stages of listening discussed in the next section and also focuses on what you do with the information you gain when you listen to others.

The Stages of Effective Listening

The listening process involves six stages: hearing, selecting, attending, understanding, evaluating, and remembering. Connected to these six stages is the final aspect of responding (see Figure 6.2).

Hearing

Hearing is the passive registering of sounds; the ILA definition of listening identifies the first part of the listening process as receiving, which happens when you hear. You may sense the sounds, but you do not allow them to penetrate beyond a superficial level. For example, when you play the radio while studying, you hear the music, but are you really listening to it? The radio provides background sounds that become listening only when you also carry out the remaining stages of the listening process.

Selecting

As mentioned in Chapter 2, we are constantly bombarded with more stimuli than we can decipher at one time. To make sense out of our environment, we must choose which stimuli we will listen to and which we will ignore. This process is called **selecting.** For example, at a party a friend may be talking to you while loud music is playing and other people are talking. In order to listen to the friend speak, you would select the friend's voice and ignore the other sounds and stimuli.

Stop reading for a moment, and listen to the sounds around you. Notice that while you were reading, you might not have been registering traffic noises, the ticking of a clock, the hum of the refrigerator motor, the sound of someone's stereo. Selecting one

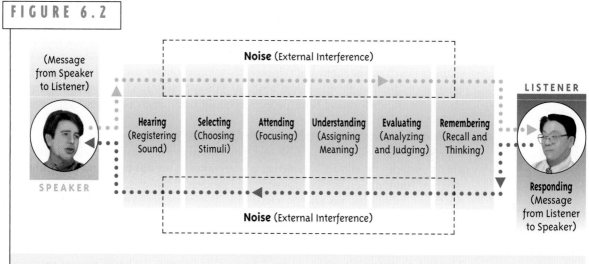

FIGURE 6.2

Stages of the Listening Process

Listening is a very complex process and involves more than simply the hearing of sounds.
It also requires selecting, attending, understanding, evaluating, remembering, and responding
to the message of the sender.

source of sound does not necessarily mean that you are fully listening to it, but it does
engage you in the second stage of the listening process.

Attending

Not only must you select what you are going to listen to, but you must also attend to
it. **Attending** is the mental process of focusing or concentrating for a period of time
on a specific stimuli that you have selected while ignoring or downplaying other competing, internal or external stimuli. Your attention span normally ranges from a few
seconds to a much longer time period. The more things you notice around you, the less
able you will be to concentrate on one single thing and listen to it effectively. Thus, it
is important that you attend to the specific stimuli (message, sound) to which you
want to listen. Attending to something does take effort and concentration, but this
alone does not constitute listening.[13]

Understanding

The main difference between hearing and listening is **understanding.** Once you have
heard, selected, and attended to sounds, you assign meaning to them. Although there
is no commonly accepted explanation of how understanding occurs, it is known
that past experiences play an important role and that you relate and compare new
sounds to those you have heard in the past. To learn calculus, for example, you
must first learn algebra. Thus, if you walk into a calculus class unprepared, you can
select and attend to what the teacher is saying. But because you are unable to interpret the teacher's message, you will not understand the material being presented.
So even though you may be hearing, selecting, and attending to what the calculus

The main difference between hearing and listening is understanding. Once we have heard, selected, and attended to sounds, we must assign meaning to them for listening to be complete. We can enhance our listening by being open and receptive to what the speaker has to say.

Making Connections

Listening Behaviors

A simple experiment illustrates what people tend to remember and for how long. For two or three minutes, read a newspaper or magazine article to a friend, and then ask the friend to repeat the key information. Do the same with several other friends. Most people will be able to report only about 50 percent of what they've heard. Then, wait twenty-four hours and ask each person to repeat the information again.

1. Discuss with your friends what you learned from the exercise.
2. Did some people do better than others? If so, why do you think they did?

Discuss in class what you learned about listening from doing this exercise.

teacher is saying, you are not prepared to understand what is being said. The inability to understand reduces your listening effectiveness.

Evaluating

In the **evaluating** stage, the listener analyzes evidence, sorts fact from opinion, determines the intent of the speaker, judges the accuracy of the speaker's statements and conclusions, and judges the accuracy of personal conclusions. Once we begin to assess the message we received and understood, we may no longer hear and attend to other incoming messages. Later in the chapter we discuss further analyzing and evaluating messages.

Remembering

When we say we are listening to someone, we may actually mean that we are paying attention to what is being said. We may not be indicating that we understand the message or that we will remember it. **Remembering** is thinking of something again. The last aspect in the complete listening process is being able to recall what was said from stored memory. It is referred to in the part of the ILA definition that relates to responding. Table 6.1 provides a comparison of the stages of listening and the ILA definition.

Unfortunately, many of us do not remember information for long. Why we remember some things and not others is not completely clear. Research beginning in 1931, and since corroborated by the ILA, suggests that we remember approximately half of the newly heard, meaningful information immediately after we hear it, but after a month we forget more than half of what we initially remembered.[14] Just as our understanding depends on the selecting and attending stages, so too does our memory. Researchers have found that 25 percent of what most people listen to can be recalled. Of that 25 percent, 80 percent is distorted or not received accurately; this

TABLE 6.1

A Comparison of the Stages of Listening with the ILA Definition of Listening (the process of receiving, constructing meaning from, and responding to spoken or nonverbal messages)

STAGES OF EFFECTIVE LISTENING	ILA DEFINITION OF LISTENING
Hearing means that we are aware of sound or that we receive stimuli.	The *process of receiving* indicates that we *hear*.
Selecting indicates that we choose to respond to some sounds and not to others. This is part of the conscious choices listeners make when sifting through the various stimuli with which they are bombarded.	In the International Listening Association (ILA) definition, the stages of selecting, attending, understanding, evaluating, and remembering may be seen as part of the *constructing meaning from* portion of the ILA definition because all four of those stages are set in motion when a listener tries to make sense of communication events.
Attending suggests that people focus on some things but not on others as they try to make sense of communication messages.	Listeners have to *do something* with those messages; they must think through, weigh, and try to internalize and personalize the information gained. Listeners, according to the ILA, first hear and then process messages so that they can follow through on them.
Understanding is a direct tie-in to the ILA definition because listeners must assign meaning to the communication behaviors they experience.	The ILA goes one step further in defining the process of listening with the phrases *responding to spoken or nonverbal messages*. The implication here is that listeners do more than think about communication events; they also remember and actively respond to others' messages, both verbal and nonverbal, and, it also suggests, according to some, that we *listen to* and respond to messages in all communication events, including Internet messages, face-to-face communication, observed behaviors, and mediated events.
Evaluating is part of thinking, analyzing, and drawing conclusions about messages.	
Remembering suggests that listeners place the information in short-term or long-term memory in order to be able to use it at some time in the future.	

leaves only 5 percent of the total message accurately received.[15] As you learned in Chapter 2, the process of perception, and especially selective perception and selective attention, may also account for loss of information: We tend to select, attend to, and, therefore, remember only information that supports our views. Other information is forgotten.

Responding: Sending Feedback

A receiver who has listened to a message can connect with the sender by verbally or nonverbally verifying the message's reception or indicating a lack of reception. This verification is referred to as responding or feedback. **Responding** is the listener's overt behavior that indicates to the speaker what has and has not been received. Examples of such behaviors are total silence (didn't hear the message, ignored the message, or was angry about what the message said), smiling or frowning (agreeing or disagreeing with the message), and asking for clarification of what was received.

Giving feedback is an important part of being an effective listener. Feedback was defined in Chapter 1 as the response to a message that a receiver sends back to a

Making Connections

Reflecting on the Stages of Listening

The six stages of the listening process are critical to effective listening in all situations. Think about a recent situation in which you were not a good listener (or someone else was not).

1. What was the situation? Did the situation itself play a role in your poor listening? Why? Why not?
2. Why do you think the listening was not effective?
3. At what stage in the listening process did you stop being effective?
4. Did the stage of listening play a role in the poor listening? Why or why not?

source. Feedback helps ensure understanding and also helps speakers determine whether they have been successful in communicating. Feedback should be appropriate to the situation, deliberate, thoughtful, and clear. When it is important that you grasp every detail of a message, you should paraphrase or repeat the information for the sender in order to verify your reception, understanding, and recall of it. This also indicates to the sender that you are actively listening and are committed to receiving the intended message.

As students, you are always providing your instructors with feedback, both consciously and unconsciously. Some of you, however, may not always be completely honest in your responses. For example, even though you may be totally confused, you may indicate through verbal and nonverbal cues that you are listening to, understanding, and agreeing with everything being said—even if the communication has made little sense to you. This behavior, unfortunately, may lead to more unclear messages and further confusion. When those who are confused admit their confusion, their instructors are more likely to improve their presentations. Active listeners always try to get the most out of the message by making sure that they have received it accurately and completely.

As you can see, listening is not simply a matter of paying attention. Listening is an extremely active and complex process that involves hearing, selecting, attending, understanding, evaluating, and remembering. Although we have discussed the stages of the process separately, all six are interdependent. All six stages are necessary for optimum listening.

The Functions of Listening

You wake in the morning to the sound of an alarm clock, the noise your roommate makes moving around in the next room, or the ring of a telephone. While you get dressed, some students talk outside your door and a fire engine wails in the street. You turn on your stereo. At breakfast you join in a heated discussion about the proposed destruction of a historic building on your campus. Then you rush off to the last lecture before an upcoming exam. In the evening you go to a concert. After the concert you meet a good friend who is really upset over receiving a low grade on a test.

Throughout this day you have listened to many different people and things for a variety of purposes. You listened to the alarm clock to get up at the right time; you listened to your friends' opinions to evaluate the proposed removal of the oldest building on campus; you listened to your professor to get information about a subject; you listened to the concert for enjoyment; you listened to your troubled friend to understand his feelings. In each case, listening served a different function and involved different skills. Let's look at each of these functions in greater detail and the listening skills that each requires.

1. Listening to Obtain Information

You probably spend most of your listening time **listening for information,** that is, listening to gain comprehension. You listen as your teacher discusses process, perception, nonverbal and verbal communication, famous speakers, and similar topics in order to learn about speech skills. Each day you listen for information such as news, weather forecasts, sports scores, directions, orders, assignments, names, numbers, and locations.

2. Listening to Evaluate

Evaluative listening is listening to judge or to analyze information. For example, a car owner who hears a squeak coming from the front end rolls down the window and does some evaluative listening. That is, the owner tries to pinpoint the exact location and cause of the bothersome noise. A teacher listens to students' speeches to discriminate between good and poor presentations and to assign grades. In most situations we all should listen critically. We should constantly judge evidence, arguments, facts, and values. We need to ask questions if we hope to be effective listeners. We are bombarded by messages asking us to believe, accept, or buy things. For our own protection, we must evaluate everything to which we listen. (Later in this chapter, specific guidelines are presented for evaluating what we hear.)

Empathic listening occurs when we listen to what someone else is experiencing and seek to understand that person's thoughts and feelings. When we empathize, we try to put ourselves in the other person's place to understand what is happening to him or her.

3. Listening with Empathy

Empathic listening occurs when you listen to what someone else is experiencing and seek to understand that person's thoughts and feelings. It is not sympathy, which means that you feel sorry for the other person. Empathy means you try to put yourself in another's place to try to understand what is happening to him or her. Most of us find it difficult to avoid making judgments when we listen to someone else's problems, but that is exactly what we must do if we hope to listen with empathy. Listening empathically can be a healing and soothing process. Empathic listening indicates that we are aware, appreciative, and understanding of another person's feelings.

Caring about someone requires a great deal of sensitivity as well as the ability to communicate that sensitivity. It is not easy to listen; it is even more difficult to listen with empathy. If, however, we fail to empathize with others, we also fail to understand them. (You will learn more about relationships and relational communication in Chapters 13 and 14.)

4. Listening for Enjoyment

When we listen purely for pleasure, personal satisfaction, and appreciation, we **listen for enjoyment.** We usually listen to music, for example, simply because we enjoy it. The same is true for most of us when we combine listening and viewing as we watch television or a movie.

Listening for enjoyment involves more than merely sitting back and letting sounds enter our ears. Listening for enjoyment also involves the thinking process. We evaluate what we hear and see to understand something or to learn more about it. As we listen to music, we try to find some personal value or relevance in the lyrics and the instrumentation. Even if we attend an opera for the first time and do not understand the language, we can enjoy the performance as we seek to understand it. In other words, listening for enjoyment uses the same process as other kinds of listening: We select, attend, understand, evaluate, and remember. We construct meaning from what we hear and respond to it in some way.

Barriers to Effective Listening

Why are most people poor listeners? The answer to this question is surprisingly complex. The quality of our listening changes from time to time and from situation to situation. A number of barriers contribute to our ineffectiveness as listeners. The context of each communication will affect how important each barrier actually is, and some of the barriers that reduce our listening effectiveness are under our control whereas others are not. The following six barriers to effective listening were identified by Ralph Nichols, who is considered the "father of listening research."[16] Nichols and other researchers have replicated his research in subsequent studies and found the same results. Although these six barriers may not be the only ones, they are the most common. And remember, listening, like communication, is a learned behavior, so we *can learn* to overcome the obstacles that interfere with our listening effectiveness.

Considering the Topic or Speaker Uninteresting

The level of interest and the amount of importance we place on a subject or a speaker usually govern how much effort we put into listening. Deciding that a subject or person is uninteresting or boring often leads us to the conclusion that the information being presented is not important. However, this is not necessarily true. What appears to be dull or insignificant may very well be vital for passing an exam, doing an assignment correctly, learning something, following your supervisor's instructions, making a sale, or learning a new way of doing something on the job. In other words, a competent listener keeps an open mind.

Criticizing the Speaker Instead of the Message

How many times have you judged a speech by the number of "ahs" and "ums" the speaker used? How many times has a speaker's volume, mispronunciations, or accent influenced your opinion? Have you ever missed a message because you were focusing on a mismatched shirt and tie, bizarre earrings, or the speaker's facial expressions or nervous behaviors?

Of course, when it is possible, speakers should do everything in their power to eliminate personal quirks that may distract attention from their message, but listeners must also share responsibility for receiving the message. An effective listener must be able to overlook the superficial elements of a person's delivery style or appearance in order to concentrate on the substance of the presentation. In short, the listener must stay involved in the message, not the speaker or the speaker's attire or behaviors.

Concentrating on Details, Not Main Ideas

Many of us listen for specific facts such as dates, names, definitions, figures, and locations, assuming that they are the important things to know. But are they? Specific facts are needed in some situations, but we often focus too much on details. As a result, we walk away with disjointed details and no idea how they relate to each other and to the total picture.

Competent listeners focus on the main or most important ideas, not on every single word. All stages of the listening process are affected adversely when we forget that general ideas may be more significant than the details that surround them. Listen carefully to your professors or your supervisors for clues as to what is most important and note when they ask you to carefully select what to write in your notes.

Avoiding Difficult Listening Situations

Most of us find it difficult to keep up with the vast amount and increasing technical complexity of the information that confronts us each day. At times we may deal with complex listening situations by giving up and ignoring what is being presented.

Concentration and energy are needed to overcome the temptation to ignore or avoid what may seem difficult and confusing. When you are faced with a difficult listening situation, the best approach is usually to ask questions. For example, physicians often use complex medical terminology when talking to patients, but patients can take the responsibility for gaining understanding. They can ask the physician to explain terms, to review procedures, and to supply missing information. The same principles apply to the classroom or to the workplace. You should never hesitate to ask about something when you don't understand it, because without understanding, you cannot learn.

Sometimes you may not listen to new and difficult information because you lack motivation, but once again, the responsibility falls on you to make the effort to listen. Try consciously and continually to listen to such communication. Each time you are successful at staying tuned in, you will acquire not only some information but also improved confidence and ability.

Tolerating or Failing to Adjust to Distractions

Distractions constantly disrupt our concentration. As listeners, we have the responsibility to adjust to, compensate for, or eliminate distractions and to focus on speakers and their messages.

We can control some distractions. If, for example, noise from another room competes with a speaker, the listener can close the door, ask the person who is creating the noise to be quiet, move closer to the speaker, or ask the speaker to talk louder.

TABLE 6.2

Ineffective and Effective Listening Habits

BAD LISTENER	GOOD LISTENER
Thinks topic or speaker is of no interest	Finds areas of interest—keeps an open mind
Focuses on the speaker's appearance and delivery	Concentrates on the content of the presentation and overlooks speaker characteristics—stays involved
Listens only for details	Listens for ideas
Avoids difficult material	Exercises the mind—prepares to listen
Is easily distracted	Resists distractions
Fakes attention	Pays attention

Some distractions must be overcome through mental rather than physical effort. A noise in the background can become a major distraction, or we can reduce it to a minor nuisance by forcing ourselves to listen more intently to the speaker. When distractions occur, we must consciously focus on selecting the appropriate messages and attending to them. We must take advantage of our ability to filter out extraneous noise and distractions and concentrate on the sounds that are important to us. If we cannot modify external noise, we must alter our internal listening behavior in order to understand the speaker's message.

Faking Attention

At one time or another everyone pretends to pay attention to something or someone. You appear to listen intently, but your mind is somewhere else. You might even smile in agreement, when all you are really doing is maintaining eye contact. In class you may pretend to take notes, although your mind may not be following what is being said.

Pretending to pay attention may become a habit. Without even realizing what you are doing, you may automatically tune out a speaker and let your mind wander. If, after a speech, you cannot recall the main purpose or the essential points presented by the speaker, you were probably faking attention. Although it may seem harmless, such deceptive behavior can lead to misunderstandings and cause people to question your credibility and sincerity.

Table 6.2 summarizes the differences between ineffective and effective listening habits.

Effective Listening

1. Effective listeners check their attention periodically. They ask themselves, "Am I paying attention?" When listeners realize that they are distracted, they should make an effort to pay attention. Good listeners recognize when they are not listening well and do whatever it takes to return their attention to the speaker.

2. Effective listeners adopt behaviors that support listening effectiveness. They demonstrate active nonverbal behaviors, such as maintaining eye contact and leaning forward toward the speaker. They mentally prepare themselves to receive the message. Effective listeners demonstrate attitudes, behaviors, and thinking that allows them to focus on others. They know that listening is an active process, requiring energy and effort on their part.

Critical Listening and Critical Thinking: Analyzing and Evaluating Messages

As listeners, our goal is more than simply understanding a message; we also try to become critical listeners. Practicing **critical listening** involves analyzing and assessing the accuracy of the information presented, determining the reasonableness of its conclusions, and evaluating its presenter. In other words, we must ask ourselves questions about the message: Is the message true? Is it based on solid evidence? Is it complete? Is it logical? What motivates the speaker to present the message?

We are constantly confronted with many choices and decisions. For example, we are exposed to numerous commercial messages each day in addition to the interpersonal messages we receive at school, home, work, and in recreational situations. We also live in an increasingly technological world. Web searches to find information for our college papers and presentations; to enhance a presentation at work; or even to learn more about a city, country, or company provide an infinite number of resources very quickly. (We discuss web searches for speeches in greater detail in Chapter 8.) Because we are limited in the amount of experience we can acquire on our own, we must depend on others to provide information and advice. Thus, we must evaluate and assess that information in order to judge its value and utility. We do this through critical thinking. Critical thinking is integrally linked to critical listening, because they are both a part of the process of gaining an understanding of our world. There are many definitions of critical thinking. One definition of **critical thinking** suggests that critical thinkers ask and answer the right questions to determine the appropriate responses to problems and issues.[17] In an earlier work Ennis defined critical thinking as the ability to analyze and assess information.[18] From these two definitions alone, you should be able to make the connection between listening and thinking. You must listen carefully and construct meaning from ideas, messages, and so forth if you are to make sense of the world around you. Critical thinking has become so important to academic institutions and to employers that more and more colleges and universities include courses or units in critical thinking in their curricula; some even pro-

As listeners, our goal is more than simply understanding a message; we also try to become critical listeners. Practicing critical listening involves judging the accuracy of the information presented, determining the reasonableness of its conclusions, and evaluating its presenter.

Making Connections

An Internet Site for Your Listening Self-Assessment

Do you want to learn more about you own listening effectiveness? Do you have five minutes? HighGain Inc., a training organization specializing in listening and other communication skills, provides an interactive Listening Self-Assessment that allows you to check your own listening (and provides an analysis) at http://www.highgain.com/SELF/index.php3. HighGain also provides a web newsletter at http://www.highgain.com/newsletter/hgenews-current.html.

vide a web page devoted to the characteristics of the critical thinker.[19] Bellevue Community College's web page identifies nine characteristics of a critical thinker, and two implications and six aspects of critical thinking. Basically, you need to remember that the link between critical thinking and critical listening is that critical thinkers have specific attitudes and mental habits. They are intellectually curious, flexible, objective, persistent, systematic, honest, and decisive. They use their critical listening abilities to assess information and choose the best options from among those available. Critical thinkers are aware of the ways they learn best and capitalize on opportunities to expand their learning abilities. One of the goals of a liberal arts education is to encourage people to think critically. We hope this text helps you develop habits of mind to help you become effective thinkers, listeners, and communicators.

Critical thinking and critical listening are closely linked. The critical thinker knows how to analyze and assess information. The critical listener knows how to make connections between messages and issues. The critical listener also uses the ability to analyze and evaluate messages to determine whether ideas are logically presented and whether the speaker is well informed and exhibits clear thinking. Critical listeners must be critical thinkers. Critical thinking and critical listening are closely related parts of a very complex process. Listening with a critical ear involves two phases: (1) assessing the speaker's values and intent and (2) judging the accuracy of the speaker's conclusions.[20]

Assessing the Speaker's Motivation

Assessing a speaker's motivation generally involves three stages of information processing: (1) making a judgment about the speaker's beliefs, (2) comparing our standards and those of the speaker, and (3) evaluating the worth of the message presented.

Values are strongly held beliefs central to the communication process and to each individual's perceptual system. They affect our perception and interpretation of both the messages we send and the messages we receive. (Values are discussed further in Chapter 12.) The first consideration in listening, therefore, is to examine the message in order to determine the speaker's values: We critically think about what the speaker is saying and how it compares to our own value system. Of course, we should not automatically dismiss a message merely because the speaker's values conflict with our own. However, any time we are confronted with a message that differs from our own views—one that asks us to do something, buy something, or behave in a certain way—we should be aware of the purpose behind it.

The second consideration is to determine whether the message urges us to conform to or go against our principles or standards. Finally, we consider how to evaluate and respond to the messages. We use our critical thinking skills to recognize and understand the motivation behind the messages we receive.

In order to be an effective listener you must know what to do and how to do it. With a desire to learn and with practice you can improve your listening.

Judging the Accuracy of the Speaker's Conclusions

In order to make accurate judgments and to critically think about important messages, ask the following questions:

- Is the speaker qualified to draw the conclusion?
- Has the speaker actually observed the concept or issue about which he or she is talking?
- Does the speaker have a vested interest in the message?
- Is there adequate evidence presented to support the conclusion?
- Is the evidence relevant to the conclusion?
- Does contrary evidence exist that refutes what has been presented?
- Does the message contain invalid or inadequate reasoning?

Making Connections

How Do Others Rate You as a Listener?

How do you think the following people would rate you as a listener? Use a scale of 0 to 100, with 100 being the highest rating.

1. Your best friend
2. Your boss or a teacher
3. Your roommate or a co-worker
4. Your parents

After you rated yourself, go to each person and ask him or her to rate you (without disclosing your rating, of course). Compare the ratings. Were they the same? If not, why?

Improving Listening Competence

With appropriate knowledge and practice, all of us can become better listeners (refer to the nearby cartoon). First, we must recognize the importance of listening effectively. Second, we must think of listening as an *active* behavior that requires conscious participation. Third, we must recognize that a willingness to work and a desire to improve are essential to increasing listening effectiveness.

In some situations, we need not listen with full attention. For example, if we listen to a CD while conversing with a friend, we're not likely to create problems by attending closely to the friend and partially to the music. However, each listener must be able to identify when total energy and involvement in the listening process are crucial. Effective listening often requires both energy and concentration; listeners need to constantly remind themselves that listening is vital to communication. People call on different listening skills, depending on whether their goal is to comprehend information, critique and evaluate messages, show empathy for others, or appreciate a performance. According to the National Communication Association, competent listeners demonstrate (1) knowledge and understanding of the listening process, (2) the ability to use appropriate and effective listening skills for a given communication situation and setting, and (3) the ability to identify and manage barriers to listening, all of which we have covered in this chapter.

Competent listeners work at listening (see the Guidelines for Competent Listening). They are prepared to listen and know what they wish to gain from their listening experiences. Competent listeners also engage in appropriate listening behaviors. They realize that being a good listener is active and complex. They know that they must pay attention if they are to listen well. They do not interrupt others, they look at the speaker, they listen to ideas, and they concentrate on what is being said.

Competent Listeners

1. Be prepared to listen. Learn to control internal and external distractions.

2. Behave like a good listener. Stop talking and let others have their say. Do not interrupt. Concentrate on what is being said, not who is saying it, or what the speaker is doing. Good listeners maintain eye contact with speakers, ask questions at appropriate times, and maintain flexibility as they carefully listen to the speaker's views.

3. Take good notes. Listen for main ideas and write down the most significant, most important points; don't attempt to write down every word. Good note taking helps listeners remember better and longer, and provides a written indication of ideas to remember. Brevity is usually best, so that you can carefully listen to the speaker and the speaker's intent. Write clearly to facilitate the review of your notes later. Review your notes as soon after the event as possible to help you recall them later. And, finally, reorganize or rearrange your notes if necessary for clarity before filing them for future reference. Do not get so involved in note taking that effective listening is lost. Note taking should be used as an aid to listening, not as a replacement for it. All six stages of the listening process are brought into play when we listen effectively. Never concentrate so hard on writing everything down that you fail to think about what is said.

Making Connections

Thinking and Listening

A student in a lecture class approaches you as you both go into the lecture hall and says, "I do not understand what's going on in this class. It's so hard to take notes? The instructor always has so much stuff on that computer screen, and then she says, 'Listen to the examples, because that's where the exam questions will come from.' I can't listen to those examples. It's all I can do to listen and look at what's on the screen and get those ideas down. What do you do? Do you have any suggestions for me?"

1. Based on what we've discussed in this chapter, what kind of advice could you give to your classmate?
2. What would you tell that person about listening?
3. What suggestions would you give about taking notes in the class where the computer-projected images *and* the teacher's examples and explanations are important?

Listening and Technology

Just as some people think that computers and technology will "destroy" families and relationships, some believe that computers, email, and the Internet will harm listening in all areas of our lives. What your authors and other communication scholars have found in our communication classrooms, however, is that technology can be used to students' advantage, if used merely as a tool. We suggested that taking notes helps us become better listeners, and appropriate technology as a delivery tool can also serve that function. Recent studies reported at ILA conventions indicate an increasing use of computer-enhanced presentations (such as PowerPoint), and an expanding student ability to take better notes helps students perform better on exams when technology and note-taking instruction are provided early and reinforced throughout the semes-

We can learn to be better listeners, but we must have not only the appropriate behaviors but also the right mental attitude to truly listen to others.

Reprinted with special permission of King Features Syndicate.

E-mail conversations are similar to other communication, especially one-to-one interactions. Interactants should carefully "listen" to each other from meaning, and "eavesdroppers" are not appreciated!

For Better or Worse © UFS. Reprinted by permission.

ter.[21] Listeners must remember to think independently. The words on the screen cannot eliminate individual choices. It's too easy to let the screen images take priority. But, as we have pointed out in this chapter, listeners must listen with their eyes, their minds, their bodies, and their ears. Students need to listen to determine where the instructor's emphases are and take notes accordingly.

 Summary

Until recently, the listening process was often taken for granted primarily because people thought that listening "just happens." Most of us now recognize that listening is a complex process that must be carefully cultivated because it is so crucial to effective communication.

Hearing is the physiological process in which sound is received by the ear. *Listening,* which requires energy, desire, and commitment, involves hearing, selecting, attending, understanding, evaluating, and remembering sounds and messages and then responding to them. *Selecting* is choosing what we are going to listen to. *Attending* is focusing on specific stimuli while ignoring or downplaying others. *Understanding* is assigning meaning to the stimuli that we have selected and attended to. *Evaluating* is analyzing and judging the information received. *Remembering* is recalling something from memory, thinking of something again. *Responding* is providing feedback to the speaker.

Listening serves four principal functions: (1) *listening for information* enables us to gain comprehension; (2) *evaluative listening* enables us to judge or analyze information; (3) *empathic listening* helps us understand what another person is thinking and feeling; and (4) *listening for enjoyment* creates pleasure, personal satisfaction, and appreciation.

Many obstacles prevent us from listening effectively. We may be indifferent to the topic or speaker, criticize the speaker instead of the message, concentrate on details rather than on main ideas, avoid difficult listening situations, permit distractions to interfere, or fake attention. Because listening is a learned behavior, we can learn to overcome bad listening habits and learn to be better listeners.

Critical listening occurs when a person judges the accuracy of the information presented, determines the reasonableness of its conclusions, and evaluates its presenter. To be effective critical listeners we must also be effective critical thinkers. *Critical thinking* is the ability to analyze and assess information. This involves assessing the values and intent of the speaker and judging the accuracy of the speaker's conclusions.

We can improve listening ability by being mentally and physically prepared to listen and by behaving like a good listener. To be a good listener, we need to stop talking, avoid interrupting, empathize with the other person, concentrate on what is being said, react to the ideas and not to the person talking, ask questions when we do not understand something, be flexible in our views, listen for main ideas, and take notes.

Technology can help you become a better listener and a better note taker. Remember that the technology is a tool, not the message. Competent listeners listen for main ideas and attend to a speaker's nonverbal cues to assess which are the most important points to consider. Competent listeners listen with their whole bodies and do everything they can to focus on what they need to know and be able to do as a result of listening to messages, however those messages are delivered or enhanced.

DISCUSSION STARTERS

1. Why do we take listening for granted?
2. What could you say to persuade someone of the importance of listening?
3. How would you go about teaching a person to be an effective listener?
4. What are the differences between listening and hearing?
5. What makes listening so much more complicated than hearing?
6. What role does memory play in the listening process?
7. Why is it important to understand the different functions of listening?
8. What does it mean to listen with empathy?
9. Why don't we listen effectively?
10. What are the three most important things to remember about note taking?
11. Based on the information in this chapter, how can you use technology to help you take notes?

NOTES

1. R. Bohlken, "Substantiating the Fact That Listening Is Proportionately Most Used Language Skill," *The Listening Post* 70 (1999): 5.
2. National Association of Colleges and Employers, Work Week, *Wall Street Journal,* February 8, 2000. Also, American Council on Education, *Spanning the Chasm: Corporate and Academic Cooperation to Improve Work-Force Preparation* (Washington, D.C.: American Council on Education, 1997).
3. A. D. Wolvin and C. G. Coakley, "A Survey of the Status of Listening Training in Some Fortune 500 Corporations," *Communication Education* 40 (1991): 152–64.
4. P. Rankin, "Listening Ability," *Proceedings of the Ohio State Educational Conference's Ninth Annual Session,* 1929; L. Barker, R. Edwards, C. Gaines, et al., "An Investigation of Proportional Time Spent in Various Communication Activities by College Students," *Journal of Applied Communication Research 8* (1980): 101–109
5. O. Hargie, C. Saunders, and D. Dickson, *Social Skills in Interpersonal Communication,* 3rd ed. (New York: Routledge, 1994).
6. Office Team Survey, 2000, cited in *Sssh! Listen Up!* HighGain, Inc. Newsletter (June 2000): 4.
7. J. Presley, "Putting It into Practice," cited in *Sssh! Listen Up!* HighGain, Inc. Newsletter (June 2000): 3.
8 A. D. Wolvin, *Listening in the Quality Organization* (Ithaca, N.Y.: Finger Lakes Press, 1999), 54.

9. A. Wolvin and C. Coakley, *Listening*, 5th ed. (Dubuque, Iowa: William C. Brown, 1998), 70.

10. A. Wolvin, "On Competent Listening," *Listening Post* 54 (July 1995): 1.

11. E. C. Glenn, "A Content Analysis of Fifty Definitions of Listening," *Journal of the International Listening Association* 3, (1989): 21–31.

12. International Listening Association Definition, 1994, in A. Wolvin, "One Competent Listening," *Listening Post* 54 (July 1995), 1.

13. T. G. Devine, "Listening Skills Schoolwide: Activities and Programs." ERIC Clearinghouse on Reading and Communication Skills (1982): ED 219–789.

14. A. G. Dietze and G. E. Jones, "Factual Memory of Secondary School Pupils for a Short Article Which They Read a Single Time," *Journal of Educational Psychology 22* (1931): 586–98, 667–767.

15. S. S. Benoit and J. W. Lee, "Listening: It Can Be Taught," *Journal of Education for Business* 63 (1986): 229–32.

16. R. Nichols, "Factors Accounting for Differences in Comprehension of Material Presented Orally in the Classroom" (Ph.D. diss., University of Iowa, 1948); R. O. Hirsch, *Listening: A Way to Process Information Aurally* (Dubuque, Iowa: Gorsuch Scarisbrick, 1979), 36–41.

17. V. R. Rugierro, *Beyond Feelings: Critical Thinking,* 6th ed. (Belmont, Calif.: Mayfield Publishing, 2000).

18. R. H. Ennis, "A Concept of Critical Thinking," *Harvard Educational Review* 32 (1962): 83–84.

19. Bellevue Community College, http://ir.bcc.ctc.edu/library/ilac/critdef.htm. Accessed on February 15, 2001.

20. E. D'Angelo, *The Teaching of Critical Thinking* (Amsterdam, The Netherlands: B. R. Gruner, 1971), 7; R. H. Ennis, "A Taxonomy of Critical Thinking Dispositions and Abilities," in *Teaching Thinking Skills: Theory and Practice,* eds. J. Baron and R. Sternberg (New York: Freeman, 1987).

21. P. E. Emmert and V. Emmert, ILA Convention Papers, 1997, 1998; M. L. Beall, ILA Convention Papers, 1997, 1998, 2001.

CHAPTER 7

Selecting a Topic and Relating to the Audience

"Imagination will often carry us to worlds that never were. But without it, we go nowhere."

—Carl Sagan

- Describe how to choose a topic for a speech.
- Assess whether a topic is appropriate for a speaker, an audience, and a speaking situation.
- Formulate the general purpose, specific purpose, and thesis of a speech.
- Determine the relationship between the speaker, the speech, and the audience.
- Explain what information a speaker should gather about an audience when preparing a speech.
- Interpret data from an audience analysis and apply this data to a specific speaking situation.

SCENARIO

Caller: My name is Jane Smith and I'm with the state retailers' association. We're having our annual conference in your city this year on Wednesday, April 20. You have a reputation as a fascinating speaker on the topic of communication, so we were wondering if you would be willing to speak at our conference.

Speaker: Let me look at my calendar. Yes, I am available on that day.

Caller: Good! We would like you to talk about the importance of communication to retailers. You would be speaking at approximately noon, during our luncheon. We would like you to speak for about thirty to forty-five minutes and then allow about fifteen minutes for questions. Is that OK?

Speaker: Yes, but I do have a few questions. How many people will be attending?

Caller: About sixty-five to seventy-five.

Speaker: Who will these people be?

Caller: They are mainly retailers—people who either own their own small businesses or manage large stores.

Speaker: Could you be more specific?

Caller: Yes. The business owners tend to have small clothing stores or sporting goods stores, something like that. The managers are employed by supermarkets or stores like Sears or Target.

Speaker: Can you be more specific about the topic you would like me to cover?

Caller: I'll have Sue Jones, our president, call you. She can give you more details. ■

Y ou may be thinking to yourself, "What does the situation in this scenario have to do with me? I will not be making any public speeches." But similar scenarios occur more often than most people think. For instance, many high schools invite members of the community to speak at career days to introduce students to different career choices. Medical doctors, sales representatives, police officers, physical therapists, architects, accountants, owners of small businesses, teachers, bank presidents, and college professors, along with others are invited to talk about their work. Presenters at these sessions often remark they never thought they would be giving such talks. Although most of us will not work full time as public speakers, each of us will likely be called on to make numerous public presentations in a variety of settings. Therefore, basic communication courses need to address the principles of public communication.

It is not unusual for students to believe that they will never have to give a speech and that learning about speech making is a waste of time. A survey of 202 randomly selected blue-collar workers in a medium-size city, however, found that almost half had given speeches to ten or more people at least once during the previous two-year period. They spoke to community groups, church groups, students in courses they were taking, and members of their unions. The more education they had and the higher their economic status, the more likely they were to make speeches. The report observed that college graduates were more likely to give speeches than nongraduates.[1]

In another survey, sixty-seven out of seventy-one top corporate executives in the United States maintained that training or competence in public speaking was essential for a person in middle management.[2] Most surveys of chief executive officers and personnel managers reveal that employers want to hire employees who know how to make effective presentations. Although public speaking isn't the only skill required for a successful career, it is considered necessary for those who wish to reach the top.

Experienced speakers, such as Senator Hillary Clinton, know the importance of being an effective speaker. They also know it is important to relate to their audience and to be prepared in advance.

Here are several examples of talks typical college students like you might give in addition to your presentations in this class:

Shawn is preparing a ten-minute oral report for his history class, based on research he has done on the Vietnam War.

Kelley, the volleyball team captain, has been asked to speak to the students at the local high school about the effects steroids have on young athletes.

As a member of Future Farmers of America, Mark will speak to a group of high school students about the importance of the organization and try to convince them to join.

Megan, a student teacher, is about to present to a seventh-grade class her first lecture on how to use BASIC computer language.

Lee, a volunteer at the Campus Multicultural Center, will give several presentations and tours to incoming international students during orientation week.

Each of these students is preparing for a public speaking event. Being able to give an effective speech presentation is important while you are in college. For example, many of you will give presentations or reports in classes, dorm meetings, fraternity or sorority meetings, sports team meetings, student government campaigns, political demonstrations, or a variety of other events that take place on a college campus. **Public speaking** is the presentation of a speech, usually prepared in advance, during

Making Connections

Thinking About Public Speaking

When Rita Mocek, who graduated in the spring of 1997 from Downer's Grove South High School, was selected to serve on a District 99 curriculum committee in the fall of 1996, she had to speak in front of a group that included her principal and district superintendent.

"Yes, it was a little intimidating," recalled Mocek. "Yet I was able to speak clearly, organize my thoughts, and express my ideas."

When Mocek was a freshman, she took a required one-semester class in speech communication. Since then, she participated on the school speech team that won four state speech championships. Consequently, she said, "I'm not afraid to speak my mind and I have more self-confidence."

The National Communication Association in Annandale, Virginia, would like every high school graduate to be adept in speaking before an audience, and has developed a set of guidelines and standards for speaking, listening, and media literacy standards in the K–12 curriculum.

Think about your own experiences and those of Rita Mocek. Then answer these questions:

1. Should a course in oral communication be required for high school graduation? Why or why not?

2. Should a course in oral communication be required for college graduation? Why or why not?

3. In what ways is oral communication vital to students' futures in a culturally diverse society, a competitive job market, and a world of constant change?

Excerpt from Jody Temkin, "Speech Classes Living Up to Talk," *The Chicago Tribune,* 20 July 1997, 10–11.

which the speaker is the central focus of an audience's attention. In Chapter 1 we stated that the ability to communicate is one of the most important skills a person can possess in our society, and speech making is a vital and significant form of communication. Beginning public speakers frequently express two concerns: the fear of not having anything worthwhile to say and nervousness at speaking in front of others. Both of these concerns are addressed in detail in this part of the text.

Learning about making presentations will not only help you become an effective speaker but it will also help you develop your writing, listening, organizing, researching, and reasoning skills. This in turn will increase your self-confidence.

Selecting a Speech Topic

Selecting a topic is the first step in preparing a speech. In these chapters on public communication, you will read about topics that were presented in a variety of classroom, business, and professional situations. As illustrated by the brief scenario at the beginning of this chapter, the choice of topics is often prompted by the situation itself, the needs of others, and the position and qualifications of the speaker. Selecting a good topic for you and the speaking situation requires thought and a systematic approach.

Selecting an Appropriate Topic

Many factors contribute to an effective speech presentation, including research, organization, wording, and delivery, but none is more important than selecting an appropriate topic. The topic and your interest and motivation in developing and presenting it are vital to your success as a speaker. The topic that is best for your audience, the assignment, and you isn't always easy to determine.

Some beginning speakers worry that they might not be able to think of something about which to talk. This concern is simply unwarranted. For example, if you read a

Many factors contribute to an effective speech presentation, including research, organization, wording, and delivery, but none are more important than selecting an appropriate topic. The topic and your interest and motivation in developing and presenting it are vital to your success as a speaker.

newspaper or magazine or watch television, you will be exposed to a variety of stimulating and interesting topics ranging from military involvement in foreign lands to health care. When a topic isn't assigned by the instructor, the trick is to identify a topic that matches *your* interests and qualifications, the interests and existing knowledge of your audience, and the requirements of the situation in which the speech is to be presented. If you are vitally concerned about the topic and have enthusiasm for sharing it with others, your concerns can be drastically reduced.

Selecting an Appropriate Topic

1. *Choose a topic that is meaningful to you.* The more meaningful a topic is to you, the more likely you are to put the necessary time and effort into researching and developing your speech. The stronger your commitment to a topic, the more enthusiastically you will present it. A speaker's commitment to a topic usually transfers to the audience members and gets them involved. The involvement of the audience in a topic can be an effective gauge of your success as a speaker. After all, the reason for giving a speech, besides completing the assignment, is to gain your listeners' attention, and this is more easily accomplished if you consider the topic to be important.

2. *Choose a topic that will allow you to convey an important thought to your audience.* The thought does not have to be a matter of extreme urgency, but it should at least be relevant to your audience's interests, have some direct affect on them, or be something that you believe the audience should know. Ask yourself the following questions:

   Will the audience want to learn more about the topic?

   Will the audience believe the topic is relevant?

   Will the audience be affected in some way by the topic, either now or in the future?

   Will the audience benefit from listening to a presentation on the topic?

   Will the audience believe you are a credible speaker on the topic?

   If you can answer yes to each of these questions about your topic, you are on your way to selecting an appropriate one.

3. *Choose a topic that is familiar and interesting to you.* Choosing a topic that is familiar and interesting to you will make the development and delivery of your speech easier. It would be easier to begin your research and development of a talk on DVD technology if you had some knowledge of DVD and the principles on which it is based. And researching and developing a speech will be more enjoyable if you are interested in the topic. You may find it enjoyable to select a topic in which you are interested but about which you know little. For example, you may have heard of in vitro fertilization (fertilization of an egg by a sperm in a test tube) but do not know the exact procedure or issues surrounding it. If a topic fascinates you and you want to learn more about it, this is a unique opportunity. Further, choosing a topic that interests you can increase the likelihood of audience interest and speaker credibility. (We discuss speaker credibility in Chapter 12.)

Techniques for Finding a Topic

If you have difficulty thinking of interesting subjects, there are some techniques that might help you: self-inventory; brainstorming; reviewing current magazines, newspapers, and television news programs; and conducting an Internet search. All four will generate a wide range of possible topics from which you can then select the most appropriate.

Self-Inventory. A **self-inventory** is a list of subjects that you know about and find interesting. The list might include books and newspaper articles you've read; television shows you watch; hobbies you enjoy; sports you participate in; and community, state, regional, national, or international issues that concern you. Here are some sources of topics that might spark your interest:

Books and Articles

Boundaries

Mein Kampf

Swim with the Sharks

Into Thin Air

The Dark Side of Camelot

Midnight in the Garden of Good and Evil

"Sleepless in America"

"Do Pets Feel?"

"Lost Cities"

Television

Poverty in America

Money in America

The twenty-first century

Community Issues

Wal Mart and small-town business

Computerized traffic lights

Homelessness

School violence

State Issues

Improving education

Expanding state prisons

Water supplies

Regional Issues

Population density

Air pollution

Wind erosion

Targeting drunk drivers

Hobbies

Beekeeping

Astrology

Taxidermy

Sports

The college football ranking system

Steroid use by athletes

Stress

The Heisman and other football awards

National Issues

Gun control

Home schooling

Hate speech

The electoral college

International Issues

Terrorism

Protecting the ozone layer

Human rights

Thin is in, everywhere

Ethnic cleansing

Another self-inventory technique involves listing things and ideas as broad categories and then narrowing them down to specific areas. For example

Athletics

Drug use by athletes

Use of steroids by athletes

Effects of steroids on athletes

Effects of steroids on college athletes

The category athletics was narrowed to a specific area, effects of steroids on college athletes, which is specific enough to be a possible speech topic. We discuss narrowing the topic later in the chapter. Anything or any idea can stimulate an appropriate topic for a speech.

Brainstorming.   Another topic selection technique that you might find useful is brainstorming. Brainstorming is a technique used to generate as many ideas as possible within a limited amount of time. Set aside a short period of time (four to six minutes) for intensive concentration, and write down all the ideas that come to mind as topics. To keep things simple, write key words or phrases only. Don't stop to think about whether the ideas are good or bad. The goal of brainstorming is to generate a lot of ideas, so every word or phrase is appropriate.

After listing as many thoughts as you can, select those that appeal to you. Then have a brainstorming session to list more ideas related to them. For example, the term *technology* could serve as the springboard for an entirely new list:

Intranets	Distance education	Robotics
Satellite dishes	Genetic engineering	Lasers
Organ transplant	Microchips	Medical research
Magnetic resonance imaging	X-rays	Superconductors
The Internet	Surfing the Web	Online courses
Genetically altered agricultural products		

With a little effort, brainstorming will help you generate a number of potential topics in a short time. And the process can be repeated over and over until a suitable topic is found.

Reviewing the Current Media.   A third way to generate topic ideas involves the popular media. The media are channels or means of communicating messages to the public, such as through newspapers, books, magazines, television, and movies. **Reviewing the current media** is an excellent way of developing a list of potential topics. Card catalogs and standard reference works summarize the print media. *The Readers' Guide to Periodical Literature* is a source of hundreds of up-to-date topics. For example, you will find listings of articles on beekeeping, athletics, education, government, finance, marketing, terrorism, crime, air safety, health, television violence, entertainment, and so on. Specialized indexes, such as those in the fields of agriculture and natural resources, business, economics and statistics, biology and life sciences, computers, education, and history, can provide thousands of suggestions. You can scan the headlines, the articles, and even the advertisements in any magazine or newspaper—*Time*,

Making Connections

A Self-Inventory

We suggested that a self-inventory is one of four useful tools for choosing an appropriate topic for a presentation. Complete the following self-inventory by supplying as many items as you can for each category. Then examine each item to determine whether it could be an appropriate topic for a speech.

Books and Newspapers

_____

_____

Television

_____

_____

Hobbies

_____

_____

State Issues

_____

_____

International Issues

_____

_____

People

_____

_____

Problems

_____

_____

Sports

_____

_____

Regional Issues

_____

_____

Community Issues

_____

_____

National Issues

_____

_____

Places

_____

_____

Values

_____

_____

Activities

_____

_____

1. Are there any patterns in the kinds of topics you chose?
2. What specific characteristics made you discard certain topics?
3. What specific characteristics made you decide to keep certain topics?

In conclusion discuss in class what you learned from this inventory exercise about selecting topics.

Making Connections

Brainstorming

Brainstorming involves simply sitting down and thinking about topics. It is an effective tool to help you find an appropriate topic for your speeches.

Use brainstorming to generate several topics you might use for your next informative speech. Take five minutes, and write down whatever ideas come to mind, without stopping to evaluate them. At the end of five minutes, look over your list and select those terms that appeal to you. Then brainstorm for another five minutes, listing topics related to them. Now look at your list and answer the following questions:

1. What criteria would you use to determine the *best* topic for your presentation?
2. Apply those criteria to the topics you've generated.
3. Using the criteria you have established, determine which topic you will use.

As you read on, compare and contrast the criteria you listed for selecting the best topic to the criteria provided in the chapter.

Newsweek, Sports Illustrated, Consumer Reports, Money, Business Week, Wall Street Journal, USA Today, or your local newspaper. A wealth of current topics are presented in television documentaries, news specials, and regular programs.

One caution should be noted about using the current media to generate speech topics. Some beginning speakers have a tendency to rely on one media source for the entire speech. A summary of an interesting article or movie is not acceptable for most classroom speaking assignments. The media are an excellent source for potential topics, but they are only a starting point from which to build. The content must be adapted to suit you and your specific audience, and most classroom assignments require a variety of sources. You should always bring something new to your topic, for example, a fresh insight or an application that is suitable to the speaking situation.

Surfing the Web. The rapid development of technology, the ever-increasing number of websites, and the amount of new information on the Web provide unique opportunities for all of us, but especially for students in a speech communication class. Using one or more of the many search engines available can provide unique topics and sources of information on the topic for the careful student. But because information is not reviewed and accepted by experts or authorities on the subject before it is placed on a web page, and because anyone who knows how to put a web page together can put it online, students need to carefully evaluate both the information presented and its source. How do you evaluate a web source? Use the same process you use when evaluating other sources and information, asking questions like these:

1. Who is the author or producer? What are the credentials of the author?
2. How reliable is the source? What is the authority or expertise of the individual or group that created this site?
3. Is the writer or producer biased? (For example, if you find information that cites a study conducted to determine whether a specific product is carcinogenic and learn that the company that commissioned the study is the top producer and marketer of that product and the study results indicate a safe product, think twice before accepting its report as a "scientific study.")
4. How complete and accurate is the information?
5. For whom is the information intended?
6. Is the web item up to date?

7. Does the item follow basic rules of grammar, spelling, and usage? Is the language used appropriately?

8. Is the webmaster identified? Or, is contact information for the author or producer provided so that you can seek additional information?

9. Check these websites for more information: "Evaluating Information on the Internet," http://milton.mse.jhu.edu:8001/research/education/net.html, and http://www.library.ucla.edu/libraries/college/instruct/web/critical.htm.

We discuss Internet research further in Chapter 8.

How you find your topic is not the critical issue, but it is important that you begin looking as soon as possible. Over the years of talking with students who have succeeded in selecting appropriate topics, one common factor emerges: They start looking for a topic immediately on receiving the assignment. Students who delay almost

Making Connections

Research on the Web

Surfing the Web to find all kinds of information has become a habit for many of us. When we are planning trips, we can access Travelocity.com or individual airlines to find the least expensive fares. Or, if travel times and dates are flexible and you are willing to wait, you may be able to find some really good airfares, car rentals, and hotels on Priceline.com. If you're driving to some new place, you can get door-to-door directions from sites such as Mapquest. If you're interested in genealogy, there are numerous sites to help you locate your ancestors, determine exactly when they entered the United States, and even on what specific ship.

"Okay," you say, "so what's your point?" We can use the Web not only to find information but also to help us choose topics for our presentations. Try the following exercise.

1. Take about two minutes to brainstorm a list of five to ten topics in which you have some interest, already know something about, want to learn something more about, or are curious about.

2. Choose four or five items that seem most interesting to you.

3. Access a search engine you have not used before or one with which you are relatively unfamiliar.

4. Click on the help area, the options area, or the icon that will help you understand how to do the most effective search.

5. Key in the words of your first topic.

6. How many hits did you get? What does this number tell you?

7. Check the first ten hits by scrolling through the list and reading the responses.

8. Pick the one that seems most interesting to you. Carefully read and evaluate that site.

9. Does this topic seem like a good one for you? If so, pursue it further. If not, go back to your list and choose the next most interesting topic and repeat the process.

This combination of personal brainstorming and web surfing can help you find topics for which there is adequate information. This process uses the Web to help you choose a topic that your web research reveals has information that you can appreciate. The Web can be a powerful tool in helping us find necessary information for the many needs we have.

always have more difficulty finding an appropriate topic. So begin your search as soon as you receive your assignment. Whenever you come across something that you think might be a good idea, write it down. The more ideas you can accumulate, the easier your job of selecting a good topic will be. Also, the earlier you choose your topic, the more time you will have to research, prepare, and practice your speech.

Assessing the Appropriateness of a Topic

Once you have identified a possible topic, the next step is to determine whether it is appropriate for you, your assignment, and your audience. Ask yourself these questions:

1. Does the topic merit the audience's attention?
2. Will the audience see a relationship between you and the topic and between the topic and themselves?
3. Will the topic meet the objectives of the assignment?
4. Does the audience have sufficient knowledge and background to understand the topic?
5. Can you make the topic understandable to everyone in the audience?
6. Is the topic of sufficient interest to you that you will be motivated to present it effectively?
7. Do you have adequate knowledge of the topic?
8. If you are not already familiar with the topic, will you be able to learn enough about it to give an informed speech?
9. Is the topic appropriate for the situation in which you will present it?

Narrowing the Topic

Once you have determined that your topic is appropriate to your audience and yourself, the next step is to decide whether it is narrow enough to fit the time limit and accomplish the goal of the assignment. This step can save you much time and trouble in the long run because a topic that is well focused is much easier to research than one that is too general. For example, you could work for years on a speech called "The Problems with American Education" and still not cover all the information exhaustively. If you restrict the scope to problems with education in the United States during the past five years, you begin to focus your search for information. You could narrow the topic even further by choosing a single problem with U.S. education during the past five years and so on. Each time you narrow your topic, you increase its potential depth.

The more abstract a topic, the more important it is to narrow it to meet the constraints of a speech situation. For example, a member of a university's speech and debate team started the process of selecting a topic for her ten-minute informative speech by expressing an interest in pop culture. To narrow the topic, she decided to examine only pop culture fads. As soon as she recognized the abundance of such fads, she began to focus on videogames. While thinking about videogames as a fad and as an element of pop culture, she decided to be even more specific and limited her attention to the effects of videogames on children. This continual narrowing of the topic enabled the student to focus her research and content development on a single, well-defined area of interest, which became more meaningful to the speaker and audience, because it contained more substance. Speakers can narrow the scope of a subject according to time limits, function, goals, location, and the requirements of a specific topic. Narrowing the topic is a skill critical to your success as a communicator not only in the classroom but also in the workplace and in the organizations of which you are a member and for which you may be called on to make a presentation.

Determining the General Purpose, Specific Purpose, and Thesis of a Speech

Once you have chosen and narrowed your topic, you need to begin thinking about how the final presentation will be structured. Speakers should begin their preparation with a clear idea of the general purpose, the specific purpose, and a specific thesis statement. In this section we briefly discuss each of these concepts. Chapter 11 provides in-depth coverage of informative speaking, and Chapter 12 is devoted to persuasive speaking.

The General Purpose

The **general purpose,** or overall goal, of a speech is usually to perform one of three overlapping functions—to inform, to persuade, or to entertain. Rarely does a speech serve only one function. Even though most classroom speech assignments are intended to emphasize a single function, the speeches themselves may contain aspects of all three functions. For example, the speech about the effects of videogames on children is meant to inform, but this does not mean that the speech cannot contain some persuasive and entertaining elements as well. If you are assigned an informative speech, however, you need to think carefully about how to organize your ideas and how to present those ideas to your listeners. If the general purpose is to inform your audience, your emphasis should be on presenting information about a new, interesting, and potentially useful and relevant topic.

For classroom speaking assignments, your general purpose is usually specified by the instructor, but for speeches outside the classroom, the occasion, what the audience knows or doesn't know about your topic, and how you want the audience to respond will determine whether you speak primarily to inform, to persuade, or to entertain.

The speaking goal is usually designed to affect the listeners in some purposeful way. The reaction of the listeners determines whether your speech has accomplished its purpose successfully.

This speaker on drug and alcohol abuse has a specific purpose in his talk to high school students in upper New York state. He uses his ambulatory mike to make his points, to demonstrate face to face his concern and his message. The audience's reaction suggest he is being successful.

Speeches That Inform. When the general purpose of your speech is to inform, you are expected to convey your knowledge of a particular subject. An **informative speech** enhances an audience's knowledge and understanding by explaining what something means, how something works, or how something

Making Connections

Informative Speaking

The speech to inform is meant to provide new ideas or perspectives on topics. People often give informative speeches in a variety of settings. Reflect about times in the past year when you have heard someone give a speech or presentation in which the speaker's purpose was to provide information that would be "potentially useful" to you, either now or at some future time.

Discuss in class the following either in groups with four or five students or with the class as a whole:

1. Identify the situation—organization, school, meeting, guest speaker in class, and so on—when you heard informative speeches.
2. Identify the topics of the messages.
3. Explain how you knew the messages were informative.
4. What did speakers do to keep listeners interested?

In concluding your discussion with your classmates, determine what makes an informative topic interesting to listeners.

is done. David Zarefsky, communication scholar, suggests that informative speeches do not specifically ask listeners to believe or do any particular thing.[3] The goal is to share information clearly and accurately while making the learning experience as enjoyable as possible for the audience. If you are assigned an informative speech, you need to think carefully about how to organize your ideas and how to present those ideas to your listeners. If the general purpose is to inform your audience, your emphasis should be on presenting information about a new, interesting, and potentially useful and relevant topic.

Whether you describe how to protect yourself during an assault, discuss a proposed apartment complex development in a rundown neighborhood, explain the important uses of an electromagnetic field, report how the university uses its parking fees, or explain how the electoral college works, you should assume that most of your audience does not already know all the information you are planning to present. The content of the speech depends heavily on what you think the audience knows and on how much you know or are able to learn about the topic. Your task as a speaker is to provide more information than the audience would normally get from reading a short article or listening to the news.

When a topic is controversial, for example, "The Death Penalty as Punishment for Heinous Crimes," speakers whose general purpose is to inform should not take sides; instead, they might provide a background on the death penalty and statistics or facts about which states use the death penalty and which forms of it: electrocution, hanging, lethal injection, and so on. The speaker presents the information and allows audience members to draw their own conclusions.

Speeches That Persuade. A **persuasive speech** attempts to change listeners' beliefs, attitudes, or behaviors by advocating or trying to gain acceptance of an idea or point of view. When speakers try to convince audience members to eat less sugar, to endorse the building of a new athletic complex, to change the way we elect U.S. presidents, to become a Big Brother or Big Sister, to ensure a safe campus or a safe neighborhood by joining a volunteer patrol group, to convince audience members that a tax increase or decrease would benefit the state, to accept as fact that UFOs actually exist, to believe that ethical behavior in the United States is on the decline, to push for or against an English-language-only bill, or to support the American Red Cross by donating blood, they are attempting to persuade. Such speakers must present evidence and arguments to justify their positions in order to win their audience over to their point of view.

The difference between information and persuasion is not always clear-cut. Convincing your parents to give or loan you money to buy a car is a persuasive goal. There are, however, differences among the following: informing them of the circumstances in which you need and would use a car, convincing them that you need the car and the money to buy it, and actually getting the money from your parents so you can buy the car. They may accept the reasons you present for needing the car and they may even agree that you need the money, but they still may not give you the money. In this example, the persuasive purpose is not only to inform and convince your parents that you need a car and the money to buy it but also for them to take action—to actually give you the money you need. Providing information is a necessary part of a persuasive speech, but its ultimate goal is action. Once your parents give you the money, you have achieved your purpose.

Whereas the focus of an informative speech is to convey information and understanding by explaining, reporting, or demonstrating your point of view, the purpose of a persuasive speech is to change beliefs or attitudes or motivate listeners to act in a specific manner. That action may be to think, to respond, or to behave in a certain way. The purpose (direction or course of action) may be to change diet, to vote, to believe that UFOs exist, to place a greater personal and societal emphasis on ethics, to approve a proposal, or to join a group.

The important and necessary ingredient that makes persuasion different from information is the action (to think, to respond, to behave) taken by the listener as a result of the message presented. The informative speech provides more knowledge about a topic, whereas the persuasive speech provides not only more information but also a direction or course of action the listener is to take.

Speeches That Entertain.   An **entertainment speech** provides enjoyment and amusement. Speeches that entertain may be dramatic or humorous in nature and often occur on special occasions, such as after a dinner or a "roast." A speech to entertain generally has three key qualities: it is light, original, and appropriate to the situation. An appropriate speech does not offend the sensibilities of the audience. The speaker may use humor but not at the expense of the audience's sense of values or ethics. Effective speakers do not use offensive language or potentially offensive jokes or situations. Audience members, unlike television viewers, are a captive audience and cannot click the remote to switch off offensive words or ideas. The speaker must use tasteful examples and stories that will not hurt anyone's feelings or violate their ethical principles.

In using humor, the speaker may create imaginative illustrations and figures of speech, twist meanings, tell amusing stories, create amusing character sketches, or tell jokes—all with the willing participation of the audience and in the spirit of the occasion. This does not mean, however, that an entertaining speech cannot be both informative and persuasive or that informative and persuasive speeches cannot be entertaining. What distinguishes these three kinds of speeches is the function (informing, persuading, or entertaining) on which the speaker places the most emphasis. The entertaining speech should, therefore, leave the audience members feeling they were entertained or amused as the primary function of the speech.

The Specific Purpose

The general purpose of a speech provides direction for its content. In the classroom, a speech's general purpose is usually specified in the assignment. Outside the classroom, it may or may not be specified. When the general purpose is not identified, you must determine it for yourself. To be a successful speaker, you must know exactly what you plan to accomplish by speaking.

Once you have determined your general purpose (to inform, to persuade, or to entertain), you are ready to determine your specific purpose. A **specific purpose** is a single phrase that defines precisely what you intend to accomplish in your speech. Recall the student who chose videogames as her topic. Her specific purpose was "to inform my listeners about the three major effects of videogames on children." The clear and concise statement tells exactly what the speaker intends to do and what she wants her audience to know.

An effective specific purpose identifies (1) the general purpose of the speech, (2) the audience, and (3) the exact topic to be covered. These three pieces of information significantly help the speaker develop and deliver the speech. Note that in the videogames example, the speaker's specific purpose cites the general purpose of the speech, which is to inform. The specific purpose also identifies the audience, which is important, because different audiences may require different information. For example, if a speech is to be presented to children only, to adults only, or to both children and adults, the content will have to be adjusted to fit the group. Thus, even though the general and specific purposes are the same, the content of the speech will vary depending on the listeners' backgrounds, knowledge, and attitudes toward the topic.

The careful writing of a specific purpose is important to all aspects of planning and developing a successful speech. The following guidelines should help you write an effective specific purpose.

Specific Purpose

1. The specific purpose should include a verb form that describes the general purpose of the speech. The inclusion of the verb form clarifies the action the speaker hopes to accomplish.

   Ineffective   Videogames and children
   Effective   To inform the audience of three effects of videogames on children

2. The specific purpose should be limited to one distinct thought or idea. The ineffective statement given here is too long and contains more than one subject. In fact, an entire speech could be developed around either area. It is best to select only one idea and refine it as the purpose for the speech.

   Ineffective   To inform the audience of the three effects of drugs and the four best ways to prevent alcohol abuse by teenagers
   Effective   To inform the audience about the three most dangerous effects of drugs on teenagers

   or

   To inform the audience about the four best ways to prevent alcohol abuse by teenagers

3. The specific purpose should not be a question. Although a question may indicate the topic, it fails to specify the general purpose of the speech.

   Ineffective   How does capital punishment affect crime rates?
   Effective   To persuade the audience that capital punishment does not deter crime

4. The specific purpose should be concise and carefully worded. The ineffective statement given here tries to cover too much material, is too general, and does not state clearly what is to be achieved by the speech.

Ineffective   The effects of a permissive society can be extremely harmful to children and can also create a society that eventually becomes de-sensitized to reality.

Effective   To persuade the audience that a permissive society limits children's views of reality

---

Formulating your general and specific purposes makes it easier to develop your speech. They will guide your thinking and planning. You should be ready to reconsider your specific purpose, however, throughout the development stages of the speech. As you research a topic, you may find information that leads you to revise your thinking. Or you may learn something about your audience members that will make you want to adjust your specific purpose to their needs.

The Thesis

The specific purpose of your speech states what you wish to accomplish or what effect you wish to have on your audience. It also serves as the foundation for the thesis of the speech. The **thesis** is a sentence that states specifically what is going to be discussed in a speech. For example, the specific purpose "to explain to my audience the four advantages of using computer-aided instruction" tells what the speaker wants to do but does not describe the content of the speech. A thesis concisely states the content: "Computer-aided instruction saves time, allows for self-pacing, provides practice, and is enjoyable." This clearly worded statement tells exactly what the four advantages of computer-aided instruction are.

Making Connections

Identifying Specific Speech Purposes

Let's practice creating specific speech purposes. The following sentences do not meet the criteria for expressing the specific purpose of a speech.

What is wrong with each of them? Improve each one, further narrowing the topics as necessary.

1. What is euthanasia?
2. To inform the audience about sailing
3. To persuade the audience that a need exists for quality education in our society
4. Skydiving can be fun.

What did you learn from this exercise about writing specific purpose statements?

If a speech's specific purpose is "to persuade the audience to contribute to the new football stadium fund," its thesis might be "The new football stadium will help the university attract better players, will generate more money through ticket sales, and will bring a renewed sense of pride to our university." The thesis gives the three main ideas that the speaker will discuss: (1) why a new stadium will attract better players, (2) why it will generate more money through ticket sales, and (3) why it will renew a sense of pride in the university. The thesis should be expressed as a full sentence, should not be in the form of a question, and should be clearly and concisely worded.

Here are two examples to show the relationship of the topic to the general purpose, specific purpose, and thesis:

Topic: Energy of the future

General purpose: To inform

Specific purpose: To inform my audience about four of the forms of energy to be used in the future

Thesis: Four of the forms of energy in our future are solar power, wind, ethanol, and nuclear power.

Topic: Maps

General purpose: To inform

Specific purpose: To inform my audience about the development and implications of maps

Thesis: I will examine maps by looking at the history of mapmaking, the uses of maps today, and the advancements influencing future maps.

You can see how the broad topic area is narrowed as the speaker moves from the specific purpose to the thesis. This narrowing procedure is a crucial step in preparing a speech.

Relating to the Audience

Selecting a topic; narrowing it; and wording its general purpose, specific purpose, and thesis require some understanding and knowledge of the target audience. Developing the content of the speech requires the same understanding and knowledge. Recall from the chapter opening scenario that the speaker asked the caller several questions about the audience. Specifically, the speaker asked about the number of people in the audience and their particular backgrounds and interests. The speaker needs such information in order to relate the topic to the audience. Because relating to the audience is so important to a speaker's success, the remainder of the chapter examines the audience's point of view, kinds of audience members, key information to learn about an audience, methods for researching audiences, and adapting a speech to an audience.

Audience analysis is the collection and interpretation of data about characteristics, attitudes, values, and beliefs of an audience. Analyzing the audience is an essential step in developing and delivering a speech. An audience becomes actively involved in a speech and reacts to the speaker, to the subject, to what is said, to how it is said, to other audience members, and to the situation. The more speakers know about the audience, the better they can adapt their speeches to them.

Understanding the Audience's Point of View

For our purposes, the **audience** refers to the collection of individuals who have come together to watch or listen to a speech. The individuals may become part of the audience for many different reasons. Each individual may have several reasons for being present, and they may come from many different backgrounds. Students, for example, come to class to listen to lectures because attendance is required to obtain a passing grade.

The reason individuals come together to form an audience is an important point that every speaker should consider when planning a speech. If people join an audience because they wish to listen to a speech, it is reasonable to assume that they also want to hear something that is meaningful to them. Most individuals ask the same basic questions about their involvement in an audience. What is in this for me? Why is this important to me? How will this affect me?

These questions suggest that your audience will judge what they hear on the basis of their past experiences and the relevance of the information presented. The more you know about your audience's past experiences, knowledge of the subject, relation to the subject, and reason for being there, the easier it will be for you to develop a speech that is meaningful to them. For example, imagine that you are an expert on reading and have been asked to give a speech entitled "How to Teach Children to Be More Effective Readers." You have spent many hours getting ready for the speech and are now prepared to present it. But are you really prepared? Have you thought about the members of your audience? Who are they? What do they know about reading? What is their attitude toward reading? Would you present the same information to professionals who teach reading, to parents who want their children to become better readers, to children who are indifferent about reading, or to a combination of all three groups? What results would you expect if you used the same approach for all three audiences? What results would you expect if you varied your approaches? Asking these questions and finding answers to them are essential preparation for an effective and successful presentation.

Captive Versus Voluntary Participants

Many kinds of people attend speeches for many reasons, but all are either captive or voluntary participants. Audience members required to listen to a particular speech are called **captive participants.** They may happen to want to hear the speech, but they have no choice but to attend. Some people may resist participation more than others.

Even though few circumstances (at least in the United States) force a person to be part of an audience, some situations demand attendance to avoid a penalty. For example, a teacher requires attendance during speech presentations, an employer requires employees to attend new product demonstrations, or a military leader orders troops to attend lectures on military maneuvers. In such situations, audience members cannot be absent and cannot leave without being noticed or penalized for doing so. To be effective, a speaker must recognize when he or she is dealing with captive participants.

In contrast to captive participants, **voluntary participants** choose to hear a particular speech because of interest or need. True volunteers attend only because of what they expect to hear. There is no other motivation or force behind their presence.

Key Audience Information

You should gather two kinds of information about your prospective audience—demographic and psychological. The more you know about your audience members, the better able you will be to adjust to them and relate your topic to them.

Demographic Analysis.   **Demographic analysis** is the collection and interpretation of basic information such as age, gender, cultural or ethnic background, education, occupation, religion, socioeconomic status, geographic location, political affiliation, voting habits, family relationships, marital and parental status, and group memberships. The more similar the demographic characteristics of members of an audience, the easier it is for a speaker to adapt to their needs and interests.

Age.   Knowing that members of the audience differ in age can help the speaker select a range of appropriate examples and evidence. An age difference between the speaker and the audience can also alter what and how messages are expressed. For example, if an audience consists of only eighteen and nineteen year olds, the speaker has only one age group with which to deal. If audience members range from fifteen to sixty-five years of age, the speaker will have to take into account several age groups and make language and content choices based on that wide range of listener ages.

Gender.   Gender is an important demographic characteristic that can present challenges. The speaker should consider the attitudes of each sex toward the other as well as the attitudes of each sex toward itself. As we indicated in several places in this text, gender-based biases should be avoided. Speakers should be sensitive to potential gender-based biases, for example, referring to women as "passive" or providing examples of women only in certain careers, such as nursing or teaching. Although some topics may still be more appropriate for one sex than the other, clear-cut distinctions are becoming increasingly rare.

Cultural or Ethnic Background.   Cultural or ethnic background is often not considered as thoroughly as it should be, even though a tremendous diversity of backgrounds exists in our society. Speakers should be sensitive to the different groups that may be present. The following communication variables are culturally determined and influence interactions between and among members of different ethnic and racial backgrounds.

Attitudes	Use of spatial relationships
Social status within the group	Meanings of words
Thought patterns	Time
Expected behaviors	Nonverbal expressions
Use of language	Beliefs
Values	Cooperation versus competition
Respect for age	Collectivism versus individualism

Each of these variables determines and regulates how an individual creates and interprets messages. Although the list is not exhaustive, it points out some of the important cultural and ethnic factors to consider as you plan a speech. Culture is dynamic and extremely important; culture helps define who individuals are in relationship to the world around them. Speakers who do not take culture into account

Making Connections

Culture and the Public Speaker

Pajaree and Dawn are discussing their upcoming assignment: a five-minute informative speech on a topic demonstrating ethical principles. Pajaree says she wants to talk about the concept of "saving face," but Dawn does not understand what this expression means and how it is appropriate for the assignment. Pajaree explains that saving face is a concept in her native culture that means a person does not purposely do anything to make another lose credibility or status. Pajaree says that she often does not ask the other students questions, because she is aware that the questions could cause people to lose face in their own minds or in the minds of others. According to Thai beliefs, ethical speakers and ethical listeners will not willingly cause another to lose face nor will they willingly lose face by making a mistake. Dawn is fascinated and asks more questions to learn about Pajaree's culture.

Each of us should be aware of cultural perspectives and how they may affect speakers and listeners in a speaking situation. Think about the cultures (or co-cultures) represented in your communication class, and then answer these questions:

1. What values do these other cultures promote?
2. How do the cultural values affect the way a person might respond to certain topics? Give some examples.
3. How can you increase your sensitivity and awareness of cultural perspectives?
4. What can you, as a speaker, do to adjust to different cultural values in your communication class?

may embarrass and insult an audience, and ultimately, themselves. Speech content should not offend values, customs, or beliefs held by members of the audience.

Education.   Although it may be impossible to find out exactly what an audience knows and understands about a specific topic, it is often possible to ascertain their general education level. Knowing whether most listeners have completed high school, college, or graduate school can help you to gauge their intellectual level and experience and to adapt your speech accordingly.

Occupation.   Knowledge about audience members' occupations can also tell you something about possible interest in and familiarity with some subjects. For example, lawyers might be interested in topics related to the law or in legal aspects of some topics.

Religion.   Speakers must be as sensitive to religion as they are to ethnicity. That is, they must recognize issues that touch on religious beliefs and treat them carefully. If you plan to speak on an issue that may have religious ramifications, you should evaluate how your message will affect audience members. Otherwise, you run a risk of offending or losing the attention of some or all of your audience. For example, choosing a quotation to support your viewpoint might be more appropriately taken from the Koran than from the King James Version of the Bible if your audience is of the Islamic faith.

Geographic Origins.   Knowing the geographic origins of your audience can help you to adapt your speech to them. For example, people from rural communities are more likely to know and care more about agricultural topics than people from large urban areas. People from the South may not be interested in problems related to heating their homes in winter, but if they live in an oil-producing state, they may be interested in the price of a barrel of oil.

Group Membership.   A group is a collection of individuals who have joined together for some common cause or purpose that may be social, professional, recreational, or charitable. Recognizing that individuals in your audience come from groups with special interests can help you relate your speech directly to their needs and concerns. Of course, it isn't always possible to reach every group in your audience, but by appealing to the largest group, you can create strong attention and interest. For example, a student who belonged to a sorority decided to inform her audience about sorority and fraternity functions other than social activities. Three-quarters of her student audience was not affiliated with a Greek group. Knowing this, she began her speech by talking about her thoughts on Greek organizations before she became a member. By first pointing out her reservations about such groups, she created a common understanding between herself and her listeners. Had her audience been three-quarters sorority and fraternity members, that kind of introduction would have been unnecessary.

Other Demographic Factors.   We earlier identified marital status, family makeup, and socioeconomic status as other possible elements of demographic analysis. Knowledge of the listeners' marriage and family status provides information about their priorities and interests. An awareness of socioeconomic status will also provide information about the interests and abilities of audience members to grasp the ideas to be presented. All in all, the more information we have about who the listeners are and what characteristics they share with us and with others will promote a better understanding of how to prepare the speech for the specific audience.

Psychological Analysis.   **Psychological analysis** is the collection of data on audience members' values, attitudes, and beliefs. A psychological analysis seeks to determine how the audience will react to the speaker, the speaker's topic, and the surroundings in which the speech is presented. In addition to the items related to demographic analysis, a psychological analysis helps the speaker become aware of what motivates listeners to attend to the message of a particular speech. The size of the audience; the physical setting for the presentation; the knowledge level of the audience; and the attitude of the audience toward the speaker, the topic, and the situation all play vital roles in the planning, development, and delivery of a speech.

Size of Audience.   The number of audience members has a considerable psychological effect on a speaking situation and strongly influences how a speech should be delivered. The larger the audience, the more difficult it is to use an informal, conversational speaking style. Size also affects the speaker's use of language, gestures, and visual aids. There is a difference between speaking to ten or thirty people, as in a typical classroom speech assignment, and speaking to several hundred people in an auditorium.

There is much to consider when speaking to small or large audiences. Audience size impacts the use of language, gestures, and visual aids. Effective speakers take audience size into account in their speech development and preparation.

The size of an audience can also affect the psychological disposition of the audience members and their relationship to each other and the speaker. For example, each member of a small audience is aware of himself or herself as a unique member of the audience, and each feels a close, intimate relationship to the speaker. As the size of the audience increases, members lose their sense of identity as unique individuals and feel more distanced from the speaker. Effective speakers know this and plan their presentations to meet the requirements of each situation.

Physical Setting. In evaluating the physical setting, consider factors such as room size, ventilation, seating arrangement, lighting, speaker's platform, and potential for using visual aids. Some professional speakers require specific settings and will refuse to give their presentations if their conditions can't be met. Unfortunately, you do not have that choice in a classroom assignment. You can, however, assess the physical setting and take full advantage of what is available to you.

The seating arrangement of your audience is often predetermined, as it is in classroom settings, but sometimes a slight modification may make your presentation more effective. For example, a speech professor was asked to address a group of thirty police officers. He purposely arrived early so he could see the room and assess the speaking conditions. The seats were arranged classroom-style: The chairs were placed in uniform rows directly in front of a raised speaker's podium, on which stood a large wooden lectern with a microphone. The professor believed that the setting was too formal and would inhibit his presentation, so he quickly rearranged the room by placing the chairs in a semicircle and moving the speaker's podium off to one side. These simple changes gave his presentation a more casual feeling and encouraged audience involvement.

The physical setting can also affect audience members' psychological disposition toward one another as well as toward the speaker. The more relaxed the physical setting, for example, the more open and comfortable audience members will feel in relation to one another and to the speaker. The proximity of audience members to one another may also have an effect. If, for example, the audience members are scattered throughout a large meeting room, they will not have the sense of inclusion that occurs in a physical setting in which the members are densely packed together. Close proximity of other people may create a feeling of belonging to the group and help the speaker reach the audience.

Knowledge Level. The extent of an audience's knowledge about a topic has a tremendous effect on the outcome of a speech. If an audience has little or no background on a topic and the speaker does not realize this, both the audience and the speaker may become frustrated. When an audience isn't ready to receive information or when the information is too technical for them to understand, the speaker must present the material in terms everyone can understand.

A speaker must also adjust a presentation to reach a knowledgeable audience. A physician addressing a medical conference would not waste time and bore the audience by explaining familiar medical terms. Even though people are apt to be more interested in subjects they know something about, an audience does not want a rehash of familiar information; they want to hear a new twist and to add to their existing knowledge. For example, a student decided to present a four- to six-minute informative speech about the lead pencil. After interviewing his classmates, the speaker noted that they all had a similar response: "What can you say about a lead pencil other than that it is made of lead and wood and is used for writing?" Based on his analysis, the student developed a creative, fascinating speech. Using a casual and entertaining style, he provided detailed information about the history of the lead pencil and its affect on society. The speech was a great success.

Relationship to the Speaker. The audience's knowledge of the speaker strongly influences how a speech should be developed and delivered. Two speech professors arrived late to a workshop they were offering on effective communication. Anxious to start, the professors said little about themselves and quickly launched into their main topic. Fifteen minutes into the presentation, they noticed that most of the participants were not paying attention and appeared confused. Finally, an audience member asked, "Who are you?" When the speakers replied that they were speech communication professors and listed their credentials and qualifications, the audience settled down and became attentive. As this example illustrates, an audience's attitude toward a speaker can make the difference between success and failure. Audience members always formulate some attitude toward a speaker.

This example also demonstrates how character (*ethos,* or ethical traits, discussed as an aspect of credibility more fully in Chapter 12) is derived from what the audience members know and believe about the speaker as well as their perceived view of the speaker's use of reasoning. Because effective speakers recognize that character, logic, and emotional appeals can affect the listeners' views of the speaker and the speech, they can adjust their presentations accordingly.

Attitudes and Values Related to the Topic. The audience's attitude and values as they relate to the topic are as significant as their knowledge of the speaker. If audience members do not relate to a topic, the speaker will have a difficult time getting them to listen. For instance, a student chose to speak on individual retirement accounts for his persuasive speech. He researched the subject thoroughly, practiced his delivery, and presented the speech in an enthusiastic manner. But his audience remained cool and uninvolved. The speaker had failed to consider the value the audience placed on the topic; the age of its members should have tipped off the speaker. Saving for retirement is not a high priority for most college students. The speaker could have made the speech more relevant by discussing young people's indifference to retirement saving and convincing them that they should become concerned now.

Attitudes Related to the Situation.   The speaker must also examine the audience's relationship to the overall situation in which the speech is presented. Why has the audience gathered? Audience members' expectations influence their attitude toward the situation, which in turn reflects on the speaker and the topic. A speaker who talks about the need to further fund social security to a group of seventeen to twenty-four year olds has chosen the wrong topic for an audience who cares little about retirement and social security, which is decades away for them. Listeners who believe a topic is not relevant to their own situations are less likely to listen to the speaker.

Ways to Learn About the Audience

The three most common ways of gathering information about an audience are observation, survey interviews, and questionnaires.

Observation.   Probably the easiest method of audience analysis is through observation. The speaker draws on accumulated experience with a particular audience and with similar groups. Through **observation,** the speaker watches audience members and notes their behaviors and characteristics. Although this approach relies strictly on the speaker's subjective impression, it can be useful.

No doubt you have already learned a great deal about your audience from classroom assignments. You already know the number of students, the number of males and females, and their approximate ages. Through introductions, general conversations, and other interactions, you have learned about their majors, group memberships, jobs, whether they commute or live on campus, and their interests. You have learned a great deal about your classmates' attitudes, interests, values, and knowledge. You know your instructor's views and expectations for your classroom performance. You also know the size of the classroom, the location of the lectern (if there is one), the seating arrangement, the availability of audiovisual equipment, and other physical features of the environment. You have obtained all of this information by observation.

Survey Interviews.   A **survey interview** is a carefully planned and executed person-to-person, question-and-answer session during which the speaker tries to discover specific information that will help in the preparation of a speech. The interviews can be done in person or over the phone. The purpose of the survey is to establish a solid base of fact from which to draw conclusions, make interpretations, and determine future courses of action. This method of audience research can be highly productive. To be most useful, however, surveys require a great deal of planning and organization, which take time and energy. (Specific interviewing skills are discussed in more detail in the next chapter.)

Questionnaires.   A **questionnaire** is a set of written questions distributed to respondents to gather desired information. The same questioning techniques used in survey interviews are also used in questionnaires. In some cases, questionnaires are more practical and take less time than interviews. They can be administered to relatively large groups of people at the same time. One advantage is that the respondents can re-

FIGURE 7.1

FIGURE 7.1

Sample Questionnaire

Questionnaires contain a set of written questions and are an excellent way of gathering information from large groups of people quickly. If done effectively, they can be practical, take less time than interviews, and provide for the anonymity of the respondent.

Directions: Check the response that indicates how strongly you agree or disagree with each statement. Do not write your name on this questionnaire.

1. Date rape on campus is a serious problem.
   _____ Strongly agree
   _____ Slightly agree
   _____ Undecided
   _____ Slightly disagree
   _____ Strongly disagree

2. Victims of date rape usually are asking for it.
   _____ Strongly agree
   _____ Slightly agree
   _____ Undecided
   _____ Slightly disagree
   _____ Strongly disagree

3. More definition and instruction on what is and what is not date rape is needed.
   _____ Strongly agree
   _____ Slightly agree
   _____ Undecided
   _____ Slightly disagree
   _____ Strongly disagree

4. The students, faculty, and administrators must do more to provide a safe campus environment for all students.
   _____ Strongly agree
   _____ Slightly agree
   _____ Undecided
   _____ Slightly disagree
   _____ Strongly disagree

main anonymous, which often leads to greater honesty and openness in answering questions. Although learning to develop good questionnaires takes much time and practice, here are some simple guidelines to help you get started:

1. Decide exactly what information you want to gather.
2. Decide on the best method for making multiple copies of your questionnaire.
3. Decide when, where, and how to distribute the questionnaire.
4. Plan the introduction to the questionnaire. Will the respondent need specific instructions?
5. Make sure your questions are clear and understandable.
6. Limit the number of possible responses to each question.
7. Keep the questionnaire as brief as possible.

Figure 7.1 shows a typical questionnaire. Note that it provides simple instructions, it is brief, the questions are clear, and the number of possible responses is limited.

Choosing the Best Information-Gathering Technique. The easiest way to find out about your audience is through observation. Your success with this method depends on the amount of experience you have with your audience and your ability to make accurate inferences. In most classroom situations, observation will yield adequate information for planning a speech, but if you seek more specific data, you may want to use a survey. A survey interview takes planning and time and is not very efficient, but it does provide an opportunity to get information in person and to probe for more data when necessary. If you are dealing with a large group of people, you may decide to gather information by using a questionnaire. Although good questionnaires take time to write, they can be administered more quickly than survey interviews and often yield more candid responses, especially to sensitive topics.

Relating and Adapting to the Audience   The goal of observing, survey interviewing, and administering questionnaires is to gather information so that you can relate and adapt your speech to those who make up your audience. Can you discern any patterns in the information you have gathered? What conclusions can you draw? How certain can you be of them? How can you use what you have learned to improve your speech? For example, if you surveyed twenty-five female and twenty-five male students on your campus using the questionnaire in Figure 7.1 and found that 75 percent of the women thought date rape was a serious problem but only 30 percent of the men thought so, how could that information help you prepare a speech to convince your audience that date rape is a serious problem on your campus?

A good questionnaire will be completed by a group of people who represent a sample of the entire population. You also need to make sure you have enough responses to make reliable generalizations about the group you are surveying. If your analysis is thorough and correct, you should have a fairly good picture of your audience—their relevant demographics; interests; knowledge levels; and attitudes toward the topic, the speaker, and the general situation. Although your findings will rarely be uniform, you should be able to reach some general conclusions. For example, you may find that 70 percent of your audience members strongly disagree that capital punishment should be used in U.S. society, 15 percent have no opinion, and 15 percent strongly agree. If your purpose is to persuade them that capital punishment should be used in U.S. society, you will need to adjust your speech to this audience. How will you get those who oppose you to listen to what you have to say? What can you say to draw in those who have no opinion or who already strongly agree with you?

Although it is never easy to win over people who oppose your views, you can try to do so by discussing their views first and then discussing your views. You should also make use of credible, unbiased sources—people are more likely to accept information from them. In addition, you should acknowledge that your listeners' views have as much merit as yours but assert that your views will lead to a better outcome.

If your research indicates that your audience has little or no opinion about the information you are presenting, you need to provoke their interest. Begin by telling why they should listen to what you have to say and by showing how the topic relates to them personally. Focus on helping them recognize the benefits and importance of your topic, and remember that clearly communicating your own enthusiasm can help generate interest.

Finally, when you are dealing with an audience that agrees with you and what you have to say, or knows a lot about your topic, you need to acknowledge what you share with them. For example, if you and your audience agree that a new auditorium should be built, note your shared agreement and then go on to talk about what can be done to get the new facility built. In the process, you might try to strengthen their beliefs about the need for the auditorium.

Making Connections

Planning a Persuasive Speech

Persuasive speeches require the speaker to try to convince listeners to think about something, accept a perspective as valid, or actually do something. In groups of four or five students discuss how a speech with the specific purpose of persuading students that a higher student fee is needed to purchase more computers for student use should be developed. A survey of the student body indicates that 30 percent favor the increase, 50 percent are moderately opposed, 10 percent are strongly opposed, and 10 percent don't care one way or the other. Discuss the following issues:

1. How can you use the survey to help plan the speech?

2. What information contained in the survey, if any, should you give the most consideration?

3. In developing the speech are there certain types of information that you should include to make the speech as persuasive as possible? Provide some examples.

4. How can the survey help you relate your speech to your listeners?

Finally, discuss what you learned from this exercise, and how it should help you in developing other speeches and relate to your specific audience members.

No matter what your audience's position on your topic may be, your research will enable you to identify it in advance. You can use this information to pursue your specific purpose and to adjust your presentation to your audience. Of course, the more information you have, the better equipped you will be to adapt your speech to your audience.

Summary

Public speaking is the presentation of a speech, usually prepared in advance, during which the speaker is the central focus of an audience's attention. The ability to speak in front of others can help advance one's career and help in the development of writing, listening, organizing, researching, and reasoning skills.

When selecting a topic, choose an area that you already know something about and that is of interest to you and your audience. Three methods of finding topics are *self-inventory,* listing your own interests; *brainstorming,* generating as many ideas as possible in a limited amount of time; and *reviewing the current media,* looking at current publications, television, movies, web sources, and so on. Once you have selected a subject, you must assess its appropriateness for you and your audience and narrow it to meet the situational and time requirements.

A speech should serve one of three *general purposes: an informative speech* enhances the audience's knowledge and understanding; a *persuasive speech* advocates or gains acceptance for the speaker's point of view; an *entertainment speech* provides enjoyment and amusement. Rarely does a speech serve a single general purpose exclusively; more often, the three purposes overlap.

Part of the narrowing and focusing of a topic is the formulation of a *specific purpose,* a single phrase that defines precisely what is to be accomplished in a speech. The clearer the specific purpose, the easier it is to plan, research, and develop a successful speech. The *thesis* focuses the topic further by detailing and forecasting exactly what is to be discussed in the speech.

Effective speakers tailor their speeches to their audience. An *audience* is a collection of individuals who have come together to watch or listen to someone or something, such as a speech. The more speakers know about their audience's past experiences, knowledge, attitudes, and reasons for attendance, the easier it is to develop speeches that are meaningful and relevant. An *audience analysis* can provide the kind of basic information a speaker needs to ensure success.

Although audience members vary greatly in personal traits and reasons for attendance, they can be divided into two categories based on the nature of their participation. *Captive participants* are audience members who are required to hear a particular speaker or speech, whereas *voluntary participants* are audience members who choose to hear a particular speaker or speech because of personal interest or need.

To be fully prepared, a speaker needs to gather demographic and psychological information about an audience. *Demographic analysis* is the collection and interpretation of basic information such as age, gender, cultural and ethnic background, education, occupation, religion, geographic location, and group membership. *Psychological analysis* is the collection and interpretation of information about values, knowledge, beliefs, and attitudes toward the speaker, the topic, and the surroundings in which the speech is presented. The size of the audience and the physical setting for the presentation also play roles in the planning, development, and delivery of a speech.

The three most common ways of gathering information about an audience are observation, survey interviews, and questionnaires. *Observation* relies on the speaker's perceptions of the audience's behaviors and characteristics. It is the easiest way to gather information about an audience, but its accuracy relies on the amount of experience a speaker has had with the audience and the speaker's ability to draw reliable conclusions. The *survey interview* is a carefully planned and executed person-to-person, question-and-answer session. A *questionnaire* is a set of written questions. It is an efficient way to obtain information from a large number of people at one time.

No matter what information-gathering technique you use, you must analyze the results to understand the audience and discover patterns that might help in the development of your speech. Once you have completed your analysis, you can use your findings to adapt your speech to suit the characteristics of your audience. As a result, your audience should have little difficulty answering the question "What's in this for me?"

DISCUSSION STARTERS

1. How can becoming an effective public speaker influence your life?
2. Name three speakers whom you find especially effective. What contributes to their effectiveness?
3. Your best friend has been asked to give a speech, but the topic has been left open. What advice would you give your friend about choosing an appropriate topic?
4. Describe the criteria you would use to determine whether a speech topic is appropriate for you and your audience.
5. Why is it necessary to formulate a general purpose and a specific purpose as you develop a speech?

6. In what ways can a demographic analysis of your audience help you in the development and delivery of a speech?

7. Which audience, in your opinion, would be easiest to address: captive participants, voluntary participants, or a mixture of both?

8. How does audience members' self-interest affect their attitudes toward a speech? What can a speaker do to take this into account?

9. What information can a psychological analysis of your audience provide?

10. Why is it important to know your audience's attitudes toward you before you give a speech?

11. You are preparing to speak on the need for stricter laws governing illegal drugs and are uncertain of your audience's views. What should you know about your audience? How would you go about getting the information you need?

12. How can you use technology to help you choose a topic?

NOTES

1. K. K. Edgerton, "Do Real People Give Speeches?" *Central States Speech Journal* 25, no. 3 (fall 1974): 233–35; R. L. Sorenson and J. C. Pearson, "Alumni Perspectives on Speech Communication Training: Implications for Communication Faculty," *Communication Education* 30 (1981): 299–307; V. Di Salvo and J. K. Larsen, "A Contingency Approach to Communication Skill Importance: The Impact of Occupation, Direction, and Position," *Journal of Business Communication* 24 (1987): 3–22; V. Di Salvo and R. Kay, "An Identification of Core Communication Skills Found in Organization-Related Careers" (unpublished paper, 1988).

2. J. D. Trent and W. C. Redding, "A Survey of Communication Opinions of Executives in Large Corporations" (unpublished special report, no. 8, Purdue University, September 1964); J. C. Benett and R. J. Olney, "Executive Priorities for Effective Communication in an Information Age," *Journal of Business Communication* 23 (1986): 13–22; P. Freston and J. Lease, "Communication Skills Training for Selected Supervisors," *Training and Development Journal* (1987): 67–70.

3. D. Zarefsky, *Public Speaking Strategies for Success* (Boston: Allyn and Bacon, 1999), 336.

CHAPTER 8

Gathering
and Using
Information

"All things begin in order, so shall they
end, and so shall they begin again."

—Sir Thomas Browne

- Identify four principal sources of information about a speech topic and indicate how each contributes to the research process.
- Determine when it is appropriate to use the interview for gathering information.
- Use the library and the World Wide Web to gather and evaluate information for a speech.
- Cite five guidelines that can make the research process more efficient and effective.
- Explain how testimony, examples, definitions, and statistics can be used to support and clarify a speaker's message and enhance the impact of a speech.

SCENARIO

Dana works part time in the radiology lab at the local hospital. She knows from her work that lasers are used in a wide range of medical situations. When she had to present an informative speech in her communication class, she decided to speak on the medical uses of the laser in the United States.

To prepare for her speech, Dana interviewed several radiologists and surgeons about their use of lasers and read several articles about the latest developments in laser technology. But when she sat down to outline her presentation, Dana realized that she still didn't have enough current information on laser technology. She decided to research her subject more thoroughly in the school library and on the World Wide Web. She found more than enough additional information to fulfill her assignment.

By the time Dana finished gathering information, she had drawn on her own experiences, spoken with other people, read the most recent printed sources she could find, and read additional information on the Web. By being so thorough in gathering information, she had taken a crucial step toward developing a first-rate speech. ■

Gathering information takes time and effort, but as Dana learned in the opening scenario, it is also one of the most rewarding aspects of developing a speech. Gathering information is rewarding, because you learn from information previously reported and can develop an interesting and effective speech. The more current the information you gather, the more likely you are to impress your audience. Because this information becomes the backbone of your speech, the speech can only be as good as your information. This chapter focuses on research and using the information you find to support and clarify what you want to say.

Gathering Information

College professors and professional speakers have said that every ten minutes of speaking time requires at least ten hours of research and preparation time. Each topic and speaking occasion will require a different amount of information, but there is no question that the more information you have, the better equipped you will be to design and develop your presentation and adapt it to your audience. Of course, quality of information matters more than quantity, especially when your time is limited. That is why it is important to develop your research skills. The more skilled you become at doing research, the better use you will make of your time.

Using Yourself as a Source of Information

If you want to make the best use of your time and gather the best information, where should you begin? Most often, with yourself. You are one of the most valuable sources of information available.

Your experiences and knowledge can contribute to the content of your speech and give you authority to speak on a subject. In the opening scenario, Dana's experiences as a part-time lab assistant gave her a solid background on her subject, helped her locate additional sources of information, bolstered her confidence in her ability to handle the subject, and added to her credibility as a speaker. Here is part of what she said:

> New technology in the health professions is allowing life expectancy to increase by several months every year. My work in a local radiology lab has given me firsthand experience in working with some of the latest medical advances and technologies. Our office recently purchased a laser scanner, which has improved the doctors' ability to read x-rays reliably and accurately. All of the lab assistants have been instructed in the use and benefits of the scanner. Today I would like to explain to you what a laser scanner is, its uses in reading x-rays, and its benefits in providing better health care for all of us.

By using her own experience and knowledge, Dana established her authority and competence with her classmates and a strong and positive relationship between herself and her topic.

An Asian student used her experiences of growing up in another culture as the basis for a speech. She talked about her people, the educational traditions of her country, and some of the unique cultural differences between her country and the United States. Your job, special situations you have encountered, hobbies, involvement in social or political causes, and other life experiences are a valuable source of information that can be used in your speeches. Probing your own knowledge of a subject can also help you organize your thoughts, develop a research plan, and, eventually, save you a great deal of time.

The Interview as a Source of Information

Of course, for most topics your firsthand experience and knowledge will not be sufficient. The interview can be a valuable tool for gathering **expert opinion** (ideas, testimony, conclusions, or judgments of witnesses or someone recognized as an authority) and the most up-to-date information. A good interviewer can often discover information that could never be obtained through any other sources.

Of course, for most topics your firsthand experience and knowledge alone will not be sufficient to develop an effective speech. The interview resource can be a valuable for gathering expert opinion and the most up-to-date information.

An **interview** is a carefully planned, person-to-person, question-and-answer session aimed at gathering information. An interview requires a constant exchange of questions and answers between two individuals. Both persons speak and listen as in a social conversation. In fact, the most frequent interviews of all are the social conversations in which we engage when we meet someone new or try to get better acquainted with someone. Therefore, an interview requires the same skills and insights as social conversation. The key difference is that the interview requires careful preparation, a decision as to what information is desired, and a clear, well-thought-out plan for obtaining that information. So, let's take a brief look at the steps involved and some questions you need to ask in the interview process.

Steps in the Interview Process

1. *Establish the purpose of the interview.* What do you want to know? What information will be most helpful? How can you learn what you need to know about the topic?

2. *Choose the interviewee.* From whom will you get the best information? The most up-to-date information? What are that person's credentials? Is the interviewee willing to openly and honestly provide that information? Is the interviewee accessible? How many people should be interviewed to get complete and accurate information?

3. *Conduct research prior to the interview.* You need background both on the interviewee and on your topic. You need to learn as much as you can on your own in order to ask intelligent questions to help you gain the best, most important information.

4. *Record the interview.* To be sure that you accurately recall information provided during the interview, you need to record it, either on tape or on paper. Choose the method that best allows you to interact with your interviewee. Use the note-taking guidelines in the accompanying Guidelines.

Recording Interviews

1. Ask permission to take notes or to tape the interview, and let interviewees know that they will have the opportunity to check the notes from time to time or that you will send the interviewee a copy of the transcribed notes.

2. If you are using a tape recorder, be sure it is in good working order and test it prior to the interview. Make sure that you know how long your tape is and how the machine operates. Set the volume appropriately before you begin. The tape recorder should be positioned as inconspicuously as possible during the interview.

3. Maintain eye contact as much as possible.

4. Take notes throughout the interview.

5. Agree to follow any "ground rules" established by the interviewee and offer the interviewee the opportunity to review the script of your speech prior to your presentation.

6. Review your notes or tape recording as soon after the interview as possible.

7. Remember to be courteous throughout the interview and to thank the interviewee for taking the time to speak with you.

5. *Prepare questions.* Carefully prepare questions in advance. Be flexible enough to ask additional questions to get more information, to probe further, or to follow an unexpected opportunity the interviewee might provide.

6. *Organize the interview.* An interview, like a speech, usually has three identifiable segments: an opening, a body, and a closing. Organize your interview, and provide a template for the interviewee's responses.

7. *Other considerations.* Factors such as appropriate dress, punctuality, and attentive listening contribute to a successful interview. Always give the interviewee your complete and undivided attention during the interview. After you check your notes or listen to the tape, if anything is unclear, contact the interviewee for clarification as soon as possible after the interview.

Making Connections

Connecting Speaking and Thinking

Interviews are an effective means of gaining up-to-date information from people who have specialized knowledge of your topic. List some people you would consider interviewing if you were planning to speak on the following topics. The first item has been completed for you.

Subject	Interviewee
High cost of insurance	Insurance agent, state director of insurance, several insurance policy holders
Air traffic safety	_____
Prison reform	_____
High cost of education	_____
Genetic engineering	_____
Corruption in athletics	_____

1. For each subject, which individuals would be likely to give you unbiased information? Why?

2. For each subject, whom would you choose to interview first? Why?

Preparing for an Interview: A Review

1. Determine the kind of information you are seeking.
2. Formulate a clear and concise general objective.
3. Select the right person for the interview.
4. Research the topic and the person before the interview.
5. Decide how you are going to record the information and prepare your equipment.
6. Prepare questions and possible probes.
7. Organize the interview: opening, body, and closing.
8. Dress appropriately.
9. Be on time.
10. Give the interviewee your undivided attention.
11. Review your notes or listen to your tape as soon as possible after the interview. Follow up appropriately, if necessary.

The Library as a Source of Information

Making use of the library requires some effort, but once you understand how the system works—and most libraries use essentially the same system—you will find that the library is one of the most useful and beneficial resources for speech preparation we have. Libraries are now much more user friendly than in the past. Many libraries have invested great sums of money to install computerized systems to help researchers find materials quickly and easily.

If you do not know how to locate material, now is the time to learn. A little time invested now will save you a great deal of time later, and you will find that the library is a convenient and pleasant place to locate information. If you do not use the library, you will be at a disadvantage not only in your speech class but in all your other classes as well.

Start by attending one of the tours or orientation sessions that many libraries offer. Some also provide educational packages with instructions on how to use the library. After your introduction to the system, you need to practice using the library. Principal sources of information in the library include: the librarian, library computer-assisted search programs, the computerized catalog, and the reference department.

The Library Computer Search. Most libraries have computer-assisted research systems, and each year these systems improve and become more user friendly.

Many universities and colleges have network systems that allow you to enter the library indexes through home or campus computers. Once you learn the appropriate log-on procedures to access the library computer, menus guide you through the steps needed to find what you want. You will learn where the materials are located and if they are available at your library.

The Card Catalog. The card catalog, an index to all the books in a library, is designed to be a quick and easy means of locating materials. The use of computer databases is

Consulting resources, such as reference librarians and computer databases, is required for most speech preparation. Do not be afraid to ask for help; this is one of the library's most important functions.

replacing the card catalog, but because not all libraries are completely computerized, you still need to understand how the card catalog works. Most card catalogs list books in three ways: by author's last name, by title, and by subject. Entries in the card catalog are arranged alphabetically.

Periodicals (magazines, professional journals, newspapers, and serials) are listed by title or may be listed by the name of the issuing body, such as Modern Language Association or American Council on the Teaching of Foreign Languages. To find a specific piece of information or magazine article, you must go to the reference department.

The Reference Department.   Most library research begins in the reference department, which contains all the books needed for easy access to specific subject areas, such as dictionaries, almanacs, biographical aids, encyclopedias, yearbooks, newspapers, atlases, bibliographies, indexes, and guides to periodical literature. If you are uncertain which to use or how to use them, ask the librarian.

There are specialized indexes for particular subjects, such as agriculture and natural resources, business and economics, statistics, biology and life sciences, computers, education, and history. The index most widely used by beginning speech students is the *Readers' Guide to Periodical Literature*. This index lists articles from more than 190 popular periodicals. Issues of the guide, published semimonthly or monthly, are bound separately for the latest publications and compiled in volumes for publications that are a year or more old.

Periodicals.   Because magazines, research journals, and newspapers have the most recently available information on a subject, they are the most often used resources for speech writing. If you want to know the latest opinions and trends on almost any social, political, or economic issue, weekly magazines and newspapers will probably be your best resources. If you are looking for specific scientific research, research journals may be your best alternative.

Magazine and newspaper articles are usually brief and written for a general audience, so they are rich sources of basic information for speeches. Given their brevity, you can read several articles in order to gather different points of view. In addition, libraries not only have local and state newspapers but they also usually subscribe to major newspapers from all over the world, which can provide you with an even broader perspective.

If you do not know what your library has to offer, take time to learn about it. The search for knowledge is never easy, but thought and preparation will enable you to find ample information about almost any speech topic.

Electronic Information Sources

Many libraries have access to an online database of current periodicals: newspapers, magazines, newsletters, transcripts, and wire information. Some libraries have access to very expensive services such as Lexis-Nexis, an electronic source of newspapers from around the world. Lexis-Nexis provides the most current information from newspapers available. In some cases, you can access Lexis-Nexis at midnight your time and read the next morning's news from another part of the world. Many libraries also have an ERIC (Educational Research Information Clearinghouse) database as well, which provides access to reviewed convention papers, a source of the most up-to-date research findings as well as opinion pieces by experts in their own fields. When searching an electronic database, you need to determine keywords and phrases to use in your search before you begin the process so that you can maximize your time and effort. Check the options for each, but, generally, the word *and* is used as a connector between keywords. This allows the database to search the available materials for the information you need. Complete directions for carrying out searches are provided by your library or may be found on the screen where your search begins. Electronic databases are a valuable source of information.

The Internet. Most colleges and universities have access to the **World Wide Web (WWW),** a global information system that allows users to access Internet information. Web searches can provide a great wealth of information quickly and easily. Remember that web information does not go through a review process, nor is it fact-checked in any way, so material on a web page is more suspect than that gathered from traditional sources. Critically weigh and verify the information you find, because much of it is unreliable. In Chapter 7, we reviewed ideas for evaluating web sources; review that section as you consider the information and the qualifications of the authors of your web sources.

To find information on the Web, conduct a search using one of the many available search engines. There are topic-based searches and site-based searches. The most common Internet search is the topic-based search. When you identify a general topic (computers, medicine, health issues, communication, and so on), you can access information about all aspects of that topic. You may, however, receive too many responses to your query and need to narrow your topic in order to find responses you can easily peruse to find information for your speech. Each search engine has a tutorial to help you get started. Among the more readily accessible are these:

Lycos (http://www.lycos.com)

AltaVista (http://www.altavista.com)

Yahoo! (Http://www.yahoo.com)

Infoseek (http://www2.infoseek.com)

Google (http://www.google.com)

Excite (http://www.excite.com)

When you find information on the Web, be sure to write down the specific bibliographic information (URL [uniform resource locator], date accessed, page number, and author or producer), print the information, save it on a floppy disk, or bookmark it. If you're using Netscape, for example, pull down the File menu to Page Setup. Click on each of the boxes so that a check mark appears in front of Document Title, Document Location, Page Number, Page Total, and Date Printed. If you create a bookmark, you will also need to save it on the hard drive or on a floppy disk. Many campus computer labs do not allow users to save information, or it may be saved only for a short period of time. In many cases you will not be able to save the URL, so be sure to print at least the first page with the URL or write it down so you can find it later.

Surfing the Web: The Internet as a Source of Information

Searching the Web can be interesting, fun, entertaining, frustrating, addicting, and educational, and it facilitates access to a wealth of information in a relatively short period of time. Web information comes from a variety of sources. Some are reliable and credible, and others are not very useful, credible, relevant, or reliable. Websites are not subject to the same evaluation and review as print sources, so it is important that you assess not only the information on a website but also the person, persons, or organization responsible for the site. It is no accident that when you key in the words *critical thinking* many of your hits (responses) will be suggestions for evaluating web sources. Several of the scores of critical thinking websites were actually titled "Thinking Critically About Web Sources" or something similar. Three of our favorite guides for evaluating web sources (because of their thoroughness and because they are from respected university libraries) are provided by Esther Grassian at the UCLA library, Elizabeth Kirk of the Milton S. Eisenhower Library of The Johns Hopkins University, and Cornell University. Each is different, yet each contains similarities. Each asks the surfer to consider specific questions about websites being accessed for information or research purposes.

Kirk (http://milton.mse.jhu.edu:8001/research/education/net.html), for example, offers four basic evaluative criteria:

1. *Author.* Who wrote the material? How do you know this person is qualified to write about this subject? Can you contact the author if you have questions?

2. *Publishing body.* Who "publishes" or sponsors the website? When you look at the web page, do you see a header or footer that shows a connection to a larger website? Is there a link on the page that takes you to the home page of the website? What can you learn from the Internet address (the URL)? Check the letters just to the left of the first backslash (/). Following are some abbreviations that provide some insight to a web source, which are used with URLs:

.edu	Refers to a U.S. college or university
.cc(state)us	Refers to a community college
.k12(state)us	Refers to a school for kindergarten through twelfth grade
.com	Refers to a business or other commercial enterprise
.org	Refers to a nonprofit organization or trade association
.mil	Refers to a military site
.gov	Refers to a government agency, official, or organization
.net	Refers to a network administration organization

   Look beyond the backslash. If you see a tilde (~) or if the URL includes terms such as "/users/" or "/people/," you may be looking at an individual's personal page within the official pages of a larger website. If it is a personal page, you may have no way of knowing whether the information on the page represents the organization. However, if you know the author's identity and qualifications (say, a librarian at an educational site), you will be able to ascertain the credibility of the personal page.

3. *Currency.* How recently was the website published, created, or updated? This information should be at the bottom of the web page or home page of the website. Does the document contain data that must be recent? Is there a date connected to that information? (For example, major league baseball standings of September 25,

2000, are no longer current.) Does the website have links to other sites that no longer work?

4. *Purpose.* Can you determine why the information is on the World Wide Web? Does the site provide information, give explanations, persuade, publicize, sell products, or entertain? Sometimes the URL will give you a clue. Part of the URL contains a function indicator, such as *gov* or *com,* that indicates the purpose of a website:

.edu or .gov	Provides factual information and explanations
.com	Promotes and sells products, or provides current news and information
.org	Influences public opinion and advocates for particular issues
.net or .com	Entertains
.info	Especially used to provide truly global general information; most current registrations are in the United States
.biz	Specifically for businesses
.name	Indicates the site is for individuals
.pro	Indicates professionals; attorneys, dentists, or medical doctors, for example, register their sites for easy access (For example, Janedoe.law.pro identifies a site belonging to attorney Jane Doe.)
.museums	Accredited museums worldwide
.aero	Globally recognized suffix for airlines, airports, computer reservation systems, and related industries
.coop	Identifies business cooperatives, such as credit unions and rural electric coops worldwide

Making Connections

Checking and Evaluating Websites

For more information on checking the accuracy and validity of websites, consider the evaluation techniques provided by professional librarians. Here are a few suggestions:

Elizabeth Kirk at The Johns Hopkins University, Maryland (cited in the text): http://milton.mse.jhu.edu:8001/research/education/net.html

Jane Alexander and Marsha Tate at Widener University, Pennsylvania: http://www.science.widener.edu/ ~ withers/

Hope Tillman at Babson College, Massachusetts: http://www.tiac.net/users/hope/findqual.html

John Henderson at Ithaca College, New York: http://www.ithaca.edu/library/Training/hott.html

Esther Grassian at UCLA, California: http://www.library.ucla.edu/libraries/college/instruct/web/critical.htm

Finally, consider one more question: How does web information compare with other available resources, such as print media? If there are discrepancies among sources, do some further checking to find the best sources of information you can. Remember, too, that websites change at the click of a mouse. You might search a specific topic and find 15,050 hits then return an hour later and find 16,589 hits. Websites are added rapidly and changed often. Also, a search engine may sample more or fewer individual sites at different times. Some of the library websites in the Making Connections box on page 207 may have changed from the initial writing to the time this book is published. Sometimes you will automatically be redirected to another site. At other times you will need to search further or find another source. This is another good reason for writing down URLs and bookmarking websites: You can go back to the exact site to get further information or direct others to a specific site.

Suggestions for Doing Research

There are no shortcuts to doing good research, but there are ways to make research more enjoyable and easier no matter what sources you choose to use. Here are several suggestions:

1. *State a clear purpose before starting your research.* Knowing what you want to find makes the job of searching easier. If, for example, the purpose of your speech is to inform your audience about the importance of maintaining a good diet, the key term in your purpose statement would be *diet.* Your search for information should begin there. Thinking of other key terms will help lead you to topics related to diet, such as *nutrition* and *health.* Considering all the possible areas of research in advance will get you started quickly and productively.

2. *Begin your research early.* Because finding appropriate materials takes time, you should start your research as soon as possible. If you wait until the last minute, you may discover that the materials you need are unavailable or that it takes longer to find them than you anticipated.

3. *Use computer searches when possible.* The computer is one of the simplest means of obtaining lists of sources on any topic. If you are unfamiliar with your library's computer system, ask a librarian for help. Librarians will gladly help you find what you need.

4. *Maintain a bibliography of sources.* As you find sources on the computer, in the card catalog, and in periodical guides, copy them in the same form onto a sheet of paper or index cards (3 × 5 inch or 4 × 6 inch). The advantage of index cards is that you can sort them quickly, either alphabetically or by importance to your speech. List each item separately and make notes about its importance to your speech presentation. Although this may seem tedious, it is essential that you keep track of the materials you find.

5. *Take notes.* Efficient and accurate note taking is a must. Once you have located information, you must either record it by hand or photocopy it for later use. Whether you quote a statement verbatim, summarize it, or paraphrase it, you must record the original information accurately and completely. Take plenty of notes, and always make sure that the source is fully and accurately indicated, as in the sample note cards

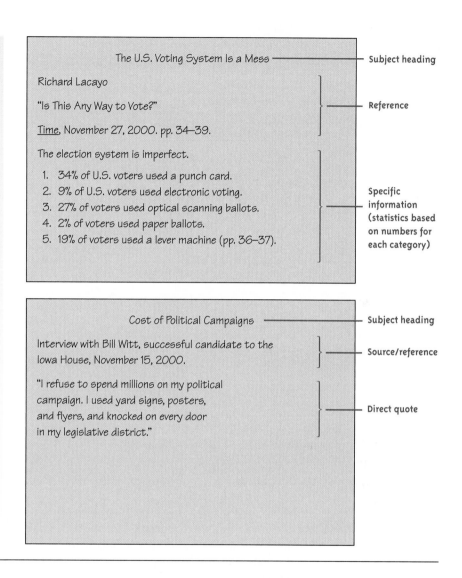

FIGURE 8.1

Sample Note Cards

Note taking, if done accurately and completely, can save you a great deal of time and effort. It is always best to take plenty of notes and to record the sources of the notes correctly.

The U.S. Voting System Is a Mess ———— Subject heading

Richard Lacayo

"Is This Any Way to Vote?"

Time, November 27, 2000. pp. 34–39.

———— Reference

The election system is imperfect.

1. 34% of U.S. voters used a punch card.
2. 9% of U.S. voters used electronic voting.
3. 27% of voters used optical scanning ballots.
4. 2% of voters used paper ballots.
5. 19% of voters used a lever machine (pp. 36–37).

———— Specific information (statistics based on numbers for each category)

Cost of Political Campaigns ———— Subject heading

Interview with Bill Witt, successful candidate to the Iowa House, November 15, 2000.

———— Source/reference

"I refuse to spend millions on my political campaign. I used yard signs, posters, and flyers, and knocked on every door in my legislative district."

———— Direct quote

in Figure 8.1. Nothing is more frustrating than having information and not being able to use it because you don't know its source and cannot return to it for additional information. The more information you record, the better. You should always have more than you need to write your speech.

Using Research to Support and Clarify Ideas

More than 2,000 years ago, Aristotle, a famous Greek scholar, wrote that there are essentially two parts to every speech—a statement and its proof. Aristotle's description is still valid today. How a speaker clarifies and supports ideas determines the quality of the speech. For example, consider the following statement:

Making Connections

Thinking About Traditional and Web Information Sources

There are many places to find information that will enhance your speeches. Using the library and the Internet, and interviewing experts are several sources discussed in this chapter. Imagine that in two weeks you will present an informative speech using visual aids in your communication class. Your professor has indicated that the topic may be of your own choosing. Follow these steps as you begin your search for information.

1. Identify the general topic area for your speech.
2. Identify the general subject of your keyword search.
3. Decide whether to use traditional library sources or electronic sources.
4. Decide when you will use library sources and when you will use web sources.
5. Identify five sites where you might find information on your topic.
6. Conduct a web search.
7. Refine your search and narrow your topic in that search.
8. Determine what criteria you will use to evaluate your information.
9. Determine what guidelines you will use as you seek information on the Web.

> Students of today are far more advanced than students of a decade ago. Today's students, for example, have access to computer technology, which has allowed them to advance at a much faster rate.

On the surface, this statement seems to be valid, but is it accurate and will an audience accept it at face value? Does the statement offer any data to help you accept the first sentence as true? What proof is provided that students who have access to computer technology have advanced more quickly than those who do not? Careful analysis shows that we need to think carefully before we accept the statement as true.

Audiences generally accept information because of the perceived believability of the speaker or the information itself. Thus, the statement would likely be more acceptable to audiences if it were made by a well-known educator and researcher than if it were made by a student. But regardless of the source, most listeners require some proof or specific data before they completely accept a statement. Consequently, effective speakers justify each main idea in their speeches with a variety of supporting and clarifying materials.

Supporting and clarifying materials bring life to a speech. They can make the content of a speech appealing, vivid, exciting, meaningful, acceptable, and more useful to listeners. Compare these two paragraphs:

> To what extent do males and females differ in the way that they learn and communicate? The sexes are psychologically similar in many respects. Although some of the differences may have a biological basis, the existing evidence is conflicting.

> To what extent do males and females differ in the way that they learn and communicate? Eleanor Maccoby and Carol Jacklin, two widely respected psychologists and authors, report in their book *The Psychology of Sex Differences* that "the sexes are psychologically much

Making Connections

Key Terms and Computer Searches

Before you key in your computer search, take a few minutes to analyze your topic and plan your approach. Warm up your brain.

One good way to begin is to break your topic down into component parts. If, for example, you are interested in finding out about violence on television and its affect on children, rather than typing "the effect of TV violence on kids" type "television and violence and children."

Next, expand your list of key terms to further define your topic. You might add "child*." Entering the * as the last character allows you to search for various words beginning "child." You can broaden your search by typing in "children or youth or teenagers or adolescents." This process allows you to clarify what you want before you begin the search process and helps you over-

come one of the obstacles of good subject researching—a narrow view of the terminology needed to define the subject.

1. Using the topic of your choice, identify and list related key terms.
2. Further define your topic by putting terms together to form appropriate phrases.
3. Next, either do a library search online or go to the library itself to do your research.
4. How successful were your searches?
5. What did you learn about typing in key words?

Adapted from B. E. Weeg and L. Gullickson, "Using UNISTAR," in M. L. Beall, *Oral Communication, A Guide,* 2nd ed. (New York: Forbes, 1999), 51–54.

---

alike in many respects." Although some of the differences in behavior—such as the superior verbal ability of girls and accelerated math skills of boys—may have a biological basis, a great deal of conflicting evidence surrounds such differences.

Which paragraph do you find to be more meaningful? More acceptable? More interesting? More useful? Why?

Consider the following statement made in a speech by a student:

Exercise is the best means of losing weight. Although many people consider exercise to be hard work, it doesn't have to be. In fact, there are a number of exercise programs that are easy, and you don't even have to sweat to lose pounds.

Sounds great, but, as they say, something that sounds too good to be true is probably not true, or, in this case, is not convincing. Most of us would question something that claims we are going to lose weight with little or no effort. The student must provide some evidence before the audience will accept such a statement.

The quantity and quality of a speaker's supporting and clarifying materials, plus the speaker's ability to use them correctly, usually makes the difference between a mediocre speech and a good one. Thus, in this section we focus on the basic kinds of supporting and clarifying materials used in speeches: testimony, examples, definitions, and statistics.

Testimony

The opinions or conclusions of witnesses or recognized authorities is referred to as **testimony.** Speakers use testimony to support or reinforce points they want their audiences to accept. The value of the testimony is related both to the listeners' opinion of its acceptability and to the speaker who presents it. Consider this opening of a student's speech:

> You try to stop yourself, but for some reason you can't! The child keeps on screaming, "Mommy, Mommy, please don't hit me anymore!" You've lost control and until your rage subsides, you can't stop, even though you know you should. Not until you are caught or you do something severely harmful is anything done about it. When it's all over, you have inflicted the worst kind of human atrocity on your own child. How do I know this? Because I used to beat my own child until I got help.

The young woman who gave this speech had her audience's attention not only because of the story she was recounting but also because she had the courage to relate what she had done and how she had overcome it. Her abuse of her own child did not enhance her believability and create acceptance for what she was saying, but her willingness to admit that she was personally involved in her topic did.

The use of testimony usually adds trustworthiness to what a speaker says—a necessity for all speakers who are not yet established as experts on their chosen speech topic. The speaker's own experience can be an excellent form of testimony as in the previous example. When the speaker's reputation and experience are insufficient, the use of a recognized and trusted authority can be invaluable in gaining listeners' acceptance.

Testimony can either support or clarify material or both. Here is an example of testimony that does both:

> The following statement by the American Automobile Association sums up experiments too numerous to mention and represents the best current professional opinion on automotive safety: "We know that seat belts, if used properly and at all times, can save hundreds of lives each year. By 'used properly' we mean that both the shoulder and seat belts must be fastened."[1]

Here the speaker adds support by citing the American Automobile Association as a source of information, and clarifies what seat belts can do, and explains the meaning of the phrase "used properly."

Testimony can be either quoted directly or paraphrased. Paraphrasing is an effective method of condensing a long text or clarifying a passage that is too technical for audience members to understand. Sometimes audience members tune out speakers who use long and complex quotations. Restating long quotations in your own words helps make the source's words fit the tone of your speech. If you paraphrase, be sure not to violate the meaning of the original statement.

Certain statements are so well phrased that they cannot be stated any better. An example is the forceful and unforgettable statement made by John F. Kennedy in his 1961 presidential inaugural address: "Ask not what your country can do for you; ask what you can do for your country." Always quote such statements word for word. Misquoting someone can be embarrassing, but even worse, it can destroy your believability. Double-check every quotation for accuracy and source, and never use a quotation out of context.

Testimony should meet two essential tests: The person whose words are cited must be qualified by virtue of skills, training, expertise, recognition, and reputation; and the expert's opinion must be acceptable and believable to your listeners.

The person you quote should be a qualified authority on the subject. For example, an athlete's endorsement of tennis shoes and a movie star's endorsement of cosmetics are fairly believable because they use such products in their work. But when

The value of testimony is related both to the listeners' opinion of the acceptability of the message and to the credibility of the speaker who presents it. Venus Williams, tennis star, is a credible spokesperson for Reebok, but she is probably not a qualified authority on many other subjects.

celebrities advertise products completely unrelated to their area of expertise, their opinions becomes less believable. Avoid using celebrities' names solely because they are well known. The best testimony comes from a person whose knowledge and experience are related to the topic and who is recognized by your listeners.

For maximum believability, testimony should also come from objective sources. The objectivity and neutrality of authorities is particularly important when your subject is controversial. For example, in trying to persuade an audience that today's automobiles are safer than those of a decade ago, it is more convincing to quote the American Automobile Association or the National Safety Council than the president of an automotive company. Listeners tend to be suspicious of opinions from a biased or self-interested source.

Using Testimony: Some Tips

1. Use testimony or expert opinion when you need additional supporting or clarifying information.
2. Cite sources completely and accurately.
3. Paraphrase long and difficult quotations in your own words.
4. Keep quotations short, accurate, and relevant to what you are saying.
5. Use recognized, qualified, unbiased, and trusted authorities.

Examples

An **example** is a simple, representative incident or model that clarifies a point. Examples are useful when you are presenting complex information to listeners who are unfamiliar with a topic and when your purpose is to inform or instruct. Brief examples, illustrations, and analogies are three kinds of examples that help make things clear for an audience.

Brief Examples.   A **brief example** is a specific instance used to introduce a topic, drive home a point, or create a desired impression. The following brief example was used to introduce a subtopic related to the main topic of computer-assisted presentations.

> Presentational computer software programs have made it possible for speakers to enhance their business presentations.

A series of brief examples can also be used to create a desired impression:

> Presentational computer software programs have made it possible for speakers to enhance their business presentations. In fact, many businesses now have a hiring requirement that future employees have specific experience in PowerPoint or similar presentation aids. Many companies provide mandatory PowerPoint workshops for their employees. Because computer technology is so prevalent in the workplace, both employers and customers rely on computer presentations to make a positive impact on clients and the general public. Knowledge of presentational programs can greatly increase the professional look of business and professional presentations, so it is in your best interest to be aware of effective strategies for incorporating this technology. Edward R. Tufte, considered the "guru of visual explanations," quoted in the February 6, 2000, edition of the *New York Times,* offers caveats about graphic presentations. He suggests that presentational aids such as PowerPoint presentations are overused, have too many flashy elements, and do not contain enough information. Dr. Tufte said, "The task is not to have 'high-impact presentations,' or 'point, click, wow' or 'power pitches.' The point is to explain something." Tufte also suggests that the goals of presentational aids should be to exchange information and demonstrate clear reasoning and problem-solving."[2] These examples of the use of computer-assisted presentations illustrate the importance of including some media or visual presentations in our personal portfolios.

Illustrations.   An **illustration,** or extended example, is a narrative, case history, or anecdote that is striking and memorable. Illustrations often exemplify concepts, conditions, or circumstances, or they demonstrate findings. If an example refers to a single item or event, it is an illustration. Because illustrations go into more detail than brief examples, they are useful in establishing proof.

An illustration lends depth and explanation to the point a speaker is trying to make. It also gives the information more meaning. An illustration may be either factual or hypothetical. A **factual illustration** tells what has actually happened; a **hypothetical illustration** tells what could or probably would happen, given a specific set of circumstances.

A hypothetical illustration, because it is speculative, asks listeners to use their imaginations. Such examples are often short stories that relate to a general principle or concept. One instructor used the following hypothetical example to help her students envision how to use their voices when delivering an emotional speech:

> Imagine that an angry mob has accused your friend of a crime—a serious crime—and that they are going to hang him because they believe he is guilty, even though you know he isn't. Your only chance to save your friend is to persuade the unruly mob that he is innocent.

This hypothetical illustration demonstrates that people who are involved in serious situations must use their voices to make their point. The speech to the mob would have to be vivid, forceful, convincing, and highly emotional.

The use of a hypothetical illustration can be particularly effective when it involves the listeners. The illustration should create a vivid picture in the listeners' minds. The more realistic the situation, the more likely it is that the listeners will become involved. A speaker should always specify whether an illustration is factual or hypothetical.

Analogies.   An **analogy** is a comparison of two things that are similar in certain essential characteristics. Analogies explain or prove the unknown by comparing it to the known.

There are two kinds of analogies. A **figurative analogy** draws comparisons between things in different categories. For example, the thermostat, whose workings are understood by most people, is commonly used to explain feedback. The thermostat reacts to the heat produced by the furnace and sends a message back to the furnace; the listener responds to the sender's message and sends a message to the sender. A **literal analogy** is a comparison of members of the same category and makes a simple comparison, for example, two universities (Florida State University and the University of Southern California), two cities (New York and Milwaukee), or two languages (Spanish and German).

Most speech topics offer many opportunities to use analogies. Generally, figurative analogies make ideas clear and vivid, whereas literal analogies supply evidence to prove points. Not only are analogies an effective and creative means of proving a point and clarifying information but they are also efficient, because they use fewer words to communicate information.

Restatements.   Speakers can and should use a variety of strategies to make their speeches memorable. Effective speakers have often used both restatement and repetition to support and clarify their ideas. A **restatement** is the expression of the same idea using different words. It may take the form of a summary, synonym, or rephrasing.

Dr. Martin Luther King Jr., Nobel prize winner and 1960s leader of the Civil Rights movement, was a brilliant and mesmerizing speaker. In 1963, he gave his famous "I Have a Dream" speech to a crowd of thousands in Washington, D.C. His rhythmic repeating of the phrase, "I have a dream," pinpointed his message and captivated the audience.

Restatement does not provide evidence, but it often has a persuasive effect. A well-planned use of restatement can add clarity, meaning, and dramatic rhythm to a message. Martin Luther King Jr., in his famous "I Have a Dream" speech, used both repetition and restatement to make his point:

> I say to you today, my friends, so even though we face the difficulties of today and tomorrow, I still have a dream. It is a dream deeply rooted in the American dream.
>
> I have a dream that one day this nation will rise up and live out the true meaning of its creed, "We hold these truths to be self-evident, that all men are created equal."
>
> I have a dream that one day on the red hills of Georgia the sons of former slaves and sons of former slave owners will be able to sit down together at the table of brotherhood.[3]

Using Examples: Some Tips

1. Use factual examples to add authenticity to your presentation. A factual example builds on the basic information presented and adds believability to both you and your speech.

2. Use examples that are realistic and relate directly to your discussion. If you try to generalize from unusual or rare situations, you risk undermining believability.

3. Use examples that are authentic, accurate, and verifiable. Always give credit to the source of an example so that your listeners can verify it.

Definitions

You must define all unfamiliar words and concepts, especially technical terms, if you want your listeners to understand and accept your speech. Nothing is more bothersome to listeners than a speaker who uses terminology they do not understand. In most cases, it is better to offer too much explanation than too little. However, do not patronize your audience by explaining the obvious. You can use several different kinds of definitions to keep your audience's attention.

A **logical definition,** the most common form used by speakers, usually contains two parts: a term's dictionary definition and the characteristics that distinguish the term from other items in the same category. For example, "*Sociology* is defined as an academic field of study—the science of society, social institutions, and social relationships. Its focus of study is the origin, development, organization, and function of human society." This definition states what sociology is, and listeners can easily infer that it differs from other academic fields, such as communication, anthropology, biology, and chemistry.

An **operational definition** explains how an object or concept works, gives the steps that make up a process, or states how conceptual terms are measured. Here are some examples:

Selective perception is the choosing of stimuli we want to perceive and the ignoring of stimuli we do not want to perceive.

The mean is the result of adding all the scores in a set of scores and dividing by the number of scores in the set.

Sex is defined as the biological differences between males and females, whereas gender is defined by masculine and feminine traits displayed by either males or females. Thus, gender is operationalized by characteristics and traits a person displays and not biological differences.

A communicative apprehensive person is defined as a person who scores 90 or above on the Personal Report of Communication Apprehension Test.

A **definition by example** clarifies a term not by describing it or giving its meaning but by mentioning or showing an example of it.

When I speak about large universities, I mean institutions such as the Universities of Wisconsin, Southern California, or Minnesota, each of which has an enrollment of more than thirty thousand students.

A scissors kick is different from other swimming kicks in that you extend both legs and open them sideways—then you cross and recross them, like scissors. Here is what it looks like. [The speaker shows a diagram displaying the scissors kick.]

Using Definitions: Some Tips

1. Define a term or concept whenever you suspect your audience may not understand what you mean or that multiple interpretations are possible.

2. Keep definitions short and to the point. Do not make your explanation more complex than necessary.

3. Use clear and concise language that your audience can easily understand. Make your definitions come alive for your audience by providing examples.

Statistics

Numerical data that show relationships or summarize or interpret many instances are known as **statistics.** Every day we are confronted with numerical analyses. We read, for example, that the earth's population is more than five billion, the gross national product increased by one-tenth of 1 percent in the past two years, the enrollment at the university declined from 23,500 to 22,100, or 17 percent of all married couples prefer to have 1.7 children. Although statistics can point out some interesting information, they can be difficult to interpret.

Statistics enable speakers to summarize a large amount of data rapidly, to analyze specific occurrences or instances, to isolate trends, and to calculate probabilities of future events. They are used to clarify and support a speaker's position. For example, consider these two statements.

> The Mormon religion is one of the fastest growing religious denominations in the United States.

> According to the *U.S. News & World Report* November 13, 2000, issue, there were 5.1 million members of the Mormon Church in the United States in 1999. These figures reflect a membership increase of 220 percent since 1970.

The first statement is broad and does not tell us how many members are enrolled in the church or the time frame for the growth. The statement is vague and difficult to defend. The second statement, because it cites a specific number, percentage, and time frame, gives listeners a clearer picture of the situation and is, thus, more convincing. In addition, the second statement uses a source to add credence to the data. Statistics can be used to emphasize the magnitude of a particular issue, as seen in the following example:

> Halabja, Iraq, the site of a 1988 chemical weapons attack, is a "living laboratory for studying the effects of chemical weapons on civilians. Today, Halabja is suffering and dangerous, its population down from 75,000 to 47,000. Unemployment is 75 percent, and 2,500 homes have yet to be rebuilt.[4]

Statistics can also be informative:

> In October 2000, Philip Morris, the No. 1 tobacco maker, posted its highest earnings gain since 1997. This despite an unprecedented 8 percent drop in tobacco consumption from 1998 to 1999, according to the November 13 issue of *U.S. News & World Report.*[5]

Making the Most of Statistics.   Following five simple guidelines will help you make the most of the statistics you've gathered.

1. *Make sure that the statistics you present in your speech are from reliable and neutral sources.* The motives of the source of any statistics must be carefully assessed. For example, if you heard two sets of data on fuel economy per gallon of gasoline—one prepared by the DaimlerChrysler Corporation and the other by the Environmental Protection Agency—which would you expect to be more reliable? Although Daimler-Chrysler's data may be perfectly accurate, listeners would tend to believe that their data are biased. It would be to a speaker's advantage, therefore, to use the more neutral source, in this case, the Environmental Protection Agency.

Many times, however, it may be difficult to identify the most neutral source. For example, whose statistics would you use if you wished to inform your audience about the U.S. strength in nuclear weapons—the Department of Defense or the Americans for Peace? Here the choice is debatable unless you intend to take a position on the issue. Remember, statistics can be used in many different ways and can, thus, influence interpretations and outcomes.

2. *Take time to explain the statistics you are using.* Interpret and relate your statistics to your listeners. Consider the following use of statistics:

> The diameter of the sun is about 865,000 miles, about 109 times the diameter of the earth. Because the sun is about 93 million miles from the earth, it does not appear larger than the moon. But the sun's diameter is 400 times as large as that of the moon. The sun is also almost 400 times farther from the earth than is the moon.
>
> If the sun were the size of a skyscraper, the earth would be the size of a person. The moon would be the size of a cocker spaniel standing next to the person.[6]

This explanation makes use of analogy and makes statistics meaningful by clearly comparing the size and distance of the sun and the moon. When using data that listeners may have difficulty understanding or visualizing, try to provide appropriate comparisons in order to make the data more meaningful.

3. *Use statistics sparingly.* Statistics are difficult to comprehend, so if you use too many, you run a high risk of boring or confusing your audience. Use statistics only when necessary, and make sure they are easy to understand. The following example would be difficult for even the most attentive listener to comprehend:

> If my new proposal is accepted, we will have at least a 20 percent increase in production efficiency and at least a 50 cent per unit cost reduction, according to our 2005 projections. This, I might add, means a 10 percent, or a minimum of 35 cents per unit, cost reduction over the next five to six years. What this all adds up to is a 15 percent increase over this time period and an eventual profit of $110,000 per year. That will also give us a 6 percent depreciation allowance.

It would be much easier to understand if the data were presented as follows:

> The new proposal, if accepted, will increase production efficiency by 20 percent or 50 cents per unit according to our 2005 projections. This would provide a minimum cost reduction of 35 cents per unit over the next five to six years and a $110,000 per year profit for a 15 percent increase over the time period.

4. *Round off large numbers when possible.* Listeners understand and remember figures better when they are not complicated. For example, it is easier to remember 10,000 than 9,987. Although it's true that the Statue of Liberty's torch rises about 305 feet and 1 inch, or 92.99 meters, above the base of the pedestal, it is less complicated to say that the torch rises about 305 feet, or 93 meters. Unless an exact figure is needed, round off most statistics to the nearest whole number.

5. *Use visual aids to present statistical information, if appropriate and possible.* Using visual aids saves explanation time and also makes statistics easier to understand.

TABLE 8.1

A Simplified Way of Presenting Statistics

	NET SALES	NET EARNINGS	DIVIDENDS PER SHARE
1st quarter	$ 44,000	$ 2,900	$0.10
2nd quarter	50,100	3,500	0.15
3rd quarter	55,000	4,500	0.20
4th quarter	56,700	5,000	0.22
Total	$205,800	$15,900	$0.67

Compare the clarity of the following paragraph with Table 8.1. Note how all the words in the verbal presentation are summed up in a simple four-column display:

> The first quarter net sales were $44,000, which created a net earning of $2,900, thus producing a 10 cent dividend per share. The second quarter net sales were $50,100, leading to a net earning of $3,500 for a 15 cent dividend per share. The third quarter net sales of $55,000 created a net earning of $4,500 for a 20 cent dividend per share. And the fourth quarter net sales of $56,700 produced a net earning of $5,000, or a 22 cent dividend per share. The total net sales were $205,800, with a total net earning of $15,900 paying a total dividend per share of 67 cents.

Figure 8.2 presents another example of how complex data can be summarized and presented in an interesting way. Note how the artwork makes it much easier for the viewer to understand the statistics about bank takeovers. (Chapter 10 discusses in more detail the use of visual aids in a speech presentation.)

FIGURE 8.2

Visualizing Statistical Data

Viewing statistical data can help summarize complex data and make it come alive to interest your audience.

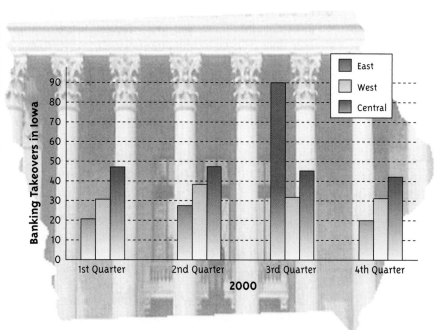

Using Statistics: Some Tips

1. Make sure that the statistics you use come from reliable and neutral sources.

2. Take the time to explain to your listeners the statistics you are using.

3. Use statistics sparingly.

4. Display statistics visually whenever possible in order to save explanation time.

Summary

Gathering information is essential in the speech development process. Many resources are available to help you locate information. Begin with yourself. Even if you are not an expert on your topic, you probably have some knowledge of it. If your personal experiences do not suffice, you can obtain information from others who have *expert opinions,* from the library, and from the Internet.

Interviews can provide more in-depth and up-to-date information than newspaper or magazine articles, information that is not covered in other published materials, and news from experts or others who have firsthand knowledge of the topic. An interview is a carefully planned, person-to-person, question-and-answer session aimed at gathering information.

There are three principal sources of information in the library: the card catalog, the computer-assisted search, and the reference department. Librarians can help you access information from these sources. You should have a working knowledge of the library and know what you want to find before you begin your search. The card catalog is an alphabetical index to all the books in the library, listed by author's last name, by title, and by subject. Periodicals are also listed by title or by the name of the issuing organization. Some computer searches can be done only by librarians, but others can be done by students. Computer searches allow access to library indexes through home or campus computers, locating information and sources not always available in your own library. If you use the Internet, search engines are helpful as you gather information for your speech. You conduct searches using subjects and keywords. Lexis-Nexis, an electronic source of the world's newspapers, provides current news coverage from around the world. Another electronic information source is the ERIC database. ERIC provides up-to-date research findings and opinion pieces by experts in their own fields. The World Wide Web offers a wealth of information. When using web sources, be sure to assess their value, using the criteria provided by reputable sources such as Elizabeth Kirk at the Milton S. Eisenhower Library: (1) identify the author, (2) evaluate the publishing body, (3) check that the source is current, and (4) determine its purpose. We also recommend that you compare web information to other sources. The reference department contains dictionaries, biographical aids, encyclopedias, yearbooks, atlases, indexes, and guides to periodical literature.

To simplify your research process, know what you want to find, begin early, record citations accurately and completely, and take clear notes of the information.

Although a speaker's believability and delivery are critically important to the success of a speech, effective research that supports and clarifies main points usually makes the difference between a good speech and a poor one. The four basic kinds of supporting and clarifying materials used in speeches are testimony, examples, definitions, and statistics.

Testimony includes the opinions or conclusions of witnesses or recognized authorities. Using testimony benefits student speakers who have not yet established themselves as experts on the topics they present. When presenting *expert opinion,* use short quotations, quote and paraphrase accurately, and use qualified and unbiased sources.

Examples are the most useful form of supporting and clarifying material. There are four kinds: the *brief example,* a specific instance used to introduce a new topic, drive home a point, or create a desired impression; the *illustration,* an extended *factual* or *hypothetical* example that is striking and memorable; the *analogy,* a *figurative* or *literal* comparison of two things that are similar in certain essential characteristics; and the *restatement,* an expression of the same idea using different words. When presenting examples, use factual cases whenever possible, relate them to the topic you are discussing, make them realistic and believable, provide verifiable sources, and give proper credit to the originator.

Speakers who are sensitive to their audiences realize the importance of defining unfamiliar terms. There are three basic forms of definitions. The *logical definition,* which is the most common, consists of a term's dictionary definition. The *operational definition* explains how an object or concept works. The *definition by example* explains terms and concepts through the use of verbal or actual examples. When using definitions, keep them short, use clear and concise language, explain every term that your audience might not understand or could misinterpret, and provide examples to clarify meanings.

Statistics enable speakers to summarize a large amount of data rapidly, to analyze specific occurrences or instances, to isolate trends, and to calculate probabilities of future events. Statistics should be accurate, meaningful to the audience, used sparingly, representative of the speaker's claims, and based on a reliable source.

DISCUSSION STARTERS

1. What advice would you give to a beginning speech student about gathering information for a speech?
2. Why is it important to examine what you know about a topic before you consult with others or use the library?
3. Why is an interview a particularly productive way of gathering information?
4. What advice would you give a person who has never conducted an interview? What would he or she need to know to be an effective interviewer?
5. You have just entered the library to research your speech topic, gun control. You want to learn as much as possible about this subject. Where would you begin?
6. How can the reference department in a library help a speaker to gather materials for a speech?
7. What advice would you give to a beginning speaker about using supporting and clarifying materials in a speech?
8. On what basis should you judge the effectiveness of a source of information in supporting a particular point of view?
9. As a receiver of information, what cautions should you take when you hear someone using statistics in a speech?
10. What advantages are there for using electronic sources to find information?
11. How should we evaluate web sources?

NOTES

1. American Automobile Association, *Buckle Up* (American Automobile Association, 1994), Omaha, Nebraska.
2. D. Corcoran, "Talking Numbers with Edward R. Tufte: Campaigning for the Charts That Teach," *New York Times,* February 6, 2000, C4.
3. From "I Have a Dream" by Martin Luther King Jr., Copyright 1963 by Martin Luther King Jr., copyright renewed 1991 by Coretta Scott King. Reprinted by arrangement with the Heirs to the Estate of Martin Luther King Jr., c/o Writers House, Inc. as agent for the proprietor.
4. W. P. Strobel, "Saddam's Lingering Atrocity," *U.S.News & World Report,* November 27, 2000, 52.
5. M. LaVelle, "Big Tobacco Rises from the Ashes," *U.S.News & World Report,* November 13, 2000, 50.
6. *The World Book Encyclopedia,* vol. 18 (Chicago: World Book, Inc., 1984), 780.

Organizing
and Outlining
Your Speech

"Unless a capacity for thinking be
accompanied by a capacity for action,
a superior mind exists in torture."

—*Benedetto Croce*

- Identify the purposes and content of the three main parts of a speech.

- Select and appropriately state the main points of a speech.

- Assess seven patterns of organization and choose the one that best suits the topic and purpose of a speech.

- Use transitions, signposts, internal previews, and internal summaries to connect the thoughts in a speech.

- Compose an effective introduction and an effective conclusion for a speech.

- Prepare a complete sequence of preliminary, full-content, and presentational outlines for a speech.

- Use websites to find examples of outlines

SCENARIO

Becci has been the office manager for a department of fifty for thirty years. She must not only complete the work assigned to her but also oversee the work of others. In an ordinary day Becci will answer the phone a hundred times, make twenty-five calls, schedule appointments for her supervisor, supervise two secretaries and three clerks, secure equipment and supplies, and distribute mail. Becci works overtime on many occasions simply to get caught up with everything. When asked about the most necessary characteristics for her job, Becci says, "I have a great clerical staff who work well together and who are excellent workers—that's very important. I drive forty miles from home to work each day, and that gives me time to plan my beginning of the day speech and organize the tasks in my mind. I have to be super organized, or we would accomplish very little in this department. I run a staff meeting each week and give a speech about what has to be done, by whom, and by when. My speech includes my appreciation for the work the staff does every day and a complete listing of what I know has to be done by the end of the week. I also talk about the unexpected items of business that come up and how we'll handle that as a staff. My speech must be planned and organized or it won't help the staff understand the importance of our work." ■

Becci is responsible for a great deal in her office. As she noted, planning and organization are key to the successful operation of her department. Becci knows from past experience that worthwhile endeavors require advanced planning and careful organization, and that her weekly speech must be very carefully planned and organized in order to get all the work done in the right way and at the right time. Even such a simple activity as baking cookies requires planning and organization—if you want the cookies to taste good, that is. The first step is to choose a recipe. This step is similar to

The thought and time you put into finding the most effective organization for your presentation will result in a speech that is interesting and makes sense to your audience.

selecting a topic for a speech. The second step is to assemble all the ingredients. This corresponds to a speaker's research. The third step is to combine the ingredients to make the batter in the order and manner described in the recipe. If you randomly put ingredients into a bowl or onto a cookie sheet and bake them, your chances of creating a delicious batch of cookies diminishes dramatically. Correspondingly, if you randomly combine pieces of information, your chances of creating a meaningful and effective speech also diminish. So, whether you are planning and organizing the workload for a department of fifty, baking cookies, or developing a speech, success is more likely if you organize the task effectively.

We have already discussed selecting a speech topic; stating the general purpose, specific purpose, and thesis; analyzing the audience; and gathering information. These are all crucial steps in the speech-making process. But for a speech to make sense, it must be organized. In this chapter we examine how to bring all the parts of your speech together through organizing and outlining.

Organizing your speech involves arranging its parts into a systematic and meaningful whole. Once you have thoroughly researched your topic, you can simplify your writing task by carefully organizing your material. All speeches are organized into three main parts: introduction, body, and conclusion. By this point, you have determined your speech's general and specific purposes and have begun to think about your thesis statement. This should help guide you in the organizing process. Because the body is the main part of any speech, containing most of its content, we recommend that students begin by working on the body and only later write the introduction and conclusion. Thus we examine the body first.

Organize the Body of Your Speech

The **body** of a speech presents the main content, and organizing it will help you formulate your thesis statement. To ensure that the body of your speech is well organized, your content must be divided into main points that are thoughtfully selected and stated; limited in number; and carefully ordered, connected, and supported.

Develop the Main Points

Well-developed **main points,** the principal subdivisions of a speech, are critical to defining your thesis statement. Assume that the specific purpose of your speech is to inform your audience about the most significant causes of the spread of viral and bacterial infections. To determine the main points and help finalize your thesis, ask yourself two questions:

1. What causes the spread of infectious diseases?
2. Which causes contribute most significantly to the spread of such infections?

By asking these questions, *if* you have thoroughly researched your subject, you can determine the main points of your speech. The following is an example:

Main Points

    I. Germs are everywhere, carried in the air, on surfaces, and by living creatures (including us).

   II. The spread of germs through different types of contact causes viral and bacterial infections.

The structure of the body of the speech will take shape around these two main points. The main points are derived from research on the causes of infection. If the research had indicated more than two factors that contribute significantly to outbreaks of infection such as colds, influenza, and strep throat, each significant cause would have been an additional main point.

Remember that every piece of information you have gathered does not constitute a main point. Main points are broad, overarching statements that help organize the many particulars you have found through research. For example, statements such as colds can be spread through sneezing, and germs can be killed with disinfectants are not main points.

Relate Main Points, Specific Purpose, and Thesis.   The main points serve as the basis for the thesis statement. Together, the specific purpose and the thesis will determine the direction of the speech. Here is the thesis resulting from the main points noted earlier:

Specific purpose: To inform the audience about the most significant causes of viral and bacterial infections.

Thesis: The presence of germs all around us and the spread of those germs cause infections such as colds, influenza, and strep throat.

Making Connections

Develop Purpose Statements and the Thesis

You have been assigned to give an informative speech in your communication class. Your instructor wants you to choose a topic that might be presented in the workplace. Choose one of the following topics. Then write a general purpose statement, a specific purpose statement, and a thesis statement for it. Explain in writing why you think these statements are appropriate for the topic. (Because you haven't researched the subject extensively, you may have to make an educated guess or two.) Then swap your list with a classmate. Evaluate each other's statements, noting what the main points of the speech might be, based on the thesis statement.

1. Making presentations about the company to community organizations
2. The benefits of company-provided health insurance
3. Positive and negative aspects of offering child care on the company premises
4. On-the-job safety measures
5. Your choice of a topic related to the workplace

Here is another example of developing purpose, thesis, and main points. Student Nicki Schneider stated her specific purpose as follows: to inform the audience of the effects of special interest groups on legislation related to drinking and driving. Here is Nicki's thesis statement: MADD (Mothers Against Drunk Drivers) is a drinking and driving awareness organization that has influenced our society, as evidenced through the organization's purpose, activities, and impact on legislation. Nicki's purpose and thesis establish three main points: the purpose, activities, and impact of MADD. She will develop these points to create the body of her speech.

Suppose you have been assigned to give a speech that will persuade your audience to adopt a particular point of view. From your research on computers and your belief that they are making our society impersonal, you decide to discuss the harmful effect computers have on interpersonal relationships. The main points for this speech do not evolve as readily as they did in the previous examples, because you are not reporting facts only but are developing what may at first seem to be a rather general, broad concept into a tightly organized, compelling argument.

As you begin to think about and research your topic, you will also refine your specific purpose. To do this, first state your general purpose: to persuade my audience that computers can be harmful to interpersonal relationships. Then ask yourself why, specifically, computers are harmful to relationships. As you generate answers, the main points of your speech will begin to emerge. You eventually pinpoint two key reasons that support your view: Computers are mere machines that cannot respond to us as other humans do, and using computers limits the amount of personal contact people have. At this point you are ready to refine your specific purpose and state your thesis and main points.

Specific purpose: To persuade my audience that computers harm interpersonal relationship development in two specific ways.

Thesis: Although computers are commonly used in college and in the workplace, they can be detrimental to relationships because they are inanimate machines and because they limit our contact with others.

Main points: (I) Computers are harmful because they demand our time and concentration, but as machines they do not respond and react as other humans do in the context of a relationship, and (II) computers are harmful because we spend so much time working with them that they seriously limit the time we spend in personal contact with others.

Present the Main Points. Main points, like the specific purpose and thesis, should be carefully developed and written. They should also be specific, vivid, relevant, and parallel in structure. (We use Roman numerals to designate main points because, as you will see later, they eventually become the main elements in the speech outline.)

Be Specific. The more specific the main points, the less confusion they will create and the more meaningful they will be to an audience. It can be easy to misunderstand a speaker who makes vague, overgeneralized statements. Each main point in a speech should also be independent of the others and simple to understand. Compare the following:

Ineffective Main Point

I. Nuclear power is the most efficient fuel used in our society, but historically it has been misunderstood by most people.

Effective Main Points

   I. Nuclear power is the most efficient fuel used in our society.

   II. Nuclear power historically has been misunderstood by most people.

As you can see the first example contains two ideas in one point, which makes it too complicated. The second example divides the two ideas into two separate points, thus making each one easier to understand.

Use Vivid Language.   In Chapter 4, we discussed the importance of language choice. When you listen to or present speeches, you become aware of language. The more vivid the main points, the more likely they are to create interest. Main points should be thought-provoking, attention-grabbing ideas that stand out from the supporting materials. It is more vivid to say "College student Brandi Russell says the proposed federal law requiring parental notification for birth control use would create a ludicrous situation for college students under age eighteen who are on their own" than to say "The proposed federal regulation requiring family planning clinics that receive federal funds to notify parents of anyone under the age of eighteen who wishes to use birth control devices would have a devastating effect on teenagers."

Vivid phrasing should not, however, become overblown or exaggerated. Such language may hurt the speaker's credibility. The limits of good taste and ethical considerations should be taken into account.

Show Relevance.   Main points that are relevant to the audience's immediate interests encourage greater involvement and empathy. For instance, instead of saying "Air pollution has reached high levels," say "Air pollution in our city has reached high levels." Using direct references to the audience, whenever possible, increases the link between you, what you are saying, and your audience. Audience members like to know how the speaker's subject relates to them and why they should listen.

Create Parallel Structure.   Main points should be expressed in parallel structure, that is, using similar grammatical patterns and wording, when possible. For example,

Not Parallel

   I. Child pornography has been a serious problem in our community.

   II. Our community is experiencing increased amounts of child pornography.

   III. Child abuse has increased because of the pornography in our community.

Parallel

   I. Child pornography has been a serious problem in our community.

   II. Child pornography has increased in our community.

   III. Child pornography has caused an increase in child abuse in our community.

Parallel structure of the main points makes material easier to develop and to remember. Audiences usually have only one opportunity to hear a speech; therefore, anything you can do to make the main points stand out from the rest of the content is to your benefit. In addition, the speaker strengthens the bond with the audience by consistently using the phrase "our community" in each of the three main points.

Limit the Number of Main Points. The number of main points in your speech will depend on at least three considerations:

1. The time available to deliver the speech
2. The content to be covered in the speech, especially the amount and complexity of the supporting materials required for each point
3. The amount of information that the audience can reasonably comprehend and remember

The time available for most classroom speeches is limited by practical considerations. As a result, most classroom speeches have no more than five main points, and the majority have two or three.

Try to balance the amount of time that you devote to each main point. For example, if you are assigned a five- to seven-minute speech, plan to allow about two minutes for the introduction and conclusion, distributing the remaining time equally among the main points. Of course, this is only a guideline. It isn't always possible to balance the main points exactly, nor should you. The nature of some speech topics requires that some main points be emphasized more than others.

An audience should be able to sort out and recall each main point. This recall is impossible if there are too many points. Common sense tells us that three points are easier to remember than five. Thus, as a speaker, you must set reasonable expectations for both you and your listeners. If you have too many main points and a limited amount of time, you will be unable to develop each point thoroughly enough to make it clear, convincing, and memorable. Instructors are not arbitrary and capricious in their demand that you stay within the time limits for your assignments; they realize that all presentations inside and outside the classroom have time limits. You need to carefully consider and adhere to the time limits for classroom speeches, because most presentations you give in the workplace, in organizations of which you are a member, and in groups in your place of worship will have a time limit.

Order the Main Points

Once you've identified your main points, you must decide the order in which to present them. This takes serious analysis, because the order determines your speech's structure and strategy. The most effective order of presentation depends on the topic, the purpose, and the audience. Several basic patterns of presentation have been recommended and used over the years: time sequence, spatial, topical, problem–solution, cause–effect (or effect–cause), and motivated sequence. Other cultures and co-cultures, however, use alternative organizational patterns that are very effective. Many Native Americans, African Americans, and women, for example, use narrative or storytelling as a way of organizing their presentations. Many speakers effectively use a combination of one or more organizational patterns in a given speech. Until you're confident in your ability to organize your thoughts, you may wish to use one primary organizational pattern in any given speech.

The Time-Sequence Pattern. In the **time-sequence pattern,** or chronological pattern, the presentation begins at a particular point in time and continues either forward or backward. The key is to follow a natural time sequence and avoid jumping haphazardly from one date to another. This pattern is especially useful for tracing the steps in a process, the relationships within a series of events, or the development of ideas. Topics such as the history of photographic technology, the steps in setting up an advertising display, and the development of the computer in today's society lend themselves to the time sequence. Here is an example of a time sequence that moves forward from a specific period of time.

Main Points

I. In 1787 the drafters of the U.S. Constitution created the electoral system.

II. In 1804 Congress enacted and the states ratified the Twelfth Amendment, providing for separate electoral votes for president and for vice president.

III. In 1877 the Electoral Commission was created because of a dispute about the 1876 election.

IV. In 1887 Congress enacted a law that gave the states almost exclusive power to resolve all controversies regarding the selection of the presidential electors.

V. In 1961 the Twenty-Third Amendment, which permits residents of the District of Columbia to vote for three electors in the same manner as the residents of the states, was adopted.

A reverse-order time sequence begins at a specific period of time and works chronologically backward. For example, a speech discussing advertising trends in the auto industry, organized in reverse-order time sequence, could start as follows:

Main Points

I. In the 1990s advertisements emphasized safety.

II. In the 1980s advertisements emphasized fuel economy.

III. In the 1970s advertisements emphasized how well a car rode.

IV. In the 1960s advertisements emphasized the size of the car.

The time-sequence pattern can also be used to explain a process. Topics such as the development of the space industry, how to make computer-presentation aids, how to use CPR in an emergency, and how to water-ski all have specific steps that must be presented in the correct sequence if the result is to be successful.

The Spatial Pattern. In a **spatial pattern** of presentation, the content of a speech is organized according to relationships in space. This method is especially appropriate for presentations describing distances, directions, or physical surroundings. For example, a spatial pattern might be used to describe each area in a factory floor plan, the floor-by-floor plans for a building, or how to get from one location to another by moving from east to west, north to south, center to outside, clockwise, and so on. A spatial pattern describes the relationships between all the main points. Here is an example of main points organized according to a spatial pattern:

Main Points

I. The southeastern part of the country was devastated by Hurricane Andrew.

II. The midwestern part of the country was devastated by flooding.

III. The southwestern part of the country was devastated by wind and fire.

IV. The northwestern part of the country was devastated by drought.

Both time-sequence and spatial patterns are well suited to informative speeches.

Former White House press secretary Jim Brady, who was shot during the attempted assassination of President Reagan, gives a persuasive speech about gun control. Speakers who are attempting to persuade often use problem-solution, cause-effect, or the motivated sequence to organize their speeches.

The Topical Pattern.   According to the **topical pattern,** the main topic is divided into a series of related subtopics. Each subtopic becomes a main point in the speech, and all main points are joined to form a coherent whole. In this way, the topical pattern is a unifying structure.

The topical pattern is most likely to be used when none of the other patterns of organization can be applied to the topic or purpose of a speech. Topics such as the benefits of running, study habits that can improve your grades, uses of the video camera, and barriers to effective listening can easily be organized using the topical pattern. Here is how the topical pattern could be used to organize the main points of a speech about the barriers to effective listening:

Main Points

 I. Language distractions are barriers to effective listening.

 II. Factual distractions are barriers to effective listening.

 III. Mental distractions are barriers to effective listening.

 IV. Physical distractions are barriers to effective listening.

When the topical pattern is used correctly, each main point is parallel in structure and related to the others. Because the topical pattern is versatile, it can be adapted to most speech purposes and can effectively present material related to a variety of topics.

The Problem–Solution Pattern.   A speech that follows the **problem-solution pattern** usually has two main points: the problem and the suggested solution. The problem is defined as a need, doubt, uncertainty, or difficulty, and the suggested solution remedies or eliminates the problem without creating other problems. A problem–solution approach could be used to address topics such as the lack of a sufficient exercise facility for students, the discovery that the new student computer labs cannot be open during the evenings, uncertainty that a new crime prevention program will work, and the belief that the university provides insufficient experiential learning opportunities for students.

The problem–solution pattern, correctly used, should do more than state a problem and a solution; it should help the audience understand both the problem and the solution and why the solution will work. For example, a speech advocating change in the university's policies toward violence might follow this problem–solution pattern:

Problem

 I. The past two semesters have seen a significant increase in violent crimes against students on campus.

Solution

 II. A volunteer security force must be instituted by students to help protect one another from violent crime on the campus.

The problem–solution pattern usually includes three to five of the following:

 1. *A definition and description of the problem,* including its symptoms and size

2. *A critical analysis of the problem,* including causes, current actions, and requirements for a solution

3. *Suggestions of possible solutions,* including a description of each solution's strengths and weaknesses

4. *A recommendation of the best solution,* including a thorough justification of its superiority over other proposed solutions

5. *A discussion of the best solution put into operation,* including a description of how the plan can be implemented

The Cause–Effect Pattern. In the **cause–effect pattern,** the speaker explains the causes of an event, problem, or issue and discusses its consequences. Causes and effects may be presented in two different sequences. A speaker may either describe certain forces or factors and then show the results that follow from them, or describe conditions or events and then point out the forces or factors that caused them.

Consider this example of using the cause–effect pattern to discuss the effects of computers on students' job placement. A speaker might begin by recounting recent developments in computer procedures that have led to a more accurate analysis of students' skills, and then show that, as a result, the number of students who have obtained first jobs in their chosen fields has increased dramatically. Or, the speaker might reverse the process and first point out that the number of jobs that students are landing in their chosen fields is the result of more accurate computer analysis of their skills.

Regardless of the exact sequence, a speech organized by cause and effect has two main points—a description of the factors that are the *cause* and a prediction of identification of the subsequent *effect,* or vice versa. Topics such as eating disorders in young adults, television violence, heart disease, and new approaches to improving memory all lend themselves to the use of the cause–effect pattern.

Using the cause–effect pattern, a speech on the need to raise taxes to support education might be arranged in either of the following ways:

Cause

 I. School officials have planned poorly, overspent, and mismanaged tax dollars since 1996.

Effect

 II. Because of the mishandling of tax dollars, tuition was raised to compensate for the resulting shortfall.

Or

Effect

 I. Without a tuition increase, several programs will have to be cut from the university.

Cause

 II. Poor planning, overspending, and mismanagement of funds by school officials have been the primary contributors to the need for a tuition increase.

Because the cause–effect pattern can be used in a variety of ways, it is a useful format for either informative or persuasive speeches. As long as the cause can be directly related to the effect that you are trying to prove, this pattern is an excellent choice

Thinking About Speeches

Siegrun has been assigned an informative presentation on a topic of her own choice in her French class next month. Siegrun has a wonderful command of the French language but believes that she needs help in organizing her speech. Because she has never been in a speech class, Siegrun asks you for help.

1. What will you tell Siegrun about general purpose, specific purpose, and thesis statements?
2. How would you explain organizational patterns?
3. What advice will you give her about choosing an organizational pattern?

for many different topics and a beneficial means of reaching your listeners.

The Motivated Sequence Pattern. A widely used pattern of organization for the persuasive speech is the **motivated sequence,** developed by Professor Alan H. Monroe of Purdue University in the 1930s.[1] This pattern is specifically designed to help the speaker combine sound logic and practical psychology and is briefly mentioned again in Chapter 12. (We cover the idea in this chapter because it is an organizational strategy, but you may wish to refer back to this section as you read Chapter 12.) The motivated sequence is particularly effective because it follows the human thinking process and motivates listeners to take action. The sequence has five steps: attention, need, satisfaction, visualization, and action.

1. *Attention.* In the first step, the persuader attempts to create an interest in the topic so that the audience will want to listen. This step takes place in the introduction and follows the guidelines for an effective presentation. The speaker is subtly saying, "Please pay attention. This is important to you."

2. *Need.* In the second step, the persuader focuses on the problem by analyzing the things that are wrong and relating them to the audience's interests, wants, or desires. At this point the speaker is saying, "This is wrong, and we must do something about it."

3. *Satisfaction.* In the third step, the persuader provides a solution or plan of action that will eliminate the problem and thus satisfy the audience's interests, wants, and desires. The speaker is saying, "What I have to offer is the way to solve the problem."

4. *Visualization.* In the fourth step, the persuader explains in detail how the solution will meet the audience's need. The speaker's message now becomes, "This is how my plan will work to solve the problem, and if you accept my solution, things will be much better."

5. *Action.* In the fifth and final step, the persuader asks the audience for a commitment to put the proposed solution to work. The speaker basically concludes by saying, "Take action!"

The following is an example of a motivated sequence outline:

Specific purpose | *To persuade my audience to act now to prevent skin cancer*

Introduction

Attention | I. Approximately 700,000 new cases of skin cancer are diagnosed every year.

	Body
Need	II. Prevention schemes are most important in dealing with skin cancer because treatment requires often painful, long-term follow-up.
Satisfaction	III. Frequent skin inspections and avoiding overexposure to the sun are two surefire ways to reduce the risk of skin cancer.
Visualization	IV. It is vital to do frequent (once every three months) self-exams on preexisting skin markings to detect any changes. Also, one must avoid the dangerous ultraviolet rays (UVR) from the sun and artificial devices such as tanning booths.
Action	V. Minimize your exposure to the sun, avoid tanning salons, inspect your skin frequently, and use fresh, proper sunscreens to prevent skin cancer from claiming your life!

The motivated sequence is most often used in persuasion. It is also commonly used by advertisers because it works well in "selling" ideas.

Choosing the Best Pattern.   We have emphasized the importance of matching the pattern of organization to your topic, specific purpose, and thesis. You must also consider another key factor—your audience. The wise speaker anticipates responses from the audience. Thus, if your audience analysis indicates that important questions or objections are likely to be raised, you should arrange your main points to meet those objections. For example, if you are advocating that a lottery be legalized in your community and are certain that your audience is likely to ask whether a lottery will bring crime into the community, you might structure your presentation as follows:

Main Points

   I. Lotteries are one of the most economical ways to raise revenues.

  II. Lotteries are cost efficient.

 III. Lotteries are crime free.

No matter what pattern you select, as a beginning speaker you should probably use only that pattern when sequencing your main points. As you become more proficient, you might wish to combine patterns.

Connect the Main Points

A conversation can move from one unrelated topic to another without losing meaning or impact, but for a speaker to communicate effectively with an audience, the thoughts in the speech must be systematically connected. The four most common connecting devices that speakers use, singly or in combination, are transitions, signposts, internal previews, and internal summaries.

Transitions.   Phrases and words used to link ideas are called **transitions.** They form a bridge between what has already been presented and what will be presented next. Transitions are typically used between the introduction and the body of a speech, between main ideas, between supporting materials and visual aids, and between the body and the conclusion. A transition can review information that has already been presented, preview information to come, or summarize key thoughts. Here are some typical transition statements that might be made in a speech:

Let me move on to my next point.

Now that I have discussed the history of the Internet, I would like to talk about its uses.

Turning now . . .

The final point I would like to make is . . .

Another example might be . . .

Keeping in mind these four items I discussed, we arrive at the following conclusion.

Signposts. Just as a traffic sign warns drivers about travel conditions, **signposts** are words, phrases, and short statements that let the audience know what is ahead. Here are some typical signposts:

Let me first illustrate . . .

My second point is . . .

To recap . . .

As you look at my chart . . .

Next . . .

Finally . . .

Questions can also be used as signposts:

Why does our tuition continue to increase?

What does this all mean for us?

How can we solve this problem?

Who, then, is responsible?

Such questions draw the audience's attention to a forthcoming answer.

A signpost not only prepares an audience for what to expect next but also alerts the audience that the upcoming information is important. For example

The most essential aspect of this is . . .

Let's look at possible solutions to . . .

The only thing you need to know is . . .

Internal Previews. Short statements called **internal previews** give advance warning, or a preview, of the point(s) to be covered. Here is an example, "Next we'll look at possible solutions to the problem of budget shortfalls."

Internal Summaries. An **internal summary** is a short review statement given at the end of a main point. For example

Let me briefly summarize what I have said so far. In a time of fewer dollars from the legislature, and rising costs, finances become very tight. For every percentage point of budget shortfall, we must raise tuition by 4 percent. We must convince the governor and the legislature to provide more funding for the university.

Support the Main Points

Main points by themselves are nothing more than assertions. An audience needs supporting and clarifying material in order to accept what a speaker says. It is crucial that each main point be supported and that the support be relevant and logically organized. When supporting materials are included, the body of a speech expands to outline form, in which the main points are followed by subpoints, which in turn may be broken into further supporting points.

Main point

Support and clarifying
material

I. Colleges in the United States are recruiting international students

   A. Colleges and universities are trying to diversify

      1. According to *U.S. News and World Report,* 11/27/2000, p. 68, there were fewer than 180,000 international undergraduate students in 1987.

      2. The number increased to 222,000 by 1993.

      3. By 1999, there were nearly 240,000 undergraduates from abroad in U.S. college classrooms.

Supporting materials should be clearly related to the specific purpose, thesis, and main points of the speech.

Organize the Introduction of Your Speech

Experienced speakers often develop their introductions after, not before, the body of the speech. An **introduction** includes opening statements that serve two important functions: motivating the audience to listen and orienting them to the subject. Thus, your introduction should prepare your audience for the main ideas of your speech by setting the stage for the topic.

Your introduction should be based on the information you gathered in your audience analysis. If your analysis was accurate and thorough, you should have a pretty good understanding of your audience's frame of reference and how it might differ from your own. Your introduction should meet these three goals:

1. Orient the audience to the topic
2. Motivate the audience to listen
3. Forecast (preview) the main points

Orient the Audience to the Topic

Decide how much background information to provide based on what your audience knows or does not know about your subject. This is the appropriate time to gain

Nobel prize author Toni Morrison is a world-renowned novelist who has many resources she can call on to arouse the interest of an audience. She might refer to the subject or occasion, tell stories, use personal and biographical information, present a startling statement, use humor, read passages from her work, or ask rhetorical questions.

attention, state your specific purpose and thesis statement, and define terms, if necessary, that are essential to understanding the speech.

Several approaches can be used to gain attention and arouse the interest of your audience, including referring to the subject or occasion, using personal references or narratives, asking rhetorical questions, presenting a startling statement, using humor, or using quotations. You should carefully choose these devices to fit the audience, occasion, and context. None is always effective, and each has limitations. For example, using humor to focus your listeners' attention on a serious topic such as cancer would not be effective. Consider the overall speech as you choose your approach, because all parts of the speech must fit together well to achieve your desired purpose.

Refer to the Subject or Occasion.   You may be asked to speak on a special occasion such as a holiday, founders' day, graduation, or an anniversary. Here is a sample attention-getter related to an occasion:

> I am honored to have been asked to give a speech in celebration of Public Education Week. This is truly a special occasion, because our public educational system has made this community what it is today.

Use Personal References or Narratives.   Whenever you can relate your own experience to a speech, do so. Personal experiences make your speech more meaningful to your audience and show them that you know your subject. Here is how a speaker used a personal experience to introduce his speech on convenience food packaging.

> In a recent investigation of my wastebasket, I discovered an empty yogurt container, a cup of microwavable Cheeze Whiz, a hand pack of Teddy Grahams, a V-8 sip box, and a single serving of raisins. It appears that I, like many Americans, have fallen into the ocean of garbage created in our society by convenience foods and their plastic packaging.[2]

Ask Rhetorical Questions.   A rhetorical question is a question for which no answer is expected. Asking rhetorical questions in an introduction usually encourages an audience to become intellectually involved. (Asking real questions is also an effective way to get your audience interested in and involved in the speech, but it is important to let the audience know that you intend to get answers from them when asking this type of question.) Such questions can also be used to create suspense. Here is one example of rhetorical questions used to involve the audience.

> Have you ever gone through a day feeling like you're missing something? What would you say if I told you that your health may be at risk if you stay up half the night? Each of us probably suffers from a sleep deficit every day even though we may not realize it. New research reported in the October 16, 2000, issue of *U.S.News and World Report* suggests that sleep is the third essential component of a long and healthy life, up there with a good diet and regular exercise.[3]

Present a Startling Statement.   A startling statement can be used when you want to shock or surprise your audience. Startling statements are extremely effective at getting attention, as shown by this example, "The harsh reality is this: party time is over!" Startling stories can also be used to get your audience's attention:

> Big Dan's Tavern certainly didn't appear to be anything special to the mother of two who crossed its threshold for the first time to make a simple purchase. Try as she may, though, she will never forget the barroom, because when the youthful mother entered it—her nightmare began. She endured more shame and terror that night than most of us probably will ever have to face. She was stripped, assaulted, and raped by four men for over an hour. She pleaded for mercy or aid and yet more than fifteen other bar patrons simply stood and watched the spectacle. One man brushed aside her pleading hands as he moved out of the way. Another helped hold her on the pool table for the convenience of the attackers. Many cheered and applauded, but no one called the police.[4]

Use Humor.   A funny story or relevant joke not only gains the attention of your audience but also relaxes them. Stories and jokes must be tied to the content of the speech and not offered simply for the sake of humor. One speaker began his talk as follows:

> The last time I gave a speech to this large a group, an audience member raised his hand in the back row and shouted, "I can't hear you." Immediately, a hand went up in the front row, and the person asked, "Can I move back there?" Now I know all of you want to hear me, so I'll try to speak loud enough so that you can understand what I have to say about becoming familiar with the room in which your speech will be made so that you know how to present your ideas.

Use Quotations.   Sometimes a quotation can grab your audience's attention, and if cited accurately, it can also add to the believability of your speech. A student talking about the future started her speech as follows.

> Lew Lehr, the former president of the 3M Company, one of the companies cited in the popular best-seller *In Search of Excellence,* wrote, "The future belongs to those who see opportunity where others see only problems." The future is ours, but we must see it as an opportunity to excel. Our college education equips us for this opportunity. Today, I want to talk to you about what the twenty-first century will bring to each of us.

Whatever you choose to gain attention and maintain interest in your introduction, it should be relevant and orient the audience to the topic.

THE FAR SIDE   By GARY LARSON

The class was quietly doing its lesson when Russell, suffering from problems at home, prepared to employ an attention-getting device.

State the Specific Purpose and Thesis.   After getting your audience's attention you need to state the specific purpose and thesis statement of your speech. Both the specific purpose and thesis statement were discussed in detail earlier in this chapter. Sometimes the specific purpose and thesis statement are best stated together; sometimes it is appropriate to state the specific purpose at the beginning and the thesis toward the end of the introduction, where it serves as a preview of the speech. By stating the specific purpose and thesis, you are orienting your topic to the audience and giving them a clear indication of where you are headed with your speech. Also, this preview is essential in helping your audience recall what you said, because they have only one opportunity to hear your message.

Motivate the Audience to Listen

Design your introductory comments to gain the attention and interest of your audience. You must hold their interest and attention throughout the entire presentation, but that task will be easier if you can capture them by making the topic significant and important to them and by establishing your credibility.

A standard way of making your topic relevant is simply to point out the reasons for presenting your speech. It is important that the audience find a reason to listen to the speech as early in the speech as possible. You should also consider whether it is necessary to establish your credibility in speaking on the topic you have selected.

Credibility refers to a speaker's believability based on the audience's evaluation of the speaker's competence, experience, and character. If, for example, Madonna (singer, entertainer, actor) wanted to speak on health care or violence in our society, she would have to establish her credibility on the subject by relating the subject to herself and by indicating how she became an expert on the topic.

Forecast the Main Points

Before you finish introducing your speech, let the audience know what you will cover in the speech itself. This is known as "forecasting" and it affords listeners a "road map" so they know where you will take them in the remainder of your speech. Forecasting helps your audience be better listeners.

Let's look at some sample introductions. The following portions show you how to orient and motivate your listeners, and forecast the main points of your speech:

Orienting material | "Employers are looking for students who have higher levels of complex, critical thinking skills," says Phil Gardner, author of the Twenty-Ninth Annual Recruiting Trends survey.

Further, Gardner says, "Not only is the labor market poised to expand, but all academic majors will benefit from the increase in hiring levels. This is very good news for college graduates. If they are qualified, they should find a job."

Motivating material

College graduates with public speaking skills and a high level of computer proficiency will be among the most highly sought job candidates this year and well into the future. As in the past, the employers surveyed said they are seeking solid communication abilities, computer aptitude, leadership, and teamwork skills. Employers now are placing more emphasis on public speaking and presentation abilities. For these reasons, it is necessary to learn more about how we can be more competent communicators.

Forecasting of main points

As in the past, today's employers are looking for specific skills. In my speech, I will describe the specific communication abilities, as well as the public speaking and presentational skills, employers identified as critical to career success.[5]

Can you label the specific parts of the previous introduction? Now look at the following example. The specific parts are labeled for you.

Orienting material (attention-getter)

Twenty-five-year-old Scott Wilson, a gardener at a Florida condominium, accidentally sprayed the herbicide he was using on his face and hands. He had used chemicals many times in the past and that's why he simply washed his face and hands and returned to work—even though his shirt was still dripping wet. Five days later, Scott Wilson was rushed to the hospital, barely breathing.

Motivating material (definition of term)

(significance of topic)

Paraquat, the herbicide that Wilson was using, kills plants within hours by disrupting the photosynthetic process, causing individual cells to collapse. Paraquat, in diluted form, is also a herbicide of choice for thousands of home gardeners. Its brand name is Ortho Spot Weed and Grass Control.[6]

The next introduction accomplishes several functions at one time—it gets attention, it relates the topic directly to the audience and to the speaker, it establishes the speaker's credibility on the topic, and it notes the main points of the speech.

Rhetorical question
Citing research to establish credibility
Relating topic to audience
Establishing credibility
Thesis and forecasting of main points

What do you fear most? Surveys conducted over the past twenty years suggest that Americans' greatest fears were death, accidents, and heights. Most, however, identify fear of public speaking as their absolute greatest fear. Most of us in this room would probably agree with this finding. Speaking is never easy, but the experiences I have had in the business world and in this class have made me more confident and a better speaker. Today I'd like to define speech anxiety, identify its causes and effects, and share ideas about how to control or reduce anxiety.

The following introduction was part of a college student's award-winning speech:

A Sample Introduction

Background and attention-getter

One year ago two of my professors, Steve and Mary, were involved in a head-on collision with a drunk driver. Steve was killed instantly. Mary was critically injured and was

Making Connections

Creating Introductions

The introduction is an important part of any presentation. Researchers tell us that the first fifteen seconds of the speech are critical to audience involvement in the presentation, and speakers need to make the introduction show the relevance of the speech topic to the audience members.

Here are three speech topics. For each topic, write a brief introduction that would gain your classmates' attention and make the topics relevant to them. Then, in the margin, mark which techniques you used to orient your classmates to each topic. Share your introductions with your classmates to see how well you did.

1. The Importance of Mammograms
2. Animal Rights
3. Rap Music

---

not expected to live. The case was especially tragic because Steve and Mary had two young daughters and no will. Without a will, the state was required to take possession of the children, despite the fact that friends and family were more than willing to raise them.

Reason to listen

Significance of topic

Relevancy

Specific purpose and thesis

Over 60 percent of all Americans die without a will, and most of us don't even consider writing a will until relatively late in life. To those of us in the prime of our lives, the thought of writing a will of our own seems morbid and unnecessary. That simply isn't true. The fact is that each of us needs some kind of will, and most of us don't have the least idea of how to go about writing one. After hearing me speak, I hope you will realize that having a will is important. Now, let's look at what a will is, why a will is necessary, the reasons people avoid writing a will, and finally, how to obtain a will.[7]

Guidelines

Develop Your Introduction

1. Keep the introduction relatively brief, making up only 5 to 10 percent of the speech's total content.

2. Allow plenty of time to prepare the introduction carefully. Because it is critical to the success of your speech, it should not be rushed or written at the last minute.

3. Make the introduction creative and interesting. To accomplish this, think of several possible introductions, and choose the most effective one.

4. As you research your speech, watch for material to use in the introduction. Keep a notebook or file of interesting quotations, stories, humorous statements, and other items that might give your opening some dazzle. But remember: A successful introduction *must* be relevant to the speech topic.

5. Develop the introduction after you have completed the main part of your speech. Relevant introductions are easier to create after you have determined the content and direction of the body.

6. Write out the introduction, word for word. This section of the speech is too important to improvise or leave to chance. In addition, knowing exactly what

you will say at the beginning of your speech will give you confidence and help you get off to a strong start. Then, practice delivering the introduction until you can present it conversationally, but flawlessly.

Organize the Conclusion of Your Speech

Your **conclusion** should focus your audience's thoughts on the specific purpose of your speech and bring your most important points together in a condensed and uniform way. Your conclusion should relate to your introduction, helping your audience make the connections between the various parts and points of the message. In persuasive speeches, you may also use your conclusion to spell out the action or policies you recommend to solve a problem. In every case, your conclusion should reinforce what you want your audience to remember.

Because your conclusion is as important as any other part of your presentation, you should give it the same amount of attention. Be especially careful to avoid adding new information in this part of the speech. Also, remember that you, as a speaker, have only one chance to get your message across to your audience. Repetition is an important strategy for helping listeners recall the important information you've presented. Your conclusion should

1. Let your listeners know that you are finishing the speech.
2. Make your thesis clear to your listeners.
3. Reinforce your purpose by reviewing your main points.
4. Leave your listeners with a memorable thought.
5. Tie everything together.

Making Connections

Writing Conclusions

The conclusion is important to you, the speaker, and to your audience. A conclusion leaves the listeners with something to "hang on to" so that they can remember your speech. Earlier you created introductions for three topics. Now, keeping in mind the guidelines we've provided, write conclusions for the topics. Identify how you might warn your classmates that the speech is ending and leave them with a memorable thought about the topic.

1. The Importance of Mammograms
2. Animal Rights
3. Rap Music

Share your conclusions with your classmates to see how well you did.

Show That You Are Finishing the Speech

You need to prepare your listeners for the end of your speech; otherwise they are "left hanging" and uncomfortable, sensing that something is missing. You should not bluntly state that you are finishing or even say, "In conclusion, ..." Instead, you should carefully and creatively indicate that the speech is winding down. An example might be, "As you have seen in this speech, there are ways we can become better listeners."

Make Your Thesis Clear

Repetition is important when you have only one chance for the listeners to hear your message. Be sure you creatively remind your listeners of your central idea, "As I stated early in my speech, effective listening is a highly valued skill that can be learned."

Review the Main Points

Repeating the main points of a speech is particularly helpful any time you want your audience to remember your main points. For example, the speaker who informed her audience about barriers to effective listening concluded her speech as follows:

> Let me review the barriers that have the most impact on our listening. They are language, factual, mental, and physical distractions. If you remember these and how they affect listening, you will be a more effective listener.

In addition to helping the audience remember your content, reviewing the speech reinforces both your purpose and the thesis statement.

End with a Memorable Thought

A memorable thought may include referring back to an attention-getting device, citing a quotation, or issuing a challenge or appeal. Citing a memorable quotation can be a good way to leave a lasting impression on your audience. When it is relevant and reinforces your thesis statement, a quotation can give your speech additional authority and help to increase your credibility. It is crucial that you always cite the source of all quoted information or any information that is not your own. (The importance of citing sources and the responsibilities of a speaker to cite sources are discussed in Chapter 10.) A student speaking on the right to die with dignity concluded her speech as follows:

> If we can adopt these two requirements, we can forever banish death as a grim reaper. As former New York Senator Jacob Javits said shortly before his death, "The right to die with dignity is profound, moral, and essential."[8]

If your purpose is to persuade, the conclusion may also include a challenge or appeal to action. The following conclusion recaps the main points and asks the listeners to take action:

> Sleep researchers are just beginning to understand what we have lost when we lose sleep. Our bodies change drastically when we're sleep deprived and there are many health risks. Our hormone levels change to the point that our energy levels are very low when we awaken and are actually comparable to the low morning levels usually associated with the elderly. Furthermore, sleep deprivation may lead to obesity, a decline in immune function, fuzzy thinking, and even to cancer risks. You need to change your schedules! You need at least eight hours of sleep. Plan your work so that you can always get a good night's rest. If you do get behind, take a nap! A short nap works best—about forty-five minutes and can

improve your health, your attitude, and your thinking. I urge you to take charge of your life. Get some sleep![9]

Develop Your Conclusion

1. The conclusion should be brief and should end with a definite summarizing statement. The conclusion should account for between 5 and 15 percent of the content of the speech.

2. The conclusion should not contain information that was *not* already mentioned in either the introduction or the body of your speech.

3. The preparation of the conclusion should not be rushed. Allow plenty of time to develop it, and write it carefully.

4. Leave your audience with an impact that will make your speech memorable. Think of several possible endings, and choose the one that best serves the purpose of your speech.

5. Write out the conclusion word for word. Then learn it well so that you can end your speech smoothly, conversationally, and confidently.

Signal your audience that your speech is nearing its end by using phrases such as "Today, we have examined . . . ," "In the past minutes we have examined . . . ," "Finally, let me say. . . ." Each prepares your audience for your concluding remarks. The following conclusion lets listeners know that the speech is nearly finished and it summarizes and synthesizes the major points covered. There is an appeal for action, and listeners are left with a memorable thought.

Signal of speech's end	Today I have shared with you some important points about skin cancer.
Summary of main points	It is important to understand the three types of skin cancer including risk factors and recognition of the tumors. Even though Americans love to get a nice tan, it is one of the most dangerous things that you can do in relation to getting skin cancer. There are some very specific things you can do in order to prevent skin cancer. First, you must minimize sun exposure by avoiding tanning salons and using fresh sunscreen appropriate for your skin type and the length of time you're in the sun. You must also be able to recognize the changes in the skin that may indicate skin cancer when you conduct self-exams every three months. With early detection most skin cancers are very curable. With a little knowledge and a little effort you can prevent skin cancer from claiming your life!
Appeal for action	
Memorable final thought	

Outline Your Speech

Outlining is one of the most difficult (and, therefore, mistakenly avoided) steps in preparing a speech. Outlining and organizing are similar terms. **Outlining** involves arranging the entire contents of a speech in a logical sequence and writing that sequence in a standardized form. The outline is often referred to as the blueprint or

Making Connections

Ordering Ideas in an Outline

For a speech entitled "Making Reading Your Hobby," rearrange the following sentences in proper outline form for the body. Make sure to arrange the content in a logical sequence. Place the number of each sentence in the proper place in the outline. (See page 256 to verify your answers.)

1. Low-cost rental libraries are numerous.
2. Reading is enjoyable.
3. It may lead to advancement in one's job.
4. Books contain exciting tales of love and adventure.
5. Many paperback books cost only $7.95 to $10.95.
6. People who read books are most successful socially.
7. Reading is profitable.
8. One meets many interesting characters in books.
9. Reading is inexpensive.

I. _____

   A. _____

   B. _____

II. _____

   A. _____

   B. _____

III. _____

   A. _____

   B. _____

skeleton of a speech. Organizing is arranging ideas or elements in a systematic and meaningful way. To organize your speech, select one of the patterns of organization discussed earlier in the chapter. Both organizing and outlining involve arranging information to form a meaningful sequence, but outlining is a more rigorous written process.

Outlining is more detailed than organizing and helps unify and clarify thinking, make relationships clear, and provide the proper balance and emphasis for each point as it relates to the specific purpose of a speech or written paper. Outlining also helps ensure that information is both accurate and relevant.

As you prepare your outline, you will gain an overview of your entire presentation. Developing an outline should help you gauge the amount of support you have for each of your main points and identify any points that need further development. The actual process of outlining usually requires three steps:

1. Create a preliminary outline that identifies the topic and the main points to be covered in the speech.
2. Expand the preliminary outline into a full-content outline that clearly and fully develops the speech's content.
3. Condense the full-content outline into a presentational outline to aid delivery.

The Preliminary Outline

A **preliminary outline** is a list of all the points that may be used in a speech. Suppose you are preparing a four- to six-minute informative speech on the development, uses, and benefits of femtosecond technology.[10] Because of the limited amount of time, you know you cannot possibly cover everything related to the topic. And, because your general purpose is to persuade, you need to focus the content of your speech in that direction. So, recalling what you have already read about topic selection, audience analysis, gathering information, and using supporting and clarifying materials, you determine your specific purpose: To inform my audience about femtosecond technology, its development, its uses, and its benefits. Based on this specific purpose, you can prepare a preliminary outline of possible main points, as shown in the following sample preliminary outline. Once your possible main points are arranged in this way, you will find it easier to analyze your thoughts. You can then decide exactly which main thoughts to include in your speech and choose the best order for presenting them. Here is what your preliminary outline might look like:

A Sample Preliminary Outline

Topic	Femtosecond technology
General purpose	To inform
Specific purpose	To inform my audience about the development of femtosecond technology and its uses and benefits

Possible main points

I. Sven Airinhouse hypothesized that there were many complex levels in a chemical reaction.

II. Professor Ahmed Zewail determined that science would have to create a faster way to measure time.

III. Zewail's research resulted in two types of machines: one capable of taking snapshots every femtosecond and a laser that can cut at a femtosecond pace.

IV. Femtosecond cutting is sharp, even, and smooth.

V. Femtosecond technology can be applied to medical and technical fields.

VI. Femtosecond technology can be used in dentistry.

VII. Femtosecond pulse laser procedure can be used to repair heart damage.

VIII. Data transmission will be enhanced by femtosecond technology.

IX. Obstacles need to be overcome.

The Full-Content Outline

A **full-content outline** is an expansion of the main points selected from the preliminary outline. The full-content outline is a detailed skeleton of a speech, with all main
and secondary points written in complete sentences. A full-content outline helps a
speaker clarify and polish his or her thoughts in the following ways:

1. It helps in the evaluation of each main point; a major point that cannot be written in a complete sentence is probably weak or invalid and does not belong in the
   speech.
2. Writing a complete sentence for each point requires thought.
3. The outline shows the flow of the speech and whether the sequence is logical and
   effective.
4. The outline helps to make each topic sentence clear and shows transitions from
   point to point.
5. The outline illustrates the relationship of each point to the specific purpose and enables the speaker to analyze how each point contributes to the total presentation.
6. The outline is a form of communication in itself that serves as an excellent summary
   of the text and can be used by others to see the main points of the presentation.

The full-content outline should close with a bibliography that lists all the
sources used in preparing the speech. The bibliography includes books, magazines,
interviews—any source that either the speaker or the listener might want to refer to
in order to learn more about the subject.

Because it serves so many purposes, a full-content outline is an essential part of
planning any speech. Writing a full-content outline is not necessarily an easy task. But
once the job is completed, the outline makes the rest of the preparation and delivery
of a speech much easier. The full-content outline of the speech on femtosecond technology shows the complete introduction and conclusion and the fully developed main
and secondary points and uses a topical pattern of organization.

Writing a Full-Content Outline

1. Cover the three main parts of your speech in your outline—introduction,
   body, and conclusion—adding appropriate transitions.
2. Identify each main point in your speech with a Roman numeral (I, II, and so
   on). Identify subpoints with capital letters, and successive levels of subpoints
   with Arabic numerals and lowercase letters.
3. Follow standard outline style to ensure consistency in symbols and indentation.
4. Use only one idea per numeral or letter.
5. State each main point as a single sentence.
6. All main points (with Roman numerals) should have subpoints (using capital
   letters). All main points and subpoints in full-content outlines should have at
   least two parts. That is, there should be no I without a II, no A without a B.
7. The body will usually contain two, three, or four items with Roman numerals.
8. Be sure the outline makes logical sense and that the different levels of numerals and letters really do represent a hierarchical arrangement of information.

Making Connections

Comparing Outlines—The Text and the Web

We have suggested that organizing and outlining are important parts of the speech process. Here is a web-based activity to provide a chance to analyze and evaluate speech outlines and speeches.

1. Access the Web.
2. Set your browser to "Ask Jeeves" at http://www.ask.com.
3. Ask Jeeves "How should I outline my speech?" You'll probably get six to eight responses.
4. Check out five of the responses, but do not include any responses that deal with outlining papers, such as "How to outline papers." What kinds of information are contained on the pages? What are the similarities between the responses to your web search and the ideas presented in the text? Differences? Who created this site? What are the qualifications of the web manager?
5. Check the "related searches" topics at the bottom of the page.
6. Go back and ask another question; this time, be more specific: "How do I outline informative speeches?"
7. If there is a "Suggested Speech Outline," click on that response.
8. Read the outline and compare its content with the guidelines provided in the text.
9. Click on "Sample Speech" at the bottom of the page, then read the speech.
10. What is the general purpose of the speech?
11. What organizational pattern is used?
12. Evaluate the introduction and conclusion of this sample speech, based on the information in this chapter.
13. Evaluate the speech and explain your rationale.

Title	**A Sample Full-Content Outline**
Topic	Development and Uses of Femtosecond Technology—A New Science to Give Us Time
General purpose	Femtosecond technology
Specific purpose	To inform
Thesis	To inform my audience about femtosecond technology, its development, its uses, and its benefits
Attention-getting	Scientists have created technology that is faster, better, and cooler and that will revolutionize everything from computers to advanced telecommunications to dentistry.
	Introduction
Explanation	In today's world, animation is big business. We have interactive CD-ROMs, DVDs, the Internet, and whatever story the people at Disney's historic revisionist department decides to debase this week! Back in earlier times, however, animation was much simpler. Each sheet of paper was a picture; moved rapidly, the pictures become an animation. Even the Disney blockbusters of today all boil down to this concept: a simple chain reaction of moving pictures. As early as the nineteenth century, scientists functioned under the same construct as animators, with all of chemistry boiled down to a series of simple chain reactions. The problem was that they could see only the individual molecules and the end product; there was no science capable of watching the reaction take

Significance of topic	place, like being unable to watch the pages turn. But, according to the February 6, 1998, *Science* magazine, researchers have finally been able to catch up with chemical reactions, literally. This new science is called femtosecond technology and is built around a new increment of time, equivalent to one quadrillionth, or .000000000000001, of a second, a femtosecond.
Thesis **Forecasting of main points**	So, why should this take time out of your day? Well, because the January 26, 1999, *Asia Pulse* magazine points out that femtosecond technology is promising to revolutionize everything from ultra-high-speed computers to advanced telecommunications to a trip to the dentist's office. So follow me to "Femtoland," where we'll first understand what a femtosecond is and how it is used; second, we'll examine femtosecond technology's applications; and finally, we'll look ahead to an everyday life that is so used to this technology it's as normal as a Disney cartoon.

Body

Main point	I. Sven Airinhouse hypothesized that there were many complex levels to chemical reactions.
Background	A. With nothing faster than a microscope, Sven could not prove it.
	B. It would take another 10 years for the femtosecond to herald a scientific breakthrough.
Transition	C. To understand its origins, we must look at two specific areas: how femtosecond technology came to be and how scientists have harnessed its power.
Second main point	II. Professor Ahmed Zewail of the California Institute of Technology looked for reasons some chemical reactions that look possible on paper do work and others do not.
Explanation	A. Zewail became convinced that the reason this discrepancy existed was simply because it was impossible to look at every stage of a reaction, making it unpredictable.
	B. For the next seven years, Zewail dedicated himself to finding a way to see every stage of a reaction.
	C. Using the most modern high-tech forms of scientific photography, Zewail could watch chemical reactions happening as quickly as a picosecond, one trillionth of a second.
Relevant supporting materials	1. This was still not fast enough to see every step.
	2. I am now about three minutes into my speech; about 180 quadrillion femtoseconds have already passed.
Third main point	III. Zewail's research resulted in two types of machines: one, a camera capable of taking snapshots of a chemical reaction every femtosecond and the other, a laser that can cut at a femtosecond pace.
Explanation	A. The machine looks like a tiny car wash.
	1. A group of molecules is placed at one end and put through the first stage, getting zapped by lasers, causing chemical reactions.
	a. At the other end, the molecules are completely different.
	b. A choice of scents is provided.

       c. A laser-powered camera snaps pictures at a femtosecond pace, creating a sort of animated film of how molecules interact and change.

     2. The same machine setup also works to cut at femtosecond pace.

       a. The laser slices through materials so rapidly there is no fray.

       b. The result is a smooth, even edge.

Significance

   B. Researchers created femtosecond technology to be able to know how chemicals react and, more important, to be able to control the reactions.

Transition

   C. When examining the current applications of this new science, it is important to look at them in two realms: medical and technical.

Fourth main point

IV. Femtosecond technology can be beneficially used in dentistry and medical applications.

Supporting materials

   A. Slow lasers that move at a nanosecond can cause teeth to crack or create random-shaped holes.

     1. Femtosecond lasers move so quickly they cause no damage to the tooth.

     2. This means fewer chances for infection, cavities, or later tooth loss.

Supporting materials

   B. Femtosecond lasers aid in vision correction, therapeutic eye surgery, and minor forms of heart surgery.

     1. Femtosecond pulse procedure allows drilling clean, small holes.

     2. Femtosecond procedures create fewer complications, faster healing, less pain, no infection, and no side effects.

Fifth main point

V. Modern technology is all about speed.

Supporting materials

   A. Computers and data transmission benefit from femtosecond technology.

     1. Computers and telecommunications instruments can now go three times faster.

     2. Optical disks will make floppies obsolete because they store more information more efficiently.

Information relevance

   B. Femtosecond technology is comparable to stepping on the moon for the first time.

Supporting materials

   C. Heart implants are currently metal.

     1. The human body often rejects metal parts.

     2. Femtosecond lasers are using different materials, including organic ones, to make transplants less painful and more successful.

   D. Laboratory researchers are experimenting with femtosecond technology for DNA Exploration and repair.

Internal summary

Scientific researchers are hoping that future development in the femtosecond laser pulse will help bring a clearer picture to this sub-atomic film strip, and become so commonplace that it is no longer expensive nor experimental.

Supporting materials

Significance of topic

Summary

Synthesis

Conclusion

Richard Johnson, noted chemist, wrote in the *Houston Chronicle,* "Dr. Zewail has given birth to a new era of chemistry." Although that may not seem important to those of us who couldn't care less about chemistry, the applications resulting from this new era will provide us with the ability to live better and longer lives. From the beginning of time, science has been measured in a series of steps. One scientist theorizes what is possible, and years later, the theories are proved true. By examining the origins of femtosecond technology, its current uses, and the applications of the future, it is clear that this was indeed the culmination of years of building from one idea to the next. Animators started out with stick figures and ended up with the seamless beauty of modern animation work. The femtosecond started with an observation and has ended up with the promise of faster, better, and just plain cooler technology. It didn't happen in a femtosecond, or even in the blink of an eye, but for scientists, that's okay. With this measurement, they have all the time in the world.

Bibliography

Asia Pulse, January 26, 1999.

Femtosecond Laser Pulses. 1999.

Houston Chronicle, May 6, 1997.

Houston Chronicle, October 27, 1998.

Laser Focus World, September 1, 1998.

London Independent, October 11, 1998.

Photochemistry and Photobiology, March, 1999.

Physics World, January 1, 1999.

PR Newswire, January 7, 1999.

Science, February 6, 1998.

Science, October 30, 1999.

The Presentational Outline

A **presentational outline** is a condensation of the full-content outline in which detail is minimized and keywords and phrases replace full sentences. This is the outline you will work from when you present your speech. The advantages of the presentational outline as a delivery aid are that it is concise, requires little space, and is comprehensible at a glance.

Your presentational outline should include your main points and sufficient clarifying and supporting material to aid you in making your presentation. The outline may also include your complete introduction and conclusion, although the choice is up to you. Keywords and phrases are important to use in a presentational outline because they will remind you of the points you want to make. Some speakers use codes, symbols, or even colors to remind them of key points, vocal pauses, changes in speaking rate, and so on. But remember, if your presentational outline is too long, complex, or detailed, you can easily get too involved in your notes and lose contact with your audience. The following example on femtosecond technology shows a concise, condensed outline.

A Sample Presentational OUtline

Topic	Development and Uses of Femtosecond Technology: A New Science to Give Us Time
General purpose	To inform
Specific purpose	To inform my audience about femtosecond technology, its development, its uses, and its benefits
Thesis	Scientists have created technology that is faster, better, and cooler and that will revolutionize everything from computers to advanced telecommunications to dentistry.
Reminders about delivery	SHARE! DON'T READ—TAKE A BREATH! SMILE AT AUDIENCE.

Introduction

I. Animation part of everyday lives.

    A. How animation works

    B. Chemistry very much like animation

    C. Rapid chemical reactions now seen with femtosecond technology

BRIEF PAUSE—TAKE A BREATH

MOVE SLIGHTLY, NATURALLY—SMILE!

II. New science, femtosecond technology, built around new increment of time, one quadrillionth, or (VA #1) .000000000000001, of a second.

SHOW VISUAL AID #1—POINT TO NUMBERS

    A. The January 26, 1999, *Asia Pulse*—femtosecond technology promising to revolutionize everything—ultrahigh-speed computers to advanced telecommunications to a trip to the dentist's office

    B. What a femtosecond is and how it is used, current applications, look ahead

PAUSE—TAKE A BREATH—MOVE SLIGHTLY

Body

I. Sven Airinhouse's hypothesis—many complex levels

    A. Sven could not prove

    B. One hundred and ten years for the femtosecond to herald a scientific breakthrough

    C. Two specific areas: how femtosecond technology came to be and how scientists have used it

PAUSE BRIEFLY

II. Professor Ahmed Zewail of the California Institute of Technology—account for discrepancies.

    A. Impossible to look at every stage of a reaction

    B. Find way to see every stage

Margin labels:

- Reminders about delivery
- Reminders about delivery
- Thesis (source)
- Help speaker remember
- Forecasting of main points of body
- Transition

    C. High-tech scientific photography—watch chemical reactions—picosecond, one trillionth of a second

        1. Still not fast enough

        2. Already spent 180 quadrillion femtoseconds

PAUSE—MOVE SLIGHTLY—LET AUDIENCE KNOW CHANGE

III. Zewail's research resulted in two types of machines: camera and laser.

    A. Machine like tiny car wash

        1. First stage

            a. Molecules completely different

            b. Choice of scents provided.

            c. Laser-powered camera

        2. Same machine setup—cuts at femtosecond pace

            a. Slices cleanly

            b. Leaves smooth, even edge

        B. Researchers seeking reactions and to control

Transition   C. Current applications: medical and technical

PAUSE

IV. Uses in dentistry and medicine

GET VISUAL AIDS READY

Supporting materials   A. Slow lasers move at nanosecond—damage teeth

SHOW VISUAL AID #2—POINT TO THE PICTURE

        1. Femtosecond lasers—move quickly no damage

        2. Fewer chances for infection, cavities, or later tooth loss

SHOW VISUAL AID #3—POINT TO IT

Supporting materials   B. Femtosecond lasers—vision correction, therapeutic eye surgery, and minor heart surgery

SHOW VISUAL AID #4—POINT OUT WHILE SPEAKING

        1. Allows drilling clean, small holes

        2. Creates fewer problems

SHOW VISUAL AID #5—POINT TO JAGGED HOLES

SLOW DOWN

Fifth main point   V. Modern technology-speed

Supporting materials   A Computers and data transmission benefit

        1. Computers and telecommunications three times faster

        2. Floppies obsolete—more information more efficiently

Information relevance	B. Comparable to first time on the moon
Supporting materials	C. Heart implants currently metal
	1. Body rejects
	2. Different materials for less pain, greater success
	D. Experiments with femtosecond for DNA exploration and repair
Internal summary	Scientific researchers and the future: clearer views, less expense, commonplace, not experimental
Delivery suggestions	<div align="center">PAUSE—LOOK AT ENTIRE AUDIENCE—SMILE.</div>
	Conclusion
Supporting materials	I. Richard Johnson, noted chemist, wrote in the *Houston Chronicle,* "Dr. Zewail has given birth to a new era of chemistry."
Significance of topic	A. The resulting applications will allow us to live better and longer lives.
Summary	B. Scientists theorizes and prove.
Synthesis	1. Uses and applications promise a better future.
	2. Scientists now have "all the time in the world!"

The presentational outline can be easily transferred onto note cards. Some speakers prefer to use note cards, and in many classroom situations students are required to use them. Figure 9.1 illustrates note cards that might be used in presenting your speech. The number of note cards and their use should be kept to a minimum. Classroom assignments sometimes specify that you use only one side of two or three cards. When this is the case, you need to adjust the amount and type of information that you include to aid you in remembering key information. The advantage of using note cards is that they are easier to handle than full sheets of paper and usually require only one hand, thus freeing the hands for gestures.

 ## Using Presentational Note Cards

1. Use only a few note cards (they are a help but cannot capture the whole speech).
2. Always number the note cards so that if they get out of order, you can reorder them quickly.
3. Write on only one side of the card.
4. Use abbreviations as much as possible.
5. Do not write out your speech—use an outline format.
6. If you prefer, write out the introduction and conclusion in their entirety.
7. List only the main points and subpoints on the cards.
8. If necessary, write out quotations, statistical data, and other information that must be cited accurately (see Figure 9.1 for sample note cards).

FIGURE 9.1

Sample Presentational Note Cards

Note cards should be easy to read. They help the speaker recall information and serve as a reminder of the speech's key ideas.

A CRUEL HOAX   1

Pause—Slow

It isn't surprising that a consumer culture that eats light food, drinks light beer, and performs light aerobics also drives, in ever-increasing numbers, light, compact vehicles. Light, compact vehicles include pickups, minivans, Jeeps, sport utility vehicles, and station wagons built on truck chassis.

The truth is that light cuisine frequently isn't, light beer frequently isn't, and light aerobics are still a sweaty proposition. As for light, compact vehicles . . . Well, Diana Richards saw the light by accident.

Diana Richards—(tell her story)

Today, I would like to tell you why safety regulations should be adopted for light and compact trucks, and passenger vehicles.

I will examine—lack of safety standards, costs to us, reasons for lack of standards, and solution to problem.

I. Light, compact vehicles are dangerous   2
   A. Exceedingly popular
      1. Ford/4.4 million vehicles
      2. Buying because of comfort—Wall Street J.
   B. Exceedingly dangerous
      1. Max Bramble story
      2. Thousands die or sustain serious injuries
         a. 1982–84 deaths doubles
         b. 35/100,000 pickups
            21/100,000 cars
   So far I have shown . . .
II. Not regulated—cost everyone money
   A. High health care cost, lost wages, increased insurance
   B. National Safety Council—$1 billion last year

III. Two reasons   3
   A. Manufacturers—safe enough
   B. Manufacturers—at fault
   (Manufacturers don't see problem. What is the solution?)
IV. Two solutions
   A. Protect ourselves
   B. Congress must act
(Must help ourselves and get Congress to pass legislation)
   VI. Absence of light, compact standards
   VII. We can adopt and enforce safety standards . . . or we ignore
        the carnage.
      A. Diana Richards and Max Bramble
      B. "Seeing the light . . . by accident"

Making Connections

Citing Web Sources

Just as you can find information on the Web and find ways to critically evaluate websites, you can also find some excellent websites to help you create your reference pages. The Modern Language Association and the American Psychological Association provide excellent print sources for this purpose. There are many websites, too, to help you create your bibliographies or reference pages. One superb source, a very complete listing of how to cite all types of sources, can be found at the Duke University Libraries, managed by Kelley A. Lawton and accessed on October 30, 2000. We have provided information on organizing and outlining; your instructor will explain the specific type of reference page you'll need to include with your outlines. This activity will help you learn more about the ways we cite sources from journals, books, newspaper articles, government documents, websites, and articles from electronic databases. Here's what you need to do:

1. Access the Web.
2. Go to http://www.lib.duke.edu/libguide/citing.htm.
3. Determine how to cite two different kinds of print sources.
4. Then, determine how to cite two different web sources.
5. Look again and see if you can learn how to cite an email "interview." If that site does not include personal or email interviews or conversations, search for another site to see if you can determine how to cite interviews. (Another site is the University of Vermont libraries at http://www.uvm.edu/.)
6. Bookmark these sites or print them so you have a handy reference to citing sources.

Summary

Organizing is the arranging of ideas and elements into a systematic and meaningful whole. Organizing requires planning, time, and know-how. Most speeches are organized into three main parts: introduction, body, and conclusion.

The *body,* which contains the main content of a speech, develops the speaker's general and specific purposes as well as the thesis statement. The body consists of the main points of a speech plus the supporting and clarifying materials. The *main points,* which are the principal subdivisions of a speech, are critical to the accomplishment of a speaker's specific purpose. Main points should relate to the specific purpose and thesis, be stated carefully, and be limited in number.

One of seven basic patterns is used in most speeches. The *time-sequence pattern* begins at a particular point in time and continues either forward or backward. The *spatial pattern* organizes the main points according to their relationship in space. The *topical pattern* divides a speech topic into a series of related subtopics. The *problem–solution pattern* first discusses a problem and then suggests solutions. The *cause–effect pattern* illustrates logical relationships between the cause of something and its subsequent effect. When we use *effect–cause* patterns, we first discuss the consequences of an event, problem, or issue and then explain the causes. The *motivated sequence pattern* combines logic and practical psychology; it involves five steps: attention, need, satisfaction, visualization, and action. The pattern of presentation should match the topic and the speaker's specific purpose.

The main points of a speech are connected to one another by transitions, signposts, internal previews, and internal summaries. *Transitions* are words and phrases used to link ideas. *Signposts* are words, phrases, and short statements that let an audience know what is coming. *Internal previews* forecast the points to be covered in the next section or in the body of the speech. *Internal summaries* are short reviews of what was said concerning each main point. Main points cannot stand alone; they must be supported and clarified.

The principal functions of the *introduction* (opening statement) are to orient the audience to the topic and to motivate them to listen. Besides orienting and motivating an audience, the introduction should establish *credibility* (believability based on the audience's evaluation of the speaker's competence, knowledge, experience, and character). The main functions of the *conclusion* (closing statements) are to focus the audience's thoughts on the specific purpose and to bring together the most important points in a condensed and uniform way.

Outlining provides a written account of the main features and ideas of a speech that can then serve as a blueprint or skeleton. The *preliminary outline* lists all possible main points and forms the basis for early decisions about a speech's content and direction. A *full-content outline* gives all the main and secondary points in full-sentence form. A *presentational outline* condenses the full-content outline into key words and phrases that aid the speaker in delivering the speech. When you have completed the outlining process, you should have an extremely clear picture of exactly what you will say and how you will say it.

DISCUSSION STARTERS

1. How can a speech's organization affect an audience?
2. Why should the main points of a speech be carefully developed and written?
3. What usually determines the number of main points in a speech?
4. What should be done to make a speech's main points more meaningful to an audience?
5. Why is it important for a speaker to understand the different patterns for ordering the main points in a speech?
6. Why is the introduction so important to a speech's overall effectiveness?
7. What should the introduction of a speech accomplish?
8. What suggestions would you give to beginning speakers about how to develop the introduction of a speech?
9. What should the conclusion of a speech accomplish?
10. What suggestions would you give to beginning speakers about how to develop the conclusion of a speech?
11. How do the three kinds of outlines differ?

ANSWERS AND EXPLANATIONS

Making Connections:
Ordering Ideas in an Outline

One set of possible answers: I. (2), A. (4), B. (8), II. (9), A. (1), B. (5), III. (7), A. (3), B. (6).

NOTES

1. B. E Gronbeck, R. E McKerrow, D. Ehninger, and A. H Monroe, *Principles and Types of Speech Communication,* 14th ed. (Glenview, Ill.: Scott, Foresman/Little, Brown Higher Education, 1999), 180–203.

2. P. K. Epp, "Convenience Food Packaging," in *Winning Orations* (Mankato, Minn.: Interstate Oratorical Association, 1991), 66.

3. S. Brink, "Sleepless Society," *U.S.News and World Report,* October 16, 2000, 62.

4. B. Randles, "My Brother's Keeper," in *Winning Orations* (1984), 70.

5. Information from "Survey: Employers Want Speaking, Computer Skills," *The (Cedar Rapids, Iowa) Gazette,* 4 December 1999, 2A.

6. M. Blashfield, "The Paradox of Paraquat," in *Winning Orations* (1984), 37.

7. L. Johnson, "Where There's a Will There's a Way," in *Winning Orations* (1986), 59.

8. B. Gerlach, "America—The Land of the Free?" in *Winning Orations* (1986), 104.

9. Brink, 62–72.

10. These outline examples are based on "Development and Uses of Femtosecond Technology: A New Science to Give Us Time," a speech by Brian S. Davis, four-time public speaking champion and University of Northern Iowa graduate student. Used by permission.

Managing Anxiety and Delivering Your Speech

My apprehensions come in crowds;

I dread the rustling of the grass;

The very shadows of the clouds

Have power to shake me as they pass:

I question things and do not find

One that will answer to my mind;

And all the world appears unkind.

—*William Wordsworth,*
"The Affliction of Margaret"

- Describe the roles of ethics, knowledge, preparation, and self-confidence in effective speech making.
- Discuss the symptoms and causes of speech anxiety and suggest five methods of controlling this problem.
- Analyze the pros and cons of the four basic methods of speech delivery.
- Identify the vocal and physical factors that contribute to an effective delivery.
- Tell how each of the most commonly used presentational aids can enhance a speech presentation, and describe the most frequently used methods of presentation.
- Specify how speakers can polish their delivery.

SCENARIO

Dionne: (seeing Mahmood standing in an empty room, talking) What are you doing?

Mahmood: I'm practicing my speech.

Dionne: Do you always practice by talking in an empty room?

Mahmood: No, not all the time, but it helps me feel more at ease.

Dionne: Don't you get nervous when you have to give a speech?

Mahmood: A little, I guess. But, if I'm prepared and I've practiced enough, it's a piece of cake. I really like speaking in front of others.

Dionne: Get out! ■

You may find it hard to believe, but the most enjoyable part of the speech-making process is the act of presenting the speech to the audience. The hard part is behind you: You've done your research and organized the speech, so now you can focus on the last step—delivery.

An important part of preparation is practice. Mahmood, in the opening scenario, is doing what every speaker should do to prepare for actually presenting a speech. Although it is not always possible to rehearse in the room in which the presentation is to be given, it is important to practice your speech in advance. Practicing the delivery will help you know what the speech sounds like, whether wording changes are needed, how effective your timing is, and whether the tone or mood seems appropriate. And the practice will instill greater confidence about giving the speech.

Qualities of Effective Speakers

By cultivating certain personal qualities, you as a speaker can enhance the likelihood that your listeners will accept your message. The most effective speakers are ethical, knowledgeable, prepared, and self-confident.

Ethics

Ethics, an individual's system of moral principles, plays a key role in communication. As speakers, we are responsible for what we tell others. We should always hold the highest ethical standards. We must communicate with honesty, sincerity, and integrity. In addition, a responsible, ethical speaker presents worthwhile and accurate information in a fair manner. David Zarefsky (1999) suggests that the ethical speaker respects the audience, topic, and occasion and takes responsibility for his or her statements.[1]

Ethical speakers do not distort or falsify evidence to misrepresent information, do not make unsupported attacks on opponents in order to discredit them, do not deceive an audience about their intention or objective in an attempt to persuade or take advantage, do not use irrelevant emotional appeals to sensationalize the message and divert attention from the facts, and do not pose as an authority when they are not.[2]

Ethical speakers always cite the sources of their information. Any time you use information and ideas that are not your own, you are obligated to cite the originator or source. The use of another person's information, language, or ideas without citing the originator or author, thus making it appear that you are the originator, is referred to as plagiarism. For example, it is unethical to use statistical data, direct quotations, or any information that you did not originate without giving credit to the originator. Most speeches, unless otherwise specified, require that you as the speaker be the originator of the speech's content. Of course, it is perfectly legitimate to use a reasonable amount of information and ideas from others, as long as you give them credit and cite your sources.

Avoiding Plagiarism

1. Do not rely on a single article as the only source of information for a speech.
2. Avoid using other people's language and ideas.
3. Get information and ideas from a variety of sources, and integrate them into your own thoughts.
4. Cite sources prior to quoting such material—"Dr. Smith, in her 1999 article on exercise, stated 'The best. . . .'"
5. Always identify your sources—"*Newsweek* last week indicated that President Bush's tax plan is . . ." or "According to Robert Jones, a leading economist, in the January 12, 1998, *Wall Street Journal,* 'Our economy is. . . .' "
6. Give credit to the originator of the ideas you use—"Fred Keller, an educational psychologist, created the instructional program that we now use in. . . ."

Similarly, listeners are also responsible for determining the truth. We expect speakers to be ethical, but as listeners we must be willing to verify the information we

Making Connections

Application of Ethics: Resignation Speeches

One of our colleagues, Marvin Jensen, a recently retired professor of communication, believes that at this time of cynicism about leaders, people need to recognize and appreciate ethical public conduct as it is reflected in statements of personal principle. One way to learn about personal principles is by reading resignation speeches. Jensen has his students read John F. Kennedy's *Profiles in Courage* as background reading for *ethos* (we discuss ethos in Chapters 7 and 12).

Here are some of Professor Jensen's suggested resignation speeches and statements to help you learn more about conscience, principles, and ethics:

■ Anthony Eden's resignation as foreign secretary of Great Britain in *Vital Speeches of the Day,* March 1, 1938 (and probably available in your library).

■ Elliot Richardson's resignation as U.S. Attorney General in the October 24, 1973, issue of the *Washington Post,* page A9.

■ Cyrus Vance's resignation as U.S. Secretary of State, as a result of his inability to support the military action undertaken by then-President Jimmy Carter. Vance's statement, letter of resignation, and President Carter's response may be found in the *New York Times,* April 29, 1980, pages A1, A14.

■ George H. W. Bush's resignation from the National Rifle Association, in a letter published in the *New York Times,* May 11, 1995, and referred to in a commencement address at the College of William and Mary, May 14, 1995, pages A1, B10.

Here's what to do:

1. Choose one of the speeches or statements.
2. Find the published version and carefully read it.
3. What does the speech tell you about the leader's principles?
4. At what point does a public official have an ethical duty to resign, rather than continue as a team member?
5. Would it have been better to remain in office or in the organization and try to change policy by private persuasion? Why or why not?
6. What did these individuals risk or lose by resigning?
7. Under what circumstances may a person's "leadership" be increased even when "power" is relinquished?
8. How do you personally feel about leaders who choose principle over power?

receive to ensure that it is accurate and valid. Zarefsky states that listeners should neither refuse to consider a message nor reject a message because it differs from their own beliefs; listeners should not blindly accept what the speaker says.[3] (See Chapter 6 for a discussion of the responsibilities of the listener.)

Knowledge

Knowledge is a speaker's greatest asset. Knowing your subject is essential if you plan to "reach" your listeners. Noted speakers are almost always avid readers. To enhance

Making Connections

Responsible Citing of Sources

TyAnn was practicing her speech in front of her friend, Jason. When she finished speaking, Jason said, "I noticed, TyAnn, that you provided information, examples, statistics, and a quotation in your speech. That's good. I did not, however, hear anything about where you got the information. In my speech class last semester, the professor told us that we needed to give credit to the people who came up with the ideas and facts we used. You've got a pretty good speech here, but you really need to cite your sources and tell your listeners where you found the information."

1. What does TyAnn need to do now?
2. How will including information on sources help her?
3. What else should Jason tell TyAnn?

your understanding of events, people, and values, you must read and observe things around you. From experience, you know that it is easier to talk about things you are familiar with than those you are not. Many colleges, universities, and businesses have identified the characteristics of an "educated person." As an educated person, you should not only know about past international, national, regional, and local events but also keep abreast of current events. You should read all kinds of books, at least one trade (professional) magazine, and one daily newspaper, in addition to listening to news broadcasts and documentaries.

In Chapter 8, we provide suggestions for completing the research part of your speech preparation. It is important that you understand that knowledge is gained from research and analysis. Too often we find that students believe they can "get away with" superficial information in their presentations. This is not the case! Classroom presentations should be prepared with the same kind of care one would give to any important project. If you want to establish your credibility as a knowledgeable person, you will gather far more information than you think is necessary to present in your speeches. What does that accomplish? More information provides you with a sound foundation for the presentation. Also, if your listeners ask questions, your solid knowledge base will allow you to answer most questions they may pose and, thus, come across as a speaker who is knowledgeable. An effective speaker will not be content to limit research and present a shallow speech. Instead, effective speakers ensure they have a solid information base for every presentation.

Preparation

People rarely make speeches without at least some preparation, and the most successful speakers are very well prepared. Poet Maya Angelou often makes speeches and gives "poetry readings" at colleges, universities, and other venues across the country. Angelou visited our respective campuses during September 2000. In her speech she discussed her preparation for the presentation. Her remarks included references to planning and practicing the entire presentation well in advance of her scheduled appearances. She indicated that the prior preparation and practice allowed her to respond to the situation and the listeners much more freely than if she had not prepared in advance.

A successful speech is somewhat like a successful business meeting or athletic event—all require planning, preparation, and work. Preparation means more than practicing the speech ahead of time. Preparation also means that speakers will think through the situation and possible snags or problems. In the example in the previous

A good speech depends on good delivery and good delivery almost always depends on practice. After organizing and writing a speech, present the speech out loud in an informal setting to a friend, making changes, if necessary, to make the speech more effective.

paragraph, we suggested that Maya Angelou carefully prepared herself before her presentations. Thus, her preparation included not only practice but also a process of thinking through all possible audience responses, so that she could effectively handle questions.

Wil Linkugel, a retired professor of speech communication at the University of Kansas, told this story, which illustrates the importance of practice:

> A student athlete was delivering a speech to the class. The student, speaking in a monotone voice, kept reading from a prepared script. Finally, Professor Linkugel interrupted the student.
>
> *Professor:* Why don't you put down your notes and just tell us what your notes say?
> *Student:* I can't do that. I'll never get it right.
> *Professor:* Let's see what you can do.
>
> The student tried speaking without his notes, but the result, although greatly improved, left much to be desired.
>
> *Student:* I'll never do this right!
> *Professor:* In practice, if you were running a pass pattern and you didn't do it right, what would your coach make you do?
> *Student:* We'd run it over again.
> *Professor:* How many times would you run it over?
> *Student:* As many times as it would take to get it right.

What message was Professor Linkugel trying to get across to the student? Is there a message in the story for you? Whether playing football or delivering a speech, for the beginner as well as the experienced speaker, preparation, practice, and knowledge of the fundamentals are important. Remember, however, that you don't want to practice so much that your speech sounds memorized or "canned." Effective speakers should sound conversational, not mechanical. Too much practice can make you lose the spark of spontaneity and will reduce your effectiveness.

Self-Confidence

Self-confidence, or the belief in oneself, is so essential to becoming an effective speaker that much of this book's content is aimed at helping you strengthen this quality. Refer back to the information in Chapter 3 to make the associations between self-image, self-concept, self-confidence, and a variety of communication situations. Because self-confidence is so strongly influenced by anxiety, we discuss this problem in detail.

Managing Speech Anxiety

The online *Encyclopaedia Britannica* (http://www.Britannica.com) defines *anxiety* as "a feeling of dread, fear, or apprehension often with no clear justification."[4] If you experience the fear of speaking before an audience—a condition known as **speech anxiety,** or stage fright—it may help to know that you are not alone. It is perfectly normal to encounter some anxiety before, during, and sometimes even after a speech. In fact, even the most experienced speakers confess to having some anxiety about speaking before a group. What should you know about stage fright? This question, for some teachers of public speaking, is controversial. If the subject is presented, will the mere mention of anxiety create unnecessary anxiety in the speaker? That is, will the discussion of stage fright bring out more anxiety in speakers than they would experience if it had never been mentioned at all? There is no evidence to suggest that discussing stage fright increases or decreases it, but it is commonly accepted that the more we know about stage fright and how to cope with it, the better able we are to *control* it.

If you have had to speak before a group, you probably know a little about speaker anxiety, one fear that many Americans identify as high on their list of fears, according to surveys.[5] The important thing to remember is that having some anxiety about giving a speech before a group is normal. Anxiety becomes a serious problem only when you cannot control it or choose not to communicate because of it.

Communication Apprehension

Communication apprehension, the most severe form of speech anxiety, was defined in Chapter 3 as anxiety syndrome associated with either real or anticipated communication with another person or persons.[6] Communication apprehension can be seen in individuals who either consciously or subconsciously have decided to remain silent. They perceive that their silence offers them greater advantages than speaking out, or that the disadvantages of communicating outweigh any potential gains they might receive. Communication apprehensive individuals fear speaking in all contexts, including one-on-one communication and small-group discussions. Among the fears of those with communication apprehension is that of speaking before a group. However, everyone who fears speaking before a group does not necessarily suffer from communication apprehension. That term refers to the much deeper problem of virtually cutting oneself off from most, if not all, communication with others.

Symptoms of Speech Anxiety

Speech anxiety refers more specifically to the fear of speaking before a group. Anxiety is a condition during which our bodies secrete hormones and adrenaline that eventually overload our physical and emotional responses. These chemical reactions are the same as those you might experience when you are waiting to see a friend you haven't seen in years or going to your first job interview. Your heart begins to beat faster, and your blood pressure begins to rise. More sugar is pumped into your system, and your stomach may begin to churn. When you experience these reactions, you may feel as if your body is operating in high gear and that little or nothing can be done about it. You have to realize that some of these feelings are perfectly normal and, for most us, will not interfere with our speech performance.

Speakers who experience speech anxiety often display the visible signs listed in Table 10.1. These behaviors can occur separately or in any combination, depending on the degree of anxiety the speaker is experiencing.

Speakers who experience speech anxiety may also make telling statements. For example, they may offer self-critical excuses or apologies such as "I'm not any good at this anyway," "I didn't really prepare for this because I didn't have enough time," or "I never was able to say this correctly." Instead of improving the situation, these

TABLE 10.1

Physical Signs Associated with Speech Anxiety

Voice	Quivering
	Too soft
	Monotonous, nonemphatic
	Too fast
Fluency	Stammering, halting
	Awkward pauses
	Hunting for words, speech blocks
Mouth and Throat	Swallowing repeatedly
	Clearing throat repeatedly
	Breathing heavily
Facial Expressions	No eye contact, rolling eyes
	Tense facial muscles, grimaces, twitches
Arms and Hands	Rigid and tense
	Fidgeting, waving hands about
Body Movement	Swaying
	Pacing
	Shuffling feet
Nonvisible Symptoms	Feeling too warm
	Having too much saliva
	Dry mouth or "cotton mouth"
	"Butterflies" in the stomach

From A. Mulac and A. R. Sherman, "Behavior Assessment of Speech Anxiety," *Quarterly Journal of Speech* 60, 2 (April 1974): 138.

comments tend to draw more attention to speakers' nervousness and thus magnify the problem.

Speakers who have speech anxiety often overestimate how much the audience notices about their behavior. The audience, however, tends to underestimate a speaker's anxiety. Audiences cannot detect, for example, a speaker who is experiencing butterflies unless the butterflies cause an observable reaction or the speaker's voice sounds nervous.

Causes of Speech Anxiety

Just as physicians can better treat an illness if they know its cause, people can better reduce and control speech anxiety if they can determine the underlying problem. Many people with speech anxiety treat only the symptoms and tend to ignore the causes, but trying to remove the symptoms without understanding the causes is usually a losing battle.

Making Connections

Communication Apprehension on the Web

Anxiety about communicating in public is both very real and quite natural. When we have to do something of importance we often have some anxiety or even fear. James McCroskey (a communication scholar from West Virginia University) and his colleagues have researched the topic of communication apprehension for the past three decades. There is so much information available that when you key in "communication apprehension" when searching the Web, you get thousands of hits. Let's see what you can learn about communication apprehension.

1. Choose any search engine (Lycos, Google, Dogpile, Savvysearch, AltaVista, AOL, etc.).
2. Key in "communication" + "apprehension" (check to make sure that this format is appropriate for the search engine you've chosen). How many responses do you get?
3. Scroll through some of the responses to see what is included.
4. Choose three sites to carefully read and evaluate.
5. How is communication apprehension defined? What are the similarities to and differences from the definition cited in the text?
6. According to information on these sites, how many people in the United States have some degree of communication apprehension?
7. Now, search for and complete one of the tests of communication apprehension. The Perceived Report of Communication Apprehension (PRCA) was originally developed by McCroskey and is cited on his web page (http://www.as.wvu.edu/~jmccrosk/jcmhp/html/) under publications. A copy of the PRCA can be found on other sites as well using one of the search engines previously noted. What is your score? What does it mean?

Severe speech anxiety begins at an early age as a result of negative feedback in the home. For example, children who are not encouraged to communicate or are punished for doing so are likely to learn that communicating is undesirable and that silence is beneficial. As these children avoid communicating, others may unknowingly contribute further to their fear by asking questions such as "Cat got your tongue?" or "You're afraid to talk, aren't you?" Such words can make the anxious children feel inadequate and, thus, perpetuate the fear and anxiety associated with communicating.

People may also develop speech anxiety if they constantly hear that speaking in front of others can be a terrible experience. Being told immediately before giving a speech, "Don't worry about it—you'll do fine," reinforces the notion that something can go wrong. If speakers believe that something can go wrong and that they might make fools of themselves, they are apt to lose confidence and develop speech anxiety.

In our society, success, winning, and "being number one" are too often considered all-important. When we can't be the most successful, we sometimes consider ourselves failures. No one likes to fail. Thus, we are apt to feel that success brings rewards and failure brings punishment. If you are a winner, you are praised, and if you are a loser, you are ridiculed. As a result, we place tremendous pressure on ourselves and others to be successful.

When we haven't been successful at something, we are often told to try again. But if the consequences of the failure are dramatic and the payoff for success doesn't seem worth the effort, we may prefer to avoid the situation. Avoidance may result in punishment, but we may perceive that as better than trying to do something and failing. Sometimes society is more lenient. For example, in a competition we assume that there will be a winner and a loser. No one likes to lose, but playing your best and losing is often acceptable. When someone makes a mistake in a speech, however, we may be more critical. Rather than acknowledge that the person is making an honest effort, we may perceive him or her as inadequate or unskilled. Consequently, the stress created by fear of making mistakes in front of others may be so great that it produces anxiety and sometimes complete avoidance of speaking situations. Among the other most common causes of speech anxiety are the following:

Fear of physical unattractiveness

Fear of social inadequacy

Fear of criticism

Fear of the unknown

Fear of speech anxiety

Conflicting emotions

Excitement from anticipation[7]

We learn to respond in specific ways when facing something that creates anxiety because we have become conditioned to do so. Each of these common reactions to a speech-making situation is *learned*. Because speech anxiety is a learned behavior, the only solution for its sufferers is to examine the potential reasons for the anxiety and learn how to use this knowledge to manage the discomfort.

Speech Anxiety and Other Cultures

Every year increasing numbers of international students and Americans whose first language is not English enter higher education in the United States. In spite of their differences, most of these students do not ask to be treated any differently than anyone else. But because of the language and cultural differences these students have experienced, they do deserve understanding and patience as they communicate with U.S. students. In a study of Asian students, Ester Yook and Bill Seiler found that most were anxious about presenting speeches. They were concerned about whether they would be understood by their audience because of their accent, tone, and pronunciation.[8] They were also concerned that if they were unable to "think in English," they might not be able to find the right word or expression needed on the spot, resulting in a humiliating experience.

Another source of anxiety for Asian students, according to Yook and Seiler, occurs because they sometimes have difficulty understanding the speech assignment fully. The potential for misunderstanding the assignment and their perceived lack of English fluency lead many Asian students to memorize their speeches. The memorization, however prevents many Asian students from being conversational in style and adds to their perceived ineffectiveness and anxiety as communicators. Communicating in front of others creates some anxiety for most of us, but being from a different culture and speaking English as a second language can create additional stress.

Native Americans represent another group who have more anxiety when speaking because of cultural differences. In the Native American culture, eye contact is limited. In speaking situations in the dominant culture, eye contact is expected. Native American students explain that they feel even more uncomfortable when they are reminded that eye contact is critical. Those from different cultural and language backgrounds don't want sympathy, but they do want their situations to be understood.

Treating Speech Anxiety

Although speaking before a group may produce stress and anxiety, few people allow their nervousness to prevent them from trying and succeeding.[9] In fact, as mentioned earlier, even well-known speakers feel some nervousness before giving a speech, but they have learned to *control* it. The key to successful control of your anxiety is the desire to control it. To cope with speech anxiety, we must realize that the potential for failure always exists, but that we can't let it stop us from trying. If we allowed the possibility of failure to overwhelm us, we probably would never do or learn anything. A child beginning to walk is a prime example of how most of our learning occurs. At first, the child wobbles, takes a small step, and falls. But when the child falls, someone is usually there to offer help, support, and encouragement to continue. In addition, the child usually is determined to walk regardless of the difficulties. Speech making, like learning to walk, involves many of the same processes. Help, support, and encouragement are important, but the essential ingredient is determination to succeed.

Most successful people will tell you that before they were successful they had some failures and moments of embarrassment. But their drive and self-confidence pushed them to try again. Some of our first speeches were not very good, and we were quite nervous about speaking in front of our classmates. However, it didn't take us long to realize that even the best speakers in the class felt the same way. The only difference was that they weren't afraid to make a mistake.

Many of us are too hard on ourselves. Some students, after giving a speech, will say that they were extremely nervous, but in fact the audience never detected any sign of nervousness whatsoever. To the audience the speaker appeared relaxed and in control.

There are no cures for speech anxiety—only ways to reduce, manage, or control it so that it does not interfere with your presentation. Experts suggest several guidelines to help you reduce your anxieties:

1. *Select a topic you enjoy and know.* The more you know about a subject, the easier it will be for you to talk about it. According to one research study, people who are highly anxious tend to be more negative in their assessments of themselves and more concerned with what others think of them. In addition, they tend to choose unfamiliar speech topics, which compounds their problem.[10] Sometimes, however, it is not possible to choose your own topic. In business settings, for example, we are often required to report information for specific situations in which the topic is selected by the circumstances. In this case, the speaker must work harder to have adequate information and to focus on accomplishing what is necessary for that situation.

2. *Be prepared.* Because anxious people are more negative in their self-assessments, they tend to spend less time preparing, convinced they are not going to succeed no matter what they do. Thus, they set themselves up for failure, which perpetuates the cycle of anxiety and failure. Preparation can break the cycle. Know your audience and become familiar with the physical surroundings in which you are going to speak (such as the room size, lighting, placement of microphone, and audiovisual equipment). This will help create confidence by reducing the unknown. In Chapter 9 we advised you that carefully organizing your speech will help you be more effective. The work you put into research, organization, and practice will also help you be more confident.

3. *Be confident.* Confidence plays a key role in controlling anxiety. We are often amazed at how many students sell themselves short. We have heard many student speakers over the years, and each of them had the ability and potential skill to be an effective speaker. Students who didn't believe that they could be successful seemed to have the most difficulty giving speeches. We have also had students who were extremely quiet in class, but when it came to speaking, they were exceptional. One student who seldom talked in class was asked how she felt after her speech, and she indicated that she was surprised at how good she felt. The first minute or so she was nervous, she said, but once she realized that she knew what she was talking about and the audience appeared to be listening, she completely forgot about her nervousness and concentrated on informing her audience. You only have to try. Even if you do not do as well as you'd like, the instructor is there to help you and your classmates, and wants you to do well.

4. *Think positively.* Visualize yourself giving a successful speech. Some students tell us it is easy to think positively but it doesn't help them give a successful speech. We, however, disagree. Positive thought does work. There is ample proof to suggest that those who think positively and visualize themselves doing well often surpass their own expectations. Thinking that you are going to do poorly, however, is a sure path to failure.

5. *Practice.* The better you know the content of your speech and your delivery plan, the more comfortable you will feel about your presentation. Few things are done well without some practice. For example, the quarterback who executes a perfect touchdown pass, the gymnast who scores a 10 in floor exercise, the actor who presents a flawless performance, the student who draws beautiful pictures, the person who passes the road test for a driver's license, and the person who gives a polished and interesting speech have spent hours—and sometimes years—in practice. Knowing that you don't have weeks, months, or years to practice your speech, you must practice as much as you can with the realization that you may not perfect all aspects of your speech. Remember that almost all speakers are somewhat nervous before a speech and that nervousness is perfectly normal.

Giving a speech and completing a pass play in a football game are not exactly the same thing, but both require similar preparation. The successful pass play requires research, organization, learning, observation, practice, willingness to work hard, ability to perform, confidence, knowing your opponent's defenses (or knowing your audience), and timing. A successful speech presentation requires all of the aforementioned factors in addition to selecting an appropriate topic.

Controlling Speech Anxiety

1. Realize that almost everyone has some anxiety about presenting a speech. You are not alone.

2. Select a topic that you are familiar with and that you enjoy, if possible.

3. Know your audience and the surroundings in which your presentation will take place.

4. Think positively. Prepare yourself mentally for success. Believe that you are going to be successful, and you probably will be.

5. Practice, and then practice more!

6. Ask your instructor for additional advice and other possible treatment programs that may be available.

7. Don't give up. Others want you to succeed, and you can if that is what you want.

If none of the strategies in the accompanying Guidelines feature help to reduce your anxiety, then you should probably seek professional help. Individuals who suffer from abnormal levels of speech anxiety should know that the negative feelings associated with communicating in front of others do not simply occur; they develop over a long period of time. Thus, these negative feelings do not always disappear easily. But speech anxiety is a problem that we can do something about with help. Most university settings have psychologists or counselors who are trained to reduce the fear of speaking in public. In some colleges there are special sections of the beginning communication course for those who are anxious about speaking in front of others.

If your school does not offer help in reducing speaking anxiety,[11] there is another alternative called systematic desensitization. **Systematic desensitization** is a technique in which relaxation is associated with an anxiety-producing situation. For example, a student who suffers from public speaking anxiety might be asked to visualize speaking in front of a class and then immediately associate the frightening experience with thoughts of relaxation. The theory behind systematic desensitization is that a mental rehearsal will associate relaxation with situations that create tension. Repetition of the association may help those suffering from anxiety learn that relaxation can replace tension and, thus, reduce their fear of speaking in public.

Overcoming anxiety in public speaking situations is not easy, but you must remember that some anxiety can be helpful and is a normal reaction to speaking in public. When we asked students how they dealt with their fear of speaking, they suggested the following:

1. Practice, and have your introduction, main points, and conclusion clear in your mind. Students believe that once they know their introductions, main points, and conclusions, it is a lot easier to remember the details.

2. Walk confidently to the speaking area. Students believe this helps create confidence. If you're confident, it is likely you will feel relaxed. In other words, positive behavior results in positive outcomes.

3. Do not start your speech until you are ready. The students suggest that having everything under control before you start to speak makes it easier to relax and concentrate on the speech, rather than on yourself.

4. Look at your audience, and focus most of the time on friendly faces. Students believe that concentrating on those who are likely to give positive feedback will help promote a good feeling about speaking.

Making Connections

Anxiety and the Speaker

Scott Gordon, one of our students and a published poet, shared this poem with his classmates. Read it and think about what Scott says about anxiety and the speaker.

Ode to Nervousness

What is this?
Do I have to?
I'll be skipped. I wish.
What am I going to do?

My heart begins to pound.
The deathly chill takes its course.
Nothing is worse than this, I have found.
Mephisto could be the only source.

As I am called upon to my fate,
My knees quiver with fear.
They'll all laugh at me, just wait.
Or, I won't gain any of their ears.

As I do what I have come to loathe,
I begin to feel calm.

My inner being begins to come out of a cove.
And the sweat disappears from my palm.

As I come to my closing and conclusion
I feel a sense of relief.
For in the faces of my counterparts there is
*   no intrusion.*
I actually feel good to my disbelief!

1. How would you describe Scott's feelings in the beginning of the poem?
2. Describe in your own words Scott's feelings once he is in front of the group?
3. In what way have Scott's feelings changed from the beginning to the end of the poem?
4. How can Scott's experience benefit you as a speaker?

"Ode to Nervousness" used with permission of Scott Gordon, UNI student, 1998.

These suggestions are probably not new, and they are not surprising, but they will help in your quest to become a successful speaker. The best thing you can do is continue to give speeches in class and take more classes that will afford opportunities to speak under the supervision of a trained instructor. You can reduce and control your fear of speaking, but you must make that happen by acting on the guidelines we've provided here.

Methods of Delivery

An effective delivery conveys the speaker's purpose and ideas clearly and interestingly so that the audience attends to and retains what was said as it was intended by the speaker. The effectiveness of a speech, therefore, depends both on what is said and how it is conveyed. No two speakers are alike. For example, it is unlikely that anyone could deliver the "I Have a Dream" speech as effectively as Martin Luther King Jr. did. This speech, widely regarded as a masterpiece, was delivered on August 28, 1963, to more than 200,000 people gathered in Washington, D.C., to participate in a peaceful demonstration furthering the cause of equal rights for African Americans. If you have heard a recording of this speech, you know how his delivery affected his audience.

Making Connections

Anxiety and You

In *The Book of Lists,* Irving Wallace and David Wallechinsky report that the majority of Americans identify fear of public speaking as their number one fear, even above death, which is one of the top ten fears. Most of us are anxious in one way or another about making presentations in public. This chapter provides some guidelines and suggestions for managing, controlling, or reducing anxiety. This exercise will further help you to remember this material. Think about how you have managed or might manage your anxiety in a given situation.

1. Identify three different ideas or strategies for managing your anxiety based on what you have read for class.

   A. _____

   B. _____

   C. _____

2. Identify three different strategies to help manage anxiety that you have heard from your instructor or other classmates.

   A. _____

   B. _____

   C. _____

3. Interview, in person or via email, another person who communicates frequently (e.g., supervisor, instructor, radio or television personality, minister, priest, rabbi, health care professional, or businessperson) and ask this professional speaker to share with you ways of dealing with anxiety. List five strategies that your interviewee uses (they may be the same or similar to the ones listed previously):

   A. _____

   B. _____

   C. _____

King had a rich baritone voice modulated by the cadences of a Southern Baptist preacher and the fervor of a crusader. Although the words of the speech can be repeated and King's style can be imitated, the setting, timing, and circumstances cannot be reconstructed. Thus, the effect that King had on that day can never be repeated.

A poorly written speech can be improved by effective delivery, and a well-written speech can be ruined by ineffective delivery. No set of rules will guarantee an effective delivery in every situation. The only consistent rule is that you must be yourself! Of course, as a beginning speaker, you probably have many questions about how to deliver a speech: How many notes should I use? Will I need a microphone? Where and

	ADVANTAGES	DISADVANTAGES
TABLE 10.2 — **Methods of Delivery: Advantages and Disadvantages**		
Impromptu	Spontaneous Flexible Conversational	No time for preparation Can be inaccurate Difficult to organize Can be stressful
Manuscript	Good for material that is technical or detailed or that requires complete preciseness High accuracy Can be timed to the second Prepared	No flexibility Great amount of preparation time Difficult to adapt to audience response May sound mechanical Lack of eye contact
Memorized	Good for short speeches Speaker can concentrate on delivery Easier to maintain eye contact Prepared	Inflexible Requires practice and repetition Speaker can forget or lose place Difficult to adapt to audience response May sound mechanical
Extemporaneous	Organized Flexible Conversational Prepared Great amount of eye contact	May be intimidating to inexperienced speakers

how should I stand? Where or at whom should I look? How many and what kinds of gestures should I use? How and when should I use my visual aids? How loudly should I speak? How fast or slow should my speaking be?

Such questions are valid, but the answers will vary from person to person and from situation to situation. In the end, effective delivery comes from practice under the direction of a competent instructor. An awareness of self and knowledge of effective delivery also help improve delivery. Although a speech may be delivered in many different ways, the four most common methods of delivery are impromptu, manuscript, memorized, and extemporaneous (see Table 10.2).

Impromptu Delivery

The delivery of a speech with little or no formal planning or preparation (no research, no organization) is called **impromptu delivery.** You have used this method many times, perhaps without even realizing it. Whenever you speak without prior preparation, whether in response to a question in class, to a sudden request at a business meeting, or to a comment made by a friend, you are using the impromptu method of delivery. The more formal or demanding the situation, the more most speakers prefer to avoid this approach. At times, however, you have no choice. In such cases, muster your self-control, relax, and concentrate on what you wish to say. The lack of preparation time distinguishes the impromptu method from other methods of delivery and forces speakers to depend solely on their ability to think on their feet.

Manuscript Delivery

Reading the speech word for word is known as **manuscript delivery.** Speakers who use this method are never at a loss for words. A speaker should use a manuscript for situations in which every word, phrase, and sentence must be stated precisely. Using a manuscript is not uncommon for politicians, clergy, teachers, and others who need to present information completely and accurately or who are likely to be quoted after their presentations. But in learning how to give a speech, manuscript delivery is often discouraged, because it invites the speaker to concentrate more on the script than the audience and reduces eye contact with the audience. Also, speakers who work from manuscripts are less able to adapt to the reactions of the audience and thus may sound mechanical. They are so busy concentrating on reading the speech that they may be unable to respond to the audience.

Manuscript Delivery

1. *Write your manuscript for the ear.* There is a difference between content written to be read silently and that to be read aloud. The silent reader can go back to a previous sentence for reference and can reread a passage if it is unclear the first time, but a person listening to a speech cannot.

2. *Prepare your manuscript in an easy-to-read format.* Type it triple-spaced. Use special marks and comments to point out areas you plan to emphasize.

3. *Think about what you are saying.* The presence of a manuscript often tempts a speaker to read words instead of thoughts. Try to sound spontaneous and give meaning to the manuscript.

4. *Read with expression and vocal emphasis.* Remember that your voice can add meaning to the words. Thus, the expressive use of your voice becomes an added dimension to the reading of the words.

5. *Practice reading out loud,* preferably with a tape recorder. The key to success is to sound as if the thoughts you are reading are fresh. The manuscript should be presented with enthusiasm, vigor, and interest.[12]

Memorized Delivery

Memorized delivery requires that you memorize your speech in its entirety, usually from a word-for-word script. This kind of delivery is used for short presentations, such as toasts, acceptance speeches, and introductions, and is also commonly used by speakers in contests and on lecture circuits. Speakers frequently memorize certain parts of their speeches, including examples, short stories, statistics, quotations, and other materials that they can call up at the appropriate time. Politicians, salespeople, tour guides, and others often have a memorized "pitch," or speech, to fit their needs.

Memorization has one advantage. You can concentrate less on what you have to say and focus more on your delivery. Of course, this is only true if you are extremely confident and have memorized your speech so completely that you don't need to think about each word. One disadvantage of memorized delivery is its lack of flexibility—it doesn't allow for much, if any, adaptation to your audience. Beginning speakers face another disadvantage: They may forget what they want to say and become embarrassed. In addition, it is difficult to deliver a memorized speech without sounding mechanical. Effective presentation of a memorized address requires a great deal of practice and confidence. The Guidelines feature about manuscript delivery applies equally to memorized delivery.

Extemporaneous Delivery

In **extemporaneous delivery,** the speaker uses a carefully prepared and researched speech but delivers it from notes, with a high degree of spontaneity. Extemporaneous delivery is the method most commonly used in speech classrooms and in other public communication situations. When you give a report at work, for example, you will probably be expected to present your remarks extemporaneously. If you are a member of a problem-solving group at your place of worship and you have been selected to present the group's deliberations, you will also be expected to deliver your remarks in an extemporaneous manner. Instructors often require extemporaneous delivery in the communication classroom because it is the best style for most instances of public speaking.

Extemporaneous delivery is situated somewhere between memorized or manuscript delivery and impromptu delivery. Speakers depend on a brief presentational outline or notes and choose the actual wording of the speech at the time of delivery.

The speaker here is using an extemporaneous delivery, a carefully prepared and researched speech, but delivers it from notes with a high degree of spontaneity.

(See Chapter 9 for a discussion of presentational outlines.) Speakers sometimes prefer to use a keyword outline, which simply outlines the points and subpoints of the speech using keywords. This helps keep the speaker organized and on track but does not allow the speaker to become too reliant on the outline or notes.

An extemporaneous speech may at first seem as difficult as an impromptu speech, but, in fact, it is much easier. Because it eliminates memorization and manuscript writing, it leaves more time for preparation and practice. Thus, once you have prepared your outline, you can begin to practice your delivery. The goal of the extemporaneous method is a conversational and spontaneous quality. Conversationality and spontaneity are two hallmarks of speech delivery that listeners find appealing. It is much easier to listen to and attend to speakers who are conversational, lively, and spontaneous. Each time you practice your speech, the wording should be somewhat different, although the content remains the same. Your objective should always be to use delivery to help you share meaningful ideas with your audience.

These are the advantages of extemporaneous delivery: It gives you better control of your presentation than the impromptu method, it allows more spontaneity and directness than the memorized and manuscript methods of delivery, and it is more adaptable to a variety of speaking situations than the other methods. Most teachers, as well as professional speakers, prefer to use the extemporaneous method because it allows them to adjust to the situation moment by moment. Extemporaneous delivery also allows audience members to become more involved in listening to the message.

Vocal and Physical Aspects of Delivery

Without solid content and valid sources, nothing is worth communicating; but without effective delivery, even the most compelling information cannot be clearly and vividly presented. Because the audience is the ultimate judge of effectiveness, you must deliver your speech well to involve them in your speech. Each audience member likes to feel as if he or she is being addressed personally. Therefore, try to think of your presentation as a conversation and your audience as your partners in dialogue. Then use your voice and body to create this impression.

Vocal Aspects

Many beginning speakers overlook the important role that voice plays in delivery. As you speak, your voice should be pleasant to listen to, relate easily and clearly to your thoughts, and express a range of emotions. Your voice should convey the meaning to your listeners that you wish to convey. Thus, the more natural, spontaneous, and effortless you appear to be, regardless of how hard you are working, the more your listener can focus on what you are saying rather than how you are saying it. Three aspects of voice that determine the effectiveness of delivery are vocal quality, intelligibility, and vocal variety.

Vocal Quality.   The overall impression that a speaker's voice makes on listeners is referred to as **vocal quality.** Voices may be harsh, nasal, thin, mellow, resonant, or full-bodied. Attitude can affect the quality of the voice and reveal to listeners whether the speaker is happy, confident, angry, fearful, or sad. Think about those times when you were supertired: How does your voice sound? Can you hide your tiredness from people listening to you? Probably not. Think about times when you were really excited about a topic. How do you think you sounded to your listeners? Generally, when we're really involved and interested in something, the voice carries energy and excitement that draws others into the conversation. Vocal quality is a highly accurate indicator of the presenter's sincerity. Also, listeners tend to believe speakers whose vocal delivery is interesting and easy to listen to are more credible speakers and will probably be more willing to listen to speakers who use their voices effectively.

Intelligibility. A speaker's **intelligibility,** the degree to which an audience can hear and understand words, is determined by vocal volume; distinctiveness of sound; accuracy of pronunciation; articulation; and stress placed on syllables, words, and phrases. The keys to high intelligibility are self-awareness and consideration for listeners.

To determine the proper volume, consider the size of the room and observe listeners' reactions. Do listeners look as if they're straining to hear you? Or is your voice too loud or booming for the size of the room?

We have all been known to mispronounce words. For example, a common word like *February* is often mispronounced as *Feb-u-ary.* Sometimes we mispronounce words out of habit, incorrect learning, or a regionalism. For example, many people pronounce *realtor* as *re-la-tor* instead of *real-tor.* When we mispronounce words, we lower our intelligibility and also run the risk of lowering our credibility. Speakers often drop off word endings, which makes it difficult to understand what is being said; the dropping of the *g* from words ending in *ing,* for example, makes it difficult for persons from other cultures to understand the words. Saying "I'm gonna tell you about . . ." instead of "I'm going to tell you about . . ." also may result in a loss of credibility. Effective speakers need to make sure that the words they use are clearly spoken, correctly used, and understandable.

Grammatical correctness is an important consideration. Not only is the classroom teacher bothered by incorrect grammar and inappropriate use of words but also in the world outside the classroom, we are judged by the way we present our ideas. This suggests that before we present a speech, we should practice it before a friend or colleague who might detect our errors, dropped sounds, grammatically incorrect words, and mispronunciations. And you should always use a dictionary to check any pronunciation of which you are not sure.

There is a difference, however, between mispronounced words and regional and ethnic dialects that affect pronunciation. The effect dialect has on an audience depends a great deal on the makeup of the audience and whether or not they understand the difference between dialect usage and standard pronunciation of words. Speakers should always strive to learn similarities and differences between their own dialects and those of others, and adapt their messages to the

---

Making Connections

Articulation

Professional television or radio announcers often improve their articulation by practicing tongue twisters such as the ones below. Begin by saying each word slowly and distinctly, and then increase your rate to a normal speaking speed.

Rubber buggy bumper wheels.

The sixth sick sheik's sheep is sick.

She sells seashells by the seashore.

At your next class session, discuss these questions in small groups.

1. What problems did you first encounter?
2. What, if anything, made it easier to complete this exercise?

Making Connections

Using Pauses

Read aloud the first sentence without any pauses and then read the second sentence with pauses.

The little boy and his dog having tired of fishing wandered slowly along the dusty path in the late afternoon.

The little boy and his dog, having tired of fishing, wandered slowly along the dusty path in the late afternoon.

Discuss the following in class:

1. Discuss the difference in emphasis caused by the pauses.
2. Discuss the importance of the use of pauses as a means of making a message more meaningful.
3. Discuss the difference in the speaker's delivery of the two sentences.

From E. C. Glenn, P. J. Glenn, and S. H. Forman, *Your Voice and Articulation,* 2nd ed. (Englewood Cliffs, N.J.: Prentice-Hall, 1989), 234.

situation. An African American student who uses Ebonics when speaking with friends, for example, needs to adjust language in the classroom and the workplace so that he or she can be easily understood by listeners.

Good articulation involves producing and saying words clearly and distinctly. Physical problems, such as cleft palate, difficulty in controlling the tongue, or a misaligned jaw, may create articulation problems that require specialized help, but most articulation problems result from laziness. We sometimes chop, slur, or mumble words, because we do not take the time to learn the words correctly. People say "gonna" instead of "going to," "didja" instead of "did you," or "dunno" instead of "don't know." Such articulation errors are often because of habit and sloppiness rather than ignorance of what is correct.

Unfortunately, many people don't realize that their articulation is sloppy or incorrect unless someone points it out to them. Listen to what you say and how you sound. Concentrate on identifying and eliminating your most common articulation errors. Correcting articulation errors can be well worth the effort; you will sound more intelligent and more professional, and you will further establish your credibility as an educated person.

We need to make two more points about intelligibility. Avoid fillers and vocal pauses, which clutter speeches. Fillers such as "um," "uh," "ah," "and uh," "like," and, "you know" can become both distracting and irritating to your listeners. Most communication instructors will note (and probably reduce your grade) when your speech has too many vocal fillers. The second point refers to the use of appropriate language. Adjust your language to suit the formal presentation. Just as you would not speak to your grandmother or a religious leader in the same way you speak with a group of your friends, you need to acknowledge the formality of the speaking situation by using appropriate language. Do not use slang terms or profanity, and do not use language and sentence structure that reduce your credibility. If you're not sure about what is and is not appropriate, check with your instructor.

Vocal Variety.   The combination of rate, force, and pitch variations that add to a speaker's overall vocal quality is called **vocal variety.** Such variety gives feeling to your delivery and adds emphasis to what you say. Your voice allows listeners to perceive subtle differences in the intent of your messages by altering rate, force, and pitch, promoting a genuine understanding between you and your audience.

Rate is the speed at which a speaker speaks—usually between 120 and 150 words per minute. Speaking at the appropriate rate requires self-awareness. A rate that is too fast, too slow, or that never changes can detract from the impact of your message. Sometimes when we're nervous, our speaking rate increases so much that we're practically unintelligible to our listeners. We must learn to control this rapid rate by breathing deeply before we begin speaking and by purposely using pauses to help us slow down and concentrate on the message.

Pauses are important. A pause can be an effective means of gaining attention, adding emphasis to an important point, and enabling listeners to follow shifts in ideas. Pauses punctuate and emphasize thoughts. Beginning speakers need to realize the important contribution of both rate and pauses to the overall effect of their presentations. Listen carefully to accomplished speakers. Notice how an effective speaker varies rate and uses pauses to set off ideas, to prepare for the next point, and to provide silent emphasis for ideas. Again, accomplished speakers tend to do this within the context of a conversational style.

Making Connections

Using Your Voice Effectively

Read the following excerpt from Lewis Carroll's "The Walrus and the Carpenter" with no vocal variety—that is, don't vary your rate, force, or pitch. Then read it using vocal variety—vary your rate, force, and pitch in order to put more meaning into the reading of the poem.

> *The sun was shining on the sea,*
>   *Shining with all his might.*
> *He did his very best to make*
>   *The billows smooth and bright—*
> *And this was odd, because it was*
>   *The middle of the night.*

Discuss in class the following:

1. What difference between the two versions did you hear?
2. What is the message behind the exercise?
3. Practice reading this exercise in pairs—take turns reading.

Force is the intensity and volume of the voice. You must choose a volume level that is comfortable for your audience. However, you can use force to communicate your ideas with confidence and vigor, to emphasize an important point, and to regain lagging interest. By learning how to use force, you can greatly increase your effectiveness as a speaker.

Pitch refers to how low or high the voice is on a tonal scale. Variety in pitch can eliminate monotony and add emphasis to keywords. Variety in pitch contributes to greater conversationality and, thus, makes it easy for the listener to maintain interest in and attention to the speaker and message.

Obviously, any change in rate, force, or pitch makes a word, phrase, or sentence stand out. The greater the amount of change or the more sudden the change is, the more emphatic the word or statement will be. You can use such contrasts to make selected ideas seem more important than the material delivered without such variations.

Physical Aspects

In Chapter 5 we discussed nonverbal communication in depth. You are encouraged to review the chapter, because much of the information about nonverbal communication will aid you in your speaking performances. Among the physical factors that can affect delivery are personal appearance, body movement, gestures, facial expressions, and eye contact. Each of these must be well coordinated and relevant to the purpose of your speech.

Personal Appearance. Personal appearance—what a speaker looks like and the way a speaker dresses, grooms, and presents himself or herself to others—is an extremely important consideration. Typical "student attire" is not always acceptable. As a general rule, you should use common sense in dressing for the occasion. For example, large, dangly earrings, "busy" printed T-shirts, and caps may distract your audience from what you are saying (and have a negative effect on the people evaluating your presentation). Most instructors frown on speakers wearing caps for a variety of other reasons as well: It is in questionable taste, and caps hide your facial expressions. First impressions are based mainly on appearance. Your audience may form quick and hard-to-change opinions about your attitude toward them and yourself. In this way, appearance can affect your credibility.

Although we do not know much about the exact role of personal appearance in communication, we do know that it does influence interpersonal responses. In some situations, appearance can have a profound impact on a speaker's self-image and, therefore, affect how the speaker communicates with others.[13] As simple, and even superficial, as it may seem, looking your best does help you convey your message. In addition, looking good makes you feel good, which ultimately will have a positive effect on your performance.

Body Movement. Body movement is closely related to personal appearance. It includes posture, which should be relaxed and natural; avoid slouching. Because an audience's attention instinctively follows moving objects, your motions should be easy and purposeful. The use of movement—stepping to the side, forward, or backward—can aid in holding attention and communicating ideas clearly. Movement can also serve as a nonverbal transition between points. Purposeful movement, along with posture, can indicate confidence and convey a positive self-image. Too much movement, or unmotivated, nervous movement, however, can distract your audience, make them think you are not poised and confident, and detract from your credibility.

Gestures. You can use **gestures**—movements of the head, arms, and hands—to help illustrate, emphasize, or clarify a point. Gestures should be spontaneous, not forced. For example, when you are talking to acquaintances about something you have strong feelings about, your gestures come naturally. If you are sad, angry, or happy, you automatically make gestures that express your emotions. To obtain equally natural gestures when giving a speech, you need to be equally involved in what you are saying. If you concentrate on getting your message across, rather than on your gestures, you will find yourself moving more freely and naturally.

When you are first learning how to give a speech, using gestures may seem a bit uncomfortable, but not using gestures may also seem uncomfortable. To overcome this problem, practice the use of gestures in front of others who are willing to offer positive suggestions to help you improve. Be assured that as you give more and more speeches, you will find that gesturing becomes more natural and easier to do. Soon, without even thinking, you'll be using strong and smooth-flowing gestures that help hold your audience's attention and add meaning to your message.

Facial Expressions. As defined in Chapter 5, facial expressions are configurations of the face that can reflect, augment, contradict, or be unrelated to a speaker's vocal delivery. They account for much of the emotional impact of a speaker's message. Your face is a very expressive part of your body. Facial expressions quickly and accurately tell your audience a lot about you. For example, whether you are serious, happy, worried, or angry, the audience will be able to "read" your face. Because your audience will infer a great deal from your facial expression, it is important to look warm and friendly. Such an expression will inform your listeners that you are interested in them and in what you are saying. Of course, your topic, your purpose, the situation, and your audience will all determine exactly what facial expressions are appropriate as you progress through your speech.

Eye Contact. The extent to which a speaker looks *directly* at audience members, making **eye contact,** is associated with facial expression. Facial expressions indicate a speaker's feelings about the message, but eye contact seems more related to a speaker's feelings about the listeners. Eye contact is the most important physical aspect of delivery, as it indicates interest and concern for others and implies self-confidence. Most speech communication teachers recommend that you look at your audience while you are speaking, not over their heads or at a spot on the wall.

Looking at members of the audience establishes a communicative bond between your listeners and you. Failure to make eye contact is the quickest way to lose listeners. Speakers who ignore their audiences are often perceived as tentative, ill at ease, insincere, or dishonest.

Eye contact with your audience should be pleasant and personal. Give your listeners the feeling that you are talking to them as individuals in a casual conversation. When speaking to a small audience (five to thirty people), try to look at each individual for a few seconds at a time. To avoid looking shifty, move your eyes gradually and smoothly from one person to another. For larger groups, it is best to scan the audience and occasionally talk to a specific member or members. Do not look over people's heads, and avoid staring, which can give the impression that you're angry or hostile. Try not to make your listeners uncomfortable. A colleague once had students fill out peer evaluations for each speaker. One student wrote, "He stared at me. I felt like he was drilling a hole through my head. It made me very nervous." The speaker should instead distribute eye contact among more audience members.

Your eyes should convey that you are confident, sincere, and speaking with conviction. The message your audience should get from your eye contact is that you care about them and about what you are saying. At first, establishing eye contact with an audience may make you uncomfortable, but as you gain experience, you will begin to feel more at ease. You will soon find that making eye contact puts you in control of the situation and helps you to answer these questions: Can they hear me? Do they understand? Are they listening?

Working to strengthen your use of positive vocal and physical behaviors and to reduce negative ones will greatly improve your delivery of a speech. Table 10.3 lists several behaviors that can detract from a speech's effectiveness. Observing yourself in front of a mirror or asking a supportive friend for feedback during a practice session will help you avoid these problems.

TABLE 10.3   Behaviors That Detract from Effective Delivery

General Delivery	Speaking too fast	*Voice*	Sing-song speech pattern
	Speaking too slowly		Monotone voice
	Sighing		Nasal twang
	Nervous smiling or laughing		Mumbling
	Choppy pacing		Speaking too softly
	Awkward pausing		Speaking too loudly
Face	Deadpan or serious look		High pitch
	Facial contortions (such as scowling)		Shrillness, stridency
	Listless or apathetic look		Lack of variety in pace, volume, or pitch
Hands	Fidgeting, waving, or other meaningless motions	*Body*	Tense, stiff posture
			Sloppy posture
	Hands in pockets or locked onto lectern		Hunched shoulders
			Wiggling
	Playing with hair		Swaying
Eyes	Shifty glances		Leaning on lectern
	Rolling movements	*Feet*	Shuffling
	Looking at the floor		Shifting weight
	Looking at one side of the room		Crossing legs
	Looking at the ceiling		
	Staring		
	Lack of sustained eye contact		

Making Connections

Technology and Speech Delivery

Technology has influenced every aspect of our lives, including the way teachers teach, students learn, and businesspeople make presentations. One of our communication colleagues, Dr. Lynn Disbrow of Sinclair Community College in Ohio, suggests that technology forces us all to be learners and that we all have to learn differently because of technology. How has technology affected the way speakers deliver their speeches? Let's Ask Jeeves.

1. Access your web browser.
2. Key in http://www.ask.com/.

3. When you get Jeeves, phrase a question such as, "How has technology affected speech delivery?"
4. Quickly look through the first few responses. Do they look like helpful answers? If so, read the responses. If not, ask another, similar question.
5. Read and compare the first ten new responses.
6. Answer the question, "How has technology affected speech delivery?"

Making Connections

Nonverbal Behavior and Effective Presentation of Information

We have stated that physical and vocal factors can play an important role in the effect of your presentation on your listeners. Your messages and your delivery can be enhanced or damaged by the way you present ideas. In an effort to analyze the behaviors of others in presenting information, take the next few days to observe professors, classmates, and others as they present information. Consider the messages (words, ideas) and the manner of presentation (physical and vocal factors of delivery). Take notes about the presenter and the presentation, and then answer these questions:

1. How did the speakers use "voice" to communicate ideas?

2. How did speakers vary their rates? What was the effect?
3. How were pauses used? When? To what effect?
4. What positive factors of physical and vocal delivery did you observe? What effect did these positive aspects have on you, the listener?
5. What negative factors of physical and vocal delivery did you observe? What effect did these negatives have on you as the listener?
6. What will you remember about presentations from this activity?

Presentational Aids

Speeches and presentations can often be strengthened by the addition of materials to help audience members focus on and remember the topic. **Presentational aids,** also referred to as visual aids or audiovisual aids, are materials and equipment, such as diagrams, models, real objects, photographs, tables, charts, graphs, and computer-generated materials, that speakers may use to enhance the content of the speech as well as the delivery. Students often think that the only time they will be required to use presentational aids is in classroom speech assignments. In reality, however, speeches using visual materials are presented quite frequently, and many speeches depend on them. For example, imagine an architect explaining the floor plans for a new high-rise office building without a drawing, model, or photograph; a company executive explaining this year's annual profits and losses compared to last year's without a chart or graph; a coach explaining a play without a diagram; a teacher telling the class where Mauritius is located without a map or globe; or a salesperson selling a product without showing it.

Our world has become extremely information oriented. Because people are constantly bombarded with information from a variety of sources, it is important to present information in a way that captures the interest and attention of listeners. This is difficult when the audience is already experiencing information overload. Good aids can help.

Such presentational aids offer many advantages. If "one picture is worth a thousand words," then presentational aids are an excellent way to strengthen and reinforce the development and proof of a point. Such aids are a special form of supporting and clarifying materials, because they combine both verbal and visual modes of presentation. When carefully designed and used, presentational aids can help a speaker do the following:

Save time

Gain attention and hold interest

Clarify and support main points

Reinforce or emphasize main points

Improve retention of information

Research has shown that audiences remember information longer when it is accompanied by visual or presentational aids.[14] In many of today's businesses, in a variety of positions, employees are required to make presentations and to use the computer to enhance their presentations. Some company managers believe that unless the presenter uses the computer for audio, visual, or audiovisual aids, the speaker is not really performing well. Although classroom teachers do not always require the use of computer-generated or computer-assisted presentational materials, it is important to realize that they are common in the workplace. More and more, educators are required to make computer-aided presentations. Even medical doctors and dentists are creating computer programs to help explain procedures, illnesses, and treatments to their patients. We'll next look at types of presentational aids and the methods of presenting them in speeches.

Choosing and Using Presentational Aids

When planning to use presentational aids, keep the following guidelines in mind:

1. *Presentational aids should serve a need.* They should never be used just for the sake of using them. In some cases visual aids are not appropriate, but in others, they can get a point across better than words alone. For example, it is easier to show an audience how to tie shoes than it is to tell them. Furthermore, it is easier to tell *and* to show them.

2. *Presentational aids should be planned and adapted to the audience and the situation.* For example, the size of the visual aid and the distance between you and your audience should be considered. The visual material should be kept simple and free from too much detail.

3. *Presentational aids should not dominate or take over a speaker's job.* They should supplement, but never replace, the speaker. Do not rely too heavily on visual aids, but instead use them to help elaborate or explain a point or idea or to create interest. In a speech, visual aids always require explanation by the speaker in order to make them meaningful.

4. *Presentational aids should look as professionally prepared as possible.* Accurate and neat materials will create a positive impression on the audience and reflect favorably on the competence of the speaker. Aids should be free from factual and spelling errors. They should also be bright, attractive, and easy to read from any spot in the audience. Audience members ought to be able to see, read, and understand the presentational aid once the speaker has carefully explained it.

5. *Presentational aids should be practical—easy to prepare, use, and transport.* Aids should not interfere with the speaker and presentation, and they should not call undue attention to themselves.

6. *Presentational aids that are not original or that contain information that is not yours require documentation.* Cite your source either directly on the aid where your audience can see it or in the context of your speech.

7. *Visuals should contain only one idea—one graph per poster, and so on.* Remember that presentational aids you provide are meant to clarify and strengthen your message. You want to limit yourself to one idea per poster, slide, chart, graph, or computer-generated screen so that your listeners will be able to focus on that one idea at the time you are talking about that point or concept. Too much information distracts your listeners.

Using aids during a presentation requires planning and coordination. They should not distract the audience or interrupt the flow of the speech. See the Guidelines feature on page 289 for ideas on using these aids.

Kinds of Presentational Aids

There are many different kinds of visual aids. Those most frequently used include posters, real objects, models, photographs, diagrams, tables, and graphs. A special discussion of computer-generated graphics, scanned pictures, digitized pictures, and digitized video clips is included in a later section.

Real Objects. A real object is any article related to the speech topic that a speaker displays or demonstrates, such as a musical instrument, piece of sporting equipment, or kind of food. Using a real object can make your topic more immediate and interesting, but it can also create problems if the object is too large, too small, or too impractical to show. Pets, for example, are often unpredictable and can be distracting before, during, and after a speech.

These melon "heads" far better illustrate to a physiology class areas
of the brain than a verbal description would. The teacher has carefully considered what the most
salient characteristics of the brain
are and has found an ideal substitute that enhances, emphasizes,
clarifies, and reinforces the brain's
main features.

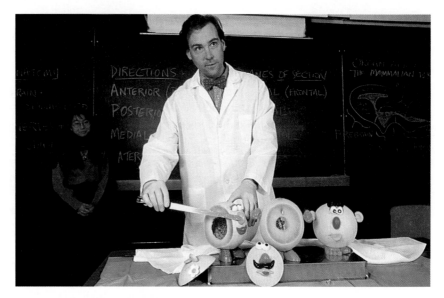

Models.   When displaying the actual article is not practical because of size or cost, a
model should be considered. A model—or representation of a real object—allows a
speaker to enlarge or shrink an object to a convenient size for display. For example, it
would be impractical to show the actual circuitry of a computer microchip, which is
no larger than a pinhead, or the inside of an actual space shuttle, which is enormous
(not to mention inaccessible). Models are appropriate in such circumstances.

Models can also be life-size. Currently, cardiopulmonary resuscitation (CPR) is a
popular and important subject. To demonstrate this procedure, speakers often use life-
size dummies of humans.

FIGURE 10.1

> **Instructor Assistant
> Area**

> **Study Area**

> **Test Area**

Classroom Layout

Simple Line Drawing

Line drawings do not need to be
elaborate or complex. In fact, line
drawings, sketches, and diagrams
can be rather simple.

Photographs and Prints.   When models are neither available nor practical, a
photograph may be used. A photograph is an excellent device for explaining details and surroundings. One student, speaking on artistic
style, brought prints of several paintings to illustrate their differences. A
student who spoke on the construction of the Egyptian pyramids showed
photos that she had taken on a vacation trip. She realized that the original photos were too small, so she had them enlarged for effective use in
the classroom. The typical photograph is usually too small to be seen
clearly unless the speaker moves through the audience or passes it
around or scans it into a computer presentation. In both instances, the
advantage of using photos is somewhat diminished because the audience
tends to pay more attention to the pictures than to what is being said.

Drawings, Sketches, and Diagrams.   When photographs or prints are unavailable, too small, or lack adequate detail, a drawing, sketch, or diagram
may be used. Don't worry if you're not artistic, because most drawings
used in classroom speeches are relatively simple. For example, Figure
10.1 is a line drawing used to describe how a classroom can be divided
in a beginning speech communication course. The diagram simply
shows the division of the room for various functions and makes a professor's explanation of a seating arrangement much easier for students
to comprehend.

FIGURE 10.2

Illustration of a Table

Tables display large amounts of data in a relatively small space. The more complex the data, the more explanation is required to make the table meaningful to your audience.

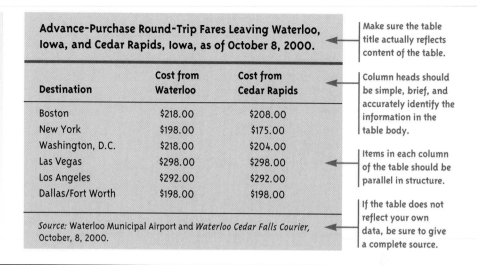

Advance-Purchase Round-Trip Fares Leaving Waterloo, Iowa, and Cedar Rapids, Iowa, as of October 8, 2000.		
Destination	**Cost from Waterloo**	**Cost from Cedar Rapids**
Boston	$218.00	$208.00
New York	$198.00	$175.00
Washington, D.C.	$218.00	$204.00
Las Vegas	$298.00	$298.00
Los Angeles	$292.00	$292.00
Dallas/Fort Worth	$198.00	$198.00

Source: Waterloo Municipal Airport and *Waterloo Cedar Falls Courier,* October, 8, 2000.

Make sure the table title actually reflects content of the table.

Column heads should be simple, brief, and accurately identify the information in the table body.

Items in each column of the table should be parallel in structure.

If the table does not reflect your own data, be sure to give a complete source.

Similarly, a speaker might use an architect's blueprint, a chart illustrating a company's organizational structure, a sketch of the basic positions of water-skiing, or a map of various segments of land. Virtually anything can be diagrammed or sketched.

Tables and Graphs.　Tables and graphs are used mainly to display statistics. A table is an orderly arrangement of data in columns to highlight similarities and differences, as shown in Figure 10.2.

Tables conveniently display large amounts of data in a relatively small space, but remember that a complex or lengthy (and perhaps boring) table will require an equally complex and lengthy explanation. As with any visual aid you decide to use, a table must be concise, simple, and clear so that the important information is easy to spot. Complex data are often better illustrated by a graph.

Graphs help to make statistical data vivid and illustrate relationships in ways that are easy for the audience to grasp. Line graphs, as illustrated in Figure 10.3, are particularly helpful for clarifying comparative data over time. Such graphs can help trace trends and show increases and decreases over a span of days, months, or years.

FIGURE 10.3

Example of Data Presented as a Line Graph

Line graphs are particularly helpful in clarifying comparative data over time.

Adapted from U.S. Census Bureau, *Statistical Abstract of the United States: 1999,* http://www.census.gov/prod/99pubs/99statab/sec10.pdf, accessed on February, 14, 2001.

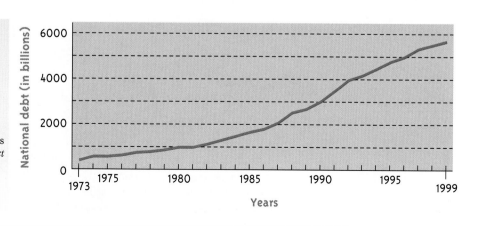

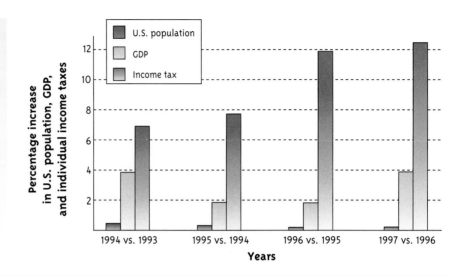

FIGURE 10.4

Example of Data Presented as a Bar Graph

Bar graphs show comparative data much more clearly and vividly than does, for example, a table.

Annual Report on the United States Government, 1997 (1998, March) Washington, DC: Congress of the U.S., House of Representatives, p. 3.

Note in Figure 10.3, for example, that the sharp upward slope of the line strongly emphasizes how dramatically the national debt increased between 1975 and 1997.

Bar graphs are another simple way to show comparisons. Note how much easier it is to compare the data depicted in the bar graph in Figure 10.4 than the data arranged in table form in Figure 10.2. Whenever possible, your visual aids should present only one or two basic relationships, so that your audience can quickly grasp your point.

Pie graphs are used to illustrate proportional divisions of a whole set of data. Each wedge of the pie represents a percentage of the whole. Pie graphs are often used to show distribution patterns and to illustrate national, state, or local budgets. Note in Figure 10.5 that the pie graph starts with a radius drawn vertically from the center to

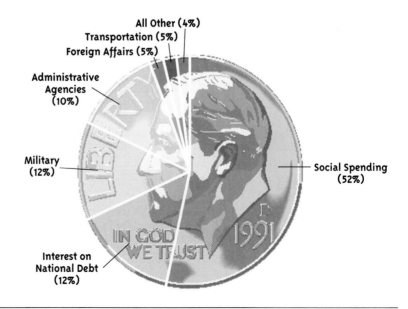

FIGURE 10.5

Example of Data Presented as a Pie Graph

A pie graph illustrates proportions of a whole set of data. Each wedge represents a percentage of the whole.

Annual Report on the United States Government, 1997 (1998, March) Washington, DC: Congress of the U.S., House of Representatives, p. 3.

the twelve o'clock position. Each segment is then drawn in clockwise, beginning with the largest and continuing down to the smallest.

Using Presentational Aids

1. Display visual materials only while you are using them. Do not distract your audience by showing your aids too early or by leaving them on display after you've finished talking about them. Even with a PowerPoint presentation, you can create a black, blank, or white screen in order not to distract your listeners.

2. Keep your presentational aids on display long enough to give everyone ample opportunity to absorb the information. Find the happy medium between "too long" and "not long enough."

3. Ensure that everyone can see your aids by making them neat, simple, large, bright, and readable. If you're using computer-generated text, the same guidelines apply. Depending on the size of the room, however, your font size should rarely be less than 36 points. For larger rooms, a 48-point or a 60-point font is desirable. The same thing applies to the television screen if you're in a distance learning classroom. Size, background, and color of text all become critical issues. For televised presentations, a blue background with either a white or yellow text color is preferable. The opposite is true for yellow or white on overhead transparencies and many posters, charts, or graphs. Light colors fade and are virtually invisible on acetate and paper products. Red and black text work better for noncomputer presentational aids, and often work better for computerized aids. Practice in the room with the equipment you'll use, well ahead of time.

4. Do not talk to your displayed objects or to the chalkboard. Discuss the content while maintaining eye contact with your audience.

5. Do not stand in front of your presentational aids. Determine where you will place or show your aids, and use a pointer or a laser to avoid blocking your audience's view.

6. Practice using your presentational aids until you feel comfortable with them. It becomes quite obvious to your listeners if you're uncomfortable and unfamiliar with the aids you've selected.

Methods of Presentation

The most frequently used methods of presentation are chalkboards, posters, projected visuals, and handouts.

Chalkboard. Although the chalkboard is the most readily available method of presenting visual aids, at least in most classrooms, some instructors will not allow you to use it. If you are unsure, check with your instructor. If it is allowed, here are several things to consider when you are planning to use a chalkboard:

1. *When to put information on the board.* Preferences vary from speaker to speaker and from instructor to instructor. Some speakers write on the board before they speak. If putting the information on the board before you speak will not interfere

with other presentations, and if you can cover what you have written (so as not to distract from other presentations), preparing the board in advance can simplify your delivery. To be safe, ask your instructor about his or her preference.

2. *How to write on the board.* This, of course, depends on the size of the room and your writing skills. Your writing should always be large enough and neat enough for everyone in the room to read. The appearance of your writing on the board communicates a message about you and your speech. Thus, you want what you write to create a positive impression.

3. *How to use the board when delivering your speech.* Even when reading from the board, you should always try to face your audience. Use a pointer, a ruler, or your outstretched arm to help guide listeners to the information on which you want them to focus. Whether writing on the board or reading from it, avoid talking to the chalkboard rather than your audience.

The chalkboard is a convenient visual device, but do not be fooled by its conveniences. If it is not used properly, it can be more of a distraction than an aid. Practice writing on the board before your speech. This will give you an idea of how it feels to write on the board. You will also be able to determine how large to write so that those sitting in the back row can see the information.

Posters.   Posters are another commonly used method of presenting information visually. The greatest advantage of posters is that they can be prepared in advance, which makes the speaker seem more efficient and professional. Many of the guidelines for writing on the chalkboard also apply to using posters. Here are three specific suggestions for using posters:

1. If an easel is not available, check to see whether there are clips on the board for hanging posters or whether you will need to use masking tape. If you must use masking tape, make large loops of tape and place them on the back of the poster in advance. Then, when you are ready to display the poster, merely place it on the board, pressing firmly on the tape loops to secure it. If you have more than one poster, you can place several of them on the board at once, or you can display each individually as you need it.
2. Make sure the poster is made of firm cardboard so that it will support itself if you have to stand it on a chalk tray or a table.
3. Posters should be displayed only when they are referred to in the speech. The rest of the time they should be turned over or covered so they don't distract the audience.

Projected Visuals.   The most common projected materials are slides, movies, overhead transparencies, and videotapes. The projection of such visuals requires planning and familiarity with the mechanical equipment. Each form has advantages and disadvantages, so knowing what each can and cannot do is vital. For example, showing slides and movies requires a totally darkened room, and the projectors may be noisy. Yet both enable you to show places and things that you could not show any other way. Films and videos add motion, color, and sound. But they can be costly and often tend to dominate a presentation by replacing the speaker for a period of time.

The most popular projected visual is the overhead transparency. These materials can be prepared in advance or created during a presentation, and whether prepared by the speaker or a professional, they are relatively inexpensive. In addition, overhead projectors are easy to use and do not require a darkened room.

When using an overhead projector, consider the following:

1. Make sure the projector is focused correctly so that everyone in the room can read what is on the transparency.
2. Cover information on the transparency until it is needed.
3. Use a pointer (pencil or pen) to direct the audience's attention to what is being discussed.
4. Practice using the overhead. Check it beforehand to make sure it is working correctly.

Mechanical devices, because of their potential for breakdown, require a backup method. It is a good idea to carry a spare bulb in case one burns out and to bring copies of visual aids in handout form.

Handouts.   Handouts can be a useful means of presenting information to your audience. If you are presenting a speech on organ donation, for example, you may want to hand out a copy of the form many states ask potential donors to carry. Or, if your speech mentions helpful persons or related organizations, a handout may list these, together with addresses or websites, so that audience members may obtain additional information. Handouts are particularly helpful if you are unable to use any other method. Among their advantages are that they can be prepared in advance and that each audience member gets a personal copy. Their main disadvantage is that they can become a distraction. Passing them out can interrupt the flow of your presentation, and audience members may pay more attention to the handouts than to the speech itself. As a result, you should use handouts only when you have no other alternatives or when you have a creative reason for doing so. In addition, you should wait until the end of the presentation to use them, if possible.

FIGURE 10.6

Advance-Purchase Round-trip Fares Leaving Waterloo, Iowa, October 8, 2000	
Destination	**Cost from Waterloo**
Boston	$218.00
New York	$198.00
Washington, D.C.	$218.00
Las Vegas	$298.00
Los Angeles	$292.00
Dallas/Fort Worth	$198.00

Source: Waterloo Municipal Airport and *Waterloo Cedar Falls Courier*, October 8, 2000.

Example of a Computer-Generated Visual Aid

Clip art from a presentational software program such as PowerPoint can also enhance your presentations.

Computer-Generated Presentational Aids

As a presentational tool, the computer has gained ever-increasing acceptance in both education and business. Many colleges and universities now require the use of computer-generated materials in a variety of presentations throughout a student's academic career. This class may be a good place to get a head start on preparing and using computer presentations. When you enter the workplace, you will be prepared to use the computer for your presentations.

Several excellent presentational software programs are available in college and university computer laboratories. Among the most popular is Microsoft's PowerPoint, which allows the presenter to select or create backgrounds, formats, layouts, colors, and tools to make a professional presentation (see Figure 10.6). Images and text can be animated to fade, dissolve, or move in from the top, the bottom, or either side of the slide. The presenter can scan in pictures, text, or other visuals (such as a brochure, a poster, a photograph), use a digital still camera, use a digital movie camera, use digitized clips from movies or other videos, and so on. The possibilities are almost endless. The kinds of materials we can create using the computer are limited only by the time, money, resources, and creativity at our disposal. The guidelines for use of other audiovisual aids apply to use of computer presentational materials, as well. There are, however, some additional suggestions you should consider if you are planning to use the computer to enhance your presentations. These are listed in the accompanying Guidelines feature.

Using Computer-Generated Aids

1. Do not overdo it! Just as you can have too many points in a speech and too many materials for traditional visual aids, you can present too much material on the computer. As a general rule, use a visual to support only 25 percent of your presentation. Select the materials carefully. Too many pictures, graphs, words, images, and animations can result in overload.

2. Make sure that the font size you use in your presentation is appropriate. Use nothing less than a 48-point font for a regular classroom. In a large lecture hall, use 60 to 72 points for headings and topics, and no less than 48 points for subpoints, quotations, and explanations.

3. Don't put too much on any given screen. It's easy to overdo it. If you put too many words or images on the "slides," people will not listen to what you have to say.

4. Remember that the computer visual is like any other visual: It is there to enhance the presentation, not to take the place of the speaker's words and ideas.

5. Practice using your computer visuals in the room in which you will present the speech, if possible, because what you see on the screen of your monitor and what people see on the screen in the presentation room may not be the same. Colors do not always enhance the material as well as they appear to on the small monitor screen. Sometimes the lighting can make a tremendous difference, and if you cannot dim the lights, you may want to change the background so that the materials are visible, clear, and easy to read anywhere in the audience. Check to see if lighting and reflections will cause problems and whether there are decreased sight lines at certain angles in the room. Also, practice to make sure you do not lose eye contact with your audience while presenting these aids. Using the computer should not distract you from staying in touch with your audience.

Developing Presentational Aids

Today many computer programs and technologies can help you develop presentational aids. If your university or college has a media center, and most do, check with the center or your instructor to learn about the most modern and easiest methods for developing visuals available to you. Certain programs and techniques will allow you to make graphics, charts, custom-made diagrams, and many other types of visual aids. Making professional-looking visual aids, whether computer-generated or traditional, is often quite simple and may require only that you become familiar with your school's offerings. Remember, too, that not every speech requires a high-tech application. In fact, many experts believe that we've gone too far in our use of graphics and images. Fewer images of higher quality, with more information, are preferable.

Polishing Your Delivery

The best way to polish your delivery is to practice, practice, practice. Practice early and often until you feel comfortable with your speech's content. Exactly how much practice you will need depends on a number of considerations, including how much experience you have had speaking before audiences, how familiar you are with your subject, and how long your speech is. There is no magic amount of time that will make your delivery perfect.

If your speech is not to be memorized, make sure to use slightly different wording in each run-through. When you memorize a speech, it's possible to master the words without mastering the content. Your goal should be to learn your speech, which will mean that you have mastered its ideas.

In practicing your delivery, it is important to start with small segments. For example, practice the introduction, then one main point at a time, and then the conclusion. After you have rehearsed each small segment several times in isolation, practice the entire speech until you have mastered the content and the ideas flow smoothly.

If possible, practice in the same room in which you will speak or under similar conditions. This helps you see how things look from the front of the class and to plan where you should place your visual aids. Your last practice session should leave you with a sense of confidence and a desire to present your speech.

Finally, concentrate on what you are saying and to whom you are saying it. Above all, be yourself.

 Summary

Ethics, an individual's system of moral principles, plays a key role in communication. Ethical speakers always cite the sources of their information. The use of another person's information, language, or ideas without citing the originator or author is referred to as *plagiarism.* In addition, ethical speakers present fair, accurate, worthwhile, and relevant information and are conscious of their responsibilities to their listeners. Effective speakers, besides being ethical, are also knowledgeable, prepared, and self-confident.

Speech anxiety, the fear of speaking before an audience, can severely undermine a speaker's self-confidence. Speech anxiety is quite common; almost everyone who speaks before a group experiences it to some extent. The important thing is to be able to control it. Speech anxiety can be reduced by selecting a topic that you know and enjoy, preparation, confidence, positive thinking, practice, and knowing the surroundings in which your presentation will take place. International students have expressed concern that their listeners will not understand them and that they will be embarrassed. Some students from co-cultures also have anxiety because their cultural norms do not fit with the expectations in mainstream culture.

Communication apprehension, an anxiety syndrome associated with either real or anticipated communication with another person or persons, is the severest form of speech anxiety. An individual who suffers from communication apprehension will actually remain silent rather than risk communicating. Everyone who fears speaking before a group does not necessarily suffer from communication apprehension. Some nervousness is natural, and if controlled, can energize your presentation. If your anxiety is such that you cannot present a speech, seek the help of your instructor, a school counselor, or use *systematic desensitization,* a technique in which relaxation is associated with an anxiety-producing situation.

A poorly written speech can be improved by effective delivery, and a well-written speech can be ruined by an ineffective delivery. Yet there are no rules that will guarantee every speaker an effective delivery in every situation. The only consistent rule is that you must be yourself.

Although a speech may be delivered in many different ways, the four most common methods of delivery are impromptu, manuscript, memorized, and extemporaneous. An *impromptu* speech is delivered without planning or preparation. The *manuscript* speech is read word for word from a script. A *memorized* speech is presented from memory, usually based on a word-for-word script. An *extemporaneous* speech is a carefully prepared and researched presentation for which the speaker uses few notes and tries to be spontaneous in choosing words.

Many beginning speakers overlook the important role that voice plays in delivery. The three essential aspects of voice are *vocal quality,* the overall impression of the voice; *intelligibility,* the clarity of the sounds and the pronunciation and articulation of the words; and *vocal variety,* the *rate, force,* and *pitch* variations that add exhuberance to a speaker's voice. In addition, many physical factors contribute to the success of a presentation. These include body movements such as stepping to the side, forward, or backward; *gestures,* the movements of head, arms, and hands to help illustrate, emphasize, or make a point; facial expressions, the configurations of the face that can reflect, augment, contradict, or be unrelated to a speaker's vocal delivery; and *eye contact,* the extent to which a speaker looks directly at audience members. Effective eye contact establishes a bond between the speaker and the audience and makes listeners believe they are each being addressed personally.

Many different kinds of presentational or visual aids can be used to enhance a speaker's words. *Presentational aids* are materials and equipment, such as diagrams, models, real objects, photographs, tables, charts, and graphs, that speakers may use to enhance the speech's content as well as its delivery. When visual aids are used as supporting and clarifying materials, they save time; gain attention; reinforce clarity, support, or emphasize main points; and improve retention. The most frequently used visual aids are real objects, models, diagrams, pictures, tables, and graphs.

The most common methods of presenting visuals are chalkboards, posters, projected visuals, and handouts. The projection of visual aids requires planning and familiarity with the mechanical device to be used. The most common projected visuals are slides, overhead transparencies, movies, and videotapes. In some classrooms, you may have access to computers and the capability to create computer-generated presentational aids. Learn computer applications, but don't overdo them in your speeches.

The best way to polish your delivery is to practice, practice, practice. The amount of time spent rehearsing a speech will determine how effective your delivery will be.

DISCUSSION STARTERS

1. Which quality of an effective speaker—ethics, knowledge, preparation, or self-confidence—would you say is the most important? Why?
2. Why do you think most people are so fearful of speaking before an audience?
3. Your best friend must give a speech and is frightened about it. What advice would you give to help your friend manage this fear?
4. What are the vocal characteristics that distinguish an effective from an ineffective speech delivery?
5. Why is the way a speech sounds to a listener more important than its content?
6. On what basis should a speaker select one method of delivery over another?
7. If you were to develop an evaluation form to assess a speaker's vocal delivery, what factors

would you include, and how would you evaluate them?

8. What nonverbal behaviors distinguish effective speakers from ineffective speakers?

9. When should a speaker use presentational aids in a speech?

10. If you were advising beginning speakers, what would you tell them about using notes in their first speech?

11. Based on the information you learned in this chapter, what advice would you give to a beginning speaker about delivery?

12. When might speakers want to be wary of computer-generated presentational aids?

NOTES

1. D. Zarefsky, *Public Speaking Strategies for Success,* 2nd ed. (Boston: Allyn and Bacon, 1999), 25.

2. J. Wenburg and W. W. Wilmot, *The Personal Communication Process* (New York: Wiley, 1973); and R. L. Johannesen, *Ethics in Human Communication,* 2nd ed. (Prospects Heights, Ill.: Waveland Press, 1983).

3. Zarefsky.

4. *Encyclopaedia Britannica,* "Anxiety," Britannica.com, Inc., 1999–2000, accessed on February 14, 2001, http://search.britannica.com/.

5. Bruskin Associates, "What Are Americans Afraid Of?" *The Bruskin Report,* 53 (1973); D. Goleman, "Social Anxiety: New Focus Leads to Insights and Therapy," *New York Times,* 18 December, 1984, C1; J. Solomon, "Executives Who Dread Public Speaking Learn to Keep Their Cool in the Spotlight," *Wall Street Journal,* 4 May 1990; and a 1993 segment of ABC's *20/20* that pointed out that the most common situation in which people are likely to experience anxiety is giving a speech.

6. J. C. McCroskey, "The Communication Apprehension Perspective," in *Avoiding Communication: Shyness, Reticence, and Communication Apprehension,* eds. J. A. Daly and J. C. McCroskey (Beverly Hills, Calif.: Sage, 1984), 13.

7. E. C. Buehler and W. Linkugel, *Speech: A First Course* (New York: HarperCollins, 1962).

8. E. Yook and W. J. Seiler, "An Investigation into the Communication Needs and Concerns of Asian Students in Speech Communication Performance Classes," *Basic Communication Course Annual* 2 (November 1990): 47–75.

9. D. W. Staacks and J. D. Stone, "An Examination of the Effect of Basic Speech Courses, Self-Concept, and Self-Disclosure on Communication Apprehension," *Communication Education* 33 (1984): 317–32; and R. S. Littlefield and T. L. Sellnow, "The Use of Self-Disclosure as a Means for Reducing Stage Fright in Beginning Speakers," *Communication Education* 36 (1987): 62–64.

10. J. A. Daly, A. L. Vangelisti, H. L. Neel, and P. D. Cavanaugh, "Pre-Performance Concerns Associated with Public Speaking Anxiety," *Communication Quarterly* 37 (1989): 39–53.

11. S. R. Glaser, "Oral Communication Apprehension and Avoidance: The Current Status of Treatment Research," *Communication Education* 30 (1981): 321–41; J. Ayres and T. S. Hopf, "Visualization: A Means of Reducing Speech Anxiety," *Communication Education* 30 (1985): 318–23; and A. M. Rossi and W. J. Seiler, "The Comparative Effectiveness of Systematic Desensitization and an Integrative Approach in Treating Public Speaking Anxiety: A Literature Review and Preliminary Investigation," *Imagination, Cognition and Personality* 9 (1989–90): 49–66.

   If your school does not have a systematic desensitization program you can write to the National Communication Association, 5105 Backlick Rd., Building E, Annandale, VA 22003, for information on how to reduce stage fright. Also, see J. Ayres and T. Hoft, *Coping with Speech Anxiety* (Norwood, N.J.: Ablex, 1994).

12. J. C. Humes, "Read a Speech Like a Pro," in *Talk Your Way to the Top* (New York: McGraw-Hill, 1980), 125–35; and J. Venlenti, *Speak Up with Confidence: How to Prepare, Learn, and Deliver Effective Speeches* (New York: Morrow, 1982), 23–26.

13. S. Chaiken, "Communicator Physical Attractiveness and Persuasion," *Journal of Personality and Social Psychology* 37 (1979): 1387–97.

14. E. P. Zayas-Baya, "Instructional Media in the Total Language Picture," *International Journal of Instructional Media* 5 (1977–78): 145–50.

Informative
Speaking

*"The desire to know is natural to good
[people].*
—*Leonardo DaVinci*

- Tell why information is powerful.
- Select an informative speech topic that focuses on objects, processes, events, or concepts.
- Gain an audience's attention by generating a need for your information and showing its relevance to their needs and interests.
- Demonstrate how to use organization and language to increase your audience's understanding of your topic.
- Explain how avoiding assumptions and personalizing information can contribute to the success of an informative speech.
- Deliver an effective informative speech.
- Be aware of evaluation criteria and use it to help you prepare and deliver the persuasive speech.

SCENARIO

Yanliu: Christine, do you know the last day we can sign up for spring semester classes?

Christine: In order to make sure that we get into those classes, the last date is December 1. If you want to take your chances, however, you can sign up any time during December.

Yanliu: I misplaced my course schedule booklet, but I knew you'd have the answer! Thanks, Christine.

Josh: I want to check out the recruiting fair here on campus to see what kinds of jobs are available and where. What do I need to do?

Susan: Contact Advising Services and ask for someone in Career Placement. They will sign you up and also get you a schedule.

Josh: Great! I'll do that right away. I know it's not until the end of the term that the Career Fair is held, but I'm anxious to find a job so I can start paying off my bills.

Lori: Professor James, I'm really interested in relational dialectics. I know that the theory can be applied to my own interpersonal relationships, but I'm a little fuzzy on exactly how to explain it. Can you help me?

Professor James: I'm delighted that you're interested in communication theory, Lori! Leslie Baxter and her associates have published many articles on relational dialectics over the years. Would you like me to give you some source citations so you can look up the articles on your own? ▪

Making Connections

Ways of Presenting Information

Instructors vary in their style of presenting information in their classes. Carefully observe two or three of your instructors, and note what they do or don't do to ensure their messages are received and understood by their students. You need not refer to them by name—your interest here is in their presentational styles and not who they are. Discuss the following in class:

1. What do the effective instructors do in their presentations to ensure that they are received and understood?
2. Describe how those qualities identified in the preceding question can be used in delivering an informative speech.
3. To conclude this exercise, discuss what a speaker must do to successfully get an audience similar to your class to receive and understand information.

In each example in the opening scenario, someone wants information and another person gives it. **Information,** according to the 1999–2000 *Merriam-Webster Dictionary,* is "the communication or reception of knowledge or intelligence," or, "knowledge obtained from investigation, study, or instruction."[1] This definition makes the act of informing seem fairly simple. Yet when you think about the amount and kinds of knowledge that you send and receive in a single day, providing information really isn't simple at all. Have you ever tried to teach someone how to perform CPR (cardiovascular pulmonary resuscitation), use a word processor, or play a card game? If you have, you know it takes time and care to present information in proper sequence and in amounts small enough to ensure that the listener understands correctly.

Teaching or informing others can be a rewarding and satisfying experience, but if you lack the required skills, it can also be frustrating. To help you in this area, we discuss how to present knowledge by means of the informative speech. This type of speech is one of the most often assigned in the speech communication classroom, because it is the most common presentation you'll make in all aspects of your life, from classroom to boardroom and everywhere in between. Knowing how to present information clearly and systematically will be a great benefit to you both personally and professionally throughout your life. You'll be grateful for the opportunity to practice informative speaking when your supervisor asks you to explain how your division works with new employees or when the local Rotary Club asks you to share ideas about computers in the classroom and the workplace. Learning what it takes to be an effective informative speaker will help you in many aspects of your life. We believe that informative speeches provide the foundation for most of the presentations people make in their lives. If you learn the fundamentals of informative speaking, you will be able to apply those concepts to other types of speeches.

Information and Power

Being informed helps reduce uncertainty. Thus, the person who possesses and controls information has power. When people need information concerning something about which they know little, they tend to turn to those who can provide the necessary information. For example, in the dialogues in this chapter's opening scenario, the person who has the desired information has the power to share it or not to share it. The greater your desire to have important information, the more valuable that infor-

The informative speech is meant to increase knowledge, whereas the purpose of the persuasive speech is to alter attitudes and behavior. Often there is a fine distinction between informative and persuasive speeches because there are elements of persuasion in an informative speech and information in a persuasive speech.

mation is to you. Thus, people who have the information you want, in a sense, gain control over you because of their power to give or withhold the knowledge you seek.

The ability to communicate information is essential in our society and will play an increasingly important role in the future. In fact, over the years we have moved from an economy based on agriculture and heavy industries, such as steel, machinery,

Making Connections

Freedom Forum Online

The Freedom Forum Online provides resources on current news related to free speech, free expression, and journalism. Stories are grouped by subject (e.g., First Amendment, free press, technology, professional journalism, etc.) with the top story in each section featured on the main page. Freedom Forum Online is a nonpartisan, international foundation dedicated to "free press, free speech, and free spirit for all people."

1. Access Freedom Forum Online at http://www.freedomforum.org/.
2. Click on one of the top stories on the main page and read the whole story.
3. Share the story you read with others and find out what they learned.

4. If you're near Washington, D.C., or Reston, Virginia, stop in and see the Newseum, a free museum dedicated to sharing all aspects of the news. You can see history through news broadcasts, be a newscaster for five minutes, or watch a live talk show as an audience member. In one area of the Newseum, you can access the current edition of your own local newspaper or any others. In other areas, you can view television newscasts from around the world. The wonders of technology are quite evident at the Newseum.

and automobile manufacturing, to an economy based on knowledge industries, such as research, health services, banking, training, and communications. During the 1950s, only about 17 percent of our labor force held information-related jobs. This figure has now increased to about 75 percent. This demand puts even more emphasis on workers' needs for greater skills in producing, storing, and delivering information. Much of the information we send and receive is written, but most is spoken. For example, teachers, trainers, consultants, media specialists, salespeople, technicians, doctors, nurses, lawyers, elected officials, and managers all depend on oral communication to succeed in their work.

Distinctions Between Informative and Persuasive Speaking

The general goal of informative speakers is to increase the knowledge of their listeners. There is a fine distinction between informing and persuading. The informative speech is meant to increase knowledge, whereas the persuasive speech is meant to alter attitudes and behavior. Information can be presented without any attempt at persuasion, but persuasion cannot be accomplished without attempting to inform.

The difference between the two is best explained through examples. A car salesperson must rely on persuasion to sell cars. However, to persuade someone to buy a car, the salesperson will probably spend a lot of time informing the customer about the advantages of buying a specific model. The salesperson might succeed in increasing the customer's knowledge and understanding of the car (informing), yet the salesperson may fail in convincing the customer to buy the car (persuading). Persuasion takes place when a person stops presenting information to increase understanding and begins to present information to alter behavior.

A math professor, in explaining a complex problem, is attempting to help students understand how the problem can be solved. The professor is not hoping to persuade the students how it should be done but is trying to help them gain the knowledge and understanding they need to find the solution on their own. Of course, the professor could add an element of persuasion if he or she tried to show that one way of solving the problem was better than another, but that would probably be less important than teaching the basic problem-solving skills.

The key to understanding the difference between information and persuasion lies in recognizing that *although information may contain some elements of persuasion, all persuasion must provide information.* Therefore, what separates an informative speech from a persuasive one is the goal of the speaker. Persuasion is discussed in more detail in the next chapter.

Topics for Informative Speeches

Surprisingly, some students believe they have little information to share with others. In actuality, most students have a wealth of information and a vast list of potential topics based on what they have learned from classes, readings, and other experiences. For example, geography, agriculture, computer science, computers in the workplace, the Internet, social science, health education, educational changes, technology in agricul-

Making Connections

Using the Web to Find Speech Topics and Examples

The Web can be an excellent source of ideas for topics as well as speech examples to help you consider what you want to accomplish in your own speeches. Here are some interesting sites with specific information to be gained from each listed.

1. An overview of the life and times of two significant leaders in the women's rights movement, Elizabeth Cady Stanton and Susan B. Anthony may be found at http://www.pbs.org/stantonanthony/.

2. The Invisible Web ("the search engine of search engines") indexes more than 10,000 databases, archives, and search engines, offering links to targeted search sources. Users can search by keyword, perform an advanced search, or browse a list of entries organized under "Hot List" by accessing http://www.invisibleweb.com/.

3. Speechtips.com provides instructions on planning, writing, and delivering a speech.

Sample speeches for a variety of situations are provided at http://www.speechtips.com/.

4. Bartleby.com is a source for free online literature, verse, and reference books. You can access complete electronic versions of the Columbia Encyclopedia, the *American Heritage Dictionary, Roget's II: The New Thesaurus, Simpson's Contemporary Quotations,* and *The American Heritage Book of English Usage* at http://www.bartleby.com/.

5. Great American Speeches, at http://www.pbs.org/greatspeeches/, is a PBS site that offers a collection of more than ninety speeches from many of the nation's "most influential and poignant speakers of the recorded age." Some of the speeches include background and audio- or videoclips.

These sites were identified by Sherwyn Morreale in Morreale's Mailbag, *Spectra,* National Communication Association newsletter (February and June, 2000).

ture, technology in the workplace, volunteerism, beneficial products from the rainforest, natural healing, first aid, art, music, physical education, political science, sociology, chemistry, health, and on-the-job experiences all offer potential topics for an informative speech.

The topic potential for an informative speech is virtually limitless. There are, however, some guidelines that you should not ignore (suggested in Chapter 7) for selecting a speech topic. They are as follows:

1. Choose a topic that will allow you to convey an important thought or action to your audience.

2. Choose a topic that is familiar and interesting to you.

3. Choose a topic that is important to you.

4. Choose a topic that will be or can be made interesting to your audience.

5. Choose a topic that can be well developed within the speech's time limit.

Communicating with others is easier when they see value in and uses for the information presented. Most audiences want the information they receive to be important and useful to them. Select a topic that will allow you to provide benefits to your audience. Sometimes a topic will speak for itself, such as "How to Make Extra Money in an Innovative and Challenging Career Field" or "Five Ways to Make College Life Easier." Both of these topics, at least in their titles, provide incentives for a typical college audience to accept them as potentially beneficial. Topics with less self-evident value such as Acela's debut on the nation's rails, may require that you clearly spell out incentives to your audience to encourage them to listen to what you have to say.

If something interests you, chances are it will also interest others. Roland, for example, has been involved with computers ever since he can remember, first with videogames and then with his own personal computer. In high school he took a few programming classes, and now, as a college major in computer science, he has learned much about the most recent technological advances in the field of graphic arts and design programming. This specialized knowledge made a natural topic for his informative speech. Yet, at the time of the assignment, Roland never even thought of it. Only after his speech professor spent some time asking him about his interests did he decide to speak on graphic design. The assignment required the use of visual aids. Roland already had many available aids to choose from, including flowcharts of his computer programs and the graphics that he and others had designed. He was also able to expand his experiences and knowledge by interviewing professors and doing more research on a subject about which he really cared.

During the past semester Cynda has been an intern volunteer for a local family crisis center. Her responsibilities include answering phone calls from troubled people and referring them to experts and organizations that can help them with their problems. Given this experience and her major in clinical psychology, Cynda wisely chose to give her informative speech on the growing role of crisis hot lines in serving the mental health needs of local communities.

Roland and Cynda are probably no different from most of you. At first they doubted that they had anything worthwhile about which to speak. Like them, if you stop to think about your past experiences and interests, you will discover that you, too, have a great deal to share with others.

Successful speakers next consider their audiences. They communicate information accurately and clearly, but most important, they make the information they present meaningful and interesting to their audience by providing new information or correcting misinformation.

Informative speech topics can be classified in many different ways. One scheme divides them into speeches about objects, processes, events, and concepts.[2]

Objects

Speeches about objects examine concrete subjects, such as people, animals, structures, and places. Here are some possible object topics:

South Park (TV show)	Martin Luther King Jr.
Barney the dinosaur	Compact discs
Scientific projects in Antarctica	Nontraditional students
Parenting issues	Single parents
Hillary Rodham Clinton	The future of space travel
Musical instruments	Electronic scoreboards
The World Wide Web	Electronic communication
Tropical rainforests	The Internet

These topics are general and must be narrowed in order to meet the guidelines of most classroom speaking situations.

Here are some specific purpose statements for informative speeches about concrete subjects, following the guidelines suggested in Chapter 7:

- To inform the audience about the latest innovations in MP3 technology
- To inform the audience about the important contributions that the nontraditional student makes in the college classroom
- To inform the audience about the role of the Internet and communication with others
- To inform the audience about the World Wide Web as an information source

Each of these purpose statements is appropriate for an informative speech.

Processes

A process topic usually focuses on a demonstration in which the speaker explains how something is done or how it takes place. Here are a few sample specific purpose statements for informative speeches about processes:

- To inform the audience about how to invest in the stock market to ensure a financially secure future
- To inform the audience about how to write a résumé
- To inform the audience about how to invest in a house while in college
- To inform the audience about how to diet with low-fat foods
- To inform the audience about how to help someone who is having a heart attack

Speeches about processes generally serve two purposes: to increase understanding and to teach someone *how to do something.* This could involve anything from how to do CPR to how to buy the right car.

Process speeches are usually organized in time-sequence (chronological) order, meaning that they proceed step by step from the beginning of the process to its end. For example, if you were to explain to your audience how to skydive, you would take them through all the necessary steps and procedures so that they would understand exactly what a sky diver does.

The demonstration of a process usually benefits from the use of a visual aid. Some processes may require an actual demonstration in order to be understood. For example, to inform listeners about how to fold napkins may require that you do the folding during the speech presentation.

Events

Informative speeches about events discuss happenings or occasions. The many possible topics include the following:

Election 2000	Cloning capabilities
Nuclear accidents	Marathons
Somalia	The fall of communism
Cancer	The NAMES Project quilt display
Baseball's moral decline	The Clothesline Display
Revitalization of America's inner cities	Chemical and biological weapons
El Niño and weather patterns	

Appropriate specific purposes for some of these topics might include the following:

- To inform the audience about the latest developments in curing cancer
- To inform the audience about the changes in specific societies because of changes in government structure
- To inform the audience about the media's impact on major sporting events, such as the college football Bowl Championship Series, the World Series, or the Super Bowl
- To inform the audience about the economic impact of weather patterns and disasters attributed to El Niño
- To inform the audience about projects that support survivors of abuse
- To inform the audience about projects that support those who have lost someone to AIDS

Concepts

Speeches about concepts deal with abstract topics such as beliefs, theories, ideas, and principles. The challenge is to make the subject matter concrete so that the audience can easily understand it. Concept-based topics include the following:

Relationship development	Learning theory
Principles of reading	Liberalism
Computer theory	Philosophy of sports
Love	Theory of rap music

These topics are too vague to be meaningful. If you were to ask a dozen people what each term or phrase means, you would probably receive a dozen different answers. Thus, the speaker is responsible for narrowing and focusing the subject so the audience understands the intended meaning. Here are specific purpose statements based on some of the general, abstract topics:

- To inform the audience about some common misconceptions regarding relationship development
- To inform the audience about two of the most common principles in learning theory
- To inform the audience about the latest sports philosophy
- To inform the audience about the theory of rap music as a specific form of social communication

Speeches about concepts take extra time and effort to develop because of their abstract nature. These topics require the use of concrete examples, definitions, and clear language.

Whether a speech is about an object, a process, an event, or a concept is not always clear because a subject may overlap these categories. Often the specific purpose that the speaker chooses to emphasize determines the category. Therefore, it is important to decide your approach to the subject and then develop your speech accordingly. If you are unsure of which approach to take, review Chapter 7 for more specific information about topic selection and how to determine which topics may be best suited for you and your audience (see the Appendix at the end of this chapter for more topics).

Making Connections

Purpose Statements and Speech Planning

As you prepare for researching, organizing, and presenting an informative speech, think about and apply the information presented in this book and by your classroom teacher.

Write a response to each of the following and discuss your responses in class as a whole or in small groups:

1. Select one or two specific purpose statements from each of the categories of informative speeches presented in this section: objects, processes, events, and concepts.
2. Refer to the section on organizational patterns in Chapter 9. Indicate which pattern of organization would be best suited for each speech purpose you have selected.

3. Refer to the section in Chapter 10 on presentational aids. Determine if visual aids would be appropriate, and justify your decision.
4. In Chapter 8 we discussed supporting materials. What forms of support would you use to help make your presentation clear to your audience?
5. In Chapter 7 we discussed the importance of the audience in topic selection and presentation. How would you relate the subject to your audience?
6. How has this exercise helped you prepare and develop an informative presentation?

Preparing and Developing an Informative Speech

The previous chapters on public communication relate directly to the principles and skills of informative speaking. All aspects of topic selection; audience analysis; information gathering; preparation of supporting and clarifying materials; and organizing, outlining, and delivering a speech are crucial to the effectiveness and eventual success of your informative presentation. In addition, you should be familiar with strategies for competing with distractions and noises, such as students arriving late, an airplane flying overhead, a lawn mower outside the window, and whispering in the audience. Such interferences cannot be ignored if you want to be successful in transmitting information to others. To achieve your main goal of increasing the audience's knowledge, you must strive to attain two subgoals: gain their attention and increase their understanding.

Gain and Maintain Audience Attention

Motivating the audience to pay attention is critical to the success of any speech (see Chapter 9 for more on motivating your audience to listen). To accomplish this, you should follow a strategy that will work well for your audience.

Generate a Need for the Information. One student wondered why the audience had not paid attention to his informative speech on the harmful effects of smoking. He had failed to consider two things when selecting and preparing his speech: No one in the class smoked, and everyone already knew, or at least thought they knew, about the harmful effects of smoking. As a result, the audience felt it was unnecessary to pay attention. If the speaker had analyzed the audience, he could have made the appropriate adjustments. Then he might have started his speech by saying the following:

> I realize that none of you smoke and that's good. I also realize that you probably know a lot about the harmful effects of smoking. But did you know that smoke from other people's cigarettes can be just as harmful to you, or even more harmful, than smoking yourself? Let me explain.

This opening attempts to pique the audience's curiosity and their need to know by asking a rhetorical question. Here are some other examples of rhetorical questions used to open speeches:

- Scientists have been working for years on the cure for the common cold, and I believe that I have found it. Do you know what I discovered?
- Do you want to know a sure way to keep a job?
- Do you know why the number of suicides among college students is on the rise?
- Why is "thin" so important in U.S. society and the world?
- What do you think is the most important skill you can learn in college?
- Why is there so much violence in our society?

Speakers can also use questions meant to generate responses from the audience as a strategy to gain and maintain audience interest and attention.

Create Information Relevance. People are much more likely to pay attention when they believe a speech relates directly to them. A speaker who gives an audience a reason to listen by relating the topic to their needs and interests creates **information relevance.** Ask yourself if the information you intend to present is relevant to your listeners, and if it is not, think about how you might make it so. One student presented an extremely well researched speech on air pollution and its effects on people. He used several excellent examples about pollution on the East and West coasts but never related them to his listeners, who were from the Midwest. To make his speech more relevant, he should have related the information to Midwesterners and why they in particular should be concerned about the effects of pollution.

Another speaker, talking about space technology and its contributions to our daily lives, used several examples to make her topic relevant and useful to her audience. In discussing products that were specifically developed for use in space, but now have become part of our everyday lives, she mentioned Velcro. She pointed out that Velcro is now commonly used on clothing, shoes, handbags, and many other items. She then held up a jacket to illustrate how Velcro works. The audience immediately recognized the relevance of her topic.

Provide a Fresh Perspective. Information that is perceived as *new* also attracts the attention of an audience. But whenever this statement is mentioned in class, some students immediately respond, "But there isn't anything new to present." Actually, discussing something new does not necessarily mean that you have to present something about which the audience has never heard. It does mean that you need to devise a new view or angle. There are subjects that we have heard discussed many times, such as AIDS, abortion, capital punishment, gun control, pollution, smoking, drugs, safe sex, and the use of seat belts. But a speaker who provides a fresh perspective on a familiar topic makes it more interesting and, thus, increases the chances of holding the audience's attention. One speaker informed the audience about illegal drugs that are medically helpful in treating certain diseases. She began her speech in the following manner:

> You have read and heard so much about cocaine, crack, heroin, and other illegal drugs that you are probably sick of the subject, but these drugs are not all bad. You may, at first, think that I am too liberal, but my mother is on drugs and I am glad of it. You see, my mother is suffering from cancer and the only relief she can get is from the small doses of heroin she receives each day to ease the pain. Today, I am going to inform you about illegal drugs that actually aid our sick and dying.

This approach is not necessarily new, but it is different. Rather than take a stand either for or against the banning of illegal drugs, the speaker focused on certain instances in which the use of illegal drugs can be beneficial. This also helped her to stay within the guidelines of the informative speech.

Focus on the Unusual. Sometimes focusing on an unusual aspect of a topic helps a speaker maintain the attention of the audience. Another speaker began her speech as follows:

> One summer day in 1948, Earle Smith borrowed $150.00 from the director of Harvard's Botanical Museum in order to join his friend in an archaeological dig in the highlands of Mexico.
>
> But these adventurers didn't discover the gold or jewels that we would associate with a great find. Instead they found 914 specimens of corn. Some of these kernels, perhaps two or three millennia old, were eventually put in hot oil, and amazingly, the oldest known corn in the world still popped. The director later wrote, "Seldom in Harvard's history has so small an investment paid so large a return."
>
> Admittedly, few of us consider corn to be anything more than a food to be eaten in the theater or at family picnics. However, the 1992 book *The Story of Corn* states that the average American ingests three pounds of corn in various forms every day. In one year, this adds up to 1,095 pounds of corn per person. That's almost 43 tons if we live to be 78.
>
> So, lend me an ear, and we'll explore corn and its relevance to human culture. To do so, we will first examine the history of corn and its importance to those who planted it. Second we'll discover the diverse roles corn plays today.[3]

Gaining and maintaining the attention of the audience is extremely important in presenting information. Audience members must believe they will benefit from receiving the information, believe it is relevant to their lives, and find it interesting enough to want to listen. Achieving this can be quite challenging to the beginning speaker, but by making your audience the central focus of the speech and using a little creativity, you can easily gain and hold their attention.

Increase Understanding of the Topic

Once you have gained your listeners' attention, you have created the opportunity to increase their understanding. Understanding is the ability to interpret, grasp, or assign meaning to an idea. You can increase your audience's understanding by organizing your presentation systematically, choosing appropriate language, and providing clear definitions.

Organize Your Presentation. In a well-organized speech, ideas are managed in a clear and orderly sequence that makes the material easy to follow and understand. Effective organization helps increase the speaker's credibility and improves the audience's comprehension and retention of information. Refer back to Chapter 9 and review the two organizational techniques that aid listeners' understanding: planned repetition and advance organizers.

Plan for Repetition. **Planned repetition** is the deliberate restating of a thought in order to increase the likelihood that the audience will understand and remember it. The repetition of information generally helps us remember things more completely. For example, we often repeat a new acquaintance's name several times to make sure that we will remember it later.

The power of repetition is so great that it is the guiding principle behind most television commercials. Although we may find it bothersome, the constant repetition of the same commercial reminds us of the product and thus increases the chances of our purchasing it. You can use this same principle in an informative speech to get your audience to remember key ideas. For example, you might say the following:

> The relationship between thought, language, and reality is called linguistic relativity—the relationship is called linguistic relativity. Once again, linguistic relativity is the relationship between thought, language, and reality.

> The combination is 37–45–72–6. That's 37–45–72–6.

You could also show the safe's combination on a computer slide presentation, put it on a poster, or write it on the board for additional repetition and emphasis. Internal summaries and previews may also include repetition to help the listener remember the points you've already made and to help them stay focused on what is to come in the speech.

Use Advance Organizers. **Advance organizers** are similar to signposts in that they signal what is coming, but they also warn that the information coming is significant. They signal the listener to pay attention.

> This is very important.
> Now get this.
> You will need to know the following.

These warnings get the attention of your audience and emphasize that the forthcoming information is both necessary and important. Teachers use advance organizers to make sure that students know what is essential. Examples include the following:

> This will probably be included on your next test.
> The following is vital if you are going to understand the overall concept.
> The next three points are crucial to your understanding of the problem.

Advance organizers also serve as previews of main points. Using advance organizers in an informative speech introduction helps your audience concentrate and focus on what is coming in the speech. For example, one speaker used the following statement in her introduction to let the audience know what was coming and what was important to meet her specific purpose: "Let's first define critical thinking, then let's examine its decline, and finally, let's learn how we can develop our own critical thinking philosophy."

Secretary of State Colin Powell is known for his use of clear and understandable language when he informs others.

Choose Language Carefully. It is extremely important to match your level of language to the knowledge your audience already possesses about your topic. If you are speaking with experts or with people who are familiar with your topic, you are free to use technical terms without explaining them, but if your audience is unfamiliar with your subject, you will need to choose your words carefully and define any special terms. In some cases, you will want to avoid technical terms altogether. This may be necessary when such terms would only confuse your audience or when your audience lacks the ability or background to understand them. Sometimes a speaker's use of too many technical terms will turn an audience off or even create hostility. A speaker should choose language carefully to avoid creating unnecessary problems. When possible, choose words that are concrete rather than words that are abstract, and use descriptions to make your points clearer.

Use Concrete Words. To increase your audience's understanding, try to use as many concrete words as possible. As discussed in Chapter 4, concrete words are symbols for specific things that can be pointed to or experienced through the senses. Thus, concrete words stand for specific places, objects, or acts: Terri Donovan, Abilene, a personal computer, writing a letter to a friend. When you use concrete language that is familiar to your listeners, they will form mental pictures similar to your own. For example, if you say that something is the size of a dime, all your listeners should form a fairly accurate picture of the size you have in mind. Because of their specificity, concrete words leave less room for misinterpretation and misunderstanding.

In contrast, abstract words refer to ideas, qualities, or relationships, such as democracy, evil, and love. Their meanings depend on the experiences and intentions of the persons using them. A speaker who says that "the local food program is good for the people" may mean either that the food in the program is nutritious or that the program as a whole is beneficial. Because of its lack of precision, abstract language may leave listeners confused about the speaker's true intent.

In a speech, one speaker stated, "There are many things I don't like about our defense spending." Because this statement is too general and vague, it had little impact on her audience. A more precise statement would have been "There are two things I don't like about our defense spending. It costs taxpayers $200 billion each year and it takes money from desperately needed education and health programs." The second statement is concrete and specific, and thus more forceful and clear.

Making Connections

Choose Concrete Language

In Chapter 4, we stated that concrete language is more meaningful and more easily understandable to listeners. Rewrite the following sentences to make them more concrete:

1. The computer is a huge benefit for students and workers.
2. The bridge was constructed of masses of steel that ran for a great distance.
3. The university provides access to all students, regardless of background or origin.
4. Sex on campus has declined dramatically for quite some time.
5. Alcohol consumption in America is dangerous.

Discuss your changes in class.

Abstract words allow listeners to choose from a wide range of personal images, whereas concrete words help listeners focus on the specific image that the speaker has in mind. Thus, as you prepare an informative speech, you should try to choose the most concrete words possible.

Use Description.   To make something more concrete, a speaker will often describe its size, quantity, shape, weight, composition, texture, color, age, strength, or fit. Words used to describe something are called **descriptors.** The more descriptors a speaker uses that relate to the listeners' experiences, the greater the likelihood that the message will be understood. Here is how Jim used descriptors in talking about the construction of a building:

> The first requirement when constructing a building is a sturdy foundation. The underlying groundwork for the foundation is called a footing. Footings are usually made of concrete and range from about one foot in depth for a house to ten feet in depth for a building with twenty floors. The width of footings ranges from one foot to the width of an entire building, depending on the soil's composition and its ability to support construction. Concrete, the result of mixing lime, cement, stone, sand, and water, is prepared for use. This mixture is gray, has the consistency of cake batter, and pours like lava coming down the side of a volcano. When concrete dries, it becomes as hard as steel.

Through his explanation, Jim gave meaning to the word *footing* by using size, quantity, color, composition, texture, and strength descriptors. His vivid, colorful language appeals to the senses, thus making a meaningful and lively presentation for his audience.

Use Definitions.   One way to ensure your audience's understanding is to define all potentially unfamiliar and complex words. Consider the importance of definitions in the following cases: Julia had been involved in computer programming and in her speech discussed flow sheets and GIGO; Daya spoke on communication apprehension, Sally on the squeal rule, and Jacques on the problem of ethnocentrism. In each

Making Connections

Bring Ideas to Life Through Description

Language choices help speakers communicate ideas in a meaningful way. How would you make the following subjects more meaningful and vivid to your listener through language choice? Write a phrase or two to describe each item.

The football stadium	The city in which the campus is located
The library on campus	The students in your speech class
The county courthouse	The main street of the city
The local antique shop	

Discuss your choices in class.

situation, many in the audience may not have understood the speaker's subject unless the basic terms were explained. For example, Julia defined *flow sheets* as written instructions that programmers use to set up step-by-step operations to be performed by the computer and *GIGO* as computer jargon meaning "garbage in, garbage out," or you get out of the computer what you put into it. Daya defined *communication apprehension* as the fear of communicating with others. Sally, in her speech, explained that a doctor uses the *squeal rule* when he or she tells the parents of a teenage girl that she is using birth control pills. *Ethnocentrism* was defined in Jacques's speech as the belief in the inherent superiority of one's own group and culture over another.

As you probably recall from Chapter 8, the most common form of definition used by speakers, the logical definition, usually contains two parts: the dictionary definition and the characteristics that distinguish the term from other members of the same category. An operational definition explains how an object or concept works, that a definition by example explains a term or a concept by using examples, either verbal or actual, to illustrate a point. In addition, there are four other methods of clearly defining a term for your listeners: using contrast, synonyms, antonyms, and etymologies.

Show Contrasts. A **contrast definition** is used to show or emphasize differences. This type of definition is helpful when you want to distinguish between similar terms. For example, a speaker discussing communication apprehension and speech anxiety differentiated one term from the other by stating that communication apprehension is a trait or global anxiety, whereas speech anxiety is a state or situational anxiety. A person suffering from communication apprehension may also have speech anxiety, but a person with speech anxiety may not necessarily have communication apprehension. A contrast definition may also point out differences in causes and effects. Thus, the speaker might point out that people with communication apprehension actively avoid all interaction with others, whereas people with speech anxiety merely feel a bit of controllable discomfort when addressing an audience.

Use Synonyms. The use of synonyms can also help clarify the meaning of a word. A **synonym** is a word, phrase, or concept that has exactly the same or nearly the same meaning as another word, term, or concept. In describing a communicative extrovert, a speaker used the phrases "willingness to talk openly," "uninhibited speech," and "ability to speak in any situation without reservation." Each phrase describes the behavior that might be exhibited by a person who is a communicative extrovert.

Use Antonyms. In contrast, an **antonym** is a word, phrase, or concept that has the opposite meaning of another word, phrase, or concept. For example, a communicative extrovert is the opposite of someone with communication apprehension. Such a person is not shy, reserved, unwilling to talk, or afraid to speak. The person greatly enjoys talking with others. Using an antonym helps the audience compare differences and leaves the audience with a memorable definition of an unfamiliar term.

Use Etymologies. An **etymology** is a form of definition that traces the origin and development of a word. One student used etymology to explain how the Olympic Games got their name. In the Greek system of telling time, an Olympiad was the period of four years that elapsed between two successive celebrations of the Olympian. This method of figuring time became common in about 300 B.C., and all events were dated from 776 B.C., the beginning of the first known Olympic Games. Such a definition provides the audience with a novel way to remember key information. The *Oxford English Dictionary* or the *Etymological Dictionary of Modern English* are excellent sources of word etymologies.

Whenever there is any possibility that your audience may not understand a term or concept, select the kind of definition that will provide the clearest explanation. In some instances, more than one kind of definition may be necessary. To err by overdefining is better than providing an inadequate definition that leaves your audience wondering what you are talking about.

Hints for Effective Informative Speaking

Almost everything covered in the text to this point is relevant to informative speaking and audience participation. Adhering to the following two additional guidelines should be particularly helpful in ensuring your success: Avoid assumptions, and personalize information.

Avoid Assumptions. A student began speaking on CPR by emphasizing how important it is in saving lives. However, she failed to explain that the acronym CPR stands for cardiovascular pulmonary resuscitation; she assumed that everyone already knew that. Most of the audience did understand, but a number of people did not. In addition, some knew what the acronym meant but did not know how the technique worked. Because at least half of the class was unfamiliar with the technique, they found the speaker's presentation confusing and frustrating. One mistaken assumption undercut all the work she had put into her speech. Follow these guidelines to avoid making assumptions:

1. Ask yourself if your listeners will already know what you are talking about. Audience analysis may be appropriate. If you are addressing your class, randomly select some of your classmates and ask them what they know about your topic and its related terminology.

2. If you believe that even one audience member may not understand, take the time to define and explain your topic.

3. If you believe that a majority of your audience already knows what you mean, say something like, "Many of you probably know what euthanasia is, but for those who don't, ..." In this way you acknowledge those who already know and help those who do not.

4. Do not make the assumption that your audience needs introductory information, especially if you have any doubts about what they know. You can always move through your basic definitions and explanations quickly if your audience seems to understand, but it is difficult to regain their interest and attention once you start talking "over their heads."

Personalize Information. When you relate your topic to your listeners so they can see its relevance for them, you are personalizing information. Judy presented a speech about nutrition and the eating habits of people in the United States. It was an interesting speech, but the audience didn't understand what it had to do with them. In revising her speech, Judy surveyed students in her residence hall and class about their eating habits. Then she personalized the information for her audience as follows.

Bad eating habits can cause problems that you may not be aware of. In a survey I took, I found that many college students like you fail to eat a variety of foods from the necessary basic food groups every day. In fact, my data indicate that 61 percent of you—that is more than half of you—do not eat balanced meals. Furthermore, I found that 50 percent of you skip breakfast at least five times a week.

What does this mean to you? According to nutrition experts, people who eat balanced meals are more motivated and less tired than people who don't eat balanced meals. In fact, those of you who drink a can of pop and eat a candy bar for breakfast—and you know who you are—are more likely to have high blood pressure, lack ambition, feel highly stressed, and be vulnerable to chronic diseases later in life.

Information that is personalized not only holds attention, but also gains interest. For example, think of your most effective instructors. Chances are that they take ordinary material and personalize it into meaningful, interesting knowledge. Listening to a string of facts can be boring and frustrating, but a speech comes to life when it contains personal illustrations.

People are also interested in others. If they were not, there would be no publications such as the *National Enquirer, Star,* and *People* and no programs such as *Who Wants to Be a Millionaire?, Survivor,* and *The Tonight Show,* or talk shows such as *Oprah.* Stories about human events are much more likely to touch listeners than are cold, harsh statistics. Thus, whenever possible, try to personalize your information and dramatize it in human terms. Relate it to specific people or situations about which your audience members know and care.

One student began an informative speech about the Heimlich maneuver, a technique used to clear the throat of someone who is choking, by relating the story of a four-year-old boy who saved his three-year-old friend. The boy, who had watched a television show in which the maneuver was used to save the life of one of the main characters, simply reenacted what he saw. By using this dramatic, real-life episode, the student was able to grab his audience's attention and prepare them for his discussion of who developed the technique, how it works, and how many lives it has saved.

Making Connections

Planning the Informative Speech

Informative speeches are required in most communication classes. Often your assignment requires a presentational aid. Although the time limit varies, such assigned speeches often have a five- to seven-minute time limit. A friend asks you for advice in choosing and researching a topic, and organizing and preparing such a speech for a "Current Issues in Communication" class.

1. What advice would you give your friend?
2. Where would you have your friend start?
3. What would you tell your friend about the unique characteristics of an informative speech?
4. How much time would you tell your friend it will take to do a good job with this project?

Personalizing Information in Your Speeches

1. Use examples and information that specifically relate to your audience.
2. Draw conclusions that your audience can identify with, and explain what the conclusions may mean for them.
3. Refer to people who are similar to your audience members, for example, single parents, nontraditional students, minority students, international students, computer science majors, commuters who must drive to campus.
4. Refer to topics and events that affect your listeners, such as campus activities, elections, state and local laws, social events, tax cuts or increases, cultural programs, and career decisions.

Developing and Preparing an Informative Speech

1. Select a topic that is appropriate for an informative speech. (Because the audience is a critical component, you may want to do an audience analysis, item 3 following, before you select a topic, or at least consider the audience during the topic selection process.)
2. Research the topic in which you are interested.
3. Analyze the audience: Narrow the topic so that it will allow you to inform your audience about something they do not already know.
4. Decide if you will be able to cover your topic adequately in the given time limit.
5. Determine your specific purpose: Word it to ensure that it meets the objective of the informative speech.
6. Organize the speech: Select and word your main points so that they are clear and meet your specific purpose.
7. Develop clarifying and supporting materials to ensure that your audience will understand everything about which you are talking.
8. Check the organization of your speech against the guidelines of effective organization specified in Chapter 9.
9. Avoid assumptions.
10. Personalize information to your listeners as much as possible.
11. Practice the delivery.
12. After delivering your speech, analyze the effectiveness of it.

The successful informative speech always considers the listeners. The speaker carefully thinks about the following questions: What do I want my listeners to learn from my speech? What will be the best way to deliver my speech so my listeners will understand and retain the information? How will I know if I was successful in accomplishing my purpose?

Evaluating the Informative Speech

Following are some of the criteria used to evaluate the competence of a speaker and the effectiveness of an informative speech. Your instructor will consider all these issues when evaluating your speech. You should be aware of them when preparing an informative speech presentation.

We have also included a speaker's self-evaluation form and a listener evaluation form (Figures 11.1 and 11.2) so that both speakers and audience members will be aware of their responsibilities to each other.

Topic

The selection of a topic should meet the following criteria:

- The topic should merit your audience's attention.
- The treatment of the topic should take into account the audience's level of knowledge of it.
- The audience should be able to see the relationship between the topic and the speaker and between the topic and themselves.
- The topic of the speech should be adequately covered in the time available. The topic should be narrow enough to be fully developed.

FIGURE 11.1

Speaker's Self-Evaluation Form

After you've completed an informative speech, take a few moments to think about your preparation and presentation. Complete the phrases on this form by stating what you would do similarly or differently, and why, if you were to give this same speech again.

Title of speech: _____.

Date and place given: _____.

My topic was_____.

My research could be improved by_____.

The organizational pattern I chose was _____.

The introduction was _____.

The body of the speech needed _____.

My conclusion seemed to be _____.

My explanation of ideas should _____.

The support I provided for my ideas was _____.

My use of language might_____.

My visual delivery was _____.

My vocal delivery needed _____.

The ways I adapted my topic, ideas, and language to this audience were _____

_____.

Things I would change are_____,

because _____.

Things I would retain are _____,

because _____.

FIGURE 11.2	

Listener's Evaluation Form

This form can be used to evaluate speeches given by your classmates. Follow your instructor's directions for providing such feedback.

Speaker _____   Topic _____

Date _____

The appropriateness of the topic for this class, assignment, and context was _____
_____.

One new or different perspective I gained was _____.

The organization of the speech was _____.

The reasons for my comments on organization are _____.

I identified the speaker's purpose as _____.

The speaker needed to explain _____.

The types of supporting materials used _____.

Presentational aids, if used, were _____.

The speaker's language should have _____.

The speaker could improve the physical aspects of delivery by _____.

The one comment I wish to make about vocal delivery is _____.

One aspect I especially liked was _____.

One area that needs improvement in the future is _____.

General Requirements

These general requirements hold for all informative speech presentations:

- The speech's purpose should be clearly to inform and should be stated as such.
- The speech should meet the time requirements set by the assignment.
- The speaker should cite sources of information other than the speaker's own.
- The speech's purpose should be relevant to the assignment and relate to the audience.
- The speech should show evidence of careful preparation.

Audience Analysis

The speaker must shape the speech to suit the audience, which often requires research (for example, determining the listeners' past experiences, beliefs, attitudes, values). The choices the speaker makes regarding content and the development of ideas should be customized for the listeners' benefit.

- The speech should reflect appropriate audience analysis.
- The speech should show the audience why the topic is important to them.
- At several points the speaker should "make contact" with the listeners by using familiar examples or showing knowledge of their preferences or experiences.

Supporting Materials

Supporting materials supply documented evidence that the information conveyed in the speech is accurate and credible.

A speaker explains to an interested group how to become a movie extra. As he tells them what they must do, he keeps in mind the objectives of being an extra, techniques in speech delivery to reinforce key points, and how to determine whether his speech is accomplishing his objectives.

- The speech should be well documented.
- The sources should be cited completely and accurately.
- The research should be up to date.
- The speaker should use adequate and sufficient clarifying materials.
- Visual aids, if used, should be appropriate, add to the audience's understanding of the speech's content, and follow the guidelines established by the assignment.

Organization

When judging the organization, the evaluator looks for a carefully planned, well-developed informative speech that takes a unified approach to the material being presented.

- The introduction should be properly developed.
  - It should orient the audience to the topic, gaining attention and arousing interest.
  - It should include a specific purpose and thesis statement.
  - It should define terms (if necessary).
  - It should be relevant.
  - It should establish credibility.
- The organization of the body should be clear and easy to follow.
  - The main points should be clear and parallel in structure.
  - The main points should be related to the purpose of the speech.
  - Transitions should provide appropriate links between ideas.
  - The organizational pattern should be appropriate.
- The conclusion should be properly developed.
  - It should reinforce the purpose by reviewing the main points.
  - It should end with a memorable thought.

Delivery

The delivery techniques provide evidence that the speaker is aware of what the audience is interested in hearing, is involved in and enthusiastic about the topic, and is interested in sharing the material with the listeners.

- The speaker's stance and posture should be appropriate.
- The speaker's eye contact with the audience should be appropriate.
- The speaker should follow the assignment in method of delivery (use of notes and number of note cards).
- The speaker's facial expressions should help convey and clarify thoughts.
- The speaker's body movements should be appropriate and effective.
- The speaker's vocal delivery should enhance the speech with appropriate volume and rate, conversational quality, enthusiastic tone, clear enunciation, appropriate pauses, and appropriate vocal variety.

Language Choice

Language choice can enhance and clarify ideas considerably.

- Language choice should be appropriate to the assignment and audience.
- Word choice should be appropriate for the college level.
- Grammar should be appropriate and show college-level competence.
- Word pronunciations should be correct.

Speakers should always analyze their presentations. We are often called on to make reports or provide information in the workplace, in the groups of which we are members, and in classrooms (ours and others). Because speaking is so prevalent, it is important that the speaker step back and carefully and critically reflect on the speech, the situation, the audience, and the performance. If we hope to become effective communicators in public settings, we need to use reflective thinking to objectively analyze what happened and how successful we were. Figure 11.1 shows a sample speaker's self-evaluation form to facilitate this reflection process.

We spend a great deal more time listening to speeches than we do making speeches, and though the focus of this book may seem to be on making effective speeches, it is also important for each of us to be a critical consumer of speeches and other presentations. Figure 11.2 provides a sample listener evaluation form to help the listener directly respond to the speaker, in writing. It is helpful for the speaker to obtain listeners' perspectives on a speech. Honest and tactful feedback can be invaluable. But it is also a good idea to closely evaluate presentations for yourself, even when you will not be passing your comments on to the speaker. Listeners are encouraged to use Figure 11.2 as a basis for creating their own evaluations and applying their own criteria to presentations.

A Sample Informative Speech with Commentary

The following transcript (with authors' commentary) is an informative speech written and delivered by Chris Lacy, University of Texas at Austin. Chris incorporates many of the strategies discussed in this chapter.[4]

Purpose

Thesis

Chris orients the listeners to the creation of a new engine, one that has fewer parts and uses sound waves, an environmentally safe method for providing power for numerous uses. He motivates the audience to listen with a vivid description of the creative process Backhaus and Swift employed in their invention. The final sentence in this introduction is the thesis statement and also provides relevance or reasons for the audience to listen to the speech, beyond the creativity of the inventors.

Chris forecasts the points to be covered in the speech: (1) the idea behind the engine and how it works, (2) current applications, and (3) what it offers in the future.

Chris creates interest and gets the listeners to pay attention with clever words, " . . . came up with their idea the old-fashioned way: They stole it." This strategy also provides support for the idea that creativity may mean using other people's ideas in a new way.

Notice that in the first three paragraphs of the speech, Chris has cited six different sources of information, ranging from CNN to a research journal, thus speaker credibility is established early in the speech and maintained throughout with citations from a variety of sources.

Thermoacoustic Stirling Heat Engine

To inform the audience about the Thermoacoustic Stirling Heat Engine (TASHE), an environmentally sound method for providing power.

With the world's concerns about pollution, global warming, and the depletion of fossil fuel reserves, this new engine is worthy of our interest.

Introduction

After watching the movie *Grease,* Scott Backhaus and Gregory Swift, two scientists at the Los Alamos National Laboratory, probably realized two things: (1) white boys can dance and (2) if you forget even one engine part, your greased lightning isn't going anywhere. So they came up with a better idea. Create an engine with fewer parts. However, no one could have guessed just how far they would go. CNN reported on June 17, 1999, that these researchers "have designed a remarkably simple, energy-efficient engine with no moving parts." The concept is based on a pretty "sound" idea. According to the July 1999 *New Energy News,* this engine, called the Thermoacoustic Stirling Heat Engine, or TASHE, uses heat to produce energy in the form of sound waves. These sound waves could be used as an environmentally sound method for powering everything from refrigerators to heating systems to power plants to, eventually, cars explains a report issued on the Discovery Channel website on October 17, 1999. *At a time when concerns are on the rise about pollution, global warming, and depleting fossil fuel reserves, the invention of this new engine certainly warrants our interest* [thesis].

To understand why *R&D* magazine named it one of the most significant inventions of 1999 we will first explore the idea behind this engine and how it works. Second, we'll discuss its current applications, before, finally, revealing what it has to offer us in the future. [Forecasting of main points.]

Body

Like any good scientists, Backhaus and Swift came up with their idea the old-fashioned way: They stole it. According to the May 27, 1999, *University Science and Research News,* their engine is partly based on the conventional Stirling heat engine, which consisted of a "cylinder in which heated air expanded to drive a piston." To achieve the power Backhaus and Swift desired for commercial applications, they wanted to replace the piston with sound waves, but prior to their discovery, most scientists dismissed sound as a possible medium of energy. A report issued on September 20, 1999, by the Macrosonix Corporation, a research company in acoustic energy, explains that at a certain point energy levels in sound waves dissipate much as the rings of water do after throwing a rock in a pond. To prevent this from happening, the two scientists from New Mexico simply changed the shape of the engine, which, as we'll learn, determines how TASHE works.

The explanation of the way the engine works fulfills Chris's forecasting of main points that the speech will offer information about the engine and how it works. Notice how Chris uses vivid sensory language with the image of the rippling water in a pond when a rock is thrown in to keep the listener aware of the topic. He further clarifies the concept by referring to how freon works in conventional appliances, but with the TASH engine, the dangers and disadvantages of freon are eliminated.

The speaker uses a personal email from one of the inventors to further explain the workings of the engine. This enhances speaker credibility while giving listeners additional information about the concept. Sensory language keeps listeners aware of what happens with this engine. The advantages of the TASH engine are identified, the speaker summarizes how the engine operates, and then moves on to the next main point: the applications.

In the sixth paragraph, Chris considers some of the current applications of the TASH engine. Although this point is not lengthy, he notes that there are advantages to this engine that are not found in conventional individual or commercial methods.

The most surprising aspect of this engine is how incredibly low-tech it is. Scott Backhaus explained via email on March 23, 2000, that the engine consists of a steel pipe shaped like a baseball bat with an oval handle at the end. Inside the pipe is compressed helium. The oval at the end of the pipe, fueled by natural gas, heats the helium, which causes the gas to expand. The gas, then, cools where it contracts. This cycle rapidly repeats, which causes the gas to resonate. The baseball bat shape of the pipe amplifies the sound waves, which increases the energy, in the same way cupping your hands over your mouth does. Imagine the vibrations you feel when you place your hand in front of a stereo speaker. Now multiply that 10 million times. Just as you can feel the energy transferred from the speaker to your hand, or to your neighbors, so too is energy transferred down the pipe to commercial devices. Fortunately though, the quarter-inch steel allows only a low hum to escape. The May 28, 1999, *Sciencenow* reports that this engine currently generates enough sound energy to power devices like refrigerators, and in the future, generators and even cars. In addition, a Department of Energy report issued on August 18, 1999, explains that TASHE, unlike conventional engines, is relatively maintenance free. Because there are no moving parts, lubrication is unnecessary, and it requires very few replacement parts.

To better understand how TASHE operates, though, we need to view it in action. Currently, scientists are using TASHE to produce environmentally friendly refrigerators for personal use and to preserve fossil fuels. The June 3, 1999, *London Daily Telegraph* reports that scientists have developed a refrigerator which uses TASHE. A conventional refrigerator works by compressing a gas, typically freon, then letting it expand. This expansion part of the process is what cools. However, freon can be detrimental to the environment and to people. The sound energy produced by TASHE can also compress and expand gases, but in this case the gas is simply air, which, most of the time, is pretty nontoxic. While keeping the milk and beer cold is great, this same process will also be able to conserve certain fossil fuels.

The May 27, 1999, issue of *Nature* indicates that researchers are beginning to use TASHE to compress and cool natural gas to a point where it liquifies. While this may not sound too exciting at first, it actually will have a profound effect on the environment. As oil is pumped out of the ground, one by-product is natural gas. A report published on June 1, 1999, by the University of California at Los Angeles notes that oil companies simply burn this gas off because in its gaseous state it is extremely difficult and expensive to transport from remote locations. Not only does burning natural gas waste valuable resources, but this practice also pollutes the air and produces greenhouse gases, which contribute to global warming. Since TASHE is made of common materials such as steel, developing it for this commercial purpose would only cost about $500,000, which is substantially less than the $1 billion required to build a plant utilizing the conventional method. Scientists believe that as TASHE improves, they will also be able to harness natural gas wasted in the same way during coal mining. Even some Republicans realize that we cannot afford to waste any of our natural resources.

As we look to the future, though, TASHE promises benefits that hit a little closer to home, primarily, generating electricity actually inside the home. First, the aforementioned *Sciencenow* indicates that this engine will be effective in generating electricity. "The acoustic energy could be harnessed to push and pull a coil around a magnet," which produces electric energy. The majority of current power plants use water, or hydropower, to accomplish this. These new power plants could be extremely beneficial in areas void of rivers and lakes, including many desert regions. Also, the relatively low cost of the engine makes it a viable power source for Third World countries. Dr. Steven Garret, a researcher in thermoacoustics at Penn State University, explains in the aforementioned *Nature* that scientists are also looking to incorporate TASHE into electric cars to generate electricity that will recharge their batteries.

Second, scientists believe TASHE will have uses in the home. The May 30, 1999, *Sunday Times* reports that a TASHE used inside the home could not only generate electricity but also heat the house and water. A big advantage of the engine is that its only emission is heat. A water tank could actually be added on to the engine to supply hot water in addition to providing heat to warm the house, significantly decreasing utility bills. Additionally, Dr. Garret explains in the previously cited Discovery Channel report that household appliances such as air conditioners will probably be available in about five years. Ultimately, whether used for commercial purposes or in the home, scientists believe TASHE could end up decreasing utility bills, making quieter, more efficient appliances, and reducing our dependence on oil-producing nations.

Conclusion

Who could have ever guessed that the one thing that has robbed countless neighbors of sleep and prevented girls in clubs from hearing my clever pick-up lines would end up paving the way to an innovative engine? Today we have explored how TASHE works and witnessed its current and future applications. Now I have a confession to make. Contrary to what *Grease* illustrates, not "all" white boys can dance. But one thing is certain, the next time any of us are working on our own greased lightning instead of asking, "Where's this go?" we may be asking, "What's that sound?"

Works Cited

Backhaus, Scott, and Gregory Swift. "A Thermoacoustic Stirling Heat Engine." *Nature,* May 27, 1999, 335–38.

*CNN news report, June 17, 1999.

*Discovery Channel report, October 17, 1999.

*Email with Scott Backhaus, March 23, 2000.

Throughout the explanation, listeners are made aware of the relevance of the topic to their lives. Chris says that not only does the engine provide future benefits to the world but it can also be used in the home. With TASH engines, each home could generate its own electricity and provide heat for the house and the water supply, with a resultant reduction in utility bills. Additional advantages include quieter and more efficient appliances.

In the final paragraph, Chris signals that the speech is coming to a close. He identifies the points covered, and leaves the listeners thinking about new applications. Although it may not be a "memorable thought," the conclusion does make the listener think and provides a link back to the introductory comments about *Grease,* greased lightning, and the innovative TASH engine.

"Energy-Efficient Engine with No Moving Parts Developed." *University and Science Research News,* May 27, 1999 available at http://unisci.com/stories/1992/0527991.htm, accessed on February 21, 2001.

Highfield, Roger. "Sound Idea Promises Cool Future." *London Daily Telegraph,* June 3, 1999, 3.

*Macrosonix Corp. report, September 20, 1999.

Lacy, Lisa. "Thermoacoustic Source Makes Electrical Power Without Moving Parts." *UCLA Daily Bruin,* June 1, 1999, 1.

Prigg, Mark. "Sound Can Power Engines." *New Energy News,* July 1999, 4–5.

Prigg, Mark. "Sound Can Power Engines." *Sunday Times,* May 30, 1999.

R&D Magazine, 1999.

*"Sound Wave-Driven Refrigerator May Offer New Way to Bring Unused Natural Gas To Mark." Department of Energy Report, August 18, 1999.

"The Ultimate Low-Maintenance Engine." *Sciencenow,* May 28, 1999.

*Reports available on request.

Analysis and Evaluation

Chris Lacy chose a technical topic about which many have never heard. Technical topics are popular for that reason—they are unusual and may have significant future relevance for listeners. He uses humor to motivate his listeners and also to ensure that the topic has information relevance. His use of language demonstrates a conversational approach to motivate his listeners to continue listening. The statement of the thesis in the first paragraph allows listeners to know his intent as a speaker and to learn the relevance of the topic. Chris's use of four specific sources within the introduction is an indication that he has done his homework and is a credible source. The final sentence of the introduction provides a forecasting of the main points to be covered in the speech.

Throughout the speech, Chris uses oral footnotes to indicate the sources from which his information came. He carefully explains how the Thermoacoustic Stirling Heat Engine works and enlightens his listeners about the process involved. His references to similar aspects or processes make the topic more meaningful because listeners are able to compare the new information with more familiar aspects.

The variety of reference materials demonstrates the large number of related topics Chris researched to make the topic relevant to his listeners. His use of numbers makes the information memorable. Chris reminds listeners of the continued relevance of TASHE and uses current research citations to show how much work has been done to find viable power sources for a world in which diminishing energy sources is a problem.

The second main point discusses current applications of TASHE. The organization of Chris's speech shows both a topical and chronological development. He covers the background and the beginnings, moves to current applications, and finally, in the third main point, dicusses future uses. The constant use of advantages of this technology reinforces the importance and relevance of the topic. Furthermore, Chris keeps the listeners' attention by talking about issues of importance: TASHE creates cost-effective energy sources for the home. The desire to decrease U.S. dependence on oil-producing nations has long been a concern of U.S. citizens and politicians. TASHE might allow us to do something about that concern.

We may think that little details such as inconsistencies are irrelevant. That, however, is not the case, because the details in a technical topic such as this one help listeners become familiar with new inventions and advances in processes affecting the world at large. Chris does not always provide sufficient information about where his information comes from. As listeners who become curious about this technical innovation that might save us money and provide more efficient cars and home appliances, we may wish to seek out the sources and learn more. Chris's failure to include the exact sources makes our work to follow up much more difficult. Also, when he discusses the cost-cutting effects, he does not tell us how much we might be able to save. Further, he does not always explain things as fully as we might wish. Although the time limitations of assignments or presentations certainly can affect a speaker's ability to develop all topics as fully as possible, when we are aware of time limits, we should cover only as much as we can fully develop and not leave too many unanswered questions for our listeners.

The first sentence of the conclusion is an attempt at humor to keep listeners with him until the very end as well as a signal that the speech is ending. If, however, listeners want to hear a more fully developed summary and synthesis, Chris leaves a lot to be desired. He does keep the audience listening by using the organizing strategies of internal previews, internal summaries, signposts, and transitions. The speech is easy to follow and holds to the forecasting that Chris laid out in the introduction. His final sentence reminds listeners that TASHE depends on sound waves.

Chris provides us with a new technical topic and explains its developmental history, its current applications, and its future uses. He organized the speech well, oriented and motivated listeners to attend, and kept listeners always aware of the relevance of the topic and his direction. Reread the speech. Determine whether you can find elements or strategies that your authors or your instructor discussed in the chapters in Part II, Connecting in the Public Context.

Summary

Information is the knowledge derived from investigation, study, or instruction. The ability to present and receive information is vital for anyone who wants to be successful. Those who possess information and can communicate it effectively possess power and command respect.

The goal of an informative speech is to increase understanding, whereas the goal of a persuasive speech is to change attitudes and behaviors. Information can be presented without attempting to persuade, but persuasion cannot be accomplished without attempting to inform.

The topic for an informative speech should be something that interests you, that you know something about, and that will interest your audience. You may talk about objects (people, animals, structures, places), processes (how something is put together, works, or is done), events (happenings, occasions), or concepts (beliefs, theories, ideas, principles).

To achieve the main goal of increasing knowledge, a speaker must focus on two subgoals: gaining the audience's attention and increasing the audience's understanding. Listeners are more likely to pay attention to information that is relevant, useful, or novel. Speakers may rely on *information relevance,* relating their information directly to the audience and, thus, giving them a reason to listen.

A speaker can increase an audience's understanding by organizing the presentation systematically, choosing appropriate language, and providing clear definitions.

Two organizational techniques that aid listeners' understanding are *planned repetition,* the deliberate repeating of a thought, and *advance organizers,* statements that warn the listener that significant information is coming.

Speakers should avoid technical language that might be unfamiliar to the audience. In addition, they should choose words that are concrete rather than abstract and use descriptors to provide even greater clarification. Concrete words stand for specific things that can be pointed to or physically experienced. Abstract words refer to ideas, qualities, or relationships. Descriptors are words that are used to describe something.

Another way to aid understanding is to define all terms that might be unfamiliar to the audience. Contrast definitions, synonyms, antonyms, and etymologies can all clarify meanings. A *contrast definition* points out differences between two objects or concepts. A *synonym* is a word, phrase, or concept that is the same or nearly the same in meaning as another word, term, or concept. An *antonym* is a word, phrase, or concept that is opposite in meaning to another word, phrase, or concept. An *etymology* traces the origin and development of a word.

In developing an effective informative speech, do not assume that your audience is already familiar with your topic and its special terminology, and when possible, personalize your speech by providing examples that touch on your listeners' needs and interests.

Speakers should always determine the criteria by which their presentations will be evaluated. The criteria included in this chapter will help you to understand general characteristics of an effective speech. A competent public communicator will think about the topic choice; the general requirements of the speech, including time limits and special needs (e.g., use of presentational aids); the results of the formal or informal audience analysis; amount, type, and quality of supporting materials; careful organization; vocal and physical delivery; and the appropriate choice of language for the presentation.

DISCUSSION STARTERS

1. Explain why information is so important in our society.
2. Why does having information give a person power?
3. In what ways have you used information to gain power?
4. What should be the prerequisites for selecting an informative speech topic?
5. What two or three informative speech topics interest you the most? Why?
6. In planning your informative speech, what should you take into consideration to ensure that you will be as effective as possible?
7. What criteria do you think are the most important in evaluating the competence of speakers delivering an informative speech?

NOTES

1. Definition of "information" from the *Merriam-Webster Dictionary,* 1999–2000, Britannica.com Inc., accessed on February 15, 2001, http://www.britannica.com/cgi-bin/dictionary.
2. This section is based on S. E. Lucas, *The Art of Public Speaking,* 6th ed. (Boston: McGraw-Hill, 1998), 343–52. The categories as cited in Lucas were described first by J. H. Bryns, *Speak for Yourself: An Introduction to Public Speaking* (New York: Random House, 1981), Chaps. 10–15.
3. Adapted from a speech developed by Janet Richards, a student at the University of Nebraska–Lincoln, 1993.
4. C. W. Lacy, University of Texas at Austin, "Thermoacoustic Stirling Heat Engine," informative speech, presented at the AFA-NIET National Tournament in April 2000.

Informative Speech Topics

Here are some possible topics for informative speeches. The items listed are not necessarily titles of specific speeches and may need to be narrowed to fit specific purposes, time limits, or other requirements set by your instructor.

New Approaches to Instruction: The Technology of Education

Investment: The Stock Market Game

Television Tabloids: Their Effect on Viewers

Lasers in the Operating Room

Library Technology: Save Time and Energy

Students at Risk: A Local Tragedy

Pedology: An Increasing Concern

Colors Communicate Emotions

Rudeness: A National Trend

Homelessness: Someone Else's Problem

Binge Drinking

How to Determine Your Career Field

Women Communicate Differently—Or Do They?

Agriculture's Newest Technologies

Animal Rights and Scientific Research

DNA: The Ultimate Fingerprint

New Telephone Technology

Genetically Altered Agricultural Products

Fraud Online

Siblings Saving Siblings

The Effects of Street Language on Society

The United States and Cultural Diversity

Native Americans: Our Real Heritage

Global Warming: Fact or Fiction?

Rejection and Its Impact on the Psyche

Software of the Future

Gangs: A Social Phenomenon

Country-Western Music

Embryo Cloning

Communication Apprehension

How to Prepare for Retirement

Adoption and the Law

How to Choose an Apartment

How to Control Stress

Advances in Automobile Safety

Videodisc Technology

The Electoral College

The Dangers of Cloning

Classical Music and Thinking

Alternative Medicine and You

CHAPTER 12

Persuasive
Speaking

"To be persuasive we must be believable;

to be believable, we must be credible;

to be credible, we must be truthful."

—Edward R. Murrow

WILL HELP YOU:

- Define persuasion and its goals.

- Explain what constitutes an appropriate topic for a persuasive speech.

- Discuss how questions of fact, value, and policy may serve as the basis of a persuasive speech.

- Tell why credibility is important in persuasive speaking.

- Develop a persuasive speech that demonstrates your ability to research, organize, and support your action goal.

- Differentiate among appeals to needs, logical appeals, and emotional appeals.

- Recognize fallacies in your own thinking and avoid them.

- Be aware of evaluation criteria for persuasive speaking and prepare your speech to fulfill those criteria successfully.

SCENARIO

If you were to analyze the communication in which you were involved during the past week, you would probably discover that many of them involve persuasion. In order to prove this point to some doubtful students, we have asked students to record their communication activities for one week. Here are some of the activities they reported:

Discussed who should be elected the next president of the United States

Tried to persuade a professor to accept a late paper without a penalty

Returned a pair of running shoes because they were defective

Listened to dozens of commercials asking me to buy, buy, buy!

Called my mother, found out she was not feeling well, told her to see a doctor

Listened to three phone calls asking me to try a new credit card

Listened to three phone services asking me to sign on with them

Tried to convince my daughter there was no money for an expensive pair of shoes

Asked my boss for a raise in salary

Discussed this whole presidential election process and what should be done about it

Was involved in a major discussion with friends regarding ethics and responsibilities among politicians

Listened to solicitors for two charitable organizations explaining why I should donate

Asked several friends to join the communication studies student association ■

Although not every situation that the students reported involved the use of persuasion, class members were surprised to discover the amount of persuasion in which they had been involved.

When you think about it, you will find that you too are involved in some form of persuasion much of the time, either as a speaker or as a listener. If you are not trying to persuade someone, someone is probably trying to persuade you. For example, you are involved in persuasion every time you ask or are asked to do or not do something and to believe or not believe something. To be more specific, some form of persuasion takes place when you ask your professor to excuse you from an exam, when you coax an employer to hire you, when you ask a friend for a loan, when someone recommends you see a certain movie, when candidates urge you to vote for them in an election, and when you talk yourself into staying home to study even though you'd rather go out with your friends.

Because persuasion is so much a part of our everyday activities, it is important to understand it thoroughly. In this chapter, we discuss how to select a persuasive speech topic, how to establish credibility, and how to prepare and develop a persuasive speech. We also provide guidelines for persuading others effectively and for being effective consumers of persuasion.

The Goal of Persuasive Speaking

Persuasion is a communication process, involving both verbal and nonverbal messages, that attempts to reinforce or change listeners' attitudes, beliefs, values, or behaviors. David Zarefsky, for example, says that persuasion means "to prompt the listeners to feel, act, or behave in a particular way."[1] Is it possible to change people's attitudes, beliefs, or values without changing their behaviors? The answer is yes. For example, you may skillfully argue that your friend should wear a seat belt and convince him that it is smart to do so. However, despite your friend's new attitude toward seat belts, he still may never put one on. Have you used persuasion effectively? The answer is debatable. You have changed your friend's attitude, but not his behavior. Which is more important?

The ultimate goal of all persuasion is action or change. Successful persuasion reinforces existing beliefs, attitudes, or behaviors; changes existing beliefs, attitudes, or behaviors; or leads to new beliefs, attitudes, or behaviors. When you want to convince someone not to change, you try to reinforce the existing belief, attitude, or behavior. At other times, you may want a person to do something different. When a speaker's main goal is to achieve change or action, the speaker will pursue one of four subgoals: adoption, discontinuance, deterrence, or continuance of a particular behavior.[2]

Persuasion is usually not a "one-shot deal"; often, persuasion occurs over time, and the effect of a persuasive message on a listener is not apparent until some time after it has been received. In other words, the listener may think about the message for a long time, and, with additional experiences, messages, and information, decide that a speaker was right. The listener may then decide to follow through on the speaker's request for action or change.

Adoption is an action subgoal that asks listeners to demonstrate their acceptance of an attitude, belief, or value by performing the behavior suggested by the speaker. For example, assume you had never liked the thought of donating blood, but one day you

Not all persuasion leads to change. People may be persuaded by an argument in theory and still not want to take action. Most skateboarders know that wearing helmets, kneepads, and wrist and hand protectors are important for safety, but some choose not to use these protective devices.

saw a television commercial pleading for blood to help the victims of a recent disaster. If the next day you donated blood, you would be displaying adoption. You still may not like the thought of giving blood, but the commercial would have persuaded you to do so. Of course, the fact that you gave blood once does not mean that you will continue to give it whenever you are asked. Your adoption of the persuasive message may be only temporary and may stop until you receive another persuasive message that convinces you to take action again.

Discontinuance is the opposite of adoption. Discontinuance is an action goal that asks listeners to demonstrate their acceptance of an attitude, belief, or value by avoiding certain behaviors. If your action subgoal is discontinuance, you want your listeners to stop doing something—running, drinking alcohol, using illegal drugs, paying high tuition, discriminating against others, eating junk food, avoiding difficult courses. You are trying to alter what you believe is negative behavior rather than encourage others to do something that you believe is a positive behavior.

Deterrence is an action subgoal that asks listeners to demonstrate their acceptance of an attitude, belief, or value by avoiding certain behaviors. Sample deterrent messages would be if you don't eat junk food, don't start now; if you don't own a gun, don't buy one; if you support busing to promote school integration, don't vote to

Making Connections

The Role of Persuasion

Do what the students in the opening scenario were asked to do: Keep a communication journal for a week. List every event in your life that involves communication. At the end of the week, mark each communication event that was characterized by persuasion. Bring your list to class, and discuss the following questions in small groups or with the whole class:

1. How well did you succeed in your efforts to persuade others?
2. How effectively did others persuade you?
3. What made your successful efforts work well? Give examples.
4. When others succeeded in persuading you, what made their efforts compelling? Give examples.
5. Describe unsuccessful efforts at persuasion, both your own and those attempted by others.

eliminate the busing law. This action subgoal is similar to discontinuance in that you do not want a negative behavior to occur; but in deterrence, you are trying to *prevent* its occurrence rather than *end* its occurrence.

Continuance is an action subgoal that asks listeners to demonstrate their acceptance of an attitude, belief, or value by continuing to perform the behavior suggested by the speaker. For example, if you jog, don't stop; continue to donate blood; keep volunteering your time to promote support groups for abused children and women; keep reading for pleasure; stay involved in extracurricular activities; keep buying from locally owned stores. This action subgoal is similar to adoption because you want a positive behavior to occur; but with continuance, you are trying to *keep* an existing behavior rather than *begin* a new behavior.

Note that the first two action subgoals, adoption and discontinuance, ask people to *change* their behavior, whereas the last two, deterrence and continuance, ask people *not to change,* but to continue doing what they are already doing or not change to something new.

Getting others to change or not to change their behaviors is not always easy. Therefore, a speaker may have to settle for a change in attitudes, beliefs, or values, as in the seat belt example. A change in attitudes, beliefs, or values, such as accepting the idea of wearing seat belts, is part of the persuasive process and must almost always occur before a change in behavior can take place. Not all persuasive speaking will lead to action, nor should persuasive speakers consider themselves failures if they do not obtain behavior change. Sometimes, as stated earlier, listeners will not immediately accept another's views, but after time and thought, the listener may decide that the persuasive message heard weeks ago was accurate and be influenced enough to change a belief, an attitude, or even a behavior. Persuasion usually occurs over time, and thus the speaker may not always be aware of whether the message was truly "persuasive." Often, listeners are persuaded only after they have heard similar messages from a

Making Connections

Persuasive Examples on the Web

Are you interested in reading some persuasive speeches or debates? There are excellent examples of both on the Web. The following sites contain some interesting speeches. Not all of the speeches are persuasive, but several are. Check them out and see if you can determine which ones are persuasive and which are not.

1. Gifts of Speech is a site dedicated to preserving speeches by contemporary influential women from around the world. It contains the texts of speeches by more than seventy women: http://www.gos.sbc.edu/.

2. Are you interested in the history of televised presidential debates? http://www.mbcnet.org/debateweb is divided into four sections: the first televised presidential debate, a history of TV debates from 1960 to 1996, the impact of TV on the political process, and resources.

These sites were identified by Sherwyn P. Morreale, Morreale's Mailbag, *Spectra,* Washington, D.C.: National Communication Association, September 2000.

variety of people, over a period of time. Especially as a beginner at persuasive speaking, you should not always expect to obtain a change in attitude, action, or behavior, but you should be able to get others to listen to what you have to say and to consider your point of view.

Topics for Persuasive Speeches

Some topics and themes lend themselves more readily to persuasive speaking than others. Especially adaptable are current and controversial subjects. The list of topics in the Appendix at the end of this chapter shows how varied the possibilities are. You will increase your likelihood of success if you follow these suggestions:

1. Select a topic that you are interested in, know something about, want to speak about, need to speak about, or are personally concerned about, whenever possible. Remember, as we said in Chapter 11, it is not always possible to choose your own topic; sometimes someone else chooses a topic for you. For example, a nursing supervisor may tell one of the nurses that he has to speak to a group of visitors about the importance of using sunblock to prevent skin cancer. Certainly, that may not be the first topic of choice for the nurse, but he does meet some of the other criteria for speaking on the subject: knowledge of the topic, awareness of the need, and a personal and professional concern about the topic.

2. Select a subject that is worthwhile and of potential concern to your audience.

3. Select a topic with a goal for influence or action. For example, the notion that exercise and eating well are good for your health may be a good persuasive theme, but if everyone in your audience is physically in good shape and healthy, could you come up with a strong persuasive strategy?

4. Select an issue that is current, but avoid one that is common knowledge or that has been discussed widely unless you plan to add a new perspective to it (see Chapter 7 for more on selecting a topic and the Appendix at the end of this chapter for a list of persuasive topics).

Persuasive speeches are often, but not always, given on topics for which two or more opposing viewpoints exist and in situations in which the speaker's point of view differs from that of the audience. For example, the speaker may want the audience to support higher tuition because it will lead to more quality instruction, but most of the audience may believe that tuition is already too high. Especially when a speaker's goal is adoption or discontinuance, there must be some difference between the speaker's view and that of the audience, or there is no need for persuasion. However, when the speaker's goal is deterrence or avoidance, the speaker's and the audience's points of view may be more closely united. In such cases the speaker's goal is to reinforce beliefs, attitudes, or behaviors that are similar to those proposed in the speech.

Sometimes speakers want their listeners to think about something from a new perspective, and they try to influence the listeners to accept a specific point of view. The speaker's goal is to persuade the listeners that one point of view is sound, valid, or worthwhile, and the speaker wants to influence the listeners to accept that specific perspective. Such speeches typically address questions of fact, questions of value, questions of policy, or any combination of the three types of questions.

Questions of Fact

A **question of fact** asks what is true and what is false. Consider these questions: Which building is the tallest in the world? Who is the richest person in the United States? Which basketball player scored the most points last season? Which university was the first to be established in the United States? Who first developed the computer and for what uses? These questions can be answered with a fact that can be verified in reference books. Because they are so cut and dried, there can be little debate about them, thus making them weak topics for a persuasive speech.

In contrast, persuasive speeches may be built on predictions of future events that will eventually become matters of fact. Consider these: Who will be the next president of the United States? Which college football team will win the national championship next year? Will there be a third world war in the next five years? Will computers replace textbooks? Although none of these questions can be answered with certainty, a persuasive speaker could build an effective case predicting the answer to each.

Persuasive speeches may also be based on complicated answers to questions of fact or justifications for answers that are unclear. Why did so many tragic air disasters occur during the past decade? Was it because of drugs? Poorly trained air traffic controllers? Overworked controllers? Outdated equipment? Insufficient rules for the use of airspace near airports? Although no one answer covers the entire situation, a speaker could build a strong argument to show that one of these factors is the primary cause of air accidents.

Finally, some persuasive speeches may attempt to answer questions of fact that are not completely verifiable: Do unidentified flying objects really exist? Can hypnotism enable a person to relive past lives? Is there intelligent life in outer space? A speech on the existence of intelligent life in outer space might be planned in this way:

Specific purpose	To persuade the audience that there is intelligent life in outer space
Thesis	There have been numerous signs of intelligent life in outer space, and the size of our universe provides us with sufficient reason to believe other intelligent life exists.
Main points	I. There have been numerous signs that there is intelligent life in outer space.
	A. The National Science Foundation, in a 1991 report, indicates that radio signals are being received from outer space.
	B. Recent sightings of UFOs by military and commercial pilots strongly suggest life in other solar systems.
	II. The size of the universe allows sufficient reason to believe that there is some form of intelligent life in outer space.
	A. Scientists suggest that we have only begun to learn about what exists beyond our solar system.
	B. There is an infinite number of solar systems beyond ours, which leaves a strong possibility that other intelligent life exists.

On the surface, questions of fact may appear more appropriate for an informative speech than for a persuasive one, but if you consider the difficulty of persuading an audience that college athletics are big business, that an earthquake will destroy the western part of the United States, or that the pyramids of Egypt were designed by an intelligence far superior to ours today, you can see that questions of fact can offer rich possibilities for persuasion.

Questions of Value

A **question of value** asks whether something is good or bad, desirable or undesirable. Value was defined in Chapter 3 as a general, relatively long-lasting ideal that guides behavior. A value requires a more judgmental response than a fact. Here are some typical questions of value: Who was the most effective political speaker during the twentieth century? Have American businesses lost their will to compete in world markets? Are today's college students better educated than college students were ten years ago? Are professional athletes the best role models for our youth? Does sex education belong in our schools? The answers to these questions are not based solely on fact, but on what each individual considers to be right or wrong, ethical or unethical, acceptable or unacceptable.

The answers to questions of value may seem to be based solely on personal opinion and subjectivity rather than on objective evidence, but this is not the case. Effective persuasive speakers will have evidence to support their positions and will be able to justify their opinions. For example, suppose a speaker contends that the social use of drugs is harmful. She might plan her speech as follows:

Specific purpose	To persuade the audience that the social use of drugs is harmful
Thesis	Social drug use is harmful because it negatively affects personal relationships and interferes with work.
Main points	I. Social use of drugs negatively affects personal relationships.
	A. According to a national survey, social drug users are involved in twice as many divorces as nonusers.
	B. Researchers have shown that the children of social drug users are more likely to be loners, have fewer friends, and eventually use drugs themselves.
	II. Social use of drugs interferes with work.
	A. The rate of absenteeism from work of social drug users is four times that of nonusers.
	B. The job turnover rate of social drug users is at least double that of nonusers.
	C. Social drug users are 30 percent less productive than nonusers doing the same job.

Values vary dramatically from one person to the next. Person A may think that rap music is bad for society, and Person B may think it is good for society; Person A may think that alcohol should be illegal on campus, and Person B may think it should be legal; Person A may believe that college sports are not necessary, and Person B may think that they are absolutely necessary. When it comes to questions of value, one person's

.

Values are complicated. The cartoon illustrates the point that values are often based on emotion and personal views and, thus, are difficult to change.

Calvin and Hobbes   by Bill Watterson

judgment is no better or worse than another's. People's values are usually complicated because they are rooted in emotion rather than reason. It is often extremely difficult to get people to change their values. A speaker's position on a question of value may be difficult to defend. Therefore, you will need to gather a great deal of research and evidence and build a strong case to support one value over another—even though you know your values are right—because your listeners believe their values are right, too.

Questions of Policy

A **question of policy** goes beyond seeking judgmental responses to seeking courses of action. Whereas a question of value asks if something is right or wrong, a question of policy asks if something should or should not be done. Should student parking on campus be more accessible? Should universities provide birth control to students? Should all students be tested for drugs before entering college? Should students be tested for basic English competencies before they graduate? Should the government provide basic health care for every U.S. citizen? Should everyone working in jobs that involve the safety of others be tested for drugs? Questions of policy involve both facts and values and are, therefore, never simple. And the answers to questions of policy are not agreed on by everyone in the same way.

Persuasive speakers can defend an existing policy, suggest modifications of an existing policy, suggest a new policy to replace an old one, or create a policy where none exists. If you defend an existing policy, you must persuade your listeners that what exists is best for the situation. If you want to modify or replace an existing policy, you must persuade your listeners that the old policy does not work and that your new one will. If you hope to create a new policy, you must persuade your audience that a policy is needed and that yours is the right one for the situation.

When discussing questions of policy, persuasive speakers usually focus on three considerations: need, plan, and suitability. If you believe that things are not fine as they are, then you must argue that there is a *need* for change. When you advocate change, you must provide a *plan,* or a solution. The plan tells the audience what you think should be done. Finally, you must defend your plan by explaining its *suitability* for the situation. Examine how student Mary Trouba used need, plan, and suitability in her persuasive speech:[3]

| Specific purpose | To persuade the audience that hate groups are a danger to society |
| Thesis | Hate groups are a danger to society because they flagrantly violate the American ideals of equality and religious tolerance. |

Need	I. Hate groups flagrantly violate the American ideals of equality and religious tolerance.

A. Hate groups are growing at an alarming rate.

B. Hate groups are employing criminal means to achieve their ends.

C. Hate groups are building a frightening capacity to inflict moral damage on society.

Plan	II. We must enact a twofold solution that includes legal and attitudinal components.

A. The first step is to take legal action to crack down on these groups.

B. The second step is to educate people about these groups.

Suitability	III. The two-step plan will control these groups and help reduce their negative impact on society.

A. Laws can prevent paramilitary groups from forming and thus reduce their impact.

B. Research has shown that people who are educated about extremist groups are less likely to join them.

Persuasive Claims

When attempting to answer questions of fact, value, and policy, we cannot always develop a formal logical answer that will irrefutably counter the objections of others. Formal rules of argument do not always determine who is right and who is wrong. Even when you supply compelling evidence to support your view, most evidence is not 100 percent clear-cut and may be interpreted in different ways. These factors make persuasive speaking especially challenging.

Making Connections

Advising a Classmate from Another Culture

Wing Keung is from China and is a student in your speech class. Your class has been assigned to present a ten-minute persuasive speech on a topic about which you have strong beliefs and for which you can find at least five different types of sources. Wing Keung is concerned because the strongest feelings he now has, he says, concern the view that everyone should study intercultural communication. Wing Keung doesn't think his topic is a good one for this assignment, and he asks you for advice.

1. What will you tell him about this topic? Why?
2. If Wing Keung keeps this topic, what does he need to do to meet the assignment?
3. What other advice, based on the chapters you've read so far, will you give Wing Keung?

Stephen Toulmin, a British philosopher, developed a model to help understand everyday persuasive arguments.[4] Although not everyone uses Toulmin's model for understanding and presenting arguments, a brief discussion of the model may be helpful, both to listeners and speakers, as a means of evaluating arguments. Toulmin's approach to supporting a persuasive position or argument involves three basic parts: claim, data, and warrant. The *claim* is what the persuader wants or hopes will be believed, accepted, or done (or, in terms of what we discussed in the previous section, whether it is a fact, a value, or a policy). Claims, however, require evidence, or what Toulmin refers to as *data*. Data are the supporting materials or evidence that should influence the listener to accept the claim as stated. Unfortunately, there is not always a clear or irrefutable relationship between the claim and the data. Thus, the persuader must explain the relationship between the claim and the data. Toulmin refers to this as the *warrant*. Here is a possible application of Toulmin's model:

Claim: Emergency room physicians are ill-prepared to treat patients.

Data: According to Dr. Emily Greene of the National Institutes of Health, almost one in every nine patients (of the more than nine million emergency room patients each year) are mistreated by inadequately trained emergency room physicians.

Warrant: Because these physicians are not certified in emergency medicine, they cause inestimable harm to the millions who seek help in our nation's emergency rooms. Furthermore, they attach additional costs to patients' bills.

According to Toulmin's model, listeners can usually respond to the claims in three ways.

1. They can accept the claim at face value. This usually occurs when it is common knowledge that the claim is probably true. For example, the statement that U.S. educational programs need improvement is generally acceptable at face value.

2. They can reject the claim outright at face value. This usually happens when the claim is clearly false, such as the claim there is no pollution in U.S. lakes and streams. It also occurs when listeners are biased against the claim or see no relationship between the claim and themselves. For example, if a claim that U.S. forests are not being depleted is made to a group trying to preserve the environment, it is unlikely they would accept this claim because of their biased views.

3. They can accept or reject the claim according to their evaluation of data and warrant. The person making the claim must provide evidence to support the claim or demonstrate that it is true.

When speakers provide evidence to support their claims, it is still up to listeners to accept the claim based on the evidence presented. Listeners essentially have three options:

1. They can accept the claim as supported by evidence.

2. They can reject the claim as not supported by the evidence.

3. They can request that the speaker provide more evidence to support the claim.

Competent speakers must develop arguments strong enough to make the claim and the supporting evidence stand on their own merits. They realize that not everyone will interpret the evidence in the same way they do, nor will everyone be convinced, even though the evidence they present may be, in their opinion, the best there is.

Establishing Credibility

The most valuable tool that you, as a persuasive speaker, can possess is credibility or believability based on the audience's evaluation of you as a speaker. At various points in this book, we have referrred to the speaker's credibility (see especially Chapters 1, 9, 10, and 11). Listeners will assess your competence, knowledge, and experience, your charisma and energy, and your character. The audience is the ultimate judge of credibility, but there is much you can do to influence their opinion. The key is to establish yourself as worthy of the listeners' attention right from the beginning of your speech.

Competence

An audience will judge your competence by the amount of knowledge, degree of involvement, and extent of experience you display. The more expertise you show in your subject, the more likely it is that your audience will accept what you have to say. You can establish your expertise in several ways:

1. *Demonstrate involvement.* One student, in urging action to avoid the chemical pollution of water, described her mother's death as a result of drinking contaminated water. Although her firsthand experiences did not in themselves make her an expert environmentalist, they clearly established her involvement in the issue.

2. *Relate experience.* One student chose to speak on the value of internships. Because he had participated in the internship program, his audience accepted him as knowledgeable and committed.

3. *Cite research.* Quoting information from written sources and interviews with experts can add weight and objectivity to your arguments. Mentioning sources that are respected by your listeners adds to your credibility and indicates that you are well read. If you were trying to persuade your audience that more women need to have yearly mammograms, from age 40 on, the following research might help to enhance your credibility.

> According to the National Center for Health Statistics, one in eight women in the United States will develop breast cancer in her lifetime. That amounts to 12.6 percent of all women who have the lifetime probability of developing breast cancer. It should be noted that men, too, can develop breast cancer, and it is just as fearsome for them as it is for women. The best ways to catch breast cancer in time are monthly self-examinations and annual mammograms beginning at age 40. Despite this, only 67 percent of women over age 40 have had one mammogram in the past two years, according to National Cancer Institute figures. (Statistics from http://www.cdc.gov/nchs/fastats/mamogram.htm)

Character

An audience's judgment of your character is based on their perceptions of your trustworthiness and ethics. The best way to establish your character is to be honest and fair.

Trustworthiness. A speaker's **trustworthiness** is the audience's perception of the speaker's reliability and dependability. Others attribute trustworthiness to us based on their past experiences with us. For example, instructors may judge our reliability according

Making Connections

Recognizing Credible Sources

Throughout the course of life we encounter people we admire and those we do not. Think about the characteristics of people whom you respect and why those characteristics inspire respect.

1. List five well-known individuals whom you believe to be highly credible.
2. Briefly describe what makes them credible.
3. Compare your names and opinions with those of your classmates. What did you learn about credibility in making the comparisons?

to whether we come to class every time it meets. Friends may evaluate our dependability according to how we have followed through on our promises. People who have had positive experiences with us are more apt to believe we are trustworthy.

Ethics.   In Chapter 1, we defined ethics as an individual's system of moral principles and stated that ethics plays a key role in communication. Though this is certainly true in communication in general, it is especially true in persuasion. Persuasive speakers who are known to be unethical or dishonest are less likely to succeed in achieving their persuasive purpose than are people recognized as ethical and honest. You must earn your reputation as an ethical person through your actions. The best way to establish yourself as an ethical speaker is to do the following:

1. *Cite sources when information is not your own, and cite them accurately.* As you develop your speech, be sure you give credit to sources of information and to ideas that are not your own. If you do not mention the sources of your information, you are guilty of plagiarism, as discussed in Chapter 10. Provide the audience with an **oral footnote,** such as "the following was taken from . . ." or "the following is a quotation from . . ." Be specific about from whom and where your information came.

2. *Do not falsify or distort information in order to make your point.* Never make up information, attribute information to a source who is not responsible for it, take quotations out of context, or distort information to meet your purpose.

3. *Show respect for your audience.* When audience members perceive that you are being respectful, even though they may not agree with your point of view, they are more likely to listen. And when they listen, you at least have a chance of persuading them. Do not try to trick audience members into accepting your point of view or to ridicule them for not agreeing with you.

Charisma

As we stated earlier, other factors influence the way the audience perceives you. Among those is **charisma,** or the appeal or attractiveness that the audience perceives in the speaker contributing to the speaker's credibility. We often associate charisma with leaders who have special appeal for large numbers of people. Charismatic speakers seem to be sincerely interested in their listeners, speak with energy and enthusiasm, and generally seem "attractive" and likable. A credible speaker will take command of the speaking situation and engage the listeners so that they know that the message is honest, well prepared, and relevant. Charismatic speakers are able to get the audience involved in their messages.

Your audience's evaluation of your credibility will ultimately determine whether they accept or reject your persuasive goals. You should remember that credibility is

Former President Bill Clinton was seen by many as being a charismatic speaker. He was often able to establish a one-to-one relationship with his audience; speak with care, energy, and enthusiasm; and inspire people to take action.

earned, that it depends on others' perceptions, and that it is not permanent. Credibility changes from topic to topic, from situation to situation, and from audience to audience, and so you must establish your credibility each time you speak.

Becoming Effective Consumers of Persuasion

We spend a great deal of our lives listening to persuasive messages of one kind or another. It is important to think about what it means to be an effective consumer of those messages. (Refer to Chapter 6 to review the role of the listener in the persuasive process.)

As listeners, we have both the right and the responsibility to get accurate, reliable, and worthwhile information. Listen carefully to the message, and ask these questions:

How knowledgeable is the speaker?

What sources has the speaker used to gain additional information?

Are these sources reliable and unbiased?

Are there real advantages to accepting this position?

Is the evidence presented in the argument worthwhile?

Can I believe the evidence?

Where can I get additional information?

Does the argument seem logical?

It pays to closely analyze and evaluate the information presented, whether we are listening to an advertisement, a telemarketer, a political candidate, a religious leader, or a financial planner. Use questions like these to evaluate information:

Is this *really* good information?

Is the information really relevant to me?

Making Connections

Source Sites for Persuasion

Students sometimes have trouble finding sources for statistics and general information to help them organize and develop their persuasive speeches. The following sites may prove helpful to you.

1. Pub List is an archive of some 150,000 periodicals. The listings contain publisher information as well as information about the periodicals themselves: http://www.publist.com.

2. A website for statistical data in the areas of agriculture, crime, demographics, economics, education, energy, environment, health, income, labor, natural resources, safety, and transportation is found at http://www.fedstats.gov/map.html.

3. Government websites may be found at http://www.firstgov.com. This URL links the user to 20,000 government websites in a streamlined search-by-topic search engine.

4. If you want to locate scholarship and resources in the area of social change, check out http://www.redrival.net/evaluation/socialchange/.

5. Findarticles.com offers free access to full-text articles published in more than 350 magazines and journals dating from 1998. You can search the database by keyword or subject category at http://www.findarticles.com/PI/index.jhtml.

6. OnlineNewspapers.com is a metasite that indexes 10,000 online newspapers from around the world. These are offered by country, province, or state with links to the newspapers' home pages: http://www.onlinenewspapers.com/.

These sites were identified by Sherwyn P. Morreale, Morreale's Mailbag, *Spectra*. Washington, D.C.: National Communication Association, October 1998, September 2000, and December 2000.

How can I learn more about this?

What additional questions should I ask to make sure that I get accurate and reliable information and sources?

Does the information really support the argument, or is it interesting but not essentially related?

Is there sufficient support for the claims and arguments?

Are there errors in the reasoning or the evidence?

Does the message basically make sense—and why or why not?

Also pay attention to the person delivering the message:

Is the speaker ethical and trustworthy? What is the evidence?

Is the speaker competent and knowledgeable? What is the evidence?

Preparing and Developing a Persuasive Speech

In a classroom situation, you typically will have only one opportunity to coax your audience to accept your persuasive purpose. Therefore, it is important to set realistic persuasive goals and to give some special thought to what is covered in Chapters 7, 8, and 9 about researching, organizing, and gathering support for your speech. Review those chapters for a complete perspective. Much of this section reinforces these earlier chapters.

Researching the Topic

Research (see Chapter 8) for a persuasive speech must be especially thorough. You'll need to gather as much information as possible about your topic, because the more you know, the better equipped you will be to support your position. When doing your research, look primarily for evidence that supports and clarifies your views. If, in the process, you discover information that contradicts your stand, make note of it and look for material that you can use to refute such information. Anticipating possible objections is especially helpful when your position is controversial and when your audience's opinions are likely to be split. If you know the arguments that may be used against you, you will be better able to support and defend your position.

Organizing the Speech

A persuasive speech requires making several special decisions that will affect its organization (see Chapter 9). Here are decisions especially related to persuasive speaking:

1. *Should you present one side or both sides of an issue?* The answer to this question depends on your audience. If your listeners basically support your position, then presenting one side may be sufficient. If their views are divided or opposed to your position, it may be more effective to present both sides. This decision also depends on your audience's knowledge of the topic and their evaluation of your credibility. If audience members are well informed and educated, presenting both sides of an argument helps minimize the effect that counterarguments can have on your audience.

2. *When should you present your strongest arguments?* Presenting your strongest arguments at either the beginning or the end of your speech is more effective than presenting them in the middle. A good strategy is to state your strongest arguments early and then repeat them toward the end. Because audience attention is most likely to wander in the middle of a speech, that is a good time to present a lot of personal examples supporting your position.

3. *What is the best way to organize your persuasive speech?* The most effective sequence of presentation depends on your topic, specific purpose, and audience. Among the patterns of organization that work well for persuasive speeches are problem–solution, cause–effect, and Monroe's motivated sequence. Each was discussed in Chapter 9.

Supporting Materials

In persuasive speeches, speakers try to influence audience members through the impressiveness of their supporting materials. Thus, they choose their supporting materials carefully to build the kind of appeal that is most likely to sway their listeners. Based on the topic and their audience analysis, persuasive speakers try to appeal to their listeners' needs, to logic, or to emotions.

Appeals to Needs.   *Appeals to needs* attempt to move people to action by calling on physical and psychological requirements and desires. Of course, different people have

David Boies, attorney for Al Gore, used logical appeals to support his proposition or claim about the uncounted ballots in Florida. His presentational aid included the justification, or statistical data that helped support his claim.

different needs, but most of us want to protect or enhance factors that affect our physical, safety, social, and self-esteem needs according to psychologist Abraham Maslow. According to Maslow's hierarchy of individual needs our lower-order needs must be satisfied before higher-order needs.[5]

Physical needs are our most basic physiological requirements, such as food, water, sleep, sex, and other physical comforts. *Safety needs* pertain to our desires for stability, order, protection from violence, freedom from stress and disease, security, and structure. *Social needs* relate to our hopes to be loved and to belong, and our needs for affection from family and friends, for membership in groups, and for the acceptance and approval of others. *Self-esteem needs* reflect our desires for recognition, respect from others, and self-respect.

Speakers can appeal to any of these needs to motivate listeners to take action. For example, a speaker trying to sell individual retirement accounts would aim his appeal at our needs for security and stability; a speaker who hoped to persuade us to lose weight would call on our needs for physical comfort, acceptance by others, and self-esteem. Our readiness to accept ideas or to take action depends heavily on the speaker's ability to relate a message to our needs.

Logical Appeals. Attempts to move people to action through the use of evidence and proof are called **logical appeals.** When speakers lead their listeners to think "Yes, that's logical" or "That makes sense," they are building a case by calling on their audience's ability to reason. To accomplish this, competent persuasive speakers use evidence such as statistics, examples, testimony, and any other supporting materials that will sway their listeners.

A logical appeal requires an ability to argue for your point of view. When you argue in persuasive speaking, you usually make a claim or state an argument or *proposition,* which is what you want your listeners to believe after you have completed your speech. A claim or proposition usually assumes that there is more than one way to do things. For example, abortion should be illegal or abortion should be legal, the electoral process should (or should not) be changed. Speakers usually try to justify such a position with reason and evidence. The *justification,* or data, involves the use of all the supporting materials you can find to support your claim or proposition, including statistics, facts, examples, testimony, pictures, objects, and so on.

In presenting their evidence, persuasive speakers guide their listeners through a carefully planned sequence of thought that clearly leads to the desired conclusion. This train of logic may fall into one of four categories: deductive reasoning, inductive reasoning, causal reasoning, or reasoning by analogy.

Deductive reasoning is a sequence of thought that moves from general information to a specific conclusion. It presents a general premise (a generalization) and a minor premise (a specific instance) that leads to a precise deduction (a conclusion about the instance). One student set up his argument as follows:

General Premise:	Heart disease is a major health concern in the Midwest.
Minor Premise:	Iowa is a part of the Midwest.
Conclusion:	Therefore, heart disease is a major health concern in Iowa.

Great care must be taken to ensure that the premises are accurate because faulty premises can lead only to a faulty conclusion. For example:

General Premise: All car salespeople are crooks.
Minor Premise: Carolyn is a car salesperson.
Conclusion: Therefore, Carolyn is a crook.

The general premise must be both accurate and defensible before deductive reasoning can be used effectively as evidence to support a position.

Inductive reasoning is the opposite of deductive reasoning—it is a sequence of thought that moves from the specific to the general. An argument based on inductive reasoning usually progresses from a series of related facts or situations to a general conclusion. A student discussing university teaching evaluations wants her listeners to agree that speech professors at her university are excellent teachers. She, therefore, leads them through the following sequence of inductive reasoning:

Facts:
1. My speech communication professor is an excellent classroom teacher.
2. The speech professor I had last semester was also an excellent classroom teacher.
3. My roommate's speech professor is an excellent classroom teacher.
4. My roommate has a friend whose speech professor is an excellent classroom teacher.

Conclusion: Speech professors at the University of Nebraska are, in general, excellent classroom teachers.

When your facts can be verified, when there are a sufficient number of facts, and when there are sufficient links between the facts and the conclusion, inductive reasoning can be an excellent way to persuade an audience of the validity of your argument.

Of course, inductive reasoning can also be misused. For example, how often have you heard general statements such as these: Athletes are intellectually void; all politicians are crooks; all farmers work hard for little gain; college causes people to become elitist; the destruction of the family unit is hurting America; the middle class is disappearing. Each of these generalizations is usually based on some past experience, but the problem is that such experiences are not always sufficient to support the conclusion.

To avoid problems when using inductive reasoning, make sure your facts are accurate and that they support your conclusion. Also, make sure your conclusion does not extend beyond the facts you have presented. You will undermine your own case if your conclusion is so general that someone can easily point out exceptions to it.

Causal reasoning is a sequence of thought that links causes with effects. Thus, it always implies or includes the word *because:* The earth's temperature is turning colder, *because* the ozone layer is thinning. As in any form of reasoning, it is necessary to support the conclusion with evidence. In the example in this paragraph, the speaker would go on to cite scientific evidence linking thinning ozone to falling temperatures. The more verifiable and valid the evidence, the more defensible the conclusion about the cause-and-effect relationship between ozone and temperature. Even though other factors may also be causes of the earth's cooling, the speaker's argument can be considered reasonable if it is based on scientific evidence that supports the speaker's point of view.

Reasoning by analogy is a sequence of thoughts that compares similar things or circumstances in order to draw a conclusion. It says, in effect, that what holds true in one case will also hold true in a similar case. Thus, in arguing that American auto manufacturers should change their approach to production, you might use the following reasoning:

General Premise: American automobile production must improve.

Minor Premise: The Japanese method of auto production has been extremely successful.

Conclusion: American auto manufacturers should adopt the Japanese method if they wish to be successful.

Analogies can be useful reasoning tools when used wisely and with appropriate support for the conclusion. The relationship in the analogy must be valid, and the conclusion should be based on the assumption that all other factors are equal. For instance, our example is based on the assumption that the Japanese method is a good way to manufacture cars and that American manufacturers could be just as successful as the Japanese. However, if the argument implied that the Japanese method's success could be traced to the workers' pride, dedication, and involvement in the production process, then similar factors would have to be applied to the American workforce. Thus, to avoid problems in drawing analogies, it is crucial to consider any dissimilarities that may refute your point.

You may wish to base your speech on a single form of reasoning, or you may prefer a combination of types of reasoning. Whatever your choice, you must remember that your argument is only as good as the evidence you use to support it.

Emotional Appeals. Attempts to move people to action by playing on their feelings—for example, by making them feel guilty, unhappy, afraid, happy, proud, sympathetic, or nostalgic—are known as **emotional appeals.** Because emotions are extremely strong motivators, this form of appeal can be highly effective. Note how the following introduction to a persuasive speech appeals to the emotions:

It is 1968, Tamaqua, Pennsylvania, where a little baby girl has just breathed her first breath. Her name is Kim. It is 1978, and ten-year-old Kim moves with her mom and dad to Florida and is enrolled in a Catholic school. It is 1985, and Kim enrolls in college. A picture-perfect all-American girl—Kim never used drugs, she studied hard, and she made the decision to remain a virgin until marriage. It is 1987, and Kim has two wisdom teeth extracted. It is 1989, and Kim is diagnosed with AIDS. It is 1990, and Kim lies on her living room sofa, her skin chalky, her body frail, and her weight 101 pounds. It is 1991, now she resembles a skeleton, her weight 65 pounds, struggling to breathe what might be her last breath. "See you tomorrow?" her father says as he carries her to bed. "Hopefully not," she replies. It's December 1991, and Kim is dead.

Kimberly Bergalis became the first-ever documented case of AIDS transmission from a health care worker to a patient in 1989, but she wasn't the last.[6]

Emotional appeals can be so powerful that they sway people to do things that might not be logical. A student's cheating on an exam, for example, can by no means be justified through logical thought, but the student may believe that she is justified from an emotional viewpoint because of parental pressure to get good grades. In fact, persuasive speakers often mix both logical and emotional appeals to achieve the strongest effect. Persuasive speakers need to be aware of the issue of ethics discussed throughout this text. A speaker must present valid, reliable information in a way that will appeal to the listeners but will not violate their rights or their responsibilities. The speaker should be fair, accurate in presenting views, careful in presenting information, and attentive to the strategies used. An ethical speaker uses emotional appeals carefully and truthfully.

Persuasive Strategies

Speakers need to use persuasive strategies to win over their listeners. First, the speaker needs to demonstrate *rhetorical sensitivity,* that is, the speaker needs to be aware of the audience and their needs, the situation, the time limits, and what listeners want and are willing to hear. The speaker is aware that listeners expect a strong, clear message to which the speaker is committed and in which the speaker believes. The speaker will also carefully adapt the message so that the listeners know that it is relevant and important to them. The audience expects the speaker to motivate them or make them want to hear the speech and learn more about the argument. The audience expects to understand the speaker's point. The audience expects the speaker to repeat and reinforce the message so that they are influenced to, at the very least, accept that the speaker has a point worth considering. All in all, the persuasive speaker will always keep the listener in mind while reinforcing the argument.

Fallacies in Argument Development

As both creators and consumers of persuasive messages, all of us must be able to analyze and evaluate others' as well as our own use of reasoning to support persuasive messages (see Chapter 6). It is especially important to avoid causing listeners to question your credibility by presenting flawed arguments. Arguments that are flawed because they do not follow the rules of logic and, therefore, are not believable are called **fallacies.** Flawed reasoning occurs all the time, and often people do not realize that they have used flawed arguments. As a critical thinker, however, it is important that you understand what fallacies are, how to recognize them, and why you should not use them or let others use them in their communication.

Many different types of fallacies are used in communication, but only the commonly used or major errors are presented here. Let's look at basic fallacies in reasoning and evidence.

Fallacies of Reason

Questionable Cause.   **Questionable cause** is a common fallacy that occurs when a speaker alleges something that does not relate to, or produce, the outcome claimed in the argument. Wanting to know what has caused certain events to occur is part of our nature.

If cheating on campus is increasing, people want to know why; if our taxes are increasing or decreasing, we want to know why; if parking spaces at work or on campus are to be eliminated, we want to know why. In our desire to know the cause of certain events or behaviors, we sometimes attribute what has happened to something that is not even related to the situation. For example, claiming that the drinking of alcohol on campus has increased this year because there is nothing else to do is a questionable cause, especially if the same number of activities exists on campus as in past years.

Ad Hominem. When someone attacks a person rather than an argument, he or she is resorting to a fallacy called an **ad hominem.** This is also referred to as "name calling." When you call someone a geek, a nerd, or a jerk in response to an argument being made, in order to diminish the relevance or significance of the argument, you are using name calling as a means to refute the argument. What is wrong with this? Such an approach is a smoke screen; it shows your inability to provide good counterarguments or evidence to challenge what the other person is claiming. Sidestepping an issue by name calling, ridiculing, or otherwise personally attacking another person can successfully diffuse an argument, but doing so usually results in a fallacious argument.

Fallacies of Evidence

Fact Versus Opinion. A major misuse of information involves the presentation of facts and opinions. Speakers who state opinions as if they are facts can be misleading and may be presenting a fallacious argument. For example, "our university's policy on drinking is too stringent" and "our university is short 250 parking spaces" are both statements of information. Which is fact, and which is opinion? The first statement is opinion, and the second is fact. How can you tell which is which? Facts can be verified—thus, the lack of parking spaces can be verified, whereas the university's policy on drinking may be stringent or not, which is a matter of opinion.

Giving opinions can be helpful in persuasive speeches or arguments, but to treat an opinion as if it were fact, or a fact as though it were an opinion, is an error in critical thinking. In either case, you will appear to claim too little or too much and, thus, raise questions about your competence and ethics.

Red Herring. Another misuse or avoidance of facts is the use of irrelevant information to divert attention from the real issue. This occurs when a speaker wishes to draw attention away from an issue that is being questioned or challenged. For example, have you ever questioned someone about something he or she did wrong, and the response you got didn't relate to the event to which you were referring? In fact, the person may change the

Making Connections

Thinking About Persuasive Speaking

Think about the insights and skills you have gained about public speaking so far. As you prepare to present a persuasive speech, consider information presented in previous chapters of this book and by your instructor in class, and address the following issues:

1. Identify four appropriate topics for your persuasive speech, and explain why these topics are appropriate for you, your audience, and the situation.
2. How might you use questions of fact, value, and policy as the basis of your speech?
3. Determine how you will establish your credibility.
4. What kinds of appeals will you make to reach the audience of your classmates?

subject or even attack your credibility to avoid discussing the issue. Irrelevant information used to divert attention away from the real issue is referred to as a **red herring** fallacy.

Hasty Generalization.   As a common critical thinking fallacy, the **hasty generalization** occurs when a speaker doesn't have sufficient data and, thus, argues or reasons from a specific example. Conclusions are drawn from insufficient data or cases. It is not uncommon to find people making generalizations based on only one or only a few examples. For instance, to argue that male students think date rape is not a problem on their campus, a speaker might cite the opinions of two or three close friends. The speaker then states the following conclusion: "In surveying people I know, I have found that most students do not believe that date rape is a problem on our campus." The argument that date rape is not a problem may sound impressive, but it does not represent a large or representative sample of students, and, thus, the claim is unjustified. The argument can be refuted as a hasty generalization.

When you develop or encounter arguments or reasoning that do not fit any of the fallacies described in the text, but you doubt the argument's validity, put the argument to the following test: Can the argument be outlined? Do the data support the claim? Is there a solid relationship between the data and the claim? It is not important to know the name of a specific type of fallacy but to analyze how arguments are developed and used in order to determine whether they are valid.

Making Effective Persuasive Speeches

1. Be realistic in setting your persuasive goal and determining what you expect to achieve.

2. Conduct as thorough an audience analysis as possible to help you choose the most appropriate strategy for accomplishing your persuasive goal.

3. Clearly identify a need so the audience recognizes that something should be done.

4. Be sure your solution is consistent with the audience's beliefs, attitudes, values, ethical standards, and experiences.

5. Make sure your solution is workable and practical so your audience can actually do or accept what you are asking of them.

6. Point out the advantages of what you offer and how those advantages will benefit your listeners. Remember that people are unlikely to accept your persuasive goal unless they see something in it for themselves.

7. Build your argument so any possible objections to your proposal by the audience will be clearly outweighed by the benefits the audience will gain if they accept your proposal.

8. Use only valid and reliable evidence to support your persuasive goal.

9. Be ethical and fair in both content and tactics.

10. Practice until you are able to present your speech without having to read it word for word.

11. Deliver your speech with enthusiasm, sincerity, and confidence.

Evaluating the Persuasive Speech

Here are some of the criteria used to evaluate the competence of the speaker and the effectiveness of a persuasive speech. Your instructor may consider these areas when evaluating your speech. You should be aware of them while preparing a persuasive speech presentation.

Topic

The selection of topic should meet the following criteria:

- The topic should merit the audience's attention.
- The audience should be able to see the relationship between the topic and speaker and between the topic and themselves.
- The topic should be able to be adequately covered in the time available. The topic should have been narrowed enough to be fully developed.

General Requirements

The following represent general requirements of most persuasive speech presentations:

- The speech's purpose should be clearly to persuade and stated as such.
- The speech should meet the time requirements set by the assignment.
- The speaker should cite sources of information that are not his or her own.
- The speech purpose should be relevant to the assignment and related to the audience.
- The speech should show evidence of careful preparation.

Audience Analysis

The speaker must shape the speech to suit the audience. This often requires research into the listeners' past experiences, beliefs, attitudes, and values. The choices the speaker makes regarding content and development of ideas should be tailored to the audience. (Chapter 7 provides details on audience analysis.)

- The speech should reflect appropriate audience analysis.
- The speaker should relate to and refer to audience members to get them involved and interested in the topic.
- The speech should include a goal, that is, the audience should be asked to think something, believe something, or take action.
- The speech should show the audience why the topic is important and relevant to them.

Supporting Materials

Supporting materials supply documented evidence that the information conveyed in the speech is accurate and credible.

- The supporting materials help the audience believe the information.
- The supporting materials should appeal to the audience's needs, logic, and emotions.
- The supporting materials should include a variety of factual statements, statistical data, personal experiences, analogies, contrasts, examples and illustrations, expert testimony, value appeals, and eyewitness accounts.
- Visual aids should be used where appropriate and helpful; they should follow guidelines established by the assignment.
- The supporting materials should be documented, cited correctly, and up to date.
- The supporting materials help the speaker establish and maintain credibility.

Organization

When judging the organization, the evaluator looks for a carefully planned, well-developed persuasive speech that takes a unified approach to the material being presented.

- The introduction should be properly developed.
  - It should orient the audience to the topic.
  - It should gain the audience's attention and arouse interest.
  - It should include a specific purpose and thesis statement.
  - It should define terms (if necessary).
  - It should motivate the audience to listen.
  - It should be relevant.
  - It should establish credibility.
- The organization of the body should be clear and easy to follow.
  - The main points should be clear and parallel in structure.
  - The main points should be related to the purpose of the speech.
  - Transitions should provide appropriate links between ideas.
  - The organizational pattern should be appropriate.
- The conclusion should be properly developed.
  - It should reinforce the purpose by reviewing the main points.
  - It should end with a memorable thought.
  - The audience should know what action is expected of them in response to the speech.

Delivery

The delivery techniques provide evidence that the speaker is aware of what the audience is interested in hearing, is involved in and enthusiastic about the topic, and is interested in sharing the material with the listeners.

- The speaker should be enthusiastic.
- The speaker should convey a persuasive attitude through focus, energy, and appropriate vocal variety.

Poet and best-selling author Maya Angelou speaks with high energy and enthusiasm to an audience on the University of Northern Iowa's campus. She is able to get her audience involved in and enthusiastic about her topic, and the enthusiasm on both sides is infectious.

- Nonverbal communication (gestures, movements, eye contact, posture, facial expression) should enhance and clarify the verbal delivery.
- The speaker should be aware of the audience's presence and reactions, and adjust delivery accordingly.
- The speaker should be confident and poised.
- The speaker should convey a sense of the topic's relevance and importance.
- The speaker's vocal delivery should enhance the speech with appropriate volume, appropriate rate, conversational quality, enthusiastic tone, clear enunciation, appropriate pauses, and appropriate vocal variety.

Language Choice

As we discussed at length in Chapter 4, effective use of language is critical to communication. It is especially essential to use language carefully when crafting a persuasive message. Clear, vivid, specific, and acceptable language should be used to enhance and clarify ideas.

- The language choice should be appropriate to the assignment and audience.
- The language should be compelling.
- The word choice should be appropriate for the speaker, topic, situation, and audience.
- Grammar should be appropriate and show both competence and an awareness of the "formal" speaking situation.
- Word pronunciations should be correct.

Speakers should evaluate their own speeches and those of others. The forms in Figures 12.1 and 12.2 can help you analyze and reflect on the speeches you give and those to which you listen.

FIGURE 12.1

Speaker's Self-Evaluation Form

On completing your persuasive speech, take a few moments to reflect on and think about all its elements. Using this form can help. Put yourself in the place of your listeners, and be specific in your comments on each aspect of the speech.

Title of speech: _____

Date and place given: _____

Topic selection _____

Research _____

Appropriateness *(to you, the classroom, the situation, the audience, the time limits)*
_____

Organization _____

The introduction _____

The body _____

The conclusion _____

Explanation and clarity of ideas _____

Soundness of the claims or arguments presented _____

Support for ideas *(Valid, worthwhile, ethical, sufficient number, clear?)*
_____

Use of language _____

Visual delivery *(movement, gestures, eye contact, posture)* _____

Vocal delivery *(conversationality, sincerity, variety, ease of listening)*
_____

The ways I adapted this speech to this audience: _____

If you made this speech again, what would you change? Why? _____

What would you retain? Why? _____

A Sample Persuasive Speech with Commentary

The following transcript (with authors' commentary) is a persuasive speech written and delivered by Holly Sisk at the AFA-NIET National Persuasive Finals at the University of Texas–Arlington, Arlington, Texas, April 5–7, 1997. Holly incorporates many of the strategies we have identified in this book.[7]

Dirty Hands Across America

Purpose

To convince the audience that dirty hands are an epidemic and to persuade them to wash up to prevent illness

Thesis

Because poor hand washing causes more deaths than auto accidents and homicides combined, we must address this public health crisis.

FIGURE 12.2

Sample Listener Evaluation Form for Persuasive Speeches

Listeners are often called on to evaluate speakers. Some instructors have listeners complete an evaluation similar to this one. It provides the speaker with invaluable information. It is also a good critical thinking exercise for the listener.

Speaker_____ Topic _____ Date _____

1. What was the speaker's specific purpose? _____

2. What was the speaker's thesis? _____

3. Which arguments did you believe? Which arguments did you have a hard time believing? Were you convinced about the claim or argument the speaker presented? Why or why not? _____
_____

4. What would it take to make you change your beliefs, attitudes, or behaviors about this topic? Do you think you might be influenced by this speaker and the stand taken in this speech? _____
_____

5. Did you hear any faulty reasoning in this speech? What kind? How could the reasoning be improved? _____

6. Did the speaker provide support for arguments, statements, and claims? What types of evidence and support were provided? _____
_____

7. Was the speaker believable? Why or why not? What could the speaker do to be more believable? _____
_____

8. Was the speaker ethical? Fair? Accurate? _____

9. What kinds of appeals were used? _____

10. Was the speaker easy to follow? Was the organization clear? _____
_____

Introduction

Holly orients her audience to the topic with a simple statement to which they can relate. She further connects with her audience with her narrative about people on a picnic. Holly has piqued interest in her story while providing a direction and focus for the topic and purpose. She uses humor and cites a source of information, *Morbidity and Mortality Weekly Report*. Holly next provides a view of her thesis and further motivates her audience to listen.

Holly cites a television program suggesting that "contaminated hands" cause extensive illness and death. The seriousness of the claim motivates the listener to attend. She further suggests that little is being done about the problem by citizens, proprietors of public facilities, or the medical community. Holly reinforces her thesis and then forecasts the points she will cover: (1) we have an epidemic, (2) the reasons for this epidemic, and (3) solutions.

The chicken salad sandwiches tasted great. At least that's what fifty picnicking Minnesotans thought in the summer of 1995. Then they woke up with, shall we say, severe gastrointestinal discomfort. Public health officials traced the outbreak to the food preparer who had changed diapers just moments before making the salad. She inadvertently added a new ingredient. As one victim said, "This gives a whole new meaning to ordering the number two." [Laughter] But ironically the September 13, 1996, *Morbidity and Mortality Weekly Report* reveals the food preparer had washed her hands, but not thoroughly enough to prevent infection. Unfortunately, hands that are unwashed or underwashed are a societal epidemic. The October 4, 1996, broadcast of ABC's *20/20* revealed that each year contaminated hands are the direct cause of more than 21 million illnesses and nearly 50,000 deaths. To make matters worse, public facilities, medical professionals,

Her language is straightforward, direct, and clear. She also uses a play on words: "Don't get caught dirty handed."

Body

In the next two sentences, Holly links the introduction and the first main point and signals her listeners about what is ahead (signpost). In the first main point, Holly reinforces the seriousness of the problem and sets up a problem—solution organizational pattern. She also uses some elements of Monroe's motivated sequence (see Chapter 10): She gets our attention and focuses on the problem that needs to be solved.

To support the point that people don't wash their hands, Holly cites a 1996 American Society for Microbiology survey. She does not, however, tell us where we can find this information. Up to this point, she has provided three specific sources, so the listener knows that she has researched her topic, but the specific source here would enhance Holly's credibility. Statistics from the survey clearly demonstrate that people do not wash their hands after using the restroom, changing diapers, or coughing or sneezing. Holly analyzes this information to suggest that the survey figures are conservative. She indicates that "even a splash in the water" counted as hand washing in the study. Her repetition of the word *conservative* is emphasized with a strong adverb *grossly*.

Here, Holly links the first subpoint, the extent of the problem, to the second subpoint, the harms caused by the problem. She brings in another set of studies, focusing on the medical community. Although this information seems relevant, valid, and sound, she does not tell us where we, the listeners, can find the results of the studies. She does, however, cite a specific and generally reliable source, the *American Medical Society Newsletter,* stating the number of illnesses and deaths associated with medical doctors' failure to wash their hands. Her language choice and "play on words" emphasize the nature and extent of the problem.

Holly relates the problem to her listeners, and elicits laughter with her appropriate use of humor. She relates a story of *E. coli* bacterial illness but does not cite the source of her information. Listeners need to know where the information came from. She makes the surprising statement that people became ill simply by touching someone who had consumed the tainted meat. The reference to a specific issue of the

and society are doing little to change this. Because *Health* magazine of December 1996 reports that poor hand washing causes more deaths than auto accidents and homicides combined, we must address this public health crisis. To do so, let's first see how dirty hands are an epidemic. Next, we uncover why few people wash up, and, finally, I will suggest some realistic solutions so you don't get caught dirty handed.

As you might imagine most people aren't willing to admit they're hygiene challenged, but they are. And the resulting epidemic can best be seen in two ways, the extent of the problem and the harms it causes.

A survey conducted in 1996 by the American Society for Microbiology found that 94 percent say they wash their hands after using the restroom, but only 60 percent actually do. Even more disgusting, 22 percent of men don't wash their hands after changing diapers. And 66 percent say after coughing or sneezing the best they can do is . . . [presenter wipes hands on her clothing]. To make matters worse, this study counted even a splash in the water as hand washing. And remember, there's a gulf between cleaning and actually washing. So at best these numbers are conservative, grossly conservative.

So OK, we don't wash up. But by golly, our good old doctors do, don't they? Well, in December 1996, a Georgetown University Consortium of forty studies on medicinal hand washing concludes that less than 40 percent of all medical professionals wash their hands between patients. The harmful effects of not washing up are substantial. The January 23, 1996, *American Medical Society Newsletter* reveals that doctors' failure to hit the suds causes 2.4 million illnesses and nearly 30,000 deaths a year. The dirty little secret in American medicine is that patients check into hospitals expecting to get better, but often get worse, because a doctor wouldn't spare forty seconds.

Now we've all heard stories of food-borne illnesses, trichinosis, salmonella, Denny's. [Laughter] Well, in 1994, more than 500 Washington state residents were stricken by the *E. coli* bacteria. But the story you probably didn't read is that forty-nine of those patients never ate the tainted meat. They simply touched someone who had. The February 9, 1996, *Wall Street Journal* reports that food poisoning cases from poor hand washing result in more than 31 million illnesses [Actually, 32 million] and nearly 4,000 deaths a year.

Wall Street Journal supports her assertion that millions of people are harmed.

In this transition, Holly helps her audience visualize the problem and focuses on who to blame: society and dysfunctional facilities.

Holly uses testimony from an expert quoted in *Commercial Appeal* to set up her second main point. She refers to a familiar axiom. In her next citation, Holly does not give us the accurate title of the publication cited. Holly states that the simple act of washing one's hands can kill antibiotic-resistant bacteria but does not provide specific data to support her claim. She offers, however, evidentiary support for her claim that hand washing will reduce the problem. But a critical listener would want more specific support to totally accept all the ramifications of Holly's thesis.

Holly's use of a CNN broadcast points up the difference between men's and women's use of hand washing. She summarizes her first subpoint by analyzing the quotation.

This statement is a transition linking the first and second subpoints in the second main point. Holly identifies the problems inherent in dysfunctional facilities. Her citation of a Centers for Disease Control official lends credibility and provides information.

In this transition, Holly explains information about a reasonable level of cleanliness, making her listeners aware that they are both a part of the problem and a part of the solution. She then moves on to identify three main solutions.

Holly identifies what one city has done to educate the public. She uses a play on words and humor to emphasize the novel approach. This strategy again draws the listener into the discussion. Holly cites a telephone interview with a public health official to support her point that Pittsburgh has reduced hand-washing related illnesses.

By now, you're probably looking at your hands and thinking, ugh. . . . But if it's so gross why don't more people wash up? The blame is twofold: societal factors and dysfunctional facilities.

As public health expert Charles Inlander told the May 14, 1996, *Commercial Appeal,* we think modern medicine can cure everything. So the old axiom, "cleanliness is next to Godliness" has lost its place. The problem with this mind-set is that as the May 1996 *Journal of Complementary Medicines* [Actually, *Journal of Alternative and Complementary Medicine*] revealed, most bacteria have evolved to the point that they resist antibiotics. But what drugs can't kill, simple hand washing can. Additionally, the Microbiology survey confirmed two facts. First, few people wash up. And second, men really are slobs. [Laughter] The September 18, 1996, broadcast of CNN's "Newsnight" reveals that men are half as likely to wash up as women are. As one man told CNN, "Men don't like, you know, care. Out with a group of guys, . . . we just want to get back to the game." As his statement suggests, when people are in a hurry, they just don't take the time to wash their hands.

But even if you want to wash your hands, dysfunctional facilities make it virtually impossible. In an effort to save money, many public restrooms have switched to faucets that dispense water only when you press on the faucet itself. But in a telephone interview on January 8, 1997, with CDC [Centers for Disease Control] official William Jarvis, he explained, "It's functionally impossible to simultaneously dispense soap, water, and wash your hands—you'd have to be a circus juggler." And when you go to dry your hands, you face another problem. Those popular handblowers are in fact havens of bacteria. They might dry your hands but they blow disease all over them.

Now we probably all know some clean hand fanatics, who won't touch doorknobs or shake hands. But you don't need to be obsessive. The solution to cleaning up our hands will require an effort on the part of public health officials, public establishments, and the public.

First, the city of Pittsburgh, Pennsylvania, has a novel idea. They were installing large hand-washing reminders inside of bathroom stalls. Talk about a captive audience. In a telephone interview on November 8, 1996, [Actually, November 7] with Allegheny County health official Susan Smith, she brags of implementing this program. Pittsburgh has seen a significant reduction in hand-washing-related illnesses.

But industry must also clean up its act. The March 28, 1996, *Health Law Reporter* explains that hospitals that implement stringent hand-washing controls see a dramatic reduction in

Holly points out that public establishments must also implement stringent hand washing controls. To develop the idea, she uses an example: the waterless cleansing system used at the Atlanta Olympics. She cites a specific issue of the *Atlanta Journal* as support.

In two sentences, Holly asks the audience to get personally involved in the solution. She identifies three specific actions each of her listeners can take to do so.

Conclusion

In her conclusion, Holly refers back to her opening statement about the Minnesotans who became ill because a food handler did not carefully wash her hands. Holly summarizes the points of her speech well and lets the audience know that she is finishing. She leaves them with a personal reason to act and a call to action. The touch of humor at the end makes a positive impression and fits the topic perfectly.

contamination. Unfortunately, less than half of all American hospitals have such programs. They need to get them.

And a good place for regular businesses to start is to follow the lead of the Atlanta Olympics. If you visited the Olympics, you noticed a waterless cleansing system outside of the portapotties. It's called chlorhexedene, an antimicrobial agent that completely cleanses the hands without the use of water or the need for hand drying. The August 28, 1996, *Atlanta Journal* reports that chlorhexedine is safe, money saving, and environmentally friendly.

But in an epidemic even a concerted effort by government and industry can't solve everything. We have to take personal action.

The September 18, 1996, *New York Times* reports that most people who wash their hands don't do so correctly. You need to wash for at least 30 seconds in warm water, and don't forget the soap. It's also very important that you be aware of where you place your hands throughout the day. We needlessly touch our eyes, nose, and mouth and in doing so we risk the spread of bacteria. Finally, chances are likely that you will visit a medical facility in the near future. Ask anyone who comes near you to wash their hands first. This includes your doctor, nurse, or pillow fluffer. We need to be willing to say, physician wash thyself.

Fifty Minnesotans probably thought they were safe, but they weren't, thanks to the carelessness of a food preparer. But she didn't realize that dirty hands are an epidemic. Or just how few people wash up. And she certainly didn't realize that a few simple steps really can protect our health. Americans have made many changes in their health over the past few years. We've stopped smoking, started having safer sex, changed our eating habits. But hand washing is a thirty-second procedure that is the number one daily thing you can do to protect your health. If the last ten minutes of reasons haven't convinced you to spare thirty seconds, hey, my hands are clean.

Analysis and Evaluation

Holly does a good job of organizing the speech and relating the topic to her audience. She orients the audience to the topic with the narrative or true story, but she also piques listener interest and curiosity when she begins her fourth sentence with the words, "Public health officials." Because she has selected a topic familiar to most listeners, she constantly refers to the fact that although the issues she raises should be common knowledge, people don't always follow through on what they "know" to be good for them. Holly does a good job of incorporating a variety of sources and motivating listeners' interest. She uses straightforward, direct, clear language and uses a play on words throughout the speech to keep listeners interested, to keep the focus on her topic, and to provide moments of levity.

This is an example of a memorized speech, delivered in the final round of the National Individual Events Tournament. The content rules call for a memorized delivery, which, as we stated in earlier chapters, can be a problem. In this speech, Holly does not provide all of the information listeners want: She does not tell us where we can find the 1996 American Society for Microbiology survey, the studies from the December 1996 Georgetown University Consortium, or the *E. coli* bacterial illness in Washington state. Inclusion of this information would enhance Holly's credibility. Also in paragraph 5, Holly incorrectly cites "more than 31 million illnesses" when the actual total reported in the *Wall Street Journal* was 32 million illnesses. In paragraph 9, Holly gave the wrong date for the interview with Allegheny County health official Susan Smith. Sometimes students think these inconsistencies are just *little details*. Little details such as these are always important to listeners but are especially important when the speaker may be evaluated by a boss, supervisor, classroom instructor, or one's co-workers.

One of the problems with Holly's speech content may be found in her second main point: She asserts that hand washing can significantly reduce illness and disease. In paragraph 10, Holly says, "Pittsburgh has seen a significant reduction in hand-washing-related illnesses," but the listener or reader has had no evidence to support that statement.

Holly provides us with a persuasive speech on a topic commonly known to most people, but she provides a new twist: Even though people know they should wash their hands, people don't, and illness and disease are spread by those dirty hands. She organized the speech well, oriented and motivated the listeners to attend to the speech, and kept listeners "tuned in" to the topic. Reread the speech to see if you can find elements or strategies that we discussed in Chapters 7 to 12.

 ## Summary

Persuasion affects us every day of our lives. If we are not attempting to persuade others, they are attempting to persuade us. An understanding of persuasion and its strategies can help us create effective persuasive messages and prepare us to analyze and comprehend the persuasive messages that we receive.

Persuasion is a process, involving both verbal and nonverbal messages, that attempts to reinforce or change attitudes, beliefs, values, or behaviors. The difference between a persuasive and an informative speech is the purpose of the speaker. The purpose of the informative speech is to have listeners understand and learn, whereas the purpose of the persuasive speech is to influence the listener in some way, either to reinforce a belief, attitude, or behavior, or to change beliefs, attitudes, or behaviors.

There are four possible action goals in persuasive speaking: (1) *Adoption* asks listeners to demonstrate their acceptance of an idea, belief, or value by performing the desired behavior; (2) *discontinuance* asks listeners to stop doing something; (3) *deterrence* asks listeners to avoid certain behaviors; and (4) *continuance* asks listeners to continue certain behaviors.

In selecting a persuasive topic, you should consider your interest in the subject, its value and concern to your audience, its potential as an action goal, and its currency. Persuasive speech topics may center on a *question of fact,* what is true and what is false; a *question of value,* whether something is good or bad, desirable or undesirable;

or a *question of policy,* what actions should be taken. When attempting to answer questions of fact, value, and policy, you cannot always develop a formal, irrefutable answer to meet the objections of others. Toulmin's model can help meet objections of others and make your argument clear to your listeners by presenting its three basic parts: claim, data, and warrant.

Credibility, a speaker's believability based on the audience's evaluation of her or his competence, experience, character, and charisma, is critical to the success of any persuasive speech. Listeners evaluate competence based on their perception of a speaker's knowledge, and they judge character based on their perception of his or her *trustworthiness* and ethics. It is important to provide within the speech an *oral footnote,* the source from which particular information comes. *Charisma* refers to the speaker's appeal or attractiveness to the audience.

Effective consumers of persuasion listen carefully to the message and ask pertinent questions to help them analyze and evaluate the message. Effective consumers of persuasion are especially concerned with good, reliable, relevant information from ethical sources. Preparing and developing a persuasive speech requires special attention to research, organization, and supporting materials. Your research must be particularly thorough and accurate. Your method of organization must also be carefully matched to your topic, specific purpose, and audience. Like an informative speech, the persuasive speech may follow a problem–solution, cause–effect, or motivated sequence pattern.

Persuasive speakers use supporting materials to build the kind of appeal that is most likely to sway their listeners. *Appeals to needs* attempt to move people to action by calling on their physical and psychological requirements and desires. *Logical appeals* use evidence and proof to support the speaker's views. In presenting a logical appeal, a speaker may use *deductive reasoning,* a sequence of thought that moves from general information to a specific conclusion; *inductive reasoning,* a sequence of thought that moves from the specific to the general; *causal reasoning,* a sequence of thought that links causes with effects and implies or includes the word *because;* and *reasoning by analogy,* a sequence of thought that compares similar things or circumstances in order to draw a conclusion. *Emotional appeals* attempt to move people to action by playing on their feelings. Emotional appeals, if properly selected, can powerfully influence people to do things that may not necessarily be logical. It is not unusual for persuasive speakers to mix both logical and emotional appeals to achieve the strongest effect.

Arguments that do not follow the rules of logic and, therefore, are not believable are called *fallacies. Questionable cause* is a common fallacy that occurs when a speaker alleges something that does not relate to, or produce, the outcome claimed in the argument. *Ad hominem* is the fallacy involved when someone attacks a person rather than the argument itself. This is also referred to as "name calling." Fact and opinion are often misused in argument. When speakers state opinions as if they are facts, they can mislead the audience and offer fallacious arguments. A *red herring* fallacy occurs when irrelevant information is used to divert attention away from the real issue. *Hasty generalization,* another type of fallacy, occurs when a speaker doesn't have sufficient data and, thus, argues or reasons from a specific example.

Persuasive speakers should consider the criteria included in this chapter in order to be more persuasive. You should think about topic choice, general requirements of the presentation, and the results of your audience analysis to ensure reaching your audience. You should also use good organization, effective delivery, and appropriate language.

DISCUSSION STARTERS

1. In what ways does persuasion affect your daily life?
2. Why is behavioral change the ultimate goal of persuasion?
3. What advice would you give to someone who was assigned to give a persuasive speech and needed to select a topic?
4. What determines whether a topic is appropriate for a persuasive speech?
5. Do you have credibility? Explain your response.
6. If people lose credibility, what can they do to regain it?
7. How can you establish credibility in a persuasive speech?
8. In what ways does organizing a persuasive speech differ from organizing an informative speech?
9. Are supporting materials used differently in a persuasive speech than they are in an informative speech? Explain your response.
10. How do you know if a speaker is being ethical based on what he or she tells you?
11. What criteria would you use to judge the effectiveness of a persuasive speech?

NOTES

1. D. Zarefsky, *Public Speaking Strategies for Success,* 2nd ed. (Boston: Allyn and Bacon, 1999), 356.
2. Adapted from W. Fotheringham, *Perspectives on Persuasion* (Boston: Allyn and Bacon, 1966), 33.
3. Adapted from a speech presented by Mary B. Trouba, reprinted with permission from *Winning Orations* (Mankato, Minn.: The Interstate Oratorical Association, 1986).
4. S. Toulmin, *The Uses of Argument* (Cambridge: Cambridge University Press, 1969), 94–145.
5. A. H. Maslow, *Motivation and Personality,* 2nd ed. (New York: Harper & Row, 1970). Maslow, in this edition, includes two additional desires or needs—the need to know and understand and an aesthetic desire—as higher stages of his hierarchy. These are often associated with subcategories of self-actualization, which is not included here.
6. Speech presented by Heather Jamison, reprinted with permission from *Winning Orations* (1992).
7. "Dirty Hands Across America," by Holly Sisk, George Mason University, from the Allyn and Bacon/AFA Student Speeches Video II, American Forensic Association National Individual Events Tournament Informative and Persuasive Finals, 1997 AFA-NIET, University of Texas–Arlington, Arlington, Texas, April 5–7, 1997.

Persuasive Speech Topics

Here are some possible topics for persuasive speeches. The items listed are not necessarily titles of specific speeches and may need to be narrowed to fit specific purposes, time limits, or other requirements set by your instructor.

Increasing Aid to Farmers

Children at Risk in Our Society

Internships Are Beneficial

Helping the Homeless

Sex Education Is Still Needed

Elderly Abuse on the Rise

Poaching of Animals

Control of Acid Rain

Tabloids Are Nothing But Rumor

Tanning Beds Can Be Fatal

Women Need Not Be Second

The Best Vacation You Can Take

All College Instructors Must Speak English Clearly

Recycling to Save the Environment

The Impact of Video Technology

Majoring in Communication

Sexual Assaults Are Increasing

Professional Athletes Are Too Greedy

Youth Programs

Cloning Must Be Curtailed

Use of the Internet Must Be Reduced

Use of the Internet Must Be Increased

Alternative Health Care Is Viable

Americans Lack Discipline

Gay Rights

Dumping of Nuclear Waste

The United States Is No Longer a World Competitor

Rap Music Can Send Important Messages

Sexual Abuse of Children

Biking: An Excellent Form of Transportation

Sunscreen Lotions and Skin Cancer

The Best Way to Make a Buck While in College

Spring Break: Do It the Inexpensive Way

Change Your Diet, Live Healthy

Improving Our Prisons

Political Involvement

Pornographic Films

Ban Small Cars

Corruption in Sports

Traditional Family Values

Plan for Your Retirement Now

The Impact of the Brady Bill

The Election Process Must Be Changed

CHAPTER

13

Interpersonal
Communication

*"Without wearing any mask we are
conscious of, we have a special face
for each friend."*
—Oliver Wendell Holmes Sr.

- Understand the relationship between interpersonal communication and meeting others.
- Analyze how motivation is related to interpersonal communication.
- Understand the connection between online and face-to-face interaction.
- Relate small talk to interpersonal communication and initiating relationships.
- Explain the connection between self-disclosure and interpersonal communication.
- Become a more competent user of self-disclosure.

SCENARIO

Thursday—the one free day Sam has during the week to do what he wants. He usually likes to spend part of the day relaxing either by sleeping in or playing tennis. Sam is a good student and is sure that he did very well on his midterm in calculus. Given that he had a good night's sleep for a change, he decided to go to the tennis courts to see if there was anybody there to play.

On his way to the courts he picked up his mail and discovered that he had received an award for his excellent grades. Sam was so pleased that he couldn't help but begin to hum out loud as he continued his walk to the tennis courts.

When he got there, Sam noticed a student from his calculus class sitting outside the courts. Sam wasn't sure of her name, but she smiled and said hello. "Hi," said Sam, "my name is Sam Jackson. You're in my calculus class, aren't you?"

"Yes I am and you're the guy that knows all the answers. By the way, my name is Marie. Do you want to play some tennis?"

Sam responded, "Sure!" As they walked onto the court Marie smiled and thought to herself, "I wonder if he is seeing anyone?" ■

Interpersonal communication usually occurs any time two people come in contact with each other. In today's technological world, for example, relationships are being initiated through chatrooms and email connections almost daily. For example, in our local newspaper the following feature was run in the Life section—"Chatroom brought them together." In the article, it explains how Shelly Zoz and Brian Davis met for the first time. In her first message to Brian, Shelly wrote, "Is it true?" He responded, "Is what true?" Before the evening was over, according to the article, they had exchanged telephone numbers. Brian said, "It was amazing. Everything just clicked between us." Shelly, in the article, was quoted as saying, "A lot of people in these chatrooms will feed you full of stuff and expect you to believe it, but he seemed honest." She went on, "We talked and talked about our feelings, and we were really on the same wavelength." Their first online encounter was in March 1999 and by May they decided to meet in person. Brian drove the 1,500 miles to Lincoln to

361

This neighborhood pick-up basketball game provides the players an opportunity to form relationships based on common interests, proximity, and athletic ability.

this is a factor

meet Shelly. They met and liked what they saw and now plan to marry. "A lot of people think meeting someone through a chatroom is totally nuts," Shelly said. "People are shocked that it worked out."[1]

Many online connections that occur between individuals and groups of individuals are limited because of the proximity of the individuals involved, but it is becoming more and more common for these types of online interactions to result in relationships. Malcolm Parks and Kory Floyd, communication scholars, surveyed twenty-four newsgroups and asked a random sample of the users if they had formed new acquaintances, friendships, or other personal relationships as a result of their interaction online. Almost two-thirds of those responding to the survey said that they had formed such relationships with someone they met on the Internet.[2] The opening scenario between Sam and Marie, however, is the most likely way that two people initiate conversations that may result in a relationship. Whether Sam and Marie's or Shelly and Brian's conversation or interaction evolves into an ongoing or lasting relationship depends on many factors such as attraction, proximity, motivation, need, and so on. Although chatrooms, email communication, and Net dating services are expedient ways to initiate conversations with strangers, they may not necessarily be the best way for us to develop relationships with others, and, in fact, they can be outright dangerous. In another newspaper article, "Caught in the Net: Proceed with Caution," Keven Koelling, a psychotherapist, says, "I've seen everything from marriages breaking down to people using the Internet as an escape from the problems they need to deal with in their marriage." In the same article, Deb Hope, a psychology professor at the University of Nebraska, said, "Chat rooms can be dangerous to people who may not have the best judgment about relationships anyway. You can end up getting involved with someone—maybe even agreeing to meet them—and really not know who they are at all." People have been exploited, taken advantage of or even victimized by someone they meet via the Internet.[3] Thus, there are many warnings about Internet interactions that should not be ignored. Communication in either situation is the overriding factor that will determine the kind of relationship Sam and Marie or Shelly and Brian develop, if any at all, and how long it will last.

Interpersonal Communication

In Chapter 1 we defined interpersonal communication as the informal exchange of information between two or more people. A **relationship** is an association between at least two people and may be described in terms of intimacy or kinship, for example, acquaintance, girlfriend, boyfriend, lover, wife, husband, mother, father, child, uncle, or cousin. Sometimes relationships are based on roles—for example, two roommates, Internet users, neighbors, boss and employee, teacher and student, doctor and patient, minister and church members. Relationships can also be described in terms of time,

"I knew her in high school" or "They just met him the other day." Finally, relationships may be based on activities or participation in events, for example, "We play volleyball together," "We go to the same synagogue," "He is in my class," "She works with me," or "We belong to the same fraternity."[4] Through our many different kinds of relationships, we satisfy our desire to connect with others and to communicate with them.

° To satisfy my needs.

The Motivation to Communicate and Form Relationships

Interpersonal communication and the relationships we form help us understand ourselves as well as others. There is no question that most of us are highly motivated to establish relationships with others. In the opening scenario, Marie, by wondering whether Sam is going with someone, shows her desire to know more about him. The phenomenon of wanting to know more about others can be explained by uncertainty reduction theory.[5] **Uncertainty reduction theory** suggests that when we meet others to whom we are attracted, our need to know about them tends to make us draw inferences from the physical data that we observe. An urge or need to reduce our uncertainty about those individuals motivates our desire for further communication with them.

Most people who have physical disabilities will tell you that they don't want special treatment. Most prefer to be treated like any other person—as a person first.

Predicted outcome value theory[6] expands on uncertainty reduction theory, providing another explanation as to why people seek to interact and to learn more about those whom they meet. **Predicted outcome value theory** suggests that people connect with others because they believe that rewards or positive outcomes will result. Thus, supporters of this theory argue that, in contrast to uncertainty reduction theory, predicted outcome value theory provides a more accurate and complete account of why people engage others initially and attempt to establish long-term relationships. Do you agree with the ideas of predicted outcome value theory, that we initiate interaction or establish relationships with others only because of the potential rewards that we will gain from them? In the next section, we discuss this issue of rewards further as an explanation of our motivation to communicate with others.

relates back to → social exchange theory, p. 368.

Each of us has many different physical and emotional needs that we wish to fulfill. Usually, our most significant communication with others is about some interpersonal need that we have or that the other person has. The more we understand our needs and the needs of others, the more competent we can become at interpersonal communication. Our personal needs and the needs of others compel us to be the individuals we are when we are by ourselves or with others. Two approaches that can help us better understand our motivation to communicate with others are William Schutz's theory of interpersonal needs and John Thibaut and Harold Kelley's social exchange theory.

Making Connections

Communicating with Persons with Disabilities

At times, we avoid communicating with certain individuals because we are uncomfortable, feel awkward, or aren't sure how to approach them. When encountering people who have a physical disability, some of us are uncertain about what to say or how to behave. Often, rather than attempting to reduce our uncertainty or fear, we may go out of our way to sidestep any interaction at all.

Most people who have physical disabilities will tell you that they don't want special treatment—most prefer to be treated like any other person, as a "person first." It is a shame that our fear of the unknown can prevent us from interacting and developing a relationship with someone.

1. Why do we enter into conversations with some individuals and not with others, especially others who may be different from us?
2. How do you feel and behave when you encounter someone with a disability?
3. What advice would you give to help reduce people's fear or uncertainty about communicating with individuals who have a disability?

4. Create a set of guidelines that you believe will facilitate more free communication between people who have and people who do not have disabilities.

If you need more information about communicating with people with disabilities, ask your instructor or go to your library to obtain the *Handbook of Communication and People with Disabilities: Research and Application,* edited by Dawn O. Braithwaite and Teresa L. Thompson (Mahwah, N.J.: Erlbaum, 2000). It is an outstanding resource that covers a wide variety of communication research and applications related to people with disabilities. You can also contact the AXIS Center for Public Awareness of People with Disabilities, 4550 Indianola Avenue, Columbus, Ohio 43214. Or stop by your college's Accommodation Resource Center or call your community's branch of the League of Human Dignity for guidelines for communicating with persons with disabilities. Another resource is the ADA Information Center's Americans with Disabilities Act home page (http://www.ada.org/). It would be worthwhile to discuss in class any guidelines you obtain.

Schutz's Theory of Interpersonal Needs

Interpersonal communication literature consistently discusses the idea that each of us needs to include others in our activities and to be included in theirs, to exert control over others and have them control us, and to give affection to others as well as receive it from them. Schutz provides insight into our communication behaviors with others via his **theory of interpersonal needs,** which consists of three needs—affection, inclusion, and control.[7] Although other needs exist, according to Schultz, most of our interpersonal behavior and motivation can be directly related to our need for affection, inclusion, and control. Almost all of us seek relationships with others, and because a majority of our communication takes place at the interpersonal level, it is essential to recognize the interpersonal needs that we all possess, regardless of background or culture. Although needs differ from person to person, from situation to situation, and from culture to culture, knowing and understanding our interpersonal needs should help us understand how they influence our interactions with others.

For most of us, our interpersonal needs do not remain static; desire and importance vary with circumstances. For instance, giving and receiving affection may be far more important in a relationship, especially as the relationship intensifies and moves toward bonding, whereas inclusion may be more significant when a relationship is coming apart. Awareness of personal needs and the needs of others also varies depending on the depth of a relationship, the timing, the context, and so forth. A mother may only become aware of her need for excessive control over her daughters when one daughter suggests that she can no longer live with so many rules. Let's look more carefully at each of the interpersonal needs and how they influence our interpersonal interactions.

① People who are personal have high self-esteem.
②: What are the factors which determine whether one is personal.

The Need for Affection. The need for affection is the need to feel likable or lovable. Every day we see people striving to fulfill this need; for example, people who join social groups or dating services are seeking to fulfill their need for belonging and love. According to Schutz's theory, a person who seems to be liked by many and, therefore, has adequately fulfilled this need is referred to as *personal*. Someone who is unable to fulfill this need is labeled either *underpersonal* or *overpersonal*.

Making Connections

Thinking About Love

How does one person go about "proving" that he or she loves another person?

According to Marilyn Vos Savant, noted lecturer, researcher, and *Parade Magazine* columnist, "It's a lot easier to prove that you don't love someone than it is to prove that you do, but one of the best 'proofs' I know in everyday life is the desire to devote time to the person with no expectation of any sort of compensation, including gratitude."

1. How does Marilyn Vos Savant's answer relate to what has been discussed in the chapter so far?
2. Explain the differences in what and how you communicate with someone whom you love (not necessarily romantic love), someone you like, someone you dislike, and someone you hate.
3. Do men and women differ in how they express love? If so, how?

Marilyn Vos Savant, "Ask Marilyn," *Parade Magazine* 21 (January 1990): 17.

Underpersonal people avoid emotional commitments or involvement with others. If we examine these individuals, we often find that they are hiding their true selves because they fear that others may not like them as they are. These people, like all other human beings, have a need for affection, but they have learned to cover it by not letting others get close to them. Some underpersonals find numerous excuses for not developing close personal relationships. Others may be friendly to everyone, but keep their friendships on a superficial level. Do you know someone who may fit this category? Why do you think this person is unwilling to get close to others?

Overpersonal individuals are the opposite of underpersonals. They need affection so badly that they often go to extremes to ensure acceptance by others. They frequently seek approval by being extremely intimate in what they communicate. They may even attempt to pay for friendship, for example, by buying things for others but never letting others buy anything for them. These individuals may be possessive and get jealous when others talk to their friends.

Personal people tend to be poised, confident, mature, and able to deal with almost everyone with whom they come in contact. Personals want to be liked, but they do not consider being liked by everyone essential for happiness. They are easy to talk with and are at ease with themselves.

The Need for Inclusion.   The interpersonal need for inclusion encompasses our needs to feel significant and worthwhile. Schutz describes individuals in terms of this need as *social, undersocial,* or *oversocial.* Undersocial people do not like being around other people because, like underpersonal individuals, they find communicating with others threatening. They tend to be shy and find initiating conversations with others difficult. Although often intelligent, undersocials are loners who prefer to do things by themselves or in large groups where they can hide in the crowd. Typically, undersocials find it difficult to speak out and generally avoid saying anything for fear of drawing attention to themselves.

Oversocial people cannot stop themselves from getting involved and communicating with others. They attempt to dominate conversations, often speak out of turn, and find it hard to keep quiet. They prefer situations in which they can take over relationships by dominating the flow of communication. The oversocial person fears being ignored by others. Sometimes oversocial people tend to be overbearing. Can you think of people who have the tendency to be oversocial? How do you react to them?

Social people have satisfied their needs for inclusion. They are capable of handling situations with or without others, and few, if any, situations make them feel uncomfortable. They have confidence in themselves and are assertive enough to speak when they feel it is necessary to do so.

The Need for Control.   Schutz's third need is for control, which is derived from responsibility and leadership. Almost all of us have some need to control others and our surroundings. However, some individuals wish to be controlled by others. The strength of this need and the way we manifest it determine whether we are *abdicrats, autocrats,* or *democrats,* according to Schutz.

Abdicrats are extremely submissive to others. They have little or no self-confidence, often perceive themselves as incompetent, take few risks, rarely make decisions on their own, and need much reinforcement to believe they are useful and capable.

Autocrats never have enough control. They try to dominate others. In a group, they are always willing to make the decisions or at least voice strong opinions about what decision ought to be made. Because autocrats have a strong need for power, they may not care whom they hurt in their search for control. They are also somewhat closed-minded, believing their own positions are the only correct ones. And they show little, if any, respect for others.

Democrats have their control needs essentially satisfied. They are comfortable as either leaders or followers, do not exaggerate either the leader's or the follower's role, and are open minded and willing to accept others' suggestions for the good of the group. They like to get things done but not at the expense of someone else.

Schutz's theory of needs clearly illustrates the reasons that motivate us to communicate with others. We develop relationships with others for many reasons. The social needs we have discussed explain a great deal about our motivation to form relationships, but there are other reasons to develop relationships: to avoid or lessen feelings of loneliness, to learn more about ourselves, and to share our lives with others. But why is it that we are attracted to some individuals more than to others? We address interpersonal attraction in more detail in Chapter 14.

Making Connections

Measuring Your Interpersonal Needs

Develop your own measuring scale using Schutz's three needs, and then measure your own interpersonal needs. Use a rating scale in which 1 represents a low need and 7 a high one. The following is an example of such a scale. Add to or change the items to better reflect how you interpret Schutz's needs or how you define your own specific needs.

Affection

1. Need to seek others' friendship	1 2 3 4 5 6 7
2. Need to keep privacy	1 2 3 4 5 6 7
3. Need to be considered likable by others	1 2 3 4 5 6 7
4. Create your own items	1 2 3 4 5 6 7

Inclusion

1. Need to be involved in groups	1 2 3 4 5 6 7
2. Need to be left alone	1 2 3 4 5 6 7
3. Need to be the center of attention	1 2 3 4 5 6 7
4. Create your own items	1 2 3 4 5 6 7

Control

1. Need to have responsibility for others	1 2 3 4 5 6 7
2. Need to tell others what to do	1 2 3 4 5 6 7
3. Need to be in charge	1 2 3 4 5 6 7
4. Create your own items	1 2 3 4 5 6 7

After adding items of your own, fill out the measuring scale based on how you perceive yourself. Then mentally select two or three different people you know (a relative, best friend, teacher, romantic partner, and so on), and complete the measuring instrument using a different color pencil for each person and your perception of how each of the individuals would rate you on each item. Compare the results. What do the results show about how you view yourself and how others see you?

If appropriate, share what you learned with a small group of your classmates, or write a one- to two-page paper expressing what you discovered about yourself. The goal is to reflect on your interpersonal needs and how they affect your communication with others.

Making Connections

It's Me That Counts

Brad and Paige have been dating for more than six months. Both agree that they have a very close relationship. After a romantic dinner at their favorite restaurant, Brad and Paige go back to Paige's apartment and are in the middle of some serious kissing when Paige says, "Brad, I want you to stop. I don't want to go any further." Brad says, "Are you kidding me? Don't you love me? I mean, it's not like we haven't been going out for six months." Paige doesn't respond immediately; she seems to have been caught off guard. Finally, she says, "Brad, I do know how you feel about me, and I do trust you, but going all the way just isn't right for me. I also don't want to end up having a kid before we are married." Brad quickly says, "But I thought you really cared about me. You know, Paige, I love you!" Paige replies, "I know, but I am not ready for sex, and I really don't want to until I am married—you have to understand that."

1. Do you think Brad's communication is motivated more out of self-interest than interest in Paige? Explain.
2. How would you describe Brad and Paige's relationship based on their interaction with each other?
3. What does the scenario teach us about motivation and communication?

○ Our goal or motivation has an impact on the way we communicate to others.

Social Exchange Theory

Tradeoffs in economics

Social psychologists John W. Thibaut and Harold H. Kelley originated the **social exchange theory,** which is based on the assumption that people consciously and deliberately weigh the costs and rewards associated with a relationship or interaction and will seek out relationships that reward them and avoid those that are costly.[8] It is Thibaut and Kelley's belief that we are motivated to develop and maintain relationships in terms of the exchange of rewards and costs. A **reward** is anything that we perceive as beneficial to our self-interest. It refers to things or relationships that bring us pleasure, satisfaction, or gratification. For example, outcomes such as good feelings, prestige, economic gain, and fulfillment of emotional needs are considered rewards. **Costs,** however, are negative rewards, things that we perceive to be not beneficial to our self-interest. They refer to outcomes, such as time, energy, and anxiety, that we do not want to incur.

In the accompanying Making Connections box, Brad's motivation is to maximize his sexual pleasure. Paige's motivation is to avoid the costs associated with premarital sex. If the scenario were to continue it might unfold as follows:

> Paige's voice carries a tinge of anger or bitterness. "Brad, I wanted to make love with you, but now I feel you are only seeking your own pleasure and don't really care about the possible consequences for me. I am the one who gets pregnant, I am the one who has to carry the baby for nine months, and, in the end, I am now the one who has to ask for common sense that would protect both of us." Brad's tone now becomes disappointed but still angry, "I'm going home!"

This scenario has implications not only for the single interaction that has occurred but for their relationship as well. The central focus of social exchange theory is on motivation.

According to the theory, we are motivated out of self-interest to act or behave in certain ways. For example, if the rewards we gain are higher than any potential costs we incur, then we regard the relationship or interaction as pleasant and satisfying. But if our reward gain (rewards minus costs) falls below a certain level, then we find the relationship unsatisfactory or unpleasant. The ratio between rewards and costs varies from person to person and from situation to situation. Thus, what is a desirable ratio of rewards and costs for one person may be much different for another person. If a relationship is healthy and satisfying, there is probably a good balance most of the time between rewards and costs, with rewards outweighing costs. Most relationships begin and prosper because the people involved benefit in some way from it.

If individuals have a number of relationships that they perceive as having a positive cost–reward ratio, they will set high-satisfaction expectations for all of the relationships they encounter. However, individuals who have few positive interactions or relationships with others are likely to set low-satisfaction expectations in their relationships and to tolerate more negativity in order to maintain the relationships they have. Abusive relationships or relationships that people stay in because they do not believe they have any alternatives are examples of the latter situation. For instance, if a person in an abusive relationship believes that the abuser is the only one who can provide security, the person being abused will be more inclined to tolerate the abuser's irritating habit of drinking too much.

As rational as the rewards–costs ratio may seem, we know from our own relationship experiences it cannot explain all of the complexities involved in forming every relationship. Nevertheless, the theory can be helpful when examining our relationships from a cost–reward perspective. For example, in relationships that are not progressing or that are stagnating, you may recognize aspects of the relationship in which the costs are greater than the rewards for you or for the other person. This recognition may encourage you and the other person to negotiate change in some aspects of the relationship before it totally deteriorates.

Relationships: Getting to Know Others and Ourselves

One of the most interesting aspects of being a human being is the way we react to other people—making acquaintances, becoming friends with a few of those acquaintances, and sometimes actively disliking others. Each of us tends to evaluate others in positive and negative terms, and they, of course, evaluate us in return.[9]

Some very specific and generally predictable factors determine whom we will get to know and how well we will get to know them. Relationships can be based on love or hate or any of the possibilities in between. Of the more than five billion people living, any one of us will come in contact with only a few. Of this small percentage, there remain hundreds of potential friends, enemies, and lovers. We, however, tend to form meaningful relationships with a small number of individuals at any given time. Researchers have often asked how we decide which relationships will become meaningful and lasting. What do you think about this question?

Learning About Others Through Online Relationships

Face-to-face interactions usually allow us to form impressions much more quickly than we might using computer-mediated communication. The likelihood of meeting

Making Connections

Relationships: What's on the Internet?

Select one of the popular search engines, such as AltaVista, GoTo, Snap, Excite, and HotBot, and do a search on the word *relationship*.

1. What do you find?
2. What does your search tell you about relationships?
3. Select a site that interest you and determine what the site has to offer and how it might help you understand relationships and interpersonal communication.
4. Prepare a brief report about the site you selected in item 3. Present or discuss your findings in class.

people and interacting with strangers, however, increases dramatically on the Internet. It only takes a few clicks before you can interact with someone on nearly any subject at any time, and the other person could be anywhere in the world. Women, it seems, are more likely to form relationships on the Internet than men. Some research suggests that 72 percent of women and 55 percent of men surveyed who interact on the Internet have formed personal relationships. Not surprisingly, the more time spent online, the more likely you are to form more relationships.[10]

There are advantages and disadvantages to interacting with people online. The advantages are that you can remain anonymous, it is generally safe because physical contact is possible only if you allow it to occur, and you can choose the time and place of that contact. On the Internet your personality or inner qualities are shared only through the words transmitted, and this can be an advantage as well as a disadvantage. Using the Internet, you generally cannot see or hear other people with whom you are communicating. We know that a person's voice and appearance provide a lot of information about that person. Without hearing the other person's voice, without seeing the other person, and without being able to touch him or her (e.g., a hand shake, a hug, a kiss, etc.), the relationship will remain a mediated relationship that allows two people to communicate, but nothing more. Of course, through technology we can hear and see images of the other person via the telephone, microphones, pictures, and minivideo cameras without ever having actual face-to-face contact. It is our belief, however, that interaction via technology can never replace face-to-face interaction or fulfill interpersonal needs. In Chapter 14, we discuss more about relationship development over the Internet.

Learning About Others Through Face-to-Face Relationships

Whether we get to know others may have little or nothing to do with their specific characteristics or ours. This is particularly true with Internet contacts. Usually, the likelihood of two people becoming acquainted has to do with contact through physical proximity and a positive rather than a negative experience at the time of the face-to-face contact. Often, the contact is not planned but occurs because of circumstances. For example, contact may take place with a person sitting next to you in an airplane, with a neighbor, a classmate, a co-worker, a member of your church, a person standing next to you in line in the cafeteria, a player on your softball team, and so on. After you encounter a person several times and easily recognize him or her, you will likely become comfortable interacting with the person or at least making small talk.

Small talk is casual conversation that is often impersonal and superficial, including an exchange of hellos or comments about the weather, newsworthy events,

a great way to test the water in meeting people.

Small talk or casual conversation is important in the development of social skills and relating to people. Casual conversation, one on one, is also a good way to learn how to establish the basis for communicating and responding.

or trivia. Most relationships begin with small talk and often depend on small talk to continue. Small talk provides an avenue for getting to know another person by talking about nonthreatening, impersonal subjects. Some people, however, believe small talk is a waste of their time, because it is based on trivial, unimportant information. Most communication scholars, however, believe that relationships develop through the exchange of small talk.

In meeting people for the first time, opening lines play a crucial role in establishing relationships. There are many prescriptions for good and bad opening lines provided by the media, friends and acquaintances, and other sources. However, most do not identify the importance of the relationship of those communicating, the context, and the nonverbal cues of the communicators.[11] For example, people meeting in a professional business setting usually shake hands and introduce themselves, whereas meeting people on an airplane is much more informal and introductions may not occur even though the conversation may become more than simply small talk.

College students and employees from several firms were asked in a research study to provide lines that might be used in order to meet someone.[12] The researchers took the lines that were provided and organized them into three categories: cute-flippant, innocuous, and direct. Following is a sampling of the lines for each of the three categories:

Cute-Flippant: Didn't I meet you in Istanbul?

Who's your dentist?

Innocuous: Where are you from?

Could you tell me what time it is?

Direct: Hi, who are you?

I don't have any anybody to introduce me, but I'd really like to get to know you.

In the second part of the study, the investigators asked males and females to indicate which category of lines they preferred and which lines would influence them the most. The study's findings concluded that most males and females prefer opening lines that are innocuous or direct, rather than cute-flippant. Some women, however, had more positive responses to innocuous lines than men did. Women also tended to view cute-flippant lines more negatively than men did. Thus, for most first-time encounters, a cute-flippant opening line is more likely to create a negative impression, especially if the target is a female. The safest strategy is to use innocuous lines—they will more often than not receive a positive response and avoid offending anyone.

Opening lines do create first impressions and play a crucial role in establishing or initiating relationships. It is usually safer to use innocuous lines—you're more likely to get a positive response.

DILBERT © UFS. Reprinted by permission.

Besides opening lines, small talk serves many functions and is a way of maintaining a sense of community or fellowship with others. We often use small talk to satisfy our need for inclusion because it requires individuals to communicate with one another. Small talk generally does not create disagreement or conflict. It does create supportiveness and affirmation, which are indispensable for people to form relationships. It generally serves as a proving ground for both new and established relationships. In this sense, it becomes an "audition for new relationships." A research study examining types of conversations people engage in found that nearly half of all the conversations with acquaintances, friends, romantic partners, family members, and others consist of relatively informal, superficial talk.[13]

Small talk is a safe way for us to let others know something about us and at the same time let us begin to learn something about them. It is a way of vying for time to determine what we wish to share with others. If something we share about ourselves isn't working, we can shift to something else about ourselves very quickly. Small talk allows us to reduce uncertainties about another person without revealing too much about ourselves. If everything seems to click in the small talk conversations, it is more likely that conversations will move from superficial to more self-revealing communication.

Small talk is also important because it can serve as an interpersonal buffer. It is usually a nonthreatening, time-killing activity devoid of the stress involved in more critical or introspective interactions. Small talk can serve as a release, escape valve, or diversion from more serious talk that requires more conscious thought and effort.[14]

If you believe you need to improve your small talk skills, consider these suggestions:[15]

1. Use the other person's name as much as possible as you converse. Knowing and recalling a person's name creates the impression that the person matters to you. To help remember a person's name listen to it, rehearse it in your mind, and, if necessary, have the person restate it or spell it for you. Think about how you feel when others remember your name—you probably feel good, and others will get the same feeling when you remember their names. Plus, it helps make small talk more comfortable.

My intuition is correct. Small talk is a good way to test the water.

Making Connections

The Importance of Small Talk

The following quotation from an analysis of a survey of married couples reveals the importance of small talk:

Small talk may save marriages, according to the findings of two social scientists. As reported in the University of California, Berkeley, Wellness Letter, *in a survey of 31 married couples (average age, early 40s; average length of marriage, 20 years) the communication valued most was not evening-long sessions hashing out their differences, but easy going, pleasant conversations about everyday events.*

Wives, in particular, interpreted this kind of open, informal chatting as an indication of mutual affection. Husbands, however, valued empathetic listening more than discussions, interpreting it as a sign of affection in their wives.

1. Why do you think men and women take these two different perspectives on the type of communication they exchange?
2. Are there any assumptions that should be considered when interpreting the findings of the survey?
3. How important is small talk in building and maintaining a relationship?

2. As discussed in Chapters 5, 6, and 10, eye contact is extremely important in effectively initiating and maintaining interaction with others. When you look at another person, you are indicating your interest in him or her. Strive for balance and comfort in eye contact when conversing with others. People in some cultures (for example, Hispanic and Japanese cultures) believe that staring or looking into someone's eyes is disrespectful. When you communicate with people from these cultures, you might focus your eyes on the face in general or on the lower part of the face—not directly on the person's eyes.

3. To effectively participate in small talk, use nonverbal behaviors (smiling, using facial expressions, and attending to body position) that indicate that you are open, positive, and interested in the other person. Positive cues such as leaning forward, smiling, and head nods are signs of caring about the other person and will help improve your small talk conversations. It is also important to use appropriate nonverbal communication when involved in small talk with individuals from different backgrounds and cultures.

4. People usually like to talk about themselves. Getting other people to talk about themselves can be a strong motivator for continuing a conversation. This is especially true if you listen carefully and ask questions such as these: Where are you from? Where did you go to high school? What do you do? Why don't you tell me about yourself? You must listen at all times and use follow-up questions to keep the person talking, if necessary.

Keep small talk casual, light, and positive. Moving too quickly to disclose personal information can be threatening and a real conversation stopper. Also try not to be negative or a whiner. If you come across as a griper, you will likely reduce the chances of future interaction. Use small talk to help reduce the uncertainty between yourself and others. By doing so, you will increase your chances of initiating and developing more lasting relationships. And as we learn about others, we also learn about ourselves and how others perceive us.

Learning About Ourselves

Through contact with others, we learn about ourselves. In Chapter 3, we defined *self-concept* as what we perceive ourselves to be and the mental picture we have of our physical, social, and psychological selves. We develop self-concept through the wide range of interactions that take place in our lives. The primary contributor to self-concept is the way others react to us. Most of us seek out both supportive and non-supportive reactions in order to perceive ourselves in as many different ways as possible, thus gaining a better understanding of who we are. The most enduring relationships are those that support and reinforce self-concept. Each relationship we form becomes a source of information, telling us who we are. The relationships that we believe are most important to us become the most influential in determining how we perceive ourselves. (For a more detailed explanation of how self-concept affects communication, see Chapter 3.)

a mirror

The most obvious reason for needing and establishing relationships with others is to share ourselves with them. We need to share our feelings about our successes in order to gain rewards or positive reactions, and about our sorrows and failures to gain reassurance that we are still all right. Relationships in which people share openly and honestly with each other are usually more likely to succeed than those that lack such candor.

Making Connections

Interpersonal Success and Failure

Take a clean sheet of paper and fold it in half lengthwise. You now have two columns. Label the column on your left "Person A: Likely to experience interpersonal failure," and label the column on your right "Person B: Likely to experience interpersonal success." In their respective columns, list the characteristics, behaviors, and strategies that you believe characterize Person A and Person B in a situation in which each approaches someone of the same sex for the first time. Then answer the following questions in class:

1. Which characteristics, behaviors, and strategies would be the same or different if Per-

son A and Person B were meeting someone of a different sex? Why?

2. Which characteristics, behaviors, and strategies would be the same or different if Person A and Person B were meeting someone from an ethnic or cultural background that differed from their own?

3. How might Person A and Person B approach others over the Internet? What behaviors and strategies might succeed or fail in this communication context?

4. What did you learn from this exercise about interpersonal communication?

To reduce uncertainty and to meet our physical and emotional needs, we must communicate who we are; we must disclose information about ourselves. When self-disclosure occurs in caring relationships, it usually results in greater self-understanding and self-improvement.

Self-Disclosure in Relationships

Relationships are built on interaction. The more sincere, honest, and open the interactions, the stronger and more lasting the relationship. Much of our interpersonal communication, however, is small talk—talk about the weather, sports, class assignments, television programs, work, movies, and so on. Such light conversation may not provide a means for us to learn who we are, to fulfill our interpersonal needs, or to grow in our relationships. Nonetheless, it does maintain an important opening to further interaction. Self-disclosure is one type of interaction that changes as a relationship becomes closer.

In order to reduce uncertainty and to meet our physical and emotional needs, we must communicate who we are; we must disclose information about ourselves. **Self-disclosure,** or the voluntary sharing of information about ourselves that another person is not likely to know, can be as simple and nonthreatening as telling our name or as complex and threatening as revealing deep feelings.

When self-disclosure occurs in caring relationships, it usually results in greater self-understanding and self-improvement. The principal benefit of self-disclosure should be personal growth. In addition, our self-disclosure to others encourages them to reciprocate and creates an atmosphere that fosters interpersonal communication and meaningful relationships.

Our use of self-disclosure is not static, and it can move back and forth from expressing our social self-identity (including our roles as students, parents, or sports fans) to very personal, intimate information about our private lives. Generally, we express our social selves early in relationships or in relatively formal settings. In any relationship there is always a tension between the need for privacy and the need for intimacy or more personal disclosure. According to some communication scholars, the dynamic between needs for privacy and intimacy creates movement in relationships.[16] When we express our personal selves with another or others, the communication moves toward the intimate end of the continuum. When we wish to maintain

Making Connections

Just Friends

The following excerpt is from an article by Patty Beutler, "Just Friends: Having a Pal of the Opposite Sex Has Many Advantages."

When Holly Pace played matchmaker last year for her girlfriend, she ended up with a best friend—her girlfriend's boyfriend. Tyler Fritz no longer goes out with that girl, but he's remained Holly's best buddy. "I love her to death," he said without reservation. He's not talking about the sort of love that makes his palms sweat or his heart pump wildly.

Instead, it's a comfortable, say-anything relationship.

1. What are the advantages to having a best friend (not a romantic relationship) of the opposite sex?
2. What are the disadvantages to having a best friend (not a romantic relationship) of the opposite sex?
3. How do your answers to these questions relate to what you have learned so far in this chapter?

our privacy by expressing only our social selves, the communication moves toward the social end of the continuum. To benefit from disclosure, we must realize that it is an ongoing process incorporated into our daily interaction with others. Ultimately, disclosure is a prerequisite for personal as well as interpersonal growth.

between relationship

The Process of Self-Disclosure: The Johari Window

One of the best ways to understand the dynamics of the self-disclosure process is to examine the **Johari Window** (see Figure 13.1). It depicts the different levels of knowledge that exist in interpersonal relationships. The model illustrates four kinds of information about a person.[17] These areas of knowledge are not rigid and unchangeable; in fact, they expand and contract over the course of the relationship based on the amount and type of information that is exchanged. We consider each area in detail.

Area I: The Open Area. The open area contains information that is known both to the self and to others, because it is readily available through observation or willingness to share. For example, when people meet for the first time, they undoubtedly note each other's height, weight, skin color, and sex. They may freely share their names, hometowns, career fields, schools, majors, and courses they are taking.

During the first meeting, individuals usually disclose minimal information about themselves. At this point the open area is relatively small. But as people get to know each other through additional interactions, this area becomes much larger, as shown in Figure 13.2.

Area II: The Blind Area. The blind area includes information that others perceive about us but that we do not recognize or acknowledge about ourselves. For example, instructors who show favoritism to certain students may not realize that their behavior is being interpreted in that way. In fact, when confronted with student evaluations that point out the problem, teachers often deny such behavior and argue that they treat everyone equally.

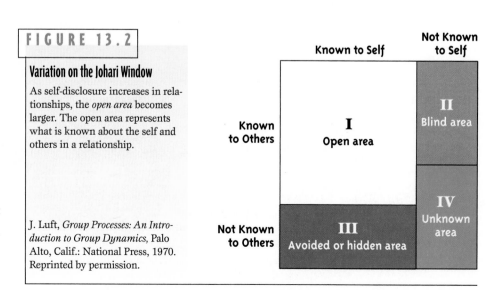

FIGURE 13.1

The Johari Window

The Johari Window illustrates four kinds of information: the open area, the blind area, the hidden area, and the unknown area. In a relationship, certain areas of information are available to and hidden from each person. What we know about others is gained primarily through self-disclosure and interpersonal communication.

J. Luft, *Group Processes: An Introduction to Group Dynamics,* Palo Alto, Calif.: National Press, 1970. Reprinted by permission.

	Known to Self	Not Known to Self
Known to Others	I Open area	II Blind area
Not Known to Others	III Avoided or hidden area	IV Unknown area

Area III: The Hidden Area.   The hidden area includes personal and private information about ourselves that we choose not to disclose to others. Others cannot know personal information unless we choose to disclose it, and we are particularly selective about disclosing such private information. As a relationship grows, more and more private information is typically shared and the hidden area shrinks.

Area IV: The Unknown Area.   The fourth window is the unknown area, which contains information that is not known to us or to others. Simply because we are human, we may submerge or repress certain information in the subconscious—perhaps a difficult part of our personality, a sexual preference, or the harm a drug is having on us physically or mentally. We may remain ignorant of these factors throughout life, or they may emerge through therapy, or through hypnosis or other consciousness-altering experiences. Another example of material in the unknown area might be an event that we seem to recall but cannot verify with certainty. Finally, we don't know about certain

FIGURE 13.2

Variation on the Johari Window

As self-disclosure increases in relationships, the *open area* becomes larger. The open area represents what is known about the self and others in a relationship.

J. Luft, *Group Processes: An Introduction to Group Dynamics,* Palo Alto, Calif.: National Press, 1970. Reprinted by permission.

	Known to Self	Not Known to Self
Known to Others	I Open area	II Blind area
Not Known to Others	III Avoided or hidden area	IV Unknown area

aspects of ourselves because they haven't had the opportunity to surface. For example, can you be sure that you can successfully give artificial respiration to someone if you have never done it before? You may think you can, but you won't really know until you actually have the occasion to try it.

Generally, the more guarded, or defensive you tend to be, the more likely you are to withhold information about yourself from others. Therefore, in your relationships the open area will tend to be smaller. The more willing you are to communicate and to encourage feedback, the larger your open area will be.

The Johari Window provides a helpful model of how the information we share with others shapes the overall relationship. It doesn't, however, explain why some people tend to disclose more than others. Researchers have found that women are more likely to disclose personal information than men are, although that is not true in all situations. For example, one research study suggests that women are likely to disclose more about themselves to intimate friends, whereas men are more likely than women to disclose personal information to strangers or casual acquaintances.[18] The choice of who will receive the disclosure is just as significant as the content of the disclosure.

Self-Disclosure and Social Penetration Theory

Social penetration theory, which was developed by social psychologists Irwin Altman and Dalmas Taylor, provides another view of how people enter relationships and how their communication moves from superficial levels to more intimate and self-revealing talk. **Social penetration theory,** according to Altman and Taylor, is the process of increasing disclosure and intimacy in a relationship.[19] Figure 13.3 illustrates this view. According to this model, self-disclosure increases gradually as the relationship develops. The figure resembles a dartboard, with the outer ring representing superficial communication and the innermost circle, or bull's-eye, representing the intimacy and depth of a close relationship. As we begin new relationships, we tend to provide information such as "Hi, I'm Bill, and I love to watch basketball." As relationships develop from casual acquaintances into friendship, conversations lend themselves to more intimate topics. When you first meet someone, the information exchanged mostly consists of biographical facts, such as your name and interests. The first levels of a casual interaction are characterized by a breadth of information that doesn't run too deep. But as the relationship becomes more intimate, it will involve more depth of

FIGURE 13.3

Social Penetration Model

The social penetration model portrays relationship development as starting with factual information and small talk. But as the relationship develops, conversations become more personal, including feelings about self and values.

From *Social Penetration: The Development of Interpersonal Relationships.* Copyright © 1973 by Irwin Altman and Dalmas Taylor.

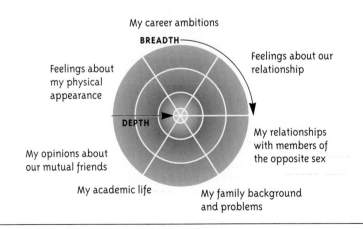

personal information. The depth is represented on the model as penetration from external factual information (the outer ring) to inner feelings (the center of the circle), revealing more about self-concept and values.

The model shows the degrees of intimacy in interpersonal communication. For example, the statements "My name is Bill" and "I love you with all my heart" express two very different levels of exchange in the development of a relationship. One is factual and the other involves a sharing of emotions and personal feelings. Once deeper levels are reached, the participants increasingly share more breadth *and* depth of personal information. Giving a person sensitive information about oneself is, in a sense, giving him or her power. Judgment is needed to determine whether the person is worthy of trust. Yet even in the best circumstances, when both parties are sincere in their wish to deepen the relationship, doing so can be challenging.

Motivation to Self-Disclose

Self-disclosure is considered by many communication scholars an important aspect in forming and maintaining in-depth relationships. As you discovered in Chapter 1, communication serves many purposes in our lives. In Chapter 3, you learned the importance of communication as it relates to self and self-concept. One function or motivation to self-disclose is to let others know who you are; the primary method of doing so is a form of self-disclosure referred to as self-presentation.

Self-Presentation. **Self-presentation** is an intentional self-disclosure tactic that we use to reveal certain aspects about ourselves for specific reasons. An example of self-presentation is the employment interview. When you are asked to talk about yourself in this situation, you discuss your background, experiences, and accomplishments, emphasizing points that would make you as attractive as possible to the interviewer in order to get the job. Another example might be telling another person something that happened to you in order to gain sympathy. In both cases you have used self-presentation to create an impression that will benefit you in some way. Self-presentation, therefore, is a form of communication that is relevant any time our social identity is being evaluated by others.[20]

Relationship Building. We self-disclose to start or maintain relationships. Self-disclosure via small talk or social conversation is one way we enter into relationships with others. The level of self-disclosure at some point can move to more intimate and self-revealing talk as the relationship develops. There are, of course, exceptions to this progression, and the depth and number of interactions can vary dramatically from one relationship to another. Also, moving from light social talk to more intimate and revealing talk does not necessarily imply that the relationship will automatically be a quality relationship.[21]

A relationship's location on the continuum between casual acquaintance and intimate confidant is determined by how people interact with each other and their specific communication behaviors. The way we communicate with another person reflects the nature and type of the relationship.

Catharsis. Self-disclosing communication can be a form of communicative release or catharsis. This is especially true when we want to rid ourselves of information that is causing tension or guilt. Catharsis provides a way of getting something off our chest to reduce stress. Although this type of self-disclosure can have positive effects on our health, the primary motivation is personal gratification.[22] One benefit of this type of

Making Connections

Self-Disclosure on the Internet

Now you can send Instant Messages back and forth with the people you want—It's hassle-free no matter how you are connected on the Internet! Private conversations and Instant Communication—to sign up today—click here.

Hundreds of chatrooms and online services offer you the ability to interact with people around the world. Think about this mode of communication as you answer the following questions:

1. Are chatrooms and email really private?
2. What precautions should be taken when sending personal information over the Internet?
3. Why is it sometimes easier to reveal personal information about yourself to someone whom you have never met in person?
4. Has the Internet become an escape from "real" relationships? In what ways?
5. Do you believe that online communication will bring about the demise of face-to-face communication?

disclosure is that it makes us better relationship partners.

Being Honest. We might self-disclose because our culture encourages us to tell it like it is. This is especially true in our intimate relationships, because we believe that withholding information from a partner is a barrier to reaching a truly open and close relationship.

Withholding Information. Although full disclosure can be cleansing, it can also be harmful and detrimental to a relationship. We have all probably heard about or experienced instances where information was deliberately withheld. There may be many reasons for withholding information, but it is usually to protect someone, to avoid a potentially negative reaction, or to avoid hurting someone. For example, if politicians know something negative is going to be revealed in the media about them, they will often break the news before the media does in an attempt to soften the negative impact and to preserve their reputations with those closest to them. In communication scholar Lawrence Rosenfeld's study of 200 male and female college students, he found that males avoid self-disclosure in order to maintain control of a relationship and to avoid having to face things about themselves. Females, according to Rosenfeld, refrain from self-disclosure in order to avoid personal hurt and problems with their relationships.[23] All of us should have someone with whom we can share our feelings and thoughts, because it is generally good for our well-being and personal satisfaction, but it is also important to understand that with self-disclosure interactions, more is not necessarily always better.

Self-disclosure is not always wise or appropriate. As we mentioned earlier, information is power. Some scholars suggest that moving relationships from a casual level to great intimacy requires rhetorical sensitivity.

Rhetorical Sensitivity

According to communication scholars Roderick Hart and Don Burks, **rhetorical sensitivity** is an alternative form of communication that can be applied to situations in which wide-open self-disclosure could be harmful. It represent a cautious approach to exchanging information while developing a relationship.[24] Rhetorically sensitive people can balance their self-interest with the interests of others. They can adjust their communication to take into account the beliefs, values, and mood of the other person. Considering the other person's views or feelings does not mean changing your own view or position, but it does mean finding an effective way to communicate your thoughts without offending or hurting the other person. Honest self-disclosure can be harmful if it is stated in a way that damages the relationship. Rhetorically sensitive individuals generally display the following attributes:

1. They accept personal complexity; they understand that every person is made up of many selves. For example, one person may be a mother, a daughter, a Republican, an Asian American, an abuse victim, a student, and a consumer.

2. They are flexible and avoid rigidity in communicating with others.

3. They do not change their own values, but they can communicate them in a variety of ways to avoid offending others.

4. They sense when it is appropriate to communicate something and when it is not.[25] Rhetorically sensitive people understand self-disclosure and know how to adapt their messages to a particular audience and situation.

Self-Disclosure and Privacy

How much is too much self-disclosure and when does it begin to invade or affect our privacy? **Privacy** is "the claim of individuals, groups, or institutions to determine for themselves when, how, and to what extent information about themselves is communicated to others."[26] These are not easy questions to answer because what may be appropriate for one situation may not be for another. Thus, an important task for people in relationships is the negotiation of privacy boundaries.[27] Privacy boundaries work in a way very similar to personal space boundaries as discussed in Chapter 5. Just as we control and protect access to our physical self, for example, how close we allow others to come to us, in the same way we control and protect our privacy boundaries. Sandra Petronio, a communication scholar and expert in the area of privacy and how we manage our privacy boundaries, states

> Revealing private information is risky because there is a potential vulnerability when revealing aspects of the self. Receiving private information from another may also result in the need for protecting oneself. In order to manage disclosing and receiving privacy information, individuals erect a metaphoric boundary to reduce the possibility of losing face and as a means of protection. Also, people use a set of rules or criteria to control the boundary and regulate the flow of private information to and from others.[28]

The process of sharing more and more personal information about one's self with another person encourages further intrusion into one's privacy whether wanted or unwanted. It would seem to be common sense but privacy boundaries are not always clear to either party in a relationship. For example, a man and a woman had been dating for several years and had been sexually intimate, but they were not married. The couple may try to control the privacy of their relationship, because revealing relational secrets could be embarrassing, or they could be fully open about their relationship. The determination of what should be kept private from each other and what should be kept private from others is usually negotiated by the mutual consent of the parties involved in the relationship. According to Petronio,

> There is a time when disclosure of some information is weighted more heavily than keeping it private. Likewise, privacy might be more heavily weighted than disclosure or secrecy. Some measure of secrecy may be considered proportionately more important than privacy and disclosure in a particular situation.[29]

When or if the boundaries of a relationship are violated or crossed, tensions may result, creating an imbalance in the relationship. Thus, negotiations between relationship partners often involve what can and should be shared and what is or should be off limits. Boundaries are erected to protect, control the flow of information, and regulate vulnerability. When one partner violates the privacy of the other, for example, attempts are made to reconstruct the privacy boundary by changing the topic or by avoiding the situation.

It also appears that men and women differ in the defensive and protective strategies they use to reduce embarrassment and maintain privacy boundaries. Men's defensive strategies include blaming the incident on something else, laughing at their own behavior, or retreating from the situation, whereas women's defensive strategies often include blaming others and criticizing themselves. No matter how privacy is defined or explained, the means by which people regulate the release of private information is through disclosure.[30]

Cultural and Gender Issues in Self-Disclosure

In general people from different cultural backgrounds tend to follow similar patterns of self-disclosure. For example, people from various cultures are likely to begin relationships with small talk and progress to more intimate levels of interaction as the relationship continues. Of course, there are differences, especially in the initial contact stage, in some cultures, but in general, as people become friends, those differences seem to diminish.

Think, however, about some of the characteristics that describe your cultural background and how they may or may not influence your communication. Do you see yourself simply as an American, or identified with some other ethnic or racial group— African American, Filipino American, Latino, Vietnamese, Korean, German or white? Do others view you the same way? How does your ethnicity affect your communication and with whom you choose to communicate? Do you use certain expressions that are understood only by members of your ethnic group? When interacting with people from a different ethnic group, how difficult is it for you to communicate? Thinking about the answers to these questions will help you understand cultural differences and why interacting with people from diverse backgrounds is much more complex than simply exchanging information. It requires thought, a recognition of differences, and some adjustments for communication to be meaningful to both parties. Not everyone thinks and communicates in exactly the same way. This may be especially important to remember when we interact with people from cultures different than our own.

Members of a majority culture typically, but not always, tend to see themselves as "normal" or "standard" rather than as different or ethnically identifiable. However, those from minority ethnic groups are much more likely to be aware of ethnic differences. There are, of course, individual differences among people within each ethnic group. These differences often form fairly stable ethnic communication patterns that have been identified by research. For example, members of some cultures are more direct than indirect, more elaborate than succinct, more personal than contextual, and more functional than emotional.

In trying to understand interpersonal communication and relationship development, keep in mind that there are many similarities in how we communicate with each other regardless of who we are. There is a bias by many to consider only interpersonal communication between men and women, and this is especially true when discussing relationships. In this chapter and the following one we use examples that involve conversations between men and women, but this is not intended to suggest that interpersonal communication between same sex individuals does not occur or that relationships develop only between men and women. Our main concern in this chapter is with interpersonal communication regardless of biological sex. In Chapter 2, we discussed gender and defined it as a social construct related to learned masculine and feminine behaviors. We often hear the words *sex* and *gender* used interchangeably in our society. What gender means is heavily dependent on cultural values and practices; it is the way a culture defines masculinity and femininity that lead to expectations about how men and women should act and communicate.

Sex is a designation based on biology, whereas gender is socially and psychologically constructed. Each of us has some of the characteristics that our culture labels masculine and some that it defines as feminine. How much of each we have determines our gender. In the United States, men are more likely to be seen as masculine and women as feminine. However, we also know that some men are more feminine than most men and that some women are more masculine than a majority of women. Gender, therefore, is considerably more complex than sex and is determined by how individuals perceive themselves and how they behave in terms of masculine and feminine tendencies. Gender is learned through interaction with others; it motivates our communication and influences the relationships we form whether another person's sex is male or female.[31]

The question that many scholars and pop psychologists are still trying to address is this: Are there really differences between the way women and men communicate? The answer is yes and no. There are many variations related to one's sex regarding experiences, sexual orientation, race, and status. There are also a great many similarities between men and women. Thus, using the terms *women* and *men* as identifiers to describe or distinguish communication between the sexes is troublesome. The terms imply sameness across all women and all men that may or may not be true. For example, to say "Women disclose their feelings more often than men do" is probably true, but it may not be true for all women or all men. Some men may disclose more feelings than some women do, and vice versa. Thus, we must be careful to avoid stereotyping solely based on biological sex differences.[32]

Some research and some authors support the notion that men and women do communicate using different sets of rules and meanings. Deborah Tannen, who was mentioned earlier in the book, has reviewed many research studies and has taken the position that women's verbal and nonverbal behaviors are different from men's. For example, she has found that men talk less personally or inclusively when compared to women and that women tend to make more validating and confirming statements than do men.[33]

Women are more likely to talk about their relationships and disclose a deeper level of intimacy, but men often do not center their talk on relational closeness.[34] Concerning relationships, men may take the attitude that "If it ain't broke, why fix it?" Women may be more likely to express the attitude "If it's going well, how can we make it go better?"

General Conclusions About Self-Disclosure

Research findings support these general conclusions about self-disclosure, whatever the interaction level obtained in a relationship:

1. Disclosure increases with increased relational intimacy.
2. Disclosure increases when rewarded—the reward outweighs the risk of disclosing.
3. Disclosure increases with the need to reduce uncertainty in a relationship.
4. Disclosure tends to be reciprocal—when one person in a relationship increases self-disclosure, the other person will typically follow suit.
5. Women tend to disclose personal information more often than men do.
6. Women seem to disclose more with those to whom they are close, whereas men seem to disclose more with those whom they trust.
7. Disclosure is culturally regulated by norms of appropriateness.

Self-disclosure research is helpful to our understanding of human communication. A review of self-disclosure research by communication scholar Arthur Bochner found that (1) people will disclose themselves to people they like; (2) people overestimate the amount of self-disclosure they actually permit; (3) self-disclosure does not automatically indicate attraction and, if inappropriate, can cause negative reactions; and (4) liking someone and wanting a relationship to continue may, in fact, discourage self-disclosure, because it may risk damaging the relationship.[35]

The open and honest sharing of our feelings, concerns, and secrets with others is at the heart of self-disclosure. This does not mean, however, that we must disclose everything or that we cannot withhold information if it is likely to hurt us or someone else. The goal is to match the amount and kind of self-disclosure to the situation.

Ultimately, self-disclosure must be based on personal judgment rather than rigid rules. The key should always be concern for both self and others. Self-disclosure is the most sensitive and beautiful form of communication that we can engage in as we develop and maintain lasting relationships. There are many reasons we sometimes find it difficult to open ourselves to others. However, when based on mutual feelings and genuine communication, relationships cannot help but grow and mature.

Appropriate Self-Disclosure

1. *Use reasoned self-disclosure.* Although open and honest relationships are desirable, it is important to recognize situational constraints. For example, as a youngster, you might have been caught shoplifting from a local store. You shoplifted only that one time. However, now you are running for public office, and you must decide whether to disclose the fact that you stole from a local store. To do so would more than likely hurt your chances of winning the election. Thus, you choose not to bring up the issue. This does not mean that you are being dishonest. In some situations and with certain individuals, not revealing a specific past behavior may be reasonable—particularly if it has little to do with the situation at hand.

2. *Make self-disclosure a two-way process.* Relationships built on one-sided exchanges are generally not very enduring, meaningful, or healthy. People are more likely to disclose information when they feel safe and when their open communication is positively received. It follows, therefore, that each party will feel safer if both are involved in the self-disclosure process. Once a mutual give-and-take is established, if one person increases self-disclosure, the other person will usually follow suit. Trust increases, self-disclosure continues, and the relationship grows in a healthy way.

3. *Make self-disclosure appropriate to the situation and the person.* When we disclose personal information about ourselves, we run the risk of being rejected. We can somewhat minimize this risk if we carefully match the disclosure to the person and the situation. Self-disclosure should be a slow process; rushing it can increase vulnerability unnecessarily. In addition, it is safest to disclose only to truly caring people and to be sensitive to both their verbal and nonverbal cues. Disclosing too much too soon or disclosing to the wrong person can lead to embarrassment and pain—and sometimes serious harm.

4. *Consider diversity.* The appropriateness and the level of self-disclosure vary by culture, group, and individual. The Japanese culture, for example, does not foster self-expression in the same way that U.S. or Korean cultures do. Consider these differences as you decide how to disclose personal information.

5. *Avoid indiscriminate self-disclosure.* Once you disclose something, you cannot take it back, though you may try to qualify what you have said.

6. *Be positive.* You should avoid being overly negative about people and issues, particularly in newly forming relationships. Negative self-disclosure can be a real turnoff as well as a tremendous drag on any relationship.

Summary

Interpersonal communication is the informal exchange of information between two or more people. A *relationship* is an association between at least two people and may be described in terms of intimacy or kinship. Interpersonal communication allows relationships to become established and to grow, satisfying our social needs.

The interpersonal phenomenon of wanting to know more about others can be explained by *uncertainty reduction theory,* which suggests that when we initially meet others to whom we are attracted, our need to know about them tends to make us draw inferences from the physical data we observe. *Predicted outcome value theory,* in contrast, suggests people connect with others because they believe there will be rewards or positive outcomes for doing so.

Many needs that we have as humans can be satisfied through communication. Two approaches that attempt to explain needs are Schutz's *theory of interpersonal needs* and Thibaut and Kelley's *social exchange theory.* According to Schutz, needs for affection, inclusion, and control determine how we communicate with others. People who have satisfied their need for affection are referred to as personal, and those who have not satisfied this need are classified as either underpersonal or overpersonal. People who have satisfied their need for inclusion are referred to as social, and those who have not are called either undersocial or oversocial. People who have satisfied their need for control are called democrats, and those who have not are called either abdicrats or autocrats.

Social exchange theory is based on the assumption that people consciously and deliberately consider the costs and rewards associated with a relationship or interaction, and that they will seek out relationships that are rewarding and avoid those that are costly. A *reward* is anything that is perceived as beneficial to our self-interest. *Costs* are negative rewards that are perceived as not beneficial to our self-interest. Both theories explain why relationships are so important to us.

If we encounter people more than once and they become recognizable, we are more likely to be comfortable interacting with them or at least making small talk with them. *Small talk* is casual conversation that is often impersonal and superficial, including hello or comments about the weather, newsworthy events, or trivia. Small talk, however, is a very important social skill.

We develop relationships to avoid or reduce loneliness, to learn about ourselves, and to share. Lasting relationships are open, a feature that allows for relatively free *self-disclosure,* which is the volunteering of information about ourselves that another person is not likely to know. The more information people reveal about themselves, the more likely they are to have a relationship that will grow and mature into a healthy and satisfying experience.

The *Johari Window* is a graphic model that depicts the development of awareness and self-disclosure in interpersonal relationships. It illustrates four kinds of information about a person. (1) The open area represents information that is known to oneself and to others; (2) the blind area represents information that others perceive about us but that we do not know; (3) the hidden area represents information about ourselves that we choose not to share with others; and (4) the unknown area represents information that is not known to us or to others. The four areas expand and contract in relationships over time and from situation to situation.

Social penetration theory provides another view of how people enter relationships and how their communication moves from superficial levels of small talk to more intimate and self-revealing talk. *Social penetration theory* involves the process of increasing disclosure and intimacy in a relationship.

We self-disclose information about ourselves because we recognize the possible advantages that we may gain from doing so. One function of communication is to let others know who we are. The primary method of making ourselves known to others is called *self-presentation*. Using this intentional tactic, we let others know certain aspects about ourselves for specific reasons. There are other reasons we self-disclose, including catharsis and being honest. At times we withhold information in order to protect ourselves or to avoid hurting someone.

Rhetorical sensitivity is an alternative form of communication that can be applied to interpersonal communication situations in which wide-open self-disclosure could be harmful to those involved. Because frankness creates vulnerability, each participant must consider situational constraints when deciding what should or should not be disclosed. *Privacy* is the claim of individuals, groups, or institutions to determine for themselves when, how, and to what extent information about themselves is communicated to others. Self-disclosure should be built on mutual sharing and should be attempted only when individuals feel safe and believe that their confidences will be received positively. People from different cultural or ethnic backgrounds tend to follow similar patterns of self-disclosure. Gender is also important in determining cultural self-identity and self-disclosure. Relationships cannot exist without taking into account gender, a social construct related to learned masculine and feminine behaviors. For relationships to grow, there must be self-disclosure.

DISCUSSION STARTERS

1. Compare and contrast the theory of interpersonal needs and social exchange theory.
2. In what ways can the Internet harm a relationship?
3. Explain in your own words how our interpersonal needs influence our relationships with others.
4. If you were to classify yourself using Schutz's categories of *personal, underpersonal,* or *overpersonal,* which would you say best describes you? Why?
5. Why do you think people stay in abusive relationships?
6. What are the advantages and disadvantages of interacting with people online?
7. Explain the importance of effective small talk.
8. What does it mean to be rhetorically sensitive?
9. Explain when it is reasonable not to self-disclose honestly.
10. Develop a list of rules for effective self-disclosure.

NOTES

1. B. Reeves, "Chat room brought them together," *Lincoln Journal Star,* 25 June 2000, sec. J, 1.
2. M. R. Parks and K. Floyd, "Making Friends in Cyberspace," *Journal of Communication* 46 (1996): 85.
3. B. Reeves, "Caught in the Net: Proceed with Caution, *Lincoln Journal Star,* 25 June 2000, sec. J, 1.
4. M. L. Knapp and A. L. Vangelisti, *Interpersonal Communication and Human Relationships,* 4th ed. (Boston: Allyn and Bacon, 2000), 34.

5. C. R. Berger and R. J. Calabrese, "Some Explorations in Initial Interactions and Beyond: Toward a Developmental Theory of Interpersonal Communication," *Human Communication Research* 1 (1975): 98–112; and C. R. Berger, "Response—Uncertain Outcome Values in Predicted Relationships: Uncertainty Reduction Theory Then and Now," *Human Communication Research* 13 (1986): 34–38.

6. M. Sunnafrank, "Predicted Outcome Value During Initial Interactions: A Reformulation of Uncertainty Reduction Theory," *Human Communication Research* 13 (1986): 3–33; K. Kellermann and R. Reynolds, "When Ignorance Is Bliss: The Role of Motivation to Reduce Uncertainty in Uncertainty Reduction Theory," *Human Communication Research* 17 (1990): 5–75; and M. Sunnafrank, "Predicted Outcome Value and Uncertainty Reduction Theories: A Test of Competing Perspectives," *Human Communication Theory* 17 (1990): 76–103.

7. W. C. Schutz, *The Interpersonal Underworld* (Palo Alto, Calif.: Science and Behavior Books, 1966), 13–20.

8. J. W. Thibaut and H. H. Kelley, *The Social Psychology of Groups,* 2nd ed. (New Brunswick, N.J.: Transaction Books, 1986), 9–30.

9. B. Park and C. Flink, "A Social Relations Analysis of Agreement in Liking Judgments," *Journal of Personality and Social Psychology* 56 (1989): 506–51.

10. M. R. Parks and K. Floyd, "Making Friends in Cyberspace," *Journal of Communication* 46 (1996): 86.

11. M. Moore, "Nonverbal Courtship Patterns in Women! Context and Consequences," *Ethology and Sociobiology* 6 (1985): 237–47.

12. C. L. Kleinke, F. B. Meeker, and R. A. Staneski, "Preference for Opening Lines: Comparing Ratings by Men and Women," *Sex Roles* 15 (1986): 585–600.

13. D. J. Goldsmith and L. A. Baxter, "Constituting Relationship Talk: A Taxonomy of Speech Events in Social and Personal Relationships," *Human Communication Research* 18 (1996): 87–114.

14. J. Levin and A. Arluke, *Gossip: The Inside Scoop* (New York: Plenum, 1987), 28–29.

15. J. S. Caputo, H. C. Hazel, and C. McMahon, *Interpersonal Communication: Competency Through Critical Thinking* (Boston: Allyn and Bacon, 1994), 98–99.

16. W. Rawlins, "Negotiating Close Friendships. The Dialectic of Conjunctive Freedoms," *Human Communication Research* 9 (1983): 255–66; and L. Baxter and B. Montgomery, *Relating: Dialogue and Dialects* (New York: Guilford, 1996), 133–39.

17. J. Luft, *Group Processes: An Introduction to Group Dynamics* (Palo Alto, Calif.: National Press, 1970), 11–14.

18. J. Stokes, A. Fuehrer, and L. Childs, "Gender Differences in Self-Disclosure to Various Target Persons," *Journal of Counseling Psychology* 27 (1980): 192–98.

19. I. Altman and D. Taylor, *Social Penetration: The Development of Interpersonal Relationships* (New York: Holt, Rinehart & Winston, 1973); and Knapp and Vangelisti, 14–20.

20. D. J. Canary and M. J. Cody, *Interpersonal Communication: A Goals-Based Approach* (New York: St. Martin's Press, 1994).

21. A. L. Sillars and M. D. Scott, "Interpersonal Perception Between Intimates: An Integrative Review," *Human Communication Research* 10 (1983): 153–76.

22. J. W. Pennebaker, *Opening Up: The Healing Power of Expressing Emotions* (New York: Guilford, 1990).

23. L. B. Rosenfeld, "Self-Disclosure Avoidance: Why I Am Afraid to Tell You Who I Am," *Communication Monographs* 46 (1979): 63–74.

24. R. P. Hart and D. M. Burks, "Rhetorical Sensitivity and Social Interaction," *Speech Monographs* 39 (1972): 75–91.

25. S. W. Littlejohn, *Theories of Human Communication,* 6th ed. (Belmont, Calif: Wadsworth, 1999), 103–4.

26. V. J. Derlega, S. Metts, S. Petronio, and S. T. Margulis, *Self-Disclosure* (Newbury Park, Calif.: Sage, 1993), 74.

27. S. Petronio, "The Boundries of Privacy: Praxis of Everyday Life," in *Balancing the Secrets of Private Disclosures,* ed. S. Petronio (Hillsdale, N.J.: Erlbaum, 2000), 9–15.

28. S. Petronio, "Communication Boundary Management: A Theoretical Model of Managing Disclosure of Private Information Between Marital Couples," *Communication Theory* 1 (1991): 311.

29. S. Petronio (2000), 14.

30. S. Petronio, "Communication Strategies to Reduce Embarrassment Differences Between Men and Women," *The Western Journal of Speech Communication* 48 (1984): 28–38.

31. J. T. Wood, *Gendered Lives: Communication, Gender, and Culture,* 3rd ed. (Belmont, Calif: Wadsworth, 1999), 22.

32. Ibid., 21–22.

33. D. Tannen, *You Just Don't Understand: Women and Men in Conversation* (New York: Morrow, 1990).

34. C. K. Riessman, *Divorce Talk: Women and Men Make Sense of Personal Relationships* (New Brunswick, N.J.: Rutgers University Press, 1990).

35. A. P. Bochner, "The Functions of Human Communicating in Interpersonal Bonding," in *Handbook of Rhetorical and Communication Theory,* eds. C. C. Arnold and J. W. Bowers (Boston: Allyn and Bacon, 1984), 554–621.

Developing Relationships

"I present myself to you in a form suitable to the relationship I wish to achieve with you."

—Luigi Pirandello

- Understand the stages of relationship development and deterioration.
- Know how dialectical tensions push and pull on relationships.
- Explain what interpersonal conflict is and how to resolve it.
- Determine when a relationship is in trouble and how to use relational repair strategies.
- Improve your interpersonal communication skills and competencies in personal and professional relationships.

SCENARIO

When Sam was eleven, his family moved from a small town in upstate New York to Los Angeles, a month or two after the LA riots. Sam suddenly found himself in a new neighborhood, new city, new state, and new school. Among the many challenges associated with such major changes in one's life are those that involve interacting with strangers, becoming acquainted with some of them, and deciding who you like and dislike.

Sam's first contact was with a fellow fifth-grader whose seat was next to his in their classroom. Terry was Chinese American, and in their initial brief conversation they exchanged names—Sam and Terry. During the first few days of school, he was the only person that Sam talked to in class, at recess, during lunch, and when they had earthquake drills and crawled under their desks for protection from falling objects. Why was Terry Sam's first friend in his new location? Could ethnic background have had anything to do with it? That seemed unlikely, because (as strange as it may sound today) Sam had never before seen anyone of Asian descent in real life—only in the movies or on TV. So why did Sam and Terry become friends? ■

A relationship has the potential to form any time two people make contact with each other, whether face-to-face or via some other medium such as the telephone or the computer. Most contacts are made accidentally, depending on factors such as classroom seating, course assignment, dorm room assignment, who happens to be online in a chatroom when we enter it, or the physical arrangement of a workplace. Where we live, sit, or work; the time we enter a chatroom; and the details of physical surroundings all increase the odds that we will come into repeated contact with some people and decrease the odds that such contact will occur with others. As a result, although this may not seem all that surprising, physical proximity and timing are very often how people meet and begin relationships with each other. The opening scenario in Chapter 13 and the opening scenario in this chapter demonstrate how some relationships are formed. Whether a relationship evolves into any kind of ongoing or lasting relationship depends on many factors, such as attraction, proximity, motivation, need, and so on—all of which were discussed in Chapter 13. Communication, however, is the overriding factor that will determine the kind of relationship that may develop and how long it may last.

Forming and Dissolving Relationships

How we progress as individuals, survive, develop intimacy, and make sense of our world depends on how we relate to others. The depth and quality of our relationships, as explained in Chapter 13, depend on the kind, amount, and effectiveness of the communication that takes place. This chapter explores why some people are interpersonally attracted to others, and the stages of growth and deterioration that most relationships go through, which are best exemplified by Mark Knapp's theory of relationship stages and Steve Duck's theory of dissolution stages. The chapter also discusses interpersonal conflict, conflict management, and how to improve interpersonal communication.

Interpersonal Attraction

Most of us develop relationships quite routinely, although the process is easier for some people than it is for others. Everyday we are enormously influenced by first impressions. We tend to make many snap judgments about people and form instant likes and dislikes. **Interpersonal attraction** is the desire to interact with someone based on a variety of factors, including physical attractiveness, personality, rewards, proximity, or similarities. Although these are perhaps obvious referents, interpersonal attraction is a very complex phenomenon. Two communication scholars, James McCroskey and Thomas McCain, identified three types of attraction: (1) social attraction ("He would fit into my circle of friends"), (2) physical attraction ("I think she's quite pretty"), and (3) task attraction ("My confidence in her ability to get the job done makes me want to work with her").[1] In other words, interpersonal attraction has a lot to do with evaluating other people along dimensions that range from like to dislike. What factors make people socially attractive to you such that you would wish to connect with them to form relationships?

Any given person (including you) is liked by some people, disliked by some, and seen as indifferent by many others. Why? This question is not easily answered, but, to some extent, differences in attraction depend on the person who is making the evaluation. Attraction also depends in part on the similarities and differences between the evaluator and the person being evaluated. Finally, the situation or context in which people interact also influences attraction.

Think about your friends and how you met them. Most of the initial contact probably occurred because of physical proximity. That is, the more convenient people are to us, the more likely we will become close friends with them. If two people find themselves in close proximity and their interactions are positive, they are likely to become friends. As acquaintances evolve from first encounters to more engaged relationships, two additional factors come into play—the need to associate with someone and reactions to observable physical attributes.

What leads to attraction and eventual friendship? There are at least six billion people on our planet, and several thousand of them could conceivably become your friends. That is exceedingly unlikely to happen, however. Any one of us is likely to be-

Making Connections

Finding the Right One

A promotion advertising "the world's largest and most successful introduction service" states, "Too many people let precious time slip by . . . just hoping that somehow that special someone will magically appear." The promotional letter goes on

If it hasn't happened for you yet as you go about your daily life—at home, work, and play—now is the time to stop waiting *and* start looking beyond your own circle of friends and activities for that special person.

The Right One® *can help you find that person. We can introduce you to many successful, intelligent and compatible singles—people who share your interestes, your goals and your values—*people who are already out there looking for you. *Since The Right One*® *reaches millions of people each month, we provide a continuous stream of new singles for our members to meet. Visit our Web Site www.therightone.com. (Advertisement sent to rural route boxholder)*

Meeting Place

Seeking country gentleman, *honest, intelligent, sensitive, shy DWF, blue/blonde, N/S, attractive, petite, enjoys dancing, walking, movies, rodeos, C&W music, reading, animals (have dog, miniature donkey). Seeking compatible male, emotionally, financially secure, for LTR.*

Is love to give, . . . *to a special lady. DWM, 32, affectionate, carpenter. Seeking S/DCF with good self-esteem, for friendship first, healthy relationship, possible romantic marriage.*

1. Why are matching services and personal ads such as these so popular in our society?
2. Write your own ad for the Meeting Place. You may wish to share your ad in a discussion.
3. Go to the home page of The Right One® (http://www.therightone.com). Look over the various links on the site. Which links did you find of interest and how does the site relate to what you have read so far?

come aware of, interact with, and get to know only a small fraction of these individuals. Of those in this relatively small subgroup, only a few will become acquaintances, fewer still will become friends, and most will remain strangers. What determines awareness, interaction, and differential attraction?

Once two people come into contact and experience relatively positive affects, they begin a transition, the initiating stages of a possible relationship. They may simply remain superficial acquaintances who exchange friendly greetings whenever they happen to encounter one another but never interact otherwise. Or they may begin to talk, learn each other's names, and exchange bits and pieces of information. At this point, they may be described as close acquaintances. Which of these two outcomes occurs depends on (1) the extent to which each person is motivated by the need to associate or the need for inclusion (referred to in Chapter 13) and (2) the way each person reacts to the observable physical attributes of the other.

The Need to Associate

Most of us feel it is very important to make new friends, spend time with existing friends, and share personal feelings with those with whom we feel close. The need to associate varies in degree from person to person. Males who have a strong need to be with others are also relatively high in self-esteem and spend more time talking to attractive females than do males who are low in their need to be with others. In the typical college classroom, male or female students who have a strong need to associate with others make more friends than do those who are more independent.[2] Of course, success in developing a relationship also depends on one's social skills and motivation to continue the relationship.

Physical Attributes

When we like—or dislike—some people at first sight, it is an indication that we have observed something about them that appears to provide information. For example, if a stranger reminds you of someone you know and like, your positive response to the person you already know is extended by association to the person you don't know at all.[3] You tend to like the stranger simply on the basis of a superficial resemblance to someone else. In other instances, the cue may not be related to a specific person in your past but to a subgroup of people to whom you respond positively—the stranger has a Wisconsin accent, for example, and you have a fondness for people from your home state. In a similar way, resemblance to a specific person you know and dislike or to a subgroup of people you dislike may cause you instantly to dislike or avoid a stranger. As discussed in Chapters 2 and 5, stereotypes are poor predictors of behavior, but, nevertheless, we find ourselves reacting to other people based on superficial characteristics.

Most of us have learned that "beauty is only skin deep," and we know that reacting to stereotypes based on appearance is meaningless. However, people do in fact respond positively to those who are very attractive and negatively to those who are very unattractive.[4] This is especially true in the early stages of interpersonal contact with strangers. In U.S. society we commonly accept or reject people based on observable characteristics such as skin color, sexual orientation, height, weight, accent, and hair color. Physical attractiveness is a very powerful message and influences many types of interpersonal evaluations, but appearance is especially crucial with respect to attraction to members of the opposite sex.[5]

In U.S. culture, both males and females are strongly influenced by attractiveness. People, in general, do respond strongly to physical attractiveness, the aesthetically appealing outward appearance, of others. This is especially true when a person judges someone's desirability as a date. It appears that attractiveness can sometimes outweigh other considerations when interacting with others. For example, in an experiment, undergraduate males were in general very eager to be accepted by an attractive female stranger—so much so that they would ingratiate themselves by expressing false attitudes in order to win the approval of attractive women. In response to unattractive women, they did the opposite and expressed false disagreements in order to avoid further interaction. Overall, males are generally more responsive to attractiveness in females than females are responsive to male attractiveness.[6]

Research shows that people in general tend to have high levels of agreement about who is or is not attractive, even across racial and ethnic lines. In most cultures, at any given time, general agreement exists as to what constitutes attractiveness and what does not. For example, most of us would find it difficult to express what attractiveness is. However, most of us "know it when we see it."[7]

How does attractiveness affect relationships and interpersonal communication? Most people, according to one research study, are afraid of being rejected by those who are more attractive than they are. Many people tend to reject others who are far less attractive than they believe themselves to be—in other words, they are saying, "I can do better than that." As a result, people tend to pair off, especially in romantic relationships, by selecting individuals whom they consider similar in attractiveness. "Mismatches" do occur, such as portrayed in the characters of Catherine (an attractive woman) and Vincent (unattractive disfigured man) in the story of "Beauty and the Beast." Why do these exceptions occur, and what explains them? If one person in a relationship is more attractive than another, for example, people tend to infer that the less attractive person in the relationship has an attribute that "balances" the mismatch, such as wealth, power, intelligence, sex appeal, or fame. For example, in "Beauty and the Beast" Vincent's appearance is unattractive, but his kindness, gentleness, and bravery make Catherine's love for him believable. Whether we wish to accept it or not, physical appearance does play a role in determining relationships. Although this attractiveness may not always predict the outcome of a relationship, research has shown that physical attractiveness is important as an attention getter.[8]

Most of us are aware that sometimes our first impressions and reasons for being attracted to another are not completely rational. Sudden lust, love at first sight, or the intense disliking of someone with whom we have had no previous contact can seem inexplicable. Many social psychologists suggest that relationship development has a lot to do with the "chemistry" between the individuals in the relationship. Either the chemistry is right and the relationship develops, or it's a mismatch and the relationship never seems to move beyond the initial stages. The chemistry explanation probably holds some truth, but many other variables influence the development of a relationship.

We are most often attracted to individuals who support us and have similar interests, attitudes, likes, and dislikes. In fact, when asked to characterize their ideal friend, people often describe someone who is similar to their perceptions of themselves. For example, those who are religious tend to seek other religious people, those

The fairy tale "Beauty and the Beast" is an ancient story that continues to hold meaning. Its theme raises the interesting question—What is the basis of attraction between people? People usually select partners whom they perceive to be similarly physically attractive or more attractive than themselves. In what cases might there be an exception to this rule?

who like sports tend to seek other sports fans, and those who like children tend to seek others who like children. Of course, opposites sometimes do attract, but relationships in which there are significant differences in important attitudes or behaviors are often strained and more likely to deteriorate than are those that have no significant disparities.

Another gender difference is exhibited in the personal ads placed by males and females who are seeking a romantic partner. It generally found that women stress their appearance and men stress their material resources.[9] It could be, of course, that those who write ads are simply echoing widespread cultural beliefs about what people assume is most appealing to the opposite sex. One research study investigated the number of replies that certain types of ad messages received.[10] In other words, do some factors in the ads attract more potential mates than others? Several interesting gender differences were found. For women, age as stated in their ads was negatively related to the number of replies—that is the older a woman was, the fewer replies. For men the opposite was true, the older a man was, the more replies he received. Also, the

[margin note: It's interesting being rich is a factor given women are financially independent now.]

higher men's stated income and educational level, the more replies. For women, in contrast, these factors were unrelated to how many responses the ad generated. Thus, a personal ad placed by a man was most effective if it indicated a mature, rich, educated individual. In ads placed by a woman, the only relevant ad content related to its effectiveness was age—the younger, the better. Interestingly, ads placed by gay men indicated a preference for younger males, and ads placed by heterosexual men indicated a preference for younger female partners. Whatever the reason, for both genders and for both heterosexuals and homosexuals, attractiveness is a positive characteristic, and numerous stereotypes are consistently associated with appearance.[11]

Coming Together on the Internet

In Chapter 13 we discussed how initial interaction on the Internet could result in relationships and the fact that those relationships are often limited in their growth because of a variety of reasons. According to Parks and Floyd, two communication scholars whose research on Internet interaction was mentioned in Chapter 13, there are conflicting theories on interpersonal communication and relationship development. Because Internet interaction is limited by fewer social cues (i.e., nonverbal communication) and potential feedback delays can lead to uncertainty (and difficulty in reducing uncertainty about the other person), the development of personal relationships might be prevented, or at least retarded.[12]

Online interactions are generally assumed to lack many of the typical characteristics of face-to-face discussions that can aid in relationship development. An important question that researchers are asking is, Are the conditions that exist in face-to-face interactions necessary for a relationship to develop into something that is ongoing or lasting? Predicted outcome value theory and social exchange theory, discussed in Chapter 13, assert that the motivation to form relationships is the forecast of a positive reward–cost ratio. In uncertainty theory, also discussed in Chapter 13, the driving force is the reduction in uncertainty about the other person and the relationship itself. None of these theories require physical contact or frequent interaction as necessary conditions for a relationship to develop. Thus, proximity and other conditions that occur in face-to-face interactions may be helpful, but they are not required for a relationship to be rewarding or fulfilling; they are not necessary for interactants to develop feelings for each other and do not affect how cyber partners treat each other.[13]

Parks and Floyd, in addition to finding that women are more likely to form relationships on the Internet than men, also found that age and martial status were not related to the likelihood of developing a personal relationship online. People who were married and divorced, according to the survey results, were equally likely to form personal relationships over the Internet. In fact, of the 176 people Parks and Floyd surveyed, about 30 percent developed personal relationships. The more in depth and personal an Internet relationship becomes the more likely it is that communication will move beyond cyberspace to more private and direct channels such as the telephone, letters, or face-to-face communication.[14] As with all relationships, Internet relationships also go through stages of coming together and coming apart.

[margin note: ✓ Model 1:]

Knapp's Stages of Coming Together

Theorists and communication scholars such as Mark Knapp[15] believe that in order for relationships to develop into something more than a brief encounter, they must go through different stages of growth. Knapp indicates that these stages do little to explain the multitude of personal and societal expectations that illustrate his model. He explains that in each case, the type of relationship that develops will depend on mutual and ongoing expectations: What is the relationship? What will it lead to? What should it lead to? What behavior is expected? Although the relationship stages in Knapp's theory are generally described as romantic in nature, he does not preclude or suggest that only romantic relationships or mixed-gender relationships are included in the model. In fact, Knapp's latest textbook, *Interpersonal Communication and Human Relationships,* co-authored with Anita Vangelisti,[16] suggests that any and all kinds of relationships, including same-sex partners, can reach the highest level of commitment. David McWhirter and Andrew Mattison, research psychologists, found that, when same-sex intimate relationships form, the same patterns or stages of development occur as with mixed-sex pairs.[17] Knapp and Vangelisti further suggest that their approach is more heavily oriented toward mixed-gender pairs but that it is not intended to exclude relationships between same-sex pairs. Although not all relationships go through the stages at the same rate or in the same way, the coming-together sequence usually progresses from initiating to experimenting, intensifying, integrating, and, ultimately, bonding.[18]

Initiating.   Initiating is the stage during which individuals meet and interact for the first time. The initial interaction may consist of a brief exchange of words, either electronically or in person, or of eye contact during which the two individuals recognize each other's existence and potential interest to meet and converse. If conversation does not begin, the initiating stage may end and the potential relationship may not progress any further. Whether the interaction continues depends on various assessments that the individuals make, for example, whether the other person is attractive or unattractive, approachable or unapproachable. A connection must be made to motivate one or both of the individuals to continue the interaction if a relationship is to develop. The decision to pursue the relationship also depends on whether the other person is open for the encounter. Is she or he in a hurry, too busy, or too involved with others?

During the initiating stage, we mentally process many impressions that lead to a key decision: "Yes, I do want to meet you" or "No, I am not interested in you." It may take less than fifteen seconds to determine whether a relationship will progress. At this stage, most of us feel extreme vulnerability and caution, even though there is considerable variance in people's initiating behaviors. The Internet seemingly is playing a larger and larger role in how people from all over the world meet and interact. People of all ages are using cyberspace to develop friendships as well as romantic relationships. This is happening because of the ease of making contact and sharing information with little or no risk.

Experimenting.   Experimenting is the stage of coming together that requires risk taking because little is known as yet about the other person. You attempt to answer the question, "Who is this person?" This stage can be extremely awkward, consisting mainly of small talk: "What's your name?" "Where are you from?" "What's your major?" "Do you know so-and-so?" Such conversation serves several important functions in the development of a relationship: (1) It uncovers similarities and interests that may lead to deeper conversation, (2) it serves as an audition for the potential friend, (3) it lets the other person know who you are and provides clues as to how he or she can get to know you better, and (4) it establishes the common ground you share with the other person.

The experimenting stage, although involving some risk, is usually pleasant, relaxed, and uncritical. Involvement and commitment are limited—and often remain

Making Connections

The Virtual Relationship

Use the Internet to develop a cyber relationship with someone. You may use email, join a list server, or enter a chatroom discussion either with existing contacts or new ones. Keep a log of all messages that you send and receive from the initial contact to help you retrace the steps in the relationship's development. It may take you several tries to find someone who is willing to interact with you over time. Answer the following questions after you have had at least eight to ten different interactions.

1. What principles from this and the previous chapter can you apply to this type of interaction?
2. What, if any, difficulties did you encounter while developing an electronically mediated relationship? How did it differ from face-to-face relationship development?
3. What did you learn about relationship development in general by using the Internet?

that way through the duration of the relationship. Most relationships do not progress beyond this stage, but this does not imply that these relationships are meaningless or useless. Relationships that remain at the experimental level can become satisfying friendships.

Intensifying.   The intensifying stage marks an increase in the participants' commitment and involvement in the relationship. Simply put, the two people become close friends. The commitment is typified by an increased sharing of more personal and private information, or self-disclosure (see Chapter 13), about oneself and one's family. For example, at this stage, it would not be unusual to share confidences such as "My mother and father are affectionate people," "I love you," "I am a sensitive person," "I once cheated on an exam," "My father is having another relationship," "I was promoted," "I drink too heavily," and "I don't use drugs."

Although the relationship deepens at this stage, there is still a sense of caution and testing to gain approval before continuing. In typical romantic relationships, we see much testing of commitment—sitting close, for instance, may occur before holding hands, hugging, or kissing. Each behavior in the relationship is engaged in order to seek approval. The relationship is beginning to mature, and the participants become more sensitive to each other's needs. During this phase, many things happen verbally:

1. Forms of address become informal—a first name, nickname, or a term of endearment is used.
2. Use of the first-person plural becomes more common—"We should do this" or "Let's do this."
3. Private symbols begin to develop—special slang or jargon or conventional language forms with mutually understood, private meanings.
4. Verbal shortcuts built on a backlog of accumulated and shared assumptions, knowledge, and experiences appear. For instance, your friend needs to be told that he or she is loved; you say that the person is important to you, but never say you love him or her.
5. More direct expressions of commitment may appear—"We really have a good thing going" or "I don't know who I'd talk to if you weren't around." Sometimes such expressions receive an echo—"I really like you a lot" or "I really like you, too, Dion."
6. Each partner acts increasingly as a helper in the other's daily process of understanding what he or she is all about—"In other words, you mean you're . . . " or "But yesterday you said you were . . ."

The integrating stage of relationship development conveys a sense of togetherness. The two people have established a deep commitment, and the relationship has become extremely important to them.

Integrating.   When integrating occurs, the relationship has a sense of togetherness. Others expect to see the individuals together, and when they do not, they often ask about the other person. The two people have established a deep commitment, and the relationship has become extremely important to them. Many assumptions take place between the individuals. For example, sharing is expected, and borrowing from the other person usually needs no formal request because it is assumed to be all right.

(ᴸᴵ) Although a strong mutual commitment characterizes this stage of a relationship, it does not mean a total giving of oneself to the other. The verbal and nonverbal expressions of the integrating stage take many forms. For example, some individuals believe their relationship is something special or unique. Some share rings, pins, pictures, and other artifacts to illustrate to themselves and others their commitment to each other. The two may begin to behave in similar ways. Still others indicate their sense of togetherness through word choice—*our* account, *our* apartment, *our* stereo, *our* car.

[handwritten margin note: There's a balance b/w these 2 positions]

Bonding.   The final stage in a relationship's development and growth is bonding, the public announcement of the commitment—as when a couple announces that they are engaged or getting married. Bonding involves the understanding that the commitment has progressed from private knowledge to public knowledge, thus, making a breakup of the relationship more difficult.

's,   The relationship at this stage is contractual in nature, even though a formal contract, such as a marriage license, is not required. Both parties must understand, however, that a relationship exists, which entails explicit and implicit agreements to hold it together. The commitment implies that the relationship is "for better or for worse" and is defined according to established norms, policies, or laws of the culture and society in which it exists.

[handwritten margin note: Model 1:]

Knapp's Stages of Coming Apart

In U.S. culture, there are no guarantees that a formal commitment will create a lasting relationship. When a relationship stops growing and differences begin to emerge, the coming-apart process begins. Some relationships may go through some or all of the stages in this process and emerge stronger than before, but when the forces that pull a relationship apart are stronger than the forces that hold it together, the alliance will end. Like the coming-together process, Knapp's coming-apart process has five stages— differentiating, circumscribing, stagnating, avoiding, and terminating.[19]

Differentiating.   In differentiating, the first stage of coming apart, the differences between the individuals are highlighted and become forces that slow or limit the growth of the relationship. The pair's communication tends to focus on how each differs from the other, and there is less tolerance of these differences. Indeed, differences that were once overlooked or negotiated now become the center of attention, putting stress on the relationship and its existence. Typically, things that were once described as "ours" now become "mine": "This is my apartment," "These are my books," and "They are my friends."

Conversations often move from mild disagreement to heated anger: "Do I have to do all the work around here? You don't do a darn thing." "Why is it that your so-called friends never clean up after themselves?" "I pay the phone bill, but you're the one who uses it the most." Conflict begins to overshadow the more positive aspects of the relationship, and the partners may become abusive to each other.

redirecting

Circumscribing. In the circumscribing stage, information exchange is reduced, and some areas of difference are completely avoided, because conversation would only lead to a deepening of the conflict. Comments during this stage may include the following: "I don't want to talk about it." "Can't you see that I'm busy?" "Why do you keep bringing up the past?" "Let's just be friends and forget it." Communication loses some of its personal qualities, is less spontaneous, and becomes increasingly superficial as the relationship becomes more strained. Interactions, in their amount and depth of disclosure, resemble those of the initiating and experimenting stages of coming together: "Have you eaten?" "Did I get any calls today?" "I saw Joe and he said to say hi."

People in the circumscribing stage often conceal their faltering relationship in public. For example, driving to a party, a couple may sit in cold silence, staring stonily into space. But once they arrive at their destination, they put on their party personalities—smiling, telling jokes, and not disagreeing with one another. When they return to the privacy of their car, they resume their cold behavior.

Stagnating. The relationship reaches a standstill at the stagnating stage. The participants avoid interaction and take care to sidestep controversy. Some people believe this is the "boring" stage of a relationship, yet they do not do anything about it. Little hope remains for the relationship once it has deteriorated to this stage, yet one of the partners may still want it to be revived.

During stagnation, both verbal and nonverbal communication tend to be thoroughly thought out, and the partners plan what to say, making interactions stylized and cold. Both persons are apt to reflect unhappiness and to act as if each is a stranger to the other.

Often the stagnation stage is relatively brief, but sometimes it is extended because of complications. For example, some people may be seriously distressed by the loss of their relationship even though they know that parting is the right decision. Others may count on the survival of the relationship, such as children, making the breakup more difficult. Others may prolong the situation in fear of experiencing additional pain and in hope of getting the relationship back on track or in an attempt to punish the other person.

Avoiding. Up to this point, the participants in the relationship are still seeing each other or sharing the same living quarters. But the fourth stage, the avoiding stage, is marked by physical distancing and eventual separation. The basic message is "I am not interested in being with you anymore." As far as the participants are concerned, the relationship is over and they have no interest in reestablishing it.

Making Connections

Troubles Talk

Think about your relationships with others and what they mean to you.

1. What concepts, principles, or characteristics in the previous chapter and this chapter can you use to describe the kind of relationship you would like to have with others?
2. Often, hurtful statements characterize relationships between partners, friends, or family members. In what ways do people hurt others through their communication behaviors?
3. In what type of relationships are hurtful messages typically given? Why?
4. Why do you think it is difficult for people who have been hurt by the communication of others to forgive or to let go of the hurt?

At times the interaction in this stage is brief, direct, unfriendly, and even antagonistic: "I really don't care to see you." "Don't call me—we have nothing to discuss." "I'm busy tonight and, for that matter, I'm going to be busy for quite some time."

Terminating.   The last stage in the breaking up of a relationship occurs when the individuals take the necessary steps to end it. Termination can be early, that is, when the relationship has barely begun, or it can occur after many years. For relationships that break up in the early stages of development, such as initiating or experimenting, the feelings of parting are usually not complex or lasting.

The interaction during this stage is self-centered and seeks to justify the termination: "I need to do something for myself—I've always put more into the relationship than I've gotten out of it." "We just have too many differences that I didn't know existed until now." "I found out that we just weren't meant for each other." When both individuals know that the relationship is ending, they say good-bye to each other in three ways—in a summary statement, in behaviors signaling the termination or limited contact, and in comments about what the relationship will be like in the future, if there is to be any relationship at all.[20]

Summary statements review the relationship and provide a rationale for its termination: "Although our love used to be very special, we both have changed over the years. We are not the same couple that we were when we first met." Ending behaviors reflect new rules of contact: "It would be good for both of us not to see so much of each other." "I wish you would stop coming over all the time." Finally, when the relationship is over, the participants state their preferences for dealing with each other in the future: "I don't want to see you anymore." "We can get together once in a while, but I only want us to be friends and nothing more." See Table 14.1 for dialogue that represents each stage of relationship development.

The stages of coming together and coming apart are complex and continuous as we move into, through, and out of relationships. Knapp and Vangelisti acknowledge that not all relationships move through each of the escalating and deescalating stages at the same pace, but they state that most relationships do go through the interaction stages systematically and sequentially. See Figure 14.1 on page 401 for a staircase model of the interaction stages developed by Knapp and Vangelisti. It illustrates that when they are coming together, people follow a process of moving up the left side of the staircase, and when they are coming apart, people commonly move down the right side. Knapp and Vangelisti also suggest that it is possible for people to skip steps during both the growth process of a relationship and the deterioration of a relationship. You may have had or heard of relationships that go from the initiating stage, "Hi, my name is," to "Let's go to your place so that we can get to know each other better." These relationships move from the initiating step right to the intensifying step. Termination may occur suddenly and without warning in this situation, thus, violating or skipping all the steps of coming apart. For example, in *Runaway Bride,* a popular movie during the late 1990s, Julia Roberts portrays a character who falls in love with several different guys, but in each case she left them standing at the altar, because she did not believe the relationship was right.

Knapp and Vangelisti also suggest that relationships can move forward and backward from one stage to the next. The direction a relationship takes depends on how one evaluates the various rewards and costs (social exchange theory—see Chapter 13) and whether the rewards outweigh the costs or vice versa, thus moving the relationship either forward or backward. The center of the staircase, according to Knapp and Vangelisti, represents the possibility of stability at a given level for a period of time.

TABLE 14.1	Knapp's Stages of Relationship Development	

PROCESS	STAGE	REPRESENTATIVE DIALOGUE
Coming together	Initiating	"Hi, how ya doin' "? "Fine. You?"
	Experimenting	"Oh, so you like to ski . . . so do I." "You do? Great. Where do you go?"
	Intensifying	"I . . . I think I love you." "I love you too."
	Integrating	"I feel so much a part of you." "Yeah, we are like one person." "What happens to you happens to me."
	Bonding	"I want to be with you always." "Let's get married."
Coming apart	Differentiating	"I just don't like big social gatherings." "Sometimes I don't understand you. This is one area where I'm certainly not like you at all."
	Circumscribing	"Did you have a good time on your trip?" "What time will dinner be ready?"
	Stagnating	"What's there to talk about?" "Right. I know what you're going to say and you know what I'm going to say."
	Avoiding	"I'm so busy, I don't know when I'll be able to see you." "If I'm not around, you'll understand."
	Terminating	"I'm leaving you . . . and don't bother trying to contact me." "Don't worry."

From Mark L. Knapp and Anita L. Vengelisti, *Interpersonal Communication and Human Relationships,* 4th ed. (Boston: Allyn and Bacon, 2000), 37. Copyright © 2000 by Allyn & Bacon. Reprinted by permission.

However, relationships are not static for very long, and, thus, it is natural for all relationships, including the most stable, to experience periods of instability. Each stage can also create its own movement, and, like most things, the stages themselves have a beginning, middle, and end.

There are at least three reasons, according to Knapp, relationships move through the stages sequentially: (1) Each stage provides information that allows movement to the next, (2) each stage enables the participants to predict what may or may not occur in the next stage, and (3) skipping a stage creates risk and uncertainty in the relationship.[21] Relationships that are happy and satisfying last, because the participants have learned to satisfy each other through their communication.

FIGURE 14.1

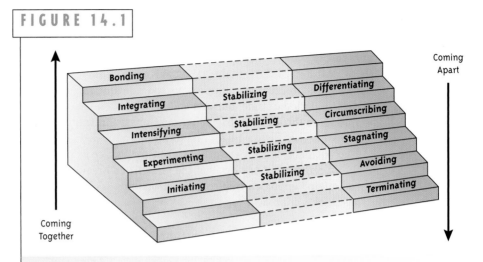

Knapp and Vangelisti's Staircase Model of Interaction

Relationship development usually follows a process of moving up the left side of the staircase, and when relationships come apart they commonly move down the right side. Relationships can also stabilize at a specific level, and the central portion of the staircase depicts that possibility.

From Mark L. Knapp and Anita L. Vangelisti, *Interpersonal Communication and Human Relationships*, 4th ed. (Boston: Allyn and Bacon, 2000), 59. Copyright © 2000 by Allyn and Bacon. Reprinted by permission.

Making Connections

Retracing a Relationship's Progress

Clearly, no two relationships are alike, nor do they all evolve in the same way. Consider a relationship that is important to you, and then complete the following steps:

1. Record the significant developments in the relationship, from the time of the first meeting to the present. Label these developments according to Knapp's stages.

2. After you have completed the labeling, imagine that your relationship is a book, and each stage or period in the relationship's history is a chapter. Create a title for each chapter, capturing that essence of the relationship during that period. You can have as many chapters as you find necessary to describe the relationship.

3. After you have titled each chapter, write a brief synopsis of what each title means. Do the chapters follow any particular pattern of development?

4. What are the similarities and differences between the stages of your relationship and Knapp's stages?

Adapted from Leslie A. Baxter, "Dialectical Contradictions in Relationships Development," *Journal of Social and Personal Relationships* (1990) 7: 69–88. Reprinted in *Contemporary Perspectives on Interpersonal Communication,* eds. Sandra Petronio, Jess K. Alberts, Michael L. Hecht, and Jerry Buley (Dubuque, Iowa: Brown & Benchmark, 1993), 92–93.

Model 2 : ## Duck's Phases of Dissolution

Communication scholar Steve Duck theorizes that dissolving relationships go through a rather complex decision-making process that does not always follow a specific order of stages, in contrast to the model of Knapp's coming-apart stages. According to Duck, relationship breakups often occur sporadically, inconsistently, and with uncertainty over a period of time, but in deciding what to do about a potential breakup, a person proceeds through the following four phases: intrapyschic, dyadic, social, and grave-dressing (see Figure 14.2). The termination of the relationship is strongly affected by the partners' social networks, and the influence of others outside the relationship is often reflected in any or all of the phases of a breakup. The uncertainty, or "on again, off again" approach that some relationships take as they dissolve, defines the phases of Duck's approach.[22]

The Intrapsychic Phase.   During the intrapsychic phase, people begin to internally assess their dissatisfaction with a relationship. This phase involves perception, assessments, and decision making about what to do about the relationship. In this phase, communication may actually decrease at times, and each of the partners may seek comfort from others outside the relationship. The intrapsychic phase is similar in some respects to Knapp's differentiating stage where differences between the individuals become noticeable to at least one of the individuals in the relationship. Communication may decrease or become more self-centered and, thus, lead to more conflict and argument rather than negotiation.

The Dyadic Phase.   In the dyadic phase, the people in the relationship discuss the status of their relationship. The interactions vary from cooperative to uncooperative in discussing the partner's unsatisfying traits or behaviors, and whether to solve the problem or to separate. There is much negotiation, persuasion, and argument during this period; each person is trying to get the other person to comply or change in some fashion. Sometimes the dyadic phase ends with an agreement to repair the relationship, but if it doesn't, the relationship may eventually move on to the next phase. The dyadic phase would be consistent with what may occur as a relationship moves through Knapp's differentiating stage to the circumscribing stage. In this phase it is likely that there is more conflict and less negotiation; the partners may also avoid subjects that may inflame the interaction. Thus, when interaction occurs during this phase in the relationship breakup, it moves toward more impersonal or formalized conversations as illustrated in Knapp's circumscribing stage.

The Social Phase.   In the social phase the relationship difficulties become more public within the context of family, friends, co-workers, or other acquaintances. Most relationships that break up, except possibly secret love affairs, do not stand completely alone and usually have an impact on others outside the dissolving relationship. For example, there is usually an effect on the children if parents separate. During this phase, the opinions and feelings of others often have an impact on what a couple eventually does. For example, children of a married couple may influence the couple to stay together in spite of their differences. The concern may become, "What kind of relationship should be continued, if any? How should it be presented to others?" Other issues include where to place blame, how to save face, how to explain what has happened, and who should be sought out for support or to provide approval for the decision.

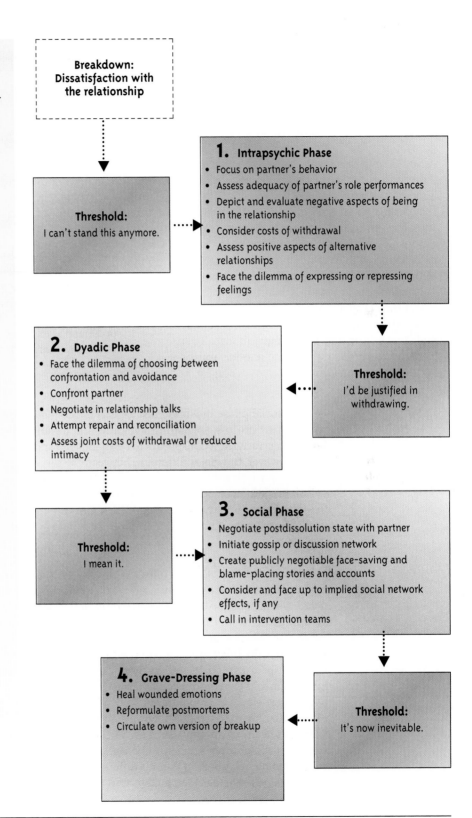

FIGURE 14.2

Duck's Dissolution Stages

When relationships break up, they go through a rather complex decision-making process that, according to Steve Duck, includes four phases of disengagement: intrapsychic, dyadic, social, and grave-dressing.

Adapted from *Personal Relationships,* by Steve Duck. Copyright © 1982 by Academic Press, Inc. Reprinted with permission of Academic Press, Inc., and the author.

Breakdown: Dissatisfaction with the relationship

Threshold: I can't stand this anymore.

1. Intrapsychic Phase
- Focus on partner's behavior
- Assess adequacy of partner's role performances
- Depict and evaluate negative aspects of being in the relationship
- Consider costs of withdrawal
- Assess positive aspects of alternative relationships
- Face the dilemma of expressing or repressing feelings

Threshold: I'd be justified in withdrawing.

2. Dyadic Phase
- Face the dilemma of choosing between confrontation and avoidance
- Confront partner
- Negotiate in relationship talks
- Attempt repair and reconciliation
- Assess joint costs of withdrawal or reduced intimacy

Threshold: I mean it.

3. Social Phase
- Negotiate postdissolution state with partner
- Initiate gossip or discussion network
- Create publicly negotiable face-saving and blame-placing stories and accounts
- Consider and face up to implied social network effects, if any
- Call in intervention teams

Threshold: It's now inevitable.

4. Grave-Dressing Phase
- Heal wounded emotions
- Reformulate postmortems
- Circulate own version of breakup

Making Connections

Thinking About Relationships

Erika was dating someone else when she started going out with Tran. A mutual friend introduced them—Erika was a first-year student and Tran was in his second year. Neither Erika nor Tran had been involved in any relationship they really cared about until now. From the first date there was an immediate attraction, and their relationship grew very intense. They were physically attracted to each other and liked to do lots of the same things together. They were becoming very comfortable together, and both would go out of their way to see each other.

Their relationship was progressing rapidly, and it was clear they were falling in love. Then Tran made plans to transfer to another university to study biochemistry, and Erika was unsure how she would handle their separation. That summer they saw each other as often as they could. By the end of the summer, however, they began to quarrel over very trivial matters; their conflicts seemed to emerge suddenly and without warning.

1. Can you name the forces that have shaped the relationship between Erika and Tran?
2. What advice would you give to Erika? To Tran?
3. Which theory of relationship stages, Duck's or Knapp's, explains Erika and Tran's relationship more thoroughly? Why?

The social phase includes most aspects of the remaining three stages of Knapp's coming-apart process: stagnating, avoiding, and termination. It is clear that the relationship has reached what appears to be an impasse and thus continuing it is most unlikely. However, the major difference between the theories of Duck and Knapp is that Duck emphasized the impact the breakup of the relationship will have on others as well as the influence others will have on the relationship. Knapp's stages do not address this issue directly. According to Duck, the individuals will seek out the approval of others, whereas Knapp is more concerned with how the individuals justify the breakup to themselves.

The Grave-Dressing Phase.   Duck names the final phase grave-dressing, because after the breakup, each partner gives an account of why the relationship ended. This phase includes some similarities to Knapp's termination stage, because it is in this stage, according to Knapp, that individuals begin to justify to others why the relationship had to end. These explanations aid in the healing process, in coping, and in the recovery from the breakup itself. It is not unusual for one or both individuals in the relationship to explain to others why the relationship dissolved. For example, if the relationship ended on friendly terms, you might hear statements such as "It just didn't work—we were too different" or "We needed time to grow, so we decided not to see each other for a while." If, however, the relationship ended on unfriendly terms, you might hear explanations such as "He always wanted things for himself—he was selfish" or "She never seemed to be satisfied with what I'd do for her." Men and women handle relationship failures differently: Women, for example, tend to confide in their friends, whereas men tend to start a new relationship as quickly as possible.[23]

Not all relationships, however, end with mutual agreement that the relationship should be terminated. You are probably aware of situations in which one partner didn't want to lose the other, but the person ending the relationship simply saw no reason to continue it. In such a case, the grave-dressing phase is usually one-sided; the person ending the relationship might say, "It just wasn't working" or "I have found someone new." Meanwhile, the person who does not want the relationship to end looks for a way to keep it going and cannot face the fact it is over. The person tries to justify to himself or herself and others that the termination is only temporary and that the other person will come to his or her senses and return.

Each phase poses certain communication challenges that Duck refers to as "social management problems." For example, in the intrapsychic phase, one must have the ability to discuss the perceived differences with one's partner. In the social phase, one must be able to discuss the breakup with others outside of the relationship. Clearly, as relationships move in and out of various phases or stages, communication plays a significant role. The more skilled the parties are at communicating, the more likely they will move through the stages smoothly (that is, if terminating a relationship can ever be considered easy).

The research of Leslie Baxter, a communication scholar, supports some of Duck's explanations regarding dissolving relationships. Baxter believes that disengagement often involves repeated attempts to limit or end relationships. They are cyclical in nature and involve different communication strategies. Moreover, the communication strategies used during the breakup of relationships involve varying degrees of directness and concern for the other person.[24] The direct strategies are explicit statements describing the desire to end the relationship, whereas the indirect strategies are more subtle in design. For example, an indirect strategy for breaking up might involve using excuses such as "I have too much homework," implying "I cannot see you now."

Someone with concern for the other person is more likely to use the indirect approach; the direct approach is much more expedient and may show little or no concern for hurting the other person. Baxter implies that strategies used in ending a relationship depend greatly on whether the breakup is one-sided or agreed on by both parties. As suggested earlier, agreed-on breakups usually involve some negotiation and face saving on behalf of both parties involved. All relationships, however, move through various stages and often move between various levels of tension or conflict.

To put it simply, relationships are often messy. This is true for even the best and most stable relationships because of the push and pull that all relationships encounter from time to time. As relationships move through the stages of growth and development toward intimacy, it is rare that there are no bumps along the way, and even the most perfect relationship has its pulls and pushes of coming together and coming apart. In fact, most romantic partners converse with each other less than a few hours a day, rarely self-disclose, often fight, on occasion become verbally and even physically violent, are rude to each other, and are more concerned with themselves than with sharing intimacies.[25] It is, therefore, not unusual that relationships don't measure up to the ideal, because most relationships—whether romantic, family, close friendship, or work-related—encounter difficult contradictions almost every day. These tensions and the conflicts that emerge from them are discussed in the following section.

Model 3:

Dialectical Theory: Push and Pull

Relationships consist of many forces that push and pull them in many different directions. These forces are referred to as *contradictions.* For example, you may want your best friend to spend more time with you, but when he or she does, you decide that you want more time to yourself. This may lead to your friend saying, "I thought you wanted to spend more time together, and now that we can, you're never around. So what do you want?" This illustrates the contradictory impulses or **dialectics** that push and pull us in conflicting directions with others. The desire for being connected and having autonomy is one of three most commonly identified dialectical tensions in the research. The other two dialectical tensions are openness–closedness and novelty–predictability.[26]

Connection–Autonomy.   Relationships require both the desire to connect to another person and the desire to retain autonomy as an individual. We want to connect to others, such as partners, friends, parents, siblings, or co-workers, but we also want to retain some control and independence or autonomy over our lives. There is a desire for our close relationships to be defined as "us," but this does not mean that we want to sacrifice our individuality or control over who we are.

When there is too much emphasis on connection or integration in a relationship, it may lead to the feeling of being smothered or consumed by a partner, friend, parent, or co-worker, such that we feel entrapped and controlled by the relationship, thus leaving us with no life of our own. Intimacy at its highest level does require a bonding that connects us with another person emotionally, intellectually, and physically, but it does not mean or require a complete loss of self. In healthy relationships, there is a reasonable balance of being connected and maintaining autonomy. Relationships that move too far in one direction or the other in terms of control versus autonomy are usually relationships that are extremely unstable and potentially destructive.

Openness–Closedness.   The second dialectic tension is the desire to be open and expressive on the one hand and closed and private on the other. In U.S. culture, we are encouraged to be open and honest with others, because we are a society that admires those who are open-minded and truthful. But even at the beginning of new relationships, when we are seeking as much information as we can about the other person, there is a counterforce that cautions against revealing too much too soon about ourselves. This tension between self-disclosing and keeping our privacy continues throughout the various stages of relationship development. We know that open expression is a necessary prerequisite in order for us to reach intimacy and bonding with another person. We also know that when we reveal ourselves to another individual we make our relationship and ourselves more vulnerable. As discussed in Chapter 13, privacy is important for a relationship to survive. All of us, therefore, face the dilemma of how much self-disclosure or honesty we should allow there to be with friends, relatives, and romantic partners and how much will be too much. Too much self-disclosure, as you learned in Chapter 13, may lead to strains on a relationship and is a sign of not being a competent, or, at the very least, a thoughtful, communicator. Relationships grow on the strength of the trust that is established between partners. When the trust that exists between partners is violated, by revealing private information or by telling a partner something he or she is not prepared to hear, the relationship is at risk for deterioration or termination.

Making Connections

Temptation: Cheating to Trade Up

The reality television show *Temptation Island* tries to provoke committed but unmarried couples into promiscuous behavior by cheating on their partners. This show is a knock-off of the popular *Survivor.* The basic assumption of *Temptation Island* is that participants should be ready to trade in a current partner should a more attractive one come along. The theme is "just go with the flow."

1. Is resisting deliberate temptation by another attractive person an effective way to prove that a relationship is strong? Explain.

2. How might we use dialectical theory to explain this show's impact on participants' relationships? On viewers' relationships?

3. What is this show communicating about relationships?

4. Discuss the ethical implications of this show and how they might affect communication in a relationship.

Novelty–Predictability. In order to develop and build healthy relationships, a certain amount of predictability is needed. Without some stability or constancy, there is too much potential for uncertainty and ambivalence for a long-term relationship to survive. Thus, we need relationships in which we know that we can count on a certain amount of predictability. Families are a central stabilizing force in most people's lives and provide an anchor for security in a very unpredictable world. Predictability is a comfort to most of us because we know what to expect. Too much predictability in some aspects of a relationship, however, may make the relationship routine and boring, thus requiring a call for something unique or different. The drive for wanting things to be consistent and predictable and the desire for novelty and difference creates a dialectical tension that requires competent communication in a relationship in order to relieve tension and prevent a destructive conflict from occurring. Pushes and pulls, or dialectic tensions, will always be part of every relationship in which we are involved, and how competently we communicate will determine whether a relationship grows, stagnates, or terminates. What can a competent communicator do to manage relationship dialectics? This question, if not answered by both partners in a relationship, will lead to conflict.

Two factors cause conflicts:
1. incompatible goals,
2. social factors

Interpersonal Conflict

Conflict, like dialectic tensions in relationships, may occur for a variety of reasons, including differences in individuals' ability to self-disclose and differences in individual perception of a situation. **Conflict,** according to William Wilmot and Joyce Hocker, "is an expressed struggle between at least two interdependent parties who perceive incompatible goals, scarce resources, and interference from others in achieving their goals."[27] The key terms in the definition are *expressed struggle, interdependent parties, incompatible goals, scarce resources,* and *interference from others.* For example, suppose you want to go to a dance on Friday evening and your friend wants to go to a movie. Both of you explain your desire for what you would like to do (expressed struggle), neither of you wants to go out alone on Friday evening (interdependent parties), you cannot go to both the dance and the movie in the same evening (incompatible goals), neither of you can afford to do both because of time and money (scarce resources), and your friend will not consider going to the dance (interference). You have incompatible goals, and one must lose for the other to win.

One study on conflict found that college students, on average, engage in some form of conflict behavior seven times a week.[28] According to the research, the more couples engage in martial conflict, the more they become verbally aggressive, and their verbal aggression often leads to physical violence.[29] The conflict may escalate, becoming more intense and hurtful, as it becomes more frequent between partners. In U.S. society, people have experienced significant increases in workplace and school conflict during the past decade. All you have to do is read a newspaper or listen to a newscast to know this is true. In fact, according to a 1998 U.S. Department of Justice report on their web site (http://www.ojp.usdoj.gov/bjs/), approximately 1,000 people on average are murdered at work each year in the United States alone.

Conflict: The Major Causes

Our definition of conflict emphasizes the existence as well as the recognition of incompatible goals. And indeed, incompatible interests are the defining features of conflicts. Yet, conflicts can fail to develop even though both sides have incompatible interests; and in other situations, conflicts occur even though the two sides don't have opposing interests—they may simply believe they exist.[30] Clearly, then, conflict involves much more than opposing views or interests. In fact, there is a growing body of research that suggests that social factors may play a role as strong as or even stronger than incompatible interests in initiating conflicts.

Faulty attributions, such as errors concerning the causes behind others' behaviors, is one social factor that may lead to conflict.[31] When individuals believe that their goals or interests have been thwarted, they generally try to determine why. Was it poor planning on their part? Was it simply a case of bad luck? Was it a lack of the appropriate resources to reach the goal? Or was it because of someone's intentional interference? If it is concluded that the latter is the reason, then the seeds for conflict may be planted—even if the other person actually had nothing to do with the situation. Thus, erroneous attributions concerning the causes of negative outcomes can and often do play an important role instigating conflicts, and sometimes result in conflicts when they readily could have been avoided.

Faulty communication is another social factor that may lead to conflict. This is evident by the fact that individuals sometimes communicate in a way that angers or annoys someone, even though it is not the communicator's intention to do so. Have you ever been harshly critized in such a way that you believed was unjustified, insensitive, unfair, and not the least helpful? If you have, you know that this type of perceived criticism leaves you feeling upset, angry, and ready to attack, thus setting the stage for conflict even though the criticism may not have been borne out of incompatible goals.

Relational repair strategies require open and honest communication and a willingness to listen to the other person with an open mind.

(iii) A third social cause of conflict may stem from our tendency to perceive our own views as objective and as reflecting reality, but to perceive others' views as biased or lacking in reality. As a result, we sometimes create conflicting views by magnifying differences between our views and those of others, especially those whom we believe are different from us.

(iv) Finally, personal traits or characteristics can lead to conflict. This is especially true of Type A individuals: those who are highly competitive, like to win, are always in a hurry, and are relatively irritable when others interfere with the reaching of goals. Type A individuals, because of their nature, are more likely to get into conflicts than Type B individuals, who are calmer and less irritable about events around them.

So what causes conflict? Conflict does not stem solely from incompatible goals. On the contrary, conflict often results from social factors such as long-standing grudges or resentment, the desire for revenge, inaccurate social perceptions, ineffective communication, and similar factors. Although the major cause of conflict may be incompatible goals, the social and cognitive causes of conflict are also factors to consider.

Conflict: Destructive and Constructive

Conflict becomes destructive when the parties involved are unwilling to negotiate their differences and instead engage in personal attacks on one another. Here are some other ways in which conflict can be destructive:

Conflict is destructive when the resolution of the conflict ends with a winner and a loser.

Conflict can be destructive if the individuals involved act too aggressively, if they withdraw from each other, if they withhold their feelings from each other, or if they accuse each other of causing their problems.

Conflict is destructive in proportion to the importance of the goals to the individuals.

Conflict creates dysfunction when it prevents us from doing our work or feeling good about ourselves.

Conflict motivates behaviors, and when it forces us to do things that we don't want to do, it is destructive.

The following statistics related to divorce in the United States illustrate that conflict can be destructive. It is estimated that more than 50 percent of the marriages in our society today will end in divorce. In addition, the rate of divorce has increased by 700 percent since 1900. It is further estimated that most divorces occur between the second and sixth years of marriage. In *USA Today,* Karen Peterson reported that the risk for divorce in second marriages is almost 70 percent. Finally, more than one-third of the children in the United States have endured the painful experience of their parents' divorce.[32]

Of course, not all divorces or separations are the result of conflict, nor is all conflict necessarily destructive. In fact, some people thrive on conflict; it motivates them to perform at extremely high levels. However, when conflict results in the termination of relationships and leaves one or both of the parties feeling foolish, inadequate, or angry, it is usually destructive.

However, the relationship should be more important than winning or losing. When appropriate, the importance of the relationship should be discussed as a part of the negotiation process. In effect, we say to one another, "We have a definite disagreement here, but no matter what, our relationship is more important than the disagreement. We are confirming the importance of the relationship when we give its survival a higher priority than winning the conflict." In order to reduce conflict and build relationships, we need to learn how to communicate effectively with each other.[33]

Conflict can sometimes be constructive and not destructive. Constructive conflict, according to Wilmot and Hocker, is characterized by a we-orientation, cooperation, and flexibility.[34] It is good to reach a solution that is mutually agreeable to all. This does not mean that we have to feel warm and fuzzy while the differences are worked out, but it does mean that conflicting parties must be willing to negotiate and cooperate to resolve differences. Constructive conflict can be frustrating and difficult as well as contentious, and it requires competent communicators who are knowledgeable, skillful, sensitive, committed, and ethical in resolving their differences.

Conflict Management: Some Useful Strategies

Because conflicts are often costly, the people involved usually want to resolve them as quickly as possible. There are several options to resolving conflicts: withdrawing, accommodating, forcing, negotiating, and collaboration.[35] Each strategy involves a different outcome, which results in relational outcomes that can be both positive and negative.

Withdrawing.   When we choose to avoid further conflict by either psychologically or physically removing ourselves from the situation, we are withdrawing. Withdrawing can be done in a number of ways, such as changing the topic, cracking jokes, ignoring, or leaving the situation altogether. Usually, when a withdrawal strategy is used, the conflict is temporarily avoided, but it really doesn't go away. Withdrawal is a temporary escape from the conflict, but both parties know that it has not been resolved.

Stonewalling is a powerful form of avoiding conflict.[36] When people exhibit stony silence, refuse to discuss problems, or physically remove themselves from another person who is complaining, disagreeing, or attacking they are said to be stonewalling. Consider the following discussion:

> *Melissa:* We need to discuss your unwillingness to set a budget. Your use of the credit card is going to bankrupt your father and me.
>
> *Tiff:* It isn't a problem and there is nothing to talk about.
>
> *Melissa:* We have got to talk about it because you are ruining our credit.
>
> *Tiff:* Get a life, I am not ruining anything. I'll pay you back. [leaves the house]

Tiff is stonewalling by withdrawing from the conflict and claiming that she has everything under control. She believes that to discuss her use of the credit card will only make the conflict between her and her mother worse. Her mother is likely becoming frustrated with Tiff's stonewalling about the use of the credit card. Stonewalling by Tiff can also communicate her disapproval, self-righteousness, indifference, and defensiveness toward her mother.

Research indicates that avoiding is a frequently used way to manage conflict. Most of us want to avoid conflict whenever we can. For example, one research study found that 50 percent of the time college students used avoiding or withdrawing strategies to keep conflict from escalating.[37] Other research studies have found that when facing conflict men use stonewalling more often than women because of their fear that they won't be able to control themselves.[38]

The only real advantage to withdrawal is that it gives time for one or both individuals involved in the conflict to think about it and to calm down before again trying to deal with the conflict. The disadvantage is that it may create more hostility and ultimately make dealing with the conflict more difficult in the long run. So, withdrawal can be a useful strategy, but it is also limited in its ability to resolve the conflict itself.

Accommodating.   Accommodating requires one person to yield or give in to another person's needs and desires. In withdrawal, the participants end up with a lose/lose situation. There is a winner and a loser in the accomodating strategy. This type of outcome often ends with such statements as "whatever" or "whatever you want, I don't care." From an individual satisfaction standpoint, the accommodating strategy requires one person to give up something, whereas the other person achieves something. Although this strategy is appropriate in certain conflict situations, such as whether to have beef or chicken for dinner, it should be used sparingly because it can have negative effects both on the individuals and the relationship itself. This is especially true, if one side always tends to accommodate the other side in order to avoid or reduce conflict.

Forcing.   Forcing is a strategy in which one person has power and dominance over another person. It may result in aggression that could include threats, criticisms, hostile remarks and jokes, ridicule, sarcasm, intimidation, fault finding, coercion, or manipulation. Extreme cases of forcing include date rape, child abuse, and sexual harassment.

This is a win/lose situation. The person with the power can claim the victory and the other person loses. However, in this situation the competition is unfair, because one individual has more control and power over the other, which ensures a victory regardless of the virtue of the other person's position.

Consider a relationship in which one person has power or control over the other. It is a relationship that is unequal and may lead to abuse. Of course, there are times when the dominance of one person could serve the relationship, such as in an emergency situation where a decision has to be made quickly. The essence of force is to pressure others to agree with something so that we get what we want. The more force we use to get others to do what we want or to agree with us, the more likely it is that resentment will increase, leading to more destructive types of conflicts.

Negotiating.   Negotiating usually involves a give-and-take process and leads to both parties ending with some satisfaction in the outcome. Negotiating is a form of compromise in which both parties must give up something in order to get something. This is interpreted by some to be a lose/lose style of conflict management.

Compromise seems to be a reasonable way to approach conflict, and it is extremely popular among many individuals, although there are potential problems with it. The most obvious problem is that the quality of the solution may be reduced—this is especially true if one of the parties in the conflict actually had a better solution that had to be compromised in order to reach agreement. Despite the negative aspects of negotiating or compromising, it may be the only possible way to approach a conflict. This is most likely true when the parties involved have equal power, if no other alternative is available, if the outcome isn't critical, if essential values are not undermined, or if the settlement is only a temporary one until a better solution can be found.

Collaboration.   Collaboration is a strategy of conflict management that requires cooperation and mutual respect. It usually involves a problem-solving approach that addresses all the concerns of both parties in order to arrive at a solution that is mutually

Making Connections

Conflict Online

Conflict can occur just as easily online as it does in face-to-face communication. Some people believe there is a tendency to communicate more forcefully and directly via the computer than in face-to-face interactions. Thus, rather than resolving conflicts or differences, the conflicts tend to escalate more readily over the computer.

1. Why do you think conflict occurs so easily online?

2. What can you do to reduce online conflicts?
3. Create a guide to improving online communication etiquette—what advice would you give in your guide to others in order to reduce or prevent online conflicts?

For help, do an Internet search using the words "online etiquette."

Making Connections

Deception in a Relationship

I (Darin) have always been a little concerned about Oliva—she is such a charmer. She told me that she was through with Aaron, her old boyfriend. We began sleeping together, spending a couple of nights plus weekends together at each other's places. Then a friend of mine told me that she saw Oliva with her "ex," and it didn't look as if they had parted ways. My friend also said that Oliva and her "ex" appeared to be intensely involved with each other. I saw Oliva today, and she didn't act differently. In fact, she acted as if everything was the same.

1. What do you think you would do in this situation?
2. What would you tell Darin to do?
3. What does a situation like this one do to a relationship?
4. Is there anything that Oliva can do to explain her behavior to Darin?
5. Are there any considerations that Darin should take into account before he jumps to conclusions?

satisfying. It is a "we" rather than a "me" approach to negotiation. In essence, collaboration is a form of compromise. It may require extra effort by both parties because more resources and considerations of new options that meet the approval of both parties may be needed.

In order for collaboration to work as a strategy, both parties must recognize that there is a conflict and they must want to find creative ways to resolve their differences. When both parties recognize that a conflict exists, they usually engage in some sort of confrontation, which is the opposite of avoidance. There are different degrees of confrontation ranging from the very violent (often depicted in the media) to the respectful. In order for collaboration to be successful, both parties must be willing to resolve their differences, treat each other as equals, be honest and open in their differences, be empathetic toward each other, and be willing to listen to each other's points of view.

The collaboration strategy is considered a win/win situation for both sides in the conflict. Both sides believe they have accomplished or gained something from the solution because of their willingness to listen to each other concerning the issues. In addition, when both parties believe they have had the opportunity to voice their opinions and they have agreed in good faith to settle the dispute, it truly is a win/win situation. The collaboration strategy to manage conflict is the best strategy for a relationship, because it shows that each party cares about the other's well-being and interests. According to Wilmot and Hocker, collaborating, as a conflict management style, produces consistently positive outcomes that leave the participants satisfied with their decisions, the process, and the growth that occurs in their interpersonal relationship.[39]

Many scholars agree that conflict is inevitable in all retionships and that conflict need not be destructive. Conflict often produces stronger and more durable relationships. Conflict in itself should not be considered negative or destructive, but a natural part of any relationship.

Signs That Show a Relationship Is in Trouble

Before we concede that a relationship is over, certain warning signs as well as some possible repair strategies might help prevent its dissolution.

Aggressive Behavior. A preliminary warning sign that a relationship is heading toward trouble is when one of the parties becomes a little too aggressive by aiming hurtful communication at the other party. All of us, at one time or another, say something that we wished we hadn't said to someone about whom we care. However, whether intentionally or not, when people communicate hurtful statements to one another with increasing frequency, it is a possible sign that their relationship is in trouble.

Lies. Another warning sign that a relationship is in trouble is when one person deceives another by lying about something. Whether the lie is significant or trivial, it weakens the relationship's foundation—which is trust. Most of the time acts of deception have consequences that people don't fully consider when justifying their reasons for lying. You can probably think of many such consequences not only for the person being deceived but also for the deceiver. A relationship built on deceit is not likely to succeed for very long.

Betrayal. Another warning sign that a relationship is in trouble is betrayal. Betrayal can happen when someone trusts another person and, in one way or another, that trust is broken. For example, if you tell a friend a personal secret and especially ask for complete confidentiality and the friend spreads the story to others, you have been betrayed. Deception and betrayal are similar; in fact, they are almost synonymous. The difference is that betrayal violates a confidence and an agreed-on expectation. Some common examples of betrayal include extramarital affairs, gossip, and harmful criticism behind someone's back.

Relationships injured by deception and betrayal are often not repairable because of the amount of hurt such breaches of trust cause. However, situations such as arguments that have gotten out of hand or misunderstandings can often be corrected or resolved. In these cases competent communication can help repair and possibly save the relationship.

Relational Repair Strategies

For situations in which both parties want to preserve the relationship, Duck has suggested the following repair tactics:

- Engage in more open and honest communication, and exhibit a willingness to listen to the other person with an open mind.
- Be willing to bring out the other person's positive side.
- Evaluate the potential rewards and costs for keeping the relationship together versus the rewards and costs for changing or ending it.
- Seek out the support of others to help keep the relationship together.
- Both parties must be willing to focus on the positive aspects of their relationship.

- Both parties must be willing to reinterpret the other's behaviors as positive and well intentioned.

- Both parties have to be willing to reduce negativity and try to keep a balanced perspective.[40]

Repairing relationships requires cooperation and mutual agreement; both parties must want to keep the relationship together in order to solve their differences. It also requires effective interpersonal communication.

Improving Communication in Relationships

The goal of this book is to encourage readers to become competent communicators. By this point you probably agree that effective communicators share these characteristics:

1. Effective communicators address issues clearly and try to avoid ambiguous or abstract statements.

2. Effective communicators are likely to treat others with respect and, thus, would not deliberately yell abuses or throw temper tantrums.

3. Effective communicators know that the use of praise, making the other person feel special, and telling them what they want to hear will most likely produce desired responses.[41]

At first glance, these statements make a lot of sense. However, probably each of us can think of times when being a little abstract or ambiguous was better than being too clear or direct in our communication. In certain situations, getting angry or throwing a tantrum may be appropriate in order to get across a point. It sometimes boils down to the difference between being honest and being brutally frank—being brutal never facilitates communication. Finally, you can probably also think of situations in which too much praise or too much agreement can lead to mistrust. Interpersonal situations may require a variety of communication strategies, some of which may violate expected norms. Although we are not endorsing unethical behaviors, disrespect, or rudeness, some situations demand unusual strategies.

The following section offers a variety of behaviors and actions that can improve interpersonal communication.

Establish Supporting and Caring Relationships

Establishing supportive and caring relationships is important to our well-being, and this process is generally easier when communication is both positive and supportive.[42] In other words, as the old cliché goes, "If you can't say something nice, don't say anything at all." One research study discusses romantic actions and verbal and nonverbal assurances that may affect commitment and satisfaction in relationships.[43] Positive strategies for romantic exchanges include the following:

1. Act cheerful and positive when talking to the other.
2. Do favors for the other, or help with tasks.

3. Initiate celebrations of special events from your shared past, such as the first time you met.

4. Do things to surprise the other.

5. Suggest that you go out to eat together at a favorite or special restaurant.

6. Create a romantic environment, perhaps with candlelight and flowers.

7. Give the other items of sentimental value, such as gifts or cards.

8. Suggest ways to spend time doing things together.

Assurances include the following verbal and nonverbal actions:

1. Physically display affection through kisses and hugs.

2. Express aloud to the other what it would be like without him or her.

3. Reminisce aloud with the other about good times you have had together in the past.

4. Say "I love you."

5. Express long-term commitment to the relationship.

6. Act in playful ways toward the other.

The research findings suggest that engaging in behaviors such as these do increase relationship commitment and satisfaction. However, it is interesting that females were more likely than males to report use of assurance and romance strategies, which suggests that females tend to undertake more relationship maintenance activity than their male partners.

Nurture a Supportive Environment

Positive and supportive communication occurs in environments that are caring, open, flexible, warm, animated, and receptive. In such environments communication is constructive and centers on the individuals and their relationship. Here are some descriptions of how people feel when constructive communication is at the center of their relationship.[44]

I feel that I can talk and that there is someone who will listen to me.

I feel accepted and supported.

I feel there is a willingness to see my point of view.

I don't feel a need or pressure to change—I am accepted for who I am.

I don't feel that I am constantly being judged or evaluated.

I feel that I am trusted.

I feel that I am treated with respect as a person.

I feel that I am treated fairly.

I feel good about myself and about us.

I feel like a responsible person.

I feel that I have control over myself.

I feel that someone is interested in me and cares about me.

I don't feel as if I have to justify everything that I do.

One of the most effective and constructive means of demonstrating care and support for someone is to invite more communication.

Invite More Communication

Many of us listen to others express their feelings and then immediately express our own. This gives the impression that we do not even acknowledge the other person's existence, let alone what he or she has said. In contrast, skilled and caring communicators usually do not respond immediately with ideas, judgments, or feelings that express their own views. Instead, they invite others to express more of their thoughts by responding with noncommittal responses such as these:

Interesting.

Uh-huh.

You did, huh.

I see.

Oh.

Really?

Or they may be more direct in asking the other person to continue, saying, for example

That's interesting. Go on.

Tell me about it.

Let's discuss it.

Tell me everything.

I understand. What else happened?

Such invitations to talk can contribute much to the development of a meaningful relationship. The willingness to listen and reserve judgment creates a positive and supportive environment that, in effect, tells people they are valuable, they are loved, and they have control over their own behavior.

Summary

In our everyday life, we are enormously influenced by first impressions and often tend to make snap judgments about people and form instant likes and dislikes. *Interpersonal attraction* is the desire to interact with someone based on a variety of factors, including physical attractiveness, personality, rewards, proximity, or similarities. Relationships, whether existing for a moment or for a lifetime, go through a series of stages of development and deterioration. Knapp's five stages of the coming-together phase are initiating, experimenting, intensifying, integrating, and bonding; the five stages of coming apart are differentiating, circumscribing, stagnating, avoiding, and terminating. All relationships move through at least some of these stages, but not all move through them in the same order or with the same intensity. Superficial relationships advance through only the first one or two stages of development and terminate without going through the entire coming-apart series. There are three reasons for the complex and continuous process of coming together and coming apart: each stage provides information for the next, each stage helps predict what may or may not occur in the next stage, and skipping a stage may create risk and uncertainty in a relationship.

According to Duck, dissolving relationships go through a complex decision-making process that does not always follow a specific series of stages. Breakups often occur sporadically, inconsistently, and with uncertainty over a period of time, but in deciding what to do about a relationship, a person typically proceeds through the following four phases: intrapyschic, dyadic, social, and grave-dressing. In the intrapsychic phase, people begin to internally assess their dissatisfaction with a relationship. In the dyadic phase, the people in the relationship discuss the status of their relationship. During the social phase, the relationship difficulties become more public within the context of family, friends, co-workers, or other acquaintances. At the final phase, grave-dressing, each partner gives an account of why the relationship has ended. Each phase requires certain communication abilities referred to as social management.

Relationships are often messy and even the most stable seem to go through various pushes and pulls, which can create tensions between partners. *Dialectics* are the contradictory impluses that push and pull us in conflicting directions with others. There are three dialectical tensions commonly mentioned in the research: connection–autonomy, openness–closedness, and novelty–predictability.

Conflict seems inevitable in all relationships. *Conflict* is an expressed struggle between at least two interdependent parties who perceive incompatible goals, scarce resources, and interference from others in achieving their goals. Conflict can be destructive if it ends only by one party's winning and the other's losing. Its destructiveness also depends on how the participants view each other during and after the conflict. Interpersonal conflict can, however, be constructive and can be resolved through self-regulation, self-expression, negotiation, and reaffirmation of the relationship. The major causes of conflict are more far-reaching than simply incompatible goals. Conflict is also caused by social factors that include faulty attributions; faulty communication; a tendency to perceive our own views as objective and as reflecting reality; and personal traits, such as being highly competitive and winning at all costs—(the Type A personality).

Managing conflict is not easy, and, in fact, resolving conflicts requires the use of a variety of strategies, including withdrawing, accommodating, forcing, negotiating, and collaboration.

There are signs that show a relationship is in trouble. They include aggressive behavior, deception, and betrayal. To help repair and possibly save relationships requires cooperation, mutual agreement, and the use of repair strategies that use effective interpersonal communication. Effective communicators address their differences clearly, respect each other, and know how to use praise in their interactions.

In a positive and supportive environment, communication between individuals usually reflects caring, openness, flexibility, warmth, animation, and receptivity. The best way to develop and maintain relationships is to invite more communication.

DISCUSSION STARTERS

1. In your opinion, what elements play the strongest role in the development of relationships? Explain.
2. What did you agree with and disagree with in the explanation of the stages of relationship development?
3. Compare and contrast Knapp's coming-apart stages with Duck's dissolution stages.
4. Describe what it takes to have a lasting relationship.

5. What happens when a relationship begins to come apart?
6. In what ways can conflict be constructive? Destructive?
7. What advice would you give to someone who wanted to improve interpersonal communication?

NOTES

1. J. C. McCroskey and T. A. McCain, "The Measurement of Interpersonal Attraction," *Speech Monographs* 41 (1974): 261–66.
2. Research and Forecasts, Inc., *The Connecticut Mutual Life Report on American Values in the '80s: The Impact of Belief* (Hartford, Conn.: Connecticut Mutual Life Insurance, 1981); B. B. Crouse and A. Mehrabian, "Affiliation of Opposite-Sexed Strangers," *Journal of Research in Personality* 11 (1977): 38–47; and D. Byrne and V. Greedlinger, "Need for Affiliation as a Predictor of Classroom Friendships" (unpublished manuscript, State University of New York at Albany, 1989).
3. S. M. Andersen and A. Baum, "Transference in Interpersonal Relations: Influences and Affect Based on Significant Representations," *Journal of Personality* 62 (1994): 459–97.
4. M. A. Collins and L. A. Zebrowitz, "The Contributions of Appearance to Occupational Outcomes in Civilian and Military Settings," *Journal of Applied Social Psychology* 25 (1995): 129–63.
5. S. Sprecher and S. Duck, "Sweet Talk: The Importance of Perceived Communication for Romatic and Friendship Attraction Experienced During a Get-Acquainted Date," *Personality and Social Psychology Bulletin* 20 (1994): 391–400.
6. T. F. Cash and R. N. Kicullen, "The Aye of the Beholder: Susceptibility to Sexism and Beautyism in the Evaluation of Managerial Applicants," *Journal of Applied Social Psychology* 15 (1985): 591–605; V. S. Folkes, "Forming Relationships and the Matching Hypothesis," *Journal of Personality and Social Psychology* 8 (1982): 631–36; E. Hatfield and S. Sprecher, *Mirror, Mirror . . . The Importance of Looks in Everyday Life* (Albany, N.Y.: SUNY Press, 1986);

Collins and Zebrowitz; Sprecher and Duck; D. Plesser-Storr, "Self-Presentation by Men to Attractive and Unattractive Women: Tactics of Ingratiation, Blasting, and Basking" (Ph.D. diss., State University of New York at Albany, 1995); and A. Feingold, "Good-Looking People Are Not What We Think: An Integration of the Experimental Literature on Physical Attractiveness Stereotyping with the Literature on Correlates of Physical Attractiveness" (unpublished manuscript, Yale University, New Haven, Conn., 1990).
7. M. R. Cunningham, A. R. Roberts, C. H. Wu, A. P. Barbee, and P. B. Druen, " 'Their Ideas of Beauty Are, on the Whole, the Same as Ours': Consistency and Variability in the Cross-Cultural Perception of Female Attractiveness," *Journal of Personality and Social Psychology* 68 (1995): 261–79; and L. Banner, *American Beauty* (New York: Knopf, 1983).
8. W. M. Bernstein, B. O. Stephenson, M. L. Snyder, and R. A. Wicklund, "Causal Ambiguity and Heterosexual Affiliation," *Journal of Experimental Social Psychology* 19 (1983): 78–92; K. H. Price and S. G. Vandenberg, "Matching for Physical Attractiveness in Married Couples," *Personality and Social Psychology* 5 (1979): 398–400; and M. Lea, "Factors Underlying Friendship: An Analysis of Responses on the Acquaintance Description Form in Relation to Wright's Friendship Model," *Journal of Social and Personal Relationships* 6 (1989): 275–92.
9. K. Deaux and R. Hanna, "Courtship in the Personal Column: The Influence of Gender and Sexual Orientation," *Sex Roles* 11 (1984): 363–75.
10. H. R. Baize Jr. and J. E. Schroeder, "Personality and Mate Selection in Personal Ads: Evolutionary

Preferences in a Public Mate Selection Process," *Journal of Social Behavior and Personality* 10 (1995): 517–36.

11. L. Mealey, "Bulking Up: The Roles of Sex and Sexual Orientation on Attempts to Manipulate Physical Attractiveness," *Journal of Sex Research* 34 (1997): 223–28.

12. M. R. Parks and K. Floyd, "Making Friends in Cyberspace," *Journal of Communication* 45 (1996): 84.

13. Ibid.

14. Ibid., 85.

15. M. Knapp, *Social Intercourse: From Greeting to Good-Bye* (Boston: Allyn and Bacon, 1978), 3–28.

16. M. L. Knapp and A. L. Vangelisti, *Interpersonal Communication and Human Relationship,* 4th ed. (Boston: Allyn and Bacon, 2000), 38.

17. D. P. McWhirter and A. M. Mattison, *The Male Couple* (Englewood Cliffs, N.J.: Prentice-Hall, 1984).

18. Knapp and Vangelisti, 39–44.

19. Ibid., 40–45.

20. M. L. Knapp, R. P. Hart, G. W. Friedrich, and G. M. Shulman, "The Rhetoric of Goodbye: Verbal and Nonverbal Correlates of Human Leave-Taking," *Speech Monographs* 40 (1973): 182–98.

21. Knapp and Vangelisti, 58–62.

22. S. W. Duck, ed., *Personal Relationships 4: Dissolving Personal Relationships* (London: Academic Press, 1982); L. A. Baxter, "Accomplishing Relationship Disengagement," in *Understanding Personal Relationships: An Interdisciplinary Approach,* eds. S. W. Duck and D. Perlman (Beverly Hills, Calif.: Sage, 1985), 243–66; S. W. Duck, *Human Relationships: An Introduction to Social Psychology* (Beverly Hills, Calif.: Sage, 1986); and S. Duck, "A Topography of Relationships Disengagement and Dissolution," in *Personal Relationships,* ed. S. Duck (London: Academic Press, 1982), 1–30.

23. K. A. Sorenson, S. M. Russel, D. J. Harkness, and J. H. Harvey, "Account-Making, Confiding, and Coping with the Ending of a Close Relationship," *Journal of Social Behavior and Personality* 8 (1993): 73–86.

24. L. A. Baxter, "Trajectories of Relationships Disengagement," *Journal of Social and Personal Relationship* 1 (1984): 29–48; and L. A. Baxter, "Strategies for Ending Relationship: Two Studies," *Western Journal of Speech Communication* 46 (1982): 223–41.

25. L. A. Baxter and B. Montgomery, *Relation: Dialogues and Dialect* (New York: Guilford, 1996).

26 J. T. Wood, "Dilectical Theory," in *Making Connections: Readings in Relational Communication,* 2nd ed., eds. Kathleen M. Galvin and Pamela J. Cooper (Los Angeles, Calif.: Roxbury, 2000), 132–38; L. A. Baxter, "Dialectical Contradictions in Relationship Development," *Journal of Social and Personal Rela-*

tionships 7 (1990): 69–88; and L. A. Baxter, "Thinking Dialogically About Communication in Interpersonal Relationships," in *Structure in Human Communication,* ed. R. Conville (Westport, Conn.: Greenwood, 1994).

27. W. Wilmot and J. Hocker, *Interpersonal Conflict,* 6th ed. (New York: McGraw-Hill, 2001), 41.

28. W. Benoit and P. Benoit, "Everyday Argument Practice of Naïve Social Actors," in *Argument and Critical Practices,* ed. J. Wenzel (Annandale, Va.: Speech Communication Association, 1987).

29. D. Cahn and S. Lloyd, *Family Violence from a Communication Perspective* (Thousand Oaks, Calif.: Sage, 1996).

30. C. K. W. DeDreu and P. A. M. Van Lang, "Impact of Social Value Orientation on Negotiator Cognition and Behavior," *Personality and Social Psychology Bulletin* 21 (1995): 1178–88; and D. Tjosvold and C. DeDrue, "Managing Conflict in Dutch Organizations: A Test of the Relevance of Deutsch's Co-operation Theory," *Journal of Applied Social Psychology* 27 (1997): 2213–27.

31. R. A. Baron, "Attributions and Organizational Conflict," in *Attribution Theory: Applications to Achievement, Mental Health, and Interpersonal Conflict,* eds. S. Graha and V. Folkes (Hillsdale, N.J.: Erlbaum, 1990), 185–204; and R. Cropanzano, ed., *Justice in the Workplace* (Hillsdale, N.J.: Erlbaum, 1993), 79–103.

32. K. M. Galvin and B. J. Brommel, *Family Communication: Cohesion and Change,* 3rd ed. (Glenview, Ill: Scott, Foresman, 1991), 7; L. Bumpass, "Children and Marital Disruption: A Replication and Update," *Demography* 21 (1984): 71–82; and H. S. Friedman, J. S. Tucker, J. E. Schwartz, L. R. Martin, C. Tomlison-Kesey, D. L. Wingard, and M. H. Criqui, "Childhood Conscientiousness and Longevity: Health Behavior and Cause of Death," *Journal of Personality and Social Psychology* 68 (1995): 696–703.

33. W. W. Wilmot, *Dyadic Communication,* 3rd ed. (New York: Random House, 1987), 230; and Wilmot and Hocker (1998), 236.

34. W. Wilmot and J. Hocker (2001), 94, 173–176.

35. A. C. Filley, *Interpersonal Conflict Resolution* (Glenview, Il.: Scott, Foresman, 1975); D. D. Cahn, "Intimate in Conflict: A Research Review," in *Intimates in Conflict: A Communication Perspective,* ed. D. D. Cahn (Hillsdale, N.J.: Erlbaum, 1990), 1–24; W. W. Cupach and D. J. Canary, *Competence in Interpersonal Conflict* (New York: McGraw-Hill, 1997); and R. Blake and J. Mouton, *The Managerial Grid* (Houston: Gulf Publishing, 1964).

36. A. L. Sillars, S. G. Coletti, D. Parry, and M. A. Rogers, "Coding Verbal Conflict Tactics: Nonverbal

and Perceptual Correlates of the 'Avoidance–Distributive–Integrative' Distinction," *Human Communication Research* 9 (1982): 83–95.

37. J. Gottman and S. Carrere, "Why Can't Men and Women Get Along? Developmental Notes and Marital Inequities," in *Communication Relational Maintenance,* eds. D. Canary and L. Stafford (New York: Academic Press, 1994).

38. J. Gottman, *Why Marriages Succeed and Fail: And How You Can Make Yours Last* (New York: Simon and Schuster, 1994); and J. Gottman, *The Marriage Clinic: A Scientifically Based Marital Therapy* (New York: Norton, 1999).

39. W. Wilmot and J. Hocker (2001), 237.

40. S. W. Duck, "A Perspective on the Repair of Personal Relationships: Repair of What, When?" in *Personal Relationships 5: Repairing Personal Relationships,* ed. S. W. Duck (New York: Macmillan, 1984).

41. Knapp and Vangelisti, (2000), 400.

42. J. M. Reisman, "Friendliness and Its Correlates," *Journal of Social and Clinical Psychology* 2 (1984): 143–55.

43. E. P. Simon and L. A. Baxter, "Attachment-Style Differences in Relationship Maintenance Strategies," *Western Journal of Communication* 57 (fall 1993): 416–30.

44. Ideas for this section are derived from a Parent Effectiveness Training workshop and from T. Gordon, *Parent Effectiveness Training* (New York: Wyden, 1970).

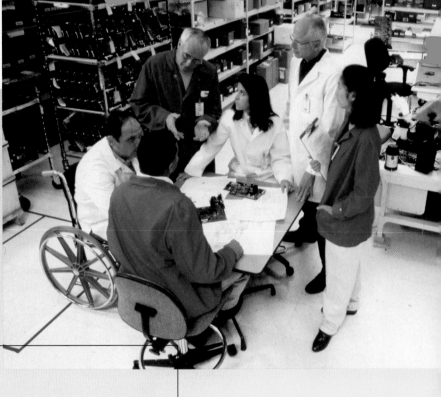

Group
and Team
Communication

"No matter how good technology is, it goes to waste if the technicians don't understand how people meet."

—Eric Richert, Vice President,
Workplace Operations and Research,
Sun Microsystems, Inc., Palo Alto,
California

- Define what a group is and how group communication is associated with the types of communication discussed in previous chapters, and explain why people join groups.

- Distinguish between the social and task-related purposes of small group communication.

- Explain the role of special types of groups, for example, project team, work team, and focus group.

- Identify the characteristics that distinguish small group communication from other forms of communication.

- Understand the disadvantages and limitations of group communication.

- Discuss the effects of gender on group communication.

- Tell what role ethical behavior has in small group communication.

- Explain how technology influences groups and group communication.

SCENARIO

The assignment is over and group X has accomplished its goal. Each member is satisfied not only with his or her work but also with the group as a whole. The meetings ran smoothly, and little, if any, time was wasted. Group Y also attained the same goal, but no one seems satisfied either with what was achieved or with the group itself. In fact, group Y's members feel that their working together as a group was a complete waste of time. How is it possible that two groups could perform the same task and yet produce such different results? ■

The answer to this question lies in the fact that many variables contribute to a group's success or failure. No two groups will produce identical results, because no two groups are identical in makeup. Furthermore, prior success cannot guarantee that a group will produce similar results in every situation. Nonetheless, understanding some key factors can increase a group's chances of achieving success.

This chapter discusses how group members communicate, defines a small group, presents the different purposes groups can serve, explores the characteristics common to all small groups, considers disadvantages of groups, explains gender differences in group communication, illustrates the importance of ethical behavior in groups, and examines how technologies influence group communication. The next chapter explores crucial aspects of small group communication: leadership, member participation, group problem-solving and decision-making methods, conflict management, and group performance evaluation.

Small Group Communication: Making the Connection

Communication is one of the major factors that influences whether a group experience is successful and satisfying. Many, if not all, of the communication principles and skills we have discussed in the previous chapters affect a group's success. For example, constructive group communication requires that its members respect one another, speak clearly, provide credible information, support others, foster a positive climate, listen effectively, and hold high ethical standards.

If each of us listed all the times we participated in group discussions during the past month, we would have evidence of how common small group activities and meetings are in our lives. The family is probably the predominant small group, but we also participate in work, professional, and social groups such as an agronomy club, a geology club, a theater club, the Association for Computing Machinery, the African People's Union, the Native American Student Congress, the Young Democrats, the College Republicans, or the Feminist Action Alliance. When we associate with other people and talk about common issues or problems, we are involved in a group.

Small group communication involves the exchange of information among a relatively small number of people, ideally five to seven, who share a common purpose, such as doing a job, solving a problem, making a decision, or sharing information. Our primary focus in this chapter and the next is small groups, so we will not include much information about large public discussion group presentations, symposiums, panels, or the comprehensive study of group dynamics.   *Have been discussed in Part II*

Group communication is so common in business, industry, and government that the average member of middle and higher management in all professions spends one-fourth to one-third of each working day in such interactions, either in person or via some form of technology. It is not surprising, therefore, that the ability to communicate effectively in small groups is essential to success in virtually every career field.

As you will soon discover, groups influence us in many ways, and the more we understand about them, the better prepared we will be to work in groups successfully.

Making Connections

Communicating in Small Groups

The brief scenario at the beginning of the chapter describes two groups—group X and group Y—and the members' level of satisfaction with their respective groups.

1. What can a group do to ensure group member satisfaction?
2. How does a group differ from a team?
3. What did you learn from the scenario about group communication?

What Is a Group?

A group is not simply a collection of people gathered in the same place. To qualify as a group, the people must be related in six ways:

1. *Perceptions:* Do the members make an impression on one another?
2. *Motivation:* Are there rewards for being together?
3. *Goals:* Do the persons have a common purpose?
4. *Organization:* Does each person have some role or task?
5. *Interdependence:* Must each person depend on the others for his or her efforts to be successful?
6. *Interaction:* Is the number of persons small enough so that each person can communicate with every other person?[1]

For our purposes, we define a **group** as a collection of individuals who influence one another, have a common purpose, take on roles, are interdependent, and interact together. If any element is not included, what exists is a collection of independent people, not a group. People standing at a corner waiting for a bus, for example, meet some of the criteria of a group. They have a common purpose (transportation), they may interact, and they may make an impression on one another. But they do not constitute a group according to our definition, because they are not interdependent and they do not take on roles. They do share certain basic goals, such as getting to a destination safely. But they don't expect to interact in the future and usually don't perceive themselves as part of a group—unless some type of emergency occurred, which would change their status radically. Deciding whether a collection of persons constitutes a true group is a complex matter.

John Brilhardt, a small group communication scholar, defines "groupness"—the necessary property that groups possess but that collections of individuals do not—as follows:

> "Groupness" emerges from the relationship among the people involved, just as "cubeness" emerges from the image of a set of planes, intersects, and angles in specific relationships to each other. One can draw a cube with twelve lines, but only if they are assembled in a definite way. Any other arrangement of the lines gives something other than a cube. Likewise, one can have a collection or set of people without having a group.[2]

A group exists as something apart from the individuals who belong to it. Just as twelve lines, when put in the proper relationship, form a cube, several individuals, when they develop particular relationships, form a group. And just as the individual

The crew team is a specialized group characterized by close-knit, interdependent relationships and made up of people with different complementary abilities and a strong sense of group identity.

identities of the lines recede to form a cube, the individual identities of group members take a back seat when "groupness" is developed.

Group Formation: Why Do People Join Groups?

Take a moment to think about all the groups to which you belong: student organizations, clubs, religious groups, social groups, work groups, informal groups of friends. Why did you join them in the first place? It doesn't take a scholar to tell you that people join groups for many reasons, and your reasons are probably similar to those that motivate others to join groups. Paul Paulus, a social psychologist, suggests that at least five common reasons explain why people join groups:

5 reasons explain why people join groups

1. Groups help satisfy important psychological and social needs, such as the need for attention and affection or the need to belong. Imagine what it would be like to be absolutely alone, in total isolation from others. Very few of us find such a prospect appealing.

2. Group membership helps people achieve goals that otherwise might not be accomplished. Groups make it easier to perform certain tasks, solve difficult problems, and make complex decisions that might overwhelm one individual.

3. Group membership can provide multiple sources of information and knowledge that might not be available to one individual.

4. Groups can help meet the need for security. The old saying that there is safety in numbers rings true in many situations; belonging to groups can provide protection and security against common enemies. For example, people join neighborhood watch groups to protect themselves from criminal activity.

5. Group membership can also contribute to an individual's positive social identity—it becomes part of a person's self-concept (see Chapter 3). Of course, the more prestigious and restrictive the groups are to which a person is admitted, the more the self-concept is bolstered.[3]

Cultural factors, such as individualistic or collective orientations, can have a profound effect on how people perceive groups and group activities. All cultures vary in the degree to which they emphasize individualism and collectivism. If you hold an **individualistic orientation,** you tend to stress self or personal goals and achievements over group goals and achievements.[4] Individualist cultures have an "I" consciousness and a tendency to focus on individual accomplishments.[5] That is, they are more likely to depend on themselves and have less commitment to group membership. For example, most North Americans value self-help, self-sufficiency, self-actualization, and personal achievements. The United States, Canada, Australia, and New Zealand are nations that tend to foster and celebrate individual accomplishments. Generally, people who have individualistic perspectives find working in groups more challenging and often frustrating.

If you hold a **collectivistic orientation,** which is more predominant in Eastern and Latin American countries such as Japan, China, Taiwan, Guatemala, and Panama, you are more likely to put aside your individual goals for the well-being of the group.[6] Collectivist cultures have a "we" consciousness and a tendency to focus on group or team accomplishments. They also have a propensity toward working in

TABLE 15.1	
Individualist and Collectivist Orientations: A Comparison of Small Groups	

INDIVIDUALIST ASSUMPTIONS	COLLECTIVISTIC ASSUMPTIONS
Individuals make better decisions than groups do.	The group's decision should supersede individual decisions.
Leaders and not the group members should do the planning.	The group should do the planning.
Individuals should be rewarded for their performance.	Reward and recognition should be shared among group members.
Competition among individual group members is good.	Teamwork is more important than competition.
The best way to get things done is to work with individuals as opposed to an entire group.	The group is the best way to accomplish goals.
Groups or teams are often perceived as a waste of time.	The commitment to the group is is strongest when the group reaches consensus.

Adapted from S. A. Beebe and J. M. Masterson, *Communicating in Small Groups,* 6th ed. (New York: Longman, 2000), 20; and J. Mole, *Mind Your Manner: Managing Business Cultures in Europe* (London: Nicholas Brealey Publishing Limited, 1995).

groups and find group work to be very rewarding and satisfying. No culture, however, is entirely individualist or collectivist. All cultures comprise a mix of individualism and collectivism, but usually one or the other dominates.[7]

How you contribute to a group may depend on whether you have an individualistic or collectivistic orientation. These two perspectives have implications for group formation and collaboration. See Table 15.1 for a comparison between individualistic and collectivistic approaches to joining and working in groups or teams.

Another force that brings people together to form groups is a *common goal.* Examples of common goals may include protesting a change in dormitory visitation rules, fighting a road expansion into a neighborhood, lobbying for a safer community, supporting a charity, or working for equal campus access for physically impaired students. The goal itself draws people into a group, even though their approaches to the goal may differ.

People, however, also avoid joining groups at times. Groups are sometimes perceived as ineffective and time-consuming; they require much work yet accomplish little. The most frequent complaint from students regarding groups is that groups are a waste of time. It is our hope that this chapter and the next will reduce the effect of negative experiences you may have encountered in the past and encourage you to participate actively in future group situations.

Purposes of Small Group Communication

Small groups may perform many tasks and solve many problems, but the purposes they serve can be grouped into two general categories: social purposes and task-related purposes.[8]

Social Purposes

Social reasons for participating in groups fall into four main categories: socialization, catharsis, therapy, and learning.

Socialization.   We often engage in small group communication when socializing with others, such as at parties or at any event where people share time and conversation. When we gather in small groups for social purposes, our goals are to strengthen our interpersonal relationships and to promote our own well-being. Such groups fulfill our interpersonal needs for inclusion and affection.

Catharsis.   Small group communication allows us to vent our emotions, including frustrations, fears, and gripes, as well as hopes and desires. When we have a chance to let others know how we feel about something, we often experience catharsis, or a release from tension. This purpose is usually accomplished in the supportive atmosphere of bull sessions or family discussions, where self-disclosure is appropriate. Cathartic group communication tends to focus on personal problems rather than on interpersonal needs.

self- help group

Therapy.   Therapeutic group sessions primarily help people alter their attitudes, feelings, or behaviors about some aspect of their personal life. For example, a therapeutic group might include people who have drinking, drug, or other problems, such as coping with the loss of a loved one. Usually, the therapeutic group is led by a professional trained in group psychotherapy or counseling.

e.g. news group

Learning and Information Sharing.   The most common reason people join small groups is to share information and to learn from one another. The sharing of information occurs in all kinds of group settings, but the most familiar ones are corporations, schools, churches, families, and service or social clubs. The underlying purpose of learning or information-sharing groups is to educate, inform, or improve understanding related to specific issues or areas of concern.

Task-Related Purposes

Small group communication is frequently used to accomplish two general tasks: decision making and problem solving.

Decision Making.   People come together in groups to make decisions on issues such as deciding which spring vacation trip to take, where to hold a dance, which play to stage, or which computer is the most practical for their needs. Discussing alternatives with others helps people decide which choice is the best not only for themselves but for the group as a whole. In addition, when everyone in the group participates in the decision-making process, all are more likely to accept the final outcome and to help carry it out. Most of us resent being told what to do, but we are more tolerant of a decision if we helped shape it.

A classic research study demonstrated the value of group decision making. The study focused on a garment factory where managers had always made decisions without seeking input from their workers. The managers decided to update some of their production techniques, but the workers were resisting the changes.

To analyze the problem, an experiment was set up in which workers were divided into groups using three different procedures: (1) a no-participation procedure, which reflected the way things had always been done—employees had no voice in planning and change; (2) a participation-through-representation procedure, in which a few employees were involved in the decision-making process; and (3) a total-participation procedure, in which all the employees were involved. In each case, whether the workers contributed or not, the final decision belonged to management. The results revealed that

1. The no-participation group continued to resist changes.
2. Both the participation groups relearned their jobs significantly faster and surpassed the previous average production levels much sooner.
3. The total-participation group performed slightly better than the participation-through-representation group.[9]

What conclusion can you draw from these results regarding decision making in groups?

Problem Solving.   Small groups can also excel at solving problems. People form problem-solving groups in almost every imaginable context—in the workplace, in government, in school, and at home. The problems they attempt to solve include how to improve health care, how to make a better product, how to perform a task more effectively or efficiently, how to stop violence, how to resolve the parking problem on campus, and how to improve a faltering relationship.

As you can see, groups can serve a variety of purposes and often will serve multiple purposes at the same time. For example, a group can solve problems while at the same time serving as a learning, social, cathartic, or therapeutic outlet for its members. It was customary in the early and middle years of the twentieth century for most people to work relatively independently of one another. Even in large organizations, people had individual responsibilities and coordinated with others only when it was necessary to do so. Recently, the value of having people work in groups has been recognized, and a group approach has been implemented in many settings, including the workplace and the classroom. This trend has taken hold not only in the United States, but also throughout the world. Just think of the many types of groups we hear about in our personal lives and in the news: cooperative learning groups, project or work teams, personal growth groups, committees, quality control groups, activity groups, and so on. Because they are so common in our society and in the classroom, we have chosen to discuss in particular the groups known as project or work teams.

Project or Work Teams

Many scholars who study groups believe there is a distinction between group involvement and team involvement.[10] A **team** is a special form of group, characterized by close-knit relationships among people with different and complementary abilities and by a strong sense of identity. Similar to groups, teams involve interaction, interdependence, common goals, personality, commitment, cohesiveness, and rules. Teams do differ, however, from groups in three ways:

Teams often consist of people with diverse abilities. The team members usually develop interdependence and have a high degree of group identity.

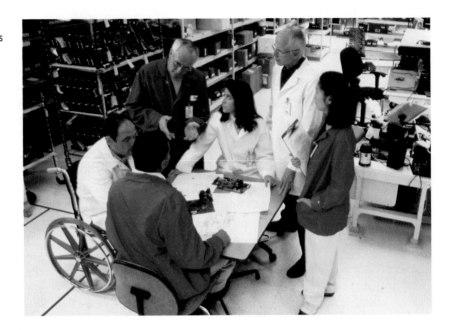

Group

Task

↑ ↑

Individual individual
   A   B

Team

Task

individual   individual B
   A   specializes
specializes   in another area.
in an area

1. Teams are more likely to consist of people with diverse abilities. For example, a surgical team performing an operation might include several surgeons, an anesthetist, and several nurses, each contributing a different skill or perspective to the task at hand. A group consists of several people, each contributing to the common goal of the group, whereas a team consists of people who have a specialization in and different perspectives on a common situation.

2. Teams usually develop more interdependence. A sports team, for example, usually cannot succeed unless all the players believe they are part of a unit.

3. Members of teams have a high degree of group identity and are more likely to identify themselves as team members than as individuals who happen to be on a team.[11]

Thus all teams consist of groups, but not all groups are teams.

Project or work teams have existed for years in almost every type of organization. Typically, project or work teams consist of a variety of individuals who get together to solve problems or make decisions. In a **project team,** these individuals are usually specialists assigned to coordinate the successful completion of an assigned task (such as finding adequate and accessible parking for all who need it). Project teams in general work quickly to determine what needs to be done, and then they do it. They also often possess little history, usually work under a deadline, and may have difficulty establishing mutually agreed-on relationships.

A **work team** is a group of people responsible for an entire work process or segment of the process that delivers a product or service to an internal or external customer. For example, a university department would be considered a work team. Their goal is to deliver instruction to students as effectively and efficiently as possible. Usually university departments have a history, they entail mutually agreed-on relationships, and the members work as a group to serve its own and the university's missions. Work teams often are subdivisions of a larger organization and can exist for

Making Connections

The Real World, the Group Meeting, and Microsoft

An article by James Fallows in *The Atlantic Monthly* (February 2000, pp. 34–38) discusses the Microsoft corporate culture and the importance of face-to-face communication. The article can be read online at http://www.theatlantic.com/issues/2000/02/002fallows.htm.

1. Briefly summarize the message of the article and determine what the author is saying about groups and their use at Microsoft? Discuss the issues in class if time permits.

2. What impressions did you get from the author as to how technology was used by groups and in day-to-day interaction in the Microsoft culture? Did this surprise you as much as it did the author? Why or why not?

3. Explain why groups and meetings are important to business organizations based on what the author describes from his Microsoft experience.

4. What are the advantages to groups as they are used at Microsoft?

an indefinite period of time or until a specific project is completed. Work teams also serve many purposes including solving problems, making decisions, socializing, and learning.

The **focus group,** a special form of work team, tries to find out what people think about specific ideas, issues, or people. A focus group usually consists of a manageable number of participants and a facilitator or leader. The facilitator runs the meeting, typically using a prepared list of questions and probes to encourage participants to contribute their ideas, beliefs, feelings, and perceptions related to the assigned topic.[12] The facilitator does not offer personal opinions or judgments, but guides group members as they express themselves. The information gathered in the focus group sessions is analyzed and then used in decision making.

Following are sample questions that might be asked of a focus group: What do college students think of binge drinking? How do nontraditional students feel about returning to the classroom? Is the government responding to the needs of Native Americans? Do the voters representing various ethnic groups in Senator Jones's district consider her trustworthy? Which of these two debaters articulated the best solution for the community's crime problem? Focus groups have been used by advertising agencies to determine which ads might appeal to certain markets and by political campaign planners to determine what issues are important for candidates to address in speeches.

Characteristics of Small Groups

Small groups have a number of characteristics in common, including interdependence, commitment, cohesiveness, group size, norms, and group culture, that make each group unique. These characteristics also determine who will join the group, how well the group will function and achieve its goals, and how the members will interact.

Making Connections

Lessons from Geese

Each of the following facts about geese contains a lesson about working in groups. Read each fact and note what its particular lesson might be. The first one has been completed for you.

Fact 1: As each goose flaps its wings, it creates an "uplift" for the birds that follow. By flying in a **V** formation, the whole flock adds 71 percent greater flying range than could be achieved if each bird flew alone.

Lesson: People who share a common direction and a sense of the group's goal can usually accomplish it more quickly and easily. Mutual support makes everyone more efficient.

Fact 2: When a goose falls out of formation, it suddenly feels the drag and resistance of flying alone. It quickly moves back into formation to take advantage of the lifting power of the bird immediately in front of it.

Lesson: _____

_____

Fact 3: When the goose tires, it rotates back into formation, and another goose flies to the front position.

Lesson: _____

_____

Fact 4: The geese flying in formation honk to encourage those up front to keep up their speed.

Lesson: _____

_____

Fact 5: When a goose gets sick or wounded or is shot down, two geese drop out of the formation and follow it down to help and protect it. They stay with it until it dies or is able to fly again. Then they launch out with another formation or catch up with the flock.

Lesson: _____

_____

The "Lessons from Geese" facts were obtained at a religious retreat. The source was listed as Anonymous.

Interdependence

Probably the most essential characteristic of a small group is **interdependence**—the fact that group members are mutually dependent. Interdependence is reflected in all the other group characteristics, for without it there would be no group. Interdependence is built on each member's willingness to subordinate his or her individual desires and goals in order to accomplish the group's goal.

Groups function best and are most satisfying for their members when each individual recognizes and respects the crucial role that interdependence plays in group processes. A group's success is indeed based on each member's cooperation and willingness to work toward a common goal.

Commitment

Another important characteristic of a group is commitment—to the task, to the group, and to the other individuals in the group. **Commitment** is the desire of group members to work together to complete their task to the satisfaction of the entire group. Members' commitment stems from interpersonal attraction; commonalty of attitudes, beliefs, and values; the fulfillment of interpersonal needs; and the rewards that the group can offer.

Commitment is important to a group's effectiveness and ultimate success. For example, how often have you been in a group in which one or two members did the work and the others did little or nothing? Those who do little or nothing lack commitment and ultimately affect the group's cohesiveness and effectiveness. Working to accomplish a difficult task even when other group members slack off reflects commitment. For a group to be truly effective, all of its members must be committed to the group, its members, and the successful completion of its task. Commitment shows that the member's desire to remain in the group is greater than the desire to leave it.

Cohesiveness

As an extension of commitment, **cohesiveness** refers to the attraction that group members feel for one another and their willingness to stick together. Consider two groups. In the first, members like one another very much, strongly desire the goals the group is seeking, and believe that they could not find another group that would better satisfy their needs. In the second, the opposite is true: Members don't care for one another, they do not share common goals, and they are actively seeking other groups to join that might offer them more rewards. Which group would exert a stronger pull on its members? The answer should be obvious—the first. The rewards for being in the first group outweigh those of leaving the group. Cohesiveness is based on each member's need to remain in the group and the group's ability to provide members with rewards, making it worthwhile to give time and energy to the group. In a sense, cohesiveness is a form of loyalty or commitment.

When Too Much Cohesiveness Is a Dangerous Thing.   Sometimes, however, individuals stick with or remain loyal to a group even when it is not in their best interest to do so. Groups can become too cohesive or committed, resulting in **groupthink**—a dysfunction in which group members see the harmony of the group as being more important than considering new ideas, critically examining their own assumptions, changing their own flawed decisions, or allowing new members to participate.[13] The following situation illustrates groupthink. Students are asked to choose one of three solutions to a certain social problem. One group is formed for each solution. Each group is asked to defend its solution and to persuade the instructor that its solution is the best. As an incentive for preparing a sound argument, students are told that the instructor will accept only one group solution as the best.

As the groups begin to organize, their members make a modest effort to pull together. Each group selects a representative to present its argument. After hearing each representative, the instructor announces that he or she is undecided as to which group offered the best solution. Therefore, all groups have one more chance to develop their arguments. The instructor also announces that students who did not like their group's solution are welcome to join another group. No one switches groups, even though some are tempted to after hearing presentations by other group representatives.

To raise the stakes, the instructor states that the groups with the second- and third-best solutions will be assigned a research project over the weekend, whereas the winning group will be exempt from this assignment. In response, the intensity within each group builds. Members pull their chairs closer together and talk more forcibly about their solution. They support one another's views more openly. The common objective has become clear and compelling—the students are motivated to persuade their instructor in order to avoid the research project. Oddly enough, this particular type of motivation can be hazardous. Groupthink is more likely to occur when a group's cohesiveness and commitment are too high and when the group is under pressure to achieve consensus at the expense of doing the best possible work. Once this collective state of mind develops, it seems that groups become unwilling and perhaps unable to change a decision, even if they realize that it is a poor one.

Research on groupthink indicates that it is a real and pervasive phenomenon that can explain some of the disastrous decisions made by groups.[14] One such outcome of groupthink occurred when a group of IBM executives in 1980 refused to consider the purchase of Microsoft's operating system from Bill Gates. The executives' decision resulted in a loss of revenues worth billions of dollars and, eventually, the emergence of a gargantuan competitor in the computer industry. In this case, the IBM executives were unwilling to consider new information. They simply thought the Microsoft operating system wouldn't work. Not one member of the executive committee was willing to go against the thinking of the group as a whole. We all now know that Bill Gates, the chairman of Microsoft, is one of the richest people in the world.

According to Irving Janis, a specialist in organizational behavior, eight symptoms lead to groupthink. They fall into three categories:

1. Overestimation of the group's power and morality

   An illusion that the group is invulnerable, which creates excessive optimism and encourages taking extreme risks

   A belief that the group will not be judged based on the ethical or moral consequences of its decisions

2. Closed-mindedness

   A tendency to rationalize or discount negative information that might lead members to reconsider their assumptions before making a decision

   Stereotypical views of other groups as too weak and stupid to warrant genuine attempts to negotiate differences

3. Pressures toward uniformity

   Individual self-censorship of differences that deviate from the group (That is, members are inclined to minimize their uniqueness and doubt the importance of their individual contributions.)

   A shared illusion of unanimity that pushes members to conform to the majority view as a result of self-censorship and the assumption that silence means consent

Pressure on group members who express arguments that differ from the majority to conform by making it clear that dissent is contrary to what is expected of all loyal members

The setting of "mindguards" against threatening information in order to protect the group members from adverse information that might shatter their shared complacency regarding their decisions[15]

Why Some Group Members Fail to Share Information with Other Members. One reason many key decisions are entrusted to groups is because it is expected that all members will share their unique information and ideas. It is further reasoned that groups will be open-minded to all ideas, even information and ideas that may be unpopular. If this belief is accepted, it is reasoned, the decisions that groups reach will be better than those that would be reached by individuals working alone. Is this actually the case? Do groups fully use the knowledge and expertise of their individual members? Research on this issue suggests that such pooling of resources may occur less often than common sense would predict.[16] What actually happens is that when groups discuss a given issue and try to reach a consensus about it, they tend to discuss information shared by most, if not all, members, rather than information that is known to only one or a few. The result is that decisions tend to reflect the shared information.[17] This is not a problem if the information that is shared leads to the best decision. But consider what happens when information that is held by a few is not shared. In this case the tendency is to discuss only the information the majority of the group knows and, thus, may prevent the group from reaching the best decision.

Why do the decisions reached by groups tend to favor majority views from the beginning? A couple of possibilities exist: (1) Decisions tend to reflect the views held by members prior to the discussion, that is members start with certain views, and these views are further strengthened during the discussion; (2) decisions are more likely to reflect the information exchanged during the discussion, and because the information exchanged is most likely the shared information, it is that information that shapes the group's decision. If the latter view is correct, then if members do bring to the surface unshared information, will the decisions be better? Several recent research studies offer support for this outcome.[18] The research found that the greater the tendency of groups to discuss information that is relevant to the decision and known to only some of the members, the more accurate the groups' final choices were. This was true even in such important contexts as medical diagnoses. Despite the potentially life-and-death nature of the decisions, teams of interns and medical students were found to pool more shared information than unshared information during group discussions. However, it was also discovered that the more they pooled unshared information (information known initially to only a few members), the more accurate the groups' diagnoses were.

What Can Be Done to Reduce Groupthink. Procedures can be used to minimize the possibility of groupthink. Here are some examples:

- Assign one group member to be a "devil's advocate" who intentionally questions and criticizes the group's actions.
- Set a guideline to prevent leaders from expressing their preferences first.
- Ensure that every group member has an opportunity to voice an opinion.
- Encourage individuals to express disagreement without being chastised by the group for doing so.[19]

punished severely.

*o One str. dealing with this is to
set the goal from the outset, &
remind members what
the goal is from time to time.*

TABLE 15.2	Group Size and Potential Interactions

NUMBER IN GROUP	POSSIBLE INTERACTIONS
2	2
3	9
4	28
5	75
6	186
7	411
8	1,056

Although cohesiveness is an important characteristic of every group, it should not lead to conformity or an unwillingness to change an unsuccessful decision or policy. Cohesiveness is a positive force when it attracts members of the group toward one another and increases effective group interaction, but it can become a negative influence if group members "go along simply to get along" or lose the ability to question group decisions.

Group Size

Group size relates to the number of participants involved in a given small group and has important ramifications for the group's effectiveness. Although there is no perfect number of members for a group, groups of certain sizes seem appropriate for certain kinds of tasks. For example, five-member groups are the most effective for dealing with intellectual tasks; coordinating, analyzing, and evaluating information; and making administrative decisions. Many small group experts recommend that groups have no fewer than three and no more than nine members. Others believe the ideal size is five to seven members.

A group that is too small may limit the information and ideas generated, whereas a group that is too large may limit the contribution that each person can make. As a group increases in size, the number of possible interactions increases dramatically (see Table 15.2). They include all the possible interactions between individual members and combinations of members. For example, in a three-person group, person A could interact with B and C separately or with B and C simultaneously. Both B and C have similar interaction possibilities, thus resulting in nine possible interactions.[20]

An important consideration in deciding on group size is that the larger the group is, the greater the variety of skills and information that will be possessed by its members. However, the advantages gained when a group has more than seven members seem to be outweighed by potential disadvantages. For example, in a certain sense ten opinions are superior to five, and twenty opinions are superior to ten. But having twice as many opinions can create twice as much potential for conflict and make consensus at least twice as difficult to reach.

In addition, some consideration should be given to the number of men and women in the group. As indicated earlier, stereotypical differences between men and women do exist in our society: Thus, when possible, it is best to form groups with an equal number of men and women or groups in which women form the majority. These two combinations tend to reduce stereotypical behavior and create a more balanced group perspective. When deciding on the most effective size for a group, remember the following points:

1. Large groups reduce the time and amount of individual interaction.

2. Large groups provide a greater opportunity for aggressive members to assert their dominance. As a result, less assertive members may feel isolated and may withdraw from the group altogether.

3. Large groups make it difficult to follow a set agenda. It is easy for someone in a large group to switch topics or introduce subjects that are not related to the group's original priorities.

Making Connections

Rules, Rules, Rules

You've been participating in small groups and have decided that in general they are a waste of your time because nothing ever seems to get accomplished, or when it does, it seems to take forever. People talk out of turn, interrupt each other, don't listen, come unprepared, and so on. Agreed-on rules can solve this problem.

1. Write a one-page paper explaining why rules are necessary to effective, efficient group interaction.
2. Develop a written list of rules for communicating in small groups, and discuss them with your classmates.

Norms

The expected and shared ways in which group members behave are called **norms.** Both informal and formal guidelines determine which behaviors are acceptable and which are not. In most group situations, the norms are informal and unwritten. In your communication class, for example, certain behaviors are expected of you. At a minimum, it is assumed that you will read your assignments, respect others' rights to speak, do your own work, and be on time for class. However, there may also be formal written rules, such as specific dates for the completion of assignments, attendance requirements, and guidelines for achieving specific grades.

For a group to function effectively, its members must agree on how things are to be done. Therefore, no matter what their size or task, groups establish norms. This is done for a variety of reasons, but the strongest one is that shared ways of behaving enable members to attain group goals and to satisfy interpersonal needs. Without guidelines for behavior, most groups would be ineffective and disorganized.

Norms also help give structure to a group. If members know what is expected of them, they are more likely to act accordingly and function more efficiently. Norms can be as simple as getting the task done or as involved as participating in complex rituals and ceremonies that must be respected if a member is to remain in the group.

In more formal situations, to increase efficiency and order, many groups use preestablished rules to guide their interaction. *Robert's Rules of Order* is the most widely used authority on conducting social, business, and government meetings. Such formal rules specify the roles of members, how meetings are to be conducted, and how topics for discussion are to be introduced, discussed, and accepted or rejected by the group's members. When it is important to maintain formal order, a group may appoint a parliamentarian to ensure that rules are correctly interpreted and followed.

Group Culture

Just like societies, organizations, and other large groups, small groups develop unique cultures. **Group culture,** according to John Brilhart and Gloria Galanes, two communication scholars, is "the pattern of values, beliefs, norms, and behaviors that are shared by group members and that shape a group's individual 'personality.' "[21] Group culture is created by many factors, including the interaction patterns of group members, the roles members are assigned, the purpose for the group, the mixture of people included in the group, members' behaviors, and norms and rules that the group follows.

The group's culture underlies all of its actions and behaviors. The culture of a group is not static—it is constantly changing and developing as it adapts to each new situation or event it confronts and to the needs of the group and its members. A group's culture is expressed in behaviors such as how its members organize it, who begins the interactions, how much interaction is allowed by any one member, who interacts with whom, how formally or informally people behave, how much or how little conflict is

Group culture is created by many factors, including the interaction patterns of the group's members, the roles members are assigned, the group's purpose, the mixture of people included in the group, members' behaviors, and norms and rules that the group follows.

allowed, how much or how little socializing takes place, how much or how little tolerance the group allows for ambiguity, and so on. These factors, as well as others, weave together to create each group's unique culture.

Disadvantages of Small Groups

Most of what we have said to this point about groups is positive, and it is true there are many advantages to groups over individuals working alone. But, there are also limitations related to groups that can ultimately lead to less effective and less satisfying outcomes.

The first disadvantage of groups is that the decision-making or problem-solving process can be time-consuming. It almost always takes longer to accomplish something when a group does it. The more members there are in a group, the more time it takes to accomplish the group's objectives. Individuals can almost always complete a task in a shorter amount of time than a group. For example, if you were to take a math problem-solving test, you'd probably read each problem silently to yourself, write notes to yourself on scratch paper, and then attempt to solve the problems. If you were in a group, you would first have to discuss each problem, decide how the problem should be solved, and then work out the solution to the problem. In other words, group work is different than individual work because there must be interaction between and among the members. How can you ensure that groups use their time wisely and effectively?

A second disadvantage is that in most groups it is not possible for all members to contribute equally. One reason for this is time, but also because each member has a different communication style and comfort level with the group, members contribute unequally. Some members may dominate and overwhelm conversations, whereas other members may not contribute at all. Also, the most verbally aggressive and dominant person in the group may not have the best ideas. In the next chapter, we discuss in more detail self-centered behaviors of group members and how to control those behaviors that hinder a group's effectiveness. What can be done to ensure that everyone has an equal opportunity to participate and contribute to the group?

A third disadvantage of groups is that members believe the workload is unfair in the group. The most frequent complaint we hear from students about working on group projects is that they believe that some group members do not do their fair share of the work. This is referred to as social loafing. **Social loafing** is the tendency for individuals to lower their work effort after they join a group.[22] For example, suppose that you and several people are helping a friend move. In order to lift the heaviest

Making Connections

Effective Groups

Several questions were implied or posed in the section on disadvantages of small groups. Write answers for them and discuss them in class.

1. How can you ensure that groups use their time wisely and effectively?
2. What can be done to ensure that everyone has an equal opportunity to participate and contribute to the group?
3. Are there other suggestions on how to deal with social loafers that are better than those suggested or that can be added to the list?
4. How can weak group members be kept from lowering the group's productivity?
5. Describe the behaviors of a successful group.

pieces, you all pitch in. Will all the people helping exert equal effort? Probably not. Some will lift as much as they can, whereas others will simply hang on, perhaps even grunting loudly in order to seem as if they are helping more than they are. Social loafers can also be irresponsible by not showing up on time or not showing up at all, because they believe others will do the work for them. Motivation seems to be the central reason for social loafing. Although there is no magical list of procedures or behaviors that will reduce social loafing, here are few suggestions: Make outputs individually identifiable, increase commitment to the task and the sense of task importance, make sure that each person's contribution is unique—not identical—to those of others, and build group cohesiveness. If these suggestions do not work, and if it is possible or reasonable, eliminate noncontributors from the group.

A fourth disadvantage is that sometimes groups may not meet their potential, because the majority of group members place pressure on the most capable members not to excel. The implication is that the weaker group members control the outcome and, therefore, require others who may want to excel to do only the minimum necessary to get the job done and no more. In fact, those members who do not cooperate and do excel beyond other group members may find themselves teased, chastised, or worse for breaking the group's norm. This phenomenon occurs when groups decide to meet the minimum expectations; it is very similar to groupthink. How can this type of situation be avoided?

Finally, people who have had only negative experiences with groups or those who do not have the communication skills to be effective in groups dislike group work. This dislike for groups has been termed the **grouphate phenomenon.**[23] For some people, group work is so distasteful that they avoid group situations whenever possible. In our experience, those who hate participating in groups the most are those who have little or no skill or lack training in how to communicate in groups. What can people do to eliminate or reduce their dislike of groups?

People who are not skilled communicators usually find group work overwhelming and unsatisfactory, because they don't know how to use communication to benefit them in solving problems, resolving conflicts, or expressing themselves.

Gender Differences in Group Communication

The differences between the way men and women communicate in groups are not clear, and the results of research are not always accurate or fair to one gender or the other. We could probably agree that most men are physically stronger than most women, but some women are stronger than some men. To say that men on average are physically stronger than women is a reasonable statement. But to say that all men are stronger than all women is not accurate, and it is not fair. Much of the research examining women and men is done by comparing averages. Thus, specific individual behaviors are usually not accounted for, leaving only averages for our consideration.

Research shows that groups consisting of both men and women are more likely to be dominated by men talking than by women talking. Men tend to demonstrate more task-related behavior than do women—that is, men tend to be more goal oriented than women and can be more impatient about moving on to the next issue or problem. Women tend to offer positive responses to others' comments, and in general, tend to express their subjective opinions more readily than men. However, men tend to be more objective in their comments than women.[24]

Because of stereotypical beliefs that exist in U.S. culture, women are sometimes perceived to be less competent than men in solving problems or making decisions. However, little, if any, difference has been found by researchers between men and women in their problem-solving abilities. The research does suggest that men appear to be better at certain kinds of problem-solving tasks than women, but that difference is reduced or eliminated when men and women work together and when all are highly motivated to solve the problem.[25]

When groups compete, it appears that, on average, women are more cooperative with their opponents than men are. Women are more likely to share resources with their opponents and are interested in fairness more than in winning. Men, on average, are more willing to engage in aggressive behavior and gain advantage through deception and deceit than women are. Also, men are more likely to be antisocial, using revenge, verbal aggression, and even physical violence, whereas women are more likely to use socially acceptable behavior such as reasoning and understanding to solve conflict.[26]

When groups are small in size, women prefer to work with other women, whereas men don't seem to have a gender preference. It is much more difficult for men to achieve cohesiveness in all-male groups than in mixed-sex groups. As U.S. culture continues to evolve, our stereotypes of men and women will change, together with the roles they play in groups. When comparing the research on men and women based on gender rather than biological sex, we are beginning to find that differences are based less on biological sex than on masculine and feminine traits. That is, individuals who have masculine traits, whether they are male or female, are more likely to be competitive and attempt to dominate and control interactions. More feminine individuals—of either sex—are less likely to display those behaviors.[27] It is important that both men and women understand the stereotypes that exist and make sure that each person who participates in a group is provided equal opportunities to participate.

Ethical Behavior in Group Communication

For groups to perform effectively, leaders and members must be ethical. There are behavioral assumptions that all people in civilized societies are expected to follow—laws, rules, standards, or agreed-on norms of a general culture. These same expectations also apply to behaviors within groups. There are, however, some special ethical concerns that all groups and group members should consider when participating in group-related activities.

1. *All group members should have the right to state an opinion or a unique perspective.* No one should be prevented from speaking openly, even when expressing unpopular views. Of course, group members must also be sensitive and responsible in making sure that their honest statements do not violate someone else's civil rights. Similarly it is inappropriate to ridicule or belittle members of the group in private or public, because they may disagree with a certain point of view. There is nothing wrong with disagreeing with another person's ideas; it is wrong, however, to attack the person instead of the idea.

2. *All group members should conduct themselves with honesty and integrity.* Members of a group should not deliberately deceive or present information that is false or untruthful. It is unacceptable to present inaccurate information in an attempt to persuade others to accept a particular viewpoint. The same principle would hold for the group itself—it would be wrong for the group to present to others results based on misrepresentation of facts. It is deceitful to persuade others to accept conclusions that are supported by misinformation. Integrity of group members individually and together as a group include other dimensions. For example, when a group makes a decision based on fair and ethical procedures, everyone should support the decision. Individual members should be willing to place the good of the group ahead of their own individual goals. The bottom line is that group members should ultimately do everything they can to benefit the group's goals.

3. *Confidential information shared in the group should remain confidential.* It is extremely unethical to share information outside of the group that members agree to keep private.

4. *Group members must use information ethically.* They should give credit to the source of the information, should not falsify data or information, and should present all relevant information and all points of view to prevent bias. Ethical use of information helps produce effective, sound results, whatever the task.

Technology and Groups

Have you ever had a problem or question that you couldn't answer or one about which you were unsure of the best answer? Did you think there must be others who know the answer or who are interested in the same issues that interest you? If so, the Internet may be your answer. A quick web search allows you to find groups of people who are interested in discussing almost any issue. If the topic that you are interested in isn't already on the Internet, then you can easily create your own website. The type of groups that are formed to discuss a particular topic on the Internet are referred to as newsgroups. A **newsgroup** is an online bulletin board where people can read and post messages about the topics of their choice. Once you post a message to a newsgroup, everyone who visits that newsgroup can read your comments and respond if they wish to do so. Newsgroups provide a vehicle whereby email messages are systematically made available to large groups of people.

The newsgroup, in a sense, resembles a gathering place similar to the local town meeting hall or restaurant where people come together to discuss subjects of mutual interest. With newsgroups, however, the communication occurs over the Internet and is electronically written, not orally discussed, as in the typical face-to-face small group arena. Similar to small groups, newsgroups revolve around specific topics, such as computers, social issues, literature and science, entertainment, hobbies, or current issues. Newsgroups provide easy access for meeting and communicating with people who share your interests from all over the world without having to leave their computers. Try accessing the following website to find newsgroups that might interest you: http://www.deja.com/usenet.

When members of formalized and established groups cannot meet in person, other forms of technology may provide a solution. Because of the cost and inconvenience of bringing people together, more and more organizations are opting to use

Making Connections

Group Success

Go back to the chapter's opening scenario, describing the experiences of group X and group Y. Group X members were very satisfied with their work and with one another, whereas group Y members were unsatisfied.

1. What do you think group X members did differently than group Y? What made them successful?
2. What recommendations would you give to group Y members to help them improve their group's experience?
3. How could technology be used by either group's members to improve their communication?

such technologies as teleconferencing, videoconferencing, or interactive computer conferencing to hold meetings. **Teleconferencing** uses telephones and speakerphones to connect people in different locations. Speakerphones enable people in different locations to interact at one given location. Although extremely cost effective, teleconferencing is limited because you cannot see those at the other locations. **Videoconferencing** is an extension of teleconferencing that includes picture and sound. It eliminates one limitation of teleconferencing in that it allows people at different locations to see each other via television. Thus, a benefit of videoconferencing is the ability of those involved in the discussion to hear and see everyone at all locations. Disadvantages of videoconferencing include its cost and the need for special equipment necessary to allow both picture and sound to be transmitted. Videoconferencing, however, is much more vulnerable to extremely frustrating equipment failures than teleconferencing.

Interactive computer conferencing is similar to videoconferencing except that the interaction occurs via computer. Although interactive computer conferencing requires special equipment and software for both sound and picture, it is far more cost effective than videoconferencing. The advantages of interactive computer conferencing include convenience, in that interaction can occur from almost any location, and the fact that only a computer and connected video camera are required. In addition, interactive computer conferencing usually does not require technicians to operate the equipment once it is installed. Its disadvantages are similar to videoconferencing in that equipment failures can occur and getting online is not always easy.

Ultimately, the success of any technology for group sharing depends on two factors: accessibility and use. We use technology to communicate within groups if the technology is readily available and if all members know how to use it effectively. When technologies are available, group members must agree on which technologies they will use, how often they will use them, and for what purposes.

In addition, if the technologies are to be empowering and useful, group members must agree on mutual expectations and rules that will guide the use of each technology. If an individual fails to check messages regularly, comes poorly prepared to teleconferences, or is not included in the exchanges by the other group members, the group will likely not be very successful. Groups that have used technology to communicate are aware that different types of technologies affect the richness and speed of their communication. Clearly, training and experience in the appropriate application of electronic communication technologies are critical to success.

Summary

Small group communication is the exchange of information that occurs among a relatively small number of persons, ideally five to seven, who share a common purpose such as doing a job or solving a problem. A *group* is a collection of individuals whose members influence one another, have a common purpose, take on roles, are interdependent, and interact with one another.

People join groups for a variety of reasons. Groups help meet both psychological and social needs, allow individuals to reach goals that they might not otherwise be able to attain, provide multiple sources of information and ideas, provide security, and can contribute to a positive social identity. Cultural orientation determines, to some extent, our predisposition to join groups and helps to form our perception of the value of groups. A culture that has an *individualistic orientation* stresses self or personal goals and achievements over group goals and achievements. A *collectivistic orientation* is more likely to stress putting aside your individual goals for the well-being of the group. A force that brings people together to form a group is a *common goal.*

Small group communication serves a wide range of purposes that can be grouped into two categories: social purposes and task-related purposes. Social purposes include socialization, catharsis, therapy, and learning; task-related purposes include decision making and problem solving. A special form of group, characterized by close-knit relationships, people with different and complementary abilities, and a strong sense of identity, is called a *team.* Similar to groups, teams involve interaction, interdependence, common goals, personality, commitment, cohesiveness, and rules. A *project team* consists of specialists assigned to coordinate the successful completion of a task. A *work team* is a group of people who are responsible for a complete work process or a segment of the process that delivers a product or service to an internal or external customer. A special form of work team is the *focus group,* which attempts to understand what people think about specific ideas, issues, or people.

Several characteristics make the small group a unique context for communication. They are *interdependence* (mutual dependence), *commitment* (the desire to work together), *cohesiveness* (attraction), group size (the number of participants), *norms* (expected and shared behavior), and *group culture* (the pattern of values, beliefs, norms, and behaviors that are shared by group members and that shape a group's individual personality). *Groupthink* is a dysfunction in which group members value the harmony of the group more than considering new ideas, hesitate to change flawed decisions, or are reluctant to allow new members to participate. Groupthink usually results when members lose individual identity and give up the individual right to free thought—even when it is not in their best interest to do so.

There are a number of disadvantages to group communication: (1) It is time-consuming—it almost always takes longer to accomplish something when it is done by a group; (2) it is not possible for all group members to contribute equally—this is partially attributed to time and to different styles of interaction; (3) some group members do not do their fair share of the work—this is referred to as *social loafing,* which is the tendency for individuals to lower their work effort after they join a group; (4) a majority of members may pressure the most capable members not to excel; and (5) some people will not work in groups because of previous negative experiences or because they do not have the communication skills to be effective in groups, which make them dislike groups—this is referred to as the *grouphate phenomenon.*

The differences between how men and women communicate and contribute to groups have not been completely clarified by research. Men tend to dominate group interaction and demonstrate more task-related behavior. Women are more patient and offer more positive responses to others' comments. Overall, men and women on average tend to differ very little in how they interact in groups.

Groups must also follow ethical principles in order to be successful. For example, all members should have the right to be heard, should conduct themselves with honesty and integrity, should keep confidential information confidential, and should treat information carefully—giving credit to sources and avoiding the use of falsified, incomplete, or biased information.

Technology is playing a larger and larger role in group interaction. We join groups to discuss the many issues and questions that we have. These groups are referred to as newsgroups. A *newsgroup* is essentially an online bulletin board where people can read and post messages about topics of their choosing. In *teleconferencing* group members use telephones and speakerphones to communicate; *videoconferencing* is an extension of teleconferencing that includes sound and picture, and *interactive computer conferencing* is similar to videoconferencing except that the interaction occurs via computer. No matter which technologies are used, thorough training and experience in the use of such tools are necessary if they are to be used effectively.

DISCUSSION STARTERS

1. Why do you think groups or teams are so widely used in our society?
2. Think of a time when you had a very positive group experience. Why was the experience positive? Consider group members, leadership, organization, environment, and time factors in your answer.
3. In your own words explain the difference between a group and a collection of individuals.
4. Which group characteristic do you think is the most important to a group's success? Why?
5. Do the advantages of belonging to groups outweigh the disadvantages? Explain.
6. How would you describe the behaviors and communication skills of an ideal group member?
7. Describe at least two norms that are operating in your class. What makes them norms?
8. Explain why groups are not very efficient in getting things done. Explain what can be done to make groups more efficient.
9. How do you think technology will change group communication?
10. Why do people join and participate in groups?
11. How does a social loafer affect a group's climate, motivation, and productivity?

NOTES

1. M. E. Shaw, *Group Dynamics: The Psychology of Small Group Behavior,* 2nd ed. (New York: McGraw-Hill, 1976), 6–10.
2. J. K. Brilhart, *Effective Group Discussion,* 5th ed. (Dubuque, Iowa: William C. Brown, 1986), 21; and J. K. Brilhart, G. J. Galanes, and K. Adams, *Effective Group Communication Theory and Practice,* 10th ed. (New York: McGraw-Hill, 2001), 8.
3. P. B. Paulus, ed., *Psychology of Group Influence,* 2nd ed. (Hillsdale, N.J.: Erlbaum, 1989).
4. B. B. Haslett and J. Ruebus, "What Differences Do Individual Differences in Groups Make?" in *The Handbook of Group Theory and Research,* 2nd ed., eds. L. R. Frey, S. Gouran, and M. S. Poole (Thousand Oaks, Calif.: Sage, 1999), 115–38; and C. H. Hui and H. C. Trandis, "Individualism–Collectivism: A Study of Cross-Cultural Research," *Journal of Cross-Cultural Psychology* 17 (1986): 225–48.
5. H. Triandis, *Individualism and Collectiveness* (Boulder, Colo.: Westview Press, 1995).
6. Ibid.
7. H. Triandis, "Cross-Cultural Studies of Individualism and Collectiveness," in *Cross-Cultural Perspective,* ed. J. Berman (Lincoln: University of Nebraska Press, 1990); and G. Hofstede, *Cultures and Organizations: Software of the Mind* (New York: McGraw-Hill, 1991).
8. R. V. Harnack, T. B. Fest, and B. S. Jones, *Group Discussion Theory and Technique,* 2nd ed. (Englewood Cliffs, N.J.: Prentice-Hall, 1977), 25–28; and J. K. Brilhart and G. J. Galanes, *Effective Group Discussion,* 7th ed. (New York: McGraw-Hill, 1998), 9–15, 133–36.
9. L. Coch and J. R. P. French Jr., "Overcoming Resistance to Change," in *Group Dynamics: Research and Theory,* 2nd ed., eds. by D. Cartwright and A. Zander (Evanston, Ill.: Row Peterson, 1960), 319–41.

10. Brilhart, Galanes, and Adams, 8.

11. G. Lumsden and D. Lumsden, *Communicating in Groups and Teams,* 2nd ed. (Belmont, Calif.: Wadsworth, 1997).

12. L. C. Lederman, "Assessing Educational Effectiveness: The Focus Group Interview as a Technique for Data Collection," *Communication Education* 39 (1990): 117–27.

13. I. L. Janis, *Groupthink: Psychological Studies of Policy Decisions and Fiascoes,* 2nd ed. (Boston: Houghton Mifflin, 1983).

14. P. E. Tetlock, R. S. Peterson, C. McGuire, S. Change, and P. Feld, "Assessing Political Group Dynamics: A Test of the Group Think Model," *Journal of Personality and Social Pyschology* 63 (1992): 403–25.

15. Janis.

16. D. Gigone and R. Hastie, "The Common Knowledge Effect: Information Sharing and Group Judgment," *Journal of Personality and Social Psychology* 65 (1993): 959–74; D. Gigone and R. Hastie, "The Impact of Information on Small Group Choice," *Journal of Personality and Social Psychology* 72 (1997): 132–40; and G. Stasser, "Pooling Unshared Information During Group Discussion," in *Group Process and Productivity,* eds. S. Worchel, W. Wood, and J. H. Simpson (Newbury Park, Calif.: Sage), 48–67.

17. D. Gigone and R. Hastie, "The Common Knowledge Effect."

18. J. R. Larson Jr., C. Christensen, T. M. Franz, and A. S. Abbott, "Diagnosing Groups: The Pooling, Management, and Impact of Shared and Unshared Case Information in Teambased Medical Decision Making," *Journal of Personality and Social Psychology* 75 (1998): 93–108; and J. R. Winquist and J. R. Larson Jr., "Information Pooling: When It Impacts Group Decision Making," *Journal of Personality and Social Psychology* 74 (1998): 317–77.

19. Brilhart and Galanes, *Effective Group Discussion,* 273–74.

20. R. Bostrum, "Patterns of Communicative Interaction in Small Groups," *Speech Monographs* 37 (1970): 257–63.

21. Brilhart and Galanes, *Effective Group Discussion,* 124.

22. S. J. Karau and K. D. Williams, "Social Loafing: A Meta-Analytic Review and Theoretical Integration," *Journal of Personality and Social Psychology* 65 (1993): 681–706; B. K. Latané and S. Harkins, "Many Hands Make Light the Work: The Causes and Consequences of Social-Loafing," *Journal of Personality and Social Psychology* 37 (1979): 822–32; and B. G. Schultz, "Improving Group Communication Performance," in *The Handbook of Group Communication Theory and Research,* eds. L. R. Frey, D. S. Gouran, and M. S. Poole (Thousand Oaks, Calif.: Sage, 1999), 371–94.

23. S. Sorensen, "Grouphate" (paper presented at the International Communication Association, Minneapolis, Minn., May 1981).

24. L. P. Stewart, A. D. Stewart, S. A. Friedley, and P. J. Cooper, *Communication Between the Sexes: Sex Differences and Sex Role Stereotypes,* 2nd ed. (Scottsdale, Ariz.: Gorsuch Scarisbrick, 1990), 43–114; D. N. Maltz and R. A. Borker, "A Cultural Approach to Male–Female Miscommunication," in *Language and Social Identity,* ed. J. J. Gumperz (Cambridge: Cambridge University Press, 1982), 195–216; and E. Baird, "Sex Differences in Group Communication: A Review of Relevant Research," *Quarterly Journal of Speech* 62 (1976): 179–92.

25. B. F. Meeker and P. A. Weitzel-O'Neil, "Sex Roles and Interpersonal Behavior in Task-Oriented Groups," *American Sociological Review* 42 (1977): 91–105; R. L. Hoffman and N. K. V. Maier, "Quality and Acceptance of Problem Solutions by Members of Homogeneous and Heterogeneous Groups," *Journal of Abnormal and Social Psychology* 62 (1961): 401–7.

26. J. C. McCroskey, V. P. Richmond, and R. A. Stewart, *One on One: The Foundations of Interpersonal Communication* (Englewood Cliffs, N.J.: Prentice-Hall, 1986), 244–47; M. E. Roloff, "The Impact of Socialization on Sex Differences in Conflict Resolution" (paper presented at the annual convention of the International Communication Association, Acapulco, Mexico, May 1980); E. A. Mabry, "Some Theoretical Implications of Female and Male Interaction in Unstructured Small Groups," *Small Group Behavior* 20 (1989): 536–50; and W. E. Jurma and B. C. Wright, "Follower Reactions to Male and Female Leaders Who Maintain or Lose Reward Power," *Small Group Research* 21 (1990): 97–112.

27. J. Bond and W. Vinacke, "Coalition in Mixed Sex Triads," *Sociometry* 24 (1961): 61–65; B. A. Fisher, "Differential Effects of Sexual Composition Interaction Patterns in Dyads," *Human Communication Research* 9 (1983): 225–38; Jurma and Wright; and D. J. Canary and B. H. Spitzberg, "Appropriateness and Effectiveness Perceptions of Conflict Strategies," *Human Communication Research* 14 (1987): 93–118.

16

Participating in Groups and Teams

"The most important quality in a leader is that of being acknowledged as such."

—André Maurois

- Understand the importance of team building.
- Describe the roles and responsibilities of small group leaders.
- Comprehend differences in men's and women's leadership styles.
- Specify the responsibilities of a small group participant.
- Describe group task roles, group building and maintenance roles, and self-centered roles.
- Understand how to conduct an efficient group meeting.
- Outline the steps in problem solving and decision making.
- Understand conflict and how to use conflict management strategies.
- Develop criteria for evaluating a small group discussion.

SCENARIO

Here is a riddle: "What is more boring than a droning professor, more tedious than peeling potatoes, and more frustrating than a perpetual busy signal when you need to reach someone by phone?"

The answer, according to many business people, is a meeting.

—Cox News Service, 1990 ∎

Why is this so? Do you think meetings have to be boring and tedious? What does this tell you about meetings? If asked, people will give a variety of reasons why they'd rather do almost anything than attend another meeting. You probably have your own list of reasons to avoid meetings—especially those that promise to be dull.

However, we all have attended meetings in which great interaction took place, time was used wisely, progress was made toward a particular goal or accomplishing a task, lots of good ideas were shared, respect for each person's contributions was shown even though disagreement sometimes occurred, differences were resolved by open discussion, and decisions were supported by everyone. People leave such meetings with a real sense of accomplishment.

What factors make the difference between an effective and an ineffective meeting? To answer this question, this chapter explores six crucial aspects of small group communication: team building, leadership, member participation, methods of group problem solving and decision making, conflict management, and evaluation.

Team Building

Not all groups will become teams or work as teams, but it is important to understand that the more a group acts or becomes like a team the more likely it is that the group will be successful. A team is likely to be more successful or effective because when people know they are part of a team they tend to cooperate more fully; they form a close-knit relationship and a strong sense of identity. As with any group or organization, a team needs a purpose and goals. It is typical for athletic teams to set goals that the team hopes to accomplish during the season. In order for groups to establish a team approach, they must first set very clear and specific goals, determine roles, and develop a team identity.

Setting Goals

Although setting clear goals requires some effort, the consequences of not setting clear and specific goals are usually frustration and low motivation among group members. The group that has little or no direction generally ends up drifting aimlessly without purpose because little is planned. The most effective groups have clear, identifiable goals, and members who understand those goals.[1] Goals that are vague, such as "campus parking is causing problems" or "crime on campus is on the rise," provide little direction as to what needs to be done. However, goals that are specific are more likely to be accomplished, for example "provide a specific solution or solutions to solve the parking congestion on campus by the end of the semester" or "develop specific actions that should be taken by the campus to help reduce the crime rate by the end of the school year."

Goals should not only be clear and specific but they should also be challenging and worthwhile. If a group believes the goals are trivial and unimportant, it will approach them with little motivation. If, however, the group understands that their decisions will result in rewards and be appreciated and worthwhile, they are more likely to take ownership of their actions and behaviors as well as be motivated to accomplish the goals.

Determining Roles

Once goals are set and understood, a group must determine the roles of its members. For a group to become a team, it requires structure. For example, a football team requires a head coach (a leader), assistant coaches (subgroups within the larger group), players who have the talent to fill the positions necessary to play the game, public relations people to promote the team, and so on. Everyone on the team has roles and assigned duties to accomplish. Football players cannot function as a team if there is no structure or if the coaches and players are uncertain of the roles they are supposed to fulfill. The same is true of any group; if the members are uncertain of their roles and there is no structure, they will not be able to function as an effective team.

Developing Identity

There is no one way to develop a group's identity. Sometimes it is assigned by the nature of the group's work and other times the group has to build its identity on its own. For example, when a department at a major university was being considered for elimination, it took on a "war room" atmosphere. The leader of the department created a campaign culture that was based on urgency and survival. The clear objective for the department under attack was to find a way to prevent the university from eliminating it. Faculty members, staff, and students bonded very quickly into a cohesive group.

Making Connections

What Makes a Leader?

List the characteristics and skills you believe a good leader must possess in order to lead a group. Then rank each characteristic, using 1 as the most important, 2 as the second most important, and so on.

Form small groups (three to seven members) to discuss each person's ranking of characteristics and skills. Together create a new ranked list of characteristics and skills for effective leaders using those generated by each person in the group and any new characteristics as determined by the group. Select one group member to write the group's top five characteristics and skills on the board and to explain why the group made these selections. After all groups have had a turn, follow these steps:

1. In an open class discussion, create a class list of the top five characteristics and skills using the group lists or any additions that may result from the class discussion.
2. How do people acquire the leadership characteristics and skills presented on the class list?
3. List five people whom you believe to be effective leaders—they can be well known or not so well known.
4. Under the names, list the characteristics and skills they possess that qualifies them for your list of effective leaders.
5. Do all these leaders have the same qualities, or are there differences? What qualities are universal among all the leaders mentioned, if any? Discuss your answers, if time permits, in class.

Leadership

__Leadership__ is an influence process that includes any behavior that helps clarify or guide the group to achieve its goals. A **leader** is a person assigned or selected, or one who emerges from a group, to guide or provide direction toward reaching the group's goals._ In most cases, only one person serves as leader, although sometimes two or more persons may share the responsibility.

Leading a Group

A leader is the person at the center of a group's attention, or the person to whom the group members address their messages. For example, in business meetings, the boss is usually the leader, and the employees center their attention on the boss, addressing their communications to him or her. At times, employees may address messages to other employees, or one employee may hold the attention of the group, but in neither situation does an employee actually become the leader of the meeting.

Another way to identify a leader is by the behaviors that he or she displays in guiding a group to its specific goal. If a person communicates a direction and the group members follow that direction to reach the goal, that person is demonstrating leadership.

Finally, a leader can be identified by his or her position or title, such as student council president, chairperson of a committee, boss, teacher, coach, captain, father, mother, and so on. But this method of identification requires caution. Even though a title signifies that a person is the stated leader, it does not mean that that person has leadership skills.

In most cases, a leader's ability to lead determines the success or failure of a group. Granted, not all successes or failures can be traced directly to the person in charge because the participants, the nature of the task to be accomplished, and the information available for completing the task also contribute to the outcome. The role of the leader in small group projects is to get the task done. To do this, the leader must be objective enough to determine how the group is functioning and whether it is progressing toward its goal. This requires, at times, the ability to "step back" and examine the group objectively.

Leaders must help address two sets of needs found in all groups. **Task needs** are related to the content of the task and all behaviors that lead to the completion of the task, including defining and assessing the task, gathering information, studying the problem, and solving the problem. **Maintenance needs** are related to organizing and developing a group such that members realize personal satisfaction from working together. Maintenance needs pertain to intangibles such as atmosphere, structure, role responsibility, praise, and social–emotional control. To meet both task and maintenance needs, leaders in small groups must perform a number of functions:

Initiating—preparing members for the discussion

Organizing—keeping members on track

Maintaining effective interaction—encouraging participation

Ensuring member satisfaction—promoting interpersonal relationships

Facilitating understanding—encouraging effective listening

Stimulating creativity and critical thinking—encouraging evaluation and improvement

Leadership Styles

In dealing with their subordinates, most leaders fall into one of two categories: **task-oriented leaders,** who gain satisfaction from performing the task, and **relationship-oriented leaders,** who gain satisfaction from establishing good interpersonal relationships.[2]

Task-oriented leaders are concerned with completing the job or solving the problem. Such leaders spend little time developing relationships unless doing so will help get the task completed more quickly. Relationship-oriented leaders emphasize people rather than the task and focus on attending to the interpersonal needs of their group's members.

Leadership style may also be classified according to how much or how little power the leader assigns to the group members. Researchers have identified three primary styles of leadership: autocratic, democratic, and laissez-faire,[3] each having a very distinctive approach to the communication that occurs within the group (see Table 16.1). However, many leaders cannot be easily classified in one of the three styles exclusively. Often effective leaders use a combination of styles or blends of the styles, which may change from one situation to the next.

Leadership style is classified by how much or how little power the leader assigns to group members. Democratic leaders, for example, guide and direct the group and, though committed to being open to all points of view, they represent only a majority or plurality of points of view of the group.

Autocratic leaders maintain complete control and make all decisions for the group. They decide what will be talked about, when it will be talked about, who may speak, and who may not. They often make decisions that affect the group without consulting its members. Autocratic leaders are able to tell others what to do, either because their position gives them the power or because the group allows them to do so.

Democratic leaders guide and direct the group but share control and remain open to all views. This leadership style allows the will of the majority to prevail even when the majority's view differs from the leader's. Because democratic leaders guide and suggest rather than prescribe and require, they make a final decision only after consulting all group members. Interaction among group members and democratic leaders is usually quite open, subject only to the constraints established by the group.

Laissez-faire leaders give complete decision-making freedom to the group or to individual members and often become figureheads who remain only minimally involved. They do not believe in taking charge and may actually feel uncomfortable in such a role. As a result, the group receives little or no direction. Some experts believe that the laissez-faire style of leadership is a contradiction in terms. It implies that a leader can be in control without leading at all.

In theory, the differences among the three styles of leadership are clear. The autocratic leader has complete control, the democratic leader shares control, and the laissez-faire leader gives up control. In practice, though, the three styles are not always so clear-cut. Most leaders do not use the same style all the time, but they vary their style to match each situation. Certain circumstances, group members, and group purposes call for direct control, whereas others require little or no control. For example, a military leader in combat and a doctor in a medical emergency will undoubtedly be

TABLE 16.1

Leadership Styles: A Comparison

AUTOCRATIC	DEMOCRATIC	LAISSEZ-FAIRE
Keeps complete control	Shares control	Gives up control
Sets policy and makes all decisions for the group	Involves members in setting policy and making decisions; does not make any decisions without consulting group members	Gives total freedom to group members to make policies and decisions; gets involved only when called on
Defines tasks and assigns them to members	May guide task assignment to be sure work is accomplished, but allows members to divide work	Completely avoids participation

Making Connections

Choosing a Leadership Style

Tia was elected chairperson of her church's administrative council. She was very pleased that others saw her as a leader, given that she was the youngest person and the only African American who had run for the position.

The committee was made up of seven members and, besides Tia, there was only one other female member. Even though this was only her third year on the church council (most members had served for longer periods), Tia felt ready to take charge, but also knew that her assignment was not going to be easy. A tremendous amount of work needed to be done in a short time, and controversial issues were involved. Despite having less experience than most members, she was confident and knew that she could do the job.

1. What advice would you give to Tia regarding her choice of leadership style?
2. What other concerns should Tia have, if any?
3. Would these concerns be different if Tia were a male? If so, why?

autocratic leaders. Such situations require immediate action, and putting decisions to a vote could create great problems.

The democratic leadership style is most often used when a leader is elected. For example, the president of the student government and the chair of a committee would probably use a democratic style. This style is most common when the leader is both a representative and a member of the group. The laissez-faire leadership style is often used when group members do not want or need a rigid structure to accomplish their goal, such as a group conducting a study session. If such a group decided that they needed a leader, they would take appropriate action, but in most cases the group does not desire or require any assistance, and so it remains leaderless.

Leaders are not always free to follow the leadership style they prefer. For example, persons who would rather be democratic or laissez-faire leaders might discover that pressures from others, the need to get things done in a certain way, or the desire to save time and energy require them to be more autocratic than they would like to be. On other occasions, when it is important for members to agree with a decision, leaders are more likely to use a democratic style. No single leadership style is perfect in all situations.

Researchers have concluded that skilled leaders have the ability to understand a situation and adapt their behaviors to meet the particular constraints of it.[4] Leadership entails the ability to determine the most appropriate style and behaviors for given situations. Here are some sample situations to which effective leadership is able to adapt:

- When group members are not committed or are unwilling to accept responsibility for implementing a decision, effective leaders use an autocratic style of leadership. For example, if a group of students have been given a class assignment in which only one student is prepared to do the work and knows what needs to be done, an autocratic style would be appropriate.

- If group members are highly committed and willing to accept responsibility for implementing a decision, effective leaders use a democratic style of leadership.

For example, if a group of responsible students is working on a classroom assignment in which all are committed and prepared, a democratic style would be an appropriate situation for a leader to use.

■ If group members are highly motivated to complete a task and have the knowledge and expertise to accomplish the task, effective leaders realize they should delegate the task to the group members and use a laissez-faire style of leadership. For example, if a group of highly talented, independent, and motivated students is working together to complete a class assignment in which each student knows his or her responsibilities, a laissez-faire style would be appropriate.

Effective leaders examine situations, understand the groups they are leading, and determine what actions need to be taken in order to accomplish a given task. Although it is impossible to say exactly which styles work best in certain situations, common sense indicates that a leader needs to be flexible in order to promote productivity and satisfaction in a given group.

Research, although not conclusive, suggests that the democratic leadership style is superior to the autocratic style in getting a task done and at the same time satisfies group members.[5] Autocratic leaders are likely to get more done, but member satisfaction is considerably lower. Probably the most significant research finding is that autocratic leaders generate more hostility and aggression among group members, whereas democratic leaders produce more originality, individuality, and independence. Groups with laissez-faire leaders accomplish less, produce work of lower quality, and waste more time.

Leadership and Gender Differences

Do male leaders and female leaders differ in their style or approach to leadership? What do you think? Marilyn Loden, in her book *Feminine Leadership or How to Succeed in Business Without Being One of the Boys,* contends that the sexes do indeed differ in terms of leadership style.[6] Loden believes that female leaders often adopt a style emphasizing cooperation and indirect means of management, whereas males tend to exhibit an "I'm in charge," directive strategy. But research on male and female leadership done by social scientists has generally found no consistent or significant difference between the sexes in terms of leadership style. The question is, Who is right?

Because of the complexity of the subject, finding the answer to this question is not simple. In a review of 150 research studies, Alice Eagly and Blair Johnson found that potential differences between male and female leadership styles had been examined on two dimensions: (1) task accomplishment versus maintenance of interpersonal relationships and (2) participative (democratic) versus directive (autocratic) leadership style.[7] Sex-role stereotypes suggest that female leaders might show more concern for interpersonal relations and tend to be more democratic in their leadership style than male leaders are. Results of Eagly and Johnson's study, however, did not support these stereotypes. Their results suggest that no evidence supports any substantial difference between males and females regarding the first dimension (task accomplishment versus maintenance of interpersonal relationships). There is, however, a significant difference between males and females regarding the second dimension (participative versus directive leadership style). Eagly and Johnson found that females were more democratic, or participative, in style than males were. What do you think accounts for this difference?

Making Connections

Are Women Better Leaders?

According to an article in *U.S.News & World Report* (January 29, 2001), more women are taking on leadership roles in government and business. The article stated that women have a greater tendency to take a holistic, contextual view of issues, whereas men tend to compartmentalize and assess the cause and effect of issues in a linear fashion. Based on what this article appears to say, women therefore are better leaders.

1. Defend or refute the article's contention that women are better leaders.

2. What does it mean to be holistic, and why would that make a person a better leader?

3. When considering the traits we generally associate with leadership, are they more likely to be masculine or feminine? Explain.

4. Who do you think is a very effective female leader? Male leader? What do they have in common? What are their differences?

According to Eagly and Johnson, the difference in leadership style may exist because—as evidence suggests—women generally possess better interpersonal skills than men do. However, this cause-and-effect connection is only speculative. Much more research must be done before a definitive conclusion can be drawn about gender differences in leadership style—and whether (and in what situations) those differences might be to a leader's advantage or disadvantage. It does appear that, in spite of the progress made regarding women in leadership roles, female leaders continue to face disadvantages in many settings. Although their behavior or style differs from that of male leaders, and in only a few minor aspects, women's leadership skills are still generally judged to be inferior to those of men.[8] Of course, we can only hope that this bias will change as gender stereotypes weaken and as more women gain leadership positions.

Member Participation

For a group to be successful, all of its members must be actively involved. Just like leaders, members of groups have certain responsibilities. The more members know about their leader's role and each other's roles, the better equipped they will be to perform. Furthermore, leaders change from time to time, so members should be ready to assume greater responsibility if doing so will benefit the group.

Roles of Group Members

Successful group outcomes depend on group members assuming various roles that are constructive and beneficial to the group's outcome. There are many roles that group members can play. Kenneth Benne and Paul Sheats, group scholars, developed a comprehensive list of roles that group members can assume.[9] Benne and Sheats classified the roles into three categories: group task, group building and maintenance, and self-centered roles.

Group task roles help the group accomplish its task or objective. They are behaviors that orient the group to the task, allow for the exchange of ideas and opinions, and motivate the group to complete the task.

Group building and maintenance roles help define a group's social atmosphere. These roles include behaviors that function to maintain a positive interpersonal climate within the group. A person who tries to maintain a peaceful, harmonious climate by mediating disagreements and resolving conflicts performs a maintenance function.

Individuals may adopt self-centered roles, which are generally counterproductive or destructive to a group, that tend to hinder group progress. In most groups, members are eager to make constructive contributions. From time to time, however, you will encounter individuals whose attitudes are not so positive. For the good of the group, it is important to recognize such people and learn how to cope with them. See Table 16.2 for various roles of group members.

Contributions of Group Members

Recognizing and handling counterproductive contributions are the responsibilities not only of the leader but also of each group member. Sometimes the best approach to these situations is to discuss them openly: "John, you sure have been quiet about this problem. What do you think?" "Sally, your jokes seem to indicate that you don't believe the issue is very serious. Why?" Sometimes conflict needs to be resolved with a vote by the group. This lets members know the position of the majority so that discussion can continue.

Comments That Are Open to Evaluation.   One of the greatest anxieties group members face is presenting their ideas for the group's evaluation. Group discussion can lead to the best possible information and the best possible decision, but this will happen only if members offer their comments for evaluation. Criticism should not be ignored or avoided. At the same time, members must remember that evaluations can be constructive only when they focus on the contribution and not on the person who originated it. It is one thing to find fault with specific data, and it is quite another thing to find fault with the person who presented the data. Criticism should be based on what is said, not on who said it. To give effective criticism, members should describe and clarify their thoughts on the topic, rather than simply finding fault. *(i) a mistake → suggest a way (ii) if there's sth. or an error to fix it not clear, ask him to clarify it*

Provocative Comments.   Comments should be made not only to bring the group closer to *or give me* its goal but also to fuel thought for further contributions. This is worthwhile even if *an example* it makes for a somewhat longer meeting. If an idea has not been fully discussed and evaluated, appropriate decisions cannot be made. Asking questions (even ones that seem trivial), challenging assumptions, presenting bold new ideas (even if they seem unusual), and disagreeing can be valuable as long as they are focused on making the final group product the best one possible.

Group participants need to study the meeting's agenda in advance so they will be prepared to contribute. Meaningful input often calls for research, so each participant should be willing to spend time and energy on advanced preparation. Probably one of the greatest weaknesses of beginning group participants is their tendency to arrive at meetings unprepared. The group must then either spend time helping them catch up or do without their contributions. Either way, valuable time, effort, and input are lost. Also, successful group outcomes depend on group-centered attitudes and behaviors, which enhance participation and member satisfaction; they include open-mindedness, a positive attitude, the ability to listen, a willingness to contribute, and preparation.

TABLE 16.2

Roles Group Members Can Play

GROUP TASK ROLES	BEHAVIORS
Initiator–contributor	Provides direction and guidance, proposes new ideas, suggests solutions, or approaches to the problem
Information seeker	Sees the need for more information, asks for clarification of ideas and relevance
Information giver	Provides information, including facts, examples, statistics, and other evidence
Opinion seeker	Asks about people's feelings and views related to the task
Opinion giver	Provides personal beliefs, opinions, or judgments about ideas being considered by the group
Elaborator	Extends information and clarifies viewpoints, ideas, and solutions
Coordinator	Clarifies and notes relationships among ideas, viewpoints, and suggestions
Orienter	Attempts to summarize what has occurred
Evaluator/critic	Makes an effort to evaluate the evidence and conclusions
Energizer	Tries to motivate to the group to take action
Recorder	Records the discussion for future reference
Tester of agreements	Determines how close the group is to reaching agreement

GROUP BUILDING AND MAINTENANCE ROLES	BEHAVIORS
Encourager	Offers praise by recognizing others' contributions
Harmonizer	Mediates disagreements, attempts to maintain positive interpersonal climate
Compromiser	Attempts to resolve conflicts by trying to find acceptable solutions to disagreements
Gatekeeper	Manages and directs the flow of communication
Standard setter	Articulates standards and goals that the group is to achieve
Follower	Goes along with the ideas and views of other group members
Feeling expresser	Highlights for the group its feelings, emotions, and attitudes

SELF-CENTERED ROLES	BEHAVIORS
Aggressor	Deflates the status of others in order to make themselves look better
Blocker	Resists, disagrees with, and opposes issues beyond reasonableness
Recognition seeker	Must be the center of attention, otherwise dissatisfied
Self-confessor	Contributes irrelevant information about self
Buffoon	Constantly jokes or engages in other kinds of horseplay
Dominator	Wants to be in charge of everything (autocrat)
Help seeker	Joins groups to satisfy personal needs
Withdrawer	Prefers not to participate at all

Adapted from K. D. Benne and P. Sheats, "Functional Roles of Group Members," *Journal of Social Issues* 4 (1948): 41–49.

Making Connections

The Buffoon

Jessica has always been fun to be around. She loves to kid and play practical jokes. The group has been fairly tolerant of her antics and at times has really had a good laugh—actually helping to reduce the group's stress level. But her recent behavior has really gotten out of control. In fact, her jokes are no longer appreciated, cause disruption, and show insensitivity to other members of the group.

No one has been willing to say anything to Jessica because they don't want to hurt her feelings. Besides, her other contributions have been excellent, and she has indispensable information regarding the problem the group is trying to solve. The situation is even more delicate because she is very sensitive and somewhat of a hothead. Members fear that if someone tells her to stop her unproductive behavior, she will leave the group.

You believe that Jessica doesn't think much of you as a leader. However, the group's morale has been steadily declining because of her, and if you don't say something to Jessica, other members may leave the group.

1. What should you do about this situation?
2. Are any ethical considerations involved in handling this problem?

Conducting a Meeting

When a group meets for the first time, the members usually begin by introducing themselves and briefly telling their reasons for joining the group or what they hope to accomplish as members.

After introductions, and depending on the nature of the group and its assigned task, members may appoint or elect a recording secretary. This person keeps a written account of the meeting's discussions that may be consulted later if necessary.

To ensure efficiency, procedures must be established, and meetings must be conducted according to a well-organized plan. The best way to accomplish this is by producing an **agenda,** a list of all topics to be discussed during a meeting. The leader usually determines the agenda, either alone or in consultation with the group members before each meeting. Sometimes, at the end of one meeting, the agenda for the next meeting is established. A typical meeting agenda might look like this:

1. Call to order
2. Introduction of new members
3. Reading, correction, and approval of minutes from previous meeting
4. Unfinished business
5. New business
6. Announcements
7. Adjournment

It takes leadership skills and an agenda to ensure an efficient meeting. Not all meetings operate in exactly the same way, but having an agenda should make any meeting run smoother.

Not all meetings operate in exactly the same way, but having an agenda should make any meeting run smoothly. Classroom groups may not follow a formal structure, but in general, they need a sense of organization and an informal agenda.

Planning and Managing a Meeting

1. Identify a purpose, plan an agenda, and distribute the agenda in advance.
2. Invite only people who need to be there (*not* everyone who might have an opinion on the topic).
3. Establish start, break, and stop times, and stick to them.
4. Assign a moderator (leader) to keep the discussion on track.
5. Decide what follow-up actions are needed after the meeting, and set deadlines for their completion.
6. Avoid holding unnecessary meetings.
7. Don't let people drone on, dominate, or avoid participation during discussions.
8. Don't allow conversations to wander off the subject.
9. Follow up to make sure that members act on decisions made at the meeting.[10]

doesn't work, & depend on others.

From Harrison Conference Services, Business Schools at the University of Georgia and Georgia State University.

 ## Problem Solving and Decision Making

Although the goal of some discussions, such as those in classrooms, is to share information, the goal of most discussions is to solve problems and make decisions: How can we raise more money for new computers? Who should be held responsible for date rape? What can be done to eliminate violence in our organization? How can we streamline production? How can we get the Hollywood media to reduce sex and violence in films and TV programs?

When solving problems and making decisions, groups must consider the alternatives and arrive at joint conclusions. To do this most effectively, they must take an organized and thorough approach to determine the exact nature of the problem and discuss its many aspects and potential solutions.

Determining the Problem

Groups are usually formed because a task needs to be accomplished. As groups are being formed, members already have an idea of their purposes and goals. In the classroom, groups are often formed to discuss particular topics in order to learn something. In communication classrooms, for example, small groups sometimes discuss subjects related to communication and sometimes simply allow students to learn about small group communication by experiencing it.

Unless your instructor assigns a topic, the first step of your group effort is to select a problem or topic. This is not always easy—after all, the topic has to be both important and interesting to everyone in the group to ensure a good discussion. A starting place might be areas that need improvement on your campus: What should be the role of athletics on the campus? Should better protection be provided for students who attend evening classes? The surrounding community is also a source for discussion topics: What can be done about public parking in the downtown area? What can the business community do to help college students get better jobs?

State, regional, and national issues can provide a broader base for topics: Can the state provide sufficient funding to the university? What should be the role of the federal government in providing loans to students? Selecting from thousands of topics and problems takes time. However, if the group does its homework, picking a topic that is agreeable to all members should not be difficult.

After a topic or problem is selected, it should be stated in the form of a question. There are four types of discussion questions: questions of fact, interpretation, value, and policy. A **question of fact** asks whether something is true or false; its answer can be verified: What is the current cost of tuition? How many students are enrolled in each of the various colleges on campus? A **question of interpretation** asks for the meaning or explanation of something: How does the economy of the state affect tuition? How can athletics contribute to a better education? A **question of value** asks whether something is good or bad, desirable or undesirable: Which college offers the best education for its students? Do coeducational dormitories provide satisfactory living conditions? A **question of policy** asks what actions should be taken: What restrictions should be placed on alcohol consumption on campus? What role should students have in evaluating instruction on campus?

Questions of fact leave little room for discussion. The answer can usually be found through research, and unless there are discrepancies in the data, no discussion is required. In contrast, questions of interpretation, value, and policy are not easily answered and thus make for good discussions. When phrasing discussion questions, whether for a classroom learning experience or another context, keep the following guidelines in mind:

1. The wording should reflect the discussion purpose or task at hand.
2. The wording should focus attention on the real problem.

3. The wording should specify whose behavior is subject to change.

4. The wording should not suggest possible solutions.

5. The wording should avoid emotional language.[10]

Discussing the Problem

In group situations, whether in the classroom or another context, it is important to determine a plan for carrying out the task or assignment. The agenda for discussing a problem, for example, usually includes the following five specific steps developed by the philosopher John Dewey: definition of the problem, analysis of the problem, suggestions of possible solutions, selection of the best solution, and putting the best solution into operation.[11] The steps developed by Dewey are referred to as "reflective thinking" steps because they provide a logical, rational, way of structuring group interaction. Here is an outline of a typical problem-solving discussion:

I. Definition of the problem

    A. *Symptoms.* How does the problem show itself, or what are the difficulties?

    B. *Size.* How large is the problem? Is it increasing or decreasing? What results can be expected if the problem is not solved?

    C. *Goal.* What general state of affairs is desired (in contrast to the present unsatisfactory one)?

II. Analysis of the problem

    A. *Causes of the problem.* What causes or conditions underlie the difficulties?

    B. *Present efforts to solve the problem.* What is being done now to deal with the problem? In what ways are these efforts unsuccessful? What hints do they provide for further attacks on the problem?

    C. *Requirements of a solution*

        1. *Direction.* Where shall we attack the problem?

            a. Would an attack on some outstanding symptom be the most fruitful approach?

            b. Is there a cause that would be worthwhile to attack? It would need these two essential characteristics:

                (1) Would its removal substantially eliminate or greatly modify the problem?

                (2) Could its removal be accomplished with facilities—personnel, equipment, finances—that are (or can be made) available?

        2. *Boundaries.* What other values—social customs, laws, institutions—must not be harmed in attempting to solve this problem?

III. Suggestions of possible solutions

    A. *One possible solution*

        1. *Nature.* What, specifically, is the plan?

        2. *Strengths.* In what ways would this plan effectively fulfill the requirements or criteria of a solution, that is, make notable progress in the direction and stay satisfactorily within the boundaries of a solution?

3. *Weaknesses.* In what ways would this plan fall short of effectively fulfilling these requirements or criteria?

B. *Another possible solution*

C. *Another possible solution*

D. *Another possible solution*

IV. Selection of the best solution

A. *Best solution (or solution with modifications).* How is this solution better than the others?

B. *Part of problem unsolved.* If the solution leaves any part unsolved, why is it still considered the best?

V. Putting the best solution into operation

A. *Major difficulties to be faced*

B. *Possible ways of overcoming difficulties*

C. *Best way to overcome difficulties*

Applying Reflective Thinking to Problem Solving and Decision Making

When solving problems and making decisions, it is always wise to incorporate a reflective thinking process that follows a plan such as the one suggested by John Dewey. The Dewey reflective thinking steps should be used as a guide to decision making, not an exact formula in approaching every problem that needs to be solved. Randy Hirokawa, a communication scholar, concluded that a systematic approach to group problem solving and decision making is better than no organized approach at all.[12] We also believe that organization and direction are important in group problem-solving interaction but inflexible, lock-step organizations can stifle or reduce a group's ability to arrive at the best solutions.

Applying Reflective Thinking to Problem Solving

1. *Clearly identify the problem you are trying to solve.* The discussion of a topic can be a good exercise, but if the discussion is not focused clearly or goals are not clearly defined as suggested earlier in the chapter, the discussion may wander without direction. For example, a group that decides to discuss the quality of public education but does not define what its purpose is for discussing the topic will likely not come to any conclusion. The group should focus on a clearly identified issue or problem, such as "How can public education be improved with limited resources?"

2. *Phrase the problem as a question to help guide the discussion.* By stating the problem or issue in the form of a question it helps the group focus and direct the discussion more easily. See the suggestions on pages 459–460 for the best way to phrase a question.

3. *Do not start suggesting solutions until you have fully analyzed the problem.* It is generally agreed by most group scholars that problems should be thoroughly researched in order to arrive at the best solutions. This will help you avoid

thinking of solutions prematurely or before you have a complete understanding of the causes, effects, and symptoms of the problem under discussion.

4. *In the definition and analysis steps of reflective thinking, do not confuse the causes of the problem with its symptoms.* Perspiration is a symptom that a person is warm or nervous. The cause for the perspiration, however, may be a stressful situation, such as having to give a speech, not dressing appropriately for weather conditions, or any number of other reasons. The key to successful problem solving is reflective thinking that examines the symptoms in search of the causes.

5. *Appoint at least one member of the group to remind others to follow the reflective thinking steps.* Although the reflective thinking steps were designed sequentially and should be followed as such, it is not unusual for groups to deviate from the order. Thus, it is a good idea to assign some members to monitor the procedures to ensure that the group does not deviate too far from its structure.

From S. A. Beebe and J. T. Masterson, *Communication in Small Groups: Principles and Practices,* 6th ed. (New York: Longman, 2000), 240–41.

Roger Firestein, a small group scholar, recommends that all members, whether leaders or participants, should help keep the group on track and periodically ask the following questions:[13]

1. Do we have sufficient evidence to support our solution?
2. Have we examined a reasonable number of alternatives?
3. Did we reexamine discarded solutions to ensure they should be discarded?
4. Have we come to closure too quickly?
5. Were we open-minded in our thinking?

Brainstorming

Sometimes groups find themselves unable to generate new ideas or to be creative in solving a particular aspect of a problem. In such cases, they may find brainstorming (also discussed in Chapter 7) helpful. **Brainstorming,** a technique used to generate as many ideas as possible within a limited amount of time, can be used during any phase of the group discussion process to produce topics, information, or solutions to problems. During the brainstorming session, group members suggest as many ideas as possible pertaining to the topic, no matter how far-fetched they might seem. One person records the ideas for later analysis. The leader lets the comments flow freely and may prompt the group by suggesting extensions of ideas that have been generated.

Productive Brainstorming

1. Don't criticize any idea, either verbally or nonverbally.
2. No idea is too wild—encourage creativity.
3. Quantity is important—the more ideas, the better.
4. Seize opportunities to improve on or to add to ideas suggested by others.

5. Record all ideas generated by the group.

6. At the end of a specified time, evaluate ideas and determine which is the best.[17]

7. Don't set too short a time limit.

8. Make brainstorming part of the group's strategy.

From A. Osborn, *Applied Imagination: Principles and Procedures of Creative Thinking* (New York: Scribner, 1953), 300–1.

The leader of a brainstorming group should create an open atmosphere that encourages creativity and spontaneity. Thus, it is important that the leader be a person of high energy who responds enthusiastically to new ideas. The leader should provide reinforcement and support to all members and encourage the members to keep contributing if they hit a dry spell. For example, the leader can use prompts such as these: "Let's generate at least two more ideas." "We've done great up to now—let's try one more time to generate some really far-out ideas."

Group members, as well as the leader, must not express disapproval (communicated by comments or looks) of any items until all ideas have been generated. Once the group has run out of ideas or time, the results should be evaluated. During this stage, members should work together to appraise each and every idea. The goal is to determine which idea or ideas merit more attention. It is appropriate to discard ideas that are unfeasible or weak, to improve undeveloped ideas, to consolidate related ideas, and to discuss further the most promising ones.

Brainstorming via Technology

In Chapter 15, we discussed ways newsgroups allow groups of individuals to communicate with each other over the Internet to share and obtain information on a

Making Connections

Stormin' with the Brain

To begin this activity, the instructor should divide the class into groups of four to six students each. Each group should select one of the following four topics:

Ways to increase diversity on campus

Incorporating technology into the classroom

Ideas to reduce alcohol consumption by students

An exciting, interesting spring break destination

Before the group discusses the agreed-on topic, each individual group member should create a list of ideas. Then the group as a whole should spend approximately ten minutes generating a list of ideas on the same topic. Make sure the group adheres to the accompanying guidelines for productive brainstorming.

1. After the group has finished the brainstorming session, discuss the value of brainstorming.

2. What did you learn about brainstorming?

variety of subjects. Similarly, groups can use electronic brainstorming, in which a group generates ideas, solutions, or strategies and inputs their thoughts onto the computer, displaying them either via a liquid crystal display (LCD) projector on a large screen to the entire group or to individual computer screens in a lab, in separate rooms, or at another location. This high-tech approach uses the same principles that face-to-face brainstorming uses except all the ideas are input on a computer instead of being written on a chalkboard or notepad. Advantages of this method include the speed of recording and the ability for group members to send their ideas simultaneously.

Another advantage according to the research is that electronic brainstorming generates more ideas than traditional brainstorming approaches.[14] It has been speculated that the increase in ideas and contributions by group members is because of the anonymity of who is generating the idea.[15] Group members feel less pressure or embarrassment about ideas that are later rejected. The ideas that are generated are considered not on the basis of who suggested them but solely on their merit and quality. Like traditional brainstorming, electronic brainstorming encourages group interaction by allowing individual group members to build on the ideas of others.

Managing Group Conflict

When you hear the word *conflict,* what comes to mind? For most people it conjures terms such as *argument, dislike, fight, stress, hate, competition, disagreement, hostility, discord, friction, disunity,* and so on. All of these words do relate to conflict. However, they illustrate only the negative side of the concept. After all, in U.S. society most people value and stress the importance of agreement and "getting along" with others. However, our society also loves competition. Sayings such as: "beat the other team at any cost" or "stick to your guns" are often cited as the American way. We as a people are competitors and we love to win. But the desires to get along with others yet to beat them in competition as well contradict each other. The idea that if one person wins, another must lose, is implanted in almost every American's mind early in life.

On the one hand, we would like to avoid conflict and preserve unity. On the other hand, we cannot experience the thrill of winning unless we enter into conflict. Is there any middle ground between these two polarities? Can conflict be resolved only by forcing someone to lose? Must conflict always hurt someone?

Whenever people come together to communicate, there is bound to be conflict. But conflict does not always have to be harmful. In fact, it can be productive and, if properly managed, can result in better decisions and solutions to problems.

Conflict and Group Communication

Communication scholars William Wilmot and Joyce Hocker suggest that communication and conflict are related in the following ways: Communication behavior often *creates* conflict, communication behavior *reflects* conflict, and communication is the *vehicle* for the productive or destructive management of conflict.[16] *Conflict,* as defined by Wilmot and Hocker, "is an expressed struggle between at least two interdependent parties who perceive incompatible goals, scarce resources, and interference from others in achieving their goals."[17] This definition has five components:

1. *"An expressed struggle"* has been communicated and understood by the parties involved in the conflict.

2. *Conflict occurs between "two interdependent parties."* If the parties were not dependent on each other, no conflict could occur. Neither person would have an interest in what the other person does. Conflict is possible only when the actions of one person can affect the other person. Conflict is a mutual activity.

3. *Conflict reflects "incompatible goals."* That is, if one person's goal is obtained, the other's will not be. In most group situations, the outcome is usually determined by group consensus. In some situations, a subgroup can produce its own results or report when the group as a whole cannot reach agreement or consensus. The subgroup, however, only represents those members in it and not the group as a whole. It is, however, rare that people working for a common goal totally oppose each other's positions. It is usually in the group's best interest to find some way to reconcile differences in order to reach a mutual decision.

4. *People perceive "scarce resources," thus limiting alternatives or choices.* For example, a committee might have to decide whether to expand the library building or remodel a deteriorating classroom building. Available funding will cover only one project. Such dynamics can create conflict. Of course, either decision will result in a positive outcome. The challenge is determining which decision will deliver the greatest benefit and getting all members to accept the decision, regardless of whether it reflects each one's preference.

Making Connections

Jerk or Hero?

Hector is always challenging Reynaldo's and Venita's ideas. He always seems to be disagreeing and asking for more explanation and evidence from Reynaldo and Venita to support what they are saying. It seems that they argue and bicker a lot whenever they are together. Reynaldo is fed up with Hector's attitude and wants to tell him to get off his case. Venita, on the other hand, appreciates Hector's way of challenging their ideas, because she recognizes that the best ideas can stand up to criticism.

This is Reynaldo's perception—"Hector is a jerk. What makes him think he can do any better!"

This is Venita's perception—"Hector is difficult but makes me think of ways to improve my ideas. I really appreciate his pushing me to come up with the best ideas."

You have just been asked to join Hector, Reynaldo, and Venita to make a difficult decision that will significantly affect the local economy.

1. What approach should Hector take when he wishes to challenge others' ideas? How will you influence him to use this approach?
2. Will Hector be a benefit or a liability to the group's discussions and decisions? Explain your response.
3. Explain why conflict might sometimes be a good thing in group communication.

5. *The parties must "perceive" that they are in conflict.* There can be no conflict unless people perceive there is one. Conflict is more than disagreement. It also involves how the disagreement is perceived and how to deal with it.

Conflict can have both beneficial and harmful results. Returning criticism for criticism will likely escalate the conflict. Both parties will ultimately try to destroy each other's credibility. However, asking for a member's reasons for a particular criticism can elicit a positive response—the person perceives the willingness to listen as an enlightened, cooperative response. Such communication can defuse a situation that is moving toward open confrontation. It also models positive communication behavior. A person who tends to argue from a polarized position may, when seeing the results of more cooperative techniques, eventually develop a more group-oriented communication style.

Effective group decision making and problem solving often depend on conflict and open disagreement. Of course, too much conflict can create unmanageable tension and heighten disagreement, resulting in personal attacks on individual group members. If personal attacks come to dominate meetings, they produce no benefits and usually lead to hurt feelings, withdrawal, and eventually to the disbanding of the group.

The benefits of group conflict, when it is understood and controlled, include a better understanding of group members and issues, better involvement and increased motivation, better decisions, and greater group cohesiveness. These benefits are more likely to occur when groups accept collaboration and compromise.

In collaboration, negotiating and problem solving are used to find a solution that fully meets the needs of all parties involved in a group conflict. In other words, each party achieves its desired results. For example, you're serving on a college curriculum committee in which the student members think that the general education course should be practical, whereas the faculty believes it should be theoretical. There is much discussion, but eventually both sides see the benefits of each view and agree that all the general education courses should include both practice and theory. The result is an ideal solution in which both students and faculty members win. The collaboration between the students and faculty generated by the conflict has resulted in a superior, integrated general education curriculum.

Compromise is a shared outcome. Compromise means conflicting parties are willing to give up part of their position to arrive at an alternative that includes parts of both parties' original positions. Compromise implies giving up something to gain something more important, so both parties involved gain from the compromise. For example, a grading appeals committee made up of two students and four faculty members has been presented with an appeal. A student believes he should have received an A, and the professor of the course insists the student got what he earned—a C. After hearing both sides, one student and two faculty members on the committee believe that the student appealing should have received an A, whereas the other student and the other two faculty members believe that the C was appropriate. A deadlock must be resolved. Through compromise, the conflicting parties agree that the student should receive a B. Neither party got exactly what it wanted, but both can agree to the compromise. The positive outcomes of conflict, according to John Brilhart and Gloria Galanes, are as follows:

1. Conflict can produce better understanding of both issues and people.

2. Conflict can increase member motivation.

3. Conflict can produce better decisions.

4. Conflict can produce greater cohesiveness among group members.[18]

Managing Conflict

In order for groups to be successful, conflict must be perceived as beneficial. It should not be avoided. In fact, we suggest that it be encouraged as long as it is created in order to produce better group decisions. Avoiding conflict, according to Brilhart and Galanes, "circumvents the very reason for engaging in group discussion."[19]

One of the primary reasons for having small groups in the first place is the notion that two heads are better than one. We also know that when people get together to discuss issues, there is bound to be conflict. If conflict is inevitable and we know it can be beneficial as well as harmful, how can we ensure that it will facilitate rather than inhibit? The answer is the use of conflict management strategies.

Principled negotiation is a procedure that helps group members negotiate consensus by collaboration through the expression of each differing need and a search for alternatives to meet those needs.[20] It is referred to as "principled" because the procedure is based on ethical principles that encourage participants to be respectful and civilized toward one another. In other words, exchanging information by asking questions instead of making demands or taking a rigid position on differences will aid in producing an agreed-on outcome. Participants must take into account other participants' views and consider them in the way they'd like their own views to be considered. Of course, not every disagreement can be resolved, and at times other approaches may have to be taken. To resolve conflict, participants must be willing to communicate about their differences and must want to find a resolution to their differences.

A legislative committee confers on a bill in a conference setting. To gain agreement on a bill, members who are not in agreement negotiate for consensus by identifying different needs and search for alternatives to meet those needs.

Ethical Behavior and Conflict

Brilhart and Galanes suggest that using ethical behaviors during a conflict situation creates a better understanding of the issues and increased cohesiveness while at the same time minimizing destructive outcomes, such as hurt feelings and personal attacks.[21] They have listed a number of helpful suggestions to aid individuals on how to behave ethically during conflicts:

1. Express disagreements openly and honestly—it is important to get disagreements on the table for discussion.

2. Stick to the issues. Be direct and get to the point.

3. Use rhetorical sensitivity when presenting your disagreements. Don't simply put down others' ideas or views.

4. Criticize the idea and not the person.

5. Base disagreements on solid evidence and good reasoning—not on rumor, emotions, or unsubstantiated information.

6. Be receptive to disagreements. Don't become defensive simply because someone disagrees with you. Keep an open mind and listen carefully.

7. Always remain calm, even if someone attacks you. Take a reasoned approach, and do not take the attack personally.

8. Look for ways to integrate ideas and to negotiate differences, whenever possible.

Evaluating Small Group Performance

To ensure success, every group must periodically evaluate its effectiveness. The evaluation can take place at any time or at the end of one task and before another begins. Evaluation is also important in classroom exercises. As students learn about group communication, they need their instructor's feedback and also to evaluate themselves. Such self-evaluation should consider the following questions:

1. Are we using our time efficiently? If not, why not?
2. Does everyone have an opportunity to participate?
3. Are some people dominating the discussion?
4. Are people listening to what others are saying?
5. Is each person bringing adequate information and research to the discussion?
6. Is the atmosphere free from personal conflict?
7. Does the group communication stay within the agenda?
8. Are the members happy about what is taking place in the discussion? If not, why not?
9. Do we set realistic goals for our meetings?
10. Do we get things accomplished? If not, why not?

For an evaluation to produce results, its findings must be made known to all members of the group. A crucial requirement for such sharing is a nonthreatening atmosphere. The leader and all the members must be willing to examine the situation without becoming defensive. The group's success is related to each member's willingness to work and cooperate with the others. If the group is not getting its job done, or if its members are unhappy, corrective steps must be taken. Otherwise people will lose interest in the group, and it may disintegrate or become unproductive and dysfunctional.

Summary

Not all groups will become teams, but groups that become like teams are often more successful than groups that do not. When group members believe they are part of a team, they tend to cooperate more because they often have set and clearly defined their goals; believe their objectives are important, meaningful, and worthwhile; have an identity or name that separates them from other teams; and have an effective leader.

Leadership is any behavior that helps to clarify, guide, or achieve the goals of a group. A *leader* is a person assigned or selected to guide or provide direction in order to reach the group's goal. Leaders are responsible for keeping things going, organizing the discussion, promoting interpersonal relationships, facilitating understanding, and stimulating creativity. In addition, they must be able to meet group members' *task needs,* needs related to getting the task completed, and *maintenance needs,* needs related to organizing and developing a group such that members realize personal satisfaction from working together. Leaders may be either *task-oriented,* concerned with completing the job or solving the problem, or *relationship-oriented,* concerned with interpersonal relationships. Leaders may also be classified as *autocratic,* maintaining complete control of the group; *democratic,* sharing control and other responsibilities; or *laissez-faire,* giving up almost all the control to the group.

The leader's approach affects the group's atmosphere and its effectiveness and efficiency in making decisions. Research indicates that the democratic leadership style is superior to the autocratic style in terms of getting the task done and satisfying group members. Autocratic leaders are able to produce more, but they seem to generate more hostility and aggression among group members. Laissez-faire groups tend to accomplish less, produce work of lower quality, and waste more time. To be most effective, a leader must know how to use all three leadership styles and how to match the appropriate style to the individual situation.

Successful groups depend on group members performing in various roles, for example, *grouptask roles,* such as initiator–contributor, information seeker, information giver, opinion seeker, opinion giver, elaborator, coordinator, orienter, evaluator/critic, energizer, recorder, and tester of agreements. *Group building and maintenance roles* help to develop a group's social atmosphere and include encouragers, harmonizers, compromisers, gatekeepers, standard setters, followers, and feeling expressers. Group members, unfortunately, at times take on *self-centered roles,* which are generally counterproductive or destructive behaviors. These self-centered roles include aggressors, blockers, recognition seekers, self-confessors, buffoons, dominators, help seekers, and withdrawers. Group members should recognize such behaviors and help the leader control them.

Planning and conducting meetings is an important step in reaching a successful outcome. To ensure efficiency, group members who are not familiar with each other should introduce themselves, and, if necessary, the group should assign or elect a leader and a recording secretary. An *agenda,* which is a list of all topics to be discussed during a meeting, should be formulated. The leader is usually responsible for setting and maintaining the agenda.

Problem solving and decision making require a systematic approach if the best conclusions are to be reached. The first step in the process of decision making is to determine the problem or topic, which should then be stated in the form of a question. Questions are of four types: a *question of fact* asks whether something is true or false; a *question of interpretation* asks for the meaning or understanding of something; a *question of value* asks whether something is good or bad, desirable or undesirable; and a *question of policy* asks what actions should be taken.

Once the discussion question is clearly formulated, it is time to select a procedure for discussing it. A common method of solving problems and making decisions includes five steps: (1) definition of the problem, (2) analysis of the problem, (3) suggestions of possible solutions, (4) selection of the best solution, and (5) putting the best solution into operation.

When a group hits a snag in the problem-solving or decision-making process, brainstorming can help generate new ideas. *Brainstorming,* a technique used to generate as many ideas as possible within a limited amount of time, can be used during any phase of the group discussion process to produce topics, information, or solutions to problems. The keys to productive brainstorming are openness and creativity.

Another efficient way to brainstorm is via the computer. Groups that brainstorm using the computer find that they are able to generate more ideas than they might using traditional brainstorming approaches.

Every time two or more people get together there is the possibility of conflict. *Conflict* is usually assumed to be harmful, but it does not have to be so. *Conflict* is an expressed struggle between at least two interdependent parties who perceive incompatible goals, scarce resources, and interference from others in achieving their goals. Conflict can be managed through effective use of communication and a technique called principled negotiation. *Principled negotiation* is a procedure that helps group members negotiate consensus by collaboration through the expression of each differing need and a search for alternatives to meet those needs.

Evaluation is a key step in ensuring a group's progress and success. For an evaluation to accomplish its purpose, the leader and all group members must be willing to accept its findings and take the appropriate corrective steps.

DISCUSSION STARTERS

1. Why is leadership so important to the success of small groups?
2. Do all leaders have leadership abilities? Explain.
3. Are there differences between male and female leadership styles? Explain.
4. What is the best way to identify a leader?
5. Which leadership style is the most appropriate for small group discussions? Why?
6. How can leadership affect small group communication?
7. What are the functions of a leader in a small group?
8. What are the responsibilities of a group participant?
9. Explain the differences between constructive and counterproductive contributions by group members.
10. Who is responsible for handling counterproductive contributions?
11. How specifically would you handle a group member who was acting the role of a buffoon?
12. How would you lead withdrawn group members back into a discussion without embarrassing them?
13. How would you organize a discussion on the following topic: What should be the role and responsibility of students in monitoring drug use on campus?
14. Describe a situation in which the use of brainstorming would be appropriate.
15. What criteria would you use to evaluate a small group discussion?

NOTES

1. C. Larson and M. LaFasto, *Teamwork: What Must Go Right, What Can Go Wrong* (Newbury Park, Calif.: Sage, 1989).
2. F. E. Fiedler, *A Theory of Leadership Effectiveness* (New York: McGraw-Hill, 1967).
3. R. K. White and R. Lippitt, *Autocracy and Democracy: An Experimental Inquiry* (New York: Harper & Row, 1960), 26–27.
4. L. G. Bolman and T. E. Deal, *Reframing Organizations: Artistry, Choice, and Leadership,* 2nd ed.

(San Francisco: Jossey-Bass, 1997); and G. Morgan, *Images of Organization,* 2nd ed. (Thousand Oaks, Calif.: Sage, 1997).
5. R. K. White and R. Lippitt, "Leader Behavior and Member Reaction in Three 'Social Climates,'" in *Group Dynamics: Research and Theory,* 2nd ed., eds. Dorwin Cartwright and Alvin Zarda (New York: Harper & Row, 1960), 527–53; L. P. Bradford and R. Lippitt, "Building a Democratic Work Group," *Personnel* 22 (1945): 142–52; and W. M. Fox, "Group

Reaction to Two Types of Conference Leadership," *Human Relations* 10 (1957): 279–89.

6. M. Loden, *Feminine Leadership or How to Succeed in Business Without Being One of the Boys* (New York: Times Books, 1985).

7. A. H. Eagly and B. T. Johnson, "Gender and Leadership Style: A Meta-Analysis," *Psychological Bulletin* 108 (1990): 233–56.

8. D. Forsyth, M. Heiney, and S. Wright, "Biases in Appraisal of Women Leaders," *Group Dynamics: Theory, Research, and Practices* 1 (1997): 98–103; S. Shackelford, W. Wood, and S. Worchel, "Behavioral Styles and the Influence of Women in Mixed-Sex Groups," *Social Psychology* 59 (1996): 284–93; and A. Eagly, S. Karau, M. Makhijani, "Gender and the Effectiveness of Leaders: A Meta-Analysis," *Journal of Personality and Social Psychology* 117 (1995): 125–45.

9. K. D. Benne and P. Sheats, "Functional Roles of Group Members," *Journal of Social Issues* 4 (1948): 41–49.

10. R. V. Harnack, T. B. Fest, and B. S. Jones, *Group Discussion: Theory and Technique,* 2nd ed. (Englewood Cliffs, N.J.: Prentice-Hall, 1997), 153–54.

11. J. Dewey, *How We Think* (Lexington, Mass.: Heath, 1933).

12. R. Y. Hirokawa, "Consensus Group Decision-Making, Quality of Decision and Group Satisfaction: An Attempt to Sort 'Fact' from 'Fiction,'" *Central States Speech Journal* 33 (1992): 407–15; and "Why Informed Groups Make Faulty Decisions: An Investigation of Possible Interaction-Based Explanation," *Small Group Behavior* 18 (1987): 3–29.

13. R. L. Firestein, "Effects of Creative Problem-Solving Training on Communication Behavior in Small Groups," *Small Group Research* 21 (November, 1990): 507–21.

14. M. C. Roy, S. Gauvin, and M. Limayem, "Electronic Group Brainstorming: The Role of Feedback on Productivity," *Small Group Research* 27 (1996): 215–47.

15. J. J. Sosik, B. J. Avolio, and S. S. Kahai, "Inspiring Group Creativity: Comparing Anonymous and Identified Electronic Brainstorming," *Small Group Research* 29 (1998) 3–31; and W. H. Cooper, R. B. Gallupe, S. Pollard, and J. Cadsby, "Some Liberating Effects of Anonymous Electronic Brainstorming," *Small Group Research* 29 (1998): 147–77.

16. W. Wilmot and J. Hocker, *Interpersonal Conflict,* 5th ed. (New York: McGraw-Hill, 1998), 35.

17. Ibid., p. 34.

18. J. K. Brilhart, G. J. Galanes, and K. Adams, *Effective Group Communication Theory and Practice,* 10th ed. (New York: McGraw-Hill, 2001), 308–10.

19. Ibid., 315.

20. R. Fisher and W. Ury, *Getting to Yes: Negotiating Agreement Without Giving In* (Boston: Houghton Mifflin, 1981).

21. J. K. Brilhart and G. J. Galanes, 318–20.

APPENDIX

Employment Interviewing: Preparing for Your Future

"You never get a second chance to make

a first impression."

—Kathryn Barbour, Fredic Berg, Maryrose Eannace, John Greene, Mary Hessig, Margot Papworth, Carol Radin, Edward Rezny, and John Suarez in The Quest: A Guide to the Job Interview *(Dubuque, Iowa: Kendall/Hunt, 1991), p. 47.*

- Use the Internet to help you prepare for the interview, research organizations, locate job openings, and get a job.
- Describe the qualities that employers seek in applicants.
- Develop a résumé that will make a good impression on prospective employers.
- Conduct yourself effectively in an employment interview.

SCENARIO

Rachelle, a mother of two children, started her college education prior to having children, but her husband and she decided that she should put her college education on hold in order to raise their children. The children are now in junior and senior high school, and Rachelle has gone back to college and is about to complete her degree in communication studies. Because she doesn't know about all the job opportunities that are available for communication majors, she turns to the Internet for help.

Bill, who is graduating in May, is looking for a public relations position with a major corporation. He has called Mr. Muller, the personnel director of S & S Enterprises, to discuss his chances of being hired by that firm.

Liz is looking for an internship in marketing in order to get some experience before she begins the real job hunt. She has contacted several different marketing firms through her university internship office and is ready to be interviewed.

Sam needs to earn a few dollars in order to make it through college. He decides to get a part-time job and is scheduled to interview with a local clothing store. ■

The students in these examples will participate in interviews that will affect the rest of their lives. In this appendix, we examine the employment interview—what you as a job hunter can expect to encounter and how you can prepare to make the best impression.[1]

Preparing for Job Hunting

The purpose of this book is to help you with the following skills: speaking, organizing, critical thinking, researching, persuading, informing, listening, discussing, making decisions, solving problems, and using nonverbal and verbal communication. Another purpose is to help you develop your leadership and interpersonal skills. After you have completed this course, it will then be up to you to continue developing

Making Connections

Thinking About Your Future

Refer back to the opening scenario, and think about what each person must be able to demonstrate in order to land a job. SKILLS! That one word means a lot to your future. The recurring theme among the experts we surveyed is an emphasis on skills and competencies, rather than on completing specific studies.

Your major alone may not make a decisive difference in your future, but the skills you master and the way you communicate them to others can carry you through a lifetime of careers.

1. What is the message in the statements?
2. What advice would you give to Rachelle, Bill, Liz, and Sam as they prepare themselves for their interviews?

J. Meyers, "The Ideal Job Candidate," *Collegiate Employment Institute Letter,* 15 July 1989, 6; and *Ford's Insider: Continuing Series of College Newspaper Supplements* (Knoxville, Tenn.: 13–30 Corporation, 1980), 14.

each skill throughout your education and your lifetime. Because employment interviews are among the most important interpersonal communication events of your life, we have devoted this appendix to them.

Most of you taking this course are probably just beginning your college education. Whether you are a recent high school graduate or have returned to school after pursuing other interests like Rachelle, the following pages on employment interviews will give you important information that will aid you in preparing for your future after graduation. Although graduation and hunting for a full-time job may seem far away, your preparation for them should begin now. You can begin by attending your university or community's career day programs. Such programs bring together undergraduates, graduate students, and alumni with employers from government, private enterprise, and nonprofit organizations. It is a time for everyone—even first-year students—to find out what organizations are looking for in potential employees. If you haven't already started to prepare for your career or first interview, you should begin now—don't wait until your senior year; that may be too late.

Career Research on the Internet

One of the most valuable tools available in preparing for the employment interview is the Internet. The Internet, via the World Wide Web, will allow you to research every aspect of the employment interview. For example, you can learn how to prepare for the interview, write a résumé, create an electronic résumé, research organizations, find job opportunities, find out what questions are commonly asked in interviews, and even get advice on what to wear to an interview. Most colleges and universities have a career and placement center that you can visit in person or contact through their home page. The career or placement center's home page can be an extremely valuable source of information. The University of Nebraska's (UNL) Career Services Center, for example, has one of the most up-to-date home pages on the Internet (see Figure A.1).

FIGURE A.1

A Sample Career Services Home Page

This figure illustrates the information provided to students by university and college career services and placement offices.

Used by permission of University of Nebraska–Lincoln Career Services.

Its Internet address is http://www.unl.edu/careers/, and it provides information pertaining to almost every aspect of careers and the employment interview. You can click any of the boxed items to explore services and resources. For example, the Job Search Preparation area leads to information on how to search for a job on the Internet, job search strategies, résumé tips and a sample résumé, how to write application letters

Making Connections

Your Personal Headhunter

Are you in search of the perfect job? There are well over a million jobs listed on the Internet currently. Of course the number of jobs and the jobs available in any specific career field does vary from day to day. If you answered yes to this question, check out some of these websites, which may help you find that perfect job:

CareerBuilder: http://www.careerbuilder.com/

CareerCity Jobs and Employment: http://www.careercity.com/

College Grad Job Hunter: http://www.collegegrad.com/

JobBank USA: http://www.jobbankusa.com/

America's Job Bank: http://www.ajb.dni.us/

CareerPath.com: http://www.careerpath.com/

CoolJobs.com: http://www.cooljobs.com/

Monster.com: http://www.monster.com/

and sample application letters, who to get as references, how to create a portfolio, information on organizations, and interviewing tips. The Internet is an incredibly valuable tool in preparing for your future career.

You should check with your college or university's career and placement center for its Internet address. You can also access a search engine and type in the word "jobs," career," or "employment." You will find a vast array of information about employers, job opportunities, and almost anything else you want to know about getting a job or starting your career with the click of a mouse.

Choosing a Career

Choosing a career may be the most important decision you will ever make. An estimated 10,000 days of your life are at stake—that's about how much time the average person spends on the job. According to some experts, there are a minimum of 42,000 career options from which college graduates can choose. Every October *U.S.News & World Report* describes "Best Jobs for the Future." This is a must-see resource for every college student.

Studying the following pages will not guarantee you the perfect job after graduation, but it should help improve your chances of getting it. There are approximately 150 million employment interviews conducted in the United States each year resulting in hundreds of thousands of jobs filled. To compete successfully for available jobs requires planning and preparation—now, rather than at the last minute. It is important that you begin the planning and preparation process for your career as early as possible in your education. Getting an early start will allow you to take advantage of all the opportunities your college and university provides in the way of extracurricular activities, which will help you develop a strong, diverse background for meeting your career objectives.

Qualities Employers Seek

Demographics of the U.S. workplace are changing more rapidly than ever as we enter a new century. Cultural diversity is more prevalent for most organizations, because we have become a global economy. Women now make up more than 50 percent of the workforce, and there is significant growth in the Hispanic and Asian American populations as well. Today, the workforce in many organizations consists of women and men of diverse cultures, languages, and ethnic backgrounds. In addition, people are living longer and working longer. What does this mean to you? No one knows for sure the answer to this question. During the past several years, the job market has grown substantially and the opportunities for employment have mushroomed to the highest numbers in U.S. history. Many companies, in order to lure top job candidates, are offering signing bonuses, stock options, tuition reimbursement, health insurance, and profit sharing. It is a seller's market today, but in spite of this growth and the vast number of job opportunities, there is still a lot of competition for the very best jobs.

During the 1970s, 1980s, and 1990s, many organizations eliminated millions of middle-management positions. Thus, advancement positions in many organizations are limited and difficult to get. In the past, college graduates who started on the ground level of an organization were almost guaranteed that working hard would move them up the organizational ladder to higher management positions. The higher management jobs are fewer, and those that are available are very competitive.

The typical company employee of the 1960s, 1970, and 1980s stayed with the same company for twenty, thirty, or forty years. Career changes during this period were two or three. Today, job security is not only a function of the type of organization but of the employee's skills and flexibility. Typical college graduates can expect to change jobs from six to eight times and make at least three career changes during their lifetime.

This does not mean that companies are not looking for long-term employees, but with changes in ownership, direction, product lines, and services that affect employment with a company, job changing has become the rule rather than the exception.[2] All of this is making organizations rethink how and who they want to hire. An August 16, 1998, *Chicago Tribune* article reported that 57 percent of the companies surveyed reported being more careful in their selection of employees to maintain and retain their workforce.[3]

Charles Stewart and William Cash Jr., communication scholars and authors of a top-selling interviewing text, suggest ten universal skills and attitudes that are essential to work in the twenty-first century. They are

1. You will need to be able to deal comfortably with numbers.
2. You will need to be computer literate.
3. You will need to be customer- and quality-oriented.
4. You will need to have a global and diverse perspective.
5. You will need to speak a second language.
6. You will need strong interpersonal skills.
7. You will need to deal with change and job ambiguity.
8. You will need to nourish a willingness to learn.
9. You will need to take on a team perspective.
10. You will need to be a problem solver.[4]

Dr. Larry Routh (email address: lrouth1@unl.edu), Director of Career Services at the University of Nebraska at Lincoln, suggests that students get as much experience in team building and working in teams as possible.[5] Companies, according to Routh, are no longer looking exclusively for people with supervisory skills as much as they are looking for individuals who can work with others. One company recruiter asks students the following question, "When you work as a part of a team what unique role do you play?" Routh said, "Hiring people who are team players is important to many companies who have downsized and have fewer management positions, because they are much more team oriented." For example, one senior student answered the question by indicating that she was the person who brought the group back to task by clarifying and pulling the group ideas to the objective. Dr. Routh suggested his strength when working on a team was the ability to brainstorm ideas. Routh's strength is quite different from the senior student's, but both are important to team success. What is your role when working with others? Is it leading, organizing, brainstorming, or something else? You need to know what your strengths are.

Internships are also important. Dr. Routh suggests that students should get involved in internships that are related to the jobs they will seek after graduation. He says that students who can say that they have done the job or similar work will have a better chance at getting a job than those with no experience.

Almost every career requires skills such as writing, speaking, reading, listening, decision making, researching, reasoning, creativity, persuasion, leadership, interpersonal communication, and organization. In addition, a number of characteristics may be important for specific jobs: achievement, aggressiveness, ambition, dependability, discipline, honesty, initiative, motivation, people orientation, persistence, responsibility, self-confidence, sensitivity, sincerity, tenacity, and tough-mindedness.[6] The way you acquire these skills and behaviors is, to a great extent, up to you. Without them, no matter how bright and knowledgeable you may be, landing a job will be extremely difficult, if not impossible. The most likely way to obtain these skills and behaviors is through courses, reading, internships, part-time or full-time employment, extracurricular activities, and participation in communication functions. Acquiring most of them requires training and practice under a qualified instructor.

Knowing what an employer is looking for in a potential employee can help an applicant prepare for an interview. Most employers that we have talked with emphasize the ability to communicate. Can the applicants speak clearly? Can they articulate what kind of person they believe themselves to be? In what kinds of work situations do they perform well? What are their strengths and weaknesses? Employers want to know about the personal qualities of the individual, so they ask questions to draw the applicant out and reveal whether the applicant has a sense of self. They look for an ability to verbalize an idea in clear, simple, understandable language. They also look for the ability to listen attentively and then the ability to respond to an idea or thought.

They also look for creativity. Is the applicant spontaneous? Some recruiters will ask "off the wall" questions just to see if this "throws" an applicant. How does an applicant respond in these tough situations? Can the applicant be creative with the answers? This is very important to most employers, because in business situations with customers, employees often have to respond to sudden changes and unfamiliar problems. Employers need to know whether an applicant can handle such situations.

What employers look for most are personal qualities—assertiveness, self-motivation, drive, ambition, and a competitive instinct. Applicants should be high achievers and want to work hard. Employers say they can usually tell about these qualities by how people present themselves and by reviewing the activities in which the applicant has been engaged. Much of this information can be found right on the job application and résumé.

Preparation for an Interview

Preparation for a job interview takes planning and some thought about what will be expected of you as an applicant. Initial job interviews average only twenty to thirty minutes in length—a short time in comparison to the time you've spent earning a college degree. Yet, these are probably the most important minutes you will spend in determining your job future. You would be surprised to learn how many applicants fail to plan adequately. Instead, they enter the interview saying essentially, "Here I am. Now what?" This gives the impression that they are indifferent—an impression that is seldom dispelled in the course of the interview. Ensuring that an impression of indifference isn't left with the employer is up to you. Make sure that you are prepared and that you present a positive picture of yourself.

Making Connections

What Every College Student Should Know to Prepare for the Job Interview

In order to learn firsthand what corporations are looking for today when they hire a college graduate, Seiler interviewed Gary Danek, who recently retired as an account executive with Procter & Gamble (P&G), a Fortune 500 corporation (http://www.pg.com). Danek, before retiring, had been with P&G for more than thirty-five years and had interviewed hundreds of college students. The Seiler and Danek interview is available on our website at www.ablongman.com/seiler.

1. Based on what you have read in the interview transcript, what could you do to make yourself a better candidate for a job?

2. If you were to give one piece of advice to someone based on the Danek interview, what would that advice be?

3. If you could ask Mr. Danek a question about what you could do to better prepare yourself for the job interview, what would that question be? Email your question to Bill Seiler (bseiler@unl.edu), and he will forward it to Mr. Danek for his response. Your question will be answered as soon as possible.

Writing a Résumé

A **résumé** (sometimes referred to as a vita) is a written document that briefly and accurately describes an individual's personal, educational, and professional qualifications and experiences. A well-written résumé increases a person's chances of making a good impression. A poorly written résumé can seriously jeopardize a person's chances, even though he or she may be well qualified. The résumé should clearly detail the experiences the applicant has had and demonstrate that he or she is an individual who takes action. For example, an assertive person might say, "I can do these things" and "I decided on this course of action," whereas a more passive person might say, "These are the experiences I have had." Employers are looking for people who demonstrate that they can do things and get them done.

Many companies are now requesting that résumés be written so they can be scanned into a computer database. This means that résumés must include keywords that describe your competencies and skills. The employer is then able quickly and efficiently to search thousands of résumés for certain keywords that describe and narrow down a long list of potentially qualified applicants for a specific job. So that a résumé can be scanned, it must be typed neatly on high-quality white bond paper. You cannot use boldface type, underlining, or bullets if a résumé is to be scanned.

 **Emailing Your Résumé to the Employer**

1. Always send it to a specific person. Determining who to send your résumé to may require some research, but the effort of locating a specific individual is

well worth it, because you will more likely get a response than if you address it to the company's personnel office or human resources department.

2. Your email memo should introduce yourself and explain what you are seeking and why. The email memo is similar to the typical cover letter that is sent via the post office. It should be brief, usually three or four paragraphs, and never more than one page. It should also be neat, contain no spelling or grammatical errors, professional in appearance, and easy to read. There are many excellent guides for writing effective cover letters that can be found on the Internet. Go to the following websites for help and samples: http://www.unl.edu/careers/tips/letters.html, http://campus.monster.com/articles/jobhunt/coverletters/, or do an Internet search using the words "cover letters." You will find many very helpful sites to guide you in writing an effective cover letter.

3. Attach your résumé to your email document rather than including it after your introductory memo. When attaching a document to an email message, it must be formatted correctly so that the person receiving the email can open it. If you are uncertain of the best format to use in sending your résumé, send an initial email requesting this information from the employer.

4. If you do not hear back from the person to whom you sent your résumé within a few days, follow with an email message asking if your message was received.

5. Thank the person for his or her time.

The personal résumé may highlight work experience (see Figure A.2) or skills (see Figure A.3). In addition, many companies also require applicants to complete an application form, which requests personal data (name, address, phone number, social security number, citizenship, and whether you have ever been convicted of a felony), job interests (position desired, data available, and salary desired), educational training (high school, college, or graduate school), references (name, occupation, phone number, and address), employment history (name, address, dates of employment, salary, positions held, and reason for leaving), and possibly voluntary information (sex, race, or ethnic identification; military service record, if you are a veteran or disabled veteran; whether you have a disability).

A résumé is an extremely powerful form of communication. Because it represents an applicant, it must be accurate, complete, and neat. The contents and layouts of résumés vary as widely as the number of individuals who apply for jobs. A general rule, and the safest, is to *keep it simple, limit it to one or two pages, and list items within each section beginning with the most current one.* Employers are busy and do not have time to read lengthy, involved reports.

Résumés reflect who you are and your qualifications for the job. Employers want to know a person's qualifications and the résumé, if done concisely and accurately, is an invaluable tool for creating a favorable impression.

By permission of Johnny Hart and Creators Syndicate, Inc.

FIGURE A.2

Self-Prepared or Personal Résumé Emphasizing Work Experience

This figure illustrates a résumé format that is used by many students. The résumé layout is fairly standard, but it may vary depending on the work experiences of the individual.

Jo Ann Doe
712 Garfield Street, Apt.2-A
Lincoln, Nebraska 00000
402/555-9797

OBJECTIVE

An administrative assistant position in a federal, state, or city government agency where I can utilize my public relations skills.

EXPERIENCE

Assistant Campaign Manager: Senator Sally Jones, Lincoln, Nebraska (July 1999–November 2000).
Directed and coordinated all public activities.
Arranged and scheduled personal appearances, debates, and media releases.
Purchased, designed, and supervised the development of campaign materials.
Recruited, trained, and supervised community volunteer groups.
Supervised a staff of 16 community volunteers.

Staff Assistant as an Intern: United Volunteer Agency, Lincoln, Nebraska (December 1997–June 1999).
Communicated the scope of Agency programs to Lincoln area businesses and community groups.
Prepared Agency filmstrips, brochures, and news releases.
Conducted public relations information sessions.

Legislative Assistant: Nebraska Legislative Session, Lincoln, Nebraska (June 1996–December 1997).
Collected, compiled, and released information briefs and legislative action profiles to public news media.
Typed and edited legislative bills.

EDUCATION

The University of Nebraska, Lincoln, Nebraska (1997–2001)
Bachelor of Arts Degree. Communication Studies and Journalism.
Grade Point Average: 3.75/4.00.

EDUCATIONAL HIGHLIGHTS

Outstanding Senior Award, Creative Writing Award, Communication Club Secretary, Phi Delta Kappa Vice President.

Related Course Work

Public Relations and Publicity	Survey of Mass Media
Social Political Communication	Interviewing
Public Speaking	Advertising Principles
Federal Grant Development	Public Opinion

Available: Immediately

References: Upon request

Most résumés include the following sections: introductory information, career objective, educational training, work experiences, extracurricular activities, and references. The *introductory information* section should include the applicant's name,

FIGURE A.3

Self-Prepared or Personal Résumé Emphasizing Skills

This figure illustrates a résumé that emphasizes a person's skills. The résumé layout is fairly standard, but it may vary depending on the work experiences and skills of the individual.

Robert L. Smith
1525 East Center Street
Los Angeles, California 00000
213/555-9797

OBJECTIVE	To help a retail company provide high customer satisfaction while managing merchandise efficiently in an entry-level management position.
SKILLS	• Resolved customer problems in retail merchandising • Organized product floor for customer convenience • Successfully dealt with wholesalers • Organized and maintained inventories • Completed college courses in management, personnel, finance, statistics, and marketing
EDUCATION	University of Southern California, Los Angeles, California, Bachelor of Science Degree: Business, May 2000, Management
HONORS	Academic Scholarships, Delta Mu Delta (Business Honorary)
ACTIVITIES and MEMBERSHIPS	President of Delta Mu Delta; Student Senator; Youth Leader of 30 member church youth group.
EXPERIENCE **February 98– present**	B. C. PRINTING, Los Angeles *Graphic Arts–Delivery Person* • Mastered all aspects of prepress operations • Effectively dealt with and resolved conflicts • Oversaw various camera procedures including working with numerous types of film and preparing press plates
January 97–98	QUALITY PRESS, INC., Los Angeles *Internship Graphic Arts– Delivery Person* • Demonstrated ability to serve and communicate with customers in a diverse office supply operation • Organized and maintained product floor and inventory
Additional Information	Paid 100% of college expenses Worked to support wife and child while attending college Computer training includes Basic, Cobol, Assembler, and Pascal
Available	Immediately
References	Available on request

address, and phone number. As an applicant, you are not required to provide information that might be discriminatory. This includes your age, sex, marital status, race, religion, and other data as set forth by the Title VII Equal Employment Opportunity Act of 1972 and other affirmative action laws. The inclusion of such facts in a résumé is up to the applicant, but it is generally advised that they be omitted.

Many placement-service directors recommend that a brief *career objective* be stated on the résumé immediately following the introductory information. The objective should be as specific as possible. For example:

My long-term objective is to become a public relations director in either a major corporation or agency. My immediate goal is to obtain experience in sales, advertising, or marketing related to that long-term objective.

Such a statement can help a potential employer understand the applicant's goals and assess whether those goals relate to a particular job opening or company.

In the *educational training* section of the résumé, the applicant should list colleges and universities attended, degrees conferred, dates of degrees, majors, minors, and special major subjects. Scholarships should be listed, and some statement about grade achievement may be included, although it is not required.

The *work experience* section should include paid and unpaid jobs held, the dates they were held, and their locations. If the applicant has held numerous part-time jobs, only a few of the most important, most recent, and most relevant jobs should be listed. Other job experience can always be discussed at the interview, if it is appropriate to do so.

In the *extracurricular activities* section, the applicant should list all offices held, all social and professional organizations that he or she was involved in, and any athletic participation. This section demonstrates the applicant's outside interests; well-roundedness; and social, leadership, and organizational skills. Such information is less important for experienced or older applicants who have demonstrated similar skills in other areas.

Making Connections

Find Résumé Guidelines on the Internet

The following Internet sites can provide helpful suggestions for preparing a résumé.

http://www.unl.edu/careers/tips/resume.html
(tips and guidelines provided by the University of Nebraska's Career Services)

http://www.dbm.com/jobguide/eresume.html
(The Riley Guide: Resumes and Cover Letters is an extremely helpful guide that discusses the myths about résumés, tells why an Internet résumé is useful, helps you prepare your résumé for the Internet, gives suggestions about posting your résumé, and provides resources for resume writing.)

http://www.provenresumes.com/
(This site provides sixty free résumé and job search workshops; it also includes a quiz to rate your résumé.)

There are many more Internet sites to help you with your résumé development; all you have to do is search the Internet.

The *reference* section should simply state that the applicant will provide references on request. In preparation, you might make a list of persons who are familiar with your work experience and professors in your major field or with whom you have taken several courses. Even though you may not be planning to apply for a job now, it is wise to get to know your professors and to make sure that they get to know you. Find appropriate times (office hours, perhaps) and reasons (discussion of a paper or an assignment) to visit with your professors so they become acquainted with you. Most professors enjoy meeting their students. Use common sense, and don't overstay your visits. Professors will find it easier to write a letter of recommendation for you, and the letter will be more personal and believable, if they know who you are.

Never put a person's name on a reference list unless you have his or her permission to do so. When asking individuals to write references for you, be prepared to hand them a copy of your résumé and to tell them what kind of job you are seeking. Contacting people to write letters of recommendation should be done as professionally and efficiently as possible. Remember that you are requesting someone to take time to help you.

References

Make a written list of at least three people who could write a letter of recommendation for you. Do not include relatives or friends. After each name on your list, answer the following questions:

1. Why is this person an appropriate reference for me?
2. What does this person know about me, my competencies, and my ability to succeed?

Share your completed list of references and information with your teacher, a career counselor, or a person who could advise you as to the appropriateness of your choices.

Because most people enjoy helping others, you should never be afraid to ask for a reference.

After you write your résumé, proofread it carefully for errors and omissions. Then ask a counselor in the career and placement office or a professor to suggest improvements. If you follow these simple steps, your completed résumé should be acceptable.

Searching the Job Market

Getting a job requires motivation, energy, hard work, and preparation. Even an applicant with superb qualifications faces tremendous competition for the best positions. According to placement service records, the average applicant spends only about three to ten hours a week searching for employment, but the person who is highly motivated will treat the search as if it were a job itself. The more time a person spends searching, the sooner and more likely he or she will be hired.

Newspaper want ads, professional magazines, placement services, former teachers, and people working in jobs you are interested in can all be good sources of job leads. However, the most productive approach to locating jobs is networking. **Networking** is the systematic contacting of people who can provide information about available jobs or who can offer jobs. Relatives, friends, classmates, colleagues, and people at social and professional gatherings are all potential sources of information. If someone does not know of any job openings himself or herself, ask if he or she knows of anyone who might. Then contact that person. In this way, your network expands from one person to another, and you gain information from each new contact. The more people you know, the better your chances are of being interviewed and the greater your opportunity for employment.

Career fairs have become very popular in recent years as a means for college students and others to learn about jobs and about the companies who are offering them. Most college campuses or the communities in which colleges and universities are located hold career fairs. They are excellent for networking as well as for making contacts with organizations for internships. Contact your career services office at your college or university and ask when the next career fair will be in your area. You should attend as many career fairs as time permits and you should begin going to them as soon as possible. You don't have to wait until your senior year to attend a career fair. By making contact with a company early in your education, you can establish a relationship with that company as well as be in the best position for getting an internship or a job after graduation.

Researching the Company via the Internet

Before arriving for an interview, you should know the full name of the company; background information on the company's history; where its headquarters, plants, offices, or stores are located; what products or services it offers; and what its economic growth has been and how its future prospects look. Such knowledge demonstrates your initiative and interest to the interviewer and can serve as a springboard for discussion. This also shows you have an interest in the company, rather than giving the impression you're "settling" for whatever job you can find.

It used to be that if you wanted to learn anything about a company you would have to write to the company for its annual report or for recruiting materials. You could also go to the library and look through publications and special directories for information related to a given company. Today, however, the Internet is the best source of company information, and although you can still go to the library or a career services office and find information, it requires much more work than a few clicks of a mouse. For example, if you wanted to learn about the IBM Corporation all you need to do is search the Internet for "IBM Corporation" and you will find the following address: http://www.ibm.com. Click on the address and you will find almost anything you'll ever want to know about IBM (see Figure A.4). The same search process should get you information on almost any company in the world.

Developing Questions to Ask the Interviewer

In preparation for your meeting, think about possible questions to ask the interviewer. Sometimes an interviewer may choose to say little or to stop talking altogether, in which case it becomes your responsibility to carry the conversation by asking

FIGURE A.4

IBM's Home Page on the World Wide Web

Reproduced by permission from IBM. Copyright 2000 by International Business Machines Corporation.

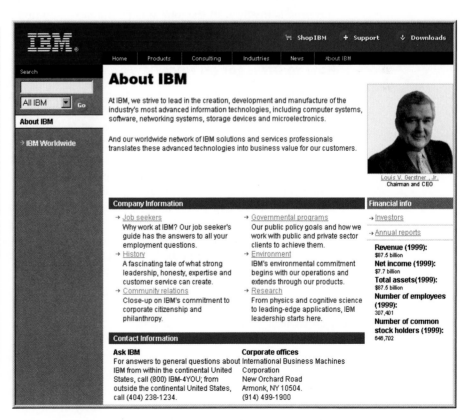

Making Connections

Learning About the Organization

Following are the names of several companies for you to research. For each one there is a question or questions to which you should be able to find the answers to by doing a search on the Internet. Report your answers to the class, if requested to do so.

1. Ford Motor Company—Approximately how many people work for the Ford Motor Company worldwide?

2. Dura Pharmaceuticals—Where is its main headquarters?
3. Oracle—When was the company started? Who is its present CEO?
4. Strong Investments Inc.—Approximately what is the amount of assets that Strong manages in billions of dollars? When was the company founded and where?

questions and continuing to emphasize your qualifications for the job. Regardless of whether the interviewer stops talking, you should have a list of questions to ask. This does not mean coming to the interview with a written list of questions, but it does mean coming prepared to ask questions such as these: What are the duties and responsibilities of the job? Does the company provide training programs? How much traveling is involved in the job? What's the next step up from the starting position? Would I be able to continue my education?

How to Dress for an Interview

Your primary goal in dressing for an interview is to feel great about the way you look while projecting an image that matches the requirements of the job and the company. Go for perfection. Wear professionally pressed clothing in natural fabrics. Although casual clothing in many settings is acceptable today, it is still wise to be conservative in what you wear. This is especially true if you do not know the culture of the organization or business. The interview is usually not the time to make a personal statement of nonconformity or disagreement with society's concept of professional image.[7] There are many excellent websites that address the issue of what is appropriate to wear to a job interview. We suggest that you do a search using the keywords "dress for the job interview." You will find many sites that provide guidelines for what to wear—we found the following site to be particularly helpful: http://www.collegegrad.com/book/15–5.shtml.

The Interview

Much of the responsibility for a successful interview rests with the interviewer, but this doesn't mean that you can merely relax and let things happen. On the contrary, research suggests that most interviewers develop a strong opinion about a job applicant in the first thirty seconds. If you do poorly at the opening, your chances of getting the job are slim, no matter how brilliantly you handle the rest of the interview. It

The employment interview is a key communication event for most people. The applicant should be prepared to discuss goals and skills and be able to clearly answer questions pertaining to why he or she is right for the job.

may seem unfair or superficial, but people do judge others on the basis of first impressions, and such impressions can be long-lasting. By all means be on time for the interview.

Frequently Asked Questions

One expert states that most applicants make two devastating mistakes when they are being questioned. First, they fail to listen to the question, and they answer a question that was not asked or give superfluous information. Second, they attempt to answer questions with virtually no preparation. Lack of preparation will reduce the chances of success for even skillful communicators. You should always take a moment to think about your answer before you respond to each question unless it is something that you have already thought through. Here are some of the most common questions interviewers ask and some possible responses to them.

1. *"What can you tell me about yourself?"* This is not an invitation to give your life history. The interviewer is looking for clues about your character, qualifications, ambitions, and motivations. The following is a good example of a positive response. "In high school, I was involved in competitive sports and I always tried to improve in each sport in which I participated. As a college student, I worked in a clothing store part time and found that I could sell things easily. The sale was important, but for me, it was even more important to make sure that the customer was satisfied. It wasn't long before customers came back to the store and specifically asked for me to help them. I'm very competitive and it means a lot to me to be the best."

2. *"Why do you want to work for us?"* This is an obvious question and, if you have done research on the company, you should be able to give a good reason. Organize your reasons into several short sentences that clearly spell out your interest. "You are a leader in the field of electronics. Your company is a Fortune 500 company. Your management is very progressive."

3. *"Why should I hire you?"* Once again, you should not be long-winded, but you should provide a summary of your qualifications. Be positive, and show that you are capable of doing the job. "Based on the internships that I have participated in and the related part-time experiences I have had, I can do the job."

4. *"How do you feel about your progress to date?"* Never apologize for what you have done. "I think I did well in school. In fact, in a number of courses I received the highest exam scores in the class." "As an intern for the X Company, I received some of the highest evaluations that had been given in years." "Considering that I played on the university's volleyball team and worked part time, I think you'll agree that I accomplished quite a bit during my four years in school."

5. *"What would you like to be doing five years from now?"* Know what you can realistically accomplish. You can find out by talking to others about what they accomplished in their first five years with a particular company. "I hope to be the best I can be at my job, and because many in this line of work are promoted to area manager, I am planning on that also."

6. *"What is your greatest weakness?"* You cannot avoid this question by saying that you do not have any; everyone has weaknesses. The best approach is to admit your weakness, but show that you are working on it and have a plan to overcome it. If possible, cite a weakness that will work to the company's advantage. "I'm not very good at detail work, but I have been working on it and I've improved dramatically over the past several years." "I'm such a perfectionist that I won't stop until a report is written just right."

7. *"What is your greatest strength?"* This is a real opportunity to "toot your own horn." Do not brag or get too egotistical, but let the employer know that you believe in yourself and that you know your strengths. "I believe that my strongest asset is my ability to stick to things to get them done. I feel a real sense of accomplishment when I finish a job and it turns out just as I'd planned. I've set some high goals for myself. For example, I want to graduate with highest distinction. And even though I had a slow start in my first year, I made up for it by doing an honor's thesis."

8. *"What goals have you set, and how did you meet them?"* This question examines your ability to plan ahead and meet your plan with specific actions. "Last year, during a magazine drive to raise money for our band trip, I set my goal at raising 20 percent more than I had the year before. I knew the drive was going to begin in September, so I started contacting people in August. I asked each of my customers from last year to give me the name of one or two new people who might also buy a magazine. I not only met my goal but I also was the top salesperson on the drive."

Interviews are now using more questions similar to this last question, based on the premise that the best predictor of future performance is past performance. This type of questioning is referred to as **behavioral-based interview questions,** which are questions that ask directly about a particular skill or trait (to which most interviewees would probably answer "yes"). The interviewer would then follow-up by asking for an example of a situation in which the interviewee could demonstrate the skill or trait that would demonstrate and support the "yes" answer they gave to the initial question. For example, in order to see if a person had decision-making skills, an interviewer might ask, "Have you had to make many difficult decisions?" The interviewee would likely respond, "yes." The follow-up question by the interviewer would attempt to solicit an example of a difficult decision the person had to make by asking something such as, "Describe a situation in which you had to make a difficult decision under pressure or when there were time limitations." For more examples of behavioral-based interview questions, go to http://edu/careers/tips/Bques.htm.

If an interviewer were to ask you any of the eight frequently asked questions, do you know how you would answer them? The key is to understand why a question is being asked. Remember, the purpose of the employment interview is to hire the best-qualified person for the job. The more often you can demonstrate through your responses to questions that you are the best qualified, the more likely you will be to get the job offer.

No matter what question you are asked, answer it honestly and succinctly. Most interviewers are looking for positive statements, well-expressed ideas, persuasiveness, and clear thinking under pressure.

If you are asked a question that violates the affirmative action laws, you can decline to answer. You might say, "I'm sorry, but I don't find that question relevant to the position being offered and it is against affirmative action laws to ask it." You may simply ask the interviewer why he or she is asking you that question. Make sure that you are tactful, but be firm in letting the interviewer know that he or she is doing something illegal.

Other Considerations

As a job applicant, you are expected to show good judgment and common sense about appearance, assertiveness, being on time, and being at the right place. Always maintain eye contact with the interviewer. Show that you are confident by looking straight at the speaker. Eye contact may not get you the job, but lack of eye contact can reduce your chances dramatically.

Most interviewers greet the applicant with a handshake. Make sure that your clasp is firm. Being jittery about the interview can result in cold, clammy hands, which create a negative impression. Therefore, try to make sure your hands are warm and dry. If this is not possible, the firm handshake will show more confidence.

When the interviewer asks you to sit down, if you have a choice, take the chair beside the desk rather than the one in front. This helps to eliminate any barriers between you and the interviewer and also makes you a little more equal, for which the interviewer will unconsciously respect you.

Before leaving, try to find out exactly what action will follow the interview and when it will happen. Shake hands as you say goodbye, and thank the interviewer for spending time with you. If you plan ahead and follow these simple suggestions, you should be able to avoid any serious problems.

Factors Leading to Rejection

Rejection is difficult for all of us to accept, but you should never give up. Being rejected by employers eight or nine times before receiving a job offer is not unusual in the present job market.[8]

Employers from numerous companies were asked, "What negative factors most often lead to the rejection of an applicant?" Here are their responses in order of frequency:

1. Negative personality or poor impression—more specifically, lack of motivation, ambition, maturity, aggressiveness, or enthusiasm
2. Inability to communicate; poor communication skills
3. Lack of competence; inadequate training
4. Low grades; poor grades in major field
5. Lack of specific goals
6. Unrealistic expectations
7. Lack of interest in type of work
8. Unwillingness to travel or relocate
9. Poor preparation for the interview
10. Lack of experience[9]

You must realize that rejection or not receiving a job offer has a lot to do with the number of people seeking jobs and the number of jobs available. You can of course enhance your chances of getting job offers by being prepared and presenting yourself in a positive and energetic way.

Factors Leading to Job Offers

An applicant who is well rounded and has good grades, some relevant work experience, a variety of extracurricular activities, an all-around pleasant personality, and effective written and oral communication skills is more likely to get job offers than those who do not possess these qualities, according to Jason Meyers of *Collegiate Employment Institute Newsletter*.[10] Meyers says, "Sounds too good to be true? Perhaps it is, but a candidate who strives to attain these qualities and who comes across as a hard-working, mature individual should have a promising career outlook."[11]

A research study, cited by Meyers in his article, asked recruiters to describe what they believed to be the qualities of a well-rounded individual. They listed maturity, ability to be part of a team, good work ethic, good decision-making skills, superior work habits, and good judgment. Another study cited by Meyers found that the most popular characteristics that recruiters sought in job applicants fit two categories: (1) quantifiable characteristics, such as grade point average, education, and work experience, and (2) interpersonal characteristics, such as communication skills, personality, and career and management skills. The study suggests that a balance of the quantifiable characteristics and interpersonal characteristics is what makes an ideal job candidate.[12]

It seems that those who are well-prepared; have effective communication skills; are mature, motivated, hard-working, team players; and can make good decisions will always be in demand. You must ask yourself how you match up to these qualities now and try to improve in those areas in which you are not as strong. You must also be able to demonstrate that you actually possess these qualities through the actions you have taken.

Summary

Choosing a career is one of the most important decisions a person can make, and a successful job interview is a crucial step in achieving that end. Planning and preparation are critical to a successful employment interview. The Internet is one the most valuable tools available in preparing for the employment interview. On the Internet, you can learn how to prepare for the interview, write a résumé, research an organization, find job opportunities, what questions are most frequently asked, and even what wear to the interview. Applicants must know their strengths and weaknesses and be able to communicate effectively with the interviewer. Getting a job requires motivation, energy, hard work, and research, plus knowing where to look and who to contact in order to obtain the necessary information.

It is not unusual for college graduates to change jobs from six to eight times and make at least three career changes during their lifetime. There are many qualities that twenty-first century employers will look for in those they hire such as an ability to deal with numbers, computer skills, a global and diverse perspective, strong interpersonal skills, willingness to learn, ability to deal with change and ambiguity, an ability to solve problems, and a team perspective. Those who have had experience through internships or jobs held while attending college are also attractive to employers.

Knowing what employers are looking for in a potential employee can help applicants prepare for interviews.

An effective *résumé* (a written document that briefly describes a person's personal, educational, and professional qualifications and experiences) can pave the way for a productive interview. In judging a résumé, employers look for thoughtfulness, creativity, accuracy, and neatness. Résumés summarize basic information about the applicant's career objective, educational training, work experience, extracurricular activities, and references.

Searching the job market requires motivation, energy, hard work, and preparation. Sources for job openings include newspaper want ads, professional magazines, placement services, former teachers, friends, and others who work in companies that have jobs that interest you. *Networking* is the systematic contacting of people who can provide information about available jobs or who can offer jobs. The more people you know, the better your chances of employment.

Before an interview, an applicant should find out about a company's background, location, products or services, growth, and prospects for the future. Using such information, the applicant can prepare possible questions to ask the interviewer.

Applicants must create a strong positive impression from the moment that they meet the interviewer. They should prepare responses to commonly asked questions, including *behavioral-based interview questions* (which are questions that ask directly about a particular skill or trait); show confidence; maintain eye contact with the interviewer; give a firm handshake, and sit, if given a choice, in the chair at the side of the desk or table rather than in front. Job applicants who prepare carefully and present themselves well can avoid some of the most common reasons for rejection.

DISCUSSION STARTERS

1. How can the Internet help you prepare for an employment interview?
2. What can you do to increase your chances of getting the best job?
3. If you were an employer, what would you look for in a job applicant?
4. What advice would you give fellow students about writing résumés?
5. Why should personal data such as age, gender, marital status, and religion be omitted from a résumé?
6. How should you go about getting references? Who should you ask?
7. What advice would you give regarding the best methods of doing a job search?
8. What should you know about a company before you are interviewed?
9. Why is it important for an applicant to ask questions of the interviewer?
10. If you were to interview someone for a job with your company, what would be some of the questions that you would ask an applicant? Why?
11. What can someone do to reduce the chances of being rejected?

NOTES

1. A special thanks to Dr. Larry R. Routh, Director of Career Services, University of Nebraska, Lincoln, for his review of the Appendix materials and for suggestions on how to use the Internet for career placement services.
2. P. L. Brill and R. Worth, *The Four Levels of Corporate Change* (New York: AMACOM, 1997), pp. 3–45; and B. A. Paternak and A. J. Viscio, *The Centerless Corporation: A New Model for Transforming Your Organization for Growth and Prosperity* (New York: Simon and Schuster, 1998).
3. "No Job Openings? Set Up an Interview Anyway," *Chicago Tribune,* 16 August, 1998, Jobs section, 6.

4. C. J. Stewart and W. B. Cash Jr., *Interviewing Principles and Practices,* 9th ed. (New York: McGraw-Hill, 2000), 263–64.

5. Interview with Dr. Larry Routh, Director of Career Services (University of Nebraska, Lincoln, September 2000).

6. Stewart and Cash, 232.

7. J. LaFevre, "How You Really Get Hired," *CPC Annual 1990/91,* 34th ed. (Bethlehem, Penn.: College Placement Council).

8. Routh.

9. *The Endicott Report: Trends in the Employment of College and University Graduates in Business and Industry* (Evanston, Ill.: The Placement Center, Northwestern University, 1980), 8. In the September 2000 interview, Dr. Routh said that the rejection reasons companies give today are not different than they were in 1980.

10. J. Meyers, "The Ideal Job Candidate," *Collegiate Employment Institute Newsletter,* 15 July, 1989, 6.

11. Ibid.

12. Ibid.

GLOSSARY

abstract word: Symbol for an idea, quality, or relationship.

adaptor: Body motion that promotes feeling at ease in communication situations.

ad hominem: A fallacy that attacks a person rather than the argument itself. This is also referred to as "name-calling."

adoption: Action goal that asks listeners to demonstrate their acceptance of attitudes, beliefs, or values by performing the behavior suggested by the speaker.

advance organizer: Statement that warns listener that significant information is coming.

affect display: Body motion that expresses emotions and feelings.

agenda: List of all topics to be discussed during a meeting.

alter-adaptors: Body movements directed at others that are learned from past experience and from the manipulation of objects.

analogy: Comparison of two things that are similar in certain essential characteristics.

androgynous: A person with both male and female traits.

antonym: Word, phrase, or concept that is opposite in meaning to another word, phrase, or concept.

appeal to needs: Attempt to move people to action by calling on their physical and psychological requirements and desires.

artifact: Ornament or possession that communicates information about a person.

attending: The mental process of focusing and concentrating on specific stimuli for a period of time while ignoring or downplaying other internal or external stimuli.

attitude: Evaluative disposition, feeling, or position about oneself, others, events, ideas, or objects.

attribution: The complex process through which we attempt to understand reasons behind others' behaviors.

attribution error: Perceive others as acting as they do because they are "that kind of person" rather than because of any external factors that may have influenced their behavior.

audience: Collection of individuals who have come together to watch or listen to someone or something, such as to listen to a speech.

audience analysis: Collection and interpretation of data about characteristics, attitudes, values, and beliefs of an audience.

autocratic leader: Leader who keeps complete control and makes all the decisions for the group.

behavioral based interview questions: Questions that ask directly about a particular skill or trait.

belief: Conviction or confidence in the truth of something that is not based on absolute proof.

body: Main content of a speech that develops the speaker's general and specific purposes.

brainstorming: A technique used to generate as many ideas as possible within a limited amount of time, which can be used during any phase of the group discussion process to produce topics, information, or solutions to problems.

brief example: Specific instance that is used to introduce a topic, drive home a point, or create a desired response.

bypassing: Misunderstanding that occurs between a sender and a receiver because of the symbolic nature of language.

captive participant: Person who is required to hear a particular speech.

causal reasoning: Sequence of thought that links causes with effects; it either implies or explicitly states the word **because.**

cause–effect pattern: Order of presentation in which the speaker first explains the causes of an event, problem, or issue and then discusses its consequences.

channel: Route (such as sound waves or light waves) by which messages flow between sources and receivers.

charisma: The appeal or attractiveness that the audience perceives in the speaker, contributing to the speaker's credibility.

chronemics: The study of how people perceive, structure, and use time as communication.

closure: Filling in of details so that a partially perceived entity appears to be complete.

cognitive complexity: The number of mental structures we use, how abstract they are and how elaborately they interact to shape our perceptions.

cohesiveness: Attraction that group members feel for each other and willingness to stick together; a form of loyalty.

collectivistic orientation: Tendency to put aside your individual goals for the well being of the group.

commitment: Desire of group members to work together to complete a task to the satisfaction of the entire group.

communication: The simultaneous sharing and creating of meaning through human symbolic action.

communications: Denotes the delivery systems for mediated and mass communication.

communication apprehension: Anxiety associated with real or anticipated communication with another person or persons.

communication competence: The ability to take part in effective communication, which is characterized by skills and understandings that enable communication partners to exchange messages successfully.

complementing: Use of nonverbal cues to complete, describe, or accent verbal cues.

conclusion: Closing statements that focus the audience's thoughts on the specific purpose of a speech and bring the most important points together in a condensed and uniform way.

concrete word: Symbol for a specific thing that can be pointed to or physically experienced.

conflict: An expressed struggle between at least two independent parties who perceive incompatible goals, scarce resources, and interference from others in achieving their goals.

connotation: Subjective meaning of a word; what a word suggests because of feelings or associations it evokes.

context: Circumstances or situation in which communication occurs.

continuance: Action goal that asks listeners to demonstrate their acceptance of an attitude, belief, or value by continuing to perform the behavior suggested by the speaker.

contrast definition: Definition that shows or emphasizes differences.

costs: Negative rewards, things that we perceive to be not beneficial to our self-interests.

credibility: Speaker's believability, based on the audience's evaluation of the speaker's competence, experience, character, and charisma.

critical listening: Listening that judges the accuracy of the information presented, determines the reasonableness of its conclusions, and evaluates its presenter.

critical thinking: The ability to analyze and assess information.

culture: The deposit of knowledge, experience, beliefs, values, actions, attitudes, meanings, hierarchies, religion, notions of time, roles, spatial relations, concepts of the universe, and artifacts acquired by a group of people in the course of generations through individual and group striving.

cultural relativism: Taking on a broader worldview and opening our minds to different cultures as merely being different and not judging them as inferior because they are different.

dating: Form of indexing that sorts people, events, ideas, and objects according to time.

decoding: Process of translating a message into the thoughts or feelings that were communicated.

deductive reasoning: Sequence of thought that moves from general information to a specific conclusion; it consists of a general premise, a minor premise, and a conclusion.

definition by example: Clarifying a term, not by describing it or giving its meaning, but by describing or showing an example of it.

deintensifying: Facial behavior response that understates reactions or emotions in order to create or maintain a favorable relationship with another.

democratic leader: Leader who guides and directs the group, but shares control and remains open to all views.

demographic analysis: Collection and interpretation of characteristics (age, gender, religion, occupation, and so on) of individuals, excluding values, attitudes, and beliefs.

denotation: Objective meaning of a word; standard dictionary definition.

descriptive feedback: The stating of the interpretation of the message received back to the sender.

descriptors: Words used to describe something.

deterrence: Action goal that asks listeners to demonstrate their acceptance of an attitude, belief, or value by avoiding certain behavior.

dialectic: Contradictory impulses that push and pull us in conflicting directions with others.

discontinuance: Action goal that asks listeners to demonstrate their alteration of an attitude, belief, or value by stopping certain behaviors.

doublespeak: The deliberate misuse of language to distort meaning.

dyadic communication: Exchange of information between two people.

emblem: Body motion that can be translated directly into words or phrases.

emotional appeal: Attempt to move people to action by playing on their feelings.

empathic listening: Listening to understand what another person is thinking and feeling.

encoding: Process by which the source expresses thoughts or feelings in words, sounds, and physical expressions, which together make up the actual message that is sent.

entertainment speech: Speech that provides enjoyment and amusement.

environment: Psychological and physical surroundings in which communication occurs.

ethics: An individual's system of moral principles.

ethnocentric: A person whose pride in his or her heritage or background leads to the conviction that he or she knows more and is better than those who differ.

etymology: Definition that traces the origin and development of a word.

euphemism: The use of an inoffensive or mild expression in place of one that may offend, cause embarrassment, or suggest something unpleasant.

evaluating: The listener analyzes evidence, sorts fact from opinion, determines the intent of the speaker, judges the accuracy of the speaker's statements and conclusions, and judges the accuracy of his or her own decisions.

evaluative listening: Listening to judge or analyze information.

example: Simple, representative incident or model that clarifies a point.

expert opinion: Opinions, testimony, or conclusions of witnesses or recognized authorities.

extemporaneous delivery: Delivery style in which the speaker carefully prepares the speech in advance, but delivers it using only a few notes and with a high degree of spontaneity.

eye behavior: A category of kinesics and a subcategory of facial expressions that includes any movement or behavior of the eyes.

eye contact: Extent to which a speaker looks directly at audience members.

facial expression: Configuration of the face that can reflect, augment, contradict, or be unrelated to a speaker's vocal delivery.

facial management techniques: Control of facial muscles in order to conceal inappropriate or unacceptable responses.

factual illustration: Report of something that exists or actually happened.

fallacy: Arguments that are flawed because they do not follow the rules of logic.

feedback: Response to a message that the receiver sends to the source.

figurative analogy: Comparison of things in different categories.

figure and ground organization: Ordering of perceptions so that some stimuli are in focus and others become the background.

focus group: A special form of work team that ascertains what people think about specific ideas, issues, or people.

force: Intensity and volume level of the voice.

friendship–warmth touch: Expression of the appreciation of the special attributes of another person.

full-content outline: Detailed skeleton of a speech with all main and secondary points written in complete sentences.

functional–professional touch: Unsympathetic, impersonal, cold, or businesslike touch.

gender: A social construct related to masculine and feminine behaviors that are learned.

gender-inclusive language: Language that does not discriminate against male or female.

general purpose: Overall goal of a speech, usually one of three overlapping functions—to inform, to persuade, or to entertain.

gesture: Movement of the head, arms, or hands that helps illustrate, emphasize, or clarify an idea.

grammar: Rules that govern how words are put together to form phrases and sentences.

group: Collection of individuals who influence one another, have a common purpose, take on roles, are interdependent, and interact together.

group culture: The pattern of values, beliefs, norms, and behaviors that is shared by group members and that shapes a group's individual personality.

grouphate phenomenon: Dislike for groups.

groupthink: A dysfunction in which group members value the harmony of the group more than new ideas, fail to critically examine ideas, hesitate to change flawed decisions, or lack willingness to allow new members to participate.

haptics: Tactile, or touch, communication; one of the most basic forms of communication.

hasty generalization: A fallacy that occurs when a speaker doesn't have sufficient data and thus argues or reasons from a specific example.

hearing: A passive physiological process in which sound is received by the ear.

high-context culture: The meaning of the communication act is inferred from the situation or location.

hypothetical illustration: Report of something that could or probably would happen, given a specific set of circumstances.

illustration: Extended example, narrative, case history, or anecdote that is striking and memorable.

illustrator: Body motion that accents, reinforces, or emphasizes an accompanying verbal message.

impression management: Creating a positive image of oneself in order to influence the perceptions of others.

impromptu delivery: Delivery style in which a speaker delivers a speech with little or no planning or preparation.

indexing: Technique to reduce indiscrimination by identifying the specific persons, ideas, events, or objects a statement refers to.

individualistic orientation: Tendency to stress self or personal goals and achievements over group goals and achievements.

indiscrimination: Neglect of individual differences and overemphasis of similarities.

inductive reasoning: Sequence of thought that moves from specific facts to a general conclusion.

information: Knowledge derived from study, experience, or instruction.

information relevance: Making information relevant to an audience, to give them a reason to listen.

informative speech: Speech that enhances an audience's knowledge and understanding by explaining what something means, how something works, or how something is done.

intelligibility: Speaker's vocal volume, distinctiveness of sound, clarity of pronunciation, articulation, and stress placed on syllables, words, and phrases.

intensifying: Facial behavior response that exaggerates expressions in order to meet the expectation of others.

intentional communication: Message that is purposely sent to a specific receiver.

interaction: Exchange of communication in which communicators take turns sending and receiving messages.

interactive computer conferencing: Similar to videoconferencing except that the interaction occurs via computer.

interdependence: Mutual dependence of group members on one another.

interference: Anything that changes the meaning of an intended message.

internal preview: Short statements that give advance warning, or preview, of the point(s) to be covered.

internal summary: Short review statement given at the end of a main point.

interpersonal attraction: The desire to interact with someone based on a variety of factors including physical attractiveness, personality, rewards, proximity, or similarities.

interpersonal communication: Informal exchange of information between two or more people.

interpretation: Assigning of meaning to stimuli.

interview: Carefully planned and executed question-and-answer session designed to exchange desired information between two parties.

intrapersonal communication: Process of understanding information within oneself.

introduction: Opening statements that orient the audience to the subject and motivate them to listen.

Johari window: Graphic model that depicts the different levels of knowledge that exist in interpersonal relationships by illustrating four kinds of information about a person: known to self, not known to self, known to others, and not known to others.

kinesics: Sometimes referred to as "body language"; any movement of the face or body that communicates a message.

laissez-faire leader: Leader who gives complete decision-making freedom to the group or to individual members.

language: Structured system of signs, sounds, gestures, and marks used and understood to express ideas and feelings among people within a community, nation, geographic area, or cultural tradition.

leader: A person assigned or selected, or who emerges from a group, to guide or provide direction toward reaching the group's goals.

leadership: An influence process that includes any behavior that helps clarify or guide the group to achieve its goals.

linguistic determinism: A theory that language determines thought.

linguistic relativity: A theory that suggests that people from different language communities perceive the world differently.

listening: The active process of receiving aural stimuli by hearing, selecting, attending, understanding, evaluating, and remembering.

listening for enjoyment: Listening for pleasure, personal satisfaction, or appreciation.

listening for information: Listening to gain comprehension.

literal analogy: Comparison of members of the same category.

logical appeal: Attempt to move people to action through the use of evidence and proof.

logical definition: Definition consisting of a term's dictionary definition and the characteristics that distinguish the term from other members of the same category.

love–intimacy touch: Usually occurs in romantic relationships; includes kissing, stroking, and other forms of highly communicative touch.

low-context culture: The meaning of the communication act is inferred from the messages being sent and not the location where the communication occurs.

main points: Principal subdivisions of a speech.

maintenance needs: Needs related to organizing and developing a group so that the members can realize personal satisfaction from working together.

manuscript delivery: Delivery style in which a speaker writes the speech in its entirety and then reads it word for word.

masking: Facial behavior response that replaces an expression of emotion with another thought to be more appropriate for the situation.

mass communication: Communicating with or to a large number of people.

mediated communication: Communication transmitted by some kind of mechanistic means, such as radio, television, telephone, or the Internet, and my be one-on-one communication.

memorized delivery: Delivery style in which a speaker memorizes a speech in its entirety from a word-for-word script.

message: Stimulus that is produced by the source.

metaphor: A figure of speech in which a word or phrase relates one object or idea to another object or idea that are not commonly linked together.

motivated sequence: Pattern of organization specifically developed for persuasive speaking that combines logic and practical psychology. Five steps are involved: **attention, need, satisfaction, visualization,** and **action.**

networking: The systematic contacting of people who can provide information about available jobs or who can offer jobs.

neutralizing: Facial behavior response that avoids showing any emotional expression in a given situation.

newsgroup: An online bulletin board where people can read and post messages about topics of their choice.

nonverbal communication: Behaviors, attributes, or objects (except words) that communicate messages that have social meaning.

norms: Expected and shared ways in which group members behave.

object-adaptor: Body motion that involves the use of an object, such as a pencil, a paper clip, or keys, for something other than its primary use.

observation: Method of collecting information about an audience in which the speaker watches audience members and notes their behaviors and characteristics.

oculesics: Study of eye movement or eye behavior.

operational definition: Definition that explains how an object or concept works, or lists the steps that make up a process.

oral footnote: Providing within the speech the source that particular information comes from: "According to *Time* magazine of September 20, 1998 . . ."

organization: Categorizing of stimuli in our environment in order to make sense of them.

organizing: Arranging of ideas and elements into a systematic and meaningful whole.

outlining: Arranging materials in a logical sequence, often referred to as the blueprint or skeleton of a speech, and writing out that sequence in a standardized form.

paralanguage: The way we vocalize, or say, the words we speak.

pendulum effect: Escalating conflict between two persons or groups that results from their use of polar terms to describe and defend their perceptions of reality.

perception: Process of selecting, organizing, and interpreting information in order to give personal meaning to the communication we receive.

perceptual set: Fixed, previously determined view of events, objects, or people.

persuasion: Communication process, involving both verbal and nonverbal messages, that attempts to reinforce or change listeners' attitudes, beliefs, values, or behavior.

persuasive speech: Speech that attempts to change listeners' attitudes or behaviors by advocating or trying to gain acceptance of the speaker's point of view.

pitch: How low or high the voice is on a tonal scale.

plagiarism: Use of another person's information, language, or ideas without citing the originator and making it appear that the user is the originator.

planned repetition: Deliberate restating of a thought in order to increase the likelihood that the audience will understand and remember it.

polarization: Tendency to view things in terms of extremes.

predicted outcome value theory: A theory that suggests people connect with others because they believe that rewards or positive outcomes will result.

preliminary outline: List of all the main points that may be used in a speech.

presentational aids: Materials and equipment, such as diagrams, models, real objects, photographs, tables, charts, and graphs, that speakers may use to enhance the speech's content as well as their delivery.

presentational outline: Condensation of the full-content outline that aids delivery by minimizing detail and listing key words and phrases in place of full sentences.

principled negotiation: A procedure that helps group members negotiate consensus by collaboration through the expression of each differing need and a search for alternatives to meet those needs.

privacy: The claim of individuals, groups, or institutions to determine for themselves when, how, and to what extent information about themselves is communicated to others.

problem–solution pattern: Order of presentation that first discusses a problem and then suggests solutions.

process: Series of actions that has no beginning or end and is constantly changing.

project team: Individuals representing different specialties who are assigned to coordinate the successful completion of an assigned task.

proxemics: Study of the use of space and of distance between individuals when they are communicating.

proximity: Grouping of two or more stimuli that are close to one another.

psychological analysis: Collection and interpretation of data about audience members' values, attitudes, and beliefs.

public communication: Transmission of a message from one person who speaks to a number of individuals who listen.

public speaking: Presentation of a speech, usually prepared in advance, during which the speaker is the central focus of an audience's attention.

question of fact: Question that asks what is true and what is false.

question of interpretation: Question that asks for the meaning or explanation of something.

question of policy: Question that asks what actions should be taken.

question of value: Question that asks whether something is good or bad, desirable or undesirable.

questionable cause: A fallacy that occurs when a speaker alleges something that does not relate to, or produce, the outcome claimed in the argument.

questionnaire: Set of written questions that is distributed to respondents to gather desired information.

rate: Speed at which a speaker speaks, normally between 120 words and 150 words per minute.

reasoning by analogy: Sequence of thought that compares similar things or circumstances in order to draw a conclusion.

receiver: Individual who analyzes and interprets the message.

red herring: A fallacy that uses irrelevant information to divert attention away from the real issue.

regulating: Use of nonverbal cues to control the flow of communication.

regulator: Body motion that controls, monitors, or maintains the interaction between speaker and listener.

relationship: An association between at least two people and may be described in terms of intimacy or kinship.

relationship-oriented leader: Leader who attempts to maintain good interpersonal relationships.

remembering: Recalling something from stored memory; thinking of something again.

repeating: Use of nonverbal cues to convey the same meaning as the verbal message.

repertoire: Wide range of communication behaviors from which effective communicators make choices.

responding: Overt verbal and nonverbal behavior by the listener indicating to the speaker what has and has not been received.

restatement: The expression of the same idea using different words.

résumé: A written document that briefly and accurately describes an individual's personal, educational, and professional qualifications and experiences.

reviewing the current media: Technique for developing a list of possible topics by looking at current publications, television, movies, and other forms of public communication.

reward: Anything that we perceive as beneficial to our self-interest.

rhetorical sensitivity: A cautious approach to self-disclosure in which the situation and factors about the other person are considered before communication begins.

Sapir-Whorf hypothesis: An explanation of how thought influences our reality and how our thought process is influenced by our language.

search engines: Programs used to find information on the World Wide Web.

selecting: In the process of listening, the stage of choosing the stimuli that will be listened to.

selection: Sorting of one stimulus from another.

selective attention: Focusing on specific stimuli while ignoring or downplaying other stimuli.

selective exposure: The deliberate choices we make to experience or to avoid particular stimuli.

selective retention: Processing, storing, and retrieving of information that we have already selected, organized, and interpreted.

self-adaptor: Body motion that is not directed at others but serves some personal need.

self-concept: A person's mental picture and evaluation of his or her physical, social, and psychological attributes.

self-disclosure: Voluntary sharing of information about the self that another person is not likely to know.

self-esteem: A person's feelings and attitudes toward himself or herself.

self-fulfilling prophecy: Expectations we have of ourselves or that others have of us help create the conditions that lead us to act in predictable ways.

self-image: A person's mental picture of himself or herself.

self-inventory: Technique for developing a list of possible topics by listing one's own interests.

self-monitoring: The willingness to change one's behavior to fit situations, awareness of one's effects on others, and the ability to regulate one's nonverbal cues and other factors to influence others' impressions.

self-presentation: An intentional tactic in which a person reveals certain aspects of himself or herself in order to accomplish specific goals.

semantics: The study of meaning, or the association of words with ideas, feelings, and contexts.

sex: The anatomical and physiological differences between males and females that are genetically determined.

sexist language: Language that creates sexual stereotypes or implies that one gender is superior to another.

sexual-arousal touch: Most intimate level of personal contact with another.

signpost: Word, phrase, or short statement that indicates to an audience the direction a speaker will take next.

similarity: Grouping of stimuli that resemble one another in size, shape, color, or other traits.

slang: Subpopulations of a language community sometimes use words or phrases in special ways unique to their group.

small group communication: Exchange of information among a relatively small number of persons, ideally five to seven, who share a common purpose, such as doing a task, solving a problem, making a decision, or sharing information.

small talk: Casual conversation that is often impersonal and superficial, including greetings, comments about the weather, newsworthy events, or trivia.

social exchange theory: A theory based on the assumption that people consciously and deliberately weigh the costs and rewards associated with a relationship or interaction.

social loafing: Tendency for individuals to lower their work effort after they join a group.

social penetration: The process of increasing disclosure and intimacy in a relationship.

social-polite touch: Touch that acknowledges another person according to the norms or rules of a society.

source: Creator of messages.

spatial pattern: Order of presentation in which the content of a speech is organized according to relationships in space.

specific purpose: Single phrase that defines precisely what is to be accomplished in a speech.

speech anxiety: Fear of speaking before an audience.

speech communication: A humanistic and scientific field of study, research, and application, focusing on how, why, and with what effects people communicate through language and nonverbal behaviors.

statistics: Numerical data that show relationships or summarize or interpret many instances.

stereotype: A categorizing of events, objects, and people without regard to unique individual characteristics and qualities.

stereotyping: The categorizing of events, objects, and people without regard to unique individual characteristics and qualities.

stimulus: Something that incites or quickens action, feeling, or thought.

substituting: Use of nonverbal cues in place of verbal messages when speaking is impossible, undesirable, or inappropriate.

survey interview: Carefully planned and executed person-to-person, question-and-answer session during which the speaker tries to discover specific information that will help in the preparation of a speech.

synonym: Word, term, or concept that is the same or nearly the same in meaning as another word, term, or concept.

system: Combination of parts interdependently acting to form a whole.

systematic desensitization: A technique in which relaxation is associated with an anxiety-producing situation.

task need: Need related to the content of a task and all behaviors that lead to the completion of it.

task-oriented leader: Leader who gains satisfaction from performing the task.

team: A special form of group that is characterized by a close-knit relationship among people with different and complementary abilities, and a strong sense of identity.

teleconferencing: Use of telephones and speakerphones to connect people in different locations.

territoriality: Need to identify certain areas of space as one's own.

testimony: Opinions or conclusions of witnesses or recognized authorities.

thesis: Sentence that states specifically what is going to be discussed in a speech.

time-sequence (chronological) pattern: Order of presentation that begins at a particular point in time and continues either forward or backward.

topical pattern: Order of presentation in which the main topic is divided into a series of related subtopics.

transaction: Exchange of communication in which the communicators act simultaneously, that is, encoding and decoding occur at the same time.

transition: Phrase or word used to link ideas.

trustworthiness: Audience's perception of a speaker's reliability and dependability.

uncertainty reduction theory: A theory suggesting that when we initially meet others to whom we are attracted, our need to know about them tends to make us draw inferences from observable physical data.

understanding: Assigning meaning to the stimuli that have been selected and attended to.

unintentional communication: Message that is not intended to be sent or is not intended for the person who receives it.

value: A general, relatively long-lasting ideal that guides behavior.

verbal immediacy: Identifies and projects the speaker's feelings and makes the message more relevant to the listener.

videoconferencing: An extension of teleconferencing that includes picture and sound.

visual aids: See *presentational aids.*

vividness: Active, direct, and fresh language that brings a sense of excitement and urgency to a message.

vocal quality: Overall impression a speaker's voice makes on his or her listeners.

vocal variety: Variations in rate, force, and pitch.

voluntary participant: Person who chooses to listen to a particular speech.

word: Symbol that stands for the object or concept that it names.

work team: A group of people responsible for an entire work process or a segment of the process that delivers a product or service to an internal or external customer.

World Wide Web: A global information system that allows users to access information from the Internet.

INDEX

Photo Credits

PRACTICE TEST

Chapter 1: Connecting Process and Principles

MULTIPLE CHOICE:

Choose the one alternative that best completes the statement or answers the question.

1 Radio, television, newspapers, magazines, books, and the World Wide Web are all examples of
   a. organizational communication
   b. small group communication
   c. mass communication
   d. interpersonal communication

2 According to the text, classical rhetoricians studied the principles of communicating effectively, including ways of composing and delivering
   a. theatrical performances
   b. persuasive speeches
   c. extemporaneous speeches
   d. comedy routines

3 _____ refers to the simultaneous sharing and creating of meaning through human symbolic action, whereas _____ refers to the deliery systems for mediated and mass communication.
   a. communications, communication
   b. interaction, speech
   c. public speaking, communications
   d. communication, communications

4 All of the following are benefits we reap from developing competent communication skills, EXCEPT
   a. advances in career deelopment
   b. personal relationships free from conflict
   c. ethical behavior
   d. an ability to communicate with diverse people

5 Aristotle suggested that communication was most powerful when the speaker's character, or _____, was engaged in presenting the truth.
   a. ethos
   b. logos
   c. pathos
   d. porthos

6 All of the following are principles of communication, EXCEPT
   a. communication is a process
   b. communication is always intentional
   c. communication is a system
   d. communication is both interactional and transactional

7 To say that communication is constantly changing is to say that communication is:
   a. transactional
   b. linear
   c. a process
   d. a system

8 Your textbook discusses the relationship between communication and ethics. One principle discussed is that unethical communication
   a. usually goes unpunished
   b. is always ineffective
   c. rarely occurs in college settings
   d. may in fact constitute effective communication

9 The human body is composed of different parts that work together to form a whole. This analogy helps demonstrate that communication is
   a. a system
   b. an interaction
   c. intentional
   d. transactional

10 Bobby and Lisa take turns exchanging information about their families during their morning chat over coffee. Their conversation demonstrates that communication is
   a. ethical
   b. multicultural
   c. unintentional
   d. an interaction
   e. none of the above

11. According to the text, competent communicators
    a. are born naturally
    b. usually choose to exchange messages unethically
    c. are able to exchange messages successfully
    d. learn to communicate rather easily

12. All of the following are basic elements of communication, EXCEPT
    a. receiver
    b. feedback
    c. context
    d. paralanguage

13. John decides to translate his feelings of anger into words and communicate them to Sue. In doing so, John enacts the process of
    a. sending
    b. encoding
    c. decoding
    d. receiving

14. An important principle related to the basic elements of communication is that
    a. you act as a source first, then a receiver
    b. you act as a receiver first, then a source
    c. you are simultaneously a source and a receiver
    d. you intentionally choose whether you want to be a source or a receiver

15. As Dr. Johnson gave her lecture on thermodynamics, her students were distracted by the sounds of police sirens outside the classroom. In this case, Dr. Johnson's discussion was interrupted by:
    a. internal interference
    b. external interference
    c. psychological interference
    d. none of the above

16. Feedback is a natural extension of effective _____.
    a. sending
    b. sense-making
    c. interference
    d. receiving

17. According to a study on feedback reported in the text, as the amount of feedback increases
    a. the accuracy of communication increases as well

    b. communication becomes more ethical
    c. the recipient's confidence in performance increases as well
    d. all of the above
    e. both A and C

18. Your textbook identified several key components of the communication process. One is defined as the psychological and physical surroundings in which communication occurs. This component is called
    a. interference
    b. channel
    c. environment
    d. context
    e. message

19. All of the following are roles performed by the sender during the communication process, EXCEPT
    a. encoding meaning into messages
    b. translating messages into meaning
    c. perceiving and reacting to a listener's responses
    d. determining the meaning of what is to be communicated

20. "Communication does not occur in a vacuum." This statement best illustrates which element of communication?
    a. environment
    b. sending
    c. receiving
    d. context

21. As spouses, Tim and Sarah often enjoy long conversations together over a cup of coffee. In these instances, Tim and Sarah are engaging in
    a. interpersonal communication
    b. public communication
    c. dyadic communication
    d. all of the above
    e. both A and C

22. According to the text, one sub-component of interpersonal communication is
    a. public speaking
    b. intrapersonal communication
    c. small-group communication
    d. organizational communication

23. All of the following are misconceptions (or myths) about communication, EXCEPT
    a. communication is a cure-all
    b. communication is irreversible

c. meaning is in the words we use
d. the more we communicate, the better off we will be

24. According to the text, which misconception about communication is probably the most serious misconception of all?
a. the notion that words contain meanings
b. the idea that more communication equals better communication
c. the notion that communication a cure-all
d. the idea that people are born with a natural ability to communicate

25. "Communication is not a panacea- in other words, communicating itself does not make the difference." This statement best refutes the misconception that:
a. communication is reversible
b. meaning is in the words we use
c. we have a natural ability to communicate
d. communication is a cure-all

26. Since words only have meaning when we give them meaning, then
a. two people can share the same meanings for all words
b. the meaning of a word cannot be separated from the person using it
c. meanings are in words rather than in the people who are using the words
d. all of the above

27. According to the text, we can distinguish different types of communication by looking at
a. the number of people involved
b. the degree of formality in which the communication occurs
c. the purpose of the communication
d. all of the above
e. A and B only

28. The classical rhetorician who noted that communication needed to be presented by "a good man speaking well" is
a. Aristotle
b. Quintilian
c. Ptolemy
d. Socrates

29. All of the following are characteristics of competent communication, EXCEPT
a. an ability to coordinate several communication tasks simultaneously
b. an ability to speak both appropriately and effectively
c. an ability to evaluate the effectiveness of a given communication after the fact
d. all of the above
e. A and B only

30. Communication that is not intended, or that is at least not consciously sent and received, is usually
a. mediated
b. verbal
c. nonverbal
d. interactional

Chapter 2: Connecting Perceptions and Communication

MULTIPLE CHOICE

Choose the one alternative that best completes the statement or answers the question.

1 _____ is pervasive because of the human psychological need to categorize and classify information.
   a. selecting
   b. discriminating
   c. organizing
   d. stereotyping

2 According to your text, _____ is at the heart of all communication
   a. cognition
   b. emotion
   c. perception
   d. classification

3 All of the following are true about the perception process, EXCEPT
   a. perception is a simple phenomenon
   b. perception is a part of everything we do
   c. what we perceive gives meaning to our experiences
   d. perceptions are relative

4 Jimmy sees a car with four wheels for the first time and is told by his parents that it is a "car." A few days later, his parents notice that he is referring to trucks and vans as "cars" rather than as "trucks" and "vans." Jimmy's inability to distinguish between different types of automobiles reflects his level of
   a. perceptual sets
   b. selective exposure
   c. awareness
   d. cognitive complexity

5 In order to perceive our surroundings, we must first
   a. classify them via our use of language
   b. be aware of them
   c. process them cognitively
   d. organize based on similarity

6 People who are high in cognitive complexity are likely to
   a. be flexible in interpreting complicated events
   b. simplify situations

   c. use "person-centered" messages when communicating with others
   d. all of the above
   e. A and C only

7 The deliberate choice of deciding to attend or to not attend a football game is called
   a. selective attention
   b. selective retention
   c. selective exposure
   d. none of the above

8 As a baseball pitcher, Roger Clemens focuses his attention on striking out the opposing batter despite the distractions from the home crowd. His ability to downplay the screaming fans from the opposing team demonstrates
   a. selective retention
   b. selective attention
   c. stimulus rejection
   d. selective exposure

9 When we categorize stimuli from our environment, we are engaged in the process of _____ data.
   a. organizing
   b. selecting
   c. perceiving
   d. conceptualizing

10 Bill and Judy had a disagreement about their finances. Judy wanted Bill to set aside more money for their savings account. Bill responded to Judy by noting that she often becomes upset when he sets aside money for his golf trips. Judy then becomes even more upset and responds that Bill is missing the point entirely. In this situation, Bill's statement illustrates what type of perception organization?
   a. figure and ground
   b. closure
   c. selective attention
   d. similarity

11 According to your text, people have a tendency to make meaningless material meaningful. This tendency is referred to as
   a. organizing
   b. selection
   c. figure and ground organization
   d. closure

12 Jack discovers that two of his co-workers live in the same apartment complex. Based on this information, Jack assumes that his co-workers have similar incomes, similar tastes in decor, and similar attitudes towards living in rental properties. Jack's perceptions of his co-workers are influenced by
a. selective retention
b. proximity
c. similarity
d. selective exposure

13 When we ignore new information and rely on past experiences, we are using a
_____.
a. selective set
b. cognitive set
c. perceptual set
d. closed set

14 All of the following statements about stereotyping are true, EXCEPT
a. Through stereotyping, we pigeonhole people.
b. Stereotyping exists in nearly every intercultural situation.
c. Stereotyping limits us from making decisions more efficiently.
d. Stereotypes ultimately impede the communication process.

15 Many communication scholars believe that the single greatest problem with human communication is the assumption that
a. our perceptions are always correct
b. our perceptions always hinder our decision-making abilities
c. all stereotypes are negative
d. stereotyping is never useful

16 On the first day of class, Michelle sees a student arriving 15 minutes late and concludes that the student must be lazy, unorganized, and irresponsible. Michelle's biased conclusions may be the result of _____.
a. closure
b. a psychological state
c. an attribution error
d. selective exposure

17 Pat, who is hot-natured, feels that 70 degrees is a perfect temperature setting for the house, whereas Steve (who happens to be cold-natured) finds 70 degrees to be way too low of a temperature setting for their

home. This example illustrates the fact that _____ influence our perceptions.
a. proximity
b. similarity
c. perceptual sets
d. physical characteristics
e. attribution errors

18 The information we receive goes through various filters and screens that sort and color what we receive and how we perceive it. In other words, our _____ influence(s) or alter(s) our perceptions of people, events, and things.
a. physical characteristics
b. psychological state
c. blinders
d. ethnocentricity

19 Which of the following characterizes the relationship between culture and communication?
a. Cultural background can affect the way in which people perceive other people.
b. Culture is an integral part of each of us and determines many of our individual characteristics.
c. Effective communication between people of diverse backgrounds occurs rather easily when both parties are unwilling to recognize that there is more than one correct viewpoint.
d. all of the above
e. A and B only

20 All of the following are true of ethnocentrism, EXCEPT
a. ethnocentrism is a natural belief that our own culture is superior to all others
b. ethnocentrism involves an inability to appreciate ideas, customs, or beliefs from other cultures
c. ethnocentrism involves judging other cultures on a superiority-inferiority scale
d. ethnocentrism is not necessarily a bad thing

21 According to communication scholars, a great deal of uncertainty surrounds the influence of _____, which is a social construct related to masculine and feminine behaviors that are learned.
a. biological sex
b. ethnocentrism
c. cultural relativism
d. gender

22 _____ is "we-oriented,"
whereas _____ is "me-oriented."
- **a.** ethnocentrism, cultural relativism
- **b.** cultural relativism, gender
- **c.** cultural relativism, ethnocentrism
- **d.** ethnocentrism, gender

23 People who are hired to create positive images of political candidates are often referred to as _____.
- **a.** spin doctors
- **b.** handlers
- **c.** cultural critiques
- **d.** all of the above
- **e.** A and B only

24 Our interpretations of different types of events are usually influenced by
- **a.** our past experiences
- **b.** our present circumstances
- **c.** the opinions of others
- **d.** all of the above

25 Ted grew up watching *The Oprah Winfrey Show*. In one particular episode, Oprah's guest shared several techniques for handling relational conflict with romantic partners. Using this information, Ted then decided to resolve his conflict with his girlfriend by following the 5-step solution discussed on Oprah's show. This example demonstrates the fact that differences in perception can be affected by
- **a.** gender
- **b.** culture
- **c.** media
- **d.** role-playing
- **e.** cultural relativism

26 Each of the following can help us improve our perception competencies, EXCEPT
- **a.** recognizing that each person's frame of reference is unique
- **b.** becoming a passive perceiver
- **c.** distinguish facts from inferences
- **d.** recognizing that people and situations change

27 One way in which we can improve our perception competencies is to
- **a.** keep an open mind
- **b.** remember that our perceptions may not be totally accurate
- **c.** be willing to change our misperceptions
- **d.** all of the above
- **e.** A and B only

28 A _____ incites or quickens action, feeling, or thought.
- **a.** concept
- **b.** frame of mind
- **c.** stimulus
- **d.** perceptual set

29 All of the following behaviors will help us to become aware of the role perceptions play in communication, EXCEPT
- **a.** taking others' perceptions into account
- **b.** assuming too much about what we perceive
- **c.** evaluating the information we receive
- **d.** checking the source of the information we receive

30 In groups containing both females and males, studies have shown each of the following differences between males and females to be true, EXCEPT
- **a.** females tend to talk for longer periods of time than males
- **b.** males take more turns at speaking
- **c.** males exert more control over the topic of conversation
- **d.** females interrupt males less frequently than males interrupt females.

Chapter 3: Connecting Self and Communication

MULTIPLE CHOICE

Choose the one alternative that best completes the statement or answers the question.

1 When Sally says, "Speech class is important," she is expressing a(n):
a. belief
b. attitude
c. value
d. position

2 _____ is our mental picture of ourselves or our social identity, whereas _____ is our feelings and attitudes toward ourselves or how we evaluate ourselves.
a. self-esteem, self-identity
b. self-esteem, self-image
c. self-image, self-esteem
d. self-image, self-identity

3 According to your text, which of the following are components of the self-concept?
a. self-awareness
b. internalized beliefs
c. interpersonal attributes
d. all of the above
e. B and C only

4 All of the following statements about self and communication are true, EXCEPT
a. what we think about ourselves is not influenced by others
b. our self-concepts and our perceptions are very closely related
c. the messages we communicate relate directly to our self-identities
d. our self-concepts influence the way we present ourselves to others

5 Which statement accurately describes the self-concept?
a. the self-concept is a fixed picture of who we think we are
b. the self-concept is relatively consistent across different contexts
c. the self-concept is a process-it's constantly changing
d. the self-concept only consists of an individual's own thoughts and feelings

6 General, relatively long-lasting ideals that guide our behavior are referred to as
a. beliefs
b. values
c. dispositions
d. attitudes

7 Which statement best describes the relationship between attitudes and beliefs?
a. attitudes include an evaluation of whether something is good or bad, whereas beliefs reflect the perception of whether something is true or false
b. attitudes include an evaluation of whether something is true or false, whereas beliefs reflect the perception of whether something is good or bad
c. attitudes are relatively enduring, whereas beliefs may change from one moment to the next
d. attitudes may change from one moment to the next, whereas beliefs are relatively enduring

8 Which of the following components is at the top of the hierarchy of self-concept?
a. social self-concept
b. general self-concept
c. physical self-concept
d. self-esteem

9 Tommy gets up to give his speech and begins to sweat profusely. As he delivers his speech, his hands tremble and his voice begins to quiver. Tommy's reactions to giving his speech reflect symptoms of
a. low self-esteem
b. an unwillingness to communicate
c. poor impression management
d. communication apprehension

10 Jack has always been told by his friends and family that he would succeed in life and become achieve whatever he sets his mind to achieve. Consequently, Jack has developed a
a. negative self-concept
b. positive self-esteem
c. positive self-concept
d. positive social self

11. Which statement best describes the relationship between the self-concept and communication?
    a. there is a linear relationship between self-concept and the way we communicate
    b. we learn to communicate first, then we develop a self-concept
    c. we develop our self-concepts first, then we become better communicators
    d. there is a reciprocal connection between self-concept and the way we communicate

12. According to personality theorists, such as Carl Rogers, our _____ is the single most important aspect of our personality.
    a. self-concept
    b. self-esteem
    c. self-determination
    d. self-image

13. Which statement best describes communication apprehension?
    a. people with communication apprehension only fear public speaking
    b. people with communication apprehension always avoid talking
    c. communication apprehension does not influence a person's self-esteem
    d. people with high communication apprehension are often perceived as shy and withdrawn

14. The anatomical and physiological differences between males and females that are genetically determined are referred to as
    a. gender
    b. sex
    c. self-concept
    d. genes

15. Which of the following statements best describes the development of our self-concepts?
    a. parental communication has very little to do with the development of our self-concepts
    b. we learn about ourselves only as we touch and speak to others
    c. we learn a great deal about ourselves by observing our own behaviors

    d. the process by which we come to know ourselves is quite different from the process by which we come to know others

16. Hannah continues to tell herself "I'm going to pass this exam . . . I'm going to pass this exam" as she prepares for her final exam in communication. Her expectations that eventually led to her passing her communication exam demonstrate
    a. impression management
    b. self-fulfilling prophecies
    c. communication apprehension
    d. gender differences

17. In an effort to boost his own image, Scott purchases a brand new suit for his upcoming date with Tammy. Scott's efforts are best described as
    a. impression management
    b. other-enhancement
    c. self-esteem enhancers
    d. self-fulfilling prophecies

18. "Honesty is the best policy" is an example of a _____, whereas "People should be honest with one another" is an example of a _____.
    a. attitude, value
    b. value, attitude
    c. value, belief
    d. belief, value

19. Impression management strategies designed to boost your own self-image are referred to as
    a. other-enhancement
    b. self-enhancement
    c. gender-enhancement
    d. self-determination

20. Which statement best describes the relationship between gender and sex?
    a. for most people, biological sex and gender identity coincide
    b. for most people, biological sex and gender identity differ
    c. half of our identities is influenced by biological sex, the other half by gender
    d. both B and C

21. According to research on sex differences, females tend to manifest greater development
    a. on the left side of the brain
    b. on the right side of the brain
    c. on both sides of the brain compared to men
    d. none of the above

22. According to your text, we develop a sense of self that includes maleness and female-ness somewhere between the ages of
    a. two and five
    b. four and seven
    c. seven and ten
    d. thirteen and sixteen

23. After the birth of their newborn baby, the doctor approaches Susan and asks "Are you looking forward to being a 'stay-at-home' mother?" to which Susan replies "Actually, I'm going back to work and David is going to be a 'stay-at-home' father." The doctor's surprise at Susan's response reflects a
    a. gender disbelief
    b. sex expectation
    c. gender expectation
    d. gender stereotype

24. In general, the gender stereotypes applied to females are _____ than those applied to males.
    a. stronger
    b. more persistent
    c. more negative
    d. all of the above
    e. B and C only

25. An overwhelming body of evidence demonstrates that sex differences in communication are the result of _____.
    a. brain differences
    b. differences in self-esteem
    c. gender expectations
    d. relational differences

26. According to your text, there is a cultural bias in the United States towards
    a. femininity
    b. masculinity
    c. androgyny
    d. none of the above

27. Today, it is estimated that between _____ and _____ percent of married women work outside of the home.
    a. 30, 40
    b. 50, 60
    c. 70, 80
    d. 80, 90

28. Men and women who have both masculine and feminine traits are referred to as
    a. undifferentiated
    b. highly apprehensive
    c. androgynous
    d. gender-benefited

29. Changing a self-concept is not easy. It usually begins with a concentrated effort to change _____.
    a. attitudes
    b. beliefs
    c. values
    d. behaviors

30. People who have a weak self-concept are more likely to
    a. compliment others
    b. be depressed
    c. be concerned with derogative sources of negative feedback
    d. all of the above
    e. both B and C

Chapter 4: Connecting Through Verbal Communication

MULTIPLE CHOICE

Choose the one alternative that best completes the statement or answers the question.

1 All of the following are variables that influence the effectiveness of language use, EXCEPT
a. accuracy
b. consistency
c. immediacy
d. vividness

2 When we use a direct, fresh language in an active voice and add a sense of excitement to what we are saying, we are using:
a. immediate language
b. accurate language
c. metaphorical language
d. vivid language

3 In _____ cultures, the meaning of the communication act is inferred from the situation, whereas in _____ cultures the meaning is often directly stated.
a. low-context, high-context
b. low-monitoring, high-monitoring
c. high-context, low-context
d. high-monitoring, low-monitoring

4 _____ is a structured system of signs, sounds, gestures, or marks that is used and understood to express ideas and feelings.
a. nonverbal communication
b. paralanguage
c. language
d. gesturing

5 Which statement accurately describes the power of language?
a. language restricts us to knowing our own experiences
b. successful communicators regard language as a "mere matter of words"
c. language is rarely useful for resolving conflicts
d. words have the power to affect our minds, feelings, and thoughts

6 According to your text, language and thought are:
a. inseparable
b. separate aspects of communication
c. symmetrical
d. none of the above

7 All of the following are elements of language, EXCEPT
a. sounds
b. grammar
c. semantics
d. all of the above are elements of language

8 Which statement best describes the relationship between language and meaning?
a. words have meaning
b. language without meaning is quite useful
c. meaning is only a small part of the language we use
d. language by itself has no meaning

9 The rules of language that govern how words may be joined into phrases and sentences are referred to as
a. semantics
b. grammar
c. syntactics
d. pragmatics

10 All of the following statements are true, EXCEPT
a. competent communicators assume others will interpret their messages accurately
b. words can be abstract or concrete
c. words typically have a denotative meaning
d. language can obscure meaning

11 _____ refers to the subjective meaning of a word (what it suggests because of feelings it evokes), whereas _____ refers to the dictionary definition of a word.
a. denotative, connotative
b. connotative, denotative
c. concrete, abstract
d. abstract, concrete

12 Words such as *right, freedom, liberty,* and *love* are examples of _____ words-words that mean different things to different people.
a. denotative
b. concrete
c. grammatical
d. abstract

13 When the authors of your text state that "meaning depends on commonalities," they really mean that
   a. the meanings of words, like words themselves, change from time to time
   b. language can be used to deliberately create ambiguous messages
   c. the more communicators have in common, the more likely they are to hold similar meanings for the words they use
   d. communication based on concrete words leaves little room for misunderstanding

14 Using the term "myocardial infarction" instead of the words "heart attack" demonstrates that
   a. language can clarify meaning
   b. language can obscure meaning
   c. language can have denotative and connotative meanings
   d. language rarely depends on commonalities

15 Judie walks up to Steve and tells him his outfit is "dope." In this case, Judie is using
   a. jargon
   b. slang
   c. denotative meaning
   d. all of the above
   e. both A and B

16 When individuals deliberately misuse language to distort meaning, they are engaging in:
   a. euphemisms
   b. doublespeak
   c. interrogation
   d. slang

17 "As the doctor entered the room, he examined the patient's forehead and ordered a head CT." This statement best demonstrates that language
   a. can be sexist
   b. can be gender neutral
   c. can clarify meaning
   d. can express commonalities

18 Language that does not discriminate against males of females is considered
   a. gender-exclusive language
   b. sexist language
   c. androgynous language
   d. gender-inclusive language

19 According to the Sapir-Whorf hypothesis
   a. thoughts determine language
   b. language determines thought
   c. thoughts determine perceptions of reality
   d. all of the above
   e. B and C only

20 According to some language scholars, our way of looking at the world around us is fundamentally _____ in nature.
   a. denotative
   b. semantical
   c. metaphorical
   d. obscure

21 "We will certainly enjoy the musical" is more _____ than saying that "People often enjoy musicals."
   a. verbally immediate
   b. vivid
   c. metaphorical
   d. accurate

22 According to Edward Hall, Japan is an example of a _____ culture, whereas the United States is an example of a _____ culture.
   a. low-context, high-context
   b. high-context, low-context
   c. semantic, pragmatic
   d. pragmatic, semantic

23 When we teach children that a four-legged animal that barks is a "dog" rather than a "cat," we are demonstrating that language is
   a. systematic
   b. arbitrary
   c. denotative
   d. reflexive

24 Which statement accurately reflects the relationship between gender and language?
   a. there is no difference in how men and women use language
   b. men use language to establish and maintain social relationships, whereas women use use language to assert status
   c. the English language is structured with an inherent bias in favor of women
   d. there are no gender-neutral pronouns in the English language

25. After class, Dr. Wilson told Billy that his paper was "in need of revisions." When Lisa asked Billy how he did on his paper later that day, Billy responded by telling Lisa that "I failed the assignment and I'm going to have to re-write the entire paper." The misunderstanding between Dr. Wilson and Billy is referred to as
    a. semantics
    b. bypassing
    c. gender-inclusive language
    d. sexist language

26. Our tendencies to refer to things in terms of good or bad, large or small, and high or low is referred to as
    a. polarization
    b. indiscrimination
    c. bypassing
    d. semantics

27. When Chad told Wes he was thinking of running for Congress, Wes responded rather negatively by stating that "Politicians are crooks and scandals." Wes' categorization of politicians is referred to as:
    a. bypassing
    b. gender-exclusive language
    c. indiscrimination
    d. polarization

28. Karla and Leah are roommates. One day after work, Karla tells Leah that it's her turn to clean the dishes. Leah responds by saying "Actually, it's your turn. I did it last time." Karla then counters by saying "No, I just cleaned the dishes last night, so it's your turn again." If Leah and Karla continue to escalate their conflict, the escalation would be referred to as:
    a. dating
    b. indiscrimination
    c. indexing
    d. the pendulum effect

29. The Sapir-Whorf hypothesis involves two theories, one of which is referred to as the theory of linguistic relativity. According to the theory of linguistic relativity,
    a. people from different language communities perceive the world differently
    b. language determines thought
    c. thought determines language
    d. people from similar language communities perceive the world differently

30. When we use a figure of speech that associates two things or ideas, not commonly linked, as a means of description, we are using _____.
    a. an abstract term
    b. a concrete term
    c. a metaphor
    d. an oxymoron

Chapter 5: Connecting Through Nonverbal Communication

MULTIPLE CHOICE

Choose the one alternative that best completes the statement or answers the question.

1 All of the following statements about non-verbal communication are true, EXCEPT
   a. the study of nonverbal communication is relatively recent
   b. 35% of the meaning of our interactions comes from nonverbal communication
   c. people often use nonverbal communication as the basis of daily decisions
   d. nonverbal communication can change the intended meaning of a message

2 To say that nonverbal communication is ambiguous is to say that
   a. we cannot assume that nonverbal messages have only one meaning
   b. we must be careful when interpreting nonverbal messages
   c. it is easy to misperceive nonverbal behaviors
   d. all of the above
   e. A and B only

3 All of the following are characteristics of nonverbal communication, EXCEPT
   a. nonverbal communication is related to culture
   b. nonverbal communication is less believable than verbal communication
   c. nonverbal communication occurs constantly
   d. nonverbal communication depends on context

4 _____, or "body language," refers to any movement of the face or body that communicates a message.
   a. proxemics
   b. haptics
   c. kinesics
   d. chronemics

5 Most scholars would agree that _____ formulate display rules that dictate when, how, and with what consequences nonverbal expressions are exhibited.
   a. schools
   b. parents
   c. individuals
   d. cultures

6 Which statement accurately describes non-verbal communication?
   a. almost all of our feelings and attitudes are expressed through nonverbal communication
   b. most of us tend to believe verbal communication, even when it contradicts the nonverbal communication
   c. nonverbal communication is only present when we decide to use it
   d. nonverbal communication occurs independently of context

7 According to your text, all of the following are communicative functions of eye contact, EXCEPT:
   a. indicating degrees of interest and arousal
   b. regulating interaction
   c. demonstrating hunger
   d. expressing emotions

8 Jay asked Bill if he was doing OK and Bill responded with a thumbs up to indicate that he was alright. In this example, Bill used a(n) _____.
   a. emblem
   b. illustrator
   c. adaptor
   d. regulator

9 In order to relieve her stress, Cynthia twiddled her pencil for hours as she studied for her final exam. Cynthia was using which type of nonverbal communication?
   a. an emblem
   b. an illustrator
   c. an adaptor
   d. an affect display

10 Which of the following behaviors is an example of a regulator?
   a. nodding your head during a conversation
   b. extending your thumb to hitch a ride
   c. jumping up and down after your team won a national championship
   d. chewing your nails to relieve some stress

11. All of the following statements about physical characteristics are true, EXCEPT
    a. physical appearance plays a significant role in our communication with others
    b. attractive people are perceived to be more successful and sociable than unattractive people
    c. attractiveness has little to do with getting a job or gaining a higher salary
    d. overweight people are often rated as older, more talkative, and more warm-hearted than people who are thin or athletic

12. When Clayton spreads his books all over the table he is occupying at the library, his nonverbal communication is referred to as
    a. territoriality
    b. proxemics
    c. chronemics
    d. all of the above
    e. both A and B

13. _____ refers to the nonverbal aspects of our verbal language.
    a. haptics
    b. chronemics
    c. kinesics
    d. paralanguage

14. All of the following are types of nonverbal communication, EXCEPT
    a. oculesics
    b. semantics
    c. alter-adaptors
    d. paralanguage

15. According to your text, all of the following are forms of haptics, EXCEPT
    a. adversarial touch
    b. social-polite touch
    c. friendship-warmth touch
    d. sexual-arousal touch

16. According to Edward T. Hall, distances from 4 to 12 feet comprise our _____ space.
    a. social
    b. intimate
    c. public
    d. personal

17. During class, Dr. Thomas approached Kelli and got right in her face to demonstrate how some people violate other people's expectations for distance. In response to his actions, Kelli stepped backwards to maintain a "safe" distance. In this example, Dr. Thomas violated Kelli's _____ space.
    a. public
    b. social
    c. personal
    d. intimate

18. Sue's friend Tara usually arrives 15 to 20 minutes late to most of their social outings. Although Sue understands that this is just a part of who Tara is, Sue's other friends perceive Tara as being lazy and irresponsible. In this instance, Tara is unintentionally communicating to Sue's friends through which form of nonverbal communication?
    a. haptics
    b. chronemics
    c. paralanguage
    d. oculesics

19. Clothes, perfume, automobiles, and other material cues that we use to communicate our age, gender, status, etc., are all examples of
    a. ornaments
    b. textiles
    c. artifacts
    d. territoriality

20. As Dawn says "yes" to her students, she shakes her head up and down. Dawn's nonverbal expressions are serving which function of nonverbal communication?
    a. complementing
    b. deceiving
    c. repeating
    d. regulating

21. All of the following are reasons why we have difficulty interpreting nonverbal messages, EXCEPT
    a. nonverbal cues are overt
    b. nonverbal cues have multiple meanings
    c. nonverbal cues are interdependent
    d. nonverbal cues depend on our perceptions of them

22. To improve our interpretation of nonverbal communication, the authors of your text suggest
    a. being observant of and sensitive to the nonverbal messages you receive
    b. dismiss nonverbal messages that you are not sure of

c. verify nonverbal messages that are inconsistent with other cues
d. all of the above
e. both A and C

23 _____ involves a willingness to change behavior to fit a given situation, an awareness of how we affect others, and the ability to regulate nonverbal cues.
a. proxemics
b. indexing
c. self-monitoring
d. regulating

24 Of the nonverbal behaviors discussed in your textbook, which behavior is considered by researchers to be the first and primary characteristic noticed by people?
a. touch
b. facial expressions
c. eye behavior
d. body movements

25 Typically, people spend _____% of the time looking at the other person's eyes during conversation.
a. 35
b. 45
c. 55
d. 75

26 At a party, Johnny wants Kathy to come across the room and visit with him, but she can't hear him because of the crowd noise. So instead of yelling for her to come over, Johnny simply waves at her, gets her attention, and then waves for her to come over and visit with him. In this example, what type of nonverbal behavior is Johnny engaging in?
a. substituting behavior
b. complementing behavior
c. regulating behavior
d. repeating behavior

27 Assuming a fighting position to signal a desire to fight, or moving toward a door to signal the end of a conversation are examples of
a. self-adaptors
b. alter-adaptors
c. illustrators
d. affect displays

28 Which statement best describes the relationship between verbal and nonverbal communication?
a. verbal communication is more believable than nonverbal communication
b. nonverbal communication is more believable than verbal communication
c. nonverbal communication is conscious and deliberate, whereas verbal verbal communication tends to be unintentional and spontaneous
d. none of the above

29 Maintaining a "poker face" is an example of
a. intensifying
b. deintensifying
c. masking
d. neutralizing

30 After returning from her fishing trip, Nancy held up her hands to indicate to her friends that she had caught a red snapper that was "This big!" In other words, Nancy used a(n) _____ to demonstrate how large the fish was.
a. regulator
b. adaptor
c. illustrator
d. emblem

Chapter 6: Connecting Listening and Thinking in the Communication Process

MULTIPLE CHOICE

Choose the one alternative that best completes the statement or answers the question.

1 Which statement accurately describes the relationship between listening and education?
   a. skills in listening and processing information are often included in formal education curriculums
   b. informal listening training is generally provided to students of all ages
   c. most organizations consider training in listening to be of little importance
   d. proportionately, listening is the most used skill

2 As students, we are expected to listen approximately _____ percent of the time.
   a. 25
   b. 40
   c. 50
   d. 65

3 _____ is an active process, whereas _____ is a passive process.
   a. Hearing, listening
   b. Listening, hearing
   c. Hearing, talking
   d. Talking, listening

4 According to your text, all of the following are functions of listening, EXCEPT
   a. listening to feign interest in conversation
   b. listening to obtain information
   c. listening for enjoyment
   d. listening to evaluate

5 According to recent figures, the average person spends how much time speaking each day?
   a. more than two-thirds of the time
   b. approximately half of the time
   c. less than one-third of the time
   d. more than three-fourths of the time

6 All of the following differences between listening and hearing are true, EXCEPT
   a. most scholars would agree that the major difference between listening and hearing is expressed by the word "passive"

   b. listening requires energy and effort, whereas hearing naturally happens
   c. a person can be excellent at hearing but be terrible at listening
   d. you must get involved and work at listening

7 All of the following are stages of effective listening, EXCEPT
   a. hearing
   b. selecting
   c. describing
   d. understanding
   e. evaluating

8 While transcribing interviews, the court reporter focused in on the defendant's voice while ignoring the background noise coming from the rest of the courtroom. Which stage of effective listening is the court reporter engaged in?
   a. evaluating
   b. attending
   c. understanding
   d. describing

9 Total silence, smiling or frowning, and asking for clarification of what was received are all examples of
   a. paraphrasing
   b. evaluating
   c. describing
   d. responding

10 According to your textbook, ILA stands for
   a. International Listening Association
   b. Inter-generational Listening Association
   c. Interdisciplinary Library Association
   d. Interdisciplinary Letters of America

11 The process of assigning meaning to the sounds we've heard and attended to is referred to as
   a. evaluating
   b. describing
   c. understanding
   d. remembering

12 Sam has just lost his grandfather. As he shares his feelings of remorse with his best friend Peter, Peter shows Sam that he is aware of his feelings of loss and that he appreciates the hurt that Sam must be going through. Which function of listening is Peter engaged in?
   a. listening for enjoyment
   b. listening with empathy
   c. listening to obtain information
   d. listening to evaluate

13 We spend the least amount of time _____.

   a. writing
   b. listening
   c. speaking
   d. hearing
   e. reading

14 All of the following statements about the functions of listening are true, EXCEPT
   a. in most situations, we should listen critically
   b. we spend time listening for information everyday
   c. listening for enjoyment involves merely sitting back and letting sounds enter our ears
   d. empathetic listening is not the same as sympathetic listening

15 According to researchers, how much information can we recall after a short period of time?
   a. 80%
   b. 50%
   c. 40%
   d. 25%

16 The process of responding really involves the process of _____.
   a. evaluating information
   b. sending feedback
   c. describing your own feelings
   d. attending to certain types of information

17 All of the following are barriers to effective listening, EXCEPT
   a. criticizing the message instead of the speaker
   b. considering the topic uninteresting
   c. faking attention
   d. failing to adjust to distractions

18 While listening to the presidential debates, Nichelle assessed the accuracy of each candidate's position and determined the reasonableness of their conclusions. In other words, Nichelle engaged in
   a. empathetic listening
   b. listening for enjoyment
   c. critical listening
   d. listening for information

19 Assessing a speaker's motivation generally involves
   a. making a judgement about the speaker's beliefs
   b. comparing our standards and those of the speaker
   c. evaluating the worth of the message presented
   d. all of the above
   e. A and C only

20 According to your textbook, listening with a critical ear involves
   a. assessing the speaker's values and intent
   b. judging the accuracy of the speaker's conclusions
   c. comparing the speaker's values to those of society
   d. all of the above
   e. A and B only

21 All of the following are ways in which we can become better listeners, EXCEPT
   a. thinking of listening as a passive activity
   b. recognizing the importance of listening effectiveness
   c. understanding that effective listening requires a desire to improve and a willingness to work
   d. recognizing that effective listening requires conscious participation

22 In order to judge the accuracy of a speaker's conclusions, we can ask all of the following questions, EXCEPT
   a. Is the speaker qualified to draw the conclusion?
   b. Will the speaker's conclusions benefit me?
   c. Is the evidence relevant to the conclusion?
   d. Does the message contain invalid or inadequate reasoning?

23 According to the authors of your text, which statement accurately describes the relationship between listening and technology?
   a. Research documents that technologies such as email and the Internet are destroying students' abilities to listen in the classroom.
   b. Technology can be used to students' advantage, if used merely as a tool.
   c. Computer-enhanced presentations (such as PowerPoint) are helping students to focus on information and to take better notes in the classroom.
   d. none of the above
   e. both B and C

24 Critical thinking is an important skill in today's world because
   a. we are constantly confronted with many choices and decisions
   b. we live in an increasingly technological world, filled with information
   c. we must depend on others to provide information and advice
   d. all of the above
   e. A and B only

25 When you are faced with a difficult listening situation, the best approach is usually to
   a. ask questions
   b. paraphrase what the speaker is saying
   c. concentrate on the details rather than the main ideas
   d. leave the scene

26 An example of a poor listening habit is
   a. to ask questions
   b. to concentrate on details rather than on main ideas
   c. adjusting to distractions
   d. criticizing the message instead of the speaker

27 As the professor lectured, Paul was momentarily distracted by the sounds of other students in the hallway. In response to the noise, Paul got up, shut the door, and returned to listening to the professor's lecture. Which of habit of effective listening did Paul best demonstrate?
   a. paying specific attention
   b. concentrating on main ideas instead of details
   c. adjusting to distractions
   d. considering the topic interesting

28 When students listen to professors lecture in class, they are primarily listening for the purpose of
   a. evaluation
   b. obtaining information
   c. enjoyment
   d. empathy

29 According to the National Communication Association, competent listeners demonstrate
   a. knowledge and understanding of the listening process
   b. an ability to use appropriate and effective listening skills for a given situation
   c. an inability to identify and manage barriers to listening
   d. all of the above
   e. A and B only

30 _____ refers to the process of choosing which stimuli we will listen to and which stimuli we will ignore.
   a. evaluating
   b. hearing
   c. selecting
   d. remembering

Chapter 7: Selecting a Topic and Relating to the Audience

MULTIPLE CHOICE

Choose the one alternative that best completes the statement or answers the question.

1 According to a survey of 202 randomly selected blue-collar workers, almost half had given speeches to
   a. church groups
   b. community groups
   c. members of their unions
   d. all of the above
   e. A and C only

2 According to your text, all of the following are techniques for finding a topic, EXCEPT
   a. audience inventories
   b. brainstorming
   c. reviewing current media
   d. surfing the web

3 All of the following are questions we can ask ourselves to assess the appropriateness of a topic, EXCEPT
   a. Will the topic meet the objectives of the assignment?
   b. Does the topic merit the audience's attention?
   c. Does the audience of full knowledge of the topic?
   d. Can you make the topic understandable to everyone in the audience?

4 Beginning public speakers frequently express two concerns,
   a. the fear of not having anything worthwhile to say and the fear of not having nice visual aids.
   b. nervousness at speaking in front of others and the fear of not having anything worthwhile to say.
   c. the fear of passing out and nervousness at speaking in front of others.
   d. the fear of not having nice visual aids and nervousness of at speaking in front of others.

5 The most important factor in presenting an effective speech presentation is
   a. researching the topic
   b. wording the speech appropriately
   c. delivery
   d. selecting an appropriate topic

6 "To persuade my audience to purchase Nike tennis shoes," is an example of a
   a. specific purpose
   b. general purpose
   c. thesis
   d. topic

7 A sentence that states specifically what is going to be discussed in a speech is referred to as a
   a. general purpose
   b. preview
   c. thesis
   d. specific purpose

8 At Kathy's wedding, Jennifer stood up and gave a humorous after-dinner speech that had the entire wedding cast laughing. Jennifer delivered a(n) _____ speech.
   a. informative
   b. persuasive
   c. entertainment
   d. extemporaneous

9 An effective specific purpose statement identifies
   a. an important reference
   b. the audience
   c. the exact topic to be covered
   d. all of the above
   e. B and C only

10 Which of the following statements accurately reflects the task of narrowing a topic?
   a. The more concrete a topic, the more important it is to narrow it to meet the constraints of a speech situation.
   b. A broad topic is much easier to research than a well-focused topic.
   c. Each time you narrow a topic, you increase its potential depth.
   d. Narrowing the topic is not that critical to your success as a communicator.

11 *The Readers' Guide to Periodical Literature* is referred to in your text as one example of
   a. brainstorming
   b. reviewing the current media
   c. creating a self-inventory
   d. surfing the web

12. Speeches usually perform one of three overlapping functions, including
    a. to inform
    b. to entertain
    c. to persuade
    d. all of the above

13. _____ is the collection of data on audience members' values, attitudes, and beliefs.
    a. voluntary participant analysis
    b. psychological analysis
    c. demographic analysis
    d. captive participant analysis

14. All of following would be included in a demographic analysis of the audience, EXCEPT
    a. age
    b. attitudes
    c. gender
    d. ethnic background

15. _____ participants are required to listen to a particular speech, whereas _____ participants choose to hear a particular speech because of interest or need.
    a. captive, voluntary
    b. informed, captive
    c. voluntary, captive
    d. voluntary, informed

16. Jeffrey gave an informative speech on cardiovascular systems in his speech class. The audience in this situation would be considered
    a. voluntary
    b. captive
    c. persuasive
    d. demographic

17. All of the following could included in an analysis of key audience information, EXCEPT
    a. size of audience
    b. whether or not they like the thesis
    c. knowledge level
    d. physical setting

18. Before delivering her speech to her class-mates, Phyllis watched her audience and noted their behaviors and characteristics. In other words, Phyllis learned about her audience through
    a. survey interviewing
    b. a questionnaire
    c. observation
    d. personal interviews

19. A carefully planned and executed person-to-person, question-and-answer session is referred to as a(n)
    a. survey interview
    b. questionnaire
    c. observation session
    d. telephone survey

20. According to your text, the goal of observing, survey interviewing, and administering questionnaires is to
    a. relax yourself and provide an easier audience to speak to
    b. give your audience a preview of what you're going to speak about
    c. provide an audience profile for the next speaker
    d. gather information so that you can adapt your speech to the audience

21. When evaluating a web site, the authors of your text suggest you should ask yourself all of the following questions, EXCEPT
    a. Are there other sites such as this one?
    b. Who is the author or producer of the site?
    c. How reliable is the source?
    d. For whom is the information intended?
    e. Is the web item up to date?

22. When your instructor does not assign a topic, the trick is to
    a. identify a topic that matches your interests and qualifications
    b. identify the interests and existing knowledge of your audience
    c. identify the requirements of the situation that the speech is intended for
    d. all of the above
    e. A and B only

23 According to recent surveys on the popularity of public speaking, researchers discovered that
   a. nongraduates were more likely than college graduates to give speeches
   b. most personnel managers want to hire employees who know how to give effective public presentations
   c. public speaking is considered a necessary skill for career advancement
   d. most corporate executives maintain that competence in public speaking is essential for a person in middle management

24 "Effective speeches have an introduction, a body, and a conclusion." This statement is an example of a
   a. thesis
   b. general purpose
   c. specific purpose
   d. topic

25 A collection of individuals who have come together to watch or listen to a speech is referred to as
   a. participants
   b. an audience
   c. a troupe
   d. speakers

26 All of the following are suggestions for relating and adapting to your audience, EXCEPT
   a. When dealing with an audience that knows a lot about your topic, you need to acknowledge what you share with them.
   b. When dealing with audiences that oppose your views, you should make use of biased sources.
   c. Acknowledge that your listeners' views have as much merit as your own.
   d. When dealing with an audience that has little or no interest in your topic, you need to provoke their interest.

27 The collection and interpretation of basic information such as age, gender, education, and religion is best described as
   a. psychological analysis
   b. captive participant analysis
   c. setting analysis
   d. demographic analysis

28 Analyzing your audience is really concerned with
   a. understanding your own point of view
   b. understanding your audience's point of view
   c. understanding the strongest point in your speech
   d. understanding the weakest point in your speech

29 Informative speeches can perform all of the following functions, EXCEPT
   a. attempting to change listeners' attitudes
   b. explaining what something means
   c. explaining how something works
   d. attempting to demonstrate how something is done

30 Which of the following statements accurately describes the difference between persuasive and informative speeches?
   a. the difference between the two is always clear-cut
   b. informative speeches seek to change listeners' behaviors, whereas the persuasive seeks to convey information and understanding
   c. the ultimate goal of persuasive speeches is action, whereas the ultimate goal of informative speeches is to generate understanding
   d. informative speeches have a call to action, whereas persuasive speeches simply demonstrate how something is done

Chapter 8: Gathering and Using Information

MULTIPLE CHOICE

Choose the one alternative that best completes the statement or answers the question.

1 According to college professors and professional speakers, every ten minutes of speaking time requires at least:
   a. 2 hours of research and preparation time
   b. 5 hours of research and preparation time
   c. 10 hours of research and preparation time
   d. 20 hours of research and preparation time

2 All of the following are electronic information sources, EXCEPT
   a. Lexis-Nexis
   b. Readers' Guide to Periodical Literature
   c. ERIC
   d. the Internet

3 According to Elizabeth Kirk, all of the following are basic criteria one should use when one evaluates an Internet source, EXCEPT
   a. the length of time a source has been posted
   b. the author of the material
   c. who publishes the website
   d. how many links the website provides

4 URL stands for
   a. uniform research library
   b. uniform resource locator
   c. united research laboratories
   d. uniform resource librarian

5 The URL ".gov" indicates that the website
   a. promotes or sells products
   b. entertains
   c. provides factual information and explanations
   d. influences public opinion and advocates for particular issues

6 All of the following are suggestions for doing research, EXCEPT
   a. use computer searches only when absolutely necessary
   b. take notes
   c. state a clear purpose before starting your research
   d. begin your search early

7 According to your text, you should use _____ as you maintain your bibliography of sources.
   a. a 5 x 7 inch notecard
   b. a 3 x 5 inch notecard
   c. a 2 x 4 inch notecard
   d. a 7 x 9 inch notecard

8 According to Aristotle, every speech has essentially which two parts?
   a. a statement and a conclusion
   b. an introduction and a conclusion
   c. a statement and its proof
   d. a conclusion and its review of the main points

9 All of the following are types of "examples" you can use to support your ideas, EXCEPT
   a. personal testimony
   b. analogies
   c. illustrations
   d. restatements

10 A _____ analogy draws comparisons between things in different categories.
   a. figurative
   b. literal
   c. metaphorical
   d. illustrative

11 Examples that refer to single items or to events that have occurred are called
   a. analogies
   b. metaphors
   c. testimonials
   d. illustrations

12 According to your textbook, all of the following are sources of information one can use when researching a speech topic, EXCEPT
   a. yourself
   b. interviews
   c. tabloids
   d. library
   e. the Internet

13 In court cases, psychologists are often asked to provide what type of information?
   a. restatements
   b. expert opinions
   c. analogies
   d. illustrations

14. Some of the steps in the interview process include
    a. establishing the purpose of the interview
    b. conducting research after the interview
    c. recording the interview
    d. all of the above
    e. A and C only

15. Audiences generally accept information because of
    a. their curiosity
    b. the perceived believability of the speaker
    c. the credibility of the information itself
    d. all of the above
    e. B and C only

16. According to your text, which of the following elements turns a mediocre speech into a good speech?
    a. a speaker's ability to use sources correctly
    b. the quantity of a speaker's supporting material
    c. the quality of a speaker's supporting material
    d. all of the above
    e. A and C only

17. The most common definition form used by speakers is the
    a. logical definition
    b. operational definition
    c. definition by example
    d. methodological definition

18. "The mean is the result of adding all the scores in a set of scores and dividing by the number of scores in the set." This statement is an example of a
    a. definition by example
    b. logical definition
    c. hierarchical definition
    d. operational definition

19. All of the following are suggestions for making the most out of statistics, EXCEPT
    a. be sure to report decimals when working with large numbers
    b. use statistics sparingly
    c. if possible, use visual aids to present statistical information
    d. take time to explain the statistics you are using

20. According to your text, the word(s) _____ is generally used as a connector between keywords when conducting a search in an electronic database.
    a. as well as
    b. but
    c. not
    d. and

21. The URL ".net" refers to a
    a. network administration organization
    b. U.S. college or university
    c. military site
    d. network of community colleges

22. When researching your topic, remember
    a. the less information you record, the better
    b. there are plenty of shortcuts to doing good research
    c. you should always have more than you need to write your speech
    d. the computer is one of the most difficult ways of obtaining sources on a topic

23. Characteristics that define what an interview is include
    a. being carefully planned
    b. involving a person-to-person interaction
    c. a question-and-answer session
    d. all of the above
    e. B and C only

24. An important difference between websites and print sources such as journals and periodicals is that
    a. only websites provide current information on different topics
    b. only print sources provide information about the author of the material
    c. print sources do not undergo the same evaluation and review process that websites go through
    d. websites do not undergo the same evaluation and review process that print sources go through

25. According to your text, _____ is an effective method of condensing a long text or clarifying a passage that is too technical for audience members to understand.
    a. testifying
    b. providing opinions
    c. paraphrasing
    d. quoting

26 "The Mormon religion is one of the fastest growing religious denominations in the United States." This statement is an example of a(n)
a. definition by example
b. statistic
c. illustration
d. analogy

27 A _____ tells what could or probably would happen, given a specific set of circumstances.
a. hypothetical analogy
b. hypothetical illustration
c. hypothetical metaphor
d. hypothetical restatement

28 According to the authors of your text, interviews differ from social conversations in that
a. interviews require little preparation
b. interviews involve a decision about what information is desired
c. interviews often occur spontaneously
d. all of the above
e. both A and C

29 A(n) _____ is the expression of the same idea using different words.
a. testimonial
b. illustration
c. analogy
d. restatement

30 All of the following are types of supporting information one can use when presenting a speech, EXCEPT
a. definitions
b. myths
c. testimony
d. statistics
e. analogies

Chapter 9: Organizing and Outlining Your Speech

MULTIPLE CHOICE

Choose the one alternative that best completes the statement or answers the question.

1 When we express main points using similar grammatical patterns and wording, we're using
   a. linear structure
   b. parallel structure
   c. vivid language
   d. time-sequence patterns

2 All of the following patterns are ways in which we can organize speeches, EXCEPT
   a. spatial pattern
   b. parallel pattern
   c. cause-effect pattern
   d. problem-solution pattern

3 According to your text, the introduction of a speech should meet all of these goals, EXCEPT
   a. tie everything together
   b. forecast the main points
   c. motivate the audience to listen
   d. orient the audience to the topic

4 "Let me first illustrate" and "My second point is" are examples of
   a. internal summaries
   b. parallel points
   c. concluding statements
   d. signposts

5 The main points of a speech should be
   a. thoughtfully selected and stated
   b. very broad in number
   c. carefully ordered and connected
   d. all of the above
   e. A and C only

6 When we arrange the parts of a speech into a systematic and meaningful whole, we are _____ the speech.
   a. researching
   b. organizing
   c. writing
   d. delivering

7 All of the following are steps included in the process of developing a body to a speech, EXCEPT
   a. developing the main points
   b. supporting the main points
   c. previewing the main points
   d. connecting the main points

8 Which of the following suggestions are given by the authors of your text when presenting the main points of a speech?
   a. be general
   b. use abstract language
   c. create parallel structure
   d. avoid relevance

9 The number of main points in your speech will depend on
   a. the time available to deliver the speech
   b. the content to be covered in the speech
   c. the amount of information the audience can comprehend and remember
   d. all of the above
   e. A and B only

10 When we divide the main topic into a series of related subtopics, we are using the _____ pattern of organizing.
   a. topical
   b. spatial
   c. problem-solution
   d. time-sequence

11 Consider the following main points:

   I. Without a tuition increase, several programs will have to be cut from the university.

   II. Poor planning, overspending, and mismanagement of funds by school officials have been the primary contributors to the need for a tuition increase.

   Which organizing pattern best describes the way in which these main points have been arranged?
   a. effect-cause pattern
   b. cause-effect pattern
   c. time-sequence pattern
   d. topical pattern

12 Alan H. Monroe developed a widely used pattern of organization for persuasive speeches known as:
   a. the topical pattern sequence
   b. the parallel structure sequence
   c. the motivated sequence
   d. the time-for-action sequence

13 "Let me move on to my next point" and "Another example might be" are examples of:
  a. signposts
  b. parallel structures
  c. internal previews
  d. transitions

14 All of the following are approaches one can use to gain the attention of an audience, EXCEPT
  a. ask rhetorical questions
  b. use personal narratives
  c. state the thesis of your speech
  d. use humor

15 A standard way of making your topic relevant is simply to point out
  a. some humorous aspects of your topic
  b. some statistics that support your views
  c. the reasons for presenting your speech
  d. all of the above

16 Michael Jordan has been a wonderful spokesperson for Nike because of his
  a. competence
  b. character
  c. credibility
  d. all of the above
  e. A and B only

17 When you offer your audience a "road map" of what you're going to talk about in your speech, you are essentially _____ the main points.
  a. forecasting
  b. previewing
  c. concluding
  d. all of the above
  e. both A and B

18 All of the following steps should be included in the conclusion of a speech, EXCEPT
  a. reviewing the main points
  b. make your thesis clear
  c. end with a memorable thought
  d. let the audience piece everything together

19 _____ involves arranging the entire contents of a speech in a logical sequence and writing that sequence in a standardized form.
  a. spacing
  b. outlining
  c. organizing
  d. researching

20 What is the difference between organizing and outlining a speech?
  a. organizing is a more rigorous written process than outlining
  b. only organizing involves arranging information to form a meaningful sequence
  c. outlining is more detailed than organizing
  d. organizing, rather than outlining, helps unify and clarify thinking

21 A full-content outline includes all of the following, EXCEPT
  a. main points written as simple bullet points
  b. secondary points written in complete sentences
  c. a bibliography
  d. an expansions of the main points selected from the preliminary outline

22 A presentational outline should include
  a. a full bibliography of all sources cited within the speech
  b. a list of all points that may or may not be used in the speech
  c. all points in complete sentences
  d. a condensed version of the full-content outline

23 A question for which no answer is expected is referred to as
  a. a concluding question
  b. a rhetorical question
  c. a question of disbelief
  d. a metaphorical question

24 "Next we'll look at possible solutions to the problem of budget shortfalls," is an example of a(n)
  a. internal summary
  b. signpost
  c. transition
  d. internal preview

25 All of the following are steps in the motivated sequence pattern, EXCEPT
  a. visualization
  b. action
  c. disbelief
  d. satisfaction

26 According to your text, the introduction to a speech serves two important functions
  a. motivating the audience to listen and orienting them to the subject
  b. motivating the audience to listen and previewing your sources
  c. establishing credibility and stating your main points
  d. orienting them to the subject and previewing your main points

27 In persuasive speeches, the conclusion should
  a. focus your audience's thoughts on the specific purpose of the speech
  b. spell out the action or policies recommended by the speaker
  c. relate to the introduction
  d. all of the above
  e. A and B only

28 All of the following are types of outlines, EXCEPT
  a. a reference outline
  b. a full-content outline
  c. a presentational outline
  d. a preliminary outline

29 A short review statement given at the end of each main point is referred to as a(n)
  a. internal summary
  b. internal preview
  c. transition
  d. signpost

30 When we present the main points of a speech in chronological order, we're using a _____ pattern of organizing.
  a. problem-solution
  b. time-sequence
  c. spatial
  d. motivated sequence

Chapter 10: Managing Anxiety and Delivering Your Speech

MULTIPLE CHOICE

Choose the one alternative that best completes the statement or answers the question.

1 All of the following are symptoms of speech anxiety, EXCEPT
   a. your heart begins to beat faster
   b. more sugar is pumped into your system
   c. your blood pressure slows down
   d. you may make telling statements such as "I'm not any good at this anyway."

2 The theory behind _____ is that a mental rehearsal will associate relaxation with situations that create tension.
   a. systematic distortion
   b. communication desensitization
   c. mental distortion
   d. systematic desensitization

3 At the beginning of class, Danielle was given a slip of paper asking her to compare and contrast the different types of speeches mentioned in her textbook. Her instructor told her that she had 2 minutes to think of what she wanted to say, and then she would have to give the speech. Since Danielle has to deliver the speech with little preparation, her speech is referred to as a
   _____ speech.
   a. impromptu
   b. extemporaneous
   c. memorized
   d. manuscript

4 Common causes of speech anxiety include all of the following, EXCEPT
   a. fear of the unknown
   b. fear of physical attractiveness
   c. fear of criticism
   d. fear of social inadequacy

5 According to your text, practicing the delivery of your speech will help you
   a. know what the speech sounds like
   b. know whether wording changes are needed
   c. know whether you are dressed appropriately
   d. all of the above
   e. A and B only

6 All of the following are qualities of effective speakers, EXCEPT
   a. unsure of themselves
   b. knowledgeable
   c. ethical
   d. prepared

7 Ethical speakers avoid all of the following behaviors, EXCEPT
   a. distorting or falsifying information
   b. citing all of the sources of their information
   c. making unsupported attacks on opponents in order to discredit them
   d. using irrelevant emotional appeals to sensationalize the message

8 According to your text, _____ is a speaker's greatest asset.
   a. a visual aid
   b. knowledge
   c. preparation
   d. a strong voice

9 Billy finds that he trembles every time he has to get up before his classmates and deliver a speech. Outside of the moments when he has to deliver a speech, however, he finds that he enjoys interacting with his fellow classmates and he even enjoys working on group projects in class. In this case, Billy suffers from
   a. communication apprehension
   b. stage fright
   c. speech anxiety
   d. all of the above
   e. B and C only

10 Experts suggest several guidelines for reducing speech anxiety, including
   a. selecting a topic that you know very little about
   b. thinking realistically about your inabilities as a speaker
   c. practicing your speech
   d. spending little time in preparation for the speech

11. Martin Luther King Jr. delivered one of the most widely regarded speeches in history known as the _____ speech
    a. "I Dream of Freedom"
    b. "I Have a Mission"
    c. "I Dream of Equality"
    d. "I Have a Dream"

12. The only consistent rule when delivering a speech is that
    a. you must have an effective visual aid
    b. you must keep the speech between 5 to 7 minutes long
    c. you must be yourself
    d. you must deliver part of the speech memorized

13. When a speaker uses a carefully prepared and researched speech, but delivers it from notes with a high degree of spontaneity, he or she is using a(n) _____ style of delivery.
    a. extemporaneous
    b. memorized
    c. impromptu
    d. manuscript

14. When President Bush delivers his "State of the Union" address using a teleprompter, his is most likely using a(n) _____ delivery.
    a. extemporaneous
    b. memorized
    c. impromptu
    d. manuscript

15. Most speakers deliver their words at a rate between
    a. 75 and 100 words per minute
    b. 120 and 150 words per minute
    c. 150 and 200 words per minute
    d. 200 and 250 words per minute

16. Pausing in your speech can serve all of the following functions, EXCEPT
    a. gaining the audience's attention
    b. de-emphasizing an important point
    c. enabling listeners to follow shifts in ideas
    d. punctuating thoughts

17. Presentational aids can help a speaker
    a. increase the length of their presentation
    b. gain attention and hold interest
    c. improve retention of information
    d. all of the above

18. When planning to use a chalkboard during your presentation, the authors of your text suggest that you consider
    a. when to put information on the board
    b. how to write on the board
    c. how to use the board when delivering your speech
    d. all of the above
    e. B and C only

19. The most frequently used methods of presentation include all of the following, EXCEPT
    a. posters
    b. handouts
    c. question and answer sessions
    d. projected visuals
    e. handouts

20. When planning to use presentational aids, you should keep all of the following guidelines in mind, EXCEPT
    a. Visuals should contain at least 2 ideas per poster.
    b. Presentational aids should be practical.
    c. Visual aids should serve a need.
    d. Visual aids should look as professional as possible.

21. Before delivering her speech, Mary asked her friend Stuart if he could see her visual aid from the back of the classroom. Mary was attempting to follow which guideline for using presentational aids?
    a. Presentational aids that are not original require documentation.
    b. Presentational aids should look professional.
    c. Presentational aids should not dominate or take over a speaker's job.
    d. Presentational aids should be adapted to the audience and the situation.

22. _____ refers to how high or low the voice is on a tonal scale.
    a. rate
    b. pitch
    c. force
    d. volume

23. A speaker's intelligibility is determined by all of the following characteristics of a speaker, EXCEPT
    a. vocal volume
    b. accuracy of pronunciation

c. the speaker's attire

d. articulation

24 According to your text, the key(s) to high intelligibility are

a. self-awareness

b. a well-researched topic

c. consideration for listeners

d. all of the above

e. A and C only

25 Which of the following statements about stage fright is true?

a. there is evidence to suggest that discussing stage fright decreases it

b. the more we know about stage fright, the less we are able to control it

c. stage fright is fairly uncommon

d. having some anxiety about giving a speech is normal

26 When we consider the overall impression that a speaker's voice makes on listeners, we are considering the _____ of the speaker.

a. vocal quality

b. vocal intonation

c. vocal resonance

d. vocal harmony

27 The authors of your text make two important points about speaker intelligibility. What are they?

a. use fillers and vocal pauses

b. adjust your language to suit the formal presentation

c. use a sentence structure that reduces credibility

d. use natural language, such as "like" and "um," throughout the speech

28 Which physical aspect of the speaker is the most physical aspect of delivery?

a. eye contact

b. gestures

c. body movement

d. personal appearance

e. vocal variety

29 A _____, or a representation of a real object, allows a speaker to enlarge or shrink an object to a convenient size for display.

a. photograph

b. drawing

c. model

d. table

30 The intensity and volume of the speaker's voice is referred to as

a. pitch

b. force

c. rate

d. vocal variety

Chapter 11: Informative Speaking

MULTIPLE CHOICE

Choose the one alternative that best completes the statement or answers the question.

1 Which of the following statements accurately describes the difference between an informative speech and a persuasive speech?
a. the persuasive speech is meant to increase knowledge, whereas the informative speech is meant to alter attitudes
b. the persuasive speech is meant to alter attitudes, whereas the informative speech is meant to increase knowledge
c. persuasion can be accomplished without attempting to inform, but informing cannot be accomplished without attempting to persuade
d. what separates the persuasive and the informative speech are the references cited by the speaker

2 Guidelines one should consider when selecting an informative topic include all of the following, EXCEPT
a. Choose a topic that can be made interesting to the audience.
b. Choose a topic that can be well developed within the speech's time limit.
c. Choose a topic that you are unfamiliar with.
d. Choose a topic that will allow you to convey an important thought to the audience.

3 The communication or reception of knowledge or intelligence is referred to as
a. understanding
b. technology
c. systems
d. information

4 According to your text, which type of presentation is the most common presentation you will make in all aspects of your life?
a. informative
b. persuasive
c. extemporaneous
d. entertainment

5 Which statement best describes the relationship between information and power?
a. Being informed helps increase uncertainty.
b. Those who possess information tend to be less powerful than those who don't.
c. The ability to communicate information is essential in our society.
d. The greater you desire to have important information, the less valuable the information is to you.

6 According to your text, what percentage of the labor force holds information-related jobs?
a. 17%
b. 30%
c. 60%
d. 75%

7 To achieve your main goal of increasing the audience's knowledge, you must strive to attain two subgoals:
a. increase their understanding and make them laugh
b. gain their attention and call them to action
c. gain their attention and increase their understanding
d. increase their understanding and call them to action

8 When your instructor uses statements such as "This will probably be included on your next text," and "The next 3 points are crucial to your understanding of the problem," he or she is using
a. signposts
b. advance organizers
c. planned repetition
d. concrete words

9 In order to maintain audience attention, you should
a. focus on the usual
b. create information relevance
c. provide a fresh perspective
d. all of the above
e. B and C only

10 A speaker who gives an audience a reason to listen by relating the topic to their needs and interests creates
    a. information relevance
    b. information attentiveness
    c. information overload
    d. information repetition

11 A speaker can clearly define a term for the audience using all of the following methods, EXCEPT
    a. using antonyms
    b. using synonyms
    c. using contrast definitions
    d. using metaphors

12 The authors of your text provide which of the following hints for effective informative speaking?
    a. avoid assumptions
    b. be sure to give a call to action
    c. personalize information
    d. none of the above
    e. both A and C

13 When evaluating an informative speech, your instructor is likely to consider all of the following criteria, EXCEPT
    a. topic
    b. organization
    c. audience analysis
    d. speaker self-esteem
    e. supporting materials

14 Which statement accurately describes the criteria used by instructors when evaluating informative speeches?
    a. Word choice is rather insignificant.
    b. The speaker's stance and posture really doesn't matter as long as the speech is well-written.
    c. The speech should meet the time requirements set by the assignment.
    d. Showing the audience why the topic is important to them is irrelevant.

15 In order to avoid making false assumptions about the audience's level of knowledge, the speaker should
    a. conduct an audience analysis
    b. take the time to define and explain the topic
    c. make the assumption that the audience needs introductory information

    d. all of the above
    e. A and B only

16 Personalizing the information in a speech yields which of the following advantages?
    a. it holds the audience's attention
    b. it gains audience interest in the topic
    c. it can make the speech come to life
    d. all of the above
    e. A and C only

17 When speakers deliberately restating a thought in order to increase the likelihood that the audience will understand and remember it, the speaker is using
    a. planned repetition
    b. advance organizers
    c. a fresh perspective
    d. information relevance

18 According to your text, the speaker can increase understanding of the topic by
    a. organizing the presentation
    b. using definitions
    c. choosing language carefully
    d. all of the above
    e. A and B only

19 According to your text, one scheme for classifying informative speech topics includes dividing them into all of the following, EXCEPT
    a. dates
    b. objects
    c. processes
    d. events

20 "To inform the audience about how to diet with low-fat foods" is an example of a specific purpose statement for an informative speech about
    a. objects
    b. structures
    c. dates
    d. processes

21 "Relationship development" and "learning theory" are examples of informative topics that deal with _____.
    a. concepts
    b. structures
    c. processes
    d. events

22. "Election 2000" and "The Fall of Communism" are speech titles that indicate that the informative speech is about
a. objects
b. dates
c. events
d. structures

23. To make something more concrete, a speaker will often describe its size, quantity, shape, and/or composition. In these instances, the speaker is using
a. abstractors
b. descriptors
c. planned repetition
d. contrasting definitions

24. In his speech on the Olympic Games, Tommy traced the origin of the word "Olympiad" in order to increase audience understanding of the games. In his speech, Tommy used a(n)
a. synonym
b. contrast definition
c. antonym
d. etymology

25. When a speaker uses a word, phrase, or concept that has the opposite meaning of another word, he or she is using a(n)
a. synonym
b. antonym
c. etymology
d. metaphor

26. According to your text, all of the following statements are true, EXCEPT
a. we spend a great deal more time making speeches than we do listening to speeches
b. speakers should always analyze their presentations
c. in order to become effective speakers, we should always analyze what happened and how successful we were
d. it is helpful for the speaker to obtain the listeners' perspectives on a speech

27. A(n) _____ is helpful when you want to distinguish between similar terms.
a. synonym
b. etymology
c. contrast definition
d. advance organizer

28. All of the following statements about advance organizers are true, EXCEPT
a. advance organizers serve as previews of main points
b. they warn that coming information is important
c. advance organizers are completely different from signposts
d. they help the audience concentrate and focus on what is coming in the speech

29. In order to choose language carefully, an effective public speaker should
a. plan for repetition
b. use concrete words
c. use description
d. all of the above
e. B and C only

30. When a speaker uses the phrase "willingness to talk openly" to describe a communication extrovert, the speaker is using a(n)
a. synonym
b. antonym
c. etymology
d. contrasting definition

Chapter 12: Persuasive Speaking

MULTIPLE CHOICE

Choose the one alternative that best completes the statement or answers the question.

1 Questions such as "Which building is the tallest building in the world?" and "Who first developed the computer and for what uses?" are questions of _____.
   a. policy
   b. fact
   c. value
   d. action

2 Questions such as "Should student parking on campus be more accessible?" and "Should all students be tested for drugs before entering college?" are questions of

_____.
   a. action
   b. fact
   c. policy
   d. value

3 According to British philosopher Stephen Toulmin, supporting a persuasive position or argument involves which of the following parts?
   a. a warrant
   b. a claim
   c. an application
   d. all of the above
   e. both A and B

4 "Public universities provide inadequate housing to students" is an example of
   a. a claim
   b. a warrant
   c. evidence
   d. data

5 According to Toulmin's model, listeners can usually respond to claims by
   a. accepting the claim at face value
   b. rejecting the claim outright at face value
   c. accepting or rejecting the claim according to their evaluation of data
   d. all of the above
   e. A and B only

6 Speaker credibility includes all of the following characteristics, EXCEPT
   a. competence
   b. character
   c. creativity
   d. charisma

7 Audiences will judge your competence by
   a. the number of celebrities you cite
   b. the amount of knowledge you possess
   c. the professional appearance of your visual aids
   d. the way in which you dress

8 A speaker's _____ is the audience's perception of the speaker's reliability and dependability.
   a. charisma
   b. loyalty
   c. trustworthiness
   d. competence

9 Which of the following statements accurately describes persuasion?
   a. the ultimate goal of persuasion is to increase audience understanding of the topic
   b. persuasion is usually not a "one-shot deal"
   c. persuasion always involves reinforcing existing beliefs, actions, or behaviors
   d. persuasion occurs rather infrequently in our everyday lives

10 According to your text, a speaker's character is usually assessed by looking at the speaker's
   a. charisma
   b. trustworthiness
   c. ethics
   d. all of the above
   e. B and C only

11 In order to become effective consumers of persuasion, the authors of your textbook suggest that we ask which of the following questions?
   a. Is this really good information?
   b. How knowledgeable is the speaker?
   c. Does the argument seem logical?
   d. all of the above

12 Statements such as "the following was taken from . . ." or "the following is a quotation from . . ." are examples of
a. oral footnotes
b. oral headers
c. signposts
d. transitions

13 When organizing a persuasive speech, you should carefully consider all of the following decisions, EXCEPT
a. whether or not to present one side or both sides of an issue
b. when you should present your strongest argument
c. what the strongest reference cited should be
d. what the best way is to organize the speech

14 When speakers lead their listeners to think "That makes sense," in essence, building a case by calling on their audience's ability to reason, speakers are using _____ appeals.
a. emotional
b. credibility
c. logical
d. need

15 Consider the following argument:

General Premise: Lung cancer is a major health concern in the South.

Minor Premise: Texas is a part of the South.

Conclusion: Therefore, lung cancer is a major health concern in Texas.

This argument is an example of which form of reasoning?
a. inductive reasoning
b. deductive reasoning
c. causal reasoning
d. reasoning by analogy

16 _____ reasoning is based on a sequence that progresses from a series of related facts to a general conclusion.
a. inductive reasoning
b. deductive reasoning
c. causal reasoning
d. reasoning by analogy

17 All of the following are fallacies of evidence, EXCEPT
a. hasty generalization
b. ad hominem
c. red herring
d. fact versus opinion

18 In order to motivate the crowd to action, Martin Luther King Jr. awakened feelings of anger in his audience at the social injustices that existed in the 1960s, as well as a sense of hope that such injustices would someday be accounted for. In other words, King used _____ appeals in his speech.
a. logical
b. emotional
c. needs
d. information

19 The best way to establish yourself as an ethical speaker is to
a. falsify and distort information in order to make your point
b. only cite sources when you feel it is absolutely necessary
c. show respect for your audience
d. be ambiguous about from whom and where your information comes from

20 A question of _____ asks whether something is good or bad, desirable or undesirable.
a. value
b. policy
c. fact
d. morals

21 Which of the following statements about the goals of persuasive speaking is accurate?
a. Adopting involves asking the audience to keep an existing behavior, whereas continuance asks the audience to begin a new behavior.
b. Adoption and discontinuance ask people to change, whereas deterrence and continuance ask people not to change.
c. Adoption and deterrence ask people to change, whereas continuance and discontinuance ask people not to change.
d. All four goals of persuasive speaking are fairly easy to accomplish.

22 When discussing questions of policy, persuasive speakers usually focus on all of the following considerations, EXCEPT
a. need
b. resources available
c. plan
d. suitability

23 According to Abraham Maslow, _____ needs relate to our hopes of being loved and to our needs for affection from friends and family.
a. social
b. self-esteem
c. safety
d. physical

24 In response to Mark's rebuttal of her argument, Sarah attempted to diminish Mark's statement by calling him a "jerk." Sarah is guilty of committing what type of fallacy?
a. ad hominem
b. questionable cause
c. hasty generalization
d. red herring

25 When a speaker states that what holds true in one case will also hold true in a similar case, he or she is using
a. logical reasoning
b. emotional appeals
c. deductive reasoning
d. reasoning by analogy

26 _____ reasoning always implies or includes the word "because."
a. inductive
b. deductive
c. causal
d. emotional

27 After citing two personal examples of friends who do not drink and drive, Lisa states that "in surveying people I know, I have found that most students on college campuses do not drink and drive." In making this claim, Lisa is guilty of which fallacy of evidence?
a. ad hominem
b. fact versus opinion
c. hasty generalization
d. red herring

28 All of the following statements about charismatic speakers are true, EXCEPT
a. Charismatic speakers seem to be sincerely interested in their listeners.
b. Charismatic speakers speak with high energy and enthusiasm.
c. We often associate charismatic speakers as having appeal for small numbers of people.
d. They generally seem attractive and likable.

29 _____ is an action subgoal that asks listeners to demonstrate their acceptance of an attitude, belief, or value by avoiding certain behaviors.
a. discontinuance
b. adoption
c. continuance
d. deterrence

30 When a speaker demonstrates "rhetorical sensitivity," he or she is being aware of
a. the audience's needs
b. the time limits
c. the situation
d. all of the above
e. B and C only

Chapter 13: Interpersonal Communication

MULTIPLE CHOICE

Choose the one alternative that best completes the statement or answers the question.

1 Our subconscious thoughts would be placed in which area of the Johari Window?
a. open area
b. blind area
c. unknown area
d. hidden area

2 Steve chooses not to tell his closest friends that he once played professional football. Steve's decision not to self-disclose this information demonstrates which area of the Johari Window?
a. blind area
b. hidden area
c. unknown area
d. open area

3 When we refer to an association between at least two people that may be described in terms of kinship or intimacy, we are referring to a(n)
a. relationship
b. interpersonal exchange
c. intimate connection
d. romantic exchange

4 In a recent survey of on-line participants in twenty-four different newsgroups, almost _____ of those responding to the survey said that they had formed different types of personal relationships with someone they met on the Internet.
a. one-third
b. half
c. two-thirds
d. three-fourths

5 Schutz's theory of interpersonal needs includes all of the following needs, EXCEPT
a. inclusion
b. affection
c. motivation
d. control

6 According to your text, relationships can based on which of the following things?
a. roles
b. time
c. participation in events

d. all of the above
e. A and C only

7 After meeting Bill for the first time, Karen found herself wanting to ask Bill questions about himself so that she could reduce her uncertainty about him. In this instance, Karen's communication with Bill might best be explained using _____ theory.
a. predicted outcome
b. uncertainty reduction
c. uncertainty induction
d. Schutz's interpersonal needs

8 Our basic need to feel likable or lovable is referred to by Schutz as our need for

_____.
a. motivation
b. inclusion
c. control
d. affection

9 After finishing her first date with Tom, Sally decides that dating Tom really isn't worth the time and energy it would take to continue the relationship. Sally's decision to discontinue the relationship could best be explained using which theory of interpersonal communication?
a. uncertainty reduction theory
b. predicted outcome value theory
c. Schutz's theory of interpersonal needs
d. social exchange theory

10 _____ theory suggests that people connect with others because they believe that rewards or positive outcomes will result.
a. predicted outcome value
b. social exchange
c. uncertainty reduction
d. social penetration

11 There are several advantages to interacting with people online, including all of the following EXCEPT
a. You can remain anonymous.
b. Interaction via technology can fulfill our interpersonal needs.
c. You can choose the time and place of contact.
d. It is generally safe because physical contact is only possible if you allow it to occur.

12 When we exchange "hellos" or comments about the weather, newsworthy events, and trivia with other people, we are engaging in
   a. affectionate communication
   b. introductory talk
   c. small talk
   d. intimate talk

13 According to your text, the primary contributor to our self-concepts is
   a. the way we process information
   b. the way others react to us
   c. the environment we are placed in
   d. the way in which we communicate to others

14 The _____ depicts the different levels of knowledge that exist in interpersonal relationships, and it illustrates four kinds of information about a person.
   a. Johari Window
   b. social penetration theory
   c. social exchange theory
   d. Social Exchange Window

15 All of the following statements about self-disclosure are true, EXCEPT
   a. Self-disclosure often results in greater self-understanding.
   b. Our use of self-disclosure is static.
   c. The principal benefit of self-disclosure is personal growth.
   d. Our self-disclosure to others encourages them to reciprocate.

16 According to Altman and Taylor, _____ is the process of increasing disclosure and intimacy in a relationship.
   a. social penetration theory
   b. social exchange theory
   c. uncertainty reduction theory
   d. predicted outcome value theory

17 When we self-disclose to rid ourselves of information that is causing tension or guilt, we are using communication as a form of
   a. self-presentation
   b. relationship building
   c. catharsis
   d. withholding information

18 According to the authors of your text, we are motivated to self-disclose to others for all of the following reasons, EXCEPT
   a. self-presentation
   b. catharsis
   c. being honest
   d. to end relationships

19 Rhetorically sensitive individuals typically display all of the following attributes, EXCEPT
   a. They are flexible in their communication with others.
   b. They know how to adapt their messages to a particular audience.
   c. They change their own values to fit the values of others.
   d. They accept personal complexity-that every person is made up of many selves.

20 Which theory uses the concepts of breadth and depth to explain how self-disclosure gradually increases as the relationship develops?
   a. uncertainty reduction theory
   b. social exchange theory
   c. social penetration theory
   d. predicted outcome value theory

21 When we begin to consider how much self-disclosure is too much self-disclosure, we are engaged in the process of negotiating _____ boundaries.
   a. rhetorically sensitive
   b. control
   c. privacy
   d. self-presentation

22 Research findings support all of the following conclusions about self-disclosure, EXCEPT
   a. Disclosure is culturally regulated by norms of appropriateness.
   b. Disclosure decreases with the need to reduce uncertainty in a relationship.
   c. Women tend to disclose personal information more often than men do.
   d. Disclosure tends to be reciprocal.

23 Which of the following statements concerning gender, sex, and self-disclosure are true?
   a. Men are more likely to talk about their relationships.

b. Women often do not center their talk on relational closeness.

c. Women and men demonstrate the same verbal and nonverbal behaviors.

d. Women disclose more with those to whom they are close, whereas men disclose more with those to whom they trust.

24 All of the following are suggestions for improving your small talk skills, EXCEPT

a. Use the other person's name as little as possible as you converse.

b. Use nonverbal behaviors that indicate that you are interested in the other person.

c. Get the other person to talk about himself or herself.

d. Maintain an adequate amount of eye contact during the conversation.

25 Outcomes in personal relationships such as good feelings, prestige, economic gain, and fulfillment of emotional needs are referred to as

a. needs of control

b. predicted outcomes

c. rewards

d. costs

26 When a person self-discloses to us in a conversation, our own self-disclosure usually

a. decreases

b. increases

c. becomes more positive

d. becomes more negative

e. none of the above

27 Jonathan is comfortable as either a leader or a follower, and he is open minded and willing to accept others' suggestions for the good of the group. Jonathan may be identified as a(n)

a. democrat

b. abdicrat

c. autocrat

d. sociocrat

28 Jeremy does not like being around other people because he finds communicating with others to be a threatening experience. According to Schutz, Jeremy could be described as

a. oversocial

b. undersocial

c. social

d. extra-social

29 All of the following statements could be considered self-disclosure, EXCEPT

a. I am a white female with blonde hair.

b. I have been married twice.

c. I am afraid of spiders.

d. I really enjoy horror films.

e. I am a fan of the Dallas Cowboys.

30 _____ is an intentional self-disclosure tactic that we use to reveal certain aspects about ourselves for specific reasons.

a. self-revelation

b. self-denial

c. self-presentation

d. self-penetration

Chapter 14: Developing Relationships

MULTIPLE CHOICE

Choose the one alternative that best completes the statement or answers the question.

1 After meeting Danielle for the first time, David decided that Danielle was someone that could fit into his circle of friends. In this instance, David is experiencing what form of attraction to Danielle?
a. task attraction
b. social attraction
c. physical attraction
d. instrumental attraction

2 Once two people come into contact and experience relatively positive effects, whether or not they continue a possible relationship depends on which two conditions?
a. each person's need to associate and the level of task attraction between them
b. the level of social attraction between them and the way each person reacts to the observable physical attributes of the other
c. each person's need to associate with the other and the way each person reacts to the observable physical attributes of the other
d. each person's need to associate and the level of social attraction between them

3 Knapp's stages of coming together include all of the following stages, EXCEPT
a. circumscribing
b. intensifying
c. integrating
d. experimenting
e. initiating

4 Lately, Kathy and Jason have been focusing on the ways in which they differ from each other, and they have found themselves becoming less tolerant of their differences. Which of Knapp's stages adequately describes Kathy and Jason's behavior?
a. terminating
b. stagnating
c. differentiating
d. circumscribing

5 All of the following statements concerning physical attributes and attraction levels are true, EXCEPT
a. People respond positively to those who are attractive and negatively to those who are unattractive.
b. People tend to have low levels of agreement about who is or who is not attractive.
c. Most people are afraid of being rejected by those who are more attractive than they are.
d. In romantic relationships, most people select individuals with whom they perceive to be similar in attractiveness.

6 According to the authors of your textbook, which statement accurately reflects the process of coming together on the Internet?
a. The process of coming together on the Internet is identical to face-to-face interaction.
b. Online interactions have just as many social cues as face-to-face interactions.
c. Online relationships do not go through the same stages of coming together and coming apart that face-to-face relationships go through.
d. The development of personal relationships online is often slowed by feedback delays that can cause uncertainty.

7 The stage in Knapp's model of coming together that essentially answers the question of "Who is this person?" is referred to as
a. experimenting
b. intensifying
c. initiating
d. bonding

8 The interaction during the "terminating" stage of coming apart involves all of the following communication behaviors, EXCEPT
a. self-centeredness
b. an attempt to justify the termination
c. an attempt to sidestep controversy
d. stating preferences for dealing with each other in the future

9 When two individuals know that their relationship is ending, they often say good-bye to each other in which of the following ways?
   a. in a summary statement
   b. in behaviors signaling limited contact
   c. in comments about what the relationship will be like in the future
   d. all of the above
   e. A and B only

10 According to Knapp, relationships move through the stages of coming together and the stages of coming apart sequentially because
   a. each stage provides information that allows movement to the next step
   b. each stage enables the participants to predict what may or may not occur in the next stage
   c. skipping a stage creates a sense of certainty in the relationship
   d. all of the above
   e. A and B only

11 According to Knapp and Vangelisti's staircase model of interaction, the center of the staircase represents the possibility of _____ at a given level for a period of time.
   a. integration
   b. transcendence
   c. stability
   d. conflict

12 Statements such as "I don't want to talk about it," and "Can't you see that I'm busy?" reflect which stage of coming apart?
   a. stagnating
   b. circumscribing
   c. avoiding
   d. terminating

13 Duck's phases of dissolution include all of the following phases, EXCEPT
   a. the interpersonal phase
   b. the dyadic phase
   c. the social phase
   d. the intrapsychic phase
   e. the grave-dressing phase

14 Dialectical tensions that are commonly identified in communication research on personal relationships include all of the following, EXCEPT
   a. openness-closedness
   b. novelty-predictability
   c. superiority-equality
   d. connection-autonomy

15 _____ is an expressed struggle between at least two interdependent parties who perceive incompatible goals, scarce resources, and interference from others in achieving their goals.
   a. dialectic
   b. conflict
   c. disagreement
   d. intensifying

16 Our desires to be expressive on the one hand and private on the other reflect which dialectical tension?
   a. openness-closedness
   b. superiority-equality
   c. connection-autonomy
   d. presence-absence

17 Conflicts may stem from several social factors, including
   a. faulty attributions
   b. faulty communication
   c. personal traits and/or characteristics
   d. all of the above
   e. A and B only

18 According to the authors of your text, which of the following warning signs signal that a relationship is in trouble?
   a. disagreements
   b. aggressive behavior
   c. lying
   d. all of the above
   e. B and C only

19 A strategy that approaches conflict management through cooperation and mutual respect, using a "we" rather than a "me" approach, is referred to as
   a. negotiating
   b. collaborating
   c. forcing
   d. accommodating

20 Leaving the situation altogether and stonewalling are examples of which form of conflict management?
   a. accommodating
   b. forcing
   c. collaborating
   d. withdrawing
   e. negotiating

21 According to your text, which form of conflict management is often interpreted as a lose/lose style of conflict management?
   a. forcing
   b. negotiating
   c. collaborating
   d. withdrawing

22 After dating Melissa for 6 months, Derek feels that their relationship has become routine. He decides to "spice" things up in their relationship by taking Melissa on a surprise cruise to the Bahamas. Derek's attempt to "spice" things up in his relationship with Melissa demonstrates which dialectical tension?
   a. novelty-predictability
   b. openness-closedness
   c. superiority-equality
   d. connection-autonomy

23 During the _____ phase of dissolution, partners consider where to place blame for the termination of the relationship, as well as how to save face and how to explain what has happened to the social network of friends and family.
   a. grave-dressing
   b. intrapsychic
   c. dyadic
   d. social

24 According to recent statistics, approximately how many marriages in our society today will end in divorce?
   a. less than 25%
   b. less than 50%
   c. more than 50%
   d. more than 75%

25 All of the following behaviors are suggested as actions that can improve interpersonal communication, EXCEPT
   a. establishing a supporting and caring relationship
   b. avoiding conflict
   c. nurturing a supportive environment
   d. inviting more communication

26 According to research on marital conflict, the more couples engage in marital conflict
   a. the more they become verbally aggressive
   b. the more likely they become to resolve important differences
   c. the more likely their verbally aggressive behavior leads to physical violence
   d. all of the above
   e. A and C only

27 All of the following are conflict management strategies one can employ, EXCEPT
   a. compromising
   b. withdrawing
   c. forcing
   d. attacking

28 There is much persuasion, negotiation, and argument during which of Duck's phases of relationship dissolution?
   a. the grave-dressing phase
   b. the dyadic phase
   c. the social phase
   d. the intrapsychic phase

29 The contradictory impulses that push and pull us in conflicting directions with others are referred to as
   a. dialectics
   b. conflict
   c. terminating
   d. intensifying

30 The public announcement of a committed couple occurs in the _____ stage.
   a. intensifying
   b. initiating
   c. integrating
   d. bonding

Chapter 15: Group and Team Communication

MULTIPLE CHOICE

Choose the one alternative that best completes the statement or answers the question.

1 According to Paul Paulus, people join groups for all of the following reasons, EXCEPT
a. Groups can help meet the need for security.
b. Groups help satisfy important social needs, such as the need for affection.
c. Group membership provides information that is usually available to most individuals.
d. Group membership can contribute to an individual's positive social identity.

2 If you hold a _____ orientation, you are more likely to put aside your individual goals for the well-being of the group.
a. individualistic
b. collectivistic
c. cathartic
d. work

3 Which small group is considered the predominant small group that most individuals participate in?
a. the family
b. school clubs
c. professional associations
d. college fraternities and sororities

4 To qualify as a group, the people in the group must be related in all of the following ways, EXCEPT
a. motivation
b. interaction
c. organization
d. independence
e. goals

5 The question "Do members make an impression on one another?" reflects which defining characteristic of a group?
a. organization
b. perceptions
c. goals
d. motivation

6 According to John Brillhardt, a small group communication scholar, "groupness" refers to
a. the number of people in a group
b. the number of leaders in a small group
c. the roles that group members play
d. the necessary property that groups possess but that collections of individuals do not

7 Sally finds working in groups to be both challenging and frustrating. As an 'A' student, she prefers to work alone in groups so that she can be responsible for her own work. Sally's orientation to working groups could best be described as
a. detrimental
b. conspicuous
c. individualistic
d. collectivistic

8 The purposes of small group communication can be grouped into two general categories. What are they?
a. informational and task-related purposes
b. social and informational purposes
c. task-related and social purposes
d. informational and organizational purposes

9 Each morning, Bill's work team gathers together for doughnuts and coffee at the local bakery before beginning their day at work. In this instance, Bill's work team is gathering together for which of the following purposes of small group communication?
a. socialization
b. therapy
c. problem solving
d. decision making

10 All of the following purposes of group communication are considered social purposes, EXCEPT
a. therapy
b. problem solving
c. socialization
d. catharsis

11 According to your text, all of the following statements concerning gender differences in group participation are true, EXCEPT
 a. Men tend to demonstrate more social behavior than women do.
 b. Men tend to be more objective in their comments than women.
 c. Women tend to offer positive responses to others' comments.
 d. Men tend to be more goal-oriented than women.

12 When groups are competing with each other,
 a. men are more cooperative with their opponents than women are.
 b. women are more likely to gain the advantage through deception and deceit.
 c. women are more likely to be antisocial.
 d. men are more willing to engage in aggressive behavior.

13 Ethical guidelines for communicating in small groups include
 a. All group members should have the right to state an opinion.
 b. Confidential information shared in the group should remain confidential.
 c. All group members should conduct themselves with honesty and integrity.
 d. all of the above

14 The advantages to interactive computer conferencing include:
 a. convenience
 b. only a computer and connected video camera are required
 c. getting online is always easy
 d. all of the above
 e. A and B only

15 Ultimately, the success of any technology for group sharing depends on what two factors?
 a. cost and accessibility
 b. accessibility and use
 c. cost and use
 d. type of personnel and accessibility

16 According to your text, teams differ from groups in all of the following ways, EXCEPT
 a. teams are less likely to consist of people with diverse abilities
 b. teams usually develop more interdependence than groups

 c. members of teams have a high degree of group identity
 d. members of teams are more likely to identify themselves as team members

17 Jake leads a special type of work team that researches what people think about specific ideas and issues. His work team is best described as a
 a. project team
 b. focus group
 c. social team
 d. information team

18 The most essential characteristic of a small group is
 a. commitment
 b. cohesiveness
 c. interdependence
 d. group size

19 In 1980, IBM executives were unwilling to consider new information regarding the Microsoft operating system Bill Gates had developed. Consequently, they missed a tremendous opportunity that resulted in a loss of revenues worth billions of dollars. Their failure to consider new information was a result of:
 a. catharsis
 b. a lack of group interdependence
 c. groupthink
 d. faulty information

20 According to your text, what size of a group tends to be the most effective for dealing with intellectual tasks and for making administrative decisions?
 a. a three-member group
 b. a five-member group
 c. a seven-member group
 d. a nine-member group

21 Group members usually develop norms for all of the following reasons, EXCEPT
 a. norms help give a group structure
 b. norms can often help increase efficiency
 c. norms can often provide some form of order
 d. norms enable group members to attain individual goals

22 In class, Steven often lowers his work effort after joining groups with fellow classmates. Steven's tendency reflects a disadvantage to working in small groups referred to as
a. groupthink
b. social loafing
c. grouphate phenomenon
d. catharsis

23 Disadvantages to working in small groups include all of the following, EXCEPT
a. the problem-solving process can be time-consuming
b. in most groups, it is not possible for all members to contribute equally
c. members believe the workload is fair in the group
d. the group may not meet its potential

24 When deciding on the most effective size for group, remember that
a. larger groups increase the amount of individual interaction
b. smaller groups provide a greater opportunity for aggressive members to assert their dominance
c. larger groups make it easier to follow a set agenda
d. smaller groups make it easier to follow a set agenda

25 According to Irving Janis, each of the following symptoms can lead to groupthink, EXCEPT
a. open-mindedness
b. an overestimation of the group's power
c. an illusion that the group is invulnerable
d. pressures toward uniformity

26 An online bulletin board where people can read and post messages about the topics of their choice is referred to as
a. a newsgroup
b. a chat room
c. interactive computer conferencing
d. a uniform resource library (URL)

27 When group members feel for one another and are willing to stick together, their group is best described as having a high degree of
a. interdependence
b. cohesiveness
c. group culture
d. groupthink

28 According to your text, group members can minimize the possibility of groupthink by using each of the following procedures, EXCEPT
a. assigning one group member to serve as "devil's advocate"
b. setting a guideline to enable leaders to express their preferences first
c. ensuring that every group member has an opportunity to voice an opinion
d. encouraging individuals to express disagreement without being chastised by the group for doing so

29 Task-related purposes for small group communication include
a. decision making
b. catharsis
c. problem solving
d. all of the above
e. A and C only

30 Characteristics that define small groups include all of the following, EXCEPT
a. norms
b. group culture
c. cohesiveness
d. social loafing
e. commitment

Chapter 16: Participating in Groups and Teams

MULTIPLE CHOICE

Choose the one alternative that best completes the statement or answers the question.

1 As a leader in his small group, Jonathan does not believe in taking charge since he feels uncomfortable as a leader. Consequently, his group receives little or no direction. Which leadership style is reflected in Jonathan's behavior?
a. democratic leadership
b. laissez-faire leadership
c. autocratic leadership
d. task-oriented leadership

2 Leaders must perform several functions in order to satisfy both task and maintenance needs including all of the following, EXCEPT
a. facilitating understanding
b. initiating
c. controlling the conversation
d. ensuring member satisfaction

3 In order for groups to establish a team approach, they must
a. set very clear and specific goals
b. determine roles
c. develop a team identity
d. all of the above
e. A and C only

4 It is important to remember all of the following points when setting group goals, EXCEPT
a. the consequences of not setting clear goals are frustration and low motivation among group members
b. the most effective groups have clear, identifiable goals
c. setting clear goals requires very little effort
d. goals that are specific are more likely to be accomplished

5 Leaders can often be identified through which of the following behaviors?
a. by looking at the person to whom the group members address their messages
b. by the behaviors a person displays in guiding a group to its specific goal

c. by considering a person's position or title
d. all of the above
e. none of the above

6 _____ leaders gain satisfaction from establishing good interpersonal relationships, whereas _____ leaders gain satisfaction from performing the task set before the group.
a. democratic, autocratic
b. autocratic, democratic
c. task-oriented, relationship-oriented
d. relationship-oriented, task-oriented

7 Which of the following statements concerning the differences among the three styles of leadership is accurate?
a. In practice, the differences among the three leadership styles is clear-cut.
b. Most leaders use the same leadership style all of the time.
c. The democratic leadership style is most often used when a leader is elected.
d. Leaders are always free to follow the leadership style they prefer.

8 When groups members are not committed or are unwilling to accept responsibility for implementing a decision, effective leaders should most likely use which leadership style?
a. autocratic leadership
b. democratic leadership
c. laissez-faire leadership
d. relationship-oriented leadership

9 According to your text, effective leaders should use a laissez-faire leadership style when
a. group members are not committed and are unwilling to accept responsibility for implementing a decision.
b. group members are highly motivated and have the knowledge and expertise to accomplish the task.
c. group members are highly committed and willing to accept responsibility for implementing a decision.
d. none of the above

10. An influence process that includes any behavior that helps clarify or guide the group to achieve its goals is referred to as
    a. leadership
    b. team-building
    c. goal-setting
    d. group maintenance

11. Task needs are related to all behaviors that lead to the completion of the task. Examples of task needs include all of the following behaviors, EXCEPT
    a. defining and assessing the task
    b. gathering information
    c. establishing a certain atmosphere in the group
    d. studying the problem

12. Which statement accurately reflects research findings on the three leadership styles?
    a. The democratic leadership style is superior to an autocratic style in getting a task done and at the same time satisfying group members.
    b. Laissez-faire leaders are likely to get more done, but member satisfaction is considerably lower.
    c. Democratic leaders generate more hostility and aggression from group members.
    d. Groups with autocratic leaders accomplish less, produce work of lower quality, and waste more time.

13. According to your text, group member roles can be classified into one of each of the following categories, EXCEPT
    a. group dissolution roles
    b. group building and maintenance roles
    c. self-centered roles
    d. group task roles

14. Juliann's reluctance to talk during group meetings and her tendency to do her own work without consulting other group members reflects what type of group member role?
    a. a group building and maintenance role
    b. a self-centered role
    c. a group dissolution role
    d. a group task role

15. Which of the following statements accurately reflects the role of criticism during group discussion?
    a. Criticism should be ignore and avoided.

b. Evaluations can be constructive when they focus on the person who offered the comment.
    c. Criticism should be based on who makes the comment, not on what the comment actually refers to.
    d. Group discussion can lead to the best possible decision when comments are offered for evaluation by other group members.

16. A list of all topics to be discussed during a meeting is referred to as a(n)
    a. outline
    b. agenda
    c. topical header
    d. series of bullet points

17. According to your text, after a topic or problem is selected, it should be stated in the form of a question. All of the following are types of discussion questions, EXCEPT
    a. questions of selection
    b. questions of interpretation
    c. questions of fact
    d. questions of policy

18. "Which college offers the best education for its students?" is a question of
    a. value
    b. fact
    c. interpretation
    d. action

19. "What restrictions should be placed on alcohol consumption on campus?" is a question of
    a. fact
    b. policy
    c. interpretation
    d. value

20. When phrasing discussion questions, one should keep all of the following guidelines in mind, EXCEPT
    a. The wording should focus attention on the real problem.
    b. The wording should avoid emotional language.
    c. The wording should suggest possible solutions.
    d. The wording should specify whose behavior is subject to change.

21 John Dewey's "reflective thinking" steps for group problem-solving include all of the following steps, EXCEPT
  a. defining the problem
  b. analyzing the problem
  c. suggesting possible solutions
  d. evaluating the effects of the selected solution

22 When brainstorming, group members should remember which of the following guidelines?
  a. Don't criticize any idea, either verbally or nonverbally.
  b. Generate only a few, key ideas that the group should consider.
  c. Record only the most important idea generated by the group.
  d. Set a fairly short time limit for brainstorming.

23 A question of interpretation asks
  a. whether something is good or bad
  b. for the meaning or explanation of something
  c. whether something is true or false
  d. what actions should be taken

24 When group members negotiate consensus by collaboration through the expression of each differing need and a search for alternatives to meet those needs, they are engaging in
  a. principled negotiation
  b. democratic participation
  c. principled participation
  d. democratic negotiation

25 According to your text, positive outcomes associated with group conflict include
  a. increased member motivation
  b. better group decisions
  c. better understanding of both issues and people
  d. all of the above

26 An adequate definition of conflict includes all of the following elements, EXCEPT
  a. an internal conflict that has not been expressed
  b. two interdependent parties
  c. a perception of scarce resources
  d. a perception of incompatible goals

27 Advantages of using electronic brainstorming during group discussions include
  a. the speed of recording is increased
  b. group members can send their ideas simultaneously
  c. producing more effective solutions to group problems
  d. all of the above
  e. A and B only

28 One of the greatest weaknesses of beginning group participants is
  a. their inability to show up on time to group meetings
  b. their inability to generate new ideas during brainstorming
  c. their tendency to arrive at meetings unprepared
  d. their tendency to assume leadership roles immediately

29 Group members consider the causes of a problem during which stage of Dewey's "reflective thinking" process?
  a. definition of the problem
  b. suggestion of possible solutions
  c. analysis of the problem
  d. selection of the best solution

30 A person who is selected or assigned to guide or provide direction toward reaching the group's goals is referred to as a(n)
  a. principled negotiator
  b. leader
  c. facilitator
  d. mediator